Justice in Paradise

MCGILL-QUEEN'S NATIVE AND NORTHERN SERIES
BRUCE G. TRIGGER, EDITOR

1 When the Whalers Were
Up North
Inuit Memories from the
Eastern Artic
Dorothy Harley Eber

2 The Challenge of Arctic
Shipping
Science, Environmental
Assessment, and Human Values
*David L. VanderZwaag and
Cynthia Lamson, Editors*

3 Lost Harvests
Prairie Indian Reserve Farmers
and Government Policy
Sarah Carter

4 Native Liberty, Crown
Sovereignty
The Existing Aboriginal Right
of Self-Government in Canada
Bruce Clark

5 Unravelling the Franklin
Mystery
Inuit Testimony
David C. Woodman

6 Otter Skins, Boston Ships, and
China Goods
The Maritime Fur Trade of the
Northwest Coast, 1785–1841
James R. Gibson

7 From Wooden Ploughs to
Welfare
The Story of the Western
Reserves
Helen Buckley

8 In Business for Ourselves
Northern Entrepreneurs
Wanda A. Wuttunee

9 For an Amerindian Autohistory
An Essay on the Foundations of
a Social Ethic
Georges E. Sioui

10 Strangers Among Us
David Woodman

11 When the North Was Red
Aboriginal Education in Soviet
Siberia
*Dennis A. Bartels and
Alice L. Bartels*

12 From Talking Chiefs to a Native
Corporate Elite
The Birth of Class and
Nationalism among Canadian
Inuit
Marybelle Mitchell

13 Cold Comfort
My Love Affair with the Arctic
Graham W. Rowley

14 The True Spirit and Original
Intent of Treaty 7
*Treaty 7 Elders and Tribal Council
with Walter Hildebrandt, Dorothy
First Rider, and Sarah Carter*

15 This Distant and Unsurveyed
Country
A Woman's Winter at Baffin
Island, 1857–1858
W. Gillies Ross

16 Images of Justice
   Dorothy Harley Eber

17 Capturing Women
   The Manipulation of Cultural
   Imagery in Canada's
   Prairie West
   Sarah Carter

18 Social and Environmental
   Impacts of the James Bay
   Hydroelectric Project
   Edited by
   James F. Horning

19 Saqiyuq
   Stories from the Lives of Three Inuit
   Women
   *Nancy Wachowich in collaboration
   with Apphia Agalakti Awa, Rhoda
   Kaukjak Katsak, and Sandra Pikujak
   Katsak*

Justice in Paradise

BRUCE CLARK

McGill-Queen's University Press
Montreal & Kingston · London · Ithaca

To Margaret

© Bruce Clark 1999
ISBN 0-7735-2001-5

Legal deposit fourth quarter 1999
Bibliothèque nationale du Québec

Printed in Canada on acid-free paper

Canada

McGill-Queen's University Press acknowledges the financial support of the Government of Canada through the Book
Publishing Industry Development Program for its activities.
We also acknowledge the support of the Canada Council for
the Arts for our publishing program.

Canadian Cataloguing in Publication Data

Clark, Bruce A., 1944–
Justice in paradise
(McGill-Queen's native and northern series; 20)
Includes index.
ISBN 0-7735-2001-5
1. Clark, Bruce A., 1944–   2. Native peoples – Legal
status, laws, etc. – Canada. 3. Indigenous peoples – Legal
status, laws, etc. 4. Rule of law. 5. Lawyers – Canada –
Biography. I. Title. II. Series.
KE416.C53A3 1999   342′.0872′092   C99-901019-0

This book was typeset by Typo Litho Composition Inc. in
10.5/13 Times.

CONTENTS

PART ONE EARLY ENCOUNTERS OF THE
PATHOLOGICAL KIND

1 Indian Places and Formative Faces 3

2 My Introduction to Indian Law and Culture 19

3 Moving Deeper into Indian Culture 35

4 My Capture by Indian Law and Culture 48

PART TWO KICKING AGAINST THE PRICKS

5 The Bear Island Trial 65

6 Getting Fired and Going Back to School 82

7 Crises at Oka and the Lil'Wat Country 95

8 The Western Shoshone in Nevada 114

PART THREE IN THE WOMB OF THE DEVIL'S SPAWN

9 Our First Trip to Europe 123

10 Our Trip to Bulgaria 133

11 Petitions to the Queen and Meetings in Central America 144

PART FOUR MEANWHILE BACK AT THE RANCH

12 The Bear Island Incident and My First Criminal Conviction 155

13 The Gustafsen Lake Story 161

14 Europe Again and More Petitions   173

15 The Mi'gmaq, the Supreme Court, and Other Matters   180

    PART FIVE   THE UNITED STATES: LAST EMPIRE, LAST HOPE

16 Mohegans of New York and Vermont   195

17 Law Society of Upper Canada v. Bruce Clark   210

18 Epitaph for a Dead Lawyer Walking   226

    Conclusion   253

    Acknowledgments   257

    Illustrations following page   259

    Appendix   261

      Liberty Island Case   267

      Plains Case   291

      Notes   325

    Legal Authorities   373

    Index   377

PART ONE

EARLY ENCOUNTERS OF THE PATHOLOGICAL KIND

CHAPTER 1

Indian Places and Formative Faces

The sense of nature's power, of its potential for cruelty or at least indifference, was thrust upon me one December night during the time I was living on Bear Island. Having resided there for over seven years, I had been forced to learn a measure of self-sufficiency while I was directly and intimately in contact with nature – just as that the old-style Indians had done.

I had learned how to drive the motor boat at night with the horizon for my reference point. The route from Bear Island to the road-access landing on the mainland was a twisting 4-mile passage between the islands. There was little margin for error because the lake, though deep, has innumerable "islands" submerged just beneath the surface. On that particular night, each time I got the boat up to speed the point of demarcation between land and sky would disappear into obscurity, lost in a haze of snow driven by winds. I slowed the boat, waiting to gain a bearing. Then, in the water immediately to my left, loomed one of the cylindrical marker buoys that identify the channel. I fixed in my mind's eye my place on the lake and opened up the throttle. Seconds later the boat abruptly stopped in mid-flight, battered by some unseen obstacle.

Dazed, I found that my shoulder had been dislocated by the impact. I was convinced that the boat must have struck one of the shoals and that I would have no time before it sank. Knowing I would have little chance in that super-cooled, just-before-freeze-up water unless I could somehow make it to shore, I grabbed the side of the boat with the hand of the dislocated shoulder and pulled back, twisting at the same time. The shoulder realigned itself as the ball joint dropped back into its socket. Pulling off my heavy winter clothing, I readied myself to jump clear of the sinking boat into the unseen water.

In the heartbeat before I jumped I realized there was no water in the boat. Slowly, I sank to the deck and sat there. The wind still howled and the snow still swirled, but the boat was not sinking. It was not even moving. I peered over the gunwale. No waves were hitting the side. I sat in shock a while longer, trying to make my brain make sense of what was happening to me. Gingerly I put a leg over the side. My foot fell on land. The boat and I were lodged on a rocky coast, some 15 feet from the shore and 5 feet higher than the water level.

The squall let up. The land was unrecognizable, the horizon uncommunicative. I knew where I should be by dead reckoning, but I was somewhere else. Dropping to my haunches, I stared at the black water. At that moment I felt an awareness of the power that was in that lake. It was not malevolent to me, just indifferent and immense. I think I recognized in that moment the same force that early people around the world, from China to Lake Superior, saw in the waters when they invested them with the spirits of dragons, Poseidons, and Gitchi Peeshoos.

In retrospect, I am beginning to comprehend why so many indigenous peoples, once they are disillusioned with nature, turn back to spit at her. The anthropologist Calvin Martin has published an explanation under the title *Keepers of the Game*: when the old-style people found they had been let down by their magic, they turned from courting the animal spirits to wholesale slaughter of the animal bodies. They inaugurated a reign of terror on them not unlike the terror to which the people themselves were being subjugated by the white man.

When I first read that thesis many years ago I joined with the chorus of critics who saw it as an academically unjustified attack on native people as conservationists. Yet I wonder now whether Martin did not capture a deeper reality than that reflected in the academic detail swirling about in the controversy raised by his hypothesis. When I reflect on the irrational invective turned against me over the years by native people whose hopes for justice I had rekindled, only to see them dashed, I recognize a deeper pool of rage into which I have been tapping. Like the anger shown against the animals whose magic failed the people, the disappointment surging from the unrequited quest for justice has often been directed at me rather than at the perpetrators, the judges, who are seemingly above the law, immune and invincible.

To some of the old-style native fatalists, the judges are like a force of nature – capricious, implacable, vicious if provoked. There is a pathology to the rule of law as it exists in relation to native North Americans and the paradise that once was theirs.

Three Indians from Moosonee, Ontario, took fortified wine to a drinking shack. One was killed and the other two were charged with his murder. The shack was just big enough to contain an iron-drum wood stove and a single mattress. The stove had been used to knock out the victim, then his back had been flayed with a piece of fishing rod. The prosecuting attorney offered to recommend sentences of two years less a day if both the accused would agree to plead guilty to a reduced charge of manslaughter. The presiding judge in chambers indicated to the other defence lawyer and me that he would be favourably inclined to go along with such a plea bargain.

When I relayed the offer to my client, he said that if he had hit the dead man with a stove or beaten him with a fishing rod he would remember, but that he had no such memory. It must, he argued, have happened after he passed out. Physically, the effort was too heavy for him. Emotionally, he was the sad, not the violent, type when drunk. He asked me what to do: plead guilty to a manslaughter he had no memory of in order to minimize the risk of a mandatory life sentence for murder, or go for an outright acquittal? I said if I were in his shoes I would plead not guilty, but it was up to him. It was his choice.

The other defence lawyer disagreed strongly. His client wanted to accept the plea bargain, which for practical purposes meant persuading my client to do the same. The lawyer pointed out that this was my first murder trial, whereas he had acted in many; and that I was twenty-nine years old and hardly out of law school, while he was a leading counsel of established mettle. Our duty as lawyers, he schooled me, is to protect our clients from imprudent decisions. I asked him to distinguish that role from advising the client to lie. "You will learn, my young friend," he answered, "that there is no such thing as absolute truth in court. Here, reality is relative." When I suggested that this was a formula for opportunism, my would-be mentor became exasperated. He felt it more accurate to say I was the opportunist, trying to establish a reputation at the client's expense by turning just another drunken Indian dust-em-up into a self-serving performance before a jury.

The prosecutor eventually accepted a plea from the other lawyer's client, who was sentenced to two years less a day for manslaughter. Then he was called as a witness against my client, who, he testified, was the real killer. The trial took place in the tiny northern Ontario town of Cochrane. When we broke for lunch, everybody went to the same diner: the defence lawyers, the prosecuting lawyers, the investigating officers, the witnesses, my client (out on his own recognizance of bail), and the judge all squeezed in together.

My client wanted to sit in a particular booth in which a couple of his friends were already seated, along with some others. He asked them to shove over and make room. No one moved. "Move it, I said," grimaced my man, "I've killed before and I'll kill again." Sure enough, when the trial reconvened after lunch, this "confession" was adduced in evidence. Rather than argue that my client had been referring to someone else he had killed, I tried to persuade the jury that he was projecting a tough-guy image. If he really had committed murder, he was not likely to blare it out in a room full of police just to get a seat at a lunch booth.

To back this aspect of our rapidly sinking defence, I grasped at calling character witnesses. One of these men, a distinguished- and trustworthy-looking Indian with the craggy-face and hawk-nose physiognomy more typical of the southern Chippewa than of the rounder-faced Cree of the far north, acknowledged that he and my client were pacific persons. I asked him to admit that even he might on occasion make a dumb remark in jest, such as a wisecrack about beating his wife, but that alone would not make him a wife-beater, only a person with a bent sense of humour. To my chagrin he answered that he did beat his wife, but only if she deserved it. The courtroom fell silent for a few seconds before the jury erupted in laughter.

In the far north there are still "bush Indians," people whose mind-set differs from that of "reserve Indians" or "city Indians," many of whom have culturally adapted. The difference can be both endearing and frustrating. My client came across as the bush Indian type. He told the jury exactly what he had told me, and he was believed simply because he was so obviously what he was. The more the prosecutor cross-examined him, the more apparent it became that he had not the guile to lie in a believable fashion. He truly did not remember, and he honestly believed himself incapable of doing what had been described. He was acquitted.

After the judge thanked and discharged the jury and told my client he was free to go, the courtroom cleared and fell silent. I was lost in thought, still at the counsel table, packing up my papers and books. From behind I heard a "pssst." There, still in the prisoner's box, was my client. "What's going on?" he whispered. "Its over," I replied. "You're free. Go home." He looked round, stepped hesitantly out of the box, and left, without another word. Later, as I descended the courthouse steps outside, he came up to me. "Can I borrow five bucks?" he said. "I'm dry, really dry." I handed over the money. On the way out of town I drove by the liquor store. He was in the parking lot with a bottle of wine.

I am sure his memory of the trial does not closely resemble mine. His took place in a parallel universe with a different plot and point, or lack of plot and point. One of the simultaneously recorded performances was real and the other, by elimination, surreal, but, given my own cultural bias, I have no way of knowing which was which.

Kenora is another small northern Ontario town, a thousand miles to the west of Cochrane, as close to the Manitoba border as Cochrane is to Quebec's. Another murder trial took place there a short time later, this time of an Indian from the tiny reserve of Ogoki Post. This reserve sits at the juncture of two great river systems, the Albany and the Ogoki, by longitude midway between Cochrane and Kenora though by latitude far to the north of both.

Into this wilderness, Canadian government employees commute by float- and ski-plane. They build instant slums to house the Indians, to keep them out of the way of whatever development would be interfered with if the Indians were al-lowed to continue practising their aboriginal economy. Ogoki Post is equipped with the typical government-issue row houses flanking a raised boardwalk. Sub-urbia in the wilderness, designed to self-destruct in five years, ensuring the sub-sidized economy of high though temporary wages for the whites and Indians who build and rebuild. Here, surrounded by billions of gallons of pristine river water, the Indians have been gifted with a sewage system adjacent to dug wells into which their sewage seeps.

Again, as at the trial in Kenora, a man was dead because of an alcohol binge party. Beyond the fact of the death, it was difficult to understand what actually had happened: everyone present had been "half-cut." The Ogoki man also pleaded not guilty to murder. A deal of two years less a day was offered, this time if he would change his plea to guilty of the reduced charge of assault with intent to cause bodily harm. But the client held firm, and for the same reason. He couldn't remember, he said.

The evidence led by the prosecutor attributed death to pressure on the brain stem resulting from a subdural hematoma resulting from a blow on the forehead that forced his brain to oscillate and bleed inside the skull. The swelling pushed the brain down into the brain-stem passage, causing death. But no one in the community could swear to remembering clearly any physical contact between my client and the dead man's head. All readily admitted that their inebriation probably dulled their recollection of events. Then, on the morning of the third day of the trial, the widow of the deceased took the stand. She began uncomfortably and evasively. An acquittal seemed assured. She paused in the middle of a sentence that was going nowhere and seemed to go inside herself. We waited. She came out of her trance with a wail of profound anguish and the tears poured down her face. She said my client had hit her husband to protect her from being beaten, that the whole thing somehow was her mistake, and she just wanted to make it all stop, to have her husband back and to free my client – as if the three of them were all victims and there was no criminal.

I asked for a recess. The prosecutor agreed to accept a changed plea of guilty to common assault, and the judge in chambers agreed that the sentence would not likely exceed three months, which had already been served awaiting trial.

Once again I had been dropped into a universe parallel to the one occupied by the native people to whom I was plying my trade. Until she wailed I thought I was winning the game, but then I recognized it for the nightmare it was – for her, and for me.

At the time of these trials I was living in Haileybury, a town of 3000 people on the west shore of Lake Temiskaming, the centre line of which forms the Ontario-Quebec border. Forty miles southwest in Ontario is an Indian reservation at Bear Island on Lake Temagami. The lake's convoluted shoreline winds like a set of fjords for more than 3000 miles, enwrapping perfectly translucent waters stretched between rocky, pine-covered hills in spider-like arms that reach outward from a central hub, at which rests Bear Island. On a clear day the smoke from Sudbury's giant nickel mine smokestack a farther 40 miles southeast can be seen rising and bending towards the lake. At night the city lights distantly reflect off the bottom of the pollution cloud like an aurora borealis.

Lake Temagami has a unique history. It is located at the juncture where the mixed forest of the Great Lakes/St Lawrence continental basin begins to change over to the predominantly coniferous forest of the more northern Hudson Bay watershed region. Wherever this kind of ecological transition zone occurs, the opportunities for plant and animal life flourish, resulting in a proliferation and vibrancy of species. The same effect at a micro-level can be seen at the margins of lands burned over by forest fires. Life is simply more abundant.

For reasons peculiar to Ontario politics, the whole Temagami region was designated a protected provincial forest around the turn of the last century. A rail line connecting Ontario's industrial and agricultural southern heartland to its northern resources ran north from Toronto, up through the Temagami region, where it split, one line continuing due north to James Bay at the southern tip of Hudson Bay and the other curving west towards Vancouver. To the extent that the old growth stands of red and white pine exist at all in northeastern North America, they exist at Lake Temagami. The region had been preserved as a counterweight to the blighted catastrophe of Sudbury.

And so Lake Temagami became a holiday destination for wealthy Torontonians and Americans from Ohio and New York and, through them, for many of the actors of the silent films in budding Hollywood. At one time, tiny Bear Island had three big dance halls virtually side by side. Sleek mahogany launches plied the waters ferrying the occupants of exclusive hotels and cottage mansions that dotted the shores of surrounding islands. Glamorous white women took as summer lovers the willing Indian braves; suave white men spent summer nights wooing no less willing Indian maidens. But the Great Depression and the Second World War ended the idyll.

The expectations of the Temagamis for a good time and the good life never quite got over the dance-hall era. Those who were left just kept right on partying. Eventually some would break into the cottages. For the most part the white people were friends who, if they had been around, would probably have shared the drinks taken. But they did not appreciate learning, after the event, of the imposition upon their hospitality. Their feelings were injured and their outrage built. The police were called in. Invariably, when rounded up by the police, the Indians openly acknowledged the events. Almost without exception, convictions were obtained on the basis of confessions which were the only evidence capable of sustaining a conviction. In a telling reversal of the values of non-native society, these Indians had no respect for the personal property of others, but when they were apprehended they insisted on telling the whole truth in spite of the consequences.

Often the sentences meted out for these offences against property dramatically exceeded those given to natives for killing other natives. For example, before I began working in the Temagami area, one of the older native men had received a sentence of four years in jail for breaking and entering into a cottage and drinking the liquor he found there. Yet in cases of Indians beating or killing other Indians, the sentences were often nominal.

I personally was benefiting and I found my job interesting. I had a 4000-square-foot house positioned to catch the dawn rising over Lake Temiskaming, good neighbours, three cars, and a 100-acre farm with a panoramic view of the same lake. Legal aid paid moderately well for my criminal trial work, and while I was away doing that, my office had three secretaries and a law clerk profitably processing real estate deals and estates. My membership in the Rotary Club and other associations ensured my success as a small-town lawyer and resulted in commercial business as well. I owned an airplane, a Piper Cherokee 235B, a variable pitch constant-speed single-engine four-seater without de-icing capability. When the weather was doubtful I had to stay on the ground. I had acquired this plane partly because it was a toy but also because it enabled me to attend remote courtrooms and visit the Indian reserves of the clients for whom I was acting. Many reserves, though inaccessible by road, have bush airstrips.

To get to the trial of the Ogoki native, for example, I flew the plane to Kenora over the north shore of Lake Superior, rather than take the somewhat more direct route through the United States south of the lake. Lake Nipigon hovers there like a balloon tethered to the northern tip of Lake Superior. As I rounded the north end of Lake Nipigon at 9000 feet, the engine stopped. At first I was enraptured by the silence and the vastness of the curving wilderness below, then it occurred to me that I should try to restart. The standard procedure in such circumstances is first to check for fuel by switching gas tanks. But both tanks were empty – the classic act of stupidity in flying that no pilot believes will ever happen to him.

I put the plane into glide mode and scanned the terrain below for crash-landing sites. There was unlimited visibility, and I had ample time to follow the checklist of steps that is part of basic pilot training. The first surge of panic subsided. There seemed to be a break in the forest at the north end of Lake Nipigon, which I took as the hub of my emergency flight path. An old airstrip was there.

I landed and coasted over to a fuel pump beside a rusty hangar. The only sound was the wind – no people, no other planes. In the silence I began to wonder how I was going to find my way out on foot. Then an old man appeared and sauntered over. He asked what I wanted and I said to fill her up. He did not want small talk, so I did not try. I paid and took off. On the rest of the flight to Kenora I got to thinking how curious it is to find yourself fitting back into space and time after feeling suspended outside them. Psychologically, I suppose, this set me up for Kenora, for my homecoming to a place of which I had no memory, other than a quasi-memory grafted on by family stories of the town where I had been born.

For the first two years of my life, my mother and father and I lived in Kenora, on the north shore of the Lake of the Woods – a lake as big as the smallest of the Great Lakes. The lake's centre line serves as the international boundary between the province of Ontario and the state of Wisconsin. The surrounding tracts of lakes and rivers, with little pieces of land separating them, are still very much wilderness Indian country in both appearance and population.

My father was an announcer and the manager at the local radio station. It was his first real job, and it had allowed him to marry my mother and rent our home on the lakeshore. He and I were close. We went boating on the lake, and on our many hikes in the bush he would carry me on his shoulders. When by accident I peed on the kitchen floor, he had trained me to get a rag and wipe it up, saying "bad dirt." Mother's sisters remarked about that scene, not necessarily approving. Mother came from an Italian, French, and Indian family of thirteen sisters and no brothers. Her sisters thought that perhaps the pee clean-up skit was some kind of man-training or male-bonding ritual; and, besides, my father was Scottish and English, a group known by the sisters to be in the thrall of strange attitudes about child rearing.

One summer evening a few of these aunts were visiting us. While mother was making dinner, father asked her to come with him for a quick dip in the lake. She said there wasn't time, so he went in alone. My aunts made a fuss over me, declaring I was the man of the house now because I had put my feet in his slippers and was shuffling around the kitchen from one aunt to another. As I basked in their attention, my father dove off the dock and drowned.

I suspect that the suddenness and completeness of his absence from my life contributed to the absolute panic I was to feel as I stared at a hole in a fence in a schoolyard in Whitehorse, Yukon, some three years later. I cannot think of any other reason why the sense of powerlessness and futility would have been so intense, so all-consuming, and so devastating. When father drowned, mother had a nervous breakdown. For a while I was trundled among various aunts who took turns caring for me while she relocated her centre. Then, it seems I became that centre.

The pieces somewhat together, she got a job as a stenographer working for the Canadian Department of National Defence in Whitehorse. The two of us set out on phase two of our life together, though mother never really left phase one behind. The song she always sang to me was "Wreck of the Old Ninety-Nine." It was about a "brave engineer who left his sweetheart so dear" to drive a locomotive. A train crash resulted and "in the wreck he was found lying, dying on the ground." With his last breath he said, "There's a little white home that I built for our own, where I dreamt we'd be happy by and by." For mother, life seemed always a quest to find that home, with her own first true love. I looked like him, her sisters said. "Little Howard," they called me. "Take care of your mother," they said. It was rewarding work, since all I had to do to succeed was let her dote on me.

One New Year's Eve in Whitehorse, mother was all dressed and perfumed to go out on the town with friends. I became despondent and then panicky at being left behind. She stayed home. We got champagne glasses and ginger ale. I pretended that I was a rich little fat bald sugar-daddy with a big cigar and she was a Cinderella who would never have to worry again about not being rich because she could have my money and a fur coat. Later, friends prevailed on her that she would never find a new mate with a demanding five year old constantly in tow. She had a new fellow on the line, or at least circling the hook. Mother put me in a residential school.

My first real memory is as intense now as the reality was when it was lived. I was lying on the ground examining the wood siding of a wall inches away. The wood had raised ridges that meandered from a base line and then back, with deep valleys shrunk in between. It had a surface that invited you to touch it, to brush it with your lips, to find in it the trapped warmth of the sun – except that the sun didn't make it so far down between the walls. The distance between the wood walls was a foot or maybe 18 inches. I was lying on the hard-packed ground separating them. Sometimes I looked at the walls of the two sheds that defined my cubby hole and put out my hand or face to them. Mostly, though, I stared at the wood, and at the wire fence that blocked the end of the corridor defined by the walls. One fence post could be seen, with a board on top and another on the bottom making the crosspieces on which had been hung a heavy-gauge wire fence that had started out green, but wasn't any more, because the paint had gone and only rust was left. There was a hole in the wire fence, as though someone had put a foot through it or maybe a two-by-four and twisted it around. The hole might have been just big enough for me to fit through, but I never actually tried. I only planned escaping. The depression and the tears, maybe outright cowardice, overwhelmed me and made me too weak to make a break for it. But I thought about it during most school recesses.

I could hear the noise of the other children. When I turned my head around to look in the other direction, away from the fence and towards the schoolyard, I could just see a set of wooden stairs that led up to the priest's living quarters on the second floor. He stood on the platform at the head of the stairs and threw peppermints down into the yard, one at time. The kids scrambled to get to them. Just as one got to the first candy, he would throw a second, and the melee would swing around after it. I turned back to stare at the hole in the fence and the wood siding.

The main problem with making a break was that I did not know which way to go once I got on the other side. If I were to stop to think I would be noticed, and a cry would go up from the children that someone had bolted. I tried to think where I could run without stopping. But my brain could not picture the route, and I was immobilized with indecision, swamped with inadequacy. The deeper fear was that, even if I did find my mother out there somewhere, she would bring me back. Mother might not want me. And, being five years old, I could not think of anyone else to whom I might go.

The schoolyard was part of a residential school maintained by a religious order primarily for Indian children. I was there because, I suppose now, it happened to be available at a time in Mother's life when it was needed. The Indian children felt the same despair as I did. It hung in the air.

In the years after I left the residential school, whenever I went to see cowboy movies, I always cheered for the Indians. When the Indians took a beating, everybody else hooted and threw flattened popcorn boxes like Frisbees. When the Indians gave it back, I hollered and threw my popcorn box alone. Occasionally I would prod my mother for information. The recollection that stuck most in her mind on the subject of natives was of the Indian women coming to Kenora and pulling their blankets about them when they needed to squat and defecate, as was permitted in the Woodlands tradition. I do not think Mother was unique in her attitude, and she never expressed any animosity towards natives. They were simply marginal to her existence.

Other newcomers apparently found the natives not merely irrelevant but an irritant. Following the "Wounded Knee" crisis in the spring of 1973, some of the non-native inhabitants of Kenora published a local newsletter entitled *Bended Elbow*. By then I was arguing as a young lawyer on the Indians' side in the North American native renaissance that seemed to be surfacing in delayed reaction to the Civil Rights movement of the 1960s.

At the residential school in 1949 the Indian students tried to tease me out of my despair. In the evenings they followed me around the common room like a troupe of Congo line dancers, cajoling me and making long faces as I prowled and paced the caged-animal circuit from window to window, expecting to see Mother coming to rescue me. The native children knew what I was going through. They had all in one way or another experienced the same thing, and far worse. For this school was intended to eradicate the culture that segregated them as savages from the benefits of civilization. Like me, many of the Indians in the residential school were desperately lonely. In contrast with my situation, where my mother had put me there, they had been taken forcibly from home. My mother had consented; the Indian children's mothers had not.

The residential school system was a bad experience, even though some of my complaints sound trivial from the perspective of secure adulthood. Once when Mother visited she brought some *Casper the Friendly Ghost* comics. She left me behind in spite of my whinging and I slept, exhausted by my overwrought state. When I woke my comics were gone. None of the nuns knew what had happened to them. After a frantic search I finally found them outside in the oil drum the school used to burn trash. Faced with this evidence, a nun explained it was she who had purloined my treasure for my own good because the comics trifled with the "Ghost." She kept them. Her power over me superseded Mother's. I alternated between desolation and fear.

When Mother next came to visit, I told on the nun. Again Mother left me behind when visiting hours ended. Late that night the head nun came to my bedside in the dormitory. She said I had better lie on my side with my hands palm-to-palm in prayer fashion forming a pillow for my head and to keep still. "Do not ever again," she commanded calmly but firmly, "tell stories to your mother against us who are helping you." I assumed the worst and put my hands under my head and kept still. I felt they could tell if I was looking around even if they were not in the room. Eventually I slept. For as long as I was there that was how I got to sleep. Oddly enough, it still works.

I never encountered sexual abuse in the residential school. When the boys showered, we did so in the presence of the nuns, but always with our underwear on. In later years I listened to testimony by several native adults who were sexually abused as children in these schools. An elderly woman recalled how as an eight year old she had been induced on several occasions to take the priest's penis into her mouth. A young man remembered being sodomized repeatedly – not brutally, but disturbingly. Both had been favoured residents and were rewarded as such in many ways. Both blocked the memories for years and eventually sought professional help.

The old woman and the young man tried to make me understand that the main point was not the sexual character of the abuse but their powerlessness – that they were disposable, owned. Both explained that the sexual aspect only obscured the overall horror for a native child thrust into white society. It was a symptom, not the problem. It was not the sexual aspect of the abuse that tore them apart inside long after the events, but the institutionalized injustice that invaded the central core of their beings. It was not the priests but the whole of the society backing them – all the power, all the force, overwhelming, omnipresent, omniscient.

There at the residential school I was an individual with adjustment problems relative to aspects of my own culture, having some of my edges rounded. The Indians were there to be broken and reformatted, emotionally, culturally, and spiritually, to be remade in the image of more "civilized" beings. I escaped. They did not. When, years later, I took up the Indians' search for justice, I listened to many stories much worse than my own. Each one would take me back to the unhappiness of my childhood and the despair would be relived, but redoubled with sadness for their greater pain.

Without exception, the native people who have shared with me the seemingly infinite variations of their personal stories of pain have all ended at the same bedrock of angst. Pain is not the problem, or suffering. These difficulties are perennial, inevitable, fatalistically accepted as part of the human condition, and stoically abided – in the Indian Way. The basic problem is the lack of respect. It diminishes and destroys the self. This contempt is the basis of the angst that is driving the native people to self-destruction. It is the institutionalized, implacable, complacent, and artful injustice of the white man that is killing the native people from within.

These experiences increasingly wore on my conscience after the trial of the Ogoki Indian. I tried to find in my past a rational explanation for the strong feelings I was experiencing after hearing the widow's cry of anguish. Was I losing objectivity and impairing my function as a lawyer? Maybe I was programmed to think of myself as a widow-rescuer, a male role model instilled by my aunts in the absence of a father figure. Maybe I was programmed by the residential school experience to identify with and be sympathetic to Indian pain.

There was something in the conjunction of the Cochrane trial, the Kenora trial, my knowledge of my Bear Island clients, and my early childhood that made me question how to fulfill my duty as a lawyer. The flight back to Haileybury from Kenora after the trial contributed to my inquiry. It took me through the United States and back into Canada at Sault Ste Marie, where Lake Superior meets Lake Huron. From there it was over the Sudbury region of northern Ontario, then to Lakes Temagami and Temiskaming close by northern Quebec.

Another returning, another set of memories and speculations to sort through as the hours alone in the plane stretched out. It was to Sudbury that Mother and I had gravitated after Whitehorse. She had been born in Sudbury and was offered a job there as a secretary for the Canadian Immigration Department. From grade four at age nine through high school at age nineteen, I was educated in Sudbury. The region is a world-renowned environmental catastrophe – a fact that influences my predilection towards the environmental dimension of the aboriginal rights issue.

The mining basin, which accounts for the city of Sudbury, was created by a huge meteorite. Extraordinarily rich mineral deposits resulted, ranging over many thousand square miles of Ontario north and east of Lake Huron. When these deposits of ore were discovered in the late 1800s, gigantic open-pit smelters were constructed. The ore was smelted in the pits by laying in huge beds of timber, clear cut from the surrounding forests that had blanketed the rolling hills of granite of the Laurentian Shield. The ore to be smelted was laid on top, then more timber, then more ore, and so on. The fires were lit and burned, relaid, relit and reburned, until eventually the smelted ore was collected from the exhausted fire pit.

Sulphur dioxide gas, a by-product of this process, rolled out over the surrounding terrain. The small plants remaining in the sea of stumpage left from the timber harvesting were killed. The rains washed away the soils. The pre-Cambrian bedrock became exposed, to look much as it must have some 12,000 years before when the glaciers had finished scraping their way north: black rock, no trees, no grasses, no plants, no topsoil. In fact, in the early stages of the American space program, the astronauts went to Sudbury to practise techniques for walking on the moon.

While I was growing up in Sudbury, Mother and I rented a basement bedsitter at the city's outskirts, half a block from these black granite hills. At dusk I liked to climb into the ranges, nestle down in their folds, and fingertip the grooved surfaces where the retreating glaciers had ground on their ponderous northward migration. All the grooves on the rock surface lined up north-south, as did the countless lakes and rivers I could see later as I piloted my plane.

When I was seven, I used to imagine myself a witness to the rains, the winds, and the frosts that were working a soil from the rock, and to the blanket of trees and ferns that would gradually spread upward from the south. Then I could see the green driven back, apprehend the noise of the clear-cutting saws, and smell the smelters' sulphur fumes. The rains and winds took back the soils. Sometimes the bedrock seemed sad for the loss of the company of that warming blanket; sometimes it just seemed strong, invincible, indifferent. There is majesty in rock laid bare as it is around Sudbury, exposed blackness set in the endless forest.

When the darkening sky and the black rock blended into one at the horizon, the far-distant creaking and clanging of the smelter trains would start up. Waiting, I lit a little pile of dry white twigs culled from nooks and crannies in the bedrock. The hand-size fire held back the cold and the dark, as it might have done for a cave person. The noise of the rail cars fluctuated in and out in intensity as the wind fluttered and gusted. The train tracks were laid on the slag formed from the dumped molten waste that fractured as it cooled into broken pottery lumps the size of tea cups. When the curtain of debris grew too far from the edge of the track to permit the fiery liquid to pour down the side of the tip, the tracks would be taken up and relaid closer to the edge, ready to receive the next creaking train adding its slag to the advancing wall.

When the noise stopped, my eyes, raised from the fire light, met absolute darkness. But, where the noise had last been heard would appear, suspended in the blackness, an orange-red eye as the first of the rail cars tipped on its side, exposing its mouth and disgorging its molten cargo. As the tapering red stalactite of lava flowed down the unseen side of the slag heap, its light faded and died to a glow. Another car would tip, then another and another, until a necklace of fifteen glowing columns was suspended in its pitch-black frame. Neon-red silhouetted against the infinite, inexorable, and devouring black occupied all the spaces of my mind.

With the exception of these night vigils and similarly intense daytime forays to Ramsay Lake, which borders Sudbury, my early school days were filled with friends and youngsters' escapades. Like many of my friends, I expected to finish high school and get a job, probably in Sudbury. But when I was twelve a door was opened to another world and other possibilities. In our elementary school at about grade seven, every student was given aptitude and intelligence tests. The woman interpreting the tests then spoke privately with the students, to help them decide whether to enrol in high school technical studies or to pursue academic courses. When I told her that I could not go to university because my mother's income as a secretary precluded that choice, she explained I would have no problem getting scholarships.

Mother joined in my dream-weaving that night. I told her I would buy her a fur coat, a car, and a house of our own – the material things that we never had. Although she thanked me, she reassured me that the only things that really mattered to her were health and happiness, and the only way to get them was by being true to ourselves. The possibility of dreams becoming reality was particularly sweet because, at that time, we were living in a one-bedroom apartment above a confectionery store which was infested with cockroaches. My challenge on arriving home, especially in the winter when it was already dark after school, was to switch on the lights and dispatch as many of the scurrying-for-cover little monsters as possible. I sometimes wonder whether I entered the practice of law because of an affinity for the cockroaches of my youth which lawyers as a class so much resemble, scurrying after the materialistic crumbs of life, heedless of idealistic head-games like justice as the application of truth to affairs.

School was interminable from age twelve to twenty-seven, when I was called to the bar to take the oath that allowed me to practise as a lawyer. Periodically I was saved from quitting school only by the gallantry and compassion of particular teachers, one of whom always seemed to be around to stop the levelling lawnmower of mass public education from cutting off my head. For me, adjusting to the petty injustices and irrationalities to which people must conform in order to function as social beings never came easily – especially since, as a lawyer-to-be, my cherished destiny was to ensure that justice in all things should triumph for all people, including me. I wanted to understand the point of whatever rule was threatening to deprive me of my liberty – to ensure that the purpose the rules were serving justified the liberty sacrificed to them. This personality "defect" forever got me into trouble as a potential nonconformist. I always did end up conforming, but rarely unquestioningly, a trait that, to some teachers, equated me with being a troublemaker, especially to those who had no imagination to question on their own.

At the age of fourteen I was shot at close range in the thigh with a 20-gage shot-gun while hunting with a school friend near his family's cottage on the French River between Lake Nipissing and Georgian Bay. He had been slogging along a few steps ahead of me on an abandoned logging road when he suddenly turned around, raised his gun, and said, "Draw, partner." Joke. Roar. I looked down at my left pant leg, which was shredded and pock-marked with hundreds of holes. "You shot me," I said. "No," he replied. "Yes." "No." We discussed this back and forth, single-word style, until I fell over on the road and he ran for help.

As I lay in the road and watched white puffy clouds whip across a bright blue fall sky, I decided I was bleeding to death. I waited. The leg was numb at first, and I really didn't feel too much. Then he arrived with his father and we started a two-hour journey out of the bush to a hospital in Sudbury, perhaps 50 miles away. I was complaining loudly and furiously to the nurses, overstating the agony that seemed to take over my being, for they declined to give me anything for pain until the doctors arrived and made decisions about operating and anesthesia. Mother walked into the operating room and up to the table on which I lay. I lied to her that I was fine and in no pain because my leg was numb, and that if I were going to die I would have died already, but I hadn't. She left. A nurse came to me and said I was a good kid for toning it down so mother wouldn't panic. Later in life, whenever things have seemed insurmountable, I have always had this memory to go back to – that I could have died but didn't, so life afterwards was a gift anyway, and if you think about another's pain your own gets pushed back, and you get credit for being good.

It is odd that I should have survived law school, which, next to military academies and Indian residential schools, is the greatest device for training people to think the same way. Every year law schools churn out thousands of minds, like model-T Fords – each one interchangeable with any of its set and capable of being serviced anywhere. Conformity is the point: creating similar minds that can communicate in similar terms in important matters such as the legal rights and obligations that provide structure to that society. By this device, great human diversity can co-exist with predictability and order in human affairs.

By the time I received my call to the bar, after earning my LLB at the University of Western Ontario, I had decided I wanted to practise in a small town. The last thing I wanted was one big client whose whims might encroach my liberty. First I wanted freedom, which to me meant many little clients. And I wanted variety, which meant no specializing. General practice was the ticket. I would make friends with young people like myself, help them with their marriage contracts, defend them when they argued and got charged for drunk driving, sue for them when their neighbour's tree fell on their house, prepare their wills, be there to console the survivor and probate the estate when one predeceased the other, and be buried in the same cemetery as those ordinary folks I had been privileged to serve.

Every year the *Law List* in Ontario publishes lawyers' names and addresses, by city, town, and village, giving the population figures and basic information about the closest courthouse, jail, and land registration office. My search for the best small town for my particular life plan began with this book. I calculated the lawyer-to-population ratios for all the small towns. With a population of 5000 and only one listed lawyer, the town of Haileybury in northern Ontario had a ratio of 2500 to 1, including me, if I went there. The other lawyer was seventy years old, a Rhodes scholar and widely reputed courtroom rascal, bon vivant, gentleman-of-the-old-school, and charmer – the perfect competitor. Almost everywhere else the field was full of aggressive, ambitious, unprincipled young opportunists. Also, the lawyer-to-population ratio elsewhere was consistently in the 700 to 1 range. I went to look Haileybury over.

An office was available on the second floor of the town bank. It had been unoccupied for twenty years, but was divided into two parts by an oak partition that was wainscoted at the bottom, but at the top allowed light to pass through panes of bumpy glass. From the outside window I could see Lake Temiskaming, headwaters of the great Ottawa River, and could almost see the creek mouth that used to carry Indians' canoes from up and down the lake westward to Lake Temagami in the early days of the fur trade. Out the door, down the stairs, and up the hill, only 50 yards away from the lake, was the district land registry office. This meant real estate transactions and agency work. Another 50 yards farther up the hill was the District Court House, a turn-of-the-century classic – highly polished battleship-brown linoleum throughout, windows and doors 12 feet high, 15-foot ceilings, dark-wood wainscoting everywhere. A farther 75 yards up the hill was the District Jail, a holding facility for a huge area of the sparsely populated and largely Indian-occupied country to the north. A real old-style jail, one in which every closing of every door clanged throughout the three-storey edifice.

I took the office, put up my shingle, and settled in for life. The real estate, wills, and estates clients trickled in slowly. Lawyers were not permitted to advertise in those days. Success depended on doing a good job and word of mouth. But from the start business at the jail was booming. My competitor left that field to me. He'd had enough of that sort of work in his forty years at the bar. So, by age twenty-nine, when city lawyers my age were still carrying senior partners' briefcases en route to serious criminal trials, I was carrying my own briefcase to them. I thought I was in heaven. It was like acting in television courtroom drama, only it was all for real – or, for a while, seemed real. The problem was that, for my Indian clients at least, it was all perfectly unreal, a drama put on by players operating on culturally foreign cue cards they could not comprehend. As the accused persons, they were supposed to be the stars of the performance, yet they were more like furniture set on the stage in a play that went on around them, but hardly involved them, in a theatre of the absurd.

CHAPTER 2

My Introduction to Indian Law and Culture

On 11 February 1973 the Temagamis of Bear Island retained me to defend their native sovereignty. According to their oral history, their ancestors had never signed a treaty. I was forced into an active search for answers to questions of whose existence I had until then had only ill-defined suspicions.

Local newspapers had announced that the Ontario government planned to build an $80 million ski resort on what it regarded as public land at Maple Mountain. But the Temagamis regarded themselves as the stewards of that mountain. In their language it is named Chee'Bai'Gin, which means "Where the spirits go." It is the place where life began again in this world after the last cycle was destroyed, the site where life's essence returns. Maple Mountain is the highest elevation in northeastern Ontario, a height of land that establishes three continental watershed regions. To the north flow the waters to James Bay. To the southwest flow the rivers to Lake Huron. To the southeast drain the waters of the upper Ottawa River, which empties into the St Lawrence River by Montreal.

The Temagamis explained to me that Chee'Bai'Gin was the first land to emerge when the waters inundating earth receded. At that time the great-feline-serpent-water-being sent forth from its earth-womb-cavern at this place a raven-person, to scout for land on which to establish the new world order. Raven returned to Serpent with a piece of clay. More land emerged and from the cave came the person-beings that graduated into the ancestors of the Temagamis: plant-people, winged-people, crawling-people, insect-people, four-legged and two-legged people, all of whom collectively and severally constitute the sound-light-spirit-being-essence made corporeal out of the earth-air-water-fire elements of tangible existence.

Intuitively I found myself drawn in sympathy to the Temagamis' Creation account. New life was generated in and emerged from the warm, wet, and dark womb of the Earth-Mother, rather than in and from the outer space of the Heavenly Father's supreme reason and calculating intellect. The Creator was envisaged as a force or principle beyond male or female, not as a bearded patriarch fashioning an Adam in his own image. In place of the phallic symbolism triumphantly broadcast by church spires and the mosque minarets, the Temagamis' serpent phalicism was set quietly at home in the earth-womb. The natives' serpent itself was generative, not corrupting like the one in mystical Eden. Their view of creation was egalitarian and respectful of all life forms, rather than hierarchical and élitist. It was not that the Temagamis were anti-Christian; many of them wore crosses around their necks. But their world-view was more tolerant and less judgmental, demanding, or punitive than the Christian tradition with which I was familiar. It was not overtly feminist at the cost of devaluing masculinity, but equally accommodating of the feminine. It was not so much balancing feminine and masculine as above the pettiness of the competition implied by the concept of balance.

The first maps of this portion of the New World, drawn in France in the 1600s, were based on what the Indians to the south and the north of Chee'Bai'Gin told the first European explorers and fur traders entering the St Lawrence and James Bay watersheds. The phrase "Pays des Sorciers" was emblazoned across the Temagami region and sufficed in place of any detail. In the early 1980s the regional archaeologist for northeastern Ontario stuck straight pins with red plastic heads into a topographical map of northeastern North America, depicting the known rock-painting sites. The Chee'Bai'Gin area was completely blotted out by the pins. No other place came close to such an intense concentration. And the natives' religious statements were recorded in the intimacy and privacy of caves, nooks, and crannies or under rock overhangs at the water's edge, again evidencing respect for the feminine principle. The religious symbols were not hung in the hard light as if in masculine challenge, but quieted away in soft, dark places.

Immediately to the south of Chee'Bai'Gin begins the northernmost reach of one of Lake Temagami's long spider-like arms. Here Wendaban, the last Temagami medicine man overtly practising magic and renowned throughout the northeast for his powers, occupied an island palisaded by bear skulls set on stakes. At the turn of the twentieth century, indigenous people from all around went there for cures and guidance, not because Wendaban made the place magic but because it was understood that the place itself was charged with power.

Bear Island, still farther to the south at the lake's hub, was said to have achieved its name because it had many berries that attracted the bears, the arch spiritual protectors of the land. Whenever the bear spirit allowed its body to be taken to sustain the human-people, those few parts of the bear that could not be consumed were reconsecrated to the adjacent waters, from which that bear's spirit would reconstitute his body and make it live again – thus fulfilling the great mystery of the cycle of a spiritual force reconstituting corporeal existence. By borrowing the bear's flesh for energy and its fur for warmth, the hunter interrupted not only the cycle of continuity that is bearness but also the cycle that is all things.

The difference between bearness and all thingsness is similar to that between the form of one circle and the form constituted by an interwoven infinity of circles. The single exists on a flat surface. If you introduce another circle into the same plane of existence, you must enter it on another dimension, since the first dimension is occupied. As you introduce the fish cycle, the insect cycle, the human cycle, and so on, eventually you create a sphere composed of all the circles that do in fact constitute collective existence in three dimensions.

This perception takes the old-style indigenous person to the threshold of his sense of reality, for the complete reality exists in a magic realm that includes dimensions that can be felt but not stated, intuited but not calculated. The full sense is reaffirmed by the ceremony that returns the bones to the spirit dimension wrapped in the regalia of honour. In this way humankind affirms its own integration in and identity with the continuity of the sphere of circles that constitutes cyclic reality, and whose identity extends beyond the material world and merges in the mystery of collective spiritual existence.

Although told to newcomers like me in terms of the bear's bones invoking the bear's spirit, or the fish's bones invoking the fish's spirit, in the Temagamis' worldview there was no set of separate spirits arrayed like the Greek pantheon of anthropomorphized gods. Human bones were treated the same way, but not every individual's bones, any more than every bear's bones or every fish's bones. Some were honoured as representative of the principle of humanness, or bearness or fishness, as the case might be. The general force that is inherent in all things animate and inanimate reconstitutes existence. A reminder of each form and facet of existence is drawn to the attention of the unified force that is the collective sum of all forces, and in this way it contains within itself each individual form and facet of existence. It is to this all-is-one-and-one-is-all worldview that the native people paid tribute to when saluting "all my relations" – the principle of unity.

Some years after I left Bear Island I sat at a potlatch on Vancouver Island. The overlord hereditary chief of the north half of the island sat beside me. As each dance and song took its turn he explained the message to me. The dances acted out how humans evolved through all the other life forms while retaining within themselves, as a continuing and integral part of their human essence, those other life forms. The chief's comments gave me a fresh understanding of the meaning of the Jungian collective unconscious and of the concept for which Einstein was reaching when he postulated the Unified Field. The magicians and the mathematicians seemed to be saying the same thing, using different languages.

And at the centre of each process of understanding seemed to be a conviction or at least an assumption that the search was for the truth. This may be the reason that traditional native people, the bush Indians, do not lie about events in court. The lie, as a way of life, threatens their definition of self at the most profound level, for it denies not merely the integrity but the continuity of life. For this reason, the negation of the absolute truth in favour of the relative truth in the new-comers' court system is life-threatening to traditional natives dragged through that system. The nature and character of the values implemented by the actors within that court system, such as the values of the other defence lawyer at the Cochrane murder trial, refuted the existence of absolute truth and challenged the essential premise of the natives' being. A lie about a fact or an event in the material world threatens the equilibrium of reality, and therefore threatens the existence of self.

But that threat does not exist relative to promises about future conduct. Promises are not material, not integrated into physical reality. They are only expressions of intent, or mental constructs. The pejorative "Indian giver" I began to suspect may have stemmed in some fashion from this phenomenon. True, empirical evidence may be adduced that native people historically have made false promises, just as non-natives have, but that does not mean that they are equally loose with statements that describe physical reality or history. To break a promise risks no cataclysm, since the promise is only an idea. The reason for the pipe ceremony at treaty-making time was explained to me as having to do with rendering promises binding. The smoke carries the thought that constitutes the promise into the fabric of Creation. Thereafter, the promise cannot be broken without risking a tear in that fabric. The idea has become structurally significant, as are assertions concerning physical facts and oral history. Literal truth is a condition of continuity, of being in these contexts. It was for this reason that I knew for certain that the Temagamis had not made treaty promises. If they had, the promises would be constitutive of their sense of reality, about which they could not possibly be lying.

The relationship among respect, truth, law, and justice increasingly became a preoccupation for me. The more I listened to the Indian Way, the more I was drawn into translating the natives' assertions into the jurisprudential context. If, I began to ask myself, the Indians have something to teach the rest of humanity about world-views in general, how might that teaching have an impact on the definition, implementation, and fulfilment of the rule of law and the quest for justice by humanity in general? My fascination with Bear Island and its Indian culture deepened with this awareness that fresh answers might be available to some of the most basic questions that have long perplexed human civilization.

The island itself happens to be only 1 square mile in area. On its south end is an Indian village of 150 people whose mostly government-built houses are strung out along the shore, another suburbia in the wilderness. Except for this south end, the rest of the island is virtually uninhabitable. Rocky hillsides drop straight into the deep water. At the water's edge of one of its shear cliff faces, tucked into a cranny under a rocky overhang, is a triangular figure painted in ochre, a red rock dye that the people said was harvested near a small lake in the southern range of the traditional territory. The figure represents the Thunderbird

Spirit. It must have been painted from a canoe, since there is no shelf on which to stand to give access to its hidden place. As always with the ancient pictographs, it was placed protectively and discreetly, and the people do not talk about it. When I happened upon it and asked, they explained the tradition, but they would not have drawn my attention to it. It was invested with magic.

Everywhere, there was magic. Like the opening line of Gerard Manly Hopkins's poem "God's Grandeur," the Temagami region was "charged with the grandeur of God." The magic was not seen by Temagami informants as things separate from and opposed to the Creator, but as an aspect of the mystery of the spiritual power or force that is God.

At the foot of every fast-moving body of water live the Mihmeh'gwessy, the little people who dwell in the rocks and for whom the wise and caring traveller will always leave a small gift of tobacco before passing by. A great split rock, named seal rock, marks the point below which lived the "great seal" that caused the phenomenon. Every rock outcropping, every stream in the delicate lacework that makes up the water network that holds the territory together, every lake that is sprinkled over the land has a name, a story, a personality, a life. Every fish, every animal, every insect, every tree, every breeze is the receptacle, the embodiment, of the spirit of its kind. Every life that is borrowed to sustain life is a gift from its possessor, on temporary loan, to be revered lest the spirit take insult and refuse to assume corporeal form capable of again being borrowed. As with the bear's bones, the bones of the fish, the deer, the moose, and the beaver, the fibers of plants, and all things taken and harvested which are not used are, with respect, submerged in order to be reconstituted by their respective spirits, to live again, and again to sustain life.

As I learned more of this viewpoint, I came to understand that the consequence of Ontario's assumption that it could use the natives' homeland would be the desecration of a sacred area. It was not only the development of Chee'Bai'Gin that for commercial purposes that the Temagamis found threatening. The remaining vestiges of the once-great stands of white and red pine, which were originally responsible for the creation of the Temagami Forest Preserve, were being threatened by the timber industry. Open-pit mining was gouging holes in the surface of the hillsides. And the devastation caused by nickel smelting in the Sudbury basin promised to be exported to the Temagami region. The Temagamis shuddered at the prospect of that blackened wasteland swallowing the green of their homeland.

The Ontario government had introduced environmental legislation that curtailed the dumping of the Sudbury smelter's daily ration of tons of sulphur dioxide gases and other processing wastes into the air. Towering smokestacks addressed the environmental problem by throwing the poisons higher into the winds, dispersing them over a wider circumference. The sulphur dioxide, mixed with moisture in the atmosphere, was being spread out over a larger area than the

Sudbury basin, to which the pollution had been restricted by the more primitive technology of earlier years. Now the pollution was being dropped on the Chee'Bai'Gin/Temagami region to the north and east of Sudbury precisely because that was how the prevailing winds blew the product of the higher smoke-stacks. In terms of tonnage, the amount of pollution rising out of Sudbury was reputed to be the equivalent of all the airborne waste produced by the New York and Chicago industrial regions combined.

In order not to have the smelter corporation excessively or inappropriately burdened with litigation complaining of cancers and property damage caused by the pollution, the Ontario government enacted a Sulphur Fumes Arbitration Act. This statute precluded any allegedly injured person or persons from seeking injunctions or obtaining damage awards that might inhibit the pollution. Besides, from the point of view of the Ontario legislation, my clients, being Indians, were not property owners in relation to their ancestral homeland. Only people holding deeds issued by Ontario were regarded under the legislation to be property owners, and only property owners could sue for damages. Indians occupying territory on the basis of aboriginal title were excluded. In any event, my Indian clients told me they did not want to seek monetary damages under the Sulphur Fumes Arbitration Act. They wanted to prevent the damage, not be compensated for it.

The problem was exacerbated when, in a move designed to appease not only the environmentalists of southern Ontario but also the voters of Sudbury, northern Ontario's most populous centre, the smelter corporation built one great big smokestack to replace the six that formerly had served as the dispersing agents. This new stack is overwhelming in its immensity. At night while the people sleep, its mighty engines increase from quarter power to three-quarters power, shaking the immediately adjacent town of Copper Cliff and vibrating the earth for miles beyond. In consequence, the pollution now leapfrogs the moonscape at Sudbury and lands directly on the greenbelt that is Chee'Bai'Gin/Temagami. My clients heard the great stack's promotional advertising with widening eyes. At the same time, they watched the published lake-pollution and fish-mortality statistics relative to their own homeland increase drastically. These statistics confirmed what they had been experiencing in fact: the arms of the lake in the northern half of their territory were dead or approaching dead; the level of acidity had gone beyond that in which fish can survive; and the rocky nature of the lake bottoms precluded the acid being biodegraded or absorbed. About half the myriad interrelated lakes in their territory, the smaller and shallower lakes, were already dead. The scientific prognosis for the balance was "death within five years at current fallout levels." In the southern half of the territory, the prognosis was "acid-dead within ten to twenty-five years."

The basic long-term survival philosophy of the Temagamis was dramatically threatened. Like many traditional Indians, their philosophy allowed for nature being able to absorb the white man's onslaught and then bounce back. On the basis of their past experiences with the fur trade and the timber and mining industries, a self-correcting sequence was taken for granted: the white man comes, he takes all the fur-bearing animals, all the trees, all the ore, and then he moves on. The mine shafts are overgrown, the trees regenerate, the animals filter back home. There is no point in trying to stop the white man, but neither is there any long-term need: Mother Earth heals herself in spite of the white man who, in that sense, is just another natural catastrophe. Wait, and all will eventually return to balance.

But now the death of the traditional fish resource was imminent. That resource was created as the one inexhaustible and sustaining source of life energy. Regardless of the trees and the animals, the Fish Spirit alone would feed the people and carry them through. Now, even the Fish Spirit was being eclipsed by the shadow of death cast upon the lands and waters by the white man. And if the acid could kill or drive away the Fish Spirit, perhaps the Tree Spirit too would not come back. Perhaps the acid would kill the soil no less than the water. Certainly the trees that the timber companies were replanting were of a completely different kind. Where once there had been magnificent stands of slow-growing white and red pine, now there were stands of the fast-growing jack pine, an ugly thing of commercial value only for the rapid rate of growth of its cellulose mass. And even then the planting was such an obvious fraud, with seedlings placed only in sight of the tourist corridors but leaving a wasteland beyond, like the false fronts on the buildings in Hollywood westerns. The crests of the hills were the only places left to remind the people of the once-great stands of pines. And they survived only because the crests were ruled off-limits to the timber harvesters. A narrow band of trees was left on the profile of those hilltops visible from the tourist corridors. This "skyline reserve" created the misleading but comforting impression that what is visible is representative of the trees, rather than lone sentinels overlooking scrub in place of forest.

If the forest could forever be changed, perhaps the Animal Spirits also would not return. Even if they did make it back, how would their spirits recognize their homeland? Would they pass on by, looking for, but never finding, their original home?

On the technical side, the first thing I had to try to do on behalf of the Temagamis was obtain a temporary injunction against the commercial development of Chee'Bai'Gin, pending the sorting out of the legal issues. The problem at first seemed insurmountable. Here I had a set of clients whose legal position, stripped to its bare essentials, was simply that they were a sovereign people in a sovereign land, subject to no power other than that of the Creator. "Show us where we gave this up," they challenged me. "Or show us where your race of people conquered ours." I could not answer their challenge. Yet I knew that if I were to file papers in the court system in which I worked, I would automatically be relinquishing the very sovereignty they had retained me to assert. The more I pondered the dilemma, the clearer it became that I could not simultaneously relay their assertion of sovereignty, which supposedly gave them exclusive jurisdiction over their homeland, and at the same time file papers which, by the very fact of being filed, acknowledged that the invaders' court system had acquired jurisdiction.

In any rule of law society, whenever a legal dispute exists between two persons, the dispute must be turned over to a third party, a stranger to the dispute, someone whose interest is not affected one way or the other by the outcome. But the court system before which I was allowed to practise clearly was not a disinterested third party vis-à-vis the legal issue of native sovereignty. The Indians' essential legal point was that their own courts had jurisdiction, not the invaders' courts. The Indians had already determined in their own councils that that legal issue was settled. Accordingly, the Temagamis wanted me to enforce their judgment, not to ask the invaders' court to make a judgment. Their legal point was that since there was no treaty, the invaders' court had no jurisdiction.

In this sense the real disputants standing toe to toe were my clients' indigenous court system versus the court system of my own race and culture. For a virtual certainty, human nature being what it is, if I were to ask my own people's court system whether it had for many years past been in the habit of usurping the jurisdiction of the native peoples' court system, my own race's court system would acquit itself. There was definitely a conflict of interest, in the sense of a clear absence of the independence and impartiality without which the rule of law cannot function.

I was forced by these unique circumstances to cast about for a way in which to use the apparatus of the white legal system without conceding jurisdiction to that system, since denying that jurisdiction was the legal point of my native clients' sovereignty position. The Land Titles Act of Ontario seemed to offer promise. This was the statute by which all land in private hands had to be registered. In it was a section referring to a "caution before first registration." The section indicated that a person could give notice of a claim relative to public land. The document recording such a claim was termed a "caution" in keeping with its function: to warn the otherwise unsuspecting purchasers, including the government, of the claim.

The caution procedure made it unnecessary to begin with a court case. It allowed the Indians to dispute the white man's jurisdiction without, by the very process of commencing action in the white court system, conceding jurisdiction. Rather, they could register a document that could effectively freeze the commercial development of Chee'Bai'Gin, but without their first having to accept the jurisdiction of the non-native court system. All the caution need say was that these Indians asserted they were still sovereign and therefore invested with an interest in the so-called public lands of Ontario. The caution document did not have to go further and ask the non-native court system to decide on the validity of that assertion. All it did was record the assertion. Nevertheless, the fact that the assertion was registered effectively warned off the developers. To raise development capital to build the ski resort at Chee'Bai'Gin, the banks advancing the money would want to take back a mortgage securing the repayment of their investment. But for there to be a mortgage, there had to be a private title against which to register it – and the existence of the caution blocked the registration of a private title.

I researched the land titles statutes and the decided judicial decisions about them in all the provinces and states of Canada, the United States, Australia, New Zealand, and South Africa. Nowhere was there a similar section to that appearing in the Ontario legislation. Correspondingly, there was no decision against us. As fitting as the caution-before-first-registration device seemed, there were still some significant technical problems with which to deal before recourse could be had to it. Foremost among them was the requirement that the caution document must be accompanied by a legal description and a survey of the land being put under caution. But my clients' ancestral territory consisted of 4000 square miles of unsurveyed wilderness. The only borders were the natural borders formed by the heights of land, which defined their internal transportation system: the network of lakes, rivers, and streams over which their ancestors had travelled in their canoes and on their toboggans and snow shoes.

Every extended family's internal property line, the line that defined the limits of its own hunting grounds, was guarded by the spirits of that land and the ancestors of those people. Their legal sanctions protecting their family property interests derived as much from the universe of magic as from the use of social force. But the natural and spiritually protected boundaries known to Indian law were not such as to satisfy the requirement of a non-native legal description within the meaning of the Land Titles Act of Ontario. And when I explored the idea of producing a survey to get a caution registered, the official land surveyors informed me that the cost of portraying the height of land and the watershed boundary, though theoretically possible, would be in the millions of dollars. My clients were poor. Their cause was financially unsupported except by me. My law practice, while producing enough to pay the basic courts costs and travel expenses, was not by any stretch of the imagination resulting in millions.

I took up the dilemma introduced by the need for a legal description and a surveyed line with the local land registrar who was charged with implementing the Land Titles Act. We got out the big map of the whole district. I asked him what he could and would accept for registration purposes in light of this cost problem. As we looked at the big map, the first thing that stood out was the small number of places that had already been surveyed and deeded. Each of these places was superimposed on the big map and each bore a number by which it could be located in one of the bound volumes containing the permanent records of ownership to all registered private lands. Each of these private parcels of land had straight line boundaries. So did the township boundaries. Before any private parcels could be created, the whole of the region had been divided into a grid of townships. Then, when portions of the townships were purchased from Ontario, the private parcels so created were deeded away by the province. The surveyors would take as their starting reference points the junctures and intersections of the township lines appearing on the grid for the whole region.

"Suppose," I asked the registrar, "that a person were to give to you a legal description that relied on the already-surveyed lines of the private parcels and the townships, and claimed a right, title, or interest in all the territory that was within the township lines but outside the private parcels?" "How so?" he responded. "Well, a legal description already exists for the townships, right?" "Right," he confirmed. "And a legal description already exists for the parcels?" "Right." "And surveyed lines already accompany those legal descriptions?" "Correct." "Now, the purpose of my providing you with a legal description and a survey of my clients' land is that, if a new deed of public land comes into the registry office for you to process, you will be able to determine whether that deed deals with land that is covered by my clients' caution." "Go on," he urged. "Well, once you know that the deed concerns lands in any of the townships listed in my clients' caution, you will know that a conflict exists. On this basis, will you accept my clients' caution for registration in your office, even though there is no survey directly of the land claimed to be subject to the Indian title?" "Yes," he said. "Why not?"

So I typed the caution document and attached to it my own affidavit swearing that my clients claimed an interest in land entitling them to give notice of their claim. The caution so typed and sworn by me was registered in August 1973. The government of Ontario did everything in its power to get rid of the caution, short of addressing the underlying issue of jurisdiction relative to arguably unpurchased lands. Beginning in 1973 and continuing until 1978, Ontario lodged technical motion after technical motion, each contending that the registration of the caution was defective and should be set aside, regardless of the underlying issue of who had jurisdiction to decide.

A great deal of political pressure was put on the Ontario government and its bureaucrats to get rid of the caution. The local member of the Legislative Assembly himself expressed the general popular outrage in response to the Indians' effrontery. "A case of goof [northern Ontario-speak for cheap fortified wine]," he publicly proclaimed as quoted in the newspapers, "was all it would have taken to buy the land from the Indians. Why is it taking so long to sort this out?" Based as it is on natural resources, the northern Ontario economy is cyclical. Mines are exhausted; forests are depleted; international markets seem arbitrarily to open and close, rise and fall. In consequence, the lives of the non-native inhabitants tend to be borne up by boom times and knocked down in bust times. For a long period it had been bust time, and now the Indians seemed to be making things worse. The Temagamis became scapegoats for the general economic malaise of the region. The local newspaper headline read, "Keep cool, Temagami," and the accompanying article exhorted the local non-native population not to take the law into its own hands. Margaret was in the hospital having just given birth to our daughter, Zoë. One night as I was leaving Bear Island to visit them, my rickety wooden boat was rammed by a launch, which did not stop. My boat sank, but I made it safely to the shore.

Two bright lights seemed to exist on the bleak horizon for this group. One was the $80 million destination ski resort on Maple Mountain. In the immediate future it meant the construction of roads and tourist facilities, and, in the long term, the ongoing business of serving the tourists. The Indians' caution seemed to have killed that economic boost. Second, there was a rumour of a major discovery of ore and the construction of a custom crusher plant and smelter in the northern sector of the cautioned area. Now, because of the Indians' caution, prospectors could no longer register mining claims even if they found them. And the money people would not finance the on-the-ground exploration necessary to complement the airborne grids compiled by the big companies. Any fundraising prospectus would have to contain a legal counsel's opinion that title to the property was clear.

I found myself standing alone at local cocktail parties, or wishing I were alone to escape the litany of complaints laid at my Indian clients' doorstep. Raised eyebrows were gradually but inexorably settling into frowns. By 1978 this native versus newcomer conflict of interest was starting to affect my law practice. The real estate, commercial, estates and wills side that is the bread and butter of any small-town practice started to thin. The time demands for rebuffing Ontario's ever-increasing and more assiduously pressed attempts to nullify the caution made the expansion into criminal law areas impossible. The Indians themselves were still destitute, and the Legal Aid Plan refused to help with their court expenses. The fact was that I was financially underwriting the natives' case, simply because there was no other funding source, and I was bound by honour, sympathy, and professional duty not to drop the case. I had no specific financial agreement with the Temagamis. We had taken each other on faith, and I assumed that if they did well in the courts, they would compensate me. Later, in 1985, they gave me, of their own free will and without any coaching from me, a promissory note for $6 million.

On 1 May 1978 the caution proceedings came to a head. A year previously the local judge had indicated that he was going to conduct an investigation into the legal basis for the Indians' assertion that they were sovereign. By taking on only an investigatory role, this judge was not about to assume a trial jurisdiction that would have, by its very terms of reference, presumed the non-existence of native sovereignty. Rather, he was merely going to investigate. Over the years I had been before this particular judge on several occasions, and in the process I had come to have faith in his prowess as a legal thinker and in his honesty as a person.

When the judge had accepted my argument that he should conduct a judicial investigation rather than a trial, the Ontario government had appealed him and lost. On 1 May 1978 his investigation began. Ontario applied for an adjournment, and the investigation was set over to 12 June. Then, on 17 May, Ontario made a pre-emptive strike to head off the investigation. It filed suit in the Supreme Court of Ontario against the Temagamis. When the investigation resumed on 12 June, Ontario made a motion that the investigation be cancelled, or at least adjourned indefinitely pending the outcome of its Supreme Court action. I opposed Ontario's application on the ground that the rules in the Supreme Court action were not identical to those pertaining to the investigation. Ontario countered this point by undertaking on the record that the Indians would not be prevented by Ontario from doing, saying, or entering into evidence anything in the Supreme Court action that they might have said or done in the investigation. Given Ontario's express and explicit undertaking, there was nothing more that could be done. The investigation was adjourned indefinitely. Subsequently, Ontario was allowed by a Supreme Court judge with impunity to renege on that undertaking.

Ontario next delivered in the Supreme Court action a statement of claim setting out the government's official position: the Temagamis' lands had, by implication, been purchased and, even if they had not, aboriginal rights could not legally be enforced against the non-native government. In short, Ontario pleaded the white man's sovereignty. I delivered on the Temagamis' behalf a statement of defence denying any implicit purchase and, more important, pleading native sovereignty as overriding the Ontario government's claim to sovereignty.

What I failed to do, because I did not at that time have the precedent and constitutional legislation to substantiated the point, was specifically object to the jurisdiction of the Supreme Court of Ontario. I carried out the Indians' instructions by pleading native sovereignty in general, which by implication would in logical terms lead to a rejection of the presumed jurisdiction of the non-native court. If the Indians were sovereign, how could the court of their competitor have jurisdiction? But I did not directly, in black and white terms, object to the assumption of that jurisdiction by the non-native court.

The same week that Ontario commenced its suit against the Indians in the Ontario Supreme Court, I was visited by federal officials from Revenue Canada. I had not yet paid the preceding year's tax bill in the sum of $15,000 and it was three months overdue. Seizing my law firm's books of account, the officials drew to my attention my own records establishing that I had just spent $19,000 out of the firm's revenues on expenses related to the files of the Temagami Indians. Normally, as they also pointed out, lawyers do not pay out of their own pockets major sums in support of clients' cases, at least not in Ontario where contingency fee arrangements were not at that time possible. Normally, lawyers obtain a deposit from the clients to cover out-of-pocket expenses.

"Do you think you are some kind of Robin Hood," asked one of the officers, "stealing from the taxpayers of Canada to pay for the Indians' case?" "Not really," I explained, "but unless I had paid the nineteen thousand dollars myself, the land claim would have foundered, been dismissed for want of prosecution, or lost for want of preparation." The officials came back with the position that it was not open for me, or anyone else in society, to decide on which debt had priority. They declared that the law was perfectly clear that the payment of income tax takes precedence over any other debts.

I had to agree that, within the context of the law as enacted by the federal government, they were absolutely correct. But my legal point, which they declined to address, was that there was a higher constitutional law at issue. "Not to us," they declared. "But what if," I persisted, "my client turns out to be right on the constitutional law? If these Indians are sovereign, in the sense that until there has been a purchase of their land, the Canadian government has no jurisdiction to tax income earned upon or in relation to that unpurchased land, then the very imposition of the tax is illegal. And your endeavour to collect the illegal tax aids and abets the illegality." Well, the officers had heard enough of "this bullshit." Talking law was one thing; telling them they could be criminals was another, and they were having no part of it. They gave me an option: "Either you drop this nonsense of underwriting the Indians' land claim instead of paying the tax outstanding, or we seize your books and send a third-party notice to all your non-native clients."

A third-party notice is a legal form under the Canadian Income Tax Act. When tax officers deliver it to someone who owes the tax debtor money, the person receiving it is required to pay what he owes to the tax debtor directly to Revenue Canada, instead of to the tax debtor. It is similar to a garnishment of wages. It is a useful tax collection device, especially where the tax debtor has no assets that can be seized and sold. By this time I had disposed of my plane and mortgaged all my other assets to raise cash to keep the Indians' cause afloat. I had no assets left. But a lawyer's reputation is his stock in trade and, if that third-party notice were to be sent out, my reputation would be destroyed. No clients would remain. They could not feel secure entrusting the sale or purchase of their home, the estates of their deceased relatives, or their commercial affairs with a lawyer whose books were subject to seizure. Aside from the financial insecurity, legal affairs are highly confidential. Nobody would want to deal with a lawyer knowing that income tax officials would be going through his books and files.

"Can you at least make us a promise to pay your back taxes by instalments, and not to fall behind again?" they asked. "It's not as simple as that," I replied. "I only wish it were. As you know, the Ontario government has just sued my Indian clients in the Ontario Supreme Court and, far from reducing expenses, the time pressure and expense of underwriting their case is going to skyrocket. If I undertake to get caught up right away, for all practical purposes it means dropping the

Indians' case. And I'm not prepared to do that." "So," they said, "you are just going to continue to borrow from the income tax department to pay for the land claim? No way. Either you pay us, or you steal from us – there is no middle ground. Non-payment is stealing. And do not tell us we are the crooks. Federal law is a sure thing. Your imagination about a higher constitutional law is just that – imagination – until the Canadian courts agree with you."

The concept that was most difficult – indeed, utterly impossible – for the officers to grasp was that Canada had no constitutional jurisdiction to tax in relation to unceded Indian territory. Part of the reason for their resistance, I suppose, is the immensity of the consequence. The unceded Indian territory in Canada is, by some estimates, 80 per cent of the country's land mass, if arguably invalid Indian treaties are included. The tax income on which the country conducts its affairs, by this reckoning, is largely stolen from trespassers in the Indian territory. Canada, like the United States, taxes on the basis of residence. The fundamental taxation idea is that a resident of the country pays tax on his or her world income, subject to tax setoffs under treaties with other countries where residence is shared and which tax on the same basis. But residence on unceded Indian territory is constitutionally illegal – indeed, criminally so – according to the Royal Proclamation of 1763. It is not just that Canada has no jurisdiction in those territories but that the taxation revenue is derived from a criminal source, thereby making the government a party to the crime. As to the illegality of such residence, the proclamation is quite clear:

And, We do further strictly enjoin and require all Persons whatever who have either wilfully or inadvertently seated themselves upon any Lands within the Countries above described or upon any other Lands which not having been ceded to or purchased by Us are still reserved to the said Indians as aforesaid forthwith to remove themselves from such Settlements.

Residence in the unceded Indian territories is *prima facie* illegal. By extension, taxation on illegal residence is itself illegal. The illegality is exacerbated when, as in Canada, the consequence of the illegal residence has been, and to some extent still is, the genocide of the native people who are ousted by the trespass. One of the forms of genocide stipulated by article 2(b) of the international Convention for the Prevention and Punishment of the Crime of Genocide, 1948, is the imposition of "serious bodily or mental harm" on a targeted group or class of people. There is no question that the illegal occupation of the Indian territories by newcomers both caused and causes such harm.

The choice was apparent: either I drop my Indian clients to concentrate on rebuilding my non-native clientele, or the income tax department would deliver the third-party notices that would obliterate all traces of that non-native clientele. "The choice," they said, "is yours." "No," I replied, "the choice is yours." On this basis we parted, they with my books, I with my honour – or at least with my impression of the conditions on which that honour was premised.

The tax officials had not been party to the private ceremony by which I had become a blood brother to the chief of the Temagamis, nor would any explanation of the significance of that event have made any difference to them. It bound me. It did not bind them. In the summer of 1973, before I registered the caution in August, the chief and I sat at my kitchen table in Haileybury. He told me of his people's rage and fear. I informed him of the risk to me, personally, of underwriting his people's land claim. At that time it was illegal for lawyers in Ontario to do so. The crime is termed "maintenance and champerty," an ancient common law tradition which holds that only people who can afford the courts should be in court. If lawyers were to underwrite litigation, the fear was that people without property would make life uncomfortable for those with property. The legal aid system had already refused to help with the cost on the ground that it could not get involved in class actions. Even more important were the judicial decisions concerning a specific provision in the Land Titles Act of Ontario with regard to cautions. Before a caution can be registered, the lawyer doing the registering has to swear that his clients have a good case. If, in due course, the clients' case is thrown out, the decisions held that the lawyer was liable in damages to anyone affected by the caution before it was thrown out. The damages flowing from freezing 4000 square miles of land promised to be substantial. It was quite clear in the summer of 1973 that, by taking the step of swearing the affidavit to register the caution, I would be crossing a Rubicon. It was equally clear that the Indians' chance of winning in the white man's system was remote, that the white man's system had the power, and that, regardless of what the law might say, power might be what counted in the final analysis. Lastly, it was also clear that the struggle could go on for many years.

The chief had raised the spectre of having no alternative. If the law would not help his people, where could he and they turn? Did I want them to follow a scorched earth policy? The burning of the forests would, from the ugliness of the resulting wasteland, undermine the provincial plan to desecrate Chee'Bai'Gin. Who would want to go on a ski holiday to stand on a mountain overlooking a wasteland? The burned forest would at least contribute to the depth of the soil, enriching it for later generations of trees.

But what about the acid rain from the Sudbury stack? It would fall on soil unprotected by any cover and, rather than gaining, the soil would be lost all the quicker. Back and forth we went – weighing in the balance the competing claims upon our honour. We were both twenty-nine years old and took ourselves very seriously. At last we agreed: the only thing consistent with both our honour and our inclination was to fight back against the perceived injustice, but with law, not violence. The problem was too big to be stopped by burning one forest in one region. To us, the injustice lay upon the whole country, smothering not just the Temagamis but Indian people from coast to coast.

We decided. We cut and bound our wrists, and paid silent tribute to the spirits of the land we were by that act pledged mutually to exhaust our lives in saving. Five years later, the night of the day the income tax officers gave me the ultimatum to drop the land claim or be professionally destroyed, I began the move of my family to Bear Island. Over that night and the next morning my staff and I packed the office. The next afternoon my family and I were gone. In the days that followed I made arrangements for the lawyer-in-training who was in my former office to accompany my other clients' files to a cooperating local lawyer. The bridges to non-native society burned behind us. Margaret and I embarked permanently on our adventure into Indian country, and the next phase of their quest for respect for their unsurrendered sovereignty.

CHAPTER 3

Moving Deeper into Indian Culture

The hurdle that faces Indians whenever they seek to raise the subject of their own sovereignty is the non-natives' assumption that if there were no white courts and no white law, there would be anarchy. People are by nature ethnocentric. The suppression of the natives' own previously established laws and courts has been in place for a long time. Added to ethnocentrism is the problem of "temporalcentrism": the feeling of inevitability and appropriateness that intuitively attaches to the way things are.

The facile assumption is that the newcomers' laws and courts were drawn into a jurisdictional vacuum. Underlying this questionable premise is the unspoken and unacknowledged racist attitude that the natives were truly savages, without laws or courts of their own. I found this to be both a very old and a very modern misconception. In the seventeenth century, before the level of contact between natives and newcomers was sufficient to disprove this assumption, philosophers such as Hobbes speculated about what life would be like in a society without laws of any kind, as if such a thing were possible, and then assumed that the New World societies fit this imagined condition. In *Leviathan* (1651) he termed the lives of the inhabitants of his hypothetical natural society "nasty, brutish and short."

As contact increased, the blatant error of that assumption could not coexist with the accumulating empirical evidence. Human societies by nature do not exist without laws. To be human is to be a social animal, and to be social involves laws. Different societies might have different laws, but no society would have no laws and still be a society. Hobbes's imaginary lawless society lived in his mind, not in the Americas.

A more accurate observation was recorded on 10 July 1764 by King George III's Lords Commissioners of Trade and Plantations. They were charged under British colonial constitutional law with overseeing legal affairs in North America. Their observation instructed the Indian superintendent for the Northern District of North America, Sir William Johnson, in the official eighteenth-century legal view of native society: "A steady and uniform attachment to, and love of, Justice and Equity is one of their first principles of Government."

Consider, for example, the Iroquoian Gayanerekowa, the Great Law of Peace. In its essentials it is no different from the law codes that governed all the native nations. Its provisions were recited at all important gatherings, which itself evidences the close and personal connection between the native people and the rule of law. The Gayanerekowa records its legal points on woven wampum belts with beads and shells, whose presence and pattern prompts the oral history. These belts are mnemonic devices that testify to sacred compacts, contracts, and oaths which constitute the law. The Great Law of Peace itself is a constitution, and, as such, it confirms the fact that indigenous people had laws of their own and governments and courts to administer them. Except for suppression, they would still have them.

As wampums 42, 72, 73, and 75 record, ownership, titles, and interests to land are regulated by law:

Among the Five Nations and their descendants there shall be the following clans: Bear, Eel, Snipe, Beaver, Hawk, Turtle, Deer, Heron, Wolf. These Clans distributed through their respective nations shall be the sole owners and holders of the soil of the country which in them is vested, by birthright. The soil of the earth from one end to the other is the property of the people who inhabit it. By birthright, the Onkwehonwe, the original beings, are the owners of the soil which they own and occupy and none other may hold it. The same law has been held from the oldest times ... The Great Creator has made us of one blood and of the same soil he made us, and as only different tongues constitute different nations he established different hunting grounds and territories and made boundary lines between them ... Whenever a member of an alien nation comes into the territory of the League and seeks refuge and permanent residence, the Statesmen of the Nation to which he comes shall extend hospitality and make him a member of the Nation. Then shall he be accorded all the rights and privileges except as mentioned here.

Certainly, the traditional native people have always tried to explain to newcomers that land was gifted by the Creator for the use of the people. This perspective on the legal source of ownership might be different, but is not a negation of ownership.

As wampums 36, 56, and 57 record, formal offices called "titles" exist to give structure to the government and the court system:

The title names of the war chiefs of the League shall be: Ayonwehs, war chief under head chief Tekarihoken (Mohawk); Kahonwaitiron, war chief under head chief Otatsheteh (Oneida); Ayentes, war chief under head chief Atotarho (Onandaga); Wewens, war chief under head chief Dekaenyon (Cayuga); Shoneratowaneh, war chief under head chief Skanyatariio (Seneca). The women heirs of each head chief's title shall be the heirs of [the] war chief's title that is associated with that head chief's title ... Five strings of shell

tied together as one shall represent the Five Nations. Each string shall represent one territory and the whole a completely united territory known as the Five Nations Territory ...
Five arrows shall be bound together very strong and shall represent one Nation each. As
the five arrows are bound, this shall symbolize the complete union of the nations. Thus are
the Five Nations completely united and unfolded together, united in one head, one body
and one mind. They, therefore, shall labour, legislate and council together for the interest
of the future generations.

The point of law and the rule of law is that the existence of law must precede
the events being regulated. Otherwise, what follows by way of sanctions applied
to the event can only be a social and political reaction, not the course of legal
justice. Although the natives' institutions for creating law in advance of events
are perceived differently, there can be no gainsaying the fact that they exist.

As wampums 58 and 59 record, respect for and fidelity to the law is definitive
of membership in the society, and no person or institution can be above the law:

If at any time anyone of the chiefs of the League choose to submit to the law of a foreign
people, he is no longer in the League and persons of his class shall be called "They have
alienated themselves" (Tehonatonkoton). Likewise, such persons who submit to the laws of
foreign nations shall forfeit all birthrights and claims upon the League of the Five Nations
and its territory ... The people have the right to correct their erring chiefs. In case a part of
the chiefs or all of them pursue a course not vouched for by the people and heed not the
third warning of their women relatives (Wasenensawenrate), then the matter shall be taken
to the General Council of the Women of the Five Nations. If the chiefs notified and warned
three times fail to heed, then the case falls into the hands of the men of the Five Nations.
The War Chiefs shall then, by right of what has gone before, exercise power and authority
to enter the open Council to warn the chief or chiefs to return from the wrong course. If the
chiefs heed the warning they shall say: "We shall reply tomorrow." If then an answer is returned in favour of justice and in accord with the Great Law, then the Chiefs shall individually pledge themselves again, by again furnishing the necessary shells for the pledge. Then
shall the War Chief or Chiefs exhort the chiefs, urging them to be just and true. Should it
happen that the chiefs refuse to heed the third warning, then two courses are open: the men
in council may decide to depose the chiefs and let them go, or club them to death with war
clubs ... Any erring chief may become submissive before the War Chief lets fall the Black
Wampum (signifying the order to carry out the sentence of death by clubbing).

As wampums 37 and 79 record, the holders of the war chief titles served as
messengers, ombudsmen, police, legal counsel, judges, and soldiers in various
contexts, both in times of peace and of hostilities:

There shall be one war chief for each nation, whose duty shall be to carry messages for his
chief and to take up arms in case of emergency. The war chiefs shall not participate in the

proceedings of the Council, but shall watch its progress and in case of an erroneous action by a chief the war chief shall receive the complaints of the people and convey the warnings of the women to the law breaker. The people who wish to convey messages to the chiefs of the League shall do so through the war chiefs of their nations. It shall always be the duty of the war chiefs to lay the cases, questions and propositions of the people's law before the Council of the League ... The invested holder of the Skanawati title shall be vested with a double office. One half of his being shall hold the statesman title of war chief. In the event of war he shall notify the five war chiefs of the League and command them to prepare for war and have the men ready at the appointed time and place for engagement with the enemy of the Great Law of Peace.

As wampums 44, 45, 93, 94, 95, 96, 97, and 98 record, government and court procedures are legalistic, formal, structured, permanent, and egalitarian, with a sexual sharing and division of jurisdiction:

The lineal descent of the people of the Five Nations shall run in the female line. Women shall be considered the progenitors of the Nations. They shall own the land and the soil. Men and women shall follow the status of their mothers ... The women heirs of the chief-tainship titles of the League shall be called Oyaner or Otiyaner for all time to come ... Whenever an especially important matter or great emergency is presented before the League Council and the nature of the matter is such as to affect the entire body of the Five Nations, then the chiefs of the League must submit the matter for the decision of the people and the decision of the people shall determine the decision of the League Council. This decision shall be a confirmation of the voice of the people ... The men of every Clan of the Five Nations shall have a Council Fire ever burning in readiness for a Council of the Clan. Whenever it seems necessary in the interest of the people for a council to be held to discuss the welfare of the Clan, the women may gather about this fire. This Council shall have the same rights as the Council of Women ... The women of every Clan of the Five Nations shall have a Council Fire ever burning in readiness for a Council of the Clan. Whenever in their opinion it seems necessary in the people's interest, they shall hold a council and their decision and recommendation shall be introduced before the Council of Chiefs by the Clan's War Chief for consideration ...

All the Clan Council Fires of a Nation or of the Five Nations may unite into one general Council Fire, or delegates from all the Council Fires may be appointed to maintain a General Council for discussing the interest of the people. The people shall have the right to make appointments and to delegate their power to others of their number. When their council shall have come to a conclusion on any matter their decision shall be reported by the War Chief or War Chiefs to the Council of the Nation or Nations as the situation may require ... Before the real people united their nations, each nation had its own Council Fire. Before the Great Peace their councils were held. The Five Council Fires shall continue to burn as before and they are not quenched. The chiefs of each Nation in the future shall settle their national affairs at the Council governed always by the laws and rules of the League and the Great Peace ... If either a nephew or a niece see an irregularity in the performance of the functions of the Great Peace and its laws, in the League Council or in the Conferring of Chief titles in an improper way, they may through their War Chief demand that such actions become subject to correction, and that the matter be made to conform to the ways presented by the law of the Great Peace.

As wampums 99 and 104 record, the law respects the old traditions and leaves open the ears of the people for improvements suggested by wise persons:

The rites and festivals of each nation shall remain undisturbed and continue as before, because they were given by the people of old times as useful and necessary for the good of men ... Whenever any man proves himself by his good life and his knowledge of good things, he shall be recognized by the chiefs as a Teacher of Peace titled Kariwiyo and the people shall hear him.

As wampums 68, 69, and 71 record, personal status is also a legal matter:

Should any member of the Five Nations, a family or a person belonging to a foreign nation submit a proposal for adoption into a clan of one of the Five Nations, he shall furnish a string of shells, a span length, as a pledge to the Clan into which he or they wish to be adopted. The Chiefs of the Nation shall then consider the proposal and render a decision ... Any member of the Five Nations who, through esteem or other feelings, wishes to adopt an individual, a family, or a number of families, may offer adoption to them and, if accepted, the matter shall be brought to the attention of the Chiefs for confirmation and the Chiefs must confirm the adoption ... When a person or family belonging to the Five Nations desires to abandon their Nation and the territory of the Five Nations, they shall inform the chiefs of their Nation and the Council of the League of the Five Nations shall take notice of it. Whenever a person or any member of the people of the Five Nations emigrate and live in a distant region away from the territory of the League of the Five Nations, the chiefs of the Five Nations at will may send a messenger carrying a broad belt of black shells and, when the messenger arrives, he shall call the people together or address them personally, displaying the belt of black shells, and they shall know that this is an order for them to return to their original homes and to their Council Fires.

I once asked a highly respected Haida elder named "Sound-of-Many-Copper-Shields," a princess of the royal line in the Queen Charlotte Islands: "What is Indian law?" Without a moment's hesitation she replied: "Respect." She made it seem so simple. I believed her, and know now she is right. All else that is worthy of the name of law flows from that jurisprudential spring. As Ralph Waldo Emerson defined "justice" as the application of truth to affairs, she defined "law" as the application of respect to affairs. Justice and law represent the juristic dimension of truth and respect.

Since truth and respect are the basis of both the mystics' intuition of the unity of creation and of the mathematicians quest for the unified field theory, and since the magistrates' function is to implement law and justice, I was led to conclude that magistrates, mystics, and mathematicians are engaged in different aspects of the same reality. Each is charged in his or her own way with the responsibility of serving, protecting, and implementing the unity of creation based on respect and truth.

Practice has flouted these principles – respect and truth – yet they have been, and remain, the legal standard. In terms of native expression, the legal principle of respect between natives and newcomers was recorded by the Two-Row Wampum belt, named in the language of the Iroquois the Gus-wen-tah. Two rows of dark beads run the length of the belt, separated by three rows of a lighter colour. The belt itself represents the river of life and time. The two dark rows, respectively, are the paths traced by the canoes of the natives and of the newcomers. The light-coloured rows represent the three elements of the relationship – peace, friendship, and respect – separating the twin and parallel sovereignties of the two peoples.

Wherever I have travelled in the Americas, without exception, all the traditional natives I have encountered have expressed that same concept as the essential basis, in their worldview, of the true legal relationship between themselves and the newcomers. I have also found in the course of my academic research that the founding law of the newcomers supports the same principles, in words, as the wampum beads represent. Like a mystery story unfolding its secrets clue by clue, I was drawn ever deeper down history's winding and intertwining two-branched root. One branch represents the history and anthropology of native nations; the second is the corresponding history and sociology of the society of the invading newcomers.

At every stage in every epoch, I found the two branches linked by elements of law, like a double helix defining the meaning, character, and integrity not only of the legal status of the native nations but, of more general significance, of the status of the rule of law in non-native society. Each time I thought I had solved the puzzle of the how and why of things present as the sum total and reconciliation of things past, the picture would become more complicated before I could see the simple theme that explained them. Once I had that theme, another set of actors or influences from an earlier time zone would force their way in. Each time this happened I would feel confused, until the theme line reasserted itself. The process turned repeatedly upon itself.

Now, in the end, it all seems so simple in terms of the principles ultimately involved. The natives were here first. The newcomers undertook legally to respect them and did not. And now the newcomers' courts are negating the rule of law by refusing publicly to address their ongoing role in the process.

In terms of legal history, the crucial year is generally taken to be 1763. Here I found myself on history's hinge, when the law of the preceding centuries was restated virtually on the eve of the demise of the First British Empire. The expression of the past, the sum of its wisdom or folly as the case may be, occurred with the promulgation of the Royal Proclamation of that year.

At first it was hard for me to relate to the modern-day legal significance of this document, yet the length of its shadow stretches to the present. As the Bible was to govern the spirits of colonists in those days, the Royal Proclamation was to govern their secular affairs. It was the fountain of all powers of government, the supreme law that determined the legality of all lesser laws. More than that, like the goddess Themis, it was the fulcrum from which were suspended the scales that balanced the destinies of natives and newcomers.

In the centuries leading up to 1763, the monarchy had begun as an absolute source of all power. Gradually Parliament had wrested that power away to the extent that, so far as England itself was concerned, the king had no real power left at all except that which Parliament expressly permitted by legislation. Not so with regard to overseas dominions: here, the king retained the absolute power to create new law. The legal basis for the claim of crown sovereignty in the New World was that the crown – the king acting with the advice and consent of his foreign policy advisers, his Privy Council – retained, by ancient prerogative, jurisdiction to settle the terms and conditions of constitutional government for his colonists.

This power to create the first constitution was like a May fly. It could live for the day on which it chose to soar, but at day's end it was spent. The king could gift the New World regions claimed by him with their first constitution, but, having done so, he had no power left to change the trajectory of the events set in motion. In 1763 King George III enacted just such a constitutive Royal Proclamation. It created the constitution for the new lands acquired by the English as a result of the French and Indian War: the war waged between Great Britain and her American colonies, together with their Indian allies, against France and her Indian allies. The English group had won in 1760 against the French-speakers, but the Indians were not ready to bury the hatchet. A great Indian warrior, orator, and conciliator rose in the interior – Pontiac – from whose perspective the contest between the English and the French was a distinction without any difference. Both were equally non-native, the adversary in the competition for jurisdiction and sovereignty.

Rallying the Algonkian-speaking inhabitants of the northeastern woodlands and the Ohio and Mississippi River valleys, the forces under his inspiration destroyed the whole chain, except for one, of the foreigners' military forts in the interior of North America. The moccasin telegraph undoubtedly broadcast the event from coast to coast on the continent. And just as certainly the fur traders and their trading ships took the news home to Europe. Alarmed, the king of Great Britain moved resolutely to win back the allegiance of the disaffected Indians. Seizing the opportunity presented by the need to provide a constitution for the territories ceded by the French in 1760, he inserted into that constitution a part relating to native rights and remedies. Citing that the better "Protection" of the Indians against "great Frauds and Abuses" was "just and reasonable and essential to our Interest and the Security of our Colonies," this constitution undertook not only to recognize and affirm but, more assiduously, to enforce the previously established constitutional common law concerning the first inhabitants in all British regions.

As the Royal Proclamation of 1763 recited, the prevalent disregard of that common law had induced the "great Dissatisfaction of the said Indians" and had led to the Pontiac War. The new constitution legislatively was intended to alleviate the Indians' dissatisfaction by enacting that, henceforth, the breech by colonial officials of the law would be prosecuted as treason and fraud. This proclamation was the set of teeth that fulfilled the king's assurance to the Indians of the crown's "protection" against the designing colonists, their governments, and their courts. The constitutional undertaking promised that the previously established law would be honoured in the enforcement – that it was not just lip service and empty promises.

In sum, the significance of the king's proclamation of 1763 is that it is the first written constitution relative to all British North America. From this overriding position of authority and influence, it affirmed the relationship of respect as the touchstone for the legal validity of all lesser laws. The Royal Proclamation achieved little that was new. It restated the previously established law that was being ignored by the colonists, and it gathered up and reiterated principles that had existed before as the unwritten common law and the law of nations.

As to that part of North America now called Canada, I discovered that the proclamation has never lapsed, even symbolically. For that part of North America now called the United States, the same principles were accepted as being implicit in the Constitution even after the American Revolution cast aside the 1763 proclamation itself as the founding constitution.

Once the king allowed the constitution to exist, the constitution thereafter governed in place of the king's will. Since under constitutional government no man can be above the law, the moment the constitution came into existence the king himself was subject to it. This cornerstone of law was laid down in 1774 by the highest constitutional court in the British Empire, the Judicial Committee of the Privy Council, in the leading case of *Campbell v. Hall*.

The 1763 proclamation confirmed the Indians' liberty from the despotism of the colonists, their governments, and their courts. It did so by zoning all territory as Indian country, except those particular regions that were purchased from the Indians. Furthermore, it enacted that, for the time being, no such purchases could occur west of the Appalachia Divide. In 1774 the highest constitutional court of the British Empire confirmed that the king no longer had despotic powers. In *Campbell v. Hall*, the governor of the royal colony of Granada pretended to raise the tax on death duties. He did so on the basis of having the power of the king delegated to him. The court held that, without the consent of the local legislature, the king himself could not have raised the tax. Therefore, the governor, standing in the king's shoes, could not do so. Because the king had enacted the Royal Proclamation of 1763 allowing the colony a legislature, taxation could be raised or changed only with the consent of the people acting through their legislature.

The crucial legal point was that, by granting the constitutional right, the king had placed himself under the same constitution. He was, at law, a constitutional sovereign – one subject to the constitution – not a tyrant above it. Yet, in 1776, the American Revolution officially began with ringing revolutionary rhetoric inveighing against the despotism of the king. The revolution was justified on the basis of a legal mirage: ridding the American colonies of the king's despotic rule, a despotism that the highest court had already nullified two years before in *Campbell v. Hall*.

A more concrete motive for the revolution was to lift the constitutional blockade that had been imposed against the colonists' expansion westward into the Indian territories. Politically powerful men such as George Washington had large tracts already carved out in anticipation of that freedom. Nevertheless, after the revolution, the United States Supreme Court confirmed the relevant principle of British constitutional law: the United States claimed the exclusive right to buy the Indian territory from the Indians when they were freely willing to sell. Until after the purchase, Congress constitutionally had no jurisdiction over the unpurchased land. The same principle had been true for the king: he had no jurisdiction over unpurchased land once he enacted the Royal Proclamation.

The American Constitution of 1789 made no express mention of aboriginal rights. All it said was that the federal government was assigned the jurisdiction to make treaties with the Indian tribes. In other words, the purchase function was a matter for the federal government, not the state governments. The Canadian Constitution said the same thing when, in 1867, a federal system with two levels of newcomer government was installed there as well.

The non-mention of aboriginal rights was legally appropriate. The Constitution, 1789, was designed to deal with the legal relationships between citizens of the United States and their governments. The Indians on yet unpurchased lands were outside that frame of reference, as were the unpurchased lands themselves. Other than by purchase, the crown before the revolution, and the Congress after, claimed no more than the exclusive right to buy. Jurisdiction followed purchase – indeed, it was the legal consequence of that event. So far as the Indians' unpurchased lands were concerned, the only jurisdiction before treaty was the jurisdiction to make the treaty, and the constitutions of both the United States and Canada assigned that jurisdiction to the federal governments. Having done so, the sum total of the newcomers' jurisdiction relative to yet unpurchased lands was exhausted.

The formative precedents of the United States Supreme Court, and in particular the trilogy of *Johnson v. McIntosh* of 1823, *Cherokee Nation v. Georgia* of 1831, and *Worcester v. Georgia* of 1832, confirmed that the United States acquired what Great Britain once had – not more, but not less. Thus, *Johnson v. McIntosh* held that the Indians enjoyed "a legal as a well as a just claim" to their yet unpurchased lands. *Worcester v. Georgia* held that the United States had no more than the legal right to continue the process established by Europe in general and Great Britain in particular:

[I]t was necessary for the nations of Europe to establish some principle which all would acknowledge, and which should decide their respective rights as between themselves. This principle, acknowledged by all Europeans ... gave the exclusive right to purchase, but did not found that right on a denial of the right of the possessor to sell. The regulation between the Europeans and the natives was determined in each case by the particular government which asserted and could maintain this preëmptive privilege in the particular place. The United States succeeded to all the claims of Great Britain, both territorial and political; but no attempt, so far as is known, has been made to enlarge them ... The King purchased their lands when they were willing to sell, at a price they were willing to take; but he never coerced a surrender of them. He also purchased their alliance and dependence by subsidies; but never intruded into the interior of their affairs, or interfered with their self-government, so far as respected themselves only.

After the revolution, access to the Judicial Committee of the Privy Council was cut off, but the need for access to some independent and impartial third-party court remained. The existence of such access is the primary cornerstone of the rule of law, the feature without which the rule of law cannot be seen to function at all. There is a section in the Constitution, 1789, which gives the US Supreme Court the jurisdiction to adjudicate legal disputes between American governments and "foreign" nations. In 1831 the Cherokee Nation did not want to go before the non-native courts with its land dispute with Georgia. Accordingly, it applied directly to the Supreme Court of the United States in the hope that that court would, in effect, stand in the shoes of the Judicial Committee of the Privy Council as an independent and impartial third-party adjudicator.

A modern example of the application of the same constitutional section as the Cherokees relied on in 1831 is the current dispute between the states of New York and New Jersey over whose boundary the Statue of Liberty lies within. The section gives states and foreign nations the right to go directly to the US Supreme Court as the trial-level adjudicator. Neither New York nor New Jersey would be happy with the boundary and the jurisdiction dispute being decided in the courts of the other. So they rely on the section giving them direct trial-level access to the Supreme Court as the third-party adjudicator. The Supreme Court appointed a fact-finder rather than hear trial evidence itself.

But the 1831 US Supreme Court in the case *Cherokee Nation v. Georgia* held that the Supreme Court of the United States did not stand in the shoes of the Judicial Committee of the Privy Council, so far at least as the Cherokee Nation was concerned. The court declined to pretend that it was independent and impartial vis-à-vis boundary and jurisdiction disputes between the native government of the Cherokees and newcomer government of the state of Georgia. By so declining, the US Supreme Court evinced a steady and uniform attachment to the principle of fundamental justice under the rule of law. For the US Supreme Court is a creature of the non-native government system, the sovereignty of which is in direct competition with the land in question. It cannot possibly be independent and impartial in relation to boundary and jurisdiction disputes between native nations and either the state or the federal governments. Nor in 1831 did it pretend otherwise.

When the US Supreme Court refused to accept jurisdiction, it did so on the basis that the Cherokees were not "foreign" nations within the meaning of the constitution's US Supreme Court original jurisdiction section, but rather were "domestic dependent" nations. By not engaging in the false premise that it could function as independent vis-à-vis legal disputes with Indians over the purchase question, the US Supreme Court was true to the long-range interest of the rule of law: engaging in the pretense of independence would have degraded the integrity of the rule of law.

It does not follow that simply because the US Supreme Court does not exercise trial-level jurisdiction in relation to native versus newcomer boundary and jurisdiction legal disputes that lower US courts have that jurisdiction. The Supreme Court in the years under Chief Justice Marshall, 1801–35, recognized and affirmed that the essential principles of previously established pre-revolution constitutional common law remain part of the fabric into which the words of the American Constitution are woven. The most essential of the definitive threads of that fabric is the principle that the native nations have sovereign jurisdiction over themselves and their territories until such time as they relinquish that sovereignty and jurisdiction by treaty, as restated by the Royal Proclamation of 1763 immediately before the revolution, and as confirmed by the constitutive precedents of the US Supreme Court in the formative years following the revolution.

Since 1831, in consequence of the case of *Cherokee Nation v. Georgia*, the protection of the Indians' sovereign jurisdiction has for practical purposes been in abeyance. When the US Supreme Court in that year declined trial-level jurisdiction as a third-party adjudicator, the Indians were left, seemingly, with no third-party adjudicator to which to turn for protection. The consequence has been negation of the law in practice, even though the law has never been amended or repealed. At constitutional common law as created by Great Britain, adopted by the United States, and inherited by Canada, the native nations were invested with sovereign jurisdiction over all territory that has not yet been purchased from them by treaty.

Following the *Worcester* case's confirmation of native sovereign jurisdiction, President Jackson refused to implement the principle. He said, reputedly, "Chief Justice Marshall has made his decision; now let him enforce it." Thus, Jackson in effect declared an illegal and unjust war on the native nations. Then, in the Appropriations Act of 1871, the United States Congress effectively declared that, regardless of US constitutional law, treaties no longer could be entered into by any president in the domestic sphere. The intent behind these presidential and congressional declarations was to convert the natives' international and constitutional right of sovereign jurisdiction into a right subject to federal legislation. Such a conversion is legally impossible except by constitutional amendment, which has never occurred.

No doubt the position occupied by President Jackson and the Congress was popular and even democratic, in the sense that, if asked, a majority of "the public" would have supported the position. But that does not make the position legal. The rule of law exists, at least in part, to take the rough edges off democracy, lest it descend into the tyranny of the mob. The law as settled cannot be changed except by a duly enacted constitutional amendment that enlarges the sum total of powers asserted by the United States under its constitution. This concept is fundamental to the rule of law, under which even judges are not above the law. As the pre-eminent legal scholar A.V. Dicey said in his 1920 Harvard Law School Lectures, judge-made law is subject to certain inherent limitations as to what the judges can and cannot achieve short of leaving behind the rule of law:

Characteristics of Judge-made Law: (1) Judge-made law is real law, though under the form of, and often described by judges no less than by jurists, as the mere interpretation of law … (2) Judge-made law is subject to certain limitations. It cannot openly declare a new principle of law. It cannot override statute law. The Courts may, by a process of interpretation, indirectly limit or possibly extend the operation of a statute, but they can not set a statute aside. Nor have they in England ever adopted the doctrine which exists, one is told, in Scotland, that a statute may become obsolete by disuse. It cannot from its very nature override any established principle of judge-made law.

The trilogy of US Supreme Court cases represented by *Johnson v. McIntosh* of 1823, *Cherokee Nation v. Georgia* of 1831, and *Worcester v. Georgia* of 1832 did not breach the rule that judge-made law "cannot openly declare a new principle of law." To the contrary, the court expressly and explicitly made clear that it was affirming a previously established principle of law. International law and constitutional law, and the rights and obligations sheltering under them, are presumed to continue until expressly repealed by an international treaty or a constitutional convention. All that the US Supreme Court did in the formative trilogy was to confirm the presumption: there was no international law treaty or constitutional law amendment, therefore aboriginal rights continued in full force and effect after, no less than as before, the revolution.

The tragedy of the American Indian sovereignty movement is that, whenever an adherent enters a law office for help in terms of the protection of aboriginal rights on lands that have never been purchased by the United States from the Indians, the case ends up being couched in terms of federal Indian law. This very context defeats the client's opening assertion of native sovereignty because it accepts the jurisdiction of the court to decide the issue. Federal Indian law is based on the false opening premise that Jackson and the Congress conferred on the federal government jurisdiction to do whatever the newcomers' governments and courts wanted to do. The assumption is made that there had been a valid repeal of the previously established constitutional law protecting the natives sovereign jurisdiction relative to territory not yet purchased by treaty.

By developing the Indian's sovereignty case in terms of federal Indian law, the lawyers to whom the natives turn continue to ignore the legal basis for the Indians' assertion. Every time the lawyer brings forward one of the myriad pieces of congressional legislation and court cases that make up federal Indian law, the lawyer is bolstering the erroneous assumption that the federal government has jurisdiction which, if true, precludes the Indians' assertion of jurisdiction under the name of native sovereignty.

CHAPTER 4

My Capture by Indian Law and Culture

For me, these general perceptions concerning the law took place in the years 1978 through 1985 during a period of residence on Bear Island. This living experience contributed as much as my voluminous reading did to the evolution of the theory of law and jurisprudence for which I had been searching.

At the time of the closing down of the law practice in Haileybury and the move to Bear Island, my son David was two. Our daughter, Zoë, was born two weeks after the move, and our son Beau fifteen months later. At first there was not a vacancy for us in any of the houses on Bear Island itself. So, after leaving the office furniture and equipment and our few personal possessions at the Indian government office on that island, we backtracked to Temagami Island, due south 1 mile across the big lake. There, with the cooperation of a local tourist camp operator, we were allotted the use of a two-room cabin on a rocky point.

Each morning for the weeks that we lived on Temagami Island I would pull-start the 20 horsepower motor on the 16-foot steel boat temporarily rented for my use and head straight across to Bear Island. Since the two islands were at the hub of the lake, winds were free to come whipping out of the mouths of the great arms. When not in the lee of one or other of the islands, the wind almost instantaneously drove waves before me that I found terrifying. At first I would tense up and fight against the waves, overcompensating for being thrown off course, and the bow would swing dangerously into the wind.

But by stages I learned about the Indian Way, and that made life easier. If the lake wanted to take the spirit of the man, it would have it in the blink of an eye. The trick was to put the lake off wanting to take you, not by panicking or getting angry, but by being steady in the face of the wind and the waves. Let them toy with you, and toy back with them in turn. If you did that, the lake would let you live, to rock you gently or shake you aggressively some other time, as its caprice might want. If your time was up and you were meant to be dedicated with respect to the Lake Spirit, it was all over. As the Moose Spirit will sometimes allow its body to be dedicated to the man, so the man must in equal dignity accept his fate, with equanimity and humour. The key was not to overreact, but to moderate the boat's speed and roll with the wind and the waves instead of fighting against them. By accepting the rhythm dictated by them, an understanding could be established with Nature, which would then be more inclined to let you live.

Standing on the point in front of the cabin on Temagami Island, I could sometimes see a storm gathering on the western horizon. The water would ruffle and stir, the sky go almost black, and the wind would hit, as if to warn: I could have taken you had you not listened, had you gone out upon the water. The really old Indians listened more than the younger ones. They knew more about the power that lurked in Nature, ready to consume them. Hardly ever, if they could avoid it, would the old people venture onto the lake in November or December, when the weather was often angry and impatient, or in April or May, when the ice was becoming treacherous.

After we had moved to Bear Island itself, we found that the Indian band office was a clearing house of information about weather, water, and ice conditions. At the risky times, everybody coming off the water or ice would drop by the office and say a few words of hello and goodbye. At first I thought how friendly. More to the point, it was an exchange of information that was essential to life's continuity. Nature is never to be trifled with: her moods are constantly to be monitored and they may change in an instant. She is alive and must always be respected in the way she wants, which means taking care to find out what she wants. Sometimes she should be placated, but never challenged or provoked. No one should ever attempt to dominate her.

When a person enters the sweat lodge, that person should speak firmly and with resolution to the Fire Spirit in the heated stones, but never beg or thank, since that would be taken as a sign of weakness, a sign that the spirit of the sycophant was ready to donate his body to the use of some more stalwart force of nature. It is Nature's Way that the weak donate themselves to feed the strong, so if you look weak, Nature will assume that you wish to donate yourself and will accommodate you.

In the same way, white people who support Indian causes are perceived as offerings for consumption. The chief with whom I had become brother put it this way: "At one time we trapped the beaver, and it was our food and clothing. But the white man came and the beaver was hunted near to extinction. So the Indian had to learn to trap new prey – the white man." We laughed together; I hardly noticed that I was a white man. It was an inside joke and I was on the inside – or would be, once skinned. He also said there was an old saying: "Beware the wolf that smiles."

Just after we moved to the island I had occasion to defend in court a member of the Bear Island community who was charged with rape. The alleged victim was a white woman. After a party on the lake, he offered her a ride to her cottage in his 16-foot wooden boat. They stopped near a little island, to which he tied up.

It was alleged that he then attempted to romance her contrary to her inclination, in the boat, in spite of the seats, the tipsiness, the increasingly tempestuous weather, and his inebriation. The defence offered was consent.

The jury eventually acquitted the accused on the rape charge, but returned a verdict of assault. But before that happened I had the unenviable task of cross-examining the victim, a strapping wilderness-canoeing girl who should, I thought, have simply pitched my scrawny client over the side of the boat. I cross-examined her whether she was really trying to tell the jury that this little man had achieved penetration in his tiny boat while bobbing in the virtual storm. She said yes. I persisted. "Surely," I put it to her, "you will acknowledge that other than your statement that this did occur, such an act of unbridled passion would appear highly improbable under normal circumstances?" "I agree," she said, "that intercourse is a highly improbable event in a small and narrow boat, but still, it happened." The courtroom gallery, mostly being people from Bear Island, burst out laughing so animatedly that the presiding judge had to call for order.

After the trial I asked one of the gallery spectators what had been so funny. "Well," he replied, "there was you and this white woman debating whether an Indian man could make love in a tiny boat in a storm." "Yes," I said, "so where's the joke." "Do you know the rocky point just east of the boat house on Bear Island?" he asked. "Of course," I answered. "And the little island about twenty feet across that sits about fifty feet off that point?" "Yes, yes," I said, "I know these places." "Well," said he, confidingly, after looking over his shoulder to make sure the coast was clear and putting his hand over his mouth to keep this between the two of us, "in our Indian language those places are called Screw Point and Fuck Island. We Bear Island boys specialize in making babies in canoes around there. A sixteen foot boat would be a piece of cake for a Bear Island man."

Oral traditions were often couched in risqué stories. For example, the lichen that grows on the exposed bedrock of the Canadian Shield was created when one of the Tricksters slid on his fanny down a rock face. He had diarrhoea, and the residue is the lichen. Many times I have overheard Indian men in different parts of North America illustrate with a similar scatological image the fact that all men are created equal: when the white man and the Indian leave the outhouse, the feces left behind smell and look the same.

Acceptance of aboriginal rights should not be based on whether one likes Indians, finds their jokes funny, or their culture worth saving. Rights exist as a matter of law, independent of value judgments about the attributes of the holder. Otherwise, the apprehension of genocide will always involve a political debate as to whether the victims are worth saving.

By the fall of 1978 a house became available on Bear Island. This was not an Indian house. Had it been, we could not have lived there because residence of non-natives is officially illegal on a reservation. The house sat on a lot that, as an exception to the rest of the island, was held by private title. When the Bear Island

Indian Reserve was created by a unilateral executive order in council in 1971, the lot on which the old HBC factor's dwelling rested was excluded. Many years before, that piece of ground had been surveyed and transferred by the government of Ontario to the Hudson's Bay Company. That transfer was long since registered in the Land Registry Office as a separate parcel of land with its own legal description and identifying parcel number. The lot and its little house had been transferred by the company to the government-sponsored Temagami Indian Band at the request of the Canadian Department of Indian Affairs. The band was therefore the registered owner of the private title, and the house, not being part of the Indian reserve, could be lived in by a white person. We moved in.

The factor (after the style in Scotland for manager) of the fur-trade post had long since stopped living there. Sale of furs now took place by centralized annual auction at a clearing house in North Bay, Ontario. Our house sat behind what once had been the old fur-trade post itself, on the southwest side of the island, facing the lake. There was a dock at the water's edge, down a steep rise from the house, and we were allowed to park there whatever boat we had on loan. The front yard had once been a lawn surrounded by a white picket fence, with a Scottish garden in one corner. It was now a sea of wild blue cornflowers. Framing the little gate and crumbling the fence were two stunted and bedraggled lombardy poplars.

The house could have been lifted from the Scottish countryside and set down into the wilderness. None of the other houses on the island was physically segregated by a fence and lawn. The fence reminded me of the one behind which I had been a five-year-old prisoner, only this time the Indians were on the other side and my family and I were alone on the inside. I removed the fence and the poplars, thinking this gesture would help close the cultural gap between my family and those we were there to serve. Though nobody said anything at the time, years later I learned that some people were still simmering with anger over what I had done. I had made a change to communal property without first explaining my motive and lobbying for the community's consensus. Rather than bringing my family closer, the physical change had widened the gap. My action was classically Euroculture: I saw an impediment to my progress and cut it down and threw it away. The conservatism of native society, its resistance to change, is deep.

Since our children's cultural lenses, in their formative socializing years, were to be ground and fitted on Bear Island, we did not want our little ones receiving culturally contrasting messages that would estrange them from the society of peers into which they would be merging their existences. Margaret and I were aware that Indian children were given much freer rein than white children. From the time of their first steps, Indian children could play wherever they wanted. With deep water only steps away, drowning was a major cause of infant death in the native society. The fatalism that characterizes native life seemed to include an acceptance of that mortality. Not that the pain of loss was any less, for children were treasured, but there was fatalism, a passivity, that precluded attempts to out-flank the omniscience of the cycles in which all life tumultuously was tumbled, some falling out before others. As so often happens when a native wanted to share his philosophy, one of the Temagami hunters painted a mind-picture for me which captured the essence of this fatalism. Sitting in a canoe in the reeds at the water's edge one day, he waited in absolute silence and immobility for the moose to come. He waited for so long that his muscles seized and he started to topple. Be-ing in spasm, he could not adjust his weight to counteract the roll, which by then was communicated to the canoe. As both he and the canoe entered the point in the roll where he knew he would soon be head first in the water, he saw a massive, antlered moose watching him across the little bay. Their eyes met for long enough for their souls to exchange places, and both in that instant knew that the Great Spirit was playing a joke on the hunter. The instant lasted an eternity and was over in a microsecond, as the hunter's face plunged under the water. Surfacing in a burst he stood, crystal droplets of water spraying in an arch from the sweep of his long hair, looking at the shore against which the moose had been silhouetted a moment before. Now there were only trees and rushes to the water's edge. Slowly he began to laugh, until he was weak from it. Had there been a moose there, or was it only the spirit of the moose teasing him, telling him he was a silly hunter who allowed himself to cramp? There was no way of knowing. But, just in case, it was better to laugh with the moose than to be laughed at by the moose. Then, later, when the hunter was stronger and wiser and more hungry, the Moose Spirit would know him for a friend and a good companion, one with whom the moose would want to share the gift of life, and so would offer his flesh as food.

Such fatalism often was a step or two beyond my cultural grasp. I outfitted David with a life vest so he could be almost as free as the native children with whom he was growing up. I inscribed the vest "David Clark. If found return to Bruce Clark, Bear Island." David remembers his childhood as the best that could ever be: freedom to roam.

As we settled into our house we discovered buried in the back of the huge linen closet a mini-library. Most of the cloth-covered books had been published between 1890 and 1914. They were adventure stories of the "white man's bur-den" sort. The men were square jawed and flinty eyed, slow speaking and un-flappable, located in the exotic backwaters of the globe. The little library was exactly what one would expect a turn-of-the-century fur-trade factor to be read-ing to wile away the interminable winter snows. And, like him, we also were en-thralled by them over that first winter in the wilderness.

Down the hill from the Indian government office was a boathouse. The office building itself had started out in the nineteenth century as a log cabin constructed of squared logs a foot and a half on the diagonal, harvested from the stands of white pine that were once common here. Later, in the 1920s, this cabin was taken over by the Lands and Forests Branch of the Department of Mines and Resources of Ontario for use as a district office from which to monitor forest fires. A second story had been added to the cabin, and the boathouse had been built at the bottom of the little hill, some 150 feet away. The boathouse also served as a floatplane base. Ironically, I discovered after I moved to the island that I had a personal and historic connection to this office. My uncle Jack Clark had been a floatplane engineer. On emigrating as a young man from Yorkshire, he had joined the Lands and Forests Branch as a mechanic on the fledgling air service established in the 1920s. They called him Knobby because, in England, everybody who was both a Clark and an engineer was called Knobby. He was written up in the history of the Ontario air service as one of the grand old-timers. His first posting had been Bear Island; his first hangar the little boathouse. The first office to which he reported was the one at the top of the hill in which I became ensconced some fifty-five years later.

From the top of this boathouse one fine spring day several boisterous native teenagers were diving or jumping into the water. Hearing the noise and laughter, I ambled down to the waterside and watched for a while. The water of Lake Temagami must be among the clearest in the world. The name itself, "Teme Augama," in Indian means deep and clear water. I walked out onto the dock. A beautiful girl broke the water surface, rising waist high, storming my senses with the blackest of shining hair and glistening skin, the whitest of teeth, and the fullest of budded breasts thrust before the delicate arching of waist and shoulders. Momentarily suspended, smiling perplexed and slightly startled, no doubt having expected to surprise one of her friends, she descended back beneath the surface of the water.

The power and the freedom of women in native culture, as portrayed in the Iroquoian Great Law, contrasts with women's role in Euro-culture. They are the repositories and guardians of Indian culture. When the first Roman Catholic priests of the sixteenth and seventeenth centuries came upon Algonkian-speakers of the eastern woodlands, they encountered women who appalled them as libertine. The priests determined to break the matrifocal and egalitarian native culture, to make it conform to the patriarchal model of Europe: God at the top, the male sex next, followed by women, then animals and plants, and so on through creation.

Not only might native women choose and change their male partners in accordance with the exigencies of nature and inclination but, over the course of a lifetime, they might change their companions as well as the roles filled by them, taking one in the springtime of their youth as first lover, yet another for the summer of their child-bearing years, and a third for the autumn of their life of matured female wisdom. In place of this natural cycle, the church consigned each native woman to a lifetime sentence of servitude to the man who owned her and whom she must obey, as man must obey God. The suppression of native women interrupted the natural cycle centred on the free Female Force. Still, the young woman who rose out of the water argued strongly for the indomitable character of that force.

After we moved to Lake Temagami that spring of 1978, I decided to revise my preparation for the defence of an upcoming court case. I set aside everything I had done to that juncture and tried to remove from my brain any particular focus or hypothesis I had. I decided to read every case and every piece of legislation concerning Indians ever promulgated in North America, and to make notes on index cards of the issues I was reading. The cards would also record the comments of the judge or legislature in relation to these issues. In the process, I would benefit from the research done by lawyers on both sides of the question as each arose historically. Previously, I had gone to the sources looking for answers to questions that my own brain had formulated. Now I was looking for the questions that others had formulated.

I started to work back in time through the legal history as revealed in the cases and the legislation. I began with all the judicial decisions decided in the previous quarter century. These were easy enough to obtain, since the modern indexing process is thoroughly and professionally done by law-book editors. By this time, I had also accumulated my own quite substantial collection of similar materials. The actual recording of the information on the cards began in earnest that first winter on the island. By a great stroke of good fortune I had an unexpected and invaluable ally. I had met the head librarian of the Law Society of Upper Canada in Toronto and had persuaded her of the importance of the native people both to Canada and to the rule of law. She was nearing retirement at the time and was something of an autocrat in her fiefdom. She gave instructions to her staff that my requests for research assistance were to be accommodated and given priority. I sent her hundreds of citations for the cases and the legislative instruments as I discovered them, and, in return, she sent back thousands of photocopied pages. From these readings I would compile another list, and so the process would continue. I learned some years later that the librarians and staff under her command could never understand why they were spending more time helping one obscure lawyer on a island in northern Ontario than the other 6000 lawyers in Ontario combined. At the end of this process I found myself back in the sixteenth century, surrounded by 12,000 index cards.

That first winter I worked on the second floor of the Indian band office building. It was really an uninsulated attic that we euphemistically called the second floor. Because it was not heated, we left open the hole in the floor which served as an access from the cabin below so the heat would rise and keep me warm, too. Our scheming made little difference, so I got the band to buy me outdoor work clothes similar to those worn by telephone company lineman: padded bib-style coveralls, long woolly underwear, and woollen gloves with the ends of the fingers missing. These were the days before computers, and every notation was handwritten on the index cards. From November to April my breath hung misted in the air.

That first winter was cold even in our house. We kept running out of oil for the outside drum that fed the space heater. The wood stove helped, but the house was not well insulated and there was no money with which to buy fuel. So, late one night, I went down to the band office, unscrewed the line feeding into that building's space heater, and started draining some fuel to transfer to the house drum. As I was bent over guiding the siphon, from behind me I heard a voice: "Working the night shift, eh?" Startled, I spun around. Whoever it was kept right on walking. Just a comment and a chuckle in passing. I'll bet every Indian on the reserve at one point or another has found himself half frozen and has nipped out on the night shift to harvest some warmth. The comment in passing made feel almost accepted as a member of the community.

It didn't help with the cold that we had to leave a window open to vent an extraordinary odour that wafted up from the crawl space under the house. Up to this juncture in our life, if a house had odd smells, or the heat did not work, or the electricity went off, we made a telephone call to have it fixed. But this house had no telephone. If it had had a telephone, there was no one to call. And if there had been anyone to call, there was no money with which to pay. Everybody on the reserve had to learn to be self-sufficient. If you were not a fixer, things were not fixed. Despairing of help, I finally wiggled into the crawl space under the house and discovered that the sewage line was interrupted. It was not broken, simply not connected. I reconnected it, but the smell did not improve. Periodically I checked again and hit various things with a hammer, to no avail. I kept up my inquiries. Three years later some government money was designated by the federal bureaucracy for plumbing purposes. On the strength of that fund, fixing our plumbing made it onto the list. The cause was detected: the holding-tank valve had been installed backwards, allowing raw sewage to leak slowly under the house. The correction was made and we breathed deeply with relief.

In addition to being out of oil that first winter, we were also out of firewood for the wood stove. When I asked where to find firewood, people looked at me oddly, as if I were expecting a firewood store. If you want firewood, you collect it yourself. But to collect it, you have to build your own ski-doo road to some spot in the bush where the wood has not already been cut. Good trees like the old dry-wood pines, or the dry white and yellow birch, are very rare. I was to learn that you never stop scanning the shoreline for them. And when you find some, you tuck the knowledge away.

You cannot just strike out across the lake to the nearest wooded shore. The lake ice is treacherous if a ski-doo road has not been marked over it. Besides, the shores all round the island are owned by white people who will call the police if you cut. I had naively thought that, in the middle of the bush, getting wood was no problem. "Well," someone finally said, "maybe there was some wood already cut down by the ball field." The ball field was on the southeastern side of the island, in an area that had at one time been meadow surrounded by boggy lowland. The surface had been built up for the playing field, and the constructions debris had been left at one edge. I investigated. Under the snow I found tree segments strewn about. They were mine for the taking. The only problem was they were frozen into the bog. I had a scaling bar from my mining days in Sudbury, a 6-foot iron lever with which mine rock could be dislodged – a perfect tool for prying wood frozen from a bog. Each segment was perhaps 4 feet long, 12 to 18 inches in diameter, and extremely heavy. I had been loaned a ski-doo and a ski-doo trailer, and I worked long hours getting this wood from bog to house.

Thinking that the hard labour was over, I heaved the axe up over my shoulder and brought it down onto the up-ended surface of a log. The axe head came zinging back at me, passed over my head and shoulder, and threw me completely off balance. No mark of any kind appeared to have been made in the wood. Chagrined, manhood in jeopardy, I swung again, with increased vigour. An interminable time later I did, eventually, gain a beachhead for the wedge. From there it was only a matter of sweat and tears, pain and suffering. Eventually the log lay vanquished, rent asunder, in two pieces. Each of these pieces proved to be as stubborn as the whole, notwithstanding my hope that the going would get easier once the initial break had been achieved.

I looked up. A small crowd of Indian people had been gathering, just standing there watching. I redoubled my efforts, which, in terms of swinging the axe, were mighty and aimed with precision. I had worked one summer as an oil pipeline labourer swinging a sledge hammer and was experienced at the movements required. I worked my way through the whole supply, but it never got any easier. Months later the Indians explained that my bog wood had been water-logged poplar. In its frozen state, it had been regarded as too heavy to handle and too impermeable to chop. That was why it had been left in the bog beside the ball field. I had provided the gallery with an afternoon's entertainment.

Later I went looking for wood that could actually be cut and split. This quest took me by ski-doo to one of the north bays of the island. Soon I ran out of ski-doo road. The going slowed. Eventually I stopped the machine and reconnoitered the shore from the centre of the bay. Having confirmed my position, I remounted. Revving the machine's engine, I felt the ski-doo dip down instead of going forward. The traction belt had dug a trench straight down to the hard ice beneath the snow and my machine now sat at least a foot and a half below the surface of the crust. On closer investigation, I found that the first 6 inches of the crust was snow, but the remaining foot was slush. Apparently this layering is normal under certain weather conditions, particularly in certain bays. Indians know this danger and keep away from such places. I was learning.

For four hours I dug away at the slush and was able to gain another 40 feet of progress towards the shore. I deduced from this effort that I would reach my goal in about three days. I was soaking wet, sweating at my body's trunk, frostbitten at the extremities, and not in a positive frame of mind. Then I remembered the story about the Indian hunter who rolled with his canoe into the water and laughed at himself. I sat on the ski-doo and reflected. I did not break into laughter, but, after pondering my predicament, I slogged my way to the shore and cut some evergreen tree branches. With them, I laid a road leading from the place where the ice was shovelled bare in front of the ski-doo, up the snowbank made by my shovelling, and onto the hard-packed surface. The machine trolled right out of there, first try.

Exhausted, I reached the shore. An Indian woman was standing outside her house and motioned me to stop. She said she had been watching my progress on and off for hours and was happy I had figured out what to do. Her house was within shouting distance of my predicament, but she had not shouted. She had waited for me to work it out for myself. I accepted her praise, and moved one more small step into the fold.

These first few years I was on Bear Island I was in shock – culture shock. Indian society is premised on self-sufficiency. My own culture, in contrast, is based on a division of labour and intense specialization. Lawyers, for example, are highly trained to do one thing very well. I was not trained to be self-sufficient. Just as some native people have difficulty adjusting to urban life, so I had trouble on the reserve.

Our family's first mentor was the mother of the lake nymph I had seen that first spring on Bear Island. Until that young woman had a baby of her own for whom grandmother would care, our family was honoured by her mother assuming an analogous grandmother role for our family. I say analogous because Margaret and I never ceased being culturally white, nor did we ever try. Our characters were completely formed by the time we lived on Bear Island. All we could do was always respect the culture of the others in whose midst we were dropped by fate and circumstances largely beyond our control or theirs.

The first time we met this woman, our first babysitter, Margaret and I were walking the path from the band office on the island's south point to our house on the west side. We heard a rustling in the bushes to our left. Looking down, we saw a pair of small feet sticking from the brush at the path's margin. Investigating, we found that the owner of the feet was neither dead nor suffering from a stroke but, rather, from partying. She was drunk. We woke her, or induced a state resembling awakeness, and took her with us back towards her house, which happened to be just beyond our own. By the time we made it to our home, Margaret on one side and I on the other, we three were friends.

Yvonne came into the house and had a few cups of tea before continuing on her way. I walked her home. A few days later she dropped back and shyly offered to help us any time we needed a babysitter. We took her up on the offer that day and on many days thereafter. There could not have been a more mothering, sweet, and gentle soul imaginable. Apart from the odd binge when the urge to party descended, for three years she stuck closely by us and we with her, until her own grandmothering duties called her away.

Eventually, after a year or so and many gallons of tea at the kitchen table with Margaret, she spoke of the trials and tribulations of a life spent on the margins of both the white and the Indian cultures. Her husband was the head of the family hunting ground that encompassed Chee'Bai'Gin. His great-grandfather was the medicine man Wendaban, whose powers had been of renown throughout the north at the turn of the century. They had all their babies while they lived in the bush on those grounds, he trapping furs and she gathering the moss for diapers and setting the nets for fish. Now some of his fingers were missing, and the remainder were bent in different directions. They had been broken in various accidents in the bush and had healed awkwardly. As his sled dogs had careened back to her at the end of a journey out on his trapline, one of his eyes had been put out by the sharp end of a tree branch. He had survived all these physical traumas and had been an outstanding trapper.

She spoke with nostalgia of the time in her life before her babies came of school age. Then they had to move to the reserve because the children, by white man's law, had to go to the white man's school on Bear Island. It did not work well. The alcohol and partying were everywhere, and both she and her husband, being old-style Indians, were ravaged by it. For a while they tried leaving their older children with relatives and returning with their pre-schoolers to the family hunting grounds. But the older children kept escaping and making their way unaided back to the camp. This separation was just too risky. Perhaps some day their children might not make it all the way back because of the cold, a hole in the ice, or some predator animal. But they had been bush raised and were wise in its ways. Nature would reclaim them only when it was their time. The even more devastating threat came from the school officials. They warned that if the children ever again ran back to their parents in the bush, they would be made wards of the white man's court and given out for adoption to more "responsible" white families. She and her husband sadly moved back to the reserve and witnessed their lives, and the lives of their children, gradually disintegrate around them. I have heard this same scenario repeated hundreds of times on reserves from the Atlantic to the Pacific.

One Christmas we were commiserating with Yvonne over the fact that none of us had any money with which to buy presents. Suddenly she had a sparkle in her eye and, giving our little ones a warm hug, wished us a merry Christmas and left. She simply went home, packed up her husband and her children and their children, and headed out for their hunting grounds. There they had the best Christmas ever. They came back strong, confident of themselves and their power over their lives. There had been no store-bought presents – only white snows, a blanket of green, outdoor fires, fresh fish, each other, and the spirits of the family ancestors to keep them company.

Another time she described community life before the 1950s, before mandatory education totally disrupted its life cycles by demanding ten months' residency on the island. At the onset of the bone-chilling November winds that made canoe travel on the big lake too risky, each extended family would return to its family hunting territory. They wintered there, on the little frozen streams deep in their own grounds. When spring thaw permitted, the families would repeat the journey back towards Bear Island for the spring gathering. On the way, families from the northern territories would camp at the maple groves to tap the sap and boil it down to sugar.

But the young people were always impatient to reach the island. Spring and romance were in the spring, at the island's south end where the boathouse, the rocky point, and the little island sit. Once back on the island, the families would gather to share their winter's experiences, to plan picnics to the local burn areas for blueberry picking, and to enjoy the fish roe during the spawning fish runs. Summer was a time when food resources were plentiful and life was sweet. Later on in the summer, some members of the group would think about setting out for larger gatherings that might today be equated with pow-wows. Through retelling the oral traditions, Yvonne explained how these mega-gatherings were important for more than recreation and procreation. They served as economic trade fairs, religious confirmations, political negotiating grounds, and judicial centres for the peaceful resolution of legal disputes that crossed family and small-group capabilities.

Each of the families had its own oral history, carefully preserved in the retelling at its own gatherings. One story was common to all family histories: the head of each family never gave the white government any right to sell the family grounds to other people. It distressed each family deeply that the government had sold the land anyway.

There is no mention of the Temagami name in any treaty, nor is there a description of a Temagami Indian reserve in any treaty. And no Temagami Indian ever signed any Indian treaty or any document attaching to any Indian treaty. In 1850 a treaty was made and signed by other Indians to the south of the Temagami territory. Between 1850, when that Robinson Treaty was made, and 1971, when the Bear Island Reserve was created by a unilateral order-in-council of the Canadian government, the Temagamis never deviated from their stance that they had not sold their lands. The federal government agreed with their position, and in the 1880s the Temagamis started agitating for a treaty of their own. But, from the first, the Ontario government stated it was free to deal with the Temagami lands as it wished.

Ontario was not concerned to justify the legal basis for that conclusion. When pressed, it answered that, whether the Temagamis were parties to any treaty or not, their aboriginal rights had been extinguished by Ontario's course of dealing with their lands. Ultimately, Ontario was of the view that it was sovereign and therefore free to ignore aboriginal rights. Faced with intransigence on the part of Ontario, the Canadian federal government bureaucracy in the late 1880s began paying some of the Temagamis the $4 annuities they would have been paid had they been parties to the 1850 treaty.

Consistent with its own historically entrenched attitude that the whole of the Temagami region, including Bear Island, was and always had been public land belonging free and clear to the province, Ontario began in 1970 to warn that the Temagamis would be evicted from the homes they had built on Bear Island. The natives were labelled as trespassers and squatters on Ontario public land, and threatened with criminal prosecution for cutting firewood to heat those homes. To assuage the Indians' panic at the threat of eviction, the federal government simply took the initiative in 1971 to act unilaterally. First, it placated Ontario by buying the island from it, as if Ontario had the right to sell. Then it placated the Indians by designating the island an official Indian "reserve" entitled to apply for benefits applicable to such places under the federal Indian Act.

The Temagamis did not take or not take any legal steps in relation to the establishment of the Bear Island Reserve. In the years leading up to the creation of the reserve, they had expressed their anxiety to the federal government at the provincial government's eviction threat. The federal government did not ask the Temagamis to agree that, if Canada were to pretend to buy the land, which Ontario had no right to sell, they would accept the island reserve as the extinguishment in law of their aboriginal rights. To the contrary, the minister of Indian affairs on Canada's behalf immediately wrote to the Temagamis to assure them that, now the immediate pressure of eviction was off, Canada would continue to press Ontario for a settlement of the long-outstanding treaty request. There was absolutely no suggestion that the request for a treaty had just been resolved by the creation of the reserve. Indeed, the very opposite was the case, as the letter confirmed.

None of the events were intended or perceived at the time as relating to the Temagamis' outstanding aboriginal rights. Nor could they, legally, have been so perceived in the absence of a "public Meeting or Assembly" of the Indians at which they expressed their "inclination to dispose" of those rights, within the meaning of those phrases in the Royal Proclamation of 1763. But when Ontario sued the Temagamis in 1978, the federal government reneged on its former position and deserted the Indians.

I learned of these events not only from the documents but from the natives themselves. Much of my listening was done over cups of tea at a kitchen table, but some took place at drinking bouts not even euphemistically called house parties. I might have been walking home from the band office and been hailed from a doorway to come over. Inside the house would be a group. Many were of the fur trapper variety who, after working a season in the bush, would come out, sell their furs for a small fortune, and spend it all on a weekend of wine, women, and song. They could not just go from bar to bar, since there were no bars on Bear Island. Instead, they delighted in chartering floatplanes to go from bar to bar in neighbouring hamlets. While the money lasted, maybe in their minds they were like the rich Americans who came up in floatplanes weighted down with booze to hunt and fish in the wilderness with them as their guides. Or maybe they were just rascals for the sake of being rascals and never needed a model to emulate. Whatever, they would be well into it by the time they hailed me over, wanting to talk. People at these parties did not use drink as a vehicle to get to some other destination. The destination was drink.

Twelve hours later the group might be sitting on the floor, backs against the walls, some passed out, others just back from having been passed out. By this time I would have passed whatever test gave them the reassurance I would not carry tales back to the ever-present white police. Criticism would invite retribution. Better to keep quiet, so far at least as the white police were concerned, and they were concerned with everything.

Invariably the talk would turn to the iniquity of the white man and the exploits of their ancestors. How they had guided a client in confidence to the best fishing places, only to find the next year that the white person did not need the Indian guide any more. Not only did he know the best location but he had returned with a big enough crowd of his own fishing buddies to fish out the hole. Or how another Indian had shown a white friend a secret outcropping of rock on his family hunting ground, only to find out that the friend had staked the land as a mining claim and was now a multimillionaire, with never so much as a by your leave or a thank you.

From tales of personal iniquity and fraud, the group sentiment gradually would swing round to the consensus that the land, all the land, was their land, and that none of the white people had asked if they could be there. When, years later, I was to read the words in the 1984 written decision of the white judge in the *Bear Island* case, pontificating that the oral history of these people was a fraudulent recent invention, I thought my head would split. Still later, in 1991, when I read the decision of the Supreme Court of Canada that these very people to whom Margaret and I had listened over so many days and nights, had supposedly accepted the reserve on Bear Island in 1971 as an extinguishment of their aboriginal rights, I cried in frustration, anger, and despair. I knew that what the judges were pretending was utterly impossible. If the Indian people had ever had it in their minds to do what the courts were pretending, there is no way that such an intent would not have come out. I would have heard, if not an admission, then at the very least some slip-up. I cried for the people on the island. The truth, their truth, is so simple; the judges' pretence so evil.

PART TWO

KICKING AGAINST
THE PRICKS

CHAPTER 5

The Bear Island Trial

I will not be naming names in my story because we are all stock characters and I do not want to create an illusion that, if different individuals had played the roles, things might have been different.

By 1980, after seven years of listening to the native elders and researching the available anthropological, historical, and legal literature bearing on native society, I felt I was in a position to make an inventory of Canada's scholars in the several academic fields that were relevant to the Bear Island Indians' case. That summer I telephoned the pre-eminent academic experts and invited them to a conference on Bear Island. At first, all were too preoccupied with other commitments to come.

In my sales pitch to convince them to rearrange their other duties, I attempted to tweak their intellectual curiosity and, perhaps, their academic vanity. I promised them the romance of an adventure into the innerscape of their own minds and the challenge of forging, with minds as knowledgeable as their own, a new understanding. The participants at this conference would be only themselves and respected Temagami elders. There would be no rehashing of conventional wisdom, no formal presenting of papers. Rather, it would be an exploration into the uncharted waters at the margins of known archeology, pre-history, history, and anthropology. The participants would attempt on the basis of fusing the separate fields of specialization to create a synergy, perhaps an alchemy, that exceeded the former sum of the separate states of knowledge. Each contributor in the cross-disciplinary set would be there to prod the others' thinking processes, to come up with questions and answers that had not yet even been formulated.

This time they all agreed to come. I was panicked with stage fright. What if nothing were to happen? Maybe I had overpromoted a performance that would never escape the mundane. As the day approached, I became increasingly apprehensive. The conference began at a set of tables drawn into a circle in the log building used by the Temagamis as a recreation centre on Bear Island. It was the most extraordinary academic experience I have ever had. The maturity, honesty, and integrity of the scholars and the elders was profound. In one room had come together the best minds, not as teachers, but as students again – there to learn from representatives of complementary disciplines. The room was alive with energy.

My function was to keep the expedition's rudder pointed in a direction that would answer the question, for legal purposes, of the probable aboriginality of my clients on their land. After five intense days I had enough knowledge and leads to allow me to approach an additional set of scholars and pose to them questions so sophisticated, from the point of view of each of their special fields of interest, as practically to guarantee their cooperation and active participation in the required cross-disciplinary research. In due course, each of the scholars would reiterate at court the knowledge present at or prompted by the research consequence to this remarkable conference.

Also in preparation for the trial, the chief justice of Ontario hand-picked a judge to oversee the pre-trial conference. The normal purpose of pre-trial conferences is for the lawyers and a judge, other than the judge who will take the trial, to get together with a view to seeing if the matter can be settled without going to trial, or, failing settlement, at least to narrow the issues that have to be thrashed out at trial. The reason the judge presiding over the pre-trial conference is precluded from taking the trial is to encourage openness at the pre-trial conference, without fear of being prejudiced if the trial must go forward. Often things are said in confidence in the privacy of the pre-trial conference that would be imprudent and even inadmissible in the publicity of the trial. If a trial judge were to hear such inadmissible evidence, a mistrial might have to be declared. For all these reasons, the published Rules of Court clearly and plainly enact that the pre-trial judge cannot also be the trial judge. The rule precluding the pre-trial judge from being the trial judge is a hard and fast rule.

During the course of the Bear Island pre-trial hearings with the appointed judge, I made the observation that it would be good to get on to the trial because the government of Canada was spending large amounts of taxpayers' money funding legal research in other land claims across the country to research an issue that the Bear Island case, without any government assistance, was positioned to resolve. The mask of judicial impartiality dropped from the judge, exposing a face livid at the Indians' effrontery in making demands and the government's stupidity in putting up with it, let alone paying for it. I was deeply shaken.

In blatant violation of the rule governing pre-trial hearings, the chief justice had stipulated that this pre-trial judge also do the trial. The outcome would be a foregone conclusion. Accordingly, I made formal applications both to the chief justice and the trial judge himself, demanding that the rule be addressed and that some other judge, any other judge, be given charge of the trial before it actually started. The judges did not acknowledge the existence of the rule, nor did they dispute what it said. They simply carried on as if they had not heard the objection. It was as if I had become invisible and the words I wrote and spoke could not be seen or heard.

I remember riding in a taxi on the way to the courthouse that first day of trial. The bottom dropped out of my stomach and my legs were shaking. But I could do absolutely nothing but carry on, as if I were being forced to watch an execution. I found myself living the same parallel reality as that spoken of by the Indians, but which I had always thought an overstatement. The law, as written, is not visible when the judges belong to a race and culture motivated to dispossess another race and culture.

The Bear Island case became a classic Indian land claim, but with one different feature. Rather than the natives suing the newcomer government, the newcomer government sued the natives. Specifically, Ontario sued the Indians for a declaration that their aboriginal rights had been extinguished. As alternative relief, Ontario asked the courts to define the precise "legal nature and character" of unextinguished aboriginal rights in general. By framing the two issues in this particular sequence, Ontario and her courts were able to evade the law entirely. For this reason the case is not only a classic land claim case but a classic in chicanery as practised by the newcomer legal establishment.

It is the legal nature and character of aboriginal rights that determines the standard by which to judge the sufficiency of any alleged act of extinguishment. Therefore, before deciding that the Temagamis' aboriginal rights had been extinguished, it was first necessary for the courts to address the law defining such rights. That was never done. What the courts eventually said was that, regardless of what the law might say about the precise nature and character of these rights, they were extinguished when the Temagamis accepted the Bear Island Reserve in 1971. If the courts had not evaded the law, they would have seen that under the law, as expressly and explicitly written, it is impossible, given the precise nature and character of aboriginal rights, that such rights be extinguished in this way.

The trial took place in Toronto in 1982–3. On the opening day of the trial I stood and made formal objection to the assumption being made by the judge and the attorney general that the Indians bore the burden of proving their aboriginality to the land in question. I asked to be allowed to demonstrate that, as a matter of law, there was no such burden of proof upon the natives. To the contrary, the law states that it is incumbent upon the newcomers, because the Indians were here first, to prove that they have purchased the land from the Indians according to a strict formula governing the mechanics of the purchase.

The crucial point of law is that in the constitutionally formative years, all territory in British North America was reserved for the Indians, "or any of them," until a treaty was made whereby the newcomers might contend they acquired the land from the Indians. And to be valid for any particular tract of territory, the purchase had to be signed publicly by the leader of the Indian group whose lands were being purchased. In the Temagami situation, there never was a signature or even a public meeting. All there ever had been were two encounters of a different kind. After a treaty had been signed by other Indians in 1850 and the Temagami Indians asked to be included, government bureaucrats added some Temagamis to the group receiving a $4 annuity charged in the government's books against that earlier treaty. Then, in 1971, the federal government unilaterally set apart Bear Island as a federally recognized reserve. That federal legislation expressly and explicitly acknowledged that the Temagamis "without their consent" had been "omitted" from the treaty.

The usual way in which newcomers get around such defects in the treaty process is to shift the burden of proof to the Indians, in the newcomers' own courts, and then make sure that the Indians are never quite able to discharge the burden falsely placed upon them in this fashion. It is as if everyone did not know that the Indians were here first, but have to keep proving it. When it comes to court, the newcomers say the Indians must prove that their ancestors were on the land when the Europeans arrived, and that their ancestors never stopped having meetings or left their homeland area. Since the Europeans' ancestors made it virtually impossible for the Indians' ancestors to hold public meetings, the Indians did not keep written records of meetings in any event, and in many regions the newcomers drove the Indians away from their homelands, it is almost impossible for the natives at this stage in history to discharge the burden of proof that the newcomers' fraudulently impose on them. This incapacity is employed to pressure the Indians into settling for whatever the newcomers want to give them, which is usually little in comparison with the value of the lands and resources that have been stolen.

My attempt at the outset of the Bear Island trial to force the court to address the law which shows that newcomer society bears the burden of proving its purchase was stonewalled in just the same way as that concerning the rule about pre-trial judges not taking the trial. The judge would not permit the issue to be argued. He would not allow the law to be presented which established that, to be valid and enforceable, a treaty of purchase must be evidenced by a written contract describing the land with precision, concluded and signed after "a public Meeting or Assembly" at which the Indians voluntarily decided they were "inclined to dispose" of their homeland.

In law, the Indians do not have to prove aboriginality, but the crown has to prove a valid treaty. In this particular case, where there was no evidence capable of satisfying the public signature preconditions to a valid extinguishment of aboriginal rights, the trial should not have lasted more than ten minutes. Yet it was one of the longest trials in Canadian history simply because the courts would not allow the law to be addressed. And the courts never did get around to addressing the legislative words that establish the legal position relied upon by my Indian clients.

The presentation of the evidence I adduced to rebut the province's allegations and to corroborate the natives' oral history of continuity from time immemorial upon their land, all of which the judge also brushed aside, stretched over one hundred days. Eventually the Supreme Court of Canada agreed that the Temagamis were indeed aboriginal in the region in question. To this extent my clients were able to discharge the burden falsely imposed upon them.

We began the proof by filling the courtroom with fifteen antique birchbark canoes, ranging from a 30-foot fur-trade cargo canoe with its grand sweeping prow curving up some 4 feet and back, to the various smaller craft from across the north, each with its own trademark configuration and internal construction features. Several canoes provably built by Temagami Indians in the Temagami region had survived in museums into the 1980s. These canoes had been commissioned shortly after the turn of the century by non-native sojourners with cottages on Lake Temagami, and had been carefully preserved indoors ever since.

I also learned of a canoe museum in east-central Ontario. Not only did it display samples of birchbark canoes that had been made by Indians inhabiting lands adjacent to the Temagami region but the curator had undertaken a lifelong study of the cultural technology of the birchbark canoe. I called him as an expert witness to testify that, unlike some forms of material culture, birchbark canoe construction was not sex or age monopolized. Men, women, and children worked jointly through every stage of these boats' creation and often drew upon community advice and assistance for specific features.

This age and sexual equality factor was crucial to the falsely imposed burden of proving aboriginality. Styles for artifacts such as baskets or quill pouches which were created by women alone were much more mobile from region to region. Intermarriage between regions was normal. As a woman left one region, she would take with her the fashion preferences in which she had been trained. Styles could also change because of contact at social gatherings, without the people themselves necessarily moving in a permanent sense. Pre-contact gatherings at Moosonee on James Bay, Montreal on the St Lawrence River, Sault Ste Marie on the rapids between Lakes Superior and Huron, and New York on the Hudson River were also fashion shows.

In cases where the construction technology was community based and shared among both sexes and all ages, it tended to be very place-specific over long periods of time. The shape of a birchbark canoe's prow, for example, was dictated by fifteen different complex construction features, each of which depended on being integrated into its adjacent part. Canoe builders could not on a whim start doing something different and still expect the whole work to be successful. Construction was a coordinated communal effort that tended to be constant over time, as contrasted with being subject to changes in fashion.

Raw technology aside, canoes were spiritual creations – they were essential to life. And every aspect of life was charged with the grandeur of the Great Spirit. Every part of the canoe construction process was blessed and dedicated to the spirits of the lands and waters where the construction was taking place. To take a specific root or tree branch for use in the construction involved a bargain with the spirit of the particular plant, with the genus to which that plant belonged, and with the entire ecological creation in which all things animate and inanimate co-habited. Part of the bargain was that the flesh and sinews of the plant would be used for the purpose for which the plant gifted itself to the Indian. To change the use without the tacit consent of the plant donor would have been a breach of the faith on which the harmonious interdependent health and survival of all was contingent. Continuity of life was precious and precarious. There was no sure way of knowing what change might give offence or injury to unseen forces in the magical universe. The safe and secure course was not to make changes. Resistance to change was a built-in feature of aboriginal culture.

The profound conservatism of this world-view was even more resistant to change in activities that were community based. While an individual might risk disturbing the balance of nature by introducing a new motif or use, any such innovation taken in relation to a canoe-building project would be perceived as a threat to the mate and to the community. Indian society was built upon consensus because continuity in the magical universe depended on this quality.

The canoes from Temagami all had square prows and bows, exactly like the ones in the pictographs found in the Temagami region. In contrast, the canoes from the regions to the south and the west all had rounded prows and bows, exactly like the ones in the pictographs found in those adjacent regions. The canoes from the regions to the north and east all had swept-back prows and bows, exactly like the ones in the pictographs found in those regions.

The present generation of Temagamis had proved graphically, using detailed genealogical charts recording birth, marriage, and adoption statistics, that they were direct descendants of the turn-of-the-century Temagami canoe builders. These people, in turn, were building the same unique style of canoe in the same area as had the pictograph makers, from a time before the coming of the white man. A material-culture link establishing the geographical continuity of the Temagami people in the specific and restricted region of the square-prowed canoe pictographs had been identified. The subjectively "soft" oral history of the "aboriginality" of the people had been corroborated by the objectively "hard" scientific material-culture evidence from the realm of archeology.

Next I called as a witness a linguistic expert. He testified that language is equally, if not more, resistant to change than culturally specific archeological artifacts. Certain features of language – the lexicon (the words) and the morphology (the ways in which the words are put together) – tend to be constant from century to century.

Throughout the eastern woodlands of North America, a "dialectic chain" exists. To illustrate, consider Western Europe: there is one dialectic chain from Holland to Austria. If you were to start at one end and go from village to village and region to region you would find that each village and region differs marginally from its next door neighbour, but can be understood by those neighbours.

Yet people in Austria cannot speak to and be understood by people in Holland, and vice versa. Though they are members of the same Germanic linguistic family, or language group, they speak dialects that have evolved in different directions. The number of word and syntax differences gradually increase in proportion to the separation in terms of time, distance, and frequency of contacts, to the point where the speakers' brains are not able to process the meanings of the sounds of distant cousins' speech. The eastern woodlands, from Wisconsin to Hudson Bay on the north and to the Atlantic Ocean at New York on the east, contain one indigenous linguistic family: the Algonkian-speakers. Although they all are in the same linguistic family, the people at Mille Lacs, Wisconsin, could probably be understood by the people at Sault Ste Marie near Lake Huron, but probably not by the people at Maliotenam on the north shore of the St Lawrence River in northern Quebec or by the Mohegans of the Hudson River drainage basin.

Scientifically, lexicological and morphological differences are measurable. A trained linguist, by analyzing the words and the structure of the language as spoken today by a given dialect group, and comparing the features found with the dictionaries and grammars prepared by the priests making first contact with the indigenous peoples of each region, can draw a map showing how long a given dialect group has been located where it is at present. The linguist can also give an expert opinion as to where the group came from, if it turns out not to be indigenous to the place it is now located. And he can specifiy the proportion of the group that is likely of immigrant bloodlines.

The time-depth element is one of the most interesting scientifically. Languages change at predictable rates, not so much with regard to words, but to the underlying structure governing how the words are put together. The linguist I called testified on the basis of examining the Algonkian dialect as spoken by the surviving Temagami elders and comparing its features with the surrounding dialects. He arrived at a firm and unambiguously expressed conclusion: the present Temagamis are descended from speakers who resided in the same region at least five hundred to one thousand years ago, and possibly much longer. This linguist's mentor, under whom he had earned his doctorate from Yale University, was hired by the Ontario government to be present in court to listen to his testimony. Nevertheless, the government lawyers, neither in cross-examination nor by independent evidence from any other linguist, challenged my linguist's expert opinion. Another link establishing the geographical continuity of the Temagami people had been identified. Another piece of evidence scientifically and independently corroborating the accuracy of the native people's oral history had been obtained.

The anthropologist witness, who for more than fifty years has specialized in northern Ontario, advised me that, in his professional experience, it was a misnomer to call the Indian hunting groups "nations." For anthropologists at least, the term denotes a solidified structure that belied the reality of life in the boreal forest. He said the essential unit of Indian life was the family. Families could switch group or band allegiances over time, cleaving for a few generations to families to the north, then to the south, and so on. In this sense, group boundaries tend to be shifting or, more precisely, oscillating, over time.

The oscillations depended primarily on the coincidence of marriage and birth patterns, and on the unpredictable emergence of a charismatic leader in a given generation under whose influence others might fall and to whose region far-flung families might be drawn into association. Even so, each extended family stuck to the same lands over the generations because there was an accumulated wisdom about the lands that made survival more probable than under a system of random roaming. By staying in the same area over time, the family acquired specialized knowledge about the dependable locations of plants for food and medicines, the best fishing places, the haunts of riverine animals. That was where the investment of the family in the same family hunting grounds over time made its return. The wisdom not just of land in general, but of the family's lands in particular, was the key to the continuity. Families with accumulated wisdom about the peculiarities and secrets of their own territory could survive where less knowledgeable though stronger people might perish. Strength will not find fish where there are none, nor catch the humble hare when the hungry wolves have taken the vulnerable large animals for themselves. Only the fish and the small animals can feed the people in the starving times, and only the people with accumulated knowledge of the land's and water's peculiarities know best and most efficiently where to look.

The process of gathering plant materials for consumption was equally highly developed, with a set of alternatives to offset scarcity caused by any particular natural cycle. An old Indian woman explained to the court how her people had a special place in the family's hunting grounds where, in the depths of winter, they would go to dig in the snow for rosehip, a powerful natural source of vitamin C. Scurvy was never a problem. Her entire hunting ground she described as one huge pantry, a larder of plant life for human consumption. All you had to know was where the different things were located. The Indian women, especially, knew those things, she said.

Such knowledge was passed from parents to children in a land totally dotted with lakes and networked with rivers and streams. The wisdom that sustained life was cumulative and family based. Indian families in the boreal forest of the Canadian Shield do not just pick up and wander off to foreign lands. The main thing to remember, both my anthropological and native mentors stressed, is that this was essentially a riverine culture. Certainly, there was a time of the year when the people pooled efforts to take big game such as the moose or woodland caribou. But the staple was fish and small riverine mammals. The ubiquitous hare would come and go in cycles, but the fish and water mammals could be relied upon for survival. With the aid of an ichthyologist (fish biologist), whose twenty-year passion was interviewing native elders of the region so he could gather and map detailed place names, we had been able to portray the complex network of riverine highways and sacred locations, well known by even the present generation of Temagamis.

The lawyers for the Ontario government called as their witness a young anthropologist who had studied some of the account books and journals kept by fur traders. On the basis of these sources, he testified that the original people of the Temagami region had all died, wandered away, or been pushed off the land, to be replaced by northward-moving Indian migrants from the southwest. When he saw a gap in the fur-trade profits at a particular post and read the local trader's report to his superiors in England that the Indians had all gone, he believed the trader. When the accounts picked up, his conclusion was that new Indians must have moved in and started trapping. Why the old Indians could not as easily have moved back he did not know and could not, in cross-examination, offer a guess. Nor had he answer for the possibility that fur-trade volume could be down for any number of reasons other than the demise or emigration of every single Indian of the tribe. That they might be trading somewhere else, that the trader might be wholesaling their furs to a competitor and shutting out his employer, that they did not like or had had an argument with the particular trader and refused to trade with him, that there was simply a dearth of furs in any given set of years – none of these possibilities were acknowledged as possibilities by Ontario's anthropologist.

The Indians' defence witness soundly rejected the fledgling anthropologist's hypothesis. All those possibilities the younger man refused to acknowledge were, the older expert testified, probabilities. The population displacement hypothesis was not supported by either the Indian elders' oral tradition or the various non-native written sources. The only point supporting the hypothesis, tenuously in his view, was evidence of discontinuity of specific Indian names in the fur-trade records. However, such discontinuity could easily be accounted for in terms other than population displacement. The same Indian might have three or four different renditions of the same name in Indian, and a similar set of alternatives arbitrarily assigned to him by various English- or French-speaking fur traders.

Naming is an especially complex issue with regard to the societies of traditional indigenous people. The giving of a person's real name is like giving a lock of hair or a fingernail. It is considered a part of the person. By an extension of the natural law that all things are in contact, the theory of magic is that a spell cast upon the severed part affects the body of which it was a constituent part. For this reason, the old-time Indians normally used aliases rather than real names and gave different aliases to different people. Any hypothesis based on the discontinuity of names in fur-trade records is therefore inherently unreliable, the defence witness testified. Besides, there are extremely large gaps in the fur-trade records, and even where records do exist, the quality of record keeping is highly variable and unreliable.

Another defence witness, a well-known historian of the ancien régime of France in America, testified that the Temagamis were allies and trading partners of the French at Lake of Two Mountains (Oka, near present-day Montreal), and that the Indian allies of the French were not subjected to the same pressure to move as were those in areas under English influence south of the Great Lakes/ St Lawrence River. The reason was simple. The French had a "fur-trade frontier," in contrast to the English "settlement frontier." The French fur trade depended on the Indians staying on their family hunting grounds, not being dispossessed, whereas the settlement policy depended up the Indians moving off the land so the farmers could put the land to a different use. The displacement of indigenous peoples that characterized the British colonists' occupation on the Atlantic coast did not hold for the region of North America claimed by the French in the interior. In consequence, the historian testified, it was almost certain that, prior to the fall of New France, the Temagamis would have occupied the same lands continuously. There was no known historical reason why they would not, and solid economic reasons that they would.

On closer examination, the same fur-trade records as those glossed over by the Ontario government's witness revealed that the sons of the same persons who had stopped trading for a few years, and in many instances the same persons themselves (though with different nicknames assigned by different traders), were back trading in later years. They could all be connected in the records back to a native person in the area before 1763. To the extent that records exist, the Temagami people never moved – the blood lines are unbroken into the eighteenth century. And before that time there are no written records of any kind, only the oral history of the Indians themselves, and it stretches back to the re-creation at Chee'Bai'Gin after the world-destroying flood.

For the trial judge, however, the fact that the Ontario government's only witness, the young anthropologist, was paid $25,000 for expressing his opinion of massive population displacement only enhanced his credibility. Why else, the judge reasoned would he be able to charge so much? In contrast, the fact that the Indians' more mature, established, and pre-eminent scholars had all, without exception, refused money for testifying – on the ground that it might taint their academic integrity – was taken by the judge as evidence of a conspiracy by them to fabricate evidence. On this basis he accepted the evidence of Ontario's witness and rejected the evidence of the Indians' witnesses.

On the basis of an uncritical acceptance of that one witness, the Ontario government lawyers argued, and the judge agreed, that the indigenous people were lying when they recounted their oral history and that the scientific evidence corroborating the oral history was fabricated or imagined by academic do-gooders.

With a blanket rejection of everything said by the natives and their numerous experts, the Ontario court eventually concluded that the Temagamis, though Indians, were not "aboriginal" to the land involved and, therefore, not entitled to assert aboriginal rights. The trial judge held:

In summary, I believe that a small, dedicated and well-meaning group of white people, in order to meet the aspirations of the current Indian defendants, has pieced together a history from written documents, archeology and analogy to other bands, and then added to that history a study of physical features and other items, together with limited pieces of oral tradition. Even the name Teme-augama Anishnabay was not used in any printed form or record of the band or registered band until 1976. This leads me to doubt the credibility of the oral evidence introduced, and affects the weight to be given to the evidence of the non-Indian witnesses.

It was certainly true, as this judge noted, that the name spelled "Teme-augama Anishnabay" was not used in any printed form or record of the band until 1976. This name is the one by which these traditional Indians identified themselves to each other. In translation from their Indian language to the English language the parts of that name are "Teme" meaning "deep," "augama" meaning "water," and "Anishnabay" meaning "people." The native people here referred to themselves as "the deep-water people." As the evidence adduced during the trial showed, from the time of first contact the newcomers employed a phonetic rendition of the same sound. The earliest Jesuit Relation, that of Father Nicolet in 1640, referred to them as the "Outimagami." The first French maps in the later 1600s placed this Outimagami group in the region of my clients' court case. In the nineteenth century the federal government bureaucracy gave them the name "Temagami Indian Band," another phonetic rendition of the same root word.

There is no reason that the "printed forms" and "records" used by this "Indian Band," all of which exist for the purpose of communicating with the Department of Indian Affairs in the English language, would use the Indian-language term Teme-augama Anishnabay. By 1976, when a land claim was in progress, the Indians did not want to be known any longer by the bureaucrats' corrupted version of their name. They wanted to be known by the name they used for themselves – just as the Inuit had recently overruled the foreign term "Eskimo."

The trial judge brushed aside the Indians' oral history of continuity going back to a great flood and he brushed aside the corroboration of that oral history by expert academic documentation and opinion – all on the basis of this imaginary inconsistency between the terms "Teme-augama Anishnabay" and "Temagami Indian Band." He held that the natives could not, to his satisfaction at least, discharge the burden of proving that their ancestors had been present on the same land continuously from at least the year 1763. On this basis, he held, the government of

Ontario did not have to prove a purchase by treaty from the Bear Island Indians. In the alternative, he ruled, even though no Bear Island Indian had ever signed any treaty of purchase, some other Indian must have done so on their behalf. Otherwise, he asked, why had the government taken over their land and added some of them to the list of annuitants receiving $4 a year under that treaty? No evidence of any such authorization was ever adduced, but the judge implied one. In a further alternative he held that even if the Temagamis had not sold their rights directly, by cashing the $4 annual cheques and not objecting when the government started calling Bear Island an Indian reserve in 1971, they had become "adhered" to a treaty the government had made with other Indians relative to those other Indians' lands.

To support this last argument, Ontario showed that a few $4 (the amount has risen slightly) government annuity cheques had been cashed. Nothing was written on those cheques that could have given them the legal character of contracts for the sale of land. They were just ordinary government cheques, with the name of the payer, the name of the payee, and the amount. From time immemorial, the crown and then the Canadian and American governments have been making subsidies to Indians quite apart from the treaty process.

No one said to the Temagamis in 1971, when the reserve was set up in the federal books, that they had an option to go away from their homes or, by continuing to live where they always had, to be taken as having accepted the 1-square mile Bear Island reserve as an extinguishment of their aboriginal rights. Quite the contrary, for immediately before and after the creation of 1971 reserve, the federal government continued to write to the Temagamis with reassurances that the federal government was still in negotiations with Ontario on their behalf to settle the aboriginal rights issue. Even if the federal government had told the Temagamis that, by not leaving Bear Island after it was unilaterally designated a reserve, they were giving up any claim to aboriginal rights, any such representation would have been fraudulent under existing law. The law is specific and clear on this point: there are no alternative ways to effect an extinguishment of aboriginal rights other than the public signature of the Chief.

When, in the course of filing documents at the trial, I brought out that particular letter from the minister of Indian Affairs reassuring the Temagamis that, after the creation of the Bear Island Reserve in 1971, their aboriginal rights were still under negotiation, the lawyers for Ontario objected, in blatant contravention of the agreement made before the judge in the adjourned caution hearing that all evidence would go in from both sides without objection as to admissibility. The federal lawyers for Canada, who had been keeping a silent watching brief, thereupon rose in haste to say that this one piece of evidence should not be admitted into evidence. Despite my strong objection that this evidence should not be kept out, but that arguments going to its weight could be argued in due course, the judge agreed with the lawyers opposing the natives. That single document was ruled inadmissible.

The federal and provincial government lawyers then argued, and the judge agreed, that since the Temagamis had not in fact vacated Bear Island after the federal government unilaterally passed the 1971 order-in-council establishing the island as an Indian reserve, they must be assumed to have agreed to being "adhered" to the 1850 treaty. There is absolutely no reason for the Temagamis to have imagined that by staying on in their homes they were making a contractual arrangement for the sale, or the perfection of the sale, of their land. Treaty negotiations for the purpose of meeting the Royal Proclamation's mandatory requirements were in progress. Ontario was threatening to evict the Indians. Canada paid Ontario to back off that threat and unilaterally set up the purchased land as a reserve, before, during, and after which the treaty negotiations relative to the Temagamis' unextinguished aboriginal rights continued without interruption. No one would have argued in 1971 that, by simply staying on in their homes, the Indians had concluded a contract for the sale of land, let alone a contract for the extinguishment of aboriginal rights – a special type of land sale having even more stringent requirements than those applicable to run-of-the-mill land sales. In fact, there was not one single feature of the creation of the reserve process that even remotely resembled a contract for the sale by them of any land. Not one single element of the mandatory requirements of either the Statute of Frauds of 1677 or of the Royal Proclamation of 1763 was met. Nevertheless, in a complete reversal of its historical position with the Temagami Indians, in the final argument at trial, federal lawyers for Canada again stood with the Ontario lawyers to advance their recent invention that by "accepting" some of the annual annuities charged in the federal account books to the 1850 treaty, and by "accepting" the Indian reserve at Bear Island, the Temagamis and the Temagami region had become "adhered" to the 1850 treaty, such that their ancient claim to their homeland had been extinguished.

Consider the most basic principle of contract law concerning land. First, any and every purchase of land must be in writing. Second, the contract must be signed by both parties to it. Third, that signed written contract must describe the specific land. Consider the indisputable facts. No contract of purchase and sale has ever been drawn up identifying the Chee'Bai'Gin/Temagami region. The 1850 treaty expressly and explicitly concerns only the lands of the Indian bands whose "chiefs and principal men" affixed their signatures at the end of it. No Temagami Indian ever signed that treaty or any document referring to it. No Temagami ever signed anything having to do with aboriginal rights. This was not a contested point. There was never any suggestion by anyone to the contrary. No contract, no signature, no description – three strikes. Three times the Ontario government misses the ball. And the umpire, the judge, appointed by Canada and paid by Ontario, calls it a game-winning home run.

The "adhesion" argument itself is a recent invention, an ex post facto excuse that thinly veils a grotesque theft and extortion. Of course, in any contractual situation, new parties are always free to come along and make a contract of purchase and sale with regard to other land than that involved in the original contract. And the second contract can take into itself the terms and conditions of the first contract. Such a new contract can be termed an "adhesion." By it, both parties to the new contract can be said to have become "adhered" to the old contract. If one of the parties was already a party to the old contract, then only the new party would be "adhered." But calling the new contract an "adhesion" does not alter its profound legal character as a contract. If the adhesion contract is for the purchase and sale of land, calling it an adhesion cannot alter the basic requirement that it describe the land being sold and be in writing and signed by the parties. Not one of those fundamental elements of contract law apply to the so-called adhesion of the Temagamis and the Temagami region to the 1850 treaty contract. No document exists describing the Temagamis as a party to any contract. Their land is nowhere described in any surrender instrument. They still, so far as I am aware, have signed absolutely nothing.

In the further alternative, said the trial judge, there is no such thing as "aboriginal rights" in any event. That phrase, he said, is a misnomer that really refers to the government's policy of treating the Indians charitably, not out of legal necessity but out of liberal generosity: "I am of the opinion that there is no legal trust relationship between the Crown and the Indians ... Prior to Confederation in 1867, the Crown in right of the Province of Canada had full power, by legislation, administrative acts and treaties, to unilaterally revoke Indian rights." On this basis, the judge held that, before the treaty, Canada had the

beneficial interest in the lands ... To summarize, prior to Confederation, the Crown had legal title to unceded Proclamation lands. The Province of Canada had a beneficial interest in and legislative competence over such lands. After Confederation and prior to cession, the Crown still had legal title, but the Province of Ontario now had a beneficial interest in the lands. It is true that the Privy Council [in the *St Catherine's* case] characterized Ontario's right as: "... the right of the provinces to beneficial interest in these lands, available to them as a source of revenue whenever the estate of the Crown is disencumbered of the Indian title." I do not read the Privy Council as holding that Ontario could not disencumber its title by legislation, but merely that Ontario's beneficial interest was subject to such aboriginal rights as were not extinguished by treaty or legislation ... Ontario could, by legislation, deal with and even alienate or dispose of its beneficial interest, for example, by the issue of patents. The right of alienation was inherent in the beneficial interest itself ... The inevitable effect of alienation would, of course, be to extinguish aboriginal interest in the patented land.

The trial judge slipped in the two words "or legislation": "Ontario's beneficial interest was subject to such aboriginal rights as were not extinguished by treaty *or legislation*." All the law up to this time had been understood to say that aboriginal rights could only be extinguished by "purchase" – that, is, "by treaty." That law has at all times been grounded on the consensus of international law as settled by *Sublimus Deus*, 1537, as incorporated into the constitutional common law and confirmed by the written constitution ever since the Royal Proclamation of 1763.

That law, like any law, can be repealed or amended, but first the legislation doing the repealing or amending must be of international or constitutional law weight. This provision is basic to the rule of law. International and constitutional law cannot be unilaterally repealed even by the Congress of the United States or the Parliament of Canada. To pretend the opposite is to overturn the rule of law itself. And to overturn the rule of law in order to steal the lands of another race and culture is an act of genocide.

The "legislation" to which the Bear Island trial judge was referring was legislation enacted unilaterally by the Legislative Assembly of the Province of Ontario. He held that Ontario, by ordinary domestic legislation, could repeal the previously established international and constitutional legislation. The consequence of that holding would be that Ontario is above the constitution from which it derives its jurisdiction. That is a legal impossibility. In short, the trial judge held that the non-native governments and courts can do whatever they want.

The Bear Island case is not an isolated instance, but typical of the chicanery of the modern judicial approach. But that result did not take away from the truth. It proved once again the wisdom of the adage that judges ought not to be allowed to judge when in a conflict of interest: *nemo potest esse simul actor et judex* [none can be both suitor and judge]. The cornerstone of the rule of law is the existence of a genuinely independent and impartial third-party court. The genius of the rule of law is that, by the simple device of a third party as adjudicator, it removes the corrupting influence of self-interest.

Since 1537, when *Sublimus Deus* repealed *Inter Cetera*, notwithstanding Ontario's atavistic legal position to the contrary, the law had always been clear and unambiguous: the newcomers' governments have never had any lawful jurisdiction over lands in the New World which have yet to be purchased from their Indian inhabitants. All they have is the right to purchase such lands when the Indians are willing to sell. As Chief Justice Marshall of the Supreme Court of the United States held in the case of *Worcester v. Georgia* in 1832: "The United States succeeded to all the claims of Great Britain, both territorial and political ... This was the exclusive right of purchasing such lands as the natives were willing to sell. The crown could not be understood to grant what the crown did not affect to claim ... The King purchased their lands when they were willing to sell, at a price they were willing to take; but he never coerced a surrender of them. He also purchased their alliance and dependence by subsidies."

Great Britain's, and therefore Canada's, Royal Proclamation of 1763 confirmed the previously established constitutional common law. This is the law attributed to Great Britain by Chief Justice Marshall, to which the United States succeeded. There has never been a repeal. Only a constitutional amendment could effect a repeal. The proclamation itself is expressly and explicitly recognized and affirmed in the most recent revision of the Canadian constitution, the Constitution Act, 1982. The proclamation is simple, clear, and plain:

And whereas it is just and reasonable and essential to our Interest and the Security of our Colonies that the several Nations or Tribes of Indians with whom We are connected and who live under our Protection should not be molested or disturbed in the Possession of such Parts of Our Dominions and Territories as not having been ceded to or purchased by Us are reserved to them or any of them as their Hunting Grounds—We do therefore with the Advice of our Privy Council declare it to be our Royal Will and Pleasure that no Governor or Commander in Chief in any of our Colonies of Quebec East Florida or West Florida do presume upon any Pretence whatever to grant Warrants of Survey or pass any Patents ... upon any Lands whatever which not having been ceded to or purchased by Us as aforesaid are reserved to the said Indians or any of them ... And We do further strictly enjoin and require all Persons whatever who have either wilfully or inadvertently seated themselves ... upon any other Lands which not having been ceded to or purchased by Us are still reserved to the said Indians as aforesaid forthwith to remove themselves from such Settlements ... And whereas Great Frauds and Abuses have been committed in purchasing Lands of the Indians to the great Prejudice of our Interests and to the great Dissatisfaction of the said Indians In order therefore to prevent such Irregularities for the future and to the end that the Indians may be convinced of our Justice and determined Resolution to remove all reasonable Cause of Discontent We do with the Advice of our Privy Council strictly enjoin and require that ... if at any Time any of the Said Indians should be inclined to dispose of the said Lands the same shall be Purchased only for Us in our Name at some public Meeting or Assembly of the said Indians.

Faced with these constitutional words at the trial of the action commenced against the Temagamis in 1978 by Ontario in the Ontario court, the trial judge in 1984 summarized as follows: "To conclude, in 1763, George III, with the advice of his United Kingdom Ministers, did not grant ownership of vast tracts of lands to Indian bands subject to a limited right of repossession by repurchase, surrender or conquest when a war had just been fought to acquire those lands. At that time, Europeans did not consider Indians to be equal to themselves and it is inconceivable that the king would have made such vast grants to undefined bands, thus restricting his European subjects from occupying these lands in the future except at great expense."

There is no basis in law for the judge's statement that "Europeans did not consider Indians to be equal to themselves." The wording of the law is to the opposite effect. Rather than deny the Indians' humanity, the law has expressly and explicitly protected aboriginal rights as the most basic of all human rights. This is what the trial judge found to be "inconceivable." And because he personally found it so, he never did address the actual wording of the law. He brushed it all aside. The same process occurred in the Ontario Court of Appeal and the Supreme Court of Canada: the law was never addressed at any stage of the Bear Island case.

CHAPTER 6

Getting Fired and Going Back to School

Shortly after the trial the Temagamis fired me in favour of retaining a large law firm that had greater experience with appeal work. The major consequence was that the issue of native sovereignty was dropped as a feature of the case. Much like the other defence lawyer at the trial of the Moosonee Indian in Cochrane, the new lawyers felt that arguing native sovereignty was a non-starter in the court system. They took the position that I was leading the Indians down the garden path by filling their heads with my own idealistic preconceptions about the rule of law. On this basis my former Temagami clients were persuaded to restrict their appeal to the facts and to leave the law alone.

The new lawyers made a strong case in the appeal that the trial judge was wrong when he said the Temagamis were not aboriginal to the land in question. Eventually, the Supreme Court of Canada ruled that the Temagamis were aboriginal to the land in question, but that it was not necessary to address the law since the Court had not been asked to address the law and the Court could not identify a clear mistake by the lower courts on the facts. On this basis it was held at the highest level of appeal that, regardless of what the law might say concerning the impossibility of extinguishing aboriginal rights by treating an acceptance of benefits and a reservation as an "adhesion," an extinguishment by "adhesion" in fact had occurred.

The trial judge's decision was handed down on 12 December 1984. Between then and 10 April 1985 I prepared the papers identifying both the factual and the legal grounds for the appeal. I was fired on 11 April at the meeting of the Temagami council called to receive my report. After the meeting began, I handed out copies of the appeal material. The six members and the secretary pushed them aside. All of them were looking down at their hands or the table, not meeting my eyes. The chief said, first, that the meeting would consider my responses to some legal opinions that he had obtained from other lawyers. I knew nothing of these opinions, but it was apparent that the others at the meeting were familiar with them. They seemed to be awaiting my response, so I read reports right then. Each of the three opinions was based on the reasons for judgment issued by the trial judge. Each one accepted at face value what the trial judge had said. These lawyers basically indicated that, in their view, they were better lawyers with bigger law firms and deeper resources, on which basis they felt they could have persuaded the judge to think differently on the facts. They had no new material to offer. Since they did not pretend to go outside the judge's reasons, they did not know what materials the trial judge had ignored, only what the judge said they were, and the judge had not addressed any of the materials that did not suit his own predilection towards shafting the Indians.

These reports drew attention to two disparaging comments the judge had made about me in his written reasons for judgment. With regard to my analysis of the law, he said: "The constitutional attack of the defendants was so broad ranging and so vague as to render the constitutional issues incomprehensible. My view of the constitutional issues raised in the action can be summarized as follows. I have already concluded that the aboriginal rights exist at the pleasure of the Crown, and that they can be extinguished by treaty, legislation or administrative acts pursuant to legislation." His second criticism concerned the evidence:

I feel obliged to comment on how disappointed I was that there was so little evidence given by the Indians themselves. Chief Potts was the principal Indian witness to give oral history. There were a few other Indians who gave minimal amounts of oral history, some of which conflicted with that given by Chief Potts. Furthermore, they did so only as a condition of my allowing hearsay evidence to be introduced by the Mr Conway with respect to alleged Iroquois battle sites. The evidence they gave in-chief was restricted to that issue, plus the statements to the effect that they knew of no treaty and that they believed that their ancestors had always lived on the Land Claim Area. In cross examination they stuck to the proposition of ancestral residence, even when some of the evidence such as that given by William Twain, indicated that some of his ancestors had moved on to the land or were white people. The knowledge of these Indian witnesses was generally limited in time to their immediate grandparents.

The only relevant question for the purposes of the legal proceeding was the oral tradition that there was no treaty. All the Indian witnesses testified on that point, and not one of them was shaken in cross-examination. I had discussed at length with the Temagamis' council and with the families the options relative to calling witnesses. The communal consensus was that the appropriate spokespersons were those who were in fact called. As in any society, some individuals more than others are the respected historians and the politically relevant representatives. These individuals were all called.

Based on the trial judge's innuendo that other Indian witnesses could have been called but were not, in an endeavour to conceal something, the lawyers providing these second opinions all suggested that they would not have made the same mistake. They said they would have called more Indian witnesses. Yet when the new lawyers took over they did not make any application to adduce additional evidence through more Indian witnesses. Given the judge's comments on that score, such an application was positively invited and almost certainly would have been allowed. But it was not made. Instead, the new lawyers were content to argue the appeal entirely on the existing record as I had adduced it.

I put it to the councillors: "Are you trying to say that you have lost confidence in me as your lawyer? If so, it is your right to dismiss me." No answer and more looking at the table. What I did not find out until later was that the steps had already been put in place to hire the new lawyers. The elected chief had, without my knowledge, been meeting with my Toronto agent, another lawyer who was a partner in a four-hundred-lawyer firm. I had spent some time expounding to my clients the virtues of this agency firm as an extension of my own capabilities, as devil's advocates of the written materials I was filing and so on. The agent must have informed the chief that his firm could not act for them if I were acting, since the firm already had a lawyer-client relationship with me, and they therefore decided to engineer my dismissal. That advice took a highly unethical and cavalier attitude to the sanctity of the relationship between my (former) agent and me, but these things happen in legal relationships no less than in politics, business, and matrimony. Treachery is a normal part of the human condition.

Having told the councillors that it was their right to dismiss me and that they should be discussing the issue among themselves, I left. I was thunderstruck. I went home to Margaret. She said she suspected something like that was coming. The island store where we shopped for all our groceries had cut off credit the day before because the band office said it was not supporting the Clark family anymore. We no longer had access to food, a ski-doo, a car, or a boat, and we had no cash or any prospects for cash. Margaret had hoped that things might change when the Indian bureaucrats saw the appeal papers I had been preparing against the clock.

An hour later the Temagamis' second chief came over to the house. The council's decision was that another law firm would be hired. I could stay on provided I would be an unpaid back-up, preparing the papers for the other firm. All decisions on legal strategy would be made by the other firm, for which it alone would be paid. I answered that the family and I, as he well knew, could not survive under those conditions. There was literally no food. He shrugged and looked down. He was just doing his job. As these events were taking place, and subsequently, the chief reported to the people that I had quit, walked out on them, and slammed the door in their faces. Everyone in the community agreed, apparently, that the chief had no choice but to accept my decision to leave them in the lurch.

I informed the second chief that I was obliged by law and by conscience to brief the incoming lawyers fully and would do that as soon as they were identified to me. In the meantime, I asked, might I borrow a vehicle to move off Bear Island. We departed that night. I left behind all my research materials for the new lawyers.

The one prize possession Margaret had was her piano, a treasure from her own childhood. We contacted the non-native teachers, a husband and wife team who ran the island's elementary school. They agreed to buy the piano for $500. That was all the money we had. I gave personal effects like my chain saw, axes, and tools to our neighbours. We left our children's books for the school. They each chose one treasure, and we packed up our family photo albums. Everything else in the house we left to our babysitter, to distribute to those she thought would have the greatest use for what was there. Only the old lady, dear Lizzie, came to say goodbye. We cried on her shoulder, and she on ours.

With the help of a neighbour to whom I gave our woodpile of dry birch, we travelled by ski-doo the 4 miles over the lake ice to the landing, where the loaned vehicle awaited us. We headed out for Margaret's parents' house in London, Ontario. The children were delighted to see their grandparents. Margaret and I were in shock. For two weeks she and I talked and struggled with the unanticipated change that had so abruptly occurred. We had not built into our personal lives any emotional safety nets to deal with such a development. On the one hand we were swamped by resentment at the Temagamis' apparent betrayal of us as individuals, but on the other we understood that they were swamped by the treachery of our whole race of people to theirs. We were frustrated by their infidelity to their own cause, but we sympathized with them over the seeming futility of that cause in a justice system controlled by their adversary.

At the end of the first week we went to church with Margaret's parents. The theme of the sermon that particular Sunday was the proposition that resentment corrodes the vessel in which it is kept. That answered our first question. The resentment had to be allowed to pass through. Having in this fashion put that particular devil behind us, we still had to plan what to do with all the knowledge we had accumulated. Should we make a clean break with the past? Back and forth we went, debating. By the end of the second week we had come to a second conclusion. If the law was as we thought, then the major injustice from its breach was much bigger than the minor injustice to us. Regardless of the impact on our individual lives, regardless of any question of personal feelings, if our society was really trashing the rule of law, we were not entitled to walk away from such a wrong. We decided that we had to make one last attempt to determine what the law really said. If we had made a mistake on the law, then we would be free of the burden of trying to implement it.

This was a watershed point for us to acknowledge. We had seen Indian society from the inside out. Once, it must have been a self-sufficient society. What was left was an almost totally dependent municipality. Once, there must have been an economy, a language, a religious tradition, a territory. Vestiges remained of each of these features, but only vestiges. If the process by which that destruction was inflicted was indeed a crime, then the continuation of the last stages of that process continues to be a crime. The fact that only a few were left to be victims does not affect the legal principle involved. If a man commits mass murder, we do not let him finish off the last remaining victims because, after all – what's a couple more? People are not supposed to discuss the political pros and cons of prosecuting criminals. At most we might debate changing the law by repealing or amending it generally, or by legislatively granting an amnesty in extraordinary political circumstances, but we do not simply look the other way. In a society based on the rule of law there are supposed to be no exceptions to the rule that people must respect the law until it is changed by due process. If we debate the social utility of the victim before enforcing the law against the criminal, we are not just aiding and abetting the crime, but destroying the rule of law itself.

Based on such considerations, Margaret and I decided that she would return to her former profession of teaching to finance my return to university. There, I would attempt once and for all to determine whether a crime was in progress against those Indians who are still culturally Indian. As for those Indians who were profiting from the crimes against the few who were still being victimized, we no longer felt a great ethical obligation. They had made their choice to accept the jurisdiction of white society and were able to take care of themselves in that context. Certainly they had no end of lawyers at their beck and call, so long as they stayed within that context, because millions of dollars were being disbursed by Canada each year to lawyers and other experts working for Indians who do not buck the system. We agreed that if, at the end of the academic process, I had verified that the law requiring the purchase of Indian land before non-natives could have access to it had remained an unbroken chain, as I believed, I would continue to attempt as a lawyer to have the law acknowledged and respected. If the law had been repealed, then it would be for others to pursue appropriate political solutions.

London, Ontario, was admirably suited for this purpose. Margaret also had attended the University of Western Ontario, and her first job as a teacher had been with the Middlesex County Board of Education, the one surrounding this city of 350,000 people. Even though it had been twelve years since Margaret had taught for the board, she was well remembered and highly regarded. She found temporary work and began teaching right away.

I went to see the dean of the Law School, who offered me employment teaching one course in aboriginal rights and another in real estate law. He was also able to offer us the temporary use of a partially furnished apartment that the school maintained in the married students' complex. The Law School had no postgraduate program, so I applied to the history department for admission to the master of arts stream. I selected as my thesis topic the legal history of aboriginal rights in Canada. I was granted scholarship funding and a teaching assistantship conducting history tutorials for undergraduate students. As I was now a registered student, we were able to rent a subsidized townhouse in the married students' residence complex.

For the last two months of the school year we enrolled David in grade three, Zoë in grade one, and Beau in kindergarten. Fortunately, the school was located right beside the complex and, while providing education for the children from the local middle-class neighbourhood, it also attempted to accommodate the special needs of children from all over the world who learned there while their parents were attending the university. When our children were asked to describe what an Indian was like, they were bewildered and completely unable to answer the question. Bear Island and the people there had been home for all their lives and they had accepted it as it was. The children were resilient and gave our lives focus. They strengthened our resolve to ensure that the Canada in which they were growing up was based on the rule of law.

Since I was doing research in constitutional history of relevance to all Indian land claims, I offered to keep the new lawyers in charge of the Bear Island case abreast of my discoveries, as well as answering any other questions they might have. They asked whether I was content with their using the research I left behind. I confirmed that was the purpose of leaving it. Aside from that, they declined my offer of assistance. Their decision not to go into the law of aboriginal rights in the Bear Island appeal process obviated the need, in their minds, for further legal research.

At this juncture I was forty-one years old. One hears stories of older people returning to university and loving it, but for me it was not like that. In terms of the conventions of historical scholarship as contrasted with legal scholarship, I was very rusty. All the students seemed to me not only brilliant and conversant with the controversies in the field of history but, in addition, competing for grades to gain entrance for a limited number of admissions and scholarships for doctoral programs. Trying to keep up with them was exhausting. And I found that teaching the two courses in the Faculty of Law took a great deal of preparation. There were lectures and tutorials to give as well as to take, and it had been sixteen years since I had been engaged in that process.

The shift from courtroom to classroom is not a natural one. I was more terrified of the students than of the judges. With the judges, I was leading the argument on my own topic and very confident of the ground. With the students, I was playing catch-up, always trying to pick up a rhythm whose beat I had long since lost.

With Margaret teaching, I also had to help with the children more than I had previously, in terms of lunches and being there when they got home from school. That fall of 1985 I became overextended and succombed to double pneumonia. Margaret took over as usual and pulled us all through that episode. I graduated with a master's degree in history and my grade average was high enough to earn acceptance into the PhD program in history with a full scholarship. Carswell, a legal publisher, agreed to publish my thesis as a book under the name *Indian Title in Canada*.

We were at another cross-roads. Without really noticing it, I found myself becoming a historian. If we were not careful we were going to end up living a normal life in some college town, working our way up the ladder of academia. Again Margaret and I had to return to the kitchen conference table. After some discussion, the consensus was that I was meant to be a lawyer, not a historian. I had not discovered any new data that dramatically changed the issue that had prompted this venture into academia. We decided to decline the history route and its scholarship.

It seemed important to be outside North America, perhaps to gain a fresh perspective. I found that the dean of law at Aberdeen University in Scotland was personally interested in taking on a doctoral candidate in the aboriginal rights field, provided the work would be done on a comparative law basis (Australia, New Zealand, Canada, and the United States). As a former Australian himself, he retained an intellectual curiosity with the law concerning indigenous peoples. In consequence, I applied for and received both admission and a scholarship to study under his mentorship.

To our delight, we discovered in the foothills of the highlands outside Aberdeen a converted blacksmith's shop for rent as a house. Its name was Smithy Croft, and it was indeed a croft – two up, two down – nestled in the hills, with cows in the backyard and windswept fields and heather in the front. We could easily imagine the smithy at work when we built a fire in the waist-high granite-slab fireplace that dominated one end of the main downstairs room. The children attended a two-room school next to a pink stucco castle, the real-life model for Walt Disney's Fantasyland motif. We had milk and fish trucks stop at our door, and our friendly postman in his small red truck always had a cheery greeting when he delivered the mail. We were enchanted with the afternoon teas, although we never quite got used to corn on our pizzas. Behind our croft was a hill, on the crest of which was a stone circle and some adjacent menhirs. They were not as big as Stonehenge, but the idea was the same. Margaret, whose Scottish blood harkened to these hills, often reflected on the aboriginal Scots. The hills over which their stone circle maintained its vigil were once covered by the seemingly endless and inexhaustible Caledonian Forest known to antiquity, but now were laid bare of their majestic pine carpet. Like the native people for whom I had worked and with whose struggle for land and identity I was linked, the Scottish warriors were also less well equipped than the invaders to conduct wars of attrition. Like the natives of the Americas, the native Scots witnessed their land invaded and their identity challenged and changed. As we rested in the hills we asked their pagan spirits for support, in the name of the original people of land everywhere. For everywhere the Christian has gone, the land and its aboriginal people have been dominated and they have suffered. We regained our strength and our courage, sheltered by those Scottish hills.

I would write up a section and then journey into Aberdeen to spend a day with my mentor going over my papers. He has a wonderful mind – his hobby was reading Chinese law in Chinese – and he was always able to hone in on the weak link in any legal argument's chain of logic. Although Margaret had received permission to teach in Scotland, we found that teaching jobs were very scarce. When she was offered a position in London, England, we considered that possibility, but then decided that it was not realistic to expect her teaching salary to provide a living for our family in London the children and I remained in Scotland. Still, my scholarship was not enough both to cover tuition and to support the family. Then, out of the blue, came a phonecall from the Middlesex Board of Education offering Margaret a teaching position in London, Ontario. We had no choice. She accepted and returned alone to Canada. We found this split-family situation difficult.

Then came the breakthrough on the law for which I had been looking for fifteen years. I was reading the shelves in the Aberdeen Law Library, taking books down and looking for leads to resolve the native sovereignty dilemma. I went to a shelf and the first book I put my hand on was entitled *Appeals to the Privy Council from the American Plantations*. It literally fell open at a page with a reference to *Mohegan Indians v. Connecticut*.

Until then, I had begun to despair that I had covered the ground so thoroughly that I was unlikely to discover a case with which I was not already familiar. The one major lead on which I had hoped to build in Aberdeen, Lord Watson, a former chancellor of the university, had proved thin. He had introduced the term "usufruct" when describing the Indian interest in a leading case in 1888. From the notes and the biographical information of this man, the greatest of the Scottish law lords, I had hoped to gain a deeper insight into the nature of the Indian interest. But the scent on that track had petered out. As the son of a Scottish minister of the church, Lord Watson would have been familiar with the glebe, a concept based on the "usufruct" idea in Roman law of having the use of the land without the ability to dispose of its ownership. This information assisted with understanding the historical process by which the concept was incorporated into the lexicon of modern aboriginal rights law. But it did not provide any solution to the problem that the domestic courts were ignoring that law in practice.

I read the pages of the book containing the reference to *Mohegan Indians v. Connecticut* with bated breath while still standing at the shelf, unwillingly to spare the time to take the book to a reading desk. Even as I read the case for the first time I knew I had come upon the evidence that would establish the guilt of the North American legal profession in the treasonable and fraudulent genocide of the Indian nations of the Americas.

As the story of the *Mohegan* case unfolded it became apparent that almost three hundred years before my own search for a solution to the problem of domestic courts ignoring aboriginal rights, a group of Indians had walked the same path. What is more, they had secured the solution that so far had evaded me. The payment for their courage and brilliance seems to have been their extermination from the face of the earth, for they were the *Last of the Mohicans* fictionalized by James Fennimore Cooper.

At the outset of this printed description of the case were identified commentaries of contemporary lawyers. The consensus in the eighteenth century was that this *Mohegan* case was the single most important case ever decided by the Judicial Committee of the Privy Council. Since the Judicial Committee was the highest constitutional court in the British Empire, its most important decision arguably settled a point of law that governed the whole of British North America. All lawyers and all judges must have been aware of that decision in the first half of the eighteenth century. Yet in fifteen years of pouring over every single decision ever decided by the domestic courts of North America since the mid-eighteenth century, and of following up every decision mentioned in any other decision, I had never before come across this precedent.

The background was as follows. In the 1550s the Mohegans occupied the Hudson River drainage basin and were related to the Algonkian-speakers from there to the Atlantic and to the north. To the west were the Iroquois-speakers, a different linguistic family. Partly in response to the trauma of the European invasion of the Hudson valley and the related incursions of the Iroquois, who were envious of the Mohegans' middle-man position in the fur trade and tired of paying the Mohegans for the privilege of passing down the Hudson to get to the European fur traders at New Amsterdam (now New York City), many Mohegans fled in the 1500s, intermarried, and conquered their fellow Algonkian-speakers to the east. In the 1600s some of these Mohegans made a land treaty with the government of Connecticut. Later, Connecticut sold portions of that land to settlers and, when the settlers moved onto the land, the Mohegans objected.

Their objection was based on an allegation that their intent in making the treaty had been to put the land in trust for the perpetual use of themselves and their descendants. Connecticut replied that its intent in making the treaty had been to purchase the land, so that it could be opened up for settlement or such other development as the government deemed best in the interests of its own citizens. The Mohegans did not want to go to war over the dispute. In the past they had always fought as allies of the British, and they wished to continue as such. In 1637 the Mohegans had even taken part in the British massacre of the Pequot Indians, a subdivision of the Mohegan network of local bands.

The Mohegans, apparently, did not wish to risk a similar massacre, but neither did they regard the General Court of Connecticut as a sufficiently independent and impartial third party for adjudication purposes. To the contrary, they regarded that court as being in a profound conflict of interest. The colonists with whom the Mohegans were in competition were of the same race and culture as the members of the court, and had appointed the judges. Besides, they reasoned, the non-native judges had jurisdiction only over land that had been purchased outright from the Indians. Therefore, for the Mohegans to concede jurisdiction to those judges was the equivalent of agreeing that the judges had acquired jurisdiction: that a valid treaty had been made extinguishing native jurisdiction. In sum, for the natives to accept the jurisdiction of their competitors' court system was to concede defeat on the very issue under contention.

The Mohegans' basic legal argument was that the government could not have jurisdiction because the land was still Indian land, even though it was held in trust. Being Indian land still, the Indians on it could not legally be bothered by government interference, which to them meant that the government had no jurisdiction. They, the Indians, alone had jurisdiction, and the only court that could have jurisdiction would be their Indian court, not a court created by their adversary, Connecticut.

The essence of contract law is that the contract records the parties' joint intention. Since a treaty is a contract, the resolution of the dispute depended on determining what each of the parties intended, to see if there was a meeting of minds even capable of creating a contract. The white judges might not have too much trouble getting inside the minds of the government negotiators. But could they get inside the minds of the Indian negotiators? The same consideration would apply if the shoe were on the other foot – if the Indian court were asked to decide. There was reasonable basis for apprehending bias if either of the two competitors' court systems was given the right to be the adjudicator.

The Mohegans applied by way of a petition to Queen Anne, asking her to appoint a third-party court to hear the outstanding treaty interpretation issue. The queen at that time had the constitutional jurisdiction to legislate constitutional law for the colonies. On the advice and consent of her Privy Councillors, Queen Anne referred the petition to the Lords Commissioners of Trade and Plantations, also known as the Board of Trade, the subcommittee of her Privy Councillors which specialized in colonial issues. The Board of Trade in turn referred the petition to the attorney general, Lord Northey, who made three recommendations. First, he recommended the creation of the third-party court. Second, he recommended that the court be by way of a permanent committee, such as the Judicial Committee of the Privy Council, only a trial-level rather than an appeal-level committee. He did not want the new court to be a one-time-only project, since it was apparent that the kind of issue presented by the Mohegans was likely to recur in colonial society. Third, recommended that a right of appeal be provided from the new trial-level committee to the appellate level of the Judicial Committee.

The Board of Trade accepted Lord Northey's recommendations and added its own recommendation that they be enacted into constitutional law by the Queen in Council. This was done on 9 March 1704. This order was of the same constitutional weight and force as the Royal Proclamation of 1763, which is also an order-in-council.

Common to both the proclamation and the order is the underlying previously established law that the Indians' liberty and the possession of their property is constitutionally protected. That has been a constant feature of natural law, international law, and the common law of the constitution ever since 1537, when the papal legislation *Sublimus Deus* acknowledged that for natural, international, and constitutional law purposes the Indians are human beings whose rights must be respected under the law.

The Order in Council (Great Britain) of 9 March 1704 in the matter of *Mohegan Indians v. Connecticut* took this previously established law as a given. The Royal Proclamation of 1763 expressly and explicitly reiterated it. The single most important fact in the history of aboriginal rights in North America has been the effective concealment by the domestic legal establishment of the existence of the Order in Council (Great Britain) of 9 March 1704 in the matter of *Mohegan Indians v. Connecticut*. By never mentioning the order, the judges and lawyers of the domestic legal establishment have managed to oversee the greatest land theft in human history, all the while pretending to be serving a rule of law society. Under the proclamation, that theft constitutes treason and fraud. But there has never been a prosecution, precisely because the criminals have also achieved a monopoly over the legal process. It is the perfect crime, precisely because the crime is masterminded by the legal establishment. The consequence of the crime has been the genocide of a race and culture.

Finding the *Mohegan* case was to me like dropping an ice crystal in a supercooled beaker of water. In that instant the entire contents of the beaker crystallizes into ice. The moment the case touched my consciousness, all the events of the previous fifteen years of my life became explicable. For years I had heard traditional native people express the viewpoint that there is no justice for the native in the newcomers' court system because the non-native judges will never address the law. My answer to that observation had always been that such a conclusion was premature. I had always argued that until you could prove that the whole truth about the law had been put before the white judges, the expression of that viewpoint sounded like paranoia. As I put it in my book *Native Liberty, Crown Sovereignty*:

I say to aboriginal peoples, however, that their fear underestimates the power and objectivity of the rule of law. The non-native legal system is not necessarily biased against natives. Judges have so far never been given the whole truth upon which to adjudge issues; they have never had put before them the necessary legislation and precedents upon which to base their decisions. The fault if any is upon the information put into the system rather than upon some racism assumed to be inherent in the system itself.

My discovery of the *Mohegan* case meant that I could go back to the native people and challenge them to give the legal system of my own race and culture a chance to demonstrate the integrity of the rule of law in our society.

This realization galvanized the writing of my thesis and, in consequence, I received my doctorate in jurisprudence degree in 1990. In 1991 my thesis was published by McGill-Queen's University Press under the title *Native Liberty, Crown Sovereignty*. The academic reviews were favourable and predicted major changes in public policy and legal forums in light of my research. In that sense, the academic community assumed, as I did, that the law would be upheld by the judges once the whole truth about the law was put before them.

With this goal in mind, I returned to North America to resume my career as a lawyer. First I contacted the Temagami chief and council and their new lawyers. They preferred not to be distracted and bothered. I wrote to every Indian band in Canada, alerting each of them to the same law. None answered, yet hundreds of bands had land claims either in progress or in the wings. Every one of those land claims was dramatically concerned with the choice of court forum. Still, there was no expression of interest in learning more about the assertion I was making relative to native sovereignty and the jurisdiction of domestic courts. The deep freeze I was receiving at first made no sense to me.

Gradually, from the reactions of Indians I met, I learned that while I had been away doing the legal research in Scotland, the Temagami chief had disseminated negative information about me across Canada. Indian bands that I had never heard of regarded me as a traitor to the cause of native sovereignty and the rule of law. They had been informed that I had deserted the Temagamis and then sued them for $6 million. The last part of the accusation was true. I had issued a writ, in 1991, to stop the six-year limitation period from expiring on a promissory note that the Temagamis had given me in 1985 for that amount. At the time I issued the writ I offered to disregard the debt if the Temagamis would accept my gift of the law and get back to defending the rule of law as we had originally agreed. The Temagami chief had not made known this latter aspect of the litigation to the other Indians in Canada. All that was known, or at least believed, was that I was evil.

The law vindicating the truth of what the old Indians had always tried to tell to stubbornly deaf white ears was now being shut out, not by the whites, but by the Indians themselves. In despair, I had to reassess my options yet again. Margaret was still teaching with the Middlesex Board, and we would not consider separating the family again. I approached a former law school classmate who practised in the London area. He expressed an interest in the Indian situation and offered me a position as counsel in his firm. I was to do normal legal work and pursue any Indian sovereignty cases that might arise. It seemed like an ideal blend.

But it was not to be. Every time I tried to reintegrate into non-native society, new sets of income tax officials would appear and give me the same ultimatum with regard to the 1978 tax bill. As each year passed, the $15,000 debt claimed by them became larger and larger. Every year penalties were added to it, and interest was calculated on the combined total of debt and accumulated penalties. By 1991 the compounded total reached a staggering $300,000. My new law firm was served with a third-party tax notice, garnisheeing 100 per cent of the income

I earned. The firm offered to pay the tax debt if, but only if I would make a long-term commitment to devote my time to normal remunerative legal work, leaving aside my former commitment to work for native sovereignty cases. With regret I turned down the offer and once again found myself out of a paying job.

I could not consent for three reasons. First, the tax debt was not, in my view, payable until the law, which arguably establishes that the government had no jurisdiction to levy the tax in the first place, had been addressed. Second, the payment of the false tax would aid and abet the genocide of native people, which was achieved by the government's general usurpation of jurisdiction in order to levy taxes in relation to residence in the unceded Indian territories. The law clearly establishes that residence in such territories is illegal. Third, a condition of the firm's payment was that I spend significantly less time on the Indian question, which to me would be tantamount indirectly to aiding and abetting the genocide by failure to act to prevent it. Given my doctoral research, I knew of the law that has been buried for two centuries, but others were not similarly aware of it.

The tax department had continued to apply pressure over the years. When I returned to university between 1985 and 1990 to read for my master's and doctoral degrees and Margaret resumed her teaching career to support the family, I could not maintain a bank account because it would have been seized by Revenue Canada by way of a third-party notice – just as in Haileybury all those years ago when a similar threat forced me to shut down my law practice. The scholarship money with which to pay the tuition and cover related expenses was paid into and disbursed from Margaret's bank account. Learning of this, the income tax department moved to garnishee her income, at the rate of 50 per cent, until the whole tax account was paid off.

Margaret could hardly keep the family going as it was, and there was no possibility of getting by on half the amount. She also was forced out of her job, as a travelling specialist in the education of gifted students in five high schools. It was at this time that events broke at Oka.

CHAPTER 7

Crises at Oka and the Lil'Wat Country

Oka, Quebec, is situated at the confluence of the Ottawa, St Lawrence, and Richelieu rivers. The municipality wanted to allow the expansion of a golf course into land bordering on the town. Indians claimed the same land under aboriginal title. The reaction of some of the Indians to the town's declaration of intent was to proclaim the area a sacred burial ground. They established barricades and trenches, and occupied a small medical counselling and first-aid building set among the pines. And they brandished guns. In sympathy, other Indians block-aded a bridge over the St Lawrence River, interrupting the access of thousands of commuters resident on the south shore to the city of Montreal. Police forces aided by army support surrounded both areas. A police officer was shot dead, whether by his own force or by the Indians was never clarified. A standoff set in, with the two sides courting public opinion through media statements. Negotiations dragged on with a series of groups purporting to have some jurisdiction to speak to some of the issues. For two months, the media circus continued.

On the eve of the Indians' surrender, the *Globe and Mail* newspaper published on its op-ed page an article I had submitted. I presented some of the evidence arguing that, in their claim for sovereignty, the Indians were on solid legal ground. Until then, the media had overwhelmingly taken for granted that the Indians were behaving illegally and, in consequence, the national debate had been entirely in terms of the moral appropriateness or inappropriateness of their actions. The fact that the Indians were armed had been treated by many reporters and commentators as evidence that the rebels were terrorists, the illegality of whose actions forfeited any moral legitimacy to their conduct.

The theme of my article was that the only weapons being brandished illegally were those of the police. I presented an overview of the legislation and the precedents that establish the law's opening position: the Indians' liberty and posses-sion is the true starting point for legal purposes, not, as popularly assumed, the non-native governments' right to police the land. Until those non-native govern-ments have shown a purchase extinguishing the Indians' previously established right to govern their unsurrendered lands in their own way, the non-native governments have no right to assume the jurisdiction to police it. In contrast, the Indians have a prima facie right to defend the land from invasion.

I did not argue that this was necessarily a good law, only that it was the law, and that until it was repealed or amended it had to be respected under the rule of law. On this basis I suggested that the police should reconsider mounting an armed invasion, in favour of submitting the jurisdictional dispute to independent and impartial third-party adjudication as required by the Order in Council (Great Britain) of 9 March 1704 in the matter of *Mohegan Indians v. Connecticut*. Later I was to argue the same point in relation to the armed Indian standoff that occurred at Gustafsen Lake in British Columbia, and with the same effect – none.

After the arrests that brought the Oka standoff to a conclusion the next day, I was asked to go to Montreal to meet with the accused Indians. The charges ranged from causing a disturbance to assault. Some fifty-five of the Mohawk alleged criminals met with me in what they regarded as a safe-house on one of the two Indian reserves involved. It was apparent, although never expressly asked or acknowledged, that this meeting house was in some fashion related to the Indians' gambling and drug industry, which to some extent has substituted for the destroyed aboriginal economy. Like the guns in the standoff, the question whether the gambling and drugs were illegal depended entirely on who had jurisdiction to make the laws in the territory in question. If there had not been a valid surrender of the Indians' liberty to govern themselves, and therefore to make and to enforce their own laws, the non-native laws prohibiting gambling and drugs were simply not applicable to the lands on which the meeting place rested.

Given the opportunity to speak to those assembled, I asked for confirmation of my impression of the purpose of their conduct. I was informed that Indian sovereignty was the point: the traditional Indian perspective that since they had never surrendered or sold their land they were entitled to defend it, by force of arms if the whites would not address the law. I agreed with their point as a pure matter of law, and gave my legal opinion that were it to be addressed in court it would have to be upheld. To this end, I said, they should object to the jurisdiction of the non-native courts to put them on trial. It would not, I advised, be necessary for them to assemble the data proving conclusively that the land had never been surrendered. The burden to prove that it had been surrendered was on the non-native police and government. They were entitled to see the non-natives' evidence on that topic before replying to it.

At first the Indians assembled decided to defend themselves on this basis by erecting as their shield an assertion of constitutional native sovereignty under the rule of law. But another lawyer present at the meeting gave a second, and contrasting, opinion, one similar to that relied upon by the other defence counsel at the Cochrane trial and by the lawyers who took over the Bear Island case from me. Regardless of what the law may say, these lawyers advised, the reality is that the non-native courts are never going to admit that, for the past century, they have been in the habit of assuming a jurisdiction that is arguably treasonable, fraudulent, and genocidal. The other lawyer recommended that the accused Indians use technical criminal law defences, such as the difficulty of identifying masked individuals.

I had to agree that if all the natives wanted was to obtain acquittals, their best strategy was to follow the other lawyer. But if they wanted to have the jurisdiction issue sorted out and have the genocide of which they complained apprehended, their best policy was to follow my route. The other lawyer came back with the argument that by our objecting to their jurisdiction, the judges would be made even more hostile than they already were, and more predisposed to convicting and giving harsh sentences. I had to agree. Still, I continued, if the accused were willing to risk their lives for the principle of native sovereignty, why would they not see the issue through now that the risk was no longer death but merely imprisonment?

While I was at the safe-house discussing with the Mohawk their court options in the aftermath of the Oka crisis, I received a telephone call from British Columbia. It was from a lawyer who had been working pro bono in solidarity with a group of Indians who were maintaining a road blockade there. The lawyer identified the group as long-time native sovereigntists who had set up their roadblock immediately on hearing news reports of the Oka crisis some two months before. The native people involved were members or supporters of the Lil'Wat Nation, one of the Salish-speaking tribes of south-central British Columbia. The situation there was reaching a crisis of its own. The lawyer had information that the police had scheduled a pre-emptive strike for the following day to break the roadblock and to arrest its participants.

I dictated to her over the phone a statement for each of the potential arrestees to read and, if they felt that it accurately expressed their position, to have available to hand to the arresting officers instead of making any statements. I agreed to be on the next plane to join them, either at the blockade site or at the jail, depending on events.

I discussed this development with the Mohawk advisers. Together we worked out a joint strategy: I would go the British Columbia and, on behalf of the Lil'Wats, enter native sovereignty objections to the assumption of jurisdiction by the non-native courts in Vancouver. The same objection would be entered in Montreal. In the result, the legal justification for the roadblocks would be focused nationally. We hoped that, if we followed this strategy, the law would be addressed rather than covered up. The international media had taken up the events at Oka, and there was a good chance they might influence the domestic media to be less cavalier in their one-sided or superficial reporting of the underlying, but so far blindsided, legal issue.

By the time my plane landed in Vancouver, a mass arrest of sixty-three of the Lil'Wat defenders had been effected. The men were held in one place, and an equal number of women warriors in another. The men's prison, Ocala, was right in Vancouver, an old-style jail like the one in Haileybury, only much bigger. My new clients were housed in one wing, consisting of two storeys of cells facing a blank wall. The cell doors were opened and the people trekked down and along to the first-floor corridor. We shook hands as they filed closer. When everybody settled down on the floor or against the wall, the lawyer who had called did the introductions. Their faces were an inspiration. Some had obviously been beaten and were hurting, but all eyes were bright and alive, engaged with minds that were in liberty's thrall. There is nothing in the world so beautiful in the human condition as that look. It lit up my own tired soul and fired my admiration, as it did their faces.

I explained the theory of their defence as I would propose it: object to the assumption of jurisdiction. They said to a man that was their own idea. The point was that their ancestors had never surrendered their sovereignty, their liberty, their possession. They wished to have this position asserted in terms that could not be mistaken. Whether they won or lost in the white courts, they wanted the truth to be brought out and the record set straight so they could create a chance for change in a situation that was strangling the life out of their people.

From that meeting I was taken to another prison holding the women. Like the men, they were strong, bright, determined, and charged with life. They supported the same proposal: fight the case on jurisdictional grounds alone. Do not be concerned about our being in prison, they said, for we want to be seen as political prisoners. All our lives we have been political prisoners hidden away in our own communities, out of sight and out of mind. We welcome the change, of having our imprisonment public, so long as we are together to hold each other up.

From there I was taken along the Sea-to-Sky Highway that wends north up the Pacific coast out of Vancouver before turning inland through the Coast Mountains to the Lil'Wat country, nestled in the plain between that range and the Lilloet Mountains. There others were waiting, those who had escaped arrest and were anxious for news of their brothers and sisters. By this time I was so tired I hardly remember anything of that journey. I know we passed by the ski resort at Whistler Mountain which had recently been constructed on the lands of the Lil'Wats without their permission, for the lights of Whistler Village were pointed out to me as we passed.

Perhaps a half-hour later the vehicle pulled to a stop. As I got out of the car I saw that we were on a country road beside a river about 75 feet wide. On the other side of the road was a huge canvas tee-pee, silhouetted against towering mountains whose white caps caught the moonlight. As I was being ushered into the tent the person guiding me along pointed to what was left at the roadside of the earth works of the now-dismantled blockade.

The tent was jammed with dark faces and shining eyes that made a passage way to permit me to approach a fire burning at the centre and sending sparks spiraling upwards through the wide-open roof flap. This sacred fire had never stopped burning since the blockade began three months before. Drumming began. Almost everyone there held in his or her hands a tambourine-like drum of stretched hide over circular frames 2 or 3 inches in depth and 18 to 24 inches in diameter. In the enclosed space of the tent the drumming and the chanting were overwhelming. I heard shouted into my ear that the assembled generations of ancestors in the mountains, the spirits of the winged, legged, crawling, and finned relatives, were being informed of my mission as copies of the document that I had dictated over the telephone were burned in the sacred fire. The document's spirit was being taken by the smoke into the mountains, the sky, and the stars. As the paper curled and twisted in the flames and the chanting in the Lil'Wat language rose, I closed my eyes and, supported by the press of the crowd, I either fell asleep or entered into a trance.

Suddenly there exploded through my senses the deafening roar of a bear, whose arms I felt curving round to envelop me. In panic I screamed an alarm and grabbed the arms of those beside me, but there was only the same sea of faces, the same flood of drumming, and a multitude of voices raised tumultuously in undulating and pounding sound. Still shaking with my fright at the bear but feeling foolish, I tried to draw the attention of the person jammed most closely into me, but it was apparent that my scream had not actually passed my lips or, if it had, it was lost in the singing. No one noticed me and I settled down. Then, as suddenly as it had begun, it was over and I found myself bundled back into the car and en route to Vancouver. The next day, preliminary court appearances were scheduled.

I dozed fitfully in the back seat as we drove, periodically listening to the conversation of the two women in front. The lawyer who had called me was driving, and her companion was one of the native women. Waking at one juncture I heard them discussing how moved they were at the power of the songs. The native woman began identifying each of the songs by repeating its tune. This one was the deer song. This, the fish. This, the partridge, and so on. I drifted off to sleep again, only to be startled awake by the tune that had surrounded the bear's roar in my dream-trance in the tent. I interrupted their conversation to ask what that song was. The bear song, they both answered in unison, turning to look at me, perplexed at the urgency with which I had made my inquiry.

The Indian woman explained that the bear spirit was the protector of the land. I found my alarm rising again. I explained to them that while that song was being sung the bear came into the tent. "Of course," they both replied. "No," I insisted, "I am not making myself clear. I mean it really came into the tent. It roared. It overwhelmed me. It was there." "Yes," they said. They were unflappable, as if it was normal for a 9-foot rearing, roaring grizzly bear to be in a tent crammed with people. I finally sat back. They exchanged looks and smiled. I drifted off to sleep again.

Shortly before dawn we arrived in Vancouver and I telephoned the Mohawk strategists in Montreal to report progress and developments. No one was available to talk with me. As the days, then weeks, rolled by, none of my calls back east were returned. Finally, Mohawk runners, or messengers, came out to Lil'Wat country. I saw them first around the courthouse and, some of them being what I considered colleagues and friends, went up them to say hello. They literally turned their backs on me and walked away.

I became aware that their purpose was to persuade the Lil'Wats not to have anything to do with me. They had been contacted by the chief of the Temagami, who said I was a white devil. They, the Mohawks, had learned to have nothing to do with me. By this time the Temagami chief had risen in the ranks of the national Indian organizations funded by the Canadian government.

Whenever the concept of native sovereignty burbled up again at the grassroots somewhere in the country, the proponents of the concept would eventually encounter one or the other of my legal texts on the topic. The risk would rise that the issue would be taken into the courts – or worse, that I would be contacted to do the taking. The antidote against the threat of my involvement infecting the grassroots Indian body politic had become, I learned, the elected leader of the Teme-augama Anishnabay. He could always be counted on to give a negative recommendation or to make a defamatory speech nipping in the bud the emergence of the law-based native sovereignty movement.

Not that it usually took all that much persuading. Invariably, the choice was clear and plain. A great deal of government money exists to pay Indians to play at politics by the rules established by the human rights industry both in and out of government. Lobbying that promotes solutions for redress of individual cases of injustice is funded; attempts that focus on the institutionalized and structural nature of the problems are not. I had been identified as the enemy of this human rights industry because I was biting the hand that rocked the cradle that kept it pacific and fed it. Besides, argued the Mohawk runners to any Lil'Wats who would listen, native sovereignty in the white man's court has no chance whatsoever. Clark is leading us all down the garden path. The "rule of law" is white-man bullshit for ways to steal from the Indians and get away with it. Clark is hung up on the rule of law and is using Indians to prove his own theories. What really matters is not to talk in the white man's courts about sovereignty but to live it, to act sovereign – and to hell with the courts. Acting sovereign means making a living being sovereign, becoming part of the Mohawk's tobacco and drug sales empire.

My erstwhile Oka clients had, apparently, decided that the advice given by the other lawyer made more pragmatic sense. As one of the Indian organizers had warned me confidentially as I was leaving Montreal: "Hey, Bruce, there are no Nelson Mandelas here."

The Oka situation in one respect was more complex than any of the others with which I had been in contact, owing to the economic influence of gambling and drug money so close to Montreal. Since the aboriginal economy of the Mohawks had been destroyed by largely illegal white interference, a certain sector of Iroquoian society has traditionally resorted to what is regarded by the non-natives as the black market – although that market is black only if a person disregards the fact that the Mohawks, for example, are arguably still sovereign.

The irony is that the vitality of the black market depends on its remaining black. The executives of this special underground economy have an interest in promoting the concept of native sovereignty as the ideological basis for recruiting other Indians to assist with the expansion of their marketing endeavour, though that does not mean that they want to see native sovereignty vindicated. Their economic interest might well be more damaged by a return to native sovereignty than by continuing with, and complaining about, the present unresolved situation. For recruitment purposes in moving drugs and staffing gambling emporiums, the siren call of sovereignty idealism is of economic value. Yet the hereditary command in Iroquoian society has long been divided over the issue of drugs and gambling, as have the elected administrators promoted by white governments to undermine the Indians' traditional governments. If ever native sovereignty were to be vindicated in the legal context, the consequence to the established interests in the existing market would be threatened by uncertainty. In short, the actual vindication of native sovereignty might be bad for the Indian drug and gambling business as it exists.

When my new Lil'Wat clients confronted me with the Mohawk runners' accusations, I recounted in full the events that had occurred at Temagami and at Montreal and left the Lil'Wats to make up their own minds. The bottom line was that some Temagamis, and now the Mohawks, had decided, for their own political and economic reasons, to jettison the native sovereignty position at least so far as the courts were concerned. And, not wanting any other groups to pick up the banner, they were performing a character assassination on me, the one lawyer ready, willing, and able to present and defend that issue in court.

In spite of the Temagamis' and the Mohawks' efforts, the Lil'Wat defenders decided that they wanted to continue to raise the issue of native sovereignty as a basis for disputing the jurisdiction of the non-native courts to put them on trial. It was not by any means a new issue to them. In 1911, long before the road connecting their country with the white settlements on the coast had been built, their ancestors had prepared and executed a "Lil'Wat Declaration" that completely mirrored all I was trying to prove. In 1927 they had sent elders to Ottawa and to England to insist that the international and constitutional law respecting their liberty be respected. In 1985 many of their people had been arrested and beaten for fishing in the way and at the time of year that was to them an aboriginal activity, though it conflicted with recently introduced federal, provincial, or municipal law. Promises were made by the white authorities to address the law, but none of them had been kept.

By 1990 the Lil'Wat defenders were tired of waiting for justice according to the rule of law and wanted to try to make it happen. Their legal defence entailed two immediate projects. First, to persuade the judge who had granted the police the injunction ordering the removal of the Lil'Wat blockade that he had no jurisdiction to have done so. Second, and at the same time, to persuade the judge who would be trying those Indians for contempt of court for not obeying that injunction that he had no jurisdiction either.

The first judge refused to give my clients an appointment at which they might present the law establishing the validity of their jurisdictional submission. To me it was inconceivable that, in a matter of such obvious importance and notoriety, the judge could simply state that he was not prepared to listen to the law going to jurisdiction. But it was that simple. Accordingly, I applied to the chief justice of British Columbia for a review, by some another judge, of the first judge's injunction and his refusal to reconsider in light of law that previously had not been presented. That application, too, was blankly and flatly refused. I attempted to appeal these arbitrary refusals to listen to law to the British Columbia Court of Appeal.

As part of the material filed in support of the application for leave to appeal, I delivered my own affidavit explaining that my clients feared that a judicial conspiracy was under way to stonewall the law simply by refusing to allow it into the court. In British Columbia, appeals in such matters cannot take place without the "leave," or the permission, of a Court of Appeal judge. The idea is to restrict the number of appeals to these that concern issues of importance. It is a filtering process that is meant to ensure that the appeals level is not swamped with trivial work that prevents significant work from getting attention.

When I went before the Court of Appeal judge to argue this motion for leave to appeal, he said he would not listen to the application, at least not that day, because of the use of the word "conspiracy" in the supporting affidavit. He wanted to reflect, he said, on whether the court should even listen to the application for leave in such circumstances. On this basis, he adjourned the matter for a few days, recommending to the lawyers for the attorney general of British Columbia, the Indians' adversary in the proceedings, that I personally be reported by them to the bar association, with a view to my potential disbarment for having used the offending word.

A report went out on the national news wire service in Canada that I had accused the British Columbia bench of conspiracy. The context of the set of resulting newspaper articles across the country was of a lawyer run amuck, making absurd and irresponsible accusations. By this time Margaret and the children had joined me in Vancouver, and she sent to the *Globe and Mail* the typed transcript of the proceedings before the Court of Appeal judge and a copy of the affidavit in question, pointing out that I had not, as erroneously reported, accused the bench of conspiracy. I had advised the court that my clients feared a conspiracy, which was the literal truth. The relevance of this fear is that in a society based on the rule of law, justice must not only be done but be seen to be done. The refusal by the courts to address the law allegedly precluding their own jurisdiction gave rise to a fear that justice was not, in fact, being done.

The Lil'Wats, like many other Indian people, have an oral tradition that small-pox blankets were purposefully introduced into their communities in the 1800s. They believe that the white man tried through the residential schools to brain-wash the Indianness out of those Indians he did not kill by biological warfare. They believe that the law not only says that their liberty and possession must be respected but states it in such clear and plain terms that no judge could possibly mistake the point of law. The reason the genocide of the native people has oc-curred and is occurring, they claim, is that the non-native judiciary is overseeing the pogrom. Because the judges so obviously do not apply the law and so bla-tantly refuse to listen to it, my clients truly did fear a judicial conspiracy to sup-press the law by being wilfully blind to its existence.

I had recorded the existence of that fear in the affidavit to explain to the non-native courts the urgency of the need for those of us engaged in the administra-tion of justice to show the Indians that their fear was groundless. The way to do that, I argued, was simply to address the law, without further delay. I was not de-manding that the judge necessarily agree with my interpretation of the law, only that he allow the Indians to adduce the law. This the judge refused to do. Instead, he began the process of getting me disbarred for attempting to raise the law.

After court that day I happened to be standing by the information desk at the entrance to the courthouse. The Court of Appeal judge in question came to the commissionaire manning the desk and exchanged a few end-of-day pleasantries. I waited for the judge to acknowledge my presence and make the same sort of pleasantries with me. It is normal for lawyers and judges to maintain a standard of civilized behaviour outside the courtroom, no matter how difficult or hard fought the points of law have been inside. He looked at me, then through me, as I stood with a smile frozen at half mast. There were only 3 or 4 feet between us. He turned his shoulder to leave, but I could see he was shaking with anger, his face red and mottled with suppressed rage. Obviously it was my unexpected presence that had upset him, yet he knew nothing of me personally other than that I had raised a point of law which he preferred not to hear.

"How," my clients were asking themselves and me, "could justice be done un-der the rule of law if the courts refuse to read the law precluding their own juris-diction?" "How could the rule of law function if the law had to be left outside the courtroom, just because it disturbed the judges' assumption about their own jurisdiction?" These were legitimately and honestly held concerns, as well they should be to all citizens in any society based on the rule of law. They fed a fear that is latent in many native people that the white courts are conspiring to stone-wall aboriginal rights. That such a fear exists is an undeniable and important fact in North American society. To suppress the fact that such fear exists and may well have a legitimate basis only serves to evidence the conspiracy.

The *Globe and Mail* published a retraction. Nevertheless, I was eventually contacted by the Law Society of Upper Canada, the bar association in my home province of Ontario. I had been reported to it for potential disbarment or other disciplinary purposes as a result of the appeal court judge's recommendation to the opposing lawyers that this be done. After I filed the relevant transcript and affidavit with the Law Society, the charge against me was dropped. Even so, the precedent had been set: from that juncture forward, every time I raised on behalf of my clients an objection to the jurisdiction of the non-native courts, rather than address the legislative words and judicial precedents which substantiate the legal accuracy of that objection, the judges refused to address the law in favour of trying behind the scenes to have me disbarred for raising the issue.

When the time was up on the appeal court judge's adjournment for him to reflect on my clients' application for leave to appeal on jurisdictional grounds, the matter came back before him. He declared that the issue was not of sufficient importance and denied leave to appeal. His reasoning was that, for the objection to be made, the Indians would have to make a land claim. A great deal of history would have to be considered concerning Indian-white relations. Only then, he thought, could the jurisdictional point be raised. That context was essential.

On behalf of my clients I attempted to explain that the whole point of their objection to jurisdiction was that the judicial assumption that there must be a land claim was false. What the judge was saying was that he would not allow the legal point that his assumption was illegal to be argued. His reason was the self-same assumption. This was the perfect catch-22. The precedents and legislative words that the judge refused to allow to be addressed established that all land was presumptively reserved for Indian use; only a treaty purchasing the Indian interest or a constitutional amendment could change that legal situation; the judges' assumption that they had jurisdiction to shift the legal burden of proof onto the Indians, by requiring them to make a land claim which the judges could then judge the validity of, was not merely illegal, but treasonably, fraudulently, and genocidally so; and the Indians are entitled to third-party adjudication and do not have to prove anything before this judge.

In reading the materials accompanying my clients' application for leave to appeal, the judge must have seen that my clients prima facie were right in law. Nothing filed by the attorney general disputed the clear and plain words of the precedents and legislation. Yet the attorney general's materials argued that the Indians' application was an insult to the intelligence and integrity of the courts and should not be dignified by having any attention paid to it whatsoever. From that juncture forward to the present time, the strategy of the attorneys general and the judges across Canada has never varied. In every single instance they have refused publicly to address the law substantiating the validity of the jurisdiction objection, while seeking behind the scenes to have me disbarred for raising the objection.

If the injunction itself could not be set aside, either by the trial level reconsidering or by an appeal level overruling, the other alternative was to raise the jurisdictional objection in the proceedings against my clients for criminal contempt of court for having broken the injunction ordering them not to block the road. There is a rule governing matters of practice and procedure in British Columbia which allows a person to dispute the jurisdiction of the court without being assumed by his appearance in court to have accepted the court's jurisdiction. The rule reiterates the common law position that exists in any event, simply because, in any rational system of law, jurisdiction is always the starting point: before a court does anything, it must be clear it has jurisdiction to do something. The jurisdictional challenge rule in British Columbia states:

Rule 14. (6) Where a person served with an originating process has not entered an appearance ... or whether or not the person has entered an appearance, alleges that (c) the court has no jurisdiction over him in the proceeding or should decline jurisdiction, the person may apply to the court for a declaration to that effect. (7) Where an application is made under ... subrule (6) of this rule, the plaintiff or petitioner shall take no further step in the proceeding against the applicant, except with leave of the court, until the application has been concluded. (8) An application made under ... subrule (6) of this rule does not constitute acceptance of the jurisdiction of this court.

My Lil'Wat clients and I next encountered the judicial chicanery whereby the non-native courts perfect the perfect crime. When we applied to challenge the jurisdiction of the court putting them on trial for breaching the injunction, we were at first informed by the trial judge that he refused to address the jurisdiction issue. As he saw it, if he were to look at the issue and discover that the law said he did not have jurisdiction, he would be implying that the injunction itself had been unenforceable all along. If he did not have jurisdiction, neither did the judge who granted the injunction. Both were Supreme Court judges. And the law says the court itself has no jurisdiction. That result would, the trial judge "reasoned," be unacceptable because it would amount to a "collateral attack" on the jurisdiction of the first judge. And it is a well-known rule that one court, other than an appeal court, cannot overrule the decision of another court. This rule is especially important in cases involving injunctions, because the thinking is that injunctions must be obeyed until they are reconsidered by the court making them, or until set aside on appeal.

Therefore, concluded the judge, the collateral attack rule that prevented him from questioning the jurisdiction of the other court, which had granted the injunction, pre-empted the rule permitting the accused to object to his jurisdiction in his own court. I pointed out to him that this was chicanery: that on the basis of wilfully blinding himself to the law not only precluding his jurisdiction but rendering its assumption to be treason, fraud, and complicity in genocide, he was going to commit those crimes. I argued that the fact of an injunction by another court did not give him the jurisdiction to commit crimes in his court.

As I have said, the trial judge at first used this collateral attack position as a basis for refusing to address the law going to jurisdiction. He changed his mind, twice. My sixty-three native clients were still in jail, having refused to sign an undertaking to come to court as a condition to being let out of jail on bail. They refused to sign anything that agreed, even marginally, that the non-native court system had jurisdiction to put them in jail in the first place. So why, they asked themselves, should they sign a paper agreeing to come to a court that itself was trespassing on unceded Indian land? As the opening stages of the trial drew closer to Christmas of 1990, and as each day the natives entered the courtroom singing their sacred songs, the profound injustice of the situation began, apparently, to wear upon the trial judge. He asked me to find a way that my clients would agree to go home for Christmas.

Accordingly I spoke with them in jail. They instructed me to inform the trial judge that the native way was to return respect with respect. If he were to release them, they said they would voluntarily return to his court to inform him of the law, if he were ready to listen to it. They would not sign a paper agreeing to this, but they would give to him personally, in open court, their word. They would show respect in this fashion to the judge, if he were in that way to show respect to them. I passed their message on. The judge responded that he would indeed meet respect with respect. He met their promise with his promise: he stated in open court that he would listen to and deal with the law they wanted to bring before him. On this basis the judge ordered that they be released from custody. Nothing need be signed. My clients accepted.

Counsel for the attorney general of British Columbia, stood to object. He reminded the trial judge of his opening position on the collateral attack rule and argued that the judge should not change his mind about applying that rule. But the trial judge said no. He reminded the prosecution counsel that not long before he himself had been in a position similar to that in which the natives now found themselves, and at that time counsel had successfully persuaded this same judge to let in all the law, so the full position would be available for appeal purposes. He informed the prosecutor that even if he, as judge, were to return to the collateral attack position at the end of the trial, the natives would at least have a complete court record on which they could argue on appeal that he had made a mistake in interpreting the law they put before him. The trial judge asked the prosecution counsel to answer how the natives would be able to argue that a mistake had been made interpreting the law if the trial judge were to refuse to consider the law, because of the collateral attack or any other rule.

My clients were satisfied with the judge's new position. On these mutually honourable and satisfactory terms and conditions they went to their homes. No better Christmas present could be imagined at this stage. The trial judge had agreed to listen to the law going to court jurisdiction and to make a ruling interpreting it. This opportunity had never happened before. Always, historically and in their own experience, whenever the issue of court jurisdiction had been raised, the non-native judges had shunted it off to the side. Always, they had told the Indians to raise that particular law on some other day, in some other context, just not now. This judge, at last, had said he would deal with the law going to that issue. True, he might end up by saying that in his view the collateral attack rule overturned the rule establishing that the court's assumption of jurisdiction was a crime. But the natives felt that the judge would be unlikely to do that, as an honourable man, once he realized that he would in effect be saying that, on a technicality, judges can get away treason, fraud, and genocide. This judge, at last, was going, openly and honestly, to deal with the words of the law that establish the treason, fraud, and genocide. It was a major breakthrough. Respect had been met with respect, and justice would be done.

Subsequently, the judge reneged on his word. Once he saw the law that proved that the natives were right, he reverted to his opening position and held, at the end of the trial, that he would not, after all, be dealing with the law they had put before him. His reason: the collateral attack rule precluded him from acknowledging the existence of and addressing that law. When the trial judge reneged in this fashion, I stood up in court to object. I pointed out that it was chicanery for the judge who had made the injunction to refuse to address the law that rendered his assumption of jurisdiction a crime; for the appeal court to refuse to consider the same law on the ground that it wanted factual history, not pure law; and now for this judge to say that the only judges who could address the law were the ones who had in this fashion arbitrarily refused to do so. I pointed out to him that the net result of this process is that the law is left outside the courtroom. He responded, appeal me.

The result, at trial, was that the Lil'Wats were convicted of being criminally in contempt of a court order, an order they could prove was null and void for lack of jurisdiction under existing law. The courts refused to apply the law, though they could not disagree with the content of that law. The sentences for this "crime" of contempt of court were virtually non-existent. Each of the convicted Indians received a sentence of one day in jail, which in practical terms meant immediate release. Punishment was not the point being made by the non-native court system. The point, clearly and plainly made by the judges, was that the law is inadmissible when it indicts the judges themselves, as a class.

I lodged an appeal. The British Columbia Court of Appeal held that the collateral attack rule precluded the raising of the challenge to jurisdiction rule. A further appeal, or at least an application for leave to appeal, was lodged in the Supreme Court of Canada. The relevant section of the Supreme Court Act reads as follows:

Section 40(1) ... an application to the Supreme Court for leave to appeal shall be made to the Court in writing and the Court shall ... grant the application if ... any question involved is, by reason of its public importance or the importance of any issue of law or any issue of mixed law and fact involved in the question, one that ought to be decided by the Supreme Court or is, for any other reason, of such a nature or significance as to warrant a decision by it.

Leave to appeal was denied on the only ground available: the issue raised – court jurisdiction relative to arguably yet unpurchased Indian lands – is not an issue of sufficient "importance" within the meaning of the section to occupy the highest court's time.

The Lil'Wat trial was the most dramatic of any in which I have been involved. Outside the Vancouver courthouse many of the native sympathizers maintained a drumming vigil. The courtroom itself was packed with native people in addition to the sixty-three defendants. Before each resumption of the sittings, the sheriff's officers allowed natives to smudge the courtroom with the purifying and fragrant smoke of smoldering cedar boughs and herbs. At every recess the spectators and the accused would stand and sing, in massed voices, the songs of prayer calling on the spirits to witness and to protect. At the close of every recess, the voices would fall silent and the heads would bow, including mine, with fists raised in silent tribute to freedom.

One voice rang through and above the rest, purer and more perfect. This voice belonged to a young warrior who had found the red path after years of wandering aimlessly in the alcohol-soaked streets of skid-row Vancouver. After the trial he withdrew into himself and into the crafts with which he managed to make enough to survive, until he, too, fell victim to the swamping despair. He died still in his twenties, another victim to the despair of institutionalized injustice. His colleagues, when I saw them after his funeral, the warriors whose flashing eyes had so inspired the moment of our first meeting at the Ocala Prison when they felt there was hope for their struggle against injustice, were changed. The spark had gone.

Even as the Lil'Wats were being put on trial for having purposefully ignored the injunction ordering them not to block the road, a timber company began construction of a new road. It was to be a mainline or trunk road for the use of logging trucks going into and from the valley on the far side of Lil'Wat Lake. This lake is accessible on its east side by the road that the Lil'Wats had been blockading. Its west side was, until recently, inaccessible except by boat. That west side was the place where the medicine men trained and were buried in the old days. A small shelf of land at the foot of towering mountains that split at this shelf gives access to a higher mountain valley. The valley rising from the shelf was blanketed with majestic old-growth forest, the dwelling place of the spirits of the medicine people as well as a habitat of the endangered spotted owl.

The logging road was intended to cross the shelf where the timber company intended to clear-cut the forest. En route were rock outcroppings, bearing the pictographs of the medicine people, which would be in the way. The Lil'Wats once again resorted to the barricades. One, a medicine man in training, placed four stakes in the ground inside a circle that he circumscribed in the road's intended path. He began his chant as the bulldozer working on the road approached. It was apparent he was not going to move, and it was possible the machine would not stop. The loggers were angry with the Indians and had made life-endangering threats to put them in their place. The medicine man told me later that he had composed himself to die, hoping to be able to blow the earth from his cupped hand into the blade of the machine as its edge entered him. But as he drew in his last breath and was poised to expel it onto the earth in his hands, the blade stopped, inches from his face. The operator shook his head, turned the machine off, dismounted, and walked away.

Back to court we went, to the white court, the one with no jurisdiction. The timber company had another injunction application. Once again, I went before the non-native court for the purpose of objecting to its assumption of the jurisdiction to grant the requested injunction in relation to land not yet purchased by the crown from the Indians. The presiding judge announced at the outset of the hearing that he would not entertain any objections based on constitutional law. He had determined that the appropriate place for going into the constitutional law could only be at a land claim trial commenced by the Indians. Much like the British Columbia Court of Appeal judge who had earlier decided that the Indians had to bring forward a large body of historical evidence, this judge also decided that a land claim by the Indians was the only context in which the jurisdictional challenge could be raised.

I attempted to point out to him that this decision also was tantamount to chicanery: that he was saying the only way in which the Indians could establish their jurisdictional point of law was to bring a land claim, the very bringing of which meant that the Indians accepted the jurisdiction whose existence they were disputing. The judge was saying to the Indians that if they wanted to deny his jurisdiction, they had to accept his jurisdiction and, having accepted his jurisdiction, they would be met with the counter argument that their acceptance waived their objection. I pointed out to the judge that the only way in which jurisdiction could be challenged without risking this counter argument of attornment was by having recourse to British Columbia Rule of Practice Number 14. As we have seen, subsection (8) of that rule provides: "An application made under ... subrule (6) of this rule does not constitute acceptance of the jurisdiction of this court."

In response, the judge just smiled at me and shrugged. He knew that what he was doing was a fraudulent abuse of process. He knew I knew. He also knew that all I could do was appeal him, and that the Court of Appeal would back him up. He was showing the Indians who was in the driver's seat: it was not law; it was the men who controlled the legal process. He was one of them; the Indians were not. And this was a them-versus-us fight.

He smiled on the assembled lawyers appearing on behalf of the timber company and the provincial and federal governments. They smiled back. It was not necessary for them to rebut the constitutional law, which they could not have done because that law so clearly and plainly vindicated the Indian position. The judge in his opening comments had absolved those lawyers of the task of even having to try. His smile invited their congratulations to him for a job well done. Their smiles gave him the stroking for which he was looking.

I filed an application for leave to appeal. The appeal court judge before whom that application went said that there was no possibility that the Court of Appeal would ever address the law going to court jurisdiction without there being a land claim trial looking into the history of land dealings in the province. In response, I argued that the history of land dealings was utterly irrelevant to the definition of the law. I openly acknowledged that the history of land dealings in British Columbia was of a provincial establishment that had discontinued making Indian land purchases very early in its history. Basically, that province followed the lead of the United States Congress, which, in 1871, enacted an Appropriations Act proclaiming an end to the treaty-making process. British Columbia came into the Canadian Confederation that same year, and ever since had occupied the same position.

Having read for a master's degree in Canadian legal history, I assured the judge that there was no room for doubt on that historical fact; that we did not need boxcar loads of research reports and days of expert testimony to point out the obvious. My clients' argument was that this history of land dealings was neutral to the definition of the law. The law fell to be determined on the basis of legislative words. As for these, having completed a doctorate in law upon that very topic, I was able to assure the judge that the legislative words left no room for doubt but that the history of land dealings was evidence of a long-standing criminal practice in which the entire legal establishment was the criminal, from the lawyers who certified the thousands upon thousands of titles to the judges who looked only at the domestic law, but never at the constitutional law on this subject.

I argued that the only point in going into the history of land dealings, which he had identified as the precondition to addressing the jurisdiction issue, was to obfuscate that issue. On the basis of what the society had in fact done, the judges wanted to be able to infer what the law was. That is not, however, how the rule of law works. The rule of law does not begin with what was done and work backward. Rather, it works forward from what the law says to an examination of what was done, to see if what was done was what should have been done. The time to address the history of land-dealing in a rule-of-law society is after the legislative words have been addressed. Once that was done, it might never be necessary to address the details of what was in fact done. Once the law was addressed, it would be obvious to everyone that the constitutionally responsible rulers and public officials, including the judges of British Columbia, had endemically broken the law for a long time.

The historical details of that process would not matter from a legal perspective. They would not be relevant to any civil claim for damages, for the Indian victims of the treason, fraud, and genocide implicit in the historical process are dead. These victims include the traditional Indians who refused, as the 1909 *Annual Report of the Department of Indian Affairs* remarked, "to recognize the benefits likely to accrue from the adoption of the white man's methods." The Indian band governments and their constituents have, historically, been the white governments' agents in the treason and fraud by which the genocide of the traditionals was implemented. The idea now of a class action by the Indian collaborators seeking civil damages for the suffering they had caused was absurd. The point of reading the law was not to punish or to compensate, but to prevent the repetition of the crimes against the last few traditionals not yet exterminated. And to rehabilitate the rule of law for the long-range good of all people.

Having heard me out to this effect, the judge granted leave to appeal, even though he had said there was no possibility whatsoever that the Court of Appeal would consider the matter as a pure law issue as requested. He added that he would be the appropriate judge before whom to bring any subsequent motions in relation to procedural matters preliminary to the actual appeal hearing. Whenever a judge makes any order, the lawyer for the client in whose favour the order was made has to type up the order, so that it can then be signed and officially entered into the records of the court. After typing the order, the lawyer sends it to the lawyer for the other side who, if he agrees that what is typed accurately reflects the judge's decision, endorses the draft "Approved as to form and content." The first lawyer then takes the approved draft order back to the court office for official processing. If the second lawyer does not agree with the wording and cannot come up with an alternative that meets with the approval of the first lawyer, the procedure is to go back to the court for the court clerk or the judge to decide. This longer process is what happened in the case in which leave to appeal had been granted to the Lil'Wats.

The clerk of the court said that she did not want to decide the dispute as to wording, so referred the matter to the judge for his decision. In these circumstances, the judge gives an appointment at which the lawyers can appear to argue their views as to what the final wording should be. The judge decides. I waited for notification of the appointment date. I kept going back to the court desk for information. At first the answer explaining the delay was that the judge was on vacation. Then it was that he was busy on backlogged work. Finally, I was informed that he had turned the whole file over to the chief justice of British Columbia for guidance on how to proceed. This was a bizarre development. Settling the terms of an order granting leave to appeal is not normally a matter that is referred to the chief justice in any court system of which I was aware. I asked the desk clerks whether they had ever heard of such a development in British Columbia. Shrugs. No comment.

For the next six months I kept checking back to find out what the chief justice was doing with the file. Nothing. It was sitting on the corner of his desk. There was nothing the clerk of the court could do other than leave a note with the chief justice that I had inquired again and was pressing for an answer. At the end of that period I received in the mail a standard form from the court office. The normal rule is that if a person who has been granted leave to appeal neglects to process the permitted appeal within six months, the court will assume that the person has decided to abandon the appeal, in which case the leave to appeal is revoked and the file is closed on the matter. The standard form I received put me on notice that a date had been fixed for a judge to decide whether to treat the appeal as abandoned on the ground that the appeal had not been perfected.

I wrote back informing the court that the only reason I had not perfected the appeal was that I could not do so until the order granting leave to appeal had been settled, and that the reason the order had not been settled was that the chief justice was neglecting to allow the appointment for the settlement of the order. My written submission assured the court in the strongest possible terms that there was absolutely no intention to abandon the appeal, that all along my clients and I had done everything permitted by the law to expedite the appeal, and that the only reason the appeal was held up was the delay caused by the chief justice of British Columbia, on whose desk the file was apparently stalled. I sought the court's help in persuading the chief justice to do his job: either to return the file to the judge who had granted leave to appeal so he could settle the order or to settle the order himself. I pleaded with the court to do so, on the ground that thousands of lives of native people across Canada as well as the integrity of the court system arguably were in jeopardy because of the delay.

My twenty-six page letter outlining the history of the delay and the accompanying plea for help in breaking the log jam went before the chief justice himself. Yet his order said there was nothing in the file to suggest that the appellants, my clients, had not decided to abandon the appeal. Accordingly, he ordered that leave to appeal was revoked.

The order granting leave to appeal had never been signed, since it was never settled, so its existence was not even formally recorded. For this reason alone it was legally impossible for the six-month limitation period for doing something pursuant to the order to have begun. Yet the chief justice threw out the appeal because the time to perfect the appeal supposedly had expired. I attempted to get him to review his decision and to change his mind. I wrote and pleaded with the judge who had granted leave to appeal to get the file back from the chief justice to apprehend the monstrous fraud that so obviously was being perpetrated. I filed several applications to appeal. Nothing. No appointments could be obtained. Increasingly in my pleas for help I began to stress the blatancy of the fraud being perpetrated by the chief justice's abuse of power. There was no getting under, over, or around the stone wall. Applications would work their way up through the court system channels, only to be put before some other judge who would then make an order saying there was no material on file to support the application, though the file was bristling with material. Again and again I was sent back to the beginning of the line, to go through all the steps once more – always with the same result.

Eventually, in desperation, I applied to the Supreme Court of Canada for leave to appeal the most recent in the line of refusals to address the spurious abandonment issue. Even though none of the judges would give me an order, I treated the refusal to make an appealable order as an order. Leave to appeal again was denied by the Supreme Court. The supporting materials showed beyond question that the chief justice of British Columbia and every other judge before whom the file had been passed had participated in an actual fraud – not merely in a judicial error, but in an actual and literal fraud. The Supreme Court of Canada once again held that no issue of "importance" was presented.

CHAPTER 8

The Western Shoshone in Nevada

During this same time period I was contacted by some indigenous people in Nevada, the land of the Western Shoshone. An unusual treaty exists relative to this people and their land. It was made in the mid-nineteenth century, just before the United States government decided in 1871 that it would no longer enter into any new Indian treaties. Unlike most treaties, the Western Shoshonees' does not read like the normal contract recording an outright sale of the land. Instead, it reads like the grant by the Indians of an undisturbed right of passage over their lands: a corridor over a portion of the land, not a sale of the possession of the whole. When I visited the region in response to a request to discuss the sovereignty-jurisdiction issue, I could guess at the reason for the difference.

In the eye of the coyote and the roadrunner, Nevada is no doubt a thing of beauty, and certainly the sagebrush-dotted and tumbleweed-swept tracts of dry scrub land were cherished by the indigenous people I was honored to meet here. But in the eye of most non-native people the landscape would appear as a difficult terrain – not quite Sudbury, Ontario, but close. The newcomers who made the Western Shoshone Treaty apparently had one objective in mind: to get across the Nevada desert to the promised land of California.

One of the indigenous people of this Nevada land, an old bachelor by the name of Dan, maintained a small and impoverished ranch together with his two sisters. For the better part of their lives they had been struggling against what they regarded as illegal encroachments on yet unpurchased Indian land by American government agents and assigns. One of their court battles had gone all the way to the Supreme Court of the United States. In that case, on the advice of their lawyers, the Dans had placed their reliance on what is the United States is called "federal Indian law." I knew the case well.

The first thing I asked them was whether they believed they were sovereign people. "Of course," they answered, "that is our point. We must be. We Indians were here on this land first, we never gave up this land, we are legally sovereign." "Then why," I asked, "did you rely in your court case upon 'federal Indian law'?

If you are sovereign, the federal government has no jurisdiction. Right?" "Right," they replied. "Well," I continued, "if the federal government has no jurisdiction relative to your land, how can you rely on 'federal Indian law' relative to that land?" Their answer, as it always is with such people, was that the lawyers had put that on the court papers: "Ask the lawyers," they said.

Just before I arrived at their ranch, a fresh confrontation had occurred. The United States Bureau of Land Management, believing the surrounding land to be its own, had begun implementing a policy of rounding up and removing the wild horses living there. The Dans regarded this as yet another outrage against sovereign Indian country. In their view it was not only illegal but immoral, for the horses were meant to run free. The only reason they could see for the roundup was that the United States had illegally leased land in the region to white ranchers who begrudged the horses the space and the wild grass that grew on it. Their belief was that the horses were being slaughtered not for survival but for profit.

In Indian law and religion, this slaughter was illegal and unconscionable. They wished to apply Indian law over and above the conflicting white policy. To this end the brother stood defiantly on the road into his ranch, across which the federal agents employed by the Bureau of Land Management proposed to drive. Their convoy of vehicles pulled up facing him. They dismounted and, as the agents approached, they observed that he was holding a gas can in his hand. He poured its contents over his body and, holding up a disposable lighter, announced that if the horses could not live in freedom, he did not want to live himself. He ordered the agents to go away. They drew closer. He ran towards the crowd of federal agents, swinging the gas can in front of him and flicking the lighter, which failed to ignite before the agents overcame him. He was then charged with the criminal offence of endangering the lives of the federal agents. It was in relation to that charge that I had been contacted.

In terms of the ordinary criminal law there was no defence. Physically the act complained of had occurred, and the element of endangerment was undeniable. It might in theory be argued in defence that the native acted under "colour of right," meaning that his actions were not criminal in intent, so long as he honestly and on reasonable and probable grounds believed he had the right and duty to do what he did. The problem with that defence was that, in their previous case, *Dan v. United States*, the Supreme Court of the United States seemingly had rejected the existence of the reasonable and probable grounds basis for believing that such a right and duty existed, at least under "federal Indian law." It was apparent that if there were to be any defence at all, it would have to be that the United States Supreme Court had no jurisdiction, not because of federal Indian law, but, rather, because there was a law both prior in time and superior in constitutional weight to federal Indian law.

I had been contacted because, by this time, I had become identified in native sovereignty circles around North America with a legal position that challenged non-native court jurisdiction generally. Before proceeding, the sisters and their brother wanted to hear from me an explanation of how my thesis supported their concept of native sovereignty. So did an Indian Council styled the Western Shoshone Nation.

Having spent more time studying United States case law than Canadian case law, simply because there was so much more of it published, I was in a position to oblige. The explanation why there is less Canadian law they found enlightening: for many years it was a criminal offence for Indians and lawyers in Canada to make land claims. In Canada in 1884 it was made a crime for Indians to engage in the sundance or the potlatch, for the newcomers' government feared that these ceremonies fed the natives' spirit of independence. Such assertiveness could lead to a court case challenging the newcomers' recent illegal invasion of the yet unpurchased Indian territories. The court case could have been appealed outside Canada to the United Kingdom, to the appellate branch of the Judicial Committee of the Privy Council. The risk was that, as an independent and impartial third-party tribunal, the Judicial Committee would actually read and respect the existing law. That law not only constitutionally precluded but rendered criminally treasonable and fraudulent the Canadian courts' and governments' premature assumption of jurisdiction in the unpurchased Indian territories.

Against this risk, in 1884 the Canadian Indian Act of 1880 was amended to provide: "Every Indian or other person who engages in or assists in celebrating the Indian festival known as the 'Potlatch' or in the Indian dance known as the 'Tamanawas' is guilty of a misdemeanour, and shall be liable to imprisonment ... and any Indian or other person who encourages, either directly or indirectly, an Indian or Indians to get up such a festival or dance ... is guilty of a like offence."

For a lawyer to have advised an Indian client that, regardless of this domestic legislation, he had a constitutional right, at least on yet unpurchased lands, to engage in the potlatch or Sundance (Tamanawas) would have been to "encourage," within the meaning of the statute, a criminal offence. The advice itself would have been a crime. In 1895 the Canadian Indian Act was further amended to reclassify the crime from a misdemeanour to one punishable by indictment, the equivalent of a federal felony in the United States. This unconstitutional preemptive strike against Indians insisting on their constitutionally guaranteed right to resist the premature jurisdictional encroachment of the newcomers' courts and governments in the yet unpurchased Indian country was bolstered when, in 1927, it was made criminal in Canada for anyone to raise money for land claims purposes.

The Indian Act of 1927 repeated the prohibition of the potlatch and Sundance in section 140, and then in section 141 added: "Every person who, without the consent of the Superintendent General expressed in writing, receives, obtains, solicits or requests from any Indian any payment or contribution or promise of any payment or contribution for the purpose of raising a fund or providing money for the prosecution of any claim which the tribe or band of Indians to which such Indian belongs, or of which he is a member, has or is represented to have for the recovery of any claim or money for the benefit of the said tribe or band, shall be guilty of an offence."

In 1949 the Canadian Supreme Court Act was amended to remove the right of all Canadians to appeal outside the domestic courts to the Judicial Committee of the Privy Council in the United Kingdom. The illusion was created that the Indians' unique constitutional right to the independent and impartial third-party court was repealed by a mere domestic law statute rather than by a constitutional amendment. Correspondingly, in 1951, the criminal law prohibition against the Sundance, the potlatch, and Indian land claims was lifted.

Never has there been a similar statutory gag order in the United States, though never, at least since 1776, has there been the same need. The United States has not, since the American Revolution, had the Privy Council or any other independent and impartial third-party court lurking in the wings, threatening to judge the domestic judges' fraud and complicity in the genocide against the indigenous people. The natives in Nevada had no trouble seeing this duplicity. They had been all the way to the Supreme Court of the United States. All the way there and back they had been talking native sovereignty, while their lawyers took opposite tack: federal Indian law.

The fact that the lawyers were white people who were themselves occupying lands illegally taken from the Indians was not lost upon the native people. Nor was the fact that the entire bar association and all its lawyers were in a structural conflict of interest on the native sovereignty issue. If the natives are sovereign, none of the federal and state laws that the lawyers make their livings applying are relevant. Prior to purchase the only law that is relevant in the unsurrendered Indian country is the Indian law. The only courts that have jurisdiction are the Indian councils. All others are trespassers and usurpers.

The Dan family in Nevada decided that the basis for the defence of the brother on the charge of endangerment would be native sovereignty, as a ground for precluding the assumption of the non-native court to put him on trial. To this end, through a cooperating local Nevada lawyer, I delivered in federal court what was styled a motion *in limine*, an American procedural equivalent to what in British Columbia had been a Rule 14 objection to the assumption of jurisdiction by the non-native court system.

At the trial itself, the presiding judge graciously accepted my qualifications as an Ontario lawyer with scholarly expertise in the field of North American law concerning aboriginal rights. At the outset he made an order allowing me officially to address the court *pro hac vice* – on this one occasion by special dispensation – even though I was not a member of the Nevada bar. I stood to thank the judge for agreeing to hear me on the law.

Then I advised him that I wished to draw his attention to the legal authorities establishing the defence that the assumption of jurisdiction over him was not merely prima facie unconstitutional but arguably complicitous in the crime of genocide. I had been speaking for perhaps fifteen seconds when the judge interrupted my introduction. Did I use the word *genocide*, he asked. "Yes," I replied. He ordered me to sit down. He said he did not want to hear any more on that topic, and that his grant to me of the right to address the court was revoked. He said I should consider myself fortunate for not being cited by him for contempt of court and held in jail. Then he left the courtroom to compose himself, his face having become highly flushed and his voice trembling with scarcely controlled anger.

During the recess I conferred with the local Nevada lawyer, who agreed to attempt to call me as an expert witness even though the judge had just revoked his permission for me to address the court *pro hac vice*. On returning to the courtroom, the judge listened to this lawyer's protestations that, although he himself was not condoning or in any way agreeing to the proposition of law that had just been put forward, the client was insisting on raising the defence on his own. The other lawyer advised the court that I was prepared to open myself to cross-examination by the prosecuting attorney, and therefore to the risk of prosecution for perjury.

This approach must have struck a responsive cord in the judge's psyche, for he allowed that I take the witness stand. We went through my academic credentials in some detail and the judge accepted my qualifications as an expert, entitled as such to give opinion evidence. I repeated the opinion, and gave a very brief overview of the legal history, legislation, and precedents justifying the opinion.

The prosecuting lawyer began his cross-examination. "Do you abide by the rule of law?" he asked.

"Yes," I answered.

"Are you familiar with the *Dan* case in the Supreme Court of the United States?"

"Yes."

"Does it not preclude what you are suggesting?"

"No, that case was decided by a non-native court system that had no jurisdiction because there was no Indian purchase relative to the land in question."

"Are you saying that the Supreme Court of the United States had no jurisdiction?"

"Yes."

"Are you saying that the Supreme Court of the United States committed a crime by assuming jurisdiction?"

"Yes."

"Are you familiar with the concept of eminent domain?"

"Yes."

"Do you not agree that the concept of eminent domain precludes the argument that you have raised?"

"No, the concept of eminent domain is a judicial recent invention designed to excuse the highjacking of the United States' Constitution by the judicial, executive and legislative branches. It is just a fancy label designed to mask the fact that the three branches have colluded in aid of taking from the Indians land that they did not any longer want to have to purchase."

The prosecuting attorney rolled his eyes in exasperation and disbelief at the judge, who rolled his eyes in exasperation and disbelief back. I was asked to vacate the witness stand. Without waiting to hear the law substantiating my opinion, the judge ruled on the spot that there was no basis in law for the defendant's objection to jurisdiction. The matter was closed. I was invited by the court to leave its presence. Mr Dan was convicted and sentenced to the minimum provided under the sentencing guidelines that bound the court.

I filed appeal papers with the 9th Circuit Court of Appeals in San Francisco, which turned down the appeal without providing reasons. I filed appeal papers with the United States Supreme Court. By this time other lawyers had contacted the executive of the Western Shoshone National Council. They suggested that they had preferential access to the United States secretary of the interior, who apparently had recently become interested in, and was sympathetic to, the Western Shoshone problems. For the purpose of discussing this issue, money was available to travel to Washington and, potentially, to pay for various court initiatives based on federal law. The figure of $75 million was mentioned as a starting figure.

I was unceremoniously dropped by the Western Shoshonees, who simply stopped returning my calls after I suggested that some of whatever money they obtained should be put towards reimbursing me and underwriting their filed appeal to the Supreme Court. To this juncture the Western Shoshonees had paid me nothing towards court costs or my expenses, let alone fees.

Once again the challenge to court jurisdiction in the defence of native sovereignty was dropped, along with me. Subsequently, I learned of several Western Shoshone initiatives in the non-native courts, none of which challenge those courts' jurisdiction, and all of which have been based on federal Indian law. Apparently, federal funding has been made available for this purpose.

Funding was not available for challenging the jurisdictional assumption that the so-called law of eminent domain, and federal Indian law has superseded the legal presumption in favour of the indigenous peoples' liberty and possession. All the organizations I contacted in the United States that I thought might have been supportive were not willing to part with money that had been collected by them. They paid their own bureaucrats to transverse the country and the world for the purpose of complaining about injustice and abuses of jurisdiction, but they would not challenge the existence of jurisdiction. The perceived urgency and drain of that perpetual lobbying process left no money with which to attempt to take legal steps aimed structurally at apprehending the injustice.

The bureaucrats and the rhetorically inclined orators of the American Indian Movement and its lobbying counterpart, the International Treaty Council, were typical in this respect. In consequence, the first appeal application I filed in the United States Supreme Court relative to native sovereignty versus eminent domain died on the vine.

PART THREE

IN THE WOMB OF THE DEVIL'S SPAWN

CHAPTER 9

Our First Trip to Europe

The law being stonewalled in North America, I decided to explore international legal remedies in Europe, where the present European blight upon North America originated five centuries earlier. Together with two Lil'Wat natives, Tsemhu'qw and Lahalus (Harold and Loretta Pascal), we departed for Europe. Our group of seven persons, plus my family's Belgian sheepdog, Rowdy, arrived in Paris shortly after midnight. Our baggage load was staggering – not with clothes, but with files and my full-size computer, monitor, and printer, and camping food we had acquired cheaply so as not to starve should support fail to emerge in Europe. We had exhausted the last of our funds on the flight.

We had no hotel reservation, so I asked at the airport for a recommendation to an economical place. A place on the island was suggested, we called, and set out. We needed five taxis, each one a micro car, to transport us and our possessions. We buzzed at breakneck speed through the empty streets like a swarm of crazed bees, each car alternating for the lead, and occasionally one darting off on an apparent shortcut the wrong way down a one-way alley, only to burst back into the swarm. This ride is the one thing we all remember. The hotel desk clerk blanched at the sight of our invasion. "Impossible," he shrugged, dismissing us. "Mange merde, cochon," I hit back, "nous sommes ici, nous restons, c'est ça," employing my best Sudbury back-street French. He must have been impressed, because we stayed, although we promised to leave the next day.

The next day I telephoned a number of European support groups. One spokesperson said that if we could make it to The Hague, he could reimburse us for the train tickets and help us find a place to stay there. We set out that night. The trainmen were knights of the grand tradition. Our luggage vastly exceeded the limits. We started to load it on three minutes before all-aboard time. "Impossible," the platform trainman shrugged. He looked at the conductor, who shrugged back. They both walked away. We finished heaving everything on just as the train started inching away. The conductor found us an empty vestibule and storage cupboard, and again left us to our own devices as we shoe-horned everything in by ourselves.

On arrival at The Hague the next morning, Margaret, the children, Rowdy, I, and all the baggage piled off the train onto the platform. But Harold and Loretta were nowhere to be seen. As the train started to pull away, their faces, looking as wide-eyed at us as we at them, appeared in the window of the train door. For some inexplicable reason this struck all of us as hysterically funny. We collapsed in laughter on the platform as their chuckling faces receded into the distance – everything in slow motion and vaguely ridiculous. We were back together soon enough. Holland is not like northern Ontario, where the next station can be hundreds of miles away. Half an hour later Harold and Loretta were reunited with us and we all proceeded to the arranged meeting place.

Our promised benefactor, himself North American Indian, had in the meantime contacted his head office back in the United States. "Hold on," was the message. "Do not help these people with accommodation or money." We had the meeting, but our contact beat around the bush long enough for us to gauge what had happened. We left. From that juncture on we discovered the reality of the Indian tour circuit in Europe.

A small percentage of Europeans have always felt a sympathy for the plight of the North American Indian. Since patronage abhors a vacuum, a steady stream of Indians is on a perpetual pilgrimage to and around Europe. Stops are arranged, at each meeting the Indians give a talk detailing the hardship of living under the white man's boot in North America. Usually, there is a local geographical concern that is specific to the speaker's tribe or band: the pollution of a particular stream or the desecration of a particular mountain. Against the specific concern, the talk will rehearse the general havoc wrought by the residential school system and the loss of culture. At the end of each talk, the hat is passed, covering the expenses of the traveller and contributing to a modest living.

We had come with a different message and our presence was perceived by those controlling the tour as an unwelcome innovation. We were horning in on the Indian tour peoples' turf and not playing by the rules of their particular game. We were there to ask the Europeans to put all their support behind one major initiative, to address and possibly solve the root cause of all the complaints. We were asking that the money be focused toward a different project than the one with which the Indian tour people were familiar. But they turned their backs to us and continued to do what they had always done.

We found a measure of solace and a very modest level of support among expatriate indigenous peoples from other parts of the world. Europe has many refugees who are indigenous people in flight from tyrannical regimes in places such as Central and South America, the Molucan Islands, and East Timor. In discussions with these people we found that indigenous people everywhere in the world had been and were still being made the victims of genocide as technologically more advanced humans competed to industrialize and develop the entire world. These people did not gasp in disbelief when we employed the word "genocide." "Of course," they reacted, "genocide is everywhere against us." They were also deeply familiar with the cocooning engaged in by the non-indigenous peoples of the world, the fraudulent pretenses in which they wrapped themselves to keep at bay from their consciousness the real consequence of the "progress" they were achieving economically. They chided us for thinking there was any point going to the United Nations or the World Court. "Do you not yet comprehend," they asked, "that these organizations exist for the purpose of creating an illusion that something is being done so that nothing will really be done? Such organizations exist for the purpose of talking solutions into the ground. They are the great sponges for absorbing the energy of humans, for diverting their energy away from acting, so that the genocide can go on. They will never enforce the law, and if you try to enforce it without them you are branded a terrorist."

We refused to be so cynical. We wanted to prove our new friends wrong, to make the international system of law and government function in a way that would apprehend the crime-in-progress against humanity, the genocide, in North America. As individuals, the expatriates wished us well, in contrast with the financed organizations, all of which shunned us once they realized we meant to accuse the North American judges with complicity in genocide.

One consequence of our financial straits was that our little entourage got to live in some very strange and interesting accommodation. With the help of a Dutch support group for indigenous people, Harold and Loretta were allotted a refugee apartment in Amsterdam. It was on the third floor of a building scheduled to be torn down. The entrance on the ground floor must have been used as a urinal for generations of derelict people. From it climbed a narrow set of stairs that tilted and leaned their way to the apartment. By dint of hard work and scrounged paint, Harold and Loretta turned it into a human habitation. My family was offered the temporary use of a Molucan family's apartment outside Amsterdam. It was empty because it had just been acquired and they were in the midst of stripping wallpaper and repainting. We were welcome to unroll our sleeping bags there if we wished.

At this juncture I was working to complete my efforts to persuade the International Court of Justice to provide a legal remedy. After winnowing out the various access routes, two possibilities remained: one a direct application to the court; the other, a referral to the court through the Human Rights Committee of the United Nations.

As designated foreign minister for the Lil'Wat nation, Harold signed a petition that I drafted for use in the court. It recited the assertion of law that Canada was breaching existing international law relative to the liberty and possession of themselves and the indigenous nations for whom they spoke, and that the consequence was genocide contrary to the international Convention for the Prevention and Punishment of the Crime of Genocide of 1948. The petition also recited the specific section of the Statute of the International Court of Justice which said that the preliminary question of that court's own jurisdiction to address the petition could only be decided by the court itself. Before I submitted the petition, I had a conversation with the assistant registrar of the court about this issue. Much as I had gone to the see the land registrar in Haileybury before I submitted the caution document for registration, I wanted to see if the way into the court could similarly be paved with bureaucratic cooperation.

Once I identified my purpose, however, the bureaucrat advised me that I was wasting my time. He said that in the 1920s the court had ruled that another Indian group could not bring a similar case before it. The door was closed. Indian nations were not "states," he said, and only states can bring cases into the court. I replied that the 1920s case law, with which I was familiar, had occurred before the present statute defining the court's current jurisdiction had come into existence, and that, in any event, the law on which reliance was now based was different from that to which reference had been made earlier.

The legislative wording of the present statute says that any "state" which accepts the court's jurisdiction over it can petition the court, but it does not define the legal meaning of that crucial word "state." Membership in the United Nations gains automatic entry to the court, but access is by no means closed to states that are not members of the United Nations. Nor has any decision of the court attempted to give an exclusive definition of that term. The Genocide Convention on which my clients relied did not even exist in the 1920s, when the predecessor to the current court closed its doors to the native nations of the Americas. Most important, in light of the Order in Council (Great Britain) of 9 March 1704 in the matter of *Mohegan Indians v. Connecticut*, which has never before been considered by the court, a North American native nation is "juristically sovereign," which means sovereign for the purposes of assessing the matter of court jurisdiction, and that is the essence of being a "state" for legal purposes.

What my clients wished the court to consider was the submission that because the 1920s' case had been based on a different statute defining the court's jurisdiction, because the genocide convention had come into existence since that time, and because the court in 1920s had not considered the crucial 1704 precedent confirming the statehood for juristic (albeit not for political) purposes of the native nations, it would therefore be appropriate for the court to address the question of its own jurisdiction, specifically by entertaining the petition submitted by Harold as the Lil'Wat foreign minister. The clincher to my argument was that the precise wording of the statute left no room for doubt that the decision whether or not to accept jurisdiction could only be taken by the court itself. It could not be taken by the court's bureaucracy, meaning either the registrar or the president of the court.

I sent in the petition. The registrar of the court sent it right back, with a covering letter that the court did not accept petitions from North American Indian nations because they are not states. I wrote back advising the registrar that he was usurping a jurisdiction that the statute expressly and explicitly gave to the court alone. The jurisdiction to decide whether the court had jurisdiction to address the petition was designated a judicial rather than bureaucratic decision. He wrote back saying the file was closed and not to write any more letters.

I telephoned the court and asked to speak with the judge overseeing procedural matters. When I explained the problem to him he agreed with me, absolutely and unequivocally, that the decision not to proceed with the petition was a judicial one that, under the statute, had to be taken by the court, of which he was a member judge, not by the bureaucracy. He directed me to resubmit the petition. I expressed my concern that it would just come bouncing back from the registrar. He said not to worry. He undertook to speak to the president of the court and to mention it to the registrar. I sent the petition back once again.

Some time later I received a letter from the president of the court saying that he had reviewed the matter with the registrar and supported the registrar. I wrote back to the president outlining the reasons why his support for the registrar was beside the point, that even his opinion as president was beside the point. The only legal point is the jurisdiction of the court itself to decide the question of its own jurisdiction. He, in his administrative role as president, was not the court. If he were the court, he would have had to justify his decisions in terms of existing law, which he had not even begun to do. The president wrote back saying that no further correspondence would be entertained.

I telephoned the judge who had directed me to resubmit the petition on the understanding that the court would, in due course, do its duty as stipulated by the statute. He agreed with me that an impropriety had certainly occurred, but, he said, the statute unfortunately contains no provision allowing for an appeal from a decision arrived at by either the registrar or the president. The fact that the bureaucratic decision was ultra vires, beyond the power of those officials to have made, does not of itself create a right of appeal. There is no tribunal to which even to direct such an appeal.

I had to agree with the judge on that point of law, and told him so. But still, I asked him, please consider what really is happening here. The bureaucrats, one of whom happens also to be a judge, are stonewalling the law. The consequence, at least arguably, is that genocide, contrary to the genocide convention, is occurring not only with impunity but with impunity aided and abetted by bureaucratic intransigence that flouts the law that is being stonewalled. The rule of law is supposed to preclude genocide in such circumstances. That is the philosophy that feeds the sentiment of "never again," the legislative intent of both the genocide convention and the system of international justice. The judge said he agreed with me in principle, but regretted that this did not give him the jurisdiction to sit in appeal from what the president and the registrar had done. We were going in circles. I said to the judge that the rule of law is not functioning in the present circumstances, and the consequence is genocide. By not acting, I told him he was aiding and abetting that crime. At that juncture he interrupted me to say that, with regret, he was unable to continue the conversation, and he hung up.

It was now necessary for me to leave The Hague for Geneva so I could implement the alternative route into the International Court: by obtaining a United Nations Human Rights Committee reference to the court of the point of jurisdictional law. Harold and Loretta remained in Amsterdam to work with a potential support group there in raising money to continue our mission.

In Geneva, I spoke with the secretary to the Human Rights Committee of the United Nations, himself a lawyer and a scholar of some renown. Together we went through the relevant legislation. He confirmed what I had suspected for many years: the committee was afraid of its own shadow. There was no way that the members were ever going to make a decision that confirmed that the United States and Canada had been and were still engaged in genocide relative to indigenous peoples.

Everybody knows, he said, that the genocide in the Americas is a fact, but no one in authority is ever going to admit it publicly, and certainly no one appointed to the Human Rights Committee, all of whom are screened before their appointment for their reasonableness in relation to the realities of world leadership. Besides, the committee was not a court. It did not exercise any judicial power whatsoever. Its jurisdiction was confined to making recommendations that governments were perfectly at liberty to ignore. It was, in short, essentially a political rather than a rule-of-law institution. On this we agreed. Nevertheless, a section of the convention establishing the committee gave it the jurisdiction to state a case that the International Court of Justice would have to consider as a matter of law, as contrasted with politics. The committee was entitled to ask that court to provide a legal opinion to settle any legal controversy that the committee felt might bear on its political function.

I suggested that I would file with the committee a petition asking it to refer the question of the court's jurisdiction to address the problem of genocide in the Americas. He agreed that the committee was constantly inundated with complaints of genocide in the Americas, about which it basically assumed it had no jurisdiction to adjudicate. When I asked him whether it was legitimate for the committee to seek clarification of a point of jurisdictional law that might help address the problem, he responded that the point was well taken and invited me to submit the appropriate papers.

I did. Twice. Nothing ever happened. The complaints were never investigated. There was never a reply. Nothing.

By then we were right out of money and had nowhere to live. We were allowed to continue only through the generosity of a young German forester. Several years earlier he had been on holiday in Canada and had hitchhiked his way into Lil'Wat country in British Columbia. He had been offered a lift by a young native man, and the invitation led to his spending the holiday in Lil'Wat country, hiking the mountain trails with some of the native people as guides, listening to their stories and to their reports about their in-progress court challenge to newcomers' jurisdiction over their unsurrendered homeland. He returned to Germany enthralled by the native struggle for sovereignty and resolved to help in any way he could. Like many Germans, he was interested in North American Indians.

As a child he had read the books by the German author Karl May, whose tales of native adventures are full of noble savage romanticism. As a forester he himself was charged with maintaining the now-precious wood lots under rigid German government rules, and he abhorred the devastation of the pristine Lil'Wat country wilderness in British Columbia, the mindless wholesale clearcutting that utterly destroyed not only the forest but the complete cycle of interrelated life forms. He could see that once the trees were gone, the soil freely washed down the mountainside to clog the rivers and obliterate the breeding habitat of the salmon; by the same means, the habitats of the multitude of woodland wildlife and birds were eradicated. As a hunter trained in the tightly structured and highly formalized German hunting style, he cherished the beauty and the freedom of the natives' hunts and the chaotic efficiency of their fish camps.

The house that his employment provided was large and, because he was a bachelor, he had two empty bedrooms. Once again we were relieved to be able to spread out our sleeping bags on the floor and set up the computer. By sharing his house with my family, he allowed his native friends' struggle for their homeland to continue on the legal front in Europe.

I had the good fortune then to meet a German lawyer in the little farming village near which the forester resided. His wife had been educated in England, and he allowed me to fax court documents back to Canada, from his home office and to use his photocopier. There was no other faxing or photocopying facility in that town or the neighbouring villages, so his interest and generosity were a blessing.

I had been working hard to learn the basics of the German language. I could order "eine kliene forella, bitte" (one small trout, if you please) in the local pizza restaurant with aplomb, but my ability to understand the reply was non-existent. No matter how hard I listened to language tapes and memorized grammar texts, I never really developed an ear for languages. Still, my German acquaintances were delighted with my clumsy attempts to speak in their language and graciously switched to English.

I longed for my children to have the continental approach to language study in school and to learn many languages as a matter of course. They were learning by osmosis and necessity, but with the abruptness and frequency of our moves and the time needed to climatize to new environments, they relied on English and marketplace German. Beau was particularly able to assimilate languages and was Margaret's interpreter on many occasions. Our situation reminded us of immigrant families we had seen in Canada as they struggled to master a new environment.

Nothing came of my quest for support for the native cause in Germany. The fall of the Berlin Wall and the opening of the eastern sector of Germany to the affluence of the West had created their own set of problems of a much more immediate nature. And the reputation of Canada and the United States as human rights leaders seemed to be imprinted indelibly on the consciousness of the Germans, the same as with all Europeans with whom I spoke. They really weren't interested to learn that their impressions were fatally flawed in the native North American context. They generally preferred to remember the Indians of their childhood readings, complete with headdresses and tomahawks. Modern tribulations held no interest for them capable of competing with their own problems and preoccupations. It was time to leave Germany.

We were then invited to stay in The Hague at a place nick-named "The Blue Envelope." At one time this large office building had been used by the Dutch government's tax department, which sent tax collection notices contained in distinctive blue envelopes. On the mere receipt of such an envelope, the bottom would drop out of the recipient's stomach. For many years past the tax building had been vacant. Homeless people had occupied it illegally and had developed a cooperative approach to their shared residence. Some of them had heard of us and our housing need via whatever grapevine exists for this type of information, and we were cordially invited to come and squat.

We were informed before arriving of codewords by which to identify ourselves. The people meeting us were in their twenties and were completely charming. Some had outrageous hair styles and colours and some unusual costumes; others were just ordinary in appearance. All were kind and caring. They arranged two rooms for us, one for the children and the other for Margaret and me. It was very cold because it was winter and there was no heating. But there were two small oil-burning apparatuses, and for the equivalent of fifty cents enough oil could be purchased from one of the inhabitants who made a business of providing this service. Sometimes we had the money to purchase heating oil, sometimes not.

The portion of the building in which we were rooming was rat infested, a feature that we tried not to allow into our consciousness until, eventually, one of the furry rascals ran over my foot. It was larger than I thought appropriate for any rat, of the non-judicial variety at least, to be. By this time the children's ages were fifteen, thirteen, and twelve. I became preoccupied with visions of this rat visiting them while they slept, infecting them with some horrible disease. We thanked our hosts and departed.

Our next rescuer lived in Switzerland. He had also visited Lil'Wat country and had videotaped a plane ride he had taken over the devastation left after the clear-cutting of a mountainside. He was horrified at the Canadian and American judges' disregard of the law and at the wanton destruction of the North American environment. Such destruction, he said, would be unthinkable in his country. We stayed briefly in his chalet and spoke at a meeting of a native interest group to which he belonged. At the meeting we described our plight and put out a plea for accommodation. A young man offered us the use of his family's summer cottage high in the Swiss Alps. Since it was still winter, his family let us have its use. The view was magnificent, and the peace of the environment very conducive to focused planning.

To our host's delight the cottage became the meeting place for me and two natives, both of whom were from rainforest environments. One represented native organizations drawn from the South American countries that rim the tropical Amazon River drainage basin. The other hailed from the Carmanah Valley on the western shore of Vancouver Island, the leading edge of the temperate rainforest of British Columbia. Both natives were working to assert their native sovereignty and attempting, by this specific means, to save their homelands' rainforests from despoliation. The efforts of the Carmarah Valley people had been sabotaged by the collaboration of the environmentalist organizations in Canada with the federal system of puppet native governments. As a result, the legal challenge to the assumption of non native jurisdiction on which I had been acting as counsel for the Carmanah Valley hereditary and traditional native people had, like all the other challenges to jurisdiction in the domestic legal system, been stonewalled. The hope of this representative, his purpose for tracking me down in Europe, was that a viable international law remedy, as an alternative to the foiled or non-existent domestic remedies within Canada, might be forged. By "remedy," as used here, I mean a legal remedy, as contrasted with the pretense offered by the Human Rights Committee of the United Nations with which these native representatives were fed up.

As a result of these meetings, I drafted and sent in to the International Court of Justice an additional petition, along with the appropriate supporting documents, again seeking to invoke the jurisdiction of that court. This new petition was on behalf of the genocidally threatened native people of the Amazon River Drainage Basin of the interior of South America and the Carmanah nation of Vancouver Island. It cited the same international law as informs the meaning of the constitutional law of both North America and South America. In it was also cited the genocide that is ongoing as a result of ignoring the existing law.

These threatened peoples also invoked the obligation of the judges of the International Court under Articles 35(2) and 36(6) of its Statute to address the issue of the court's own jurisdiction relative to the native nations of the Americas in light of the legal research done since the 1920s. But as had been the case with the Lil'Wat petition to the court, the legal process was frustrated at the bureaucratic level. The registrar of the court refused to open a file on the matter and place it before the court. The president of the court, the judge acting for the time being as the administrator of process, again backed up the registrar, without addressing the law. In spite of the legislation expressly to the contrary, the issue of court jurisdiction was withheld from the court and stonewalled.

Again it became time to move on. When I spoke with Harold and Loretta, I found them to be disillusioned by the lack of response in Europe to their homeland's desperate situation and to their challenge to the domestic courts. They felt they had exhausted their attempts to raise awareness and money in Holland and were anxious to return to their family in Canada. And so they left for home.

Our family then moved into their refugee apartment in Amsterdam, where we assessed strategy. The conclusion was inevitable: politics, not law, also governed in the international arena, and the United States and Canada had the politics and diplomacy in their pocket. The condemned building in which the apartment was located was scheduled to be the next in the block to be demolished, so we, too, returned home to Canada, daunted but not yet permanently defeated.

CHAPTER 10

Our Trip to Bulgaria

One native client in British Columbia wanted to cut and market timber: he firmly maintained that this was one of his aboriginal rights. I informed him that he had the right, but the government and the court had the power. There was nothing I could do to protect that right other than continue to press in as many court forums as possible for a hearing into the law which, so far, had wilfully been blindsided by the Canadian courts as well as by the International Court of Justice and the Human Rights Committee of the United Nations.

My client was not satisfied with that answer. He was not alone. Other Indian clients in British Columbia and Ontario also began to press the point that they wanted to trade directly with Europe and Japan relative to their natural resource products from their as yet unsurrendered native land. Legally I had to inform them as well that there was nothing in principle to preclude such a trade, though the reality of power politics was against it.

From earliest times international and constitutional law had insisted that the Indians could sell the land only to the discovering European nation, or to its successor nation-state such as Canada or the United States. When the law said that those countries had the right to buy, the law meant that no one else had that right. There was no question of allowing for a bidding war for the land itself. The Indians were not to be molested or disturbed on their lands that had not been sold. There they could do whatever they wanted; it was nobody's business but their own. I was not aware of any legal reason why Indians could not cut timber or have timber cut on yet unsurrendered land. I was aware of much law that said that once it was cut, it was a chattel that could be sold as such without breaking the rule precluding the sale of land.

At this juncture, some of the Bear Island people rehired me. They had cut timber on the land they claimed was never surrendered. By this time the historical researcher with whom I had worked most closely when preparing the Bear Island case for trial a decade previously had been made chairman of a board of management appointed by the Temagamis' council and the Ontario government.

The board purported to exercise a jurisdiction granted by Ontario which my particular Bear Island clients denied, on the ground of native sovereignty. They wanted to cut the timber so they would have funds with which to fight for native sovereignty.

Immediately after they had cut the logs the Temagami chief called the researcher, who in turn called in lawyers. They asked the non-native court for an injunction. I opposed the injunction on the basis of the existing law identified above, but the judge refused to read the law. The injunction was granted because the Temagami council sided with the Ontario government to defeat the exposition of the law guaranteeing native sovereignty and jurisdiction.

When the injunction was breached by the Bear Islanders who had re-retained me to resurrect their native sovereignty position, they were charged with contempt of court. In their defence I brought out the law. The judge refused once again to look at the law. There were appeals. The appeal courts refused to read the law, and the Supreme Court of Canada once again denied leave to appeal, on 6 July 1995, on the ground that no issue of "importance" was presented.

In discussing this problem with the British Columbia native, another idea occurred to me. Aside from any of the legal forums approached so far, the arbitration and court procedures provided by international commercial conventions were untried as yet. In legal theory, it was possible for my native clients to make international contracts for the sale of their timber to foreign companies and governments. When the governments of British Columbia, Ontario, and Canada illegally interfered with the fulfilment of the terms of these international contracts, the breach theoretically could be submitted to the international dispute resolution mechanisms applicable to commercial ventures.

We could not simply go out and hire a team of international commercial lawyers on both sides of the Atlantic to assist. This court venture was only one aspect of a set of perhaps twenty-five court proceedings within Canada in which I was representing traditional natives. All were attempting to focus the same issue and the same law. Limited resources had to be spread round. The expense of engaging and then instructing international commercial lawyers, and rounding up contracting partners, would by a large factor have exceeded the total resources we could apply to seeking all the solutions.

Then an unexpected solution presented itself. After a court appearance in British Columbia one day a university student approached me. In part his purpose was to arrange for me to give a speech at his university, but he also wanted to talk. He explained his interest in what I was doing in terms of a struggle for liberty under the rule of law, to which his own personal background had sensitized him. He had escaped from Bulgaria during the communist era and emigrated to Canada, where he had been granted political asylum. "The Canadians just do not seem to comprehend," he said, "how dangerous is the fire with which they are playing when they ignore their own law the way they are doing." He told me how in the communist world they had started out after their revolution with a set of perfect-sounding laws, and how grotesquely officialdom there had managed to bring about a situation where the laws as written meant nothing in practice. Policy had triumphed over law, which to him meant that the rule of men had triumphed over the rule of law. The result had been tyranny, dictatorship. "By ignoring the rule of law as they are so obviously doing," he said, "the Canadian judges are opening a Pandora's box of pure evil. Once you destroy the rule of law to steal the Indians' lands, you have won the lands but you have destroyed a thing even more valuable. Vigilant respect for the rule of law is the only safeguard against the creeping in of tyranny. It is not what the laws say, for all countries have high-sounding laws. It is what the judges do with the laws that matter."

As a spectator in the British Columbia court, he had just witnessed the judges purposefully ignoring the laws on which Canada in theory was founded. This observation made him afraid for his new-found homeland, for he was en route to acquiring his Canadian citizenship – for him a passionately cherished passport to true freedom. "Eventually," he said, "they will get around to destroying you personally." He said he had seen it too many times before in his own country. It was something the students all knew and talked about in Bulgaria, and in the other Iron Curtain countries in the years before the change. "Eventually, if you try to insist on the law when those wielding power do not wish to hear of that law, they will strike you down. When that starts to happen," he said, "if you need a place to rest away from the storm, feel free to go to Bulgaria. My family will take care of you. All the water buffalo yogurt and goat cheese you can eat. You will get strong again, maybe live forever."

At first I was sceptical. I still believed very deeply it was impossible that the judges would continue to ignore the law. I still thought it was just a matter of time before I found the way to express the law with sufficient clarity to make them see, even though they might not want to see. I had always believed that a person should never lose patience if his audience did not understand his point because it is the responsibility of the person sending the message to make it easily understandable, not the responsibility of the recipient to decipher.

But even my wilfully blind faith, not just in judicial integrity but in the integrity of Canada and the United States as countries, began to weaken. By 1993 the media had not once reported the simple legal issue, juridical jurisdiction, that I was attempting to raise on behalf of my Indian clients. Not once had there been mention of the fact that I had a doctorate in law bearing directly on the point. Without exception, the news reports were in terms that I was bald and had funny glasses, was "controversial," and made outrageous and unsupported accusations of judicial crimes in a context where the accusations did not seem rationally connected with the particular legal proceedings in progress. The fact was never mentioned that in each instance the accusations were in support of a formal objection to the given court's assumption of jurisdiction in proceedings concerning some dimension of aboriginal rights, and were supported by written documentation setting out in clear and plain terms the law justifying the objection. In the context of the news reporting, a reader could only conclude that I was blurting out completely absurd and unsupported irresponsible accusations in court at totally incongruous and inappropriate times.

The constant barrage of deep judicial bias and animosity in conjunction with the wholly misleading yellow journalism was having an effect on my family and on our security. The children had begun to notice a frisson in school against them, and Margaret and I became concerned that the increasingly frustrated loggers in British Columbia might attempt some form of self-help to rid themselves of the pariah I had been made out to be. We were, in short, at ebb tide emotionally and spiritually. Our Bulgarian-Canadian friend's offer of refuge started to seem inviting.

Combined with my new clients' wish to investigate the possibilities for European contracts for the sale of Indian timber, a move to Europe began to make sense in terms of legal strategy. We could live virtually free in Bulgaria, assisted by the Bulgarian student's family. Bread was selling there we were told at pennies a loaf. I discussed this option with my clients, and especially with the BC native who had enough money to make a timber operation a viable option. It was agreed that the family and I would go to Bulgaria to attempt to establish commercial and court contacts for putting into operation the plan to have recourse to commercial arbitration and litigation.

When we landed in Sofia, Bulgaria, the hospitality shown to us by a friend of our friend extended to her moving out of her one-bedroom apartment and into her father's place so we could stay in her home. She spoke a little English and was an invaluable source of information about how her country functioned. After a short while, long enough for our daughter, aged fifteen by this time, and our new friend's eighteen-year-old son to become interested in each other despite the language barrier, we moved from the heat of lowland Sophia to the cool of the Balkan mountain town of Gabrovo.

There is a definite sense of place in Bulgaria. Much as the natives of North America have a deep physical attachment to their land, so the Bulgarians identify their heritage with their physical location in their homeland. We found that although Bulgaria is a relatively small country, it encompasses many different geographical regions, and the inhabitants of each are fiercely proud of belonging to their own particular region. The roots of this loyalty stretch far back in time. In Gabrovo, for example, there are traces of a Roman fort, one of the four observation points built on the heights of land overlooking the pass through the Balkan Mountains. The pass had been crucial because it was part of the ancient trade route between the Orient and Western Europe, just as the trucking route today comes up from the east, through Istanbul, which is still the gateway to the Orient, through Gabrovo and its still arduous mountain pass, and on its way to Western Europe.

In Gabrovo, most of the cottages and homes, along with their gardens, had been torn down during the Bulgarians' experiment with communism. With sadness but with zeal they had been replaced with identical and uniformly ugly cement-block apartment buildings that do not reflect the pride and individual personalities of the owners. Our apartment, actually our Canadian-Bulgarian friend's former apartment, was in one of these structures. From there we could walk downtown to the shops and the outside market. As in most Bulgarian towns, no cars are allowed in the main shopping area, which is reserved for the pleasure of browsing or sitting in the sidewalk cafés to enjoy a delicious Turkish coffee and a Coca-Cola. Such an arrangement is conducive to slowing life down.

Margaret learned first hand about the whimsical availability of items once seen in a stall or shop, never to be seen again. And we all enjoyed the custom of standing in line outside the bread shop, waiting for the fragrant loaves to be taken from the ovens. We always had to buy two loaves at a time, because one would be eaten piping hot and fresh from the oven on the walk back home. I was alone in my choice of treat: water-buffalo yogurt. It was the most wonderful yogurt I had ever tasted: thick, creamy, and delicious. At first we had to drive up a mountain pass (Shipka) to a special shop to buy it, and then for a while it was available in a market stall, but eventually I could not find it at all. When I tried to track some down at the farm that had the water buffaloes, I was told that the Germans were taking all their product at a better rate than they could sell it for at home. It seemed mindboggling to come to the land of special yogurt only to learn that the entire product was now being routed to Germany.

We also learned about seasonal eating, just as the native North Americans used to do. In Bulgaria when a crop is harvested, it is eaten until it has run its course and the next crop is ready. Summer was eagerly awaited because freezers were a rare luxury and canned goods very limited. Most families had parents or grandparents who lived in the surrounding villages, where the family gardens were carefully tended. Huge once-communal farms had not been operational since the fall of communism, and it is a slow process to return the land to those who had owned it before the land was requisitioned for cooperative purposes. The equipment to run a farm or even a garden was antiquated, and the cost of modern replacements prohibitive. It was normal to see a horse and hand-guided plough being used to turn the soil.

Everywhere you turned there were wonderful bigger-than-life-size statues to be seen. Some of them honoured great-grandfathers who, with the help of the Russians, had been instrumental in throwing off the yoke of five hundred years of Turkish domination. Others honoured the resistance fighters of the Second World War who had belonged to the communist underground in their struggle to overthrow the fascist government that followed their fledgling attempts at democracy, once they were freed from the Turks. And yet others were works of art to be enjoyed, such as the growling bear and the timid fawn carved in stone in a walking park in Gabrovo. All the statues were a delight to discover as they recorded some of the local history.

I will always regret not ignoring the social taboos and strong warnings from my Bulgarian friends against my desire to talk with the gypsies. They had a series of houses on our walk downtown and, as we walked past their encampment, I always thought that the children seemed the happiest I had seen anywhere and that, in the midst of seeming disarray, there was laughter. On occasion we would hear the sound of their accordion as gypsy family members walked up our street on their collection rounds. As someone would toss from their balcony clothing or other items no longer needed, the trained bear would dance their thank you and the children would scurry to pick up the new treasures. Somehow their sense of freedom and abandon was very appealing to me, and I would very much have liked to listen to their tales.

Although the language of instruction was Bulgarian, with the assistance of a new friend who taught English there we enrolled our sons in the local Mathematica Gymnasium. Beau, then fourteen years old, with his gift for languages, had been an invaluable aid to Margaret in the local marketplaces during our travels. Now he settled in to untangle yet another puzzle, this one encompassing the additional challenge of a whole new alphabet and a very different cultural background. To his delight he became a hero to students of all ages because he was also a wizard at arcade video games. To the young people, one of the advantages of the new commerce with the West, besides pirated music CDs and dubbed movie videos, was the sudden availability of arcade games. Beau spent many satisfying hours learning the language while sharing the secrets and skills of mastering Mortal Kombat.

David, then seventeen, was more resistant to learning languages, but had no qualms about instructing his fellow students in English. The standard of education was very high in Gabrovo, and even in the mathematics school studying English and Russian was an integral part of the curriculum. David had a genuine challenge, trying to explain our idioms and humour to his Bulgarian friends.

Zoë was already applying her strong sense of independence. With the guidance of our friend in Sofia, she arranged to study at a famous ceramics school in a town not far away from Gabrovo. She had always had an interest in art, and she persuaded us that the artistic medium would help her learn not only the language but the culture of Bulgaria. It wasn't altogether altruistic, since her new boyfriend was a senior student at the school. We agreed that she could move into the very basic student accommodation and begin her studies. We didn't see much evidence of her artistic accomplishments or of her language skills, although her friend's English improved by leaps and bounds. Still, it was an experience for her to be away from home, especially in a foreign environment.

With the family settled in, I turned to the task of implementing my clients' instructions. I found that Bulgaria had an extensive timber and furniture industry of its own, but in woods different from those harvested in North America. Its markets tended to be Arabia and points south, and to a lesser extent France, Germany, and England. It was conceivable that the North American fir and pine woods could be marketed through their hardwood channels. Shipping costs to and from Bulgaria's Black Sea ports were as low as could be obtained anywhere. And Bulgaria turned out to be the world's third-largest exporter of tobacco. The possibility opened of importing Bulgarian tobacco for sale in the unsurrendered Indian territories at a fraction of the cost of domestic North American tobacco.

In short, it was readily apparent that contractual relationships on which to mount the commercial test cases would be possible and could be profitable. The native Canadian investor and some of his nephews flew over to Bulgaria to meet with the legal and commercial people who might form the nucleus of a joint venture or ventures. At first they sensed a brotherly familiarity with the gypsy encampment at the outskirts of the airport facilities, and they felt an aura of rascally adventure at being in an East-block country. But Bulgaria quickly became a dismal culture shock for them. They ran hard up against the different foods and customs of the Bulgarians. One of the most difficult to accept was the Turkish toilets. Although the millionaire native still used an outhouse at home, he was aghast at having to crouch to use the toilet in Bulgaria. And the handhold he thought made it a little easier to balance his aging frame he learned, to his dismay, was where the toilet paper should have been. People are expected to have their own supply, which North American tourists do not learn until it is too late for personal convenience. Although my family had become more flexible in our journeys, unfamiliar inconveniences seemed to build up and my Indian clients preferred to be off to Switzerland – a logical destination, since the bank with the money was there.

After exploring the possibilities together, the decision was taken that the sum of $200,000 would be given to me as a fund for the underwriting of the expenses of the European legal and commercial campaign. Against this fund I would draw as required from time to time. My native clients and I booked into the same hotel in Zurich, arranging to meet for breakfast and then go together to the bank to complete the arrangements. In the morning my Indian clients were gone. They had checked out. I caught up with them at the bank. They gave me $10,000 and a speech about how I was trying to steal from them.

I returned, crestfallen, to Bulgaria. While that money lasted I tried various other ways to raise the money to permit the project to go ahead. But nothing was forthcoming. The international commerce tactic for focusing the sovereignty jurisdiction legal issue died on the vine as well.

While I had been working to find alternative ways to finance the trade experiment and to keep our family fed, I received a panic call from another group of Temagamis. Apparently they had gone into the offices of the Teme-augama Anishnabay

Council to search for and seize copies of certain documents. They believed these documents would establish that the council, by collaborating with the Ontario government, had sold out the people. They wanted this evidence for use in future legal proceedings in which they hoped to reopen the native sovereignty issue that had been side-tacked in the Bear Island case. The council members had called in the non-native police, who charged these renewed clients of mine with the criminal offence of breaking and entering. Once again, the police and the courts rallied to the defence of the Indian collaborators who were invoking the jurisdiction of the white courts against their own native people.

I prepared the necessary court papers for filing relative to the court jurisdiction issue. Since my clients' court date was imminent, I had to fax more than thirty pages. The capability to fax from Bulgaria was in its infancy, and was certainly a novelty from our town. Bright and early the next morning Margaret and I walked to the main post office, papers in hand. Bureaucratic paperwork was voluminous in Bulgaria and waiting in line a fact of life, but after a relatively brief wait we filled out the required forms and handed in our stack of pages to be faxed. The operator who handled faxing requests was aghast. She informed us that it would take several days for the task to be completed. It was our turn to be aghast.

By now I could communicate my ideas in Bulgarian and could understand the other side of the conversation if the person spoke slowly and clearly. We had become familiar faces at the post office because long-distance phonecalls were made from there and the operators found us a bit of a novelty. This particular operator patiently explained that their post office had a low priority access to the international phone lines, that businesses in Sofia had top priority to fax lines. Between breakdowns and access to the lines, it would be optimistic to suggest a shorter time frame.

We explained in turn that some native people in Canada desperately needed the papers to file before the judge so they would not be put in jail. She became interested in the dilemma and promised to do her best throughout the day to send as much as possible. We spent a lot of time in the post office over the next few hours, in case she needed clarification on page order. She was true to her word, attempting frequently to secure a working connection. By the end of that day more than twenty of the pages had made it through, an unheard-of success rate. On our last visit of the day, as a thank you, we brought in to our operator a special kind of sweet cake. She insisted that Margaret and I join her, and the colleague who had assisted her, in the celebration. We perched on stools at a desk behind the counter of the closed post office, sipping Bulgarian raakia (plum brandy) from grinningly produced shot glasses and eating a Bulgarian treat.

This impromptu celebration epitomized the hospitality of the Bulgarians we encountered. My Temagami clients soon received all the pages and duly filed them at their next court appearance. They challenged the non-native court jurisdiction from the outset, on the pure law issue, and raised no other defence. The judge set their court date for trial in Haileybury, Ontario, within three weeks. We had many telephone conversations in preparation for their appearance. Since they were not offering alternative defences, the facts of the charge were not contested. That meant that the people did not have to speak in court other than to object to jurisdiction and to adopt the filed papers as their own. But it is intimidating to be in court in any event, and to be without a lawyer to speak on their behalf became too much for them.

They pleaded with me to return to be present in court with them. I knew their fears and decided that somehow I must find a way to be at their side. Again out of the blue came the funding to allow the trip. Other developments in British Columbia persuaded another group of natives there to send enough money to bring us back to Canada. I notified my Temagami clients that I would be able to be with them, and they expressed their relief.

Just before setting out on the return journey I happened one morning to be hiking in the Balkan Mountains adjacent to Gabrovo. As the dawn began filtering through the mist, I found myself standing in front of a giant statue of hands clasped in a shake of friendship. Above and between them was a torch of bronze, rather like that lifted by the Statue of Liberty. From the hands a winding concrete staircase led up the mountainside, to a destination hidden in the mist. I started up the path. Gradually the mist parted to reveal the concrete footings of what looked like a circular spaceship – gigantic, awe-inspiring, breathtaking. I stood, mesmerized by this architectural marvel, the existence of which nobody had mentioned to me. I found this omission remarkable because I had been to taken to a great many fascinating historical sites reflective of Bulgaria's rich past, sitting as it does at the crossroads of empires and religions.

I lingered at the site. Later in the morning, workmen came and began to use a welding torch on the huge bronze doors that led into the base of the building. I approached them and, in my halting Bulgarian, identified myself. They did not want to talk, which was very unusual. I had found that, without exception, the Bulgarian people were open, gregarious, and generous. They love to talk, especially about their country. These workmen did not. They reacted as if I was from the KGB or the CIA.

I retired to a spot on the square fronting the doors and took in once again the vista presented by the structure. After a while all the workmen left except for one. He came over to me. In a combination of words and signs he undertook to let me inside the building. We entered into a fantasyland of icon art expressing communist motifs. At its centre was a huge circular meeting hall, like a Greek amphitheatre. An interior wall encircled the last row of tiered seats, all focused down to the sunken platform at the centre of the huge room. The wall was covered with mosaics of the demigods of communism – bushy-bearded Marx, bald-headed Lenin, and so on. One of the portraits was unfinished. The scaffolding of the artists, whose work had been interrupted halfway through drafting the head, remained in place ready for completing a work that would never be finished. The portrait was of the man who had been Bulgaria's leader at the crash of communism. When coupled with the event that caused the stoppage, the very fact that the portrait was suspended in mid-work made it remarkable – like a breath taken in, with the power to exhale suddenly frozen in time.

On the outside of the inner rotunda wall was another ring of icon art whose pictures and colours were defined by thousands of ceramic squares – that blend of Islamic and Christian art that is common in the Orthodox Church. The form was ancient, yet the subjects of the pictures portrayed the struggle for liberty in the communist mode: strong-jawed, bright-eyed, resolute faces of young men and women, arms linked or thrusting into the air the machine guns of liberty they had wrested from tyrants. There were pictures of smoking factories, hospitals, and giant dams – everything much larger than life, everything boasting of dawn and immortality, yet everything dead.

The outside wall of the rotunda was constructed entirely in glass. Perched on a Balkan mountain, the vista was incredible. To the north, as far as the eye could see, was the great plain left in geological times by the ancestor of the present Danube River. It had woven its passage from the mountains of Austria through Eastern Europe to the Black Sea, leaving the rich soils that had fed the ancient peoples of Bulgaria before the Roman Empire. To the south another agricultural plain opened, the home of the Thracians whose stolen lands had become the bread basket of the Roman Empire. Here could be seen the endless fields of roses which the sultans of the Ottoman Empire had planted for the fragrances to grace their harems, and which now produced 95 per cent of the rose attar for fine perfumes the world over. To the west ran the chain of mountains that eventually turned north towards Yugoslavia, the Balkan blood lands. To the east the Balkan range tapers to yet a third agricultural plain, the lowlands of the Black Sea coast. Everywhere close by are rich and tall stands of hardwood forest.

Perhaps softened by my obvious delight in the structure, the workman explained, very slowly to accommodate my faltering grasp of his language, something of the history of this remarkable edifice. At tremendous cost to the entire Bulgarian economy, it had been constructed on the eve of the fall. Its purpose had been to stand as a grand meeting place for the communist world. Hence the prefacing statue of the hands clasped in friendship, or, I suppose more accurately, comradeship. The oriental/communist art was a tribute not only to the politicians but to the ideals they were supposed to have, but never did serve. When communism fell, some of its opponents had rallied at the building and fired into its body hundreds of rounds of machine-gun fire, so hated a symbol had it become of the cruel hoax that communism as practised in their country had been. Yet for others in Bulgaria the building remained a tribute to a sublime ideal, the corruption of which in practice only added poignancy to the hopes and dreams that human inadequacy had dashed.

To me, the building was perfect for a new world court. Simply by being in the Balkans, it was at the centre of the world's greatest testing ground for the need for the rule of law to triumph. Everything about the building cried out triumph, while at the same time proclaiming the futility of heroic ideals that do not live up to their promise. Like the human condition itself, the structure was a paradox, an enigma, a vision of paradise endlessly gained and lost. The hands were human hands, not necessarily communist human hands. The meeting place here was on the line where Christianity met Islam. Beside the building ran the mountain pass that, in ancient times, connected the oriental and occidental civilizations. Like Bulgaria itself, it was neither east nor west, but perhaps a meeting place for both.

CHAPTER 11

Petitions to the Queen and Meetings in Central America

We returned to Canada from Bulgaria in the spring of 1994. In addition to dealing in the domestic courts with the renewed Temagami endeavour, during this period I consolidated all my clients' outstanding cases from the various regions of Canada in one combined application to the Supreme Court of Canada. While that application was proceeding apace, I planned and carried out a third excursion to Europe.

Up to this point, my clients had been asking the domestic courts to address the legislative words which established that, as natives occupying arguably unceded land, they have a constitutionally guaranteed right of access to a third-party court outside the domestic legal system. In support of this principle, they relied on the endorsement made constitutionally by Queen Anne in 1704 in response to the petition of the Mohegan Indians. At this juncture, however, my clients decided to follow more literally in the moccasin-steps of the Mohegans: they would petition Queen Elizabeth II directly, just as the Mohegans had Queen Anne.

In addition, it occurred to my clients that the problem of genocide was easier for Canadians and Americans to identify when the focus was Central and South America. In recent years the North American public had been exposed to several motion pictures set in those regions in which the genocidal impact of the ecological assault on the tropical rainforest was portrayed.

The strategic question became, why not link the North American natives' struggle for the right of third-party adjudication to the struggle for survival of their native brothers and sisters of Central and South America? Certainly, I had been attempting to make that linkage in my arguments in the domestic and international court systems, but I had done so at the intellectual, abstract level. What was needed, my clients and I came to think, was a tangible linkage, a connection that would carry the eye of the North American public, and hence the judiciary, from the genocide in Central and South America to their own backyard in North America.

On 3 January 1995 a petition to Queen Elizabeth II was executed by representatives of my clients in North America. Several weeks later, on 27 March, I wrote to the queen's private secretary, Sir Robert Fellowes, as follows:

The petitioners respectfully request an audience with Her Majesty for the purpose personally of presenting to her the original of the enclosed true copy of their petition.

Since the petition on its face identifies as its objective the apprehension of the crimes allegedly in progress of misprision of treason and fraud and complicity in crimes related to genocide by Her Majesty's Canadian Chief Justices, may I prevail upon you to attempt to expedite the said application for an appointment?

Since the Government of Canada is alleged to be the prime mover in the allegedly genocidal subornation of Her Majesty's Canadian Courts, may I also prevail upon you not to refer this application to the Governor General of Canada, but rather to regard it as a matter appropriately referable directly to Her Majesty? In this connection I have to ask you to draw to our Queen's attention the Monarchy's constitutionally binding [see *Campbell v. Hall* (1774), 98 English Reports 848, 895–9] undertaking by imperial order in council dated 7 October 1763 of "Protection" toward the Indian nations or tribes. On this strictly legal basis the petitioners' position respectfully must be that under the rule of law Her Majesty has not only the political right, but more importantly the juridical duty, to receive their petition.

The presentation of the petition to Her Majesty will be made and, if invited, spoken to by a native or natives trained from an indigenous North American perspective in the tradition of what in Euro-culture might analogously be seen as a hereditary duty and the diplomacy of appropriate expression. This is important, because in virtue of this petition the rule of law is being asked to function in a cross-cultural context, and the measure of that rule's viability and integrity in such context will to some extent be gauged by Her Majesty's response.

For example: in terms of the records of the European cultural tradition, I can assure you upon the basis of empiricism and academic analysis that for the purposes of existing international and constitutional law some Amerindians are vested with exclusive juridical jurisdiction over yet unsurrendered Hunting Grounds; secondly, that in relation to legal disputes over whether a given tract of land in fact still is unsurrendered those Amerindians are vested with a due process right of access to the Queen in Council (U.K.) as an independent and impartial tribunal not staffed by their jurisdictional competitors on this continent; and, finally, that the contrary premature assumption and exercise of jurisdiction by those competitors constitutes a usurpation that is treasonable, fraudulent and complicitous in crimes related to genocide.

The Amerindians seeking to present the petition herein have arrived at a similar opinion of law, aided by a process fundamentally different from the one with which it is likely that a modern-day Euro-culture person is apt to be familiar. For example, they possess artifacts which they wish to exhibit that they say were personally given to their ancestors by previous British Monarchs, as earnests both to symbolize and to bind the Indians' perpetual due process right of access to the Queen on the jurisdiction issue. They also enjoy oral traditions, prophecies and visions which are quite outside our Euro-cultural empirical-analytical tradition, but which nevertheless contribute to the meaning of their legal relationship with others, including with Her Majesty and Her Majesty's Governments. To me, these earnests, traditions, prophecies and visions appear to evidence an understanding of a legal relationship that is remarkably similar to that described above upon the basis of the empirical-analytical tradition.

I do not mean to suggest, by remarking as I have the petitioners' employment of intuitive standards, that the traditional Indians did not and do not respect the rule of law's rational basis, but rather that when they deliberate in council as courts they supplement reason with intuition, whereas we of the Euro-culture tradition tend in contrast to deny the role of intuition, as if it were a subjective cloud upon objective reason in our courts' deliberations. This difference is at the heart of the Canadian domestic courts' genocidal function. They assume, erroneously, that the lives of the traditionals were and hence by implication are (as the Chief Justice of British Columbia stated recently in a reported decision) "nasty, brutish and short." On this basis the Canadian judges' rationalize their own premature judicial invasion of the Indians' Hunting Grounds, as an innocent, necessary, helpful and inevitable occupation of a juridical vacuum. As a variant of the *terra nullius* pretext, that attitude denies the humanity of the traditional Indians. This institutionalized disrespect for their humanity is a cancer to the traditionals' body politic, to which can be attributed the social malaise that is symptomized by the Indians' tragic mortality rates.

The judicially-driven genocidal process in Canada is not, however, irreversible. The falseness of the premise underlying the judicial invasion being established, the existing natural, international, common and constitutional law that the erroneous premise through Canadian judicial willful blindness preempts will, as law, be allowed to rule. Ironically bearing witness to that falseness, a commemorative plaque "prepared in consultation with the Alberta Court of Appeal" and entitled "The Spirit of Aboriginal Justice" is appended to that Court's building. It observes:

"The First Peoples of North America have always had their own systems of justice. Community, family and personal disputes arose when there was a spiritual imbalance among those involved. Dispute resolution brought things back into harmony through a reconciliation of everyone involved. Aboriginal justice always found ways for offenders to be re-accepted by society. Each First Nation had its own traditions. While detailed practices of the justice system varied among the different Nations of southern Alberta, some principles were common to all. Disputing people would meet in the presence of elders whose wisdom and understanding helped everyone find a solution to the problem. A ceremonial pipe was lit and each person – the elders, then each party – smoked and prayed to the Creator for guidance. Each person spoke without interruption. A person could not lie in the presence of a pipe and was bound by any agreement made in its presence. The discussion would continue until a resolution was agreeable. Sometimes, at the conclusion of the agreement, the elders would put sacred paint on the people to give them the inner strength to carry out the agreement."

Similarly, on behalf of George III the Lords of Trade at Whitehall on 10 July 1764 informed the Superintendent of Indian Affairs for the Northern District of North America that "a steady and uniform attachment to, and love of Justice and Equity is one of their [the Indians'] first principles of Government."

As an institution that spans and unites Canada's contrasting indigenous and transplanted cultural traditions, the Queen may wish to hear something from both, and then to ensure that the subordinate institution to which she refers the detailed work of fact find-finding, assessing and reporting similarly is capable in an unbiased fashion in attending to the different cultural records of the same legal relationship.

The petitioners' strictly legal submission is that this is not only Her Majesty's right but her legislatively undertaken and legally binding duty, failing fulfillment of which she will by necessary implication have been suborned into aiding and abetting genocide, contrary to the rule of law.

From that juncture on, the exchange of correspondence assumed the form of the queen's secretary saying that "constitutional convention" precluded the queen from acting on the petition without the consent of the Canadian government. I pointed out to him that "constitutional law" said something that "constitutional convention" did not say. Ever since 1704, constitutional law has said that the king or queen, as the case may be, is under a duty to staff the trial-level Judicial Committee of the Privy Council as required by petition. I noted for the queen that when convention and law conflict, law must prevail. That this is how law "rules" in accordance with the "rule of law." I argued that the justification for the continued existence of the monarchy is precisely this function of ensuring that law does indeed rule. In Canadian legal theory the queen is supposed to be the fail-safe device that precludes any government from highjacking the constitution and committing genocide – in theory, but not in practice.

I also delivered an appeal to the appellate level of the Judicial Committee of the Privy Council from a decision on 6 July 1995 of the Supreme Court of Canada to stonewall the law. The bureaucracy of the Judicial Committee refused to accept the appeal papers, on the ground that in 1949 Canada had enacted legislation abolishing appeals to the Judicial Committee. I replied to the bureaucracy that such a repeal could not legally have applied to the Indians' right of appeal, precisely because that particular due process right is uniquely entrenched constitutionally. A normal domestic law enactment such as the 1949 statute could not possibly have repealed a conflicting constitutional enactment – at least, not in a rule-of-law society.

Once again, the court bureaucracy refused to allow this jurisdictional question to go before the court. Once again, the law was placed beneath political convention. In anticipation of this happening, and in an attempt to forestall it from happening, I travelled to England for the purpose of meeting with the registrar of the Judicial Committee of the Privy Council. He was a very pleasant, very upper-class English type of man, at least according to my own shamefully stereotyped image of what to expect. He told me how as a young man he had worked in the northern reaches of British Columbia on various manual labour jobs, how much he loved the geography and appreciated its native people. But, he added, "You must know, of course, that I cannot help you. Appeals from Canada to the Privy Council were abolished in 1949."

I replied that I did know there was a domestic law amendment to the Supreme Court Act to that effect. As a matter of existing constitutional law, however, the said domestic law amendment was inapplicable to the natives' aboriginal rights jurisdiction of native sovereignty on arguably unceded territory – unless domestic law can repeal constitutional law, which is a legal impossibility. I added that I was not asking the registrar to decide the point of constitutional law. I was only asking him not to stonewall it bureaucratically by refusing to place it before the Judicial Committee for argument and judicial decision in accordance with the rule of law. "I can undertake to you," he said, "to present your application for leave to appeal to the Court, and it will make the decision, not me." I thanked him. That was all I had hoped to achieve.

Eventually, the court itself refused to listen. The court's refusal was based on the assumption that the right of appeal had been abolished by domestic legislation, and it refused to listen to any argument contrary to that prejudgment. The judges' minds were made up, and they were not going to allow the constitutional law to which they were unwilling to listen to get in the way of their assumption based on domestic law.

My Central and South America journey was aided by a coincidence. During this last period in Canada my family and I were residing in Ottawa, largely because that is where the Supreme Court of Canada sits. In the neighbourhood was a commercial dry-cleaning business where two very diligent, charming, and gregarious Spanish-speaking young women from Honduras worked. We chatted, and Margaret and I had a few coffees with them at the espresso bar next door. It turned out that they were of Mayan descent – and proud of it. They expressed unbridled support for the cause in which Margaret and I were engaged and offered to help in any way they could. Their aged father was scheduled to visit them shortly, and they added that he had devoted his life sympathies to the same underlying cause and would want to talk.

The father was equally charming, in a grand and paternalistic Latin-American style. He had contacts with the indigenous peoples' organizations of Central America. It was agreed that one of his daughters, who was an excellent translator, and I would meet him in Honduras to follow up on these connections.

I stayed with his family in Tegucigalpa, the capital. There I met under his auspices with the main indigenous people's organization of Honduras. At first they were very suspicious, but things opened up when I asked whether they were collaborators like the native organizations funded by the Canadian and American governments. At this suggestion, they looked at each other around the table and burst out laughing. The silence was broken. Rapidly they took turns explaining to me that in Central America the non-native governments do not fund native organizations, as they do in Canada and the United States.

We support ourselves on nothing, they said, except a little help from Europe. But we know what you mean by the collaborators. Every time one of us is sponsored by a European group to go to an international conference, the Canadian and American Indians are there throwing money around, staying in the best hotels and picking up girls. We cry because our people are being murdered, and we have no money to help. They are busy meeting people and having a good time, and that leaves no time for us. They find us boring and awkward, and are interested only in passing resolutions and arranging for the next follow-up conference, at which nothing will be done, except talk, as always.

As a result of my meetings with the Honduran indigenous people's organization, I drafted a petition that was signed in July 1995 by the medicine people designated by the organization for the purpose. At this point in history, a common law of international human rights is evolving rapidly. We hoped that by sending this petition to each of the national courts of Europe, one of them would be persuaded to establish the remedies precedent at common law.

IN THE COURTS OF EUROPE

Between:

Medicine Men and Women of the Americas,

Petitioners,

and:

Countries of Europe,

Respondents.

PETITION

We, the petitioners identified in Schedule "A", are medicine men and women.

The reasonable and probable consequence, and therefore presumably the "intent," of the occupation by others of our territories before our people are ready, willing and able to accommodate it is "genocide" under article 2(b) of the Convention for the Prevention and Punishment of the Crime of Genocide, 1948.

The silence as well as the interference of the non-indigenous courts of the Americas is "complicity in genocide" under article 3(e), contrary to the consensus of natural, international and constitutional law established by the old countries of Europe but broken by the new countries of the Americas.

- Sublimus Deus, 1537 (Christian Europe).
- New Laws for the Government of the Indies & the Preservation of the Indians, 1543 (Spain), article 7.

- Treaty of Capitulation of New France at Montreal, 1760 (France), article 40.
- Royal Proclamation of 1763 (England), paragraphs 1–2 of part 2 and paragraphs 1–6 of part 4.
- Royal Regulation of 1772 (Spain), article 6.
- Worcester v. Georgia, 6 Peters Reports 515, 542 (United States Supreme Court 1832)
- Treaty of Cession of Russian-America, 1867 (Russia), articles 1 and 6.

THEREFORE the petitioners ask each Court to acknowledge the law.
DATED at Tegucigalpa, July 15, 1995.

From Tegucigalpa I travelled on to Guatemala City, where a meeting of all indigenous peoples' organizations in Central America was scheduled soon to begin. I was allowed to speak at this gathering, after which the following declaration was drafted and signed:

DECLARATION OF THE INDIGENOUS COUNCIL OF CENTRAL AMERICA IN SUPPORT OF THE INDIGENOUS NATIONS OF NORTH AMERICA

As Central America is the bridge between North America and South America so also will the Central American Indigenous Council accept the invitation from the autochthonous people of the north to link them with those to the south and to support them in their demands.

Indigenous natural law comprehends that the source of all law, the law by which to test the validity of all other laws, is synonymous with the concept of respect. This profound jurisprudential perception was corroborated in 1537 by the papal legislation Sublimus Deus and, in consequence, this principle is the foundation both of the international law of the world and the constitutional law of all the countries of the Americas.

Contrary to this natural law, international law, and constitutional law all the countries of the Americas commit genocide and ecocide, to the grave injury of the body and spirit of humanity and the world natural environment.

Therefore this council declares its solidarity with the Tegucigalpa Declaration made July 15, 1995, and recommends its acceptance and implementation.

Guatemala City, this 18th day of July, 1995.

The Indigenous Council of Central America was anxious to have the declaration endorsed by representatives of the medicine people of South America, so asked me to attend a conference of the United Nations Working Group for Indigenous People, scheduled for later in the summer in Geneva. I would be accompanied by a leading medicine man from Alberta, Canada, and his daughter. The Alberta medicine man was most disillusioned with the conference. It was dominated by non-native United Nations personnel and by natives who lived in Europe off the avails of the human-rights industry. No one at this forum was willing even to consider challenging the complicity in genocide of the United States and Canada. Nor was anyone interested in accusing the European countries of complicity, owing to their trade in natural resource products taken with genocidal consequences from the natives' unceded lands in the Americas. As a result, the same native person who had signed the Amazonia petition to the International Court of Justice ended up signing the Tegucigalpa petition to the national courts of Europe as a representative of some South American medicine people.

The petition to the courts of Europe seeking a declaration acknowledging the natives' right in principle to rely on the existing law precluding genocide, to obtain injunctions against the governments and corporations of Europe which receive the natural resources stolen from the natives at genocidal consequence, fell upon deaf or indifferent judicial ears. All simply declined jurisdiction, and not one permitted the jurisdictional point to be argued. The only chief justice of any European country who replied positively was the Lord Chancellor of Great Britain, who suggested, as an alternative to relying on existing law, that my clients lobby the British Parliament politically for a new law. This my clients declined to do, preferring their old lamp of law to a new political endeavour.

My sojourn in Central America was another awakening. For many years I had heard stories of murder and torture being practised against the native people there. It is a virtual truism among aboriginal rights cognoscenti that North America employs the iron fist covered by the velvet glove, and that in Central and South America the velvet glove is not worn.

The first night I spent in Tegucigalpa I stayed in a downtown hotel. I walked the streets. It was a hot Friday night. Everywhere, the passion of the people was on the surface. I do not know the reason; maybe it was a holiday, or maybe it is always like that. I walked past armed militia carrying huge submachine guns down the middle of main street. Outside banks, guards armed with still more machine guns stood in casual slouches of nonchalance and threadbare machismo. I passed fights between teenage men who were flashing knives and wielding broken pieces of wood.

Everybody I spoke with was helpful and gracious, but not far underneath the surface I sensed an inner rage, at least in the males. Of course, it was Friday night and the liquor had been flowing. Monday morning was pacific. But still, the first impression of raw human energy in turbulence so close to the surface was startling and has stayed with me. Perhaps my apprehension was heightened by the repeated warnings from my hosts not to let anyone know I was working for indigenous people. "You could be killed," they warned. "You don't understand the way it is here concerning *los Indios*."

Once before I felt that same troubled human passion and power impregnate the atmosphere. When I was fourteen years old and living in Sudbury, a dispute arose between two rival unions. In the beginning the International Nickel Company and

Falconbridge Nickel Mines, the two transnational corporate giants of the Sudbury basin, were both unionized by the International Union of Mine, Mill and Smelter Workers. Then the union known as Steel Workers of America sought to replace Mine Mill. The competition was acrimonious, with charges and counter-charges of "Commie Rats" and "Mafia Goons." The dispute came on the heals of a very long strike, which in itself placed the whole city in a pressure cooker of emotional stress.

At the time I was living with my mother in an apartment about five hundred yards from the Mine Mill union hall. From the front window I could see down the hill to the front of the hall. At about midnight one Friday night, I heard a ruckus. From the window I could see men gathered under the street lights. Tucking away mother's admonition to take care, I went down the hill to check things out. Men had been drinking and were milling about. Some shouted insults at other men inside the hall. The gist was that those inside should come outside and let those outside take over possession of the hall, as the truer representatives of the workers. A face appeared at one of the windows and snarled back a response. Rocks flew up to the window and shattered it. A group of men started bashing at the big entrance doors with a log. When the doors gave in, the men, pressed by a large and still gathering crowd, rushed in, only to be repelled by water directed by power hoses from the top of stairs. I was in the vanguard, and saw the terrified faces of the men steering the gush of water. I tumbled out of the entrance back into the street, sickened and weakened. A sheriff appeared and read the Riot Act, which made the failure to disperse immediately a criminal offence. The crowd wavered. The sheriff held his breath – and his ground. The crowd dispersed. But the faces of the men inside the hall have haunted me ever since. I was part of a mob, throbbing, thriving, thrilling with its energy. And I was weak with shame and fear for what I had become. Like fire, the power of humanity can so easily get out of hand and destroy.

PART FOUR

MEANWHILE,
BACK AT THE RANCH

The Bear Island Incident
and My First Criminal Conviction

After I left Bear Island in 1985, the researcher with whom I had been working continued in the Temagamis' employment. Soon after, he discovered a letter in the archives which raised the possibility of arguing that some of the elected chiefs of the Temagamis, including the current chief, had been engaged in the concealment from the courts of evidence that, if disclosed, would justify a reconsideration by the Supreme Court of Canada of its decision that the Temagamis' aboriginal rights had been extinguished.

The new evidence consisted of a nineteenth-century letter written to one of the Indian agents from the Temagami chief, in which he used the phrase "when I signed the treaty." It is clear that he had not signed the treaty in his own hand because every mark could be accounted for and his was not among them. Nevertheless, his use of the phrase raised a probability that his particular family hunting grounds had been sold to the crown by the chief of the Indian band whose hunting grounds adjoined his, and to whose sister he was married. Band allegiance was generally flexible in northeastern North America. The Temagami chief in 1850 would also have been a principal man or sub-chief of his wife's band to the south, and in that capacity he appeared to have participated in the treaty of 1850. Other evidence established that he was with a party of Nipissings, his wife's band, when the initial treaty payments were physically handed out, and he himself was recorded as having received at least a sub-chief's remuneration.

By saying "when I signed the treaty," the chief may have been referring to the signature of his brother-in-law which, in Indian law, could be the equivalent of his own, at least to the lands joined to both bands by intermarriage of the hereditary lines. This arrangement would not in Indian law, or in white law for that matter, have effected a sale of the hunting grounds of the other Temagami families. The chief's wife's band was invited to participate in the treaty, whereas the Temagami band was not. This interpretation fit with the historical fact that the other Temagami families were absolutely certain they had never participated in any treaty, while the Ontario government all along felt that some, at least, had.

There is no doubt that those other Temagami families were entitled to know about the letter that had been concealed so they could adduce this new evidence.

The difficulty was that the present Temagami chief claimed as his particular hunting grounds the area that the 1850 Temagami chief potentially had sold as a Nipissing sub-chief. As the result, the present chief was labouring under a personal conflict of interest so far as the disclosure of this letter was concerned. Disclosure might well result in a finding that some, but not others, of the Temagamis still had unsurrendered aboriginal rights, and that the present chief was one of the have-nots.

The researcher who discovered the letter told the present chief and the new lawyers about his discovery, and he informed me they told him to conceal it as an irrelevancy. He became worried that if the letter ever did become public, he might be scapegoated as having concealed it from them. He asked me what to do. I told him to send a copy by registered mail to the present chief and the lawyers, so he would have a record of the fact of his disclosure, at least to them, of what he had found. Some years later, I informed those Temagamis who had re-retained me of the existence and contents of the letter, and they decided they wanted to see a copy of it. When they asked the chief and the lawyers, they were informed there was no such letter. That is why my clients broke into their own band administration office: to secure a copy of this letter, so they could apprehend the apparent fraud of the chief and the lawyers. In addition to representing these clients in defence, I filed an application on their behalf in the Ontario court seeking an order to compel the production of the letter.

The chief and council, their lawyers, and the non-native government lawyers combined to oppose the application, not on its merits, but on the basis of alleging that I, personally, was in a conflict of interest and should be enjoined from acting for any Temagami Indians. In short, it was apparent that the federal and provincial government lawyers and the lawyers for the chief and council were conspiring to conceal evidence from the courts. When I sought permission to adduce evidence of this fraud in the Ontario court, the judge ordered me not to address the court.

This particular judge's name was Roberts and he was the son of Kelso Roberts, the Ontario attorney general who, in the late 1960s and early 1970s, had threatened the Temagamis with prosecution for taking firewood and with eviction from their homes on Bear Island. It was in response to that threat that the Temagamis had pleaded with Ottawa for protection, and the federal government had, in 1971, established the Bear Island reserve. I asked Judge Roberts to consider evidence showing that he, personally, was in a conflict of interest and should disqualify himself. Instead, he immediately issued an injunction prohibiting me from mentioning the possibility of judicial crime and for acting for any Temagami Indian in the future, and on this basis ordered me removed from the courtroom. This scene occurred in Sudbury, Ontario.

From there I went back directly to Haileybury. Some of my Temagami clients said they were going to enter the researcher's house and seize the letter. I intercepted them and said I should do it, because they would just be arrested and possibly beaten up, to no avail. After much discussion, I contacted the local police and asked them to accompany me, for the purpose of apprehending a fraud in progress by securing evidence at risk of destruction.

The police did accompany me, although not for that purpose. Rather, the officer said I would be arrested for trespass if I placed my foot on the researcher's property. I pointed out to the officer that the researcher's so-called property was situated on unceded Indian land and that, by refusing to assist in securing evidence at risk of destruction, he was aiding and abetting not only the researcher's alleged fraud but also the treason, fraud, and genocide being committed by the legal establishment.

I informed the officer, for the purposes of setting up a test case, that in spite of his warning I proposed to place my foot on the researcher's sidewalk. I invited him to arrest me, so that together we could at least ensure that the jurisdiction issue was placed before the courts. I informed him that if he attempted to impede me, I would place him under citizen's arrest for his own crime of complicity in genocide. I then put my foot where he pointed it should not be placed, a few inches off the main sidewalk on the researcher's sidewalk, turning slightly as I did so and presenting my back to him. The officer took my elbow and completed the turn so he could put me in a headlock from behind. I did not struggle, because I was content with the arrangement. He put handcuffs on me and led me away. At the station, rather than being charged with trespass, the charge laid was for assault. The officer said that in placing my foot on the sidewalk, my shoulder had bumped into his shoulder. I did not recall any such bump.

We went to court on this basis as an agreed set of facts. I accepted the facts and agreed, for test-case purposes, that my shoulder had bumped his. I asked the court to address the law going to jurisdiction and to base the decision on that alone. The trial judge declined to address the law going to jurisdiction, but he did make a finding on jurisdiction. He found that he did have jurisdiction because he had been exercising it for some time, and therefore it was ridiculous to allege that he did not have it. He held that it would be a waste of the court's time to listen to my argument. Since the facts were not contested, the judge automatically registered a conviction and I was immediately released from custody. The sentence was time already served, which meant no additional jail time.

I appealed. The appeal was heard by the judge who, twenty years before, had been the other defence counsel when I was involved in the murder trial at Cochrane. He also declined to address the law going to jurisdiction on the ground there was no such law and, since the facts were not contested, he confirmed the conviction. I appealed to the Court of Appeal, where the same thing happened. I applied to the Supreme Court of Canada, where leave to appeal was denied on the ground that no issue of importance was presented.

I was now, officially, a criminal, an ex-con. And not just of any crime, but of the extremely serious crime of police assault. And the law had still not been addressed at any stage of the proceedings.

In spite of this letter, or perhaps because of it, the new lawyers acting for the Temagamis went before the Supreme Court of Canada where, both in writing and orally, they informed the court there was no evidence in existence that established any basis for alleging the participation of any Temagami Indian in the 1850 treaty. Lying to the appeal courts is the most serious form of contempt of court imaginable. It is not a cosmetic matter, such as improper language or clothing. It is a form of contempt that strikes at the heart of the entire legal system, which is premised on the faith that lawyers, as officers of the courts, will not knowingly lie to the courts. At the time that misrepresentation was made, the lawyers had seen the nineteenth-century letter of the Temagami chief containing the phrase "when I signed the treaty."

I reported the lawyers' illegal concealment of the new evidence to the Law Society of Upper Canada, which refused to investigate on the ground that the new lawyers had sent in a confidential letter alleging they had done nothing wrong. Instead, the Law Society decided to take steps leading to disbarment against me: not only was I a convicted criminal but I was insulting the legal establishment by remarking on its treason, fraud, and complicity in genocide.

When the Bear Island case was being argued in the Supreme Court of Canada, a number of provincial attorneys general intervened against the Indians for the purpose of minimizing any impact the case might have on their own jurisdictional and proprietary position. One of these interveners against the Bear Island natives was the attorney general of British Columbia. The lawyer acting for him was the Vancouver partner of the Toronto law firm arguing the case for the Temagami Indians. That same Vancouver law firm was also acting for the attorney general of British Columbia in a case currently before the BC court, *Delgamuukw v. British Columbia*. To summarize, in the Bear Island case in Ontario, one law partner was acting for the Indians in a case set to determine the nature of aboriginal rights. In the *Delgamuukw* case in British Columbia, the first lawyer's partner was acting against the Indians in another case set to determine the nature of aboriginal rights. The British Columbia partner then intervened in the Bear Island case in the Supreme Court of Canada. And in that court the Ontario partner who was acting for the Indians dropped from the case the law vindicating native sovereignty and jurisdiction.

Conflicts of interest do not come any clearer than that. When I pointed this pattern out to the Law Society, it once again did not perceive the existence of any possible basis for a conflict-of-interest investigation. Instead, the disciplinary staff of the Law Society of Upper Canada undertook a massive effort to have me disbarred for openly identifying the sovereignty-jurisdiction issue in the courts on behalf of my Indian clients across four provinces.

If ever a classic case were presented for asking the courts to reconsider a judgment, these developments in the Bear Island case appeared to be the candidate. Not only had the lawyers concealed from the client the fact that the central issue of law had been dropped but the person from whom the lawyers were taking their instructions and the lawyers themselves had literally been caught lying to some of their clients and to the appeal courts about the existence of concealed and crucial evidence.

What makes the case a classic are two iron-clad rules. First, the law concerning court jurisdiction: if a court makes a decision relative to territory or an issue over which it has no jurisdiction, the decision is automatically a nullity. Any person whose rights or obligations are affected by such a decision is entitled to rely on the law precluding the jurisdiction if ever and whenever someone else attempts to enforce the decision. All the person who is objecting need do is to raise and prove the jurisdictional law. Of course, if that law had been raised and overruled in arriving at the decision, then the objection is not possible. But that was not the situation in the Bear Island case. There, as the Supreme Court of Canada said, the appeal had been restricted to the facts. Jurisdiction was never addressed.

The second rule is that, aside from jurisdictional objections to enforcement of any decision, it is always possible for a person who is affected by the decision to allege fraud upon either a party to the case or the court that made the decision. The axiom is that fraud vitiates all. The courts can never and will never, in theory at least, allow themselves to be made into the means whereby a fraud is implemented.

In the Bear Island case all the bases were covered, so far as getting the decision set aside, or at least looked into for this purpose. As a matter of law alone, in virtue of my legal research, it was apparent that Ontario had sued the Temagamis in the wrong court system. The action should have been lodged before the constitutionally designated independent and impartial third party, the trial level committee of the Judicial Committee of the Privy Council, as established by the Order in Council (Great Britain) of 9 March 1704 in the matter of *Mohegan Indians v. Connecticut*. Instead, it had been lodged before the interested and therefore presumptively biased Supreme Court of Ontario. Moreover, three distinct frauds had been perpetrated. First was the fraud that exists by operation of the constitutional law whenever, contrary to the Royal Proclamation of 1763, any official prematurely assumes jurisdiction relative to the Indian land question. Second was the actual fraud of the lawyers and the Indian chief on the Indian people of not disclosing the dropping of the jurisdiction issue or the after-discovered letter containing the phrase "when I signed the treaty." Third was the fraud on the appeal courts of asserting that there was no evidence of any Temagami person participating in the treaty, while keeping concealed the actual evidence putting the barefaced lie to that express and explicit statement.

On behalf of the Temagami Indians who had contacted me, who were a majority of the Temagami Hunting Ground families, I packaged this information in several related forms. I submitted one such package to the Ontario court as part of a motion to set aside the Bear Island case on grounds both of the lack of jurisdiction of the non-native court system and the several frauds identified above. Another I submitted to the same court in response to an application by the government of Ontario to have the Land Titles Act caution that I had registered in 1973 vacated. A third I submitted to the Supreme Court of Canada, asking it to reconsider its decision in the Bear Island case. A fourth I submitted to the Law Society of Upper Canada as part of the complaint against the lawyers, for prejudicing my clients by their own fraudulent dropping of the law and concealment of evidence, while under the undisclosed conflict of interest concerning their partnership with the British Columbia law firm that had intervened for the purpose of defeating native sovereignty.

When the matter came before the first judge, the lawyers for the Indian bureaucrats and the attorney general for Ontario came together for the purpose of asking the court not to listen to me. The reason, they said, that I should not be heard was that I was in a conflict of interest. They never explained exactly what the conflict was, although from the context it seemed that my work for the Temagamis from 1973 to 1985 made me privy to information that I ought to be, but supposedly was not, keeping confidential.

That innuendo was invalid, since the information that I was disclosing was all either a matter of public record in the court case or evidence or law discovered after 1985. The absurdity of the situation was that the lawyers who, on the basis of my clients' uncontradicted sworn affidavit evidence, had committed and were still actively engaged in actual fraud, and who were now suborning the court into persisting in a treasonable, fraudulent, and genocidal assumption of jurisdiction, had the effrontery to base their challenge on the ethics of the lawyer exposing their actual fraud.

The lawyers did not have to argue very hard or long. The presiding judge could not agree with them more. He was positively squirming in his seat, waiting for the chance to shut out of his hearing the law that proved he was engaged in treason, fraud, and genocide. Even before they said anything he blurted out: "I am not going to listen to an allegation that the Supreme Court of Ontario has been engaged in crimes." He took from the outset the same position as every other judge before whom I have ever raised the jurisdiction issue: he refused to address the law because he did not like the conclusion to which the law led.

CHAPTER 13

The Gustafsen Lake Story

The last hope for the rule of law in any society is the ordinary citizen. When all else fails, it is always open for the citizen who observes a crime in progress to effect a citizen's arrest. For this purpose, subsequent to my release from the Ontario prison, I went to British Columbia to attend at the opening of the hearing of *Delgamuukw v. British Columbia* in the British Columbia Court of Appeal. I stood at the outset and advised the assembled panel of five judges that they had been suborned by the parties before them into assuming a jurisdiction that was treasonable, fraudulent, and genocidal. To apprehend the offence, but even more to prevent the court's condoning of the offence and thereby encouraging others to repeat it, I advised the judges that I was there to effect a citizen's arrest of them for those crimes.

The president of the panel asked me to leave. The last stone having been overturned in my attempt to force the legal system to address existing law, I did just that. There was never any possibility that I physically could have followed the arrest with actual custody. That was not the legal point. The legal point was exhausting legal remedies, all possible legal remedies, up to and including that of citizen's arrest.

But I remained involved in events in British Columbia. In the summer of 1995 a group of eighteen natives drew public attention to Gustafsen Lake in the north of the province. One of these natives had been a signatory to the petition I had sent to Queen Elizabeth on 3 January 1995, in which she was asked to reconvene the third-party court established by the Order in Council (Great Britain) of 9 March 1704 in the matter of *Mohegan Indians v. Connecticut,* for the purpose of apprehending complicity in genocide of the Canadian judiciary and governments.

Apparently, the natives' frustration with the stonewalling of the law had passed a point of no return. I had reported from Europe to the Wolverine, the nom de guerre acquired by William "Jones" Ignace during the Gustafsen Lake event, that the queen refused to address the petition on the ground that the Canadian government so instructed her, and that the Judicial Committee of her Privy

Council in England did likewise in relation to the proposed appeal from the Supreme Court of Canada, the latter on the legally impossible ground that, by ordinary general domestic legislation, the Canadian parliament had supposedly repealed the natives' special constitutional law remedy. The natives' hope had been that the queen or her Privy Council would do their constitutional duty of protecting the rule of law, rather than aid and abet the genocide through the political convention of not offending Canada. When that role was declined, the pretence could no longer be maintained that the queen or her Privy Council is above political expediency and complicity in genocide. Appeasement remains the norm when major powers practise the ultimate crime.

Next, the Supreme Court of Canada refused on 4 May and 6 July 1995 to address the law going to jurisdiction in any of the fresh set of eleven cases I brought before it from British Columbia, Alberta, Quebec, and Ontario. In every instance, the applications for leave to appeal or to reconsider were dismissed on the ground that no issue of "importance" was presented.

At this juncture, a rancher in northern British Columbia decided to evict a group of Indians who had been using a portion of his ranch at Gustafsen Lake to conduct Sundance ceremonies. The rancher ran cattle on a spread of some 100,000 acres of high plains scrub and pasture. The Sundance site used perhaps 2 acres. In any given year the number of cows that might have been inconvenienced by the Indians presence was perhaps two or three. The entire ranch was unceded: it had never been purchased by the crown from the Indians as required by international and constitutional law. Nevertheless, title had been granted under provincial legislation to the predecessors of the rancher. Tiring of the natives' presence on "his" land, the rancher sent some armed ranch-hands to visit the signatory to the petition to the queen. They saluted him as "red nigger" and threatened to "string him up" if he did not "hit the road pronto, Tonto." Other Indians and some non-native supporters rallied to his defence by arming themselves with hunting rifles with which to repel, if necessary, any attempts by the ranch-hands to implement the threat forcibly. The natives also sought police help. In a knee-jerk response the police sided with the rancher, contacted the Canadian army for armoured personnel carriers, and laid siege to the Indian encampment with some five hundred police officers and military advisers. Some 77,000 thousand rounds of police ammunition were poured into the Indian encampment before they surrendered.

Throughout, I was acting as the Indians' legal counsel, in an attempt to persuade the authorities to concede the Indians demand: to address publicly the international and constitutional law relevant to the issue of the natives' legal rights of liberty and possession and their legal remedy of third-party adjudication in relation to such rights.

The police and the news media conducted a massive and coordinated smear campaign, presenting the Indians as "terrorists" and never once mentioning that all they were asking for was that existing law be addressed. One of the more literary pieces appeared as a full-page newspaper spread in *The Province* on 31 August under the headline "Cast from The Good, The Bad and The Ugly." Accompanying the article was a photograph of me with the caption: "Bruce Clark, lawyer for the native renegades, is under investigation by the Law Society of Upper Canada, pondering a call to have him disbarred for numerous alleged outrages." The article itself said:

I have to say I'm thoroughly enjoying The Percy ["red nigger"] Rosette Show. Great stuff, isn't it – homesteading rancher, gun-toting renegades, tight-lipped lawmen and something about ... a queen.

He's something else, that Percy. Four years swinging around a pole on a rope connected to a stick piercing my breastbone and I'd have some pretty wicked visions too. I don't think I'd take them quite so seriously, mind you. Not only is Percy's sundance ceremony a U.S. import, he's decided to set up shop on someone else's turf. A double indignity, surely.

Poor Lyle James, he just wanted to do a bit of big-country ranching. Now he's stuck with Percy's bizarre vision of a New World Order, a fence he didn't need and two camps of heavily armed men geared up for a gunfight. And who said the western was dead genre?

This frontier adventure is a ratings sweeper – the plots are twisted, the characters are of the steadfast-and-true school of method acting, the settings rugged and remote. Oh yeah, The Good, The Bad and The Ugly ... The lawmen in this story should have gone in there two months ago and arrested Percy and his rebel brigade for trespass. This isn't Wounded Knee, it's not Oka, this is an illegal occupation of a rancher's land. Ditch the tactful sensitivity to the native land-claims issue 'cause it doesn't apply to this showdown. While Sgt. Montague of the RCMP keeps his lips tight and face poker, these nut bars are having a gay old time ordering cigarettes and 'canned goods' while taking potshots at his fellow lawmen.

Other native bands have disavowed The Defenders of the Shuswap Nation (a.k.a. Percy and crew). Even Ovide Mercredi, grand chief of the Assembly of First Nations, is calling for the psychologists. He knows what he's dealing with – forget the body bags, this is a straightjacket job. The Bad in this story, well that's pretty obvious – 30 militants including a troupe of non-native radicals previously occupied with less volatile issues, namely bears and whales. Seems they want immunity from criminal prosecution and an audience with the Queen. Ah, roger that. That's double negative, rebel leader. You can't shoot cops in this country and walk away. And the Queen, well that's just plain silly.

Now the ugly in this frontier adventure – Bruce Clark, shades down. What's with those specs, man. And that bald pate! He looks like an unwholesome fusion of Max Headroom and Lex Luther sporting Geordie's visor. Clark's as nutty as the rest. The Ottawa lawyer was advising his renegade clients to stand their ground. When Mercredi was asked what the problems were in negotiating an end to the standoff, he replied: "Bruce Clark."

Clark's a rather colorful character. The Law Society's discipline committee is currently calling to have him disbarred. Something about assaulting an Ontario provincial police officer, trying to illegally make citizen's arrests and sassing off judges, calling them racists and agents of genocide. Oh, and that goes for the government and the police as well, all part of the same conspiracy. Forty instances of professional misconduct at last count. The 51-year old lawyer hasn't even got his occasional-appearance certificate for B.C. which would allow him to practice here. He can advise but he can't represent his wayward clients. Yep, its a great saga. The Percy Rosette Show. Stranger that fiction for sure.

When this article made reference to the fact that "other native bands have disavowed The Defenders of the Shuswap Nation (a.k.a. Percy and crew)" and to the fact that "even Ovide Mercredi, grand chief of the Assembly of First Nations, is calling for the psychologists," the article was referring to the elected band councils and their national organization headed by Mr Mercredi. Since the 1870s, puppet governments have been bought and paid for as the whites' agents in the genocide of natives who would not give up on their international and constitutional law rights, who would not accept, as good Indians supposedly should, the federal benefits and programs in lieu of the international and constitutional law rights. This article disseminated the standard North American yellow journalism propaganda. It employed the Indian collaborators' words and deeds to discredit the cause of those natives who were taking a stand both for their rights and the integrity of the rule of law. It achieved this smear because of the failure to address the issue underlying the physical conflict – the jurisprudential conflict between international and constitutional law on the one hand and ordinary domestic law on the other.

The name-calling in the article was not pointless or gratuitous. It was calculated to personalize a general issue of importance by trivialization of the issue's proponents. It was consciously designed to sidetrack the legal legitimacy of the natives' allegation of treason, fraud, and genocide on the part of the non-native legal establishment. Later, at the ensuing trial, the evidence was that the police consistently manipulated the media with the media's willing participation. The police even videotaped their own strategy conferences, including one where the supervising police officer says to his subordinates, "Kill this Clark. Smear the prick and everyone with him."

Rather than deal with any of the actual words of the legislation on which the crucial underlying issues of jurisdiction and genocide turn, the news media, like the judges who misuse the term "scandalous" and the police who misuse the term "terrorists," brushed the law aside with the equally pejorative epithet "silly." Instead of informing the public, this article, like the entire barrage of media coverage, parroted the judges' and the police's hate propaganda, which aids, abets, and perpetuates the name-callers' crimes in progress.

I made an attempt to trace the source for that newspaper columnist's confidence that I was going to be disbarred. I learned that when he and others contacted the Law Society of Upper Canada, they were put through to the Discipline

Department, which assured, indeed promised, all inquirers that I "would be disbarred by Christmas." The information was widely published across Canada. As a result, many Canadians were led to think of me as a disbarred lawyer and to discredit me on this false basis.

The natives holed up inside the Indian encampment sent out the following signed demand, a demand ignored by the police, the media, and all levels of white government and their Indian collaborators:

The Sundancers at Gustafsen Lake have one demand: that the petition dated January 3, 1995 be addressed publicly by an independent and impartial third-party tribunal, one that is neither Canadian nor Indian, such as the special constitutional court established by Queen Anne at the request of the Mohegan Indians to which court the petition is addressed: (a) is the popular assumption that the Canadian courts and police have jurisdiction legal? (b) or is that assumption criminally treasonable, fraudulent and complicitous in the genocide of the aboriginal peoples of Canada as alleged in the petition?

Instead of dealing with the legal basis for this demand, which was the basis for the Standoff, the media slavishly reiterated the police accusation that the people inside the Indian encampment were "terrorists." A terrorist is one who flouts legal process by such activities as blowing up innocent civilians to gain political ends. In contrast, the purpose of the Indians and their supporters at Gustafsen Lake was to insist on respect for the legal process that the authorities were, with genocidal consequence, evading. They did not attempt to use force to kill, wound, or maim. Rather, they promised to defend themselves against force with force unless and until the legal establishment would agree in principle to address the jurisdiction issue and the law on which they relied. The attorney general of British Columbia replied publicly that he would never concede to any demand from "terrorists."

If the Indians had wanted to kill, wound, or maim anybody, they would have done so. They would not have occupied a defensive position. The people they put at risk were themselves, and then only to the extent that the police and their political masters refused to allow the legal issue underlying the events to be resolved according to the rule of law.

In theory, the genocide convention of 1948 has removed the age-old police defence of "just following orders." Accordingly, I wrote to the police to ask them not merely to follow the orders of the attorney general of British Columbia but, rather, to make an independent assessment of their own legal obligations. I set out the relevant legislative words defining that obligation and pointed out that, by ignoring that constitutional duty in favour of enforcing the prematurely (prior to treaty) encroaching laws of the provincial and federal governments, the police were standing the rule of law on its head and aiding and abetting treason, fraud, and genocide.

I asked the police to join with me and my clients, specifically by petitioning the federal and provincial governments to submit the legal issue to the appropriate tribunal for resolution of the dispute under the auspices of the rule of law. I pleaded with the police not to prejudge the issue of their own jurisdiction by using force that could lead to loss of life. The head of the Royal Canadian Mounted Police eventually wrote me a letter, replying without saying anything.

The actual Gustafsen Lake standoff dragged on for over two months. During its course, the police ushered me in to the surrounded Indian encampment to speak with my clients, on the off-chance I might negotiate a surrender. The clients rejected that possibility out of hand. Later, when I drove into the village, I saw a group of white people gathered on one side of the street bearing signs that proclaimed, "We support our police." On the other side of the street was an old Indian couple, native sovereigntists, whom I had known and cherished for years. The woman had earlier taught me that law equals respect. I stopped the car and asked the couple what was happening. "Bruce," they said hurriedly, "go. It's not safe for you here. These people are crazy." A few of the placard holders ran over to the car and one yelled, "Crook, get out of here, you crook." Television cameras rushed over to encircle the car, and a voice animating one of the microphones shoved in my face demanded, "What do you say to this, Clark?" I answered, "It appears some citizens are exercising their right of free speech."

The problem came after I met the police. All the barely suppressed rage and frustration that can exist with pent-up power was broiling and ready to lash out, waiting for an opportunity and an excuse. The police were floating on it, surfing on the waves of popular adulation. The same mob scent was in the air. This time, the mob on the outside was the white people and their police; the endangered and vulnerable people on the inside were my native clients.

Weeks later the police siege started to pay off, as the first handful of my clients began to trickle out. They were arrested. I went to see them in the jail and found the atmosphere there one of raw mob mentality and barely suppressed rage. The police refused to let me see my clients, on the ground that they had supposedly hired other lawyers soon after they were taken into custody. I asked to be allowed to meet with my clients so they could confirm or deny my dismissal themselves. The police refused me access.

The next day my clients were to be arraigned in court. It is crucial in jurisdictional defences that the client say nothing other than raise his objection to jurisdiction. Even by pleading not guilty, an accused can later be held to have acknowledged the jurisdiction of the tribunal to assess the question of guilt or innocence. The strategy of the police and the attorney general was to encourage my clients to accept legal aid duty counsel to get bail, and thus begin the process of steering them into defences other than challenging jurisdiction.

When I went to the courthouse for the arraignment the next morning, the mob mentality manifested itself in irrational brutality on the part both of the judge and his weapon, the police. Police literally and physically blocked my way. They told me there was no room left in the courtroom. It was filled with media reporters. I managed to step around the police blockade, being assaulted by them in the process, and walked to the counsel table in the courtroom. The judge entered. I stood to identify myself.

The judge announced that I was not acting for any of the accused persons he would be dealing with that day because they all had other lawyers. I asked the judge to have the accused persons brought into the courtroom so they could accept or deny his proposition that I had been dismissed by them. The judge refused. I filed a formal motion disputing the court's jurisdiction. I had to fling it onto the desk of the court clerk because she declined to take it from my hand and, when she looked up at the judge, he shook his head. When the Canadian Press reported this incident across Canada, the story had me throwing papers at the judge and striking him in the chest.

As I continued to attempt to address the court from the counsel table, I was pushed from behind by a police officer. Because the police have no business being near the counsel table, I said to the judge, "Please ask this man to stop pushing me." The judge replied that he was holding me, not the police officer, in contempt of court. As those words were leaving the judge's lips I was surrounded by a group of police, who fell on me and pushed me to the floor. I struggled as best I could against this outrage, but was not very effective. The transaction was over in a matter of seconds. The police put handcuffs on me and removed me from the courtroom. Subsequently, I was formally charged with criminal contempt of court and resisting arrest.

From that juncture forward I was kept in jail and, in consequence, denied access to my clients throughout the crucial stages of their prosecution. My arrest for contempt occurred on a Friday. Over the ensuing weekend I was kept in custody and subjected by the police to sleep deprivation and other degrading indignities. They positioned a police radio outside my cell door and left it on at full volume all night, even though there was no one monitoring it. I was not given a blanket, and the temperature was turned down. I was left in solitary confinement, without my glasses, though I am very myopic, and without adequate clothing with which to conserve body heat.

Eventually I was heartened by the voices of my clients coming from another cell block in the same building. Although we were not allowed to have the usual lawyer-client conferences, we could hear each other as we yelled encouragement back and forth. I heard them demanding to see their lawyer, Bruce Clark. There was no doubt, in their minds at least, as to who was representing them as their legal counsel.

When taken before the same judge the following Monday, I was not only handcuffed but paraded in front of the national media in leg shackles as well. While I was waiting in the holding cell adjacent to the court for my case to be

called, one of the officers who had been assigned to negotiate the Indians' surrender and whom I had got to know in the process, came to see me. He said he
just wanted to talk and to see how I was.

I asked him whether he had read my letter to the police commissioner. He affirmed that he had. I asked him why he had made the choice he did, to apply the
domestic law over the conflicting international and constitutional law. "We were
advised," he said, "that the only way you could get to the queen's Privy Council
was on a nation-to-nation basis with England, that Canada's consent to that was
required, and that Canada would never consent." I said to him, "Can't you hear
your own words? Listen to them. You have not said that your superiors have identified an error in my statement of the law. You have not disputed that the Indians
are right in law. You have just said that, regardless of their rights, they have no
remedy to enforce those rights because Canada controls the machinery of justice.
You have just said that the answer provided by your superiors is that you can
break the law because Canada can politically get away with stonewalling the Indians' legal remedy." "Yes, Bruce," he said, "maybe that is what it boils down to. I
don't look at it that way, but maybe that is what it is all about." "How do you look
at it?" I asked. "Bruce", he said, "I've just got a job to do, and I do it the best I
can." He turned and walked away from my cell.

In court a few minutes later the judge gave me a chance to apologize, and by
doing so gain my freedom. I told him that the words I had used in court to describe the criminality of his assumption of jurisdiction were not my words but
the law's. The judge's request for an apology hinged upon my repudiating my
clients' allegation that the judge's assumption of jurisdiction was treasonable,
fraudulent, and genocidal. In response, I apologized for my use of the term "kangaroo court" in relation to his court but explained that my clients' point of law
was not mine to abandon just to secure my own comfort. I asked again for the
opportunity to substantiate their legal point by reference to the actual legislative
words creating the law on which I relied. I also asked him, the next time he was
on an Indian reservation and admiring the bright faces of the youngsters he saw,
to ask himself why it had to be that their life expectancy was much more
abridged than his grandchildren's and to look inside himself for the answer.

The judge ordered me taken in custody to a psychiatric hospital for the criminally insane. He said he wanted to know if I was suffering from a "mental disor-
der" before proceeding any further. In the interval, while my head was being
shrunk, my clients had their first appearances in court. They were conveniently
supplied with legal aid lawyers who, not being crazy like me, did not raise the jurisdiction issue. My clients were let out on bail.

On balance, my sojourn in the psychiatric hospital was much less harrowing
than the time spent in police custody. The police were not neutral, as the hospital
staff were. Rather, the police were malicious, and they were false to the principle
for which in theory they stand: the protection of the rule of law. In contrast, the

staff at the psychiatric institute were true to their own official purpose: they just did their job, without fraudulently engaging in the manipulation of appearances. They were there to observe and to report, which was all they did.

At first the shock of finding myself in a psychiatric hospital for criminals was intimidating. On arrival, all articles of clothing were taken and I was required to take a bath in sight of the staff. In the circumstances, that was no doubt a rational process, for many of the persons sent there are a risk to themselves and need to be watched. They must be clean, for their own protection and for the staff and the other inmates. But it was jarring to my sense of self. I felt owned, disposable, degraded. Immediately afterwards I was introduced into the ward – fifteen single beds in two rows along the walls.

Not since my childhood stay in the Indian residential school in Whitehorse had I been introduced under compulsion to that configuration. For a few minutes the identical sense of terror, panic, and despair that I had experienced as a child came rushing back. I thought of calling Margaret, but realized that even if I could get through to her I would achieve nothing more than forcing her to live through a nightmare she was powerless to do anything about. I stood still and hung on. After a few minutes the irrational swirling panic subsided.

After that, the experience was manageable. Many of my fellow inmates were fascinating people. The challenge of overcoming the childhood panic for me was a good thing, for it laid a ghost to rest relative to a most unsettling childhood experience. To that extent I had the good fortune to gain strength from my forced stay in the psychiatric hospital.

I had time to reflect on that telling conversation with the police officer in my prison cell. It was ironic that I should go from the cell where the officer acknowledged the irrelevancy of the law and the paramountcy of raw power to the police, through a court, en route to a psychiatric institution, all because my belief in the paramountcy of law over power made me seem mad – to the judge at least. After a week in custody of the four weeks the judge had ordered, the official report of the hospital psychiatrist certified that there was nothing wrong with me mentally. I was, accordingly, released from custody by another judge.

Once released, I had discussions with my eighteen Gustafsen Lake clients, each of whom signed and filed at their next court appearances the following document:

I wish it to be known that a great deal of pressure by the fostering of hope of advantage and fear of prejudice has been put upon me by the police, other lawyers and judges, to dismiss/not to retain Bruce Clark in favour of hiring lawyers less ready, willing and able to raise and to defend the point of law that I want raised and defended. One argument has been that Bruce Clark is crazy for thinking that the rule of law has a chance when it is the domestic judiciary as an institution that has been breaking the law for over a century ...

I do not want the charges/proceedings against me dropped at this particular juncture in time. Rather, I first want the crucial issue of jurisdiction addressed – to see if the laying of

the charges/bringing of the proceedings was legal in the first place. In my view the laying
of the charges/bringing of the proceedings was ultra vires, treasonable, fraudulent, complicitous in genocide and calculated extortionately to pressure the Indians not to stand up
for their legal rights ... I contend that not to resist genocide when you are given the chance
is to condone genocide – that there is no "neutral" or "reasonable" ground that euphemistically can be occupied between appeasement and confrontation that does not merely pro-
long those crimes.

Pending the resolution according to the rule of law of the said juridical jurisdiction issue, I hereby also authorize and direct Bruce Clark to seek to obtain a stay of the proceedings against me under the (allegedly ultra vires in relation specifically to unceded
Hunting Grounds) Criminal Code of Canada or any other domestic law. Bruce Clark further is authorized and directed to subrogate my personal interests (such as in "getting
off" in relation to the ultra vires "criminal charges" against me) to the one interest that is
of paramount concern to the generations of aboriginal peoples yet unborn: honoring the
due process right of access to the independent and impartial third-party Court designated for constitutional law purposes by the Imperial Order in Council of 9 July 1704 as
recognized and affirmed by the Imperial Order in Council of 7 October 1763, sections
109 and 129 of the Constitution Act, 1867 and sections 25(a) and 35(1) of the Constitution Act, 1982.

In furtherance of securing the said due process right, Bruce Clark further is authorized and
directed to continue to attempt to draw to the attention of the judges of the domestic courts of
Canada both the Indian law that guarantees Indian juristic sovereignty prior to its surrender
by treaty, and, also, the non-Indian constitutional law that not only supports the said Indian
law but renders its breach the crimes by the judges of 'Misprision of Treason' and 'Fraud'
within the meaning of the aforesaid Imperial Order in Council of 7 October 1763.

To the extent that the said due process right treasonably and fraudulently as aforesaid is
delayed upon any pretext whatsoever by the said judges, the said Bruce Clark is authorized
and directed to lay charges against those judges of "complicity in genocide" before the appropriate "international penal tribunal" within the meaning of those phrases as used in articles 3(e) and 4 of the *Convention for the Prevention and Punishment of the Crime of
Genocide, 1948*. To the extent that Her Majesty the Queen has been suborned by the Canadian Government into not performing her constitutional duty of placing the above mentioned jurisdiction issue before the above mentioned constitutional Court as required by
the Indians' petition dated 3 January 1995, the said Bruce Clark further is authorized and
directed to seek to appeal the Queen's decision to the European Court of Human Rights or
an international penal tribunal on the ground that by committing complicity in genocide
that decision arguably is in breach, as well, of the European Charter of Human Rights.
Bruce Clark further is authorized and directed to seek injunctions in the national courts of
the nations constituting the European Community precluding the trade by European na-
tionals in products harvested from unsurrendered Indian lands in breach of the law precluding "complicity in genocide" as aforesaid and, in due course, to appeal against any
denial of such injunctive relief to the said European Court of Human Rights.

It was in accordance with those instructions that, as I will recount in chapter 14, we departed once again for Europe in the fall of 1995 to seek the specified legal remedies in the international arena. While there, I continued to correspond with the authorities in Canada about the contempt-of-court charge outstanding against me. Ordinarily a different judge from the one laying the complaint is assigned to hear contempt cases. But the same judge who had ordered my incarceration in the forensic institute and who had charged me with contempt was also determined to hear the contempt charge itself. In response to my plea that the law going to jurisdiction be addressed, he stated: "Any thought that the contempt charge might be withdrawn, vanished when he [Clark] refused to accept the jurisdiction of the court." He issued a Canada-wide warrant for my arrest, to be brought back before him personally.

While we were in Europe, the majority of my Gustafsen Lake clients and their supporters began putting it about that I had "abandoned" them to save myself. I heard from other sources in Canada that I was being portrayed as the "evil general" behind the events, sending, from my position of safety, unwitting and innocent Indians into battle.

The old medicine man from Alberta, who had been the main supplier of funding for my 1995 travelling in North and Central America and in Europe, and who was also the spiritual mentor and financier for the Sundance circle at Gustafsen Lake, literally joined with the police and the lawyers to concentrate blame on me and even to have me disbarred. He filed affidavits that were so patently false that even the Law Society of Upper Canada, which was anxious to find something, anything, against me, could not take them seriously. He swore, for example, that I tricked him into signing documents written in the English language in which were assertions of native sovereignty, while I supposedly knew that he knew no English and was comfortable only in the Stoney language. Yet the same affidavits in which he made such allegations also appended as exhibits court transcripts of him carrying on sophisticated conversations in English with Alberta Court of Appeal judges at a hearing where the judges were trying to get him to back off his native sovereignty point.

This medicine man swore that he knew nothing of the native sovereignty agenda I supposedly was pursuing on my own, while omitting to mention that he had travelled with me to Geneva for the purpose of speaking to that issue himself and rallying South American Indian allies to that cause, all of which was done in English. He swore that he had no idea what motivated the Gustafsen Lake event, when in fact he, his eldest son, and his daughter appear on a videotape of the early stages of the standoff, where his son is brandishing a rifle while proclaiming his intent to fight to the finish for justice and liberty for the native people.

The medicine man, his son, and his daughter were never prosecuted. On the contrary, the medicine man was celebrated by the police and the media as the one who ended the standoff by bringing the defenders out of their encampment and surrendering to the police. My belief that medicine men might be more faithful to the principle of truth took a beating, but it should not have been a surprise. Native medicine men are made of the same stuff as everyone else, including all the frailties and fears that characterize the human condition. The Indian named Percy, whose labelling by the ranch-hands as "red nigger" had ignited the Gustafsen Lake event, was the son-in-law of this medicine man. He, too, for personal advantage, sold out most of his comrades who had been involved at Gustafsen Lake. Yet, ironically, both the medicine man and Percy were the fomenters no less than the spiritual leaders of the Gustafsen Lake event, just as the Wolverine was regarded as the warrior leader.

In December 1995 Margaret, the boys, and I landed back in North America at New York City. There I learned for certain that, while I had been in Europe attempting to fulfill the instructions of all my Indian clients, the majority of the Gustafsen Lake contingent had, unbeknownst to me, decided to change lawyers. The strategy of the legal establishment remains, as it has been for over a century, simply to blindside the law that indicts what the legal establishment is doing. Having demonized, criminalized, and effectively driven me, the messenger of the law that it prefers not to have to address, from the country, the legal establishment in Canada successfully encouraged my clients to get other lawyers, whose services would be paid for by the non-native government legal aid plan. As a result, my clients were steered away from the law that establishes the legal establishment's crimes. No other lawyers, so far as I am aware, are prepared to cite that law and accept the consequences that the citing entails.

Only three of my Gustafsen Lake clients remained constant with their opening position and with the written instructions they had given me. The others all denied even knowing why they were at Gustafsen Lake, other than that they were going along with me and with the minority who did not change sides.

CHAPTER 14

Europe Again and More Petitions

My fourth trip to Europe, in 1995, was partly as a result of events at Gustafsen Lake and partly to follow the instructions of my Central American clients. My clients wanted me to build on the petition we had sent to the national courts of Europe. Specifically, they instructed me to commence actions seeking injunctions in Europe to compel European companies not to act as receivers of stolen goods by trading in natural resource products taken from yet unpurchased Indian land. That trade arguably aids and abets the genocide of the wilderness people. Genocide is the natural and probable consequence of the despoliation of the wilderness in which such people live. As such, the trade demonstrably constitutes complicity in genocide contrary to articles 2(b) and 3(e) of the Convention for the Prevention and Punishment of the Crime of Genocide of 1948.

Under articles 4 and 6, the complicity can be apprehended in the national courts of any of the countries in which the transnational trade in the spoils of the crime is carried on. It is in this sense that European consumers are in the position of receiving stolen goods. One crime is committed by the theft in country A. Second crime is committed in country B when the stolen goods are received and processed.

When this trip to Europe became imperative for the family, my daughter, Zoë, refused to move again. At sixteen, she had found a school and a routine she was desperate to maintain. She had acquired a best girlfriend and a new boyfriend, both of whom were distraught at the prospect of losing her. It was a major shock to Margaret, the boys, and I, but we had to trust her right and her ability to try her wings. She stayed in Ottawa, living on welfare, which was doubly disturbing. My mother had managed to raise me working as a secretary and never had to go on welfare, and here was I, a fifty-year-old lawyer, unable to do the same. We missed Zoë dreadfully, but were impressed by her strength and dignity against what must have seemed overwhelming forces tearing at her cocoon of rationality.

Once again, the Alberta medicine man provided the funding for the work in Europe – at least initially. While drafting and sending back to Canada the court jurisdiction documents, we also travelled from capital to capital in support of our

cause. Suddenly, however, the money ceased and our benefactor stopped returning our calls. I was stonewalled once again, mainly because of money, but partly
because of the Europeans' impression that genocide in the North American context is by definition impossible. Without money it was not possible to retain European counsel to assist in formatting the necessary documents to initiate the
injunction applications in the various national courts.

A benefactor promised the use of a few rooms in Rome and sent us travel
money. When we arrived in Italy we found he had changed his mind because of
negative communications from some of the non-native Gustafsen Lake clients.
They had switched to other lawyers, whose strategy was to seek to exculpate
these clients by portraying them as innocent dupes of my supposed "evil genius." Our return tickets got us to New York. Arriving without funds or prospects, a sympathizer put us up for the winter by sharing the little he had.

I made a fresh plea to organizations for help in apprehending the ecogenocide in
the Americas on the basis of existing law, but a wall of silence resounded. The serious implementation of existing law entails pointing an accusatory finger at Canada
and the United States, and existing organizations are not willing to do that. Their
task is restricted to wilful blindness to the ecogenocide in those two countries, in
favour of pointing an accusatory finger at the Third World governments that carry
out ecogenocide elsewhere. Their fundraising is directed towards collecting money
so they can pay their executives to lobby for new laws, not to risk offending their financial sources by trying to implement the existing law.

Typical letters, to which there were no responses, follow:

December 18, 1995

The Chairperson
Goldman Environmental Foundation
One Lombard Street
San Francisco, CA 94111

Dear Chairperson:

Earlier today I read with interest your foundation's announcement in the New York
Times concerning the Ken Saro-Wiwa Fund. Congratulations for a step well taken. I hope
the response is as gratifying as it should be.

As the enclosed materials portray, a rule of law solution to the global problem of ecogenocide arguably already exists under the Convention for the Prevention and Punishment
of the Crime of Genocide, 1948.

Necessarily incidental to the implementation of such a solution is the rescuing of the
rule of law from its antithesis, international political expediency, pursuant to which emi-

nent countries such as Canada and the United States foster genocide trials elsewhere while keeping the book closed on genocide in the Americas, in which my native American clients are ongoing victims.

The set of court cases in progress and proposed may, as discussed in these materials, in part achieve and in part hasten the genuine inauguration of the rule of law and the salvation of some of the threatened enclaves.

May I ask you to consider helping me to implement the suggested solution? Thank you for listening.

November 13, 1995

The World Conservation Union
Plantage Middenlaan 2b
1018 DD Amsterdam
Holland

Dear Sir:

I have just read a legal opinion that I understand was commissioned jointly by your organization and the World Wildlife Fund and subsequently published as: W.D. Droogsma, J.H. Jans, and R. Uylenburg, *Legal Means for Restricting the Import of Non-Sustainably Produced (Tropical) Timber: Aspects of International and European law*, Amsterdam, Center for Environmental Law, January, 1994.

With great respect for the erudition and scholarship in terms of the legal instruments which the opinion's authors identified as being relevant, I have to submit that in terms of existing law they omitted from their analysis the only legal instrument that actually answers the commissioned question. None of the instruments examined (GATT's legal rules, the EEC, ITTA, cites and the Lomé Agreements) provide an existing solution under the auspices of the rule of law. At most, each examined instrument represents a context into which, in future, the politicians might place a legal remedy.

Unfortunately, by the time the world's community of nations finds the necessary political will to amend the instruments examined to provide such a remedy, the forests and the indigenous people whose existence depends upon them may well both be relegated to history. May I offer a second legal opinion? I believe that the Convention for the Prevention and Punishment of the Crime of Genocide, 1948 does provide an existing legal remedy. I act as counsel for several different indigenous peoples' groups and individuals that have instructed me to pursue this remedy. The accompanying pages will give you an overview.

In order to avoid conflicts of interest I have restricted my client base to the sorcerers or medicine people. Precisely because they are medicine people my clients are outside the commercial economy. In contrast with others in their villages they refuse, even moderately, to collaborate in the "ecocide" that entails the genocide of their cultural part of the greater indigenous population. Therefore they have no money. Can you help in any way? I do not have a European address, yet, but for the immediate present can receive messages via the [following] Amsterdam telephone numbers ...

Copies to:
World Wildlife Fund, P.O. Box 7, Ziest 3700 AA, Netherlands
World Wildlife Fund, 1250 – 24th Street North West, Washington (DC)
Greenpeace International, Keizersgracht 174, Amsterdam, Netherlands.

November 15, 1995

Amnesty International
1 Easton Street
London WC1X 8JD
England

Dear Sir:

My purpose in writing is to seek Amnesty's help for a special initiative coordinated to force the rule of law to serve 3 closely related interests:

- Amnesty's: of preventing the world-wide abuse of the criminal law process for political and financial objectives;
- Environmentalists': of preventing the eradication of the last wildernesses;
- Traditionalist Indigenous Peoples': of preventing the genocidal infliction upon themselves of incarceration and death in consequence of the aforesaid:
  - world-wide abuse of the criminal law process for political and financial objectives, and
  - eradication of the last wildernesses.

Enclosed please find a description of the initiative, in the form of a covering letter generally seeking support upon the basis of a "prospectus" and some select newspaper articles.

In years passed I have made (albeit somewhat differently focused) approaches to Amnesty, to environmentalist organizations and to Indian organizations. Amnesty consistently has declined to help on the ground that its particular mandate is rather narrowly defined in terms of ad hoc curative lobbying for public opinion that will influence governments to release or at least deal more humanely with unjustly detained individuals, as contrasted with anticipatory preventative underwriting of any specific class-action court case(s) designed structurally to preempt abuse. Somewhat similarly, the environmentalist organizations have tended to reply that their own focus is ecologically or wildlife oriented, as contrasted with the concern specifically for human demographics. Indian organizations tend to be "organized" upon the basis of funding provided by non-native governments or corporations, whose interest generally is to impose constraints that preclude active anti-ecogenocide court cases. Sponsored Indian organizations tend in consequence to have been oriented toward pragmatically searching out means whereby their constituents can share in the profits from the ecogenocide, rather than to eradicate the ecogenocide, the latter seemingly being an impossible, indeed quixotic task.

Nevertheless, the juncture in history at which the cross-disciplinary endeavour of uniting the interests of Amnesty, the Environmentalists and the Indigenous Peoples seems not only more urgently necessary today, but more within humanity's grasp. Is this a proposition that the directors of your organization might be ready, willing and able at this time to consider embracing?

Along with each of the above letters I sent a general letter seeking support in Europe:

November 11, 1995

Dear Reader:

The quest, to the support of which you respectfully are being asked to consider contributing, is to forge a fresh or at least refreshed legal remedy for a legal right that already exists. Existing law already says that genocide is a crime against all humanity. It defines genocide to include the intentional imposition, by constitutionally responsible rulers or public officials, of serious bodily or mental harm upon a religious, ethnical, racial or other identifiable group. Existing law also already says that treason and fraud occur when constitutionally responsible rulers or public officials contribute to or allow the occupation by non-natives of the territories of the Americas' indigenous peoples before the natives' existing aboriginal rights have been purchased from them.

Most importantly the rule of law says that where there is a right there must be a remedy. What then is the remedy to apprehend the genocide that is still occurring in consequence of the treasonable and fraudulent invasion of the Americas? As the accompanying prospectus attempts to make apparent, legal remedies are extraordinarily elusive. I have been searching them out for 24 years. Over the course of the past 5 of these in particular, that is since discovering while reading for my doctorate that the indigenous people have a vested due process right to take their case before an independent and impartial third-party court, I have run into an hysterical counter-reaction on the part of Canadian judges. In case after case these judges have evaded the issue, to the utter degradation and negation of the rule of law. The one feature that is common to each of the cases has been the presence of me, as legal counsel for the victimized indigenous people and their persecuted supporters. For this reason the most expeditious manner in which to portray the sum total of these events has been to use portions of the record from the disbarment proceedings against me, as the educating device. I do not by doing so mean to focus attention on my own personal plight. What has happened and is happening to me pales into insignificance when set beside the tragedies and horror stories that, after the centuries of genocidal pressure, comprise the heartbreaking reality of a race of people held to hostage, ridicule, contempt and condescension in their own stolen homeland.

In sum, at present, because of the seeming absence of a remedy, the crimes of genocide, treason and fraud are occurring with apparent impunity. The reason this is so is that the judiciary of each country in which those crimes are ongoing is not ready, willing and able to act against them.

Indeed, the judges are the crucial "constitutionally responsible rulers or public officials" without whose connivance the crimes would be impossible. To the extent that the rule of law is capable of evolving into a meaningful antidote to the scourge of genocide, the answer, therefore, seems to be to hold the judges accountable for not performing their duty as guardians of the rule of law.

The answer to the perennial questions – if not you, who? if not now, when? – is: the judges, and, now.

In aid of holding the judges of the world accountable generally to do their duty, Canada has become a laboratory. This is appropriate. Canada is identified in world public opinion as a rule of law bastion. The fact that genocide, treason and fraud are the norm there, of all places, not only puts the rule of law to one of its most daunting possible challenges but, for that very reason, makes the triumph of the rule of law over genocide that much more viable as a precedent for all the world. Unfortunately, the fire upon which the remedy must be forged is cold. It must be kindled by court actions destined to do what courts alone can do: supply rule of law remedies compelling, by court orders, respect for existing rights under existing law. It is this function that obviates the need for political agitation and the threat of violence as the preferred agents in the struggle against injustice.

Court actions must continue to be pursued in Canada, and in the other countries of the Americas. At present I happen to be the only lawyer who appears ready, willing and able to undertake that task, since the consequence of its undertaking is professional ruin and imprisonment, even in Canada, and, in some countries, I fear, torture or death.

Secondly, complementary actions must be commenced in the national courts of Europe, so as to force the judges of those courts first to acknowledge that, by buying the natural resources that have been stolen from the indigenous peoples, their countries and citizens are being receivers of stolen goods. As such, those countries and those citizens are aiders and abettors in the crimes of genocide, treason and fraud committed in the harvesting of the stolen goods. Injunctions to prevent this aiding and abetting by Europeans are within Europe's national courts' jurisdiction over European territory where the goods physically are received, and over the European citizens who receive them. If the national courts of Europe do the same as the national courts of Canada, which is to evade the issue, the judges of those courts, like the judges in Canada themselves, will become the sine qua non of those crimes' continuity. Their resulting complicity in the crimes can and will be appealed to the European Court of Human Rights.

Thirdly, international legal tribunals do exist, notably the International Court of Justice. Although this court has for many years occupied a politically opportune position by declining even to consider the question of its own potential jurisdiction, that jurisdiction issue can be raised for reassessment.

In short, since the world's community of nations is not sufficiently mature as yet to be ready, willing and able to constitute a general international penal tribunal to address the genocide problem, the only solution is to press into service the national courts of the countries of the world. I have started with those of Canada, whose judges prefer willfully to blind themselves (and hence others) to the issue and hence to the legislative words that establish those judges' own criminal involvement. I now must take the issue into the courts of the leading industrial powers of Europe.

This will cost money. If law firms other than mine were ready, willing and able to act, the cost would be in the millions of dollars each year. As matters stand, even for me alone to travel to and from the juridical capitals of the countries involved, do the work myself on a low overhead basis with the confidential assistance of national lawyers who can not in safety or security allow themselves to become more publicly involved, communicate progress or its lack to the indigenous people clients and to their supporters throughout the Americas and wherever else they may be, and to support my own family with bare necessaries of life, cumulatively will entail hundreds of thousands of dollars per year. It is this to which you are being asked to contribute financial support to the extent that your interest and other, no doubt onerous, commitments permit.

Financial support aside, the project also can benefit from an increased measure of public awareness of the profound simplicity of the issue of ecogenocide: – when the public allows the last wildernesses to die, the public condones the despair and deaths of the "wild" people whose autochthonous cultures are inseparable from wilderness. An increased public awareness and disapproval of this fact can serve as a conscience for judges. The present judicial excuse for inaction, which is that European judges can not act because to do so would interfere with the sovereignty of the foreign countries who are doing the actual killing, can not so comfortably as at present be maintained against a public made aware that without Europe's purchase of the genocidally stolen goods there would be no genocide of the variety with which we are concerned in this project.

Thank you for reading, and for thinking about the option of employing existing law more positively and assertively to prevent ecogenocide. Please telephone or write for clarification or elaboration.

There were no replies to any of these several requests for help. This lack of direct response is, of course, a form of response, only negative. When I was younger I found it inconceivable that genocide could have taken place against the Jews and the gypsies while the world sat by. Now I understood.

CHAPTER 15

The Mi'gmaq, the Supreme Court, and Other Matters

On our return from our aborted trip to Europe in December 1995, we wintered in New York State and then went on to Quebec. I had been contacted jointly by an elected chief and a hereditary chief who, on behalf of the Mi'gmaq Nation, were co-operating with each other in an attempt to defend the issue of native sovereignty and jurisdiction. This group of Mi'gmaq occupies as a reserve a modest acreage on the north shore of the Restigouche River, which constitutes the border between Quebec and New Brunswick. Its original and still unceded ancestral homeland is the entire drainage basin of the river, and includes the Gaspé Peninsula of Quebec and much of the northwest interior of New Brunswick.

After discussions with these people and other natives of the Atlantic region, I made an attempt to draft a confederated native court order that would address the law that the non-native courts so assiduously were evading. On 2 February 1997 that order was formally adopted by the sachems of chiefs of four of the leading native nations of the east. In essence, it exercised the natives' unrelinquished jurisdiction to convict the newcomer court system for its complicity in genocide and ordered it to stop.

JUDGMENT

Upon taking judicial notice of the suppression and genocide of the native people caused by the prematurely assumed jurisdiction of the newcomer courts, and in accordance with the accompanying reasons for judgment, this native court declares:

1. Court jurisdiction prima facie territorially is vested in the native courts and precluded from the newcomer courts; and

2. That in the event the newcomer courts are unable to agree with and help to uphold this declaration of right, this court invites the newcomer courts to join with this court in referring the contested jurisdictional issue for independent and impartial third party court adjudication in the international arena; or, in the alternative

3. That in the event the newcomer courts or their governments wish to submit evidence, law or argument to this native court so as to deny the premises, findings or law as

expressed herein or in the accompanying reasons for judgment, they are welcome to do so upon notifying this court of that intent.

REASONS FOR JUDGMENT

Humankind can, so easily as just doing it, choose to turn away from the Injustice Way of the past. And set its future course upon the Justice Way.

To this native court, as we hope and trust the newcomers' courts will learn to understand and respect, the Justice Way is one and the same as the Nature Way or the Native Way. It is the way of natural law.

Until recently when native people spoke of the Nature Way or the Native Way, there was hardly any basis for a communicative connection with the newcomers. The newcomers seemed unable to hear. It was rather like what Friedrich Wilhelm Nietzsche said: "No one can draw more out of things, books included, than he already knows. A man has no ears for that to which experience has given him no access."

When the newcomers began laying waste the forests of the new world, some natives could hear the sounds of the trees screaming in the face of the onslaught. But the newcomers could not hear. And if they were told, they dismissed the stories as fanciful. Yet science now discloses that plants do communicate and the medium appears to be sounds or chemicals beyond the normal reach of human sensory perception. We are told that when giraffes eat the leaves of acacia trees, the trees downwind produce chemicals that make their leaves inedible. Native medicine people could hear, sense or feel the resonances of dimensions of reality beyond the imagination of the newcomers, who dismissed their accounts as hallucinations or charlatanry. Yet since Einstein and Picasso, mathematicians, physicists, musicians and artists have ventured far beyond abstractionism and the theory of relativity – into quantum mechanics, unified field theory and hyperspace – making some of the "wildest dreams" of the ancient magicians and prophets seem like simple foresight.

Science, education and knowledge have evolved to the point where humanity is on the brink of discovering what it already knew, before the alienation of humankind from nature: there is a unity and a harmony that science no less than religion can suspect or feel even if not quite yet fully understand.

If that intuition can be translated into experience for modern humankind, it will be in virtue of tapping into the collective unconscious that unites humanity at its genetic roots. It will entail a rediscovery of what some few native people have never lost, but which was once common for all of humanity, before the sense of awe based upon respect was superseded by the conceit of the dominance of nature.

The native prophecies forecast this time. They also forecast that when this time did come humankind and nature would be on the cusp of annihilation and despoliation.

Before the European invasion of North America native society was true to its natural law principles. People, earth, sky and water were free and unpolluted. The jurisdiction of the native courts helped to maintain this condition; for the native courts oversaw the application in practice of the natural law principles.

In contrast with the prominence of the court function, the government function was relatively minor, except in time of war. In peacetime it was not thought necessary to survival in good health for native society to be very much engaged in the making of new and detailed laws. Rather, the harmonious application in practice of the old laws, the finite set of natural law principles, sufficed to maintain the balance.

After the European invasion the policy and practice of some of the newcomers was to covet the earth, sky and water by eradicating, or at least transforming, native society. The aboriginal people became victims of genocide; and the earth, sky and water of genocide's companion: ecocide.

Since native society was held together by the court function, eradicating or transforming native society meant suppressing native society's court function. The specific way has been to substitute, prematurely and therefore illegally, the jurisdiction of the newcomers' own courts, and in a complementary and distracting way to foster native preoccupation with new governmental functions.

To this end, the newcomer governments and courts in the United States and Canada constitute and promote Indian governments that are federally organized, recognized and funded, to the virtual exclusion of the native courts in the traditional jurisdiction context. These federally organized and recognized native governments function as the newcomers' agents in the application of federal law. That application is in many regions illegal, because premature, and of genocidal and ecological consequence.

By being premature, the territorial application of federal law can be contrary to natural law, international law and constitutional law. It depends upon whether the native people have consented. Purchase is, and ever since the European invasion began has been, the specific legal means for ascertaining the consent.

Furthermore, the sufficiency of the consent – the evidence and deliberation of its existence – is itself governed by specific positive law.

In essence, territory is off-limits to newcomers until it has been purchased by the newcomers' governments from the natives. And purchase is a question of mixed fact and law ...

Since the courts of the natives and the courts of the newcomers equally are interested in the answer to the purchase question, each court system, including this court, equally is biased in addressing and resolving it. For this reason, the law is that this question can only be answered as to any given territory by an outsider – an independent and impartial third party court – one the existence of whose jurisdiction does not itself turn upon a prejudgment of the very issue in contention: which court system, native or newcomer, has jurisdiction?

The assumption by the newcomers' courts that they have the jurisdiction to decide the question of their own jurisdiction when in competition with the jurisdiction of the natives' courts is the means to the genocide and the ecocide. That assumption is how those crimes against humanity and nature are perfected in North America.

And because of the influence of the United States and Canada upon world affairs, the successful and consistent apprehension of those crimes in the global village will not occur unless and until those crimes are apprehended here, at home ...

The time has come for the native courts, with respect, to remind the newcomers' courts of the natural law basis for all law, for the good of all natives and newcomers alike, and for the health of their shared environment ...

The simple point is that natural law, international law and constitutional law rights, once conceded, cannot easily be withdrawn by tyrants or substitute tyrants. The withdrawing, if it is to occur at all, can only be achieved by the people. The form of the withdrawal can only be by way of formal international law convention and constitutional law repeal. This feature is common to native and newcomer law and government, and is probably a universal characteristic of democratic human social organization ...

The issue of jurisdictional competence is so very central and important to this question because an erroneous assumption appears to have crept into and to have infected the North American judicial system, with disastrous consequences for the moral structure and physical integrity of North American society in general. Setting affairs right, now, depends upon examining that erroneous character of that assumption in light of existing natural, international and constitutional law, and correcting the identified mistake. This is the purpose, ultimately, of the present renewal of the long-suppressed jurisdiction of the native court system, as represented by these reasons for judgment.

Existing natural law, international law and constitutional law more adequately should have tempered the newcomers' conduct toward both the native North Americans and the North American environment. Lamentably, the newcomers often have been and in some regions still are in breach of natural, international and constitutional law. When the newcomers systematically and in a coordinated fashion breach the natural, international and constitutional law in any given region, they do so by applying domestic rules of conduct that pretend to be law, but which are not really law, precisely because they conflict with the anterior and superior natural law, international law and constitutional law.

When this occurs the rule of law is in abeyance, overrun by mere policy and practice masquerading as law. To the extent that this anti-law domestic "law" is allowed to supersede the consensus of natural law, international law and constitutional law, the rule of law is negated, and the harmonious survival of humankind in nature is jeopardized ...

It would be beneficial for all of humanity were the newcomers' society in North America now to address and correct its historic breach of the existing law. Society can do this by conforming to the existing law, or by due process repealing or amending the existing law. It can adopt a combination of both devices. But society cannot, legally, do this by having its courts rise above the existing law.

To do that strikes an unmistakable and undeniable posture of opportunism and lawlessness, of might being right; a posture that is so close to the heart of the society as to set a standard which negates the moral structure which makes and keeps the society a society. It is in this sense that Hume was being precise for legal purposes when he identified the true application of law under the system of third party adjudication as "the origin of civil government and society."

North American society leads humanity's evolutionary advance in the field of human and environmental rights, and neither genocide nor ecocide will be apprehended generally in the world so long as the leading exponents of its apprehension, the United States and Canada, continue to stonewall the issue at home. The addressing of this issue, in accordance with the rule of law, will signal a new beginning for humanity, a rational basis upon which to have hope for the harmonious survival of humankind in nature. With the passing of the genocide can pass from history the ecological assault upon the planet, that excess which arises in consequence of the same immature, immoderate and uncontrolled attitude in human society as that which results in the genocide.

For these purposes the native people presently feel the need to re-institute, in practice, their original natural law right of jurisdiction, at least in regions where Indian treaties relinquishing that original right either have not yet been made or, if made, made invalidly, such as under fraud, duress or undue influence, or where there has been a failure of consideration ...

When that happens vis-à-vis North America, humankind will have made an evolutionary advance of structural consequence. Human evolution has moved beyond genetic mutation. Its future lies in the evolution of human institutions. Preeminent among these institutions is the rule of law administered by third party adjudication: the pragmatic guarantor of justice as applied truth, of law as applied respect, and of order as dependably stabilized liberty.

The natives wish it to be well understood that by identifying the truth and seeking respect in this fashion they do not seek to dispossess the trespassing newcomers, whose governments and courts have in the past usurped the natives' original jurisdiction and thereby denied the natives' humanity.

The natives and their traditional courts accept the facts of history as being irreversibly albeit illegally accomplished, but nevertheless seek for the future a more balanced native and newcomer relationship, one that more faithfully conforms, in alternative ways, with the spirit of the law and justice which all too often has been breached. In contemplation is a viable and modern service economy, in place and in stead of the illegally destroyed aboriginal economy, in circumstances where the new economy respects the integrity and the sanctity of the land, in perpetuity.

This native court turns now to the details of the international law and constitutional law ...

All we ask is that the newcomer judges recognize the possibility of their own complicity in genocide and, correspondingly, their own incapacity to sit in judgment of themselves.

They can not possibly adjudicate any aspect of the issue of native rights, without implicitly adjudicating their own accountability for the genocide that has resulted, and is resulting, from their complicity in elevating federal law and policy over the conflicting natural law, international law and constitutional law.

For this reason, the *Order in Council (Great Britain) of 9 March 1704* is not only good law, but necessary to the integrity of the rule of law. Without third party adjudication, the rule of law itself will not only be a hoax, but be seen to be a hoax. That can not be allowed.

It must be opposed, not only for the native people but for all people, for all depend upon the integrity of the rule of law, upon its fidelity to justice as applied truth and law as applied respect and order based upon those two features under the system of third party adjudication ...

When all that is relevant to the issue of native rights in North America that can be said, has been said, it is apparent that principle and practice have taken different roads. Principle has taken the high road, practice the low. And the crucial perception is not to allow the volume, the detail, the ingenious character of the fraud perpetrated by the practice to obscure the simple fact of the fraud. The fraudulent practice is not self-legitimizing. It is not evidence of the law, but of the breach of the law.

For 500 years, the consensus of natural law, international law and constitutional law has been straightforward and unvarying. The law, what it actually says, has remained true to itself, and to the human species and the environment that the law exists to serve. But what the newcomers have actually done, that is the opposite of what the law says should have been done.

All along the law has said that because the natives were here first, and are humans, until territory has been purchased from them by the newcomers, the natives have the territorial jurisdiction.

In some regions, it is true, the newcomers' governments did make proper and valid written purchases, and can produce them to prove it.

But in many other regions the newcomers' governments simply allowed in the lawyers, the judges and the police before the purchase validly was completed. Thus the legal establishment acted as a unit – to perfect the greatest and most massive fraud in human history.

Like a finely tuned machine, the lawyers, judges and police successfully have thus held the law at bay in North America, equally in the United States and Canada and, so far at least, have been able to get away with it, not because they legally were capable of changing the law, but rather because illegally they abused their usurped jurisdiction to stonewall the law.

When the legal establishment prematurely, and therefore illegally, invaded any given region, the legal establishment immediately entrenched itself and consolidated its own position. The newcomer lawyers hung up their shingles and started doing land deals and certifying titles. They themselves lived in houses and raised families upon territory not yet purchased, as required by law, from the natives. When natives complained, to whom could they turn for legal redress? The judges were, and still are, elevated lawyers. Like the newcomer lawyers, the newcomer judges themselves, physically, and literally, were and are trespassers upon the yet unpurchased territory. So were, and are, the newcomer police.

If and when the natives complain, the mass of complaints fall upon the lawyers' psychologically pre-programmed ears. If and when the natives turn to the common law remedy of self-help, they are arrested as trouble makers, and taken before judges who are in a profound conflict of interest. They end up stigmatized, trivialized and discredited as criminals.

No illustration could be clearer, plainer or more poignant than that remarked above as provided by the Supreme Court of Canada, which court itself physically and literally is situate upon territory that has never been purchased from the Algonquin speakers of the Ottawa Valley drainage basin. When the traditional government of the Algonquin nation challenged that trespass, in the course of applying to intervene in the reference regarding Quebec secession, on January 17, 1997 the Supreme Court of Canada denied that nation

intervenor status. It did so on the basis of allowing an objection made by a federally organized, recognized and funded Indian Act government, located only on one small portion of
the vast Algonquin traditional territory. The particular federally organized native government objected to the intervention of the traditional government which, in contrast, was not
federally recognized. Indeed, the practical purpose of federal organization and recognition
has been to preclude and to silence the traditional form of government. In sum, the federal
government illegally placed both the Supreme Court of Canada and the objecting native
puppet government upon the yet unpurchased territory of the hereditary government of the
Algonquin Nation. Then, the two trespassing usurpers, the Court and its native collabora-
tor, acted in concert so as to exclude the position of the traditional government. In this
fashion the literal trespass of the Supreme Court of Canada upon yet unpurchased native
territory has been obscured. The transparently false illusion is that the Supreme Court of
Canada might be independent and impartial with regard to the Mi'gmaq intervention
which it did permit ...

In such a situation the newcomer society of the perpetrators is victimized along with the
native society of the victims. As the slave owner is debased by the institution of slavery, so
also is the society inflicting genocide itself inflicted.

In North America the corruption of the society thus begins at the top. The people at the
bottom, the ordinary newcomers and natives, speak through the natural law, the international law and the constitutional law. The consensus of that law is a projection of their collective good will. But their voice is not heard – because the legal establishment at the top
of the society will not listen to the law. The lawyers, judges and police have usurped jurisdiction, and they employ the usurped jurisdiction to stonewall the law.

The message reaches to every office, every boardroom, every schoolyard, every place of
worship, everywhere: might is right.

This message corrupts. It eats at the heart and sinew of the society, of all the societies,
newcomer and native alike, for even the native society is conscripted into aiding and abetting its own genocide.

If the newcomers' courts cannot agree upon the merits of these reasons, the disagreement between their contrary reasoning and this court reasoning must, under existing law,
be submitted for third party adjudication in the international arena.

All that we therefore ask the newcomers' courts to do is not to set upon us and our people the newcomers' police, in place and instead of submitting the dispute, if any, between
us as courts, to the third part adjudication of yet a third court system.

If, when objectively applying the rule of law as an independent and impartial outsider,
the third party finds that this native court is wrong, we can live with that. We are prepared
to abide by the rule of law, and ask only the same of the newcomers and their courts.

What we can no longer bear to live with, for the injustice of it is causing anguish that
spells genocide and ecocide, is the denial of our right both of jurisdiction and third party
adjudication to vindicate it.

Therefore, all that we ask the newcomers' courts in comity to do is recognize and affirm
that at law natives have rights to arguably yet unceded territory, plus the right to third party

adjudication of the question whether it is in fact ceded. We therefore invite the newcomers' courts: "Agree with this native court, or at least let an independent and impartial third party objectively decide our disagreement, in accordance with the rule of law."

Once that fair and just solution has been declared by both native and newcomer court systems, the people of both cultures and their politicians can move onward and upward toward agreeing upon the identity of the third party adjudicator for the promising millennium ahead. The era of the Native Way, the Nature Way, the Justice Way will have been reconstituted, for the good of all humankind and its environment ...

The legal establishment of North America is in the profoundest possible conflict of interest. It has an interest in upholding the integrity of the rule of law. But it has a conflicting interest in evading accountability for its own complicity in genocide for derogating from the substance of the law.

When the North American judiciary of the newcomers permits the former interest to override the latter interest, on that day humankind will have made an evolutionary advance of structural significance. That day will dawn when the newcomer judiciary listens to, and actually hears, the traditional native judiciary.

We have, therefore, attempted, by publishing these reasons for judgment, to allow the traditional native voice to be heard.

I returned to British Columbia in the spring of 1997 to defend my three remaining Gustafsen Lake clients. The criminal trials of these defendants, held in the Supreme Court of British Columbia, provided the first opportunity to test the argument presented by the Mi'gmaq native court order. For this purpose I wrote to the prosecuting attorney's office of British Columbia, explaining that I was en route to the province for that purpose and that I intended to meet the judge who wanted to put me on trial for contempt. The police met my plane on landing and placed me under arrest. Bail was denied on the ground that I was likely to flee. No one seemed to notice or care that I had just travelled 2000 miles to seek out my trial, not to flee from it.

For the show-cause hearing, I was taken before the judge who had originally cited me for contempt. He wanted to try me on the charge, even though a new judge is normally brought in at this stage of contempt proceedings. I offered to make the apology that earlier he had stipulated as the condition for having the charge withdrawn, as is also the normal procedure where lawyers are charged and the heat of the courtroom battle has had time to cool. I added, however, that I could not couple my apology with a waiver of my native clients' right to object to the judge's assumption of jurisdiction as being treasonable, fraudulent, and complicitous in genocide.

Rather than mollify the judge, my statement in court incensed him. He indicated that the point was not my apology or jurisdiction over me personally; rather, it was the contempt shown to the court by my opinion of the law. That was what had to be retracted. I declined to do that, and, for the actual trial,

requested the appointment of another judge to address the law going to jurisdiction, since this judge had already indicated that he was not prepared to listen
to that law. The judge refused and, instead, convicted me on the spot – without
arraigning me, without taking a plea, and without allowing full defence evidence.

The judge sentenced me to three months' imprisonment. I appealed to the
Court of Appeal, which refused to address the law going to jurisdiction, and on
this basis confirmed the conviction. I applied to the Supreme Court of Canada
for leave to appeal further, but leave was denied on the ground that no issue of
"importance" was presented.

While I was serving my sentence of three months in jail (one of which was
served while on electronic surveillance), I applied once again to the Law Society
of British Columbia for an occasional appearance certificate, so that, on my release, I could represent my Gustafsen Lake clients at their trial. The Law Society
refused to grant the certificate, on the ground that I was a convicted criminal who
was disrespectful of the courts. As an alternative, I arranged for my clients to
subpoena me as their witness. The subpoena was served on me in jail, and a
court order was obtained compelling the warden to transfer me in custody to the
jail adjacent to the courthouse where the Gustafsen Lake trial was in progress.
By this route I found myself in the same cell block as the two imprisoned Indians
who were still my clients.

I testified as a witness at the Gustafsen Lake trial for two weeks about the advice I had given my clients leading up to and during the Gustafsen Lake event.
The confederated native court order and its reasons were accepted in evidence as
a summation of that advice.

When I finished testifying, the trial judge instructed the jury to disregard what
I had explained about the law because, he said, I was wrong on the law. He did
not identify a mistake but, rather, informed the jury that it was up to him to decide the law and for them to take his decision as a given. He further advised the
jury that my clients did not, in fact, actually believe what I had told them about
the law, and so were not entitled to be acquitted on the ground of honest, though
mistaken, belief. As for the issue of native liberty and possession pending crown
purchase, his instructions to the jury were that it was settled law that my theory
was invalid; that the rancher was entitled to possession rather than the natives,
regardless of the fact there was not any Indian treaty; and that non-native society,
including the jury itself, did have jurisdiction to convict.

On these bases, the jury carried out the judge's instructions and convicted all
accused persons of mischief charges while armed, and for various trespass-related
offences. The Indians, it seems, have no rights on their yet unceded homelands.

The British Columbia Court of Appeal dismissed the appeal that I filed relative to the court jurisdiction issue, on the ground that the issue was pre-empted
from consideration by the Court of Appeal's previous judgment in the case

Delgamuukw v. British Columbia. On 14 May 1998 the Supreme Court of Canada denied leave to appeal, on the ground that the issue raised was not of "importance." My two Indian clients were given four-year sentences. The Wolverine, when all his time in jail awaiting trial is taken into consideration, ended up serving the equivalent of a seven-year sentence for a conviction for criminal mischief and trespass on unceded Indian territory. In Ontario, in contrast, the police officer who negligently shot and killed the Indian Dudley George, who was demonstrating to protect an ancient native graveyard from desecration near Kettle Point on Lake Huron, received eighteen months, all of which were accounted for by community service rather than actual imprisonment.

While I was preparing the Supreme Court of Canada appeal papers in relation to the Gustafsen Lake case and the reconsideration papers in relation to the Bear Island case, the Canadian attorney general delivered a set of questions to the Supreme Court of Canada, requiring the judges of that court to render an advisory opinion as to the legality of Quebec secession. Two of the native signatories to the confederated native court order, as traditional judges, had ancestral territory in Quebec. They instructed me to intervene in the reference for the purpose of advising the Supreme Court of Canada of the law precluding, or at least qualifying, that court's jurisdiction vis-à-vis that portion of Canada as arguably remained unceded Indian territory. The natives' argument was that under international and constitutional law as enacted by Order in Council (Great Britain) of 9 March 1704 in the matter of *Mohegan Indians v. Connecticut*, only an independent and impartial third-party tribunal could adjudicate jurisdictional disputes in relation to any territory on which native jurisdiction itself arguably still exists, not having been surrendered in accordance with the purchase formula constitutionally stipulated by the Royal Proclamation of 1763. The argument continued that, since the Supreme Court of Canada was constituted and staffed entirely under federal, as contrasted with constitutional legislation, it was not a third-party adjudicator.

On 17 January 1997 the chief justice of Canada responded to me in court, saying: "[W]e will be helped through you by the views of the traditional chiefs ... if you are right on the Mi'gmaq, if your position is right as regards the Mi'gmaqs, it will apply to the Algonquins and I guess to all Indians." At last, it seemed, the stonewall was crumbling. But this hope proved to be a mirage. After granting leave to make the argument, the chief justice of Canada soon precluded the law in support of the argument from actually being addressed. Specifically, he denied my clients' motion to focus the court jurisdiction issue as a preliminary constitutional question that had to be answered independently of the secession question on its merits. And so the natives for whom I was acting withdrew from the reference.

The second factor that led to my distancing myself from the Quebec Secession Reference was a change in the leadership of the Mi'qmaq Indian nation instructing me. The *Indian Act* chief of that group had been elected at least in part on the basis of a campaign stressing native sovereignty, which has always been a popular cause at the Listuguj (Restigouche) reserve. In early 1981, when the so-called Salmon War had occurred, some four hundred Quebec Provincial Police had raided the reserve, confiscating Indian nets, beating native people, and in general terrorizing the community. The Indians' offence, taking a miniscule proportion of the fish relative to the share cornered by the non-native commercial and sport fishery, was condemned by a large group of the non-native public, who liked the sound of "one law for all." This attitude generally negates the special legal status and rights that aboriginal rights entail.

Although the Listuguj natives have a reserve, it had been set apart for federal law purposes by a unilateral executive act rather than in the context of a treaty contract pursuant to which the Indians might arguably have voluntarily relinquished their aboriginal rights to the non-reserve remainder of their original homeland. The treaty that did exist was not an extinguishment treaty contract, but rather an eighteenth-century mutual confirmation between natives and newcomers of segregated peace and friendship. Instead of extinguishing aboriginal rights, this treaty, along with similar ones in the Canadian Atlantic provinces, much of New England, southeastern New York, British Columbia, and California, essentially relates to unceded Indian territory.

The first few court contests in which I was involved for the Restigouche natives repeated the same pattern I had experienced elsewhere. The local non-native judges at first were pleasant, and then, when they realized I had the law to back up my allegation that their assumption of jurisdiction was not only unconstitutional but criminally treasonable, fraudulent, and genocidal, they adopted punitive measures against me to forestall the law from being addressed.

The bar associations of both Quebec and New Brunswick denied me occasional appearance certificates on the ground that I was "under investigation" by the bar association in my home province of Ontario. When the Listuguj native hereditary leader went to a court hearing without me in New Brunswick, armed with the written material I had prepared for him to present to the court, the non-native judge not only refused to address the law but penalized him by imposing a $2000 punitive award in costs against him for having the effrontery to raise the issue, which he dismissed out of hand. The particular case was a quieting of titles application to clear ambiguities in relation to a piece of property on the site of the Listuguj natives' original prehistoric village. When the Europeans came, they pushed the Indians off this preferred site on the south, or New Brunswick, side of the Restigouche River and the Indians were forced to relocate on the north shore, in Quebec. If ever there a land ownership case suitable for testing the jurisdiction issue, this was it.

While this familiar coordinated assault by the newcomers' bench and bar was proceeding apace, the federal government's Indian Affairs department let the elected chief know that federal funding and assistance of various kinds would dry up if the Indian band persisted with me, but that otherwise they would continue to flow. The department even offered to hire and pay for other lawyers, ones more amenable to constructive engagement with the federal government and is chest of treasures. In short, the normal carrot-and-stick approach, which had been employed so successfully elsewhere in Canada, was shifted to the Restigouche region. I was dropped by both the hereditary and the elected chiefs.

While these events were happening in New Brunswick and Quebec, the Gustafsen Lake case of *R. v. Ignace, Franklin and Pitawanakwat* from British Columbia and the Bear Island case from Ontario were nearing their combined day of reckoning in the Supreme Court of Canada. I became convinced that the only hope for justice in the Gustafsen Lake appeal would be for the Temagami Indian Band and the Teme-augma Anishnabai to support the personal application by my Temagami client, Verna Friday, to reopen the Bear Island case. Accordingly, on the eve of disposition of the Supreme Court applications in the Bear Island and Gustafsen Lake cases I sent Verna the following letter, which she in turn presented to the Temagami Indian Band and the Teme-augma Anishnabai:

March 8, 1998

Dear Verna:

Rather than deal with the law identified in your application to set aside the *Bear Island* case, Ontario has alleged that no single hunting grounds family acting alone can point out that the non-native courts had no jurisdiction.

If Ontario's argument succeeds, Ontario will get away with the treasonable, fraudulent and genocidal theft of the Temagami lands not because it is legal but because the Temagamis other than your family declined to insist upon the law as it is stipulated by the *Order in Council (Great Britain) of 9 March 1704*. If Ontario gets away with these crimes, natives such as Wolverine, who continues to suffer for the corruption and complicity of others, and the rule of law itself everywhere in Canada will be sacrificed.

In the past you have told me that the band and nation will not cooperate with you because I sued them and I act for you. Accordingly, I have discontinued my legal proceedings against the band and nation and its traditional families and I hereby waive any right to sue again.

Verna said that when she presented the letter, no one was willing to talk, that it was as if they were afraid or confused about what to do. In any event, they did nothing. In consequence, my attempt to rehabilitate the rule of law by relinquishing my claim to remuneration was to no avail. Since the Temagamis have helped to sink the international and constitutional law in Canada, they may expect a pay-off from the federal and provincial governments. That is how the system works. They may be paid off, or they may find the reward for appeasement turn to dust.

On 14 May 1998 the Supreme Court of Canada denied leave in both the Gustafsen Lake and Bear Island cases. Margaret and I were thus at the seeming end of the road, so far as our endeavour to rehabilitate the rule of law and apprehend the genocide in process in Canada is concerned. The newcomers' legal establishment had with finality signaled the triumph of denial over truth, and the patience of the Indians to serve as a battering ram to knock the denial down had been exhausted. Margaret and I personally were precluded from earning an income with which to survive in Canada because the Canadian tax department was stalking us for payment of accumulated interest and penalties on the $15,000 tax that, back in 1977, I paid to the Indians rather than to Canada. I expected to be arrested on that or some other trumped-up pretext at any time, and it was apparent that if I were to be arrested, the likelihood was that I would be imprisoned. For a certainty, the jurisdiction issue that I would have to raise in my defence would be stonewalled.

After twenty-five years of trying, I had failed to make the rule of law function for the Indians, and I could not make it work for me either when I found myself in the Indians' shoes. As generation after generation of Indians had been criminalized because of the criminal and wilful blindness of the Canadian legal establishment to the rule of law, so my family and I were added to the casualty list of wasted people.

PART FIVE

THE UNITED STATES: LAST EMPIRE, LAST HOPE

CHAPTER 16

Mohegans of New York and Vermont

Meanwhile, Margaret and I had been summoned from across the border by the Passamaquoddies of Maine and the Mohegans (or Mohicans) of the Hudson River drainage basin of New York and Vermont.

It has been the nature of previous empires to rise and then fall. Native mystics are not convinced that this cyclical pattern of the past necessarily ensures that the future will also be that way. They warn that the capacity of nature to regenerate is approaching a point of exhaustion beyond which, if pushed farther, it will not be able to recover. They caution that unless the American empire finds the true path of justice and elects to walk on it, there will not be another chance, for there will not be a living planet. To these mystics, the injustice ushered in to nature and to the natural people with the European invasion of North America is on the brink of obliterating all traces of the true path, rendering it undiscoverable.

From this perspective, the United States is not only the most recent empire but the last. It will either lead the world into an era of justice or plunge it into such a darkness of injustice as to preclude recovery. Ecogenocide in America occurred because the good law precluding it was ignored in practice, not because the law was bad. The greatest crime against humankind and nature yet seen in world history began with the suppression of the law guaranteeing the natives liberty and possession. The crime will be apprehended if and when that law is allowed to surface.

My last attempt to jump start the rule of law began in the world's imperial capital, New York, much as Margaret and I had experienced it so often before in Alberta, British Columbia, California, New Brunswick, Nevada, Ontario, and Quebec. The same pattern, in essence, also happened in the Passamaquoddy country of northern Maine. I was invited to reopen the Maine Settlement Act and treaty of the early 1980s, on the ground that the process those documents recorded was a modern edition of the nineteenth-century gun-to-the-head treaties and, as such, unenforceable as against the Maine natives, who, by this juncture, were sorely disillusioned with the settlement. The Passamaquoddies found themselves cut off from the sea, and the former freedom of their fishery, because the Maine Settlement contains an omnibus clause by which they surrendered *all* their aboriginal rights, wherever located, in exchange for money and other contractual considerations. The money, by the mid-1990s, was largely spent, and many Passamaquoddies wanted the sense of freedom back.

I was able to obtain from the lawyer who had represented the Passamaquoddies at the time of the Maine Settlement an affidavit in which he acknowledged that he had not been aware, and accordingly had not informed his clients, of their right to third-party adjudication in light of the Order in Council (Great Britain) of 9 March 1704 in the matter of *Mohegan Indians v. Connecticut*. The Passamaquoddies were prepared and indeed anxious, they said, to go to court and testify that they never would have signed the Maine Settlement if they had been informed of their right to the third-party adjudication. The reason they signed, they told me, was that their legal staff told them they had no chance of winning in court against the United States in the United States's own courts. Third-party adjudication put a new slant, for them, on their prospect of justice under the rule of law.

Moreover, the Passamaquoddies' case as presented in the 1970s and 1980s had been based on the federal Indian Nonintercourse Act of 1790. That statute provides that treaties other than those with the federal government are invalid. The eighteenth-century treaty of surrender, on which it was assumed that native rights in Maine had been extinguished, was signed by the natives and by the State of Maine, but not by the federal government. The Second Circuit Court of Appeals confirmed the Passamaquoddies' argument that the federal Indian Nonintercourse Act rendered the eighteenth-century treaty void, arguably reviving the native rights previously assumed to have been extinguished under that treaty.

The reason, the Passamaquoddies said, that they accepted the Maine Settlement was that they were advised by their non-native legal counsel that the prospect of the United States Supreme Court upholding the Second Circuit, and thereby effectively giving Maine back to the Indians, was a non-starter. Their lawyer's advice had been to take the settlement deal on offer, rather than pursue their litigation in the enemy's own court system and, inevitably, lose. In contrast, the case I was invited to prepare for the Passamaquoddies eschewed federal law, including reliance on the Indian Nonintercourse Act, for the reason that reliance on federal law and the assertion of unsurrendered native sovereignty is a self-defeating contradiction in terms and concepts.

The Passamaquoddies decided to take a run at voiding the Maine Settlement on the grounds of fraud, allegedly having been duped both to their remedy of third-party adjudication and to the supposed need to rely on federal law when asserting native sovereignty. My clients took the position that they wanted to reopen the Maine Settlement based on their right of third-party adjudication. The third-party adjudicator would then be presented with the international and constitutional law (as contrasted with the federal law) basis for the allegedly still-existing aboriginal rights of liberty and exclusive possession.

Again we fell victim to the familiar train of events. The Maine judge whom we first came before to raise the law declined to do so, preferring to concentrate on attacking me for supposedly practising law illegally in the State of Maine. No lawyer in Maine was ready, willing, and able to present and defend the law that had to be addressed in support of the natives' legal argument. As usual, the judge's point was to preclude the message by precluding the messenger. At the same time, the Passamaquoddies' local lawyer raised the specter of losing what was left of the Maine Settlement benefits with nothing to substitute. It does not matter what this law says, he argued to his clients, it is never going to be applied in the non-native courts of the federal and state governments. Those courts are never going to allow the right of third-party adjudication to be addressed. In short, the rule of law is a hoax.

That is an easy argument for lawyers to make to Indian clients whom they want to steer away from the native sovereignty issue because of the conflict of interest under which those lawyers labour in relation to that issue. It is easy because Indians, from centuries of experience, are already convinced that the rule of law is a hoax. Lawyers are preaching to the converted. The Indians know that the international and constitutional law on which America is founded recognizes the Indians' priority of occupation. This occupation means that the newcomers' only original jurisdiction is that to purchase, as stipulated by the Royal Proclamation of 1763 and as confirmed by Chief Justice Marshall of the Supreme Court of the United States in 1832 in *Worcester v. Georgia*. But the natives also know that this law is like jam tomorrow, jam yesterday, never jam today, because the newcomers' bench and bar have a monopolistic control of the jam jar.

The upshot was that, as everywhere else I have been in North America, when the going got rough, rather than stick to their international and constitutional law guns, the Passamaquoddies dumped me, and therefore the law of which I was the messenger. Or, perhaps, it would be more accurate to say that the hope I had kindled in them that the rule of law might at last really function in the aboriginal rights context was dashed by events, and, with it, my utility. When their case was called in the Maine court and the judge refused to let me speak, they negotiated a deal behind my back with the prosecution to have the particular charges dropped in exchange for dismissing me from background participation.

I moved to the outskirts of the village of Granville in New York State to live with Margaret and David in the garage of the sachem of the last of the Mohegans – or at least with the man who identified himself to me as the heir of that tradition. The financial burden of the legal struggle in which he was engaged, and which he invited me to join, had persuaded him to try to raise money for its prosecution by operating an Indian bingo in Granville. Once he advertised, the attorney general of New York applied to the Supreme Court of New York for an injunction. I appeared before that court, and, in contrast with the Maine and Nevada courts and the Ninth Circuit Court of Appeals in San Francisco, was allowed by the presiding judge to address the court *pro hac vice* (for this occasion only). Bemusedly he asked me from the bench if I was actually saying to him that he, indeed the Supreme Court of New York itself, had no jurisdiction in New York. I told him that the international and constitutional law was saying so, not to all of New York, but rather to those regions of New York that arguably remained unceded by the Indians. On this basis I offered to place that law before him and let it speak for itself. He said, sceptically, but smiling and pleasantly, that he looked forward to seeing that supposed law and to dealing with it in due course. It was clear to all present in the courtroom that in dealing with my allegation of law, he would enjoy the intellectual challenge of exposing its absurdity.

I presented the law, in writing. He reserved judgment for a month while he poured over it, at the end of which time he neglected to deal with the law presented, or even, in fact, to mention it. All he said was that the bingo was precluded because the sachem had not obtained a bingo licence from the town, as if one were not only needed but as if there were no international and constitutional law arguments that might cast doubt on the assumed need. The international and constitutional law that the judge had so looked forward to addressing had suddenly become invisible. The issue itself simply evaporated, and was not even acknowledged to exist in his final judgment.

Rather than appeal that decision of the New York Supreme Court, the Mohegans (the terms Mahicans, Mohicans, and Mohegans are used interchangeably, for they are different phonetic renditions of the same Algonkian-language word) decided to submit a petition to the president of the United States in accordance with the First Amendment of the Constitution. Accordingly, on 20 August 1997 the sachem wrote to President Clinton "pursuant to the *1st Amendment* right '*to petition the Government for a redress of grievances*.'" He asked the president for "a letter from you acknowledging the existence of the Western Mohegan Tribe & Nation of New York so that we can fulfill our rightful role as participants in the life of the Hudson River valley," on the basis that "we are the valley's original inhabitants, witnesses to its conversion from paradise to wasteland, and now to the beginnings of its return to ecological health, as its economy shifts from industrial to recreational tourism." Most crucially, he added, "I am not writing so that this native nation can become a welfare recipient of programs and services under federal law. These we do not want and will not accept. I am writing so that we can regain our liberty under anterior and superior natural, international and constitutional law, and on the basis of that liberty to work in harmony with the newcomers for a better future for us all in this society of natives and newcomers and their reviving nature-based economy."

The New York Mohegans' First Amendment petition for relief from genocide recounted their oral history that "the Mohegan tribe originally consisted of the council fires of 9, later 8, autonomous Mohegan nations, all of whom annually met at a great council fire on Schodac Island just south of the present city of Albany near the center of the Hudson River drainage basin, our ancestral home-land." It explained that "oftentimes our several Mohegan nations were given different names by different outside groups encountering them, such as the Dutch or the English or even neighboring native tribes. For example, the Smithsonian Institution's *Handbook of American Indians* (1907) gives 49 different phonetic renditions for us ranging from the Dutch-speakers' term 'Magicians' to the English-speakers' 'Mohegans' both meaning 'Wolf People,' and including the 'Pequots' meaning 'Destroyers,' who speak the identical and unique Y-dialect of the Algonkian linguistic family." And that "in consequence of the trauma of the European invasion, a diaspora of much of our Mohegan tribe occurred. Some members migrated or fled eastward down the Connecticut River system immediately to the east of the Hudson River drainage basin, into Connecticut and Massachusetts. From thence some others carried on eventually to Wisconsin. Some individuals blended with adjacent and distant native peoples and acquired citizenship in other native nations. Other Mohegans stayed behind in what is now New York State, but went underground into anonymity for reasons of survival."

The letter respectfully submitted that "the existing natural, international and constitutional law which this great country confirmed following its Revolution still forbids the taking of land in the absence of an Indian treaty, regardless of the statement to the contrary made by the federal *Appropriations Act of 1871* ... In sum, the native Americans' life, liberty and pursuit of happiness continues to shelter under the consensus of natural, international and constitutional law that precludes usurpation, confiscation and enslavement by newcomer Americans." The petition concluded: "But it is legally impossible for an act of Congress to repeal a previously vested natural, international and constitutional law right in the absence of an empowering constitutional amendment. And it is equally impossible for subsequent judicial decisions to overrule a constitutional principle previously settled by an original and authoritative precedent."

On this basis, the petitioning letter argued:

As a matter of bureaucratic assumption and convention, the adjective "*federal*" in the crucial phrase "*federal recognition*" is taken to signify that the recognition specifically be by the federal Bureau of Indian Affairs (BIA) or Congress. That signification imports the act of state doctrine: the legal principle which holds that no legal remedy attaches to any given right unless the government chooses in addition to acknowledge the status of the entity to assert that right. More simply put, the United States says: we respect the native sovereignty of those native nations that we recognize as native nations. It is just that we do not actually acknowledge any native groups as "nations." We have not done so since the *Appropriations Act of 1871* precluded the making of Indian treaties that by definition recognize native groups as "nations."

From 1871 to the present, *"federal recognition"* bureaucratically has in fact been extended only to those native groups that relinquish their national status and accept in its place municipality status. This pre-condition to *"federal recognition"* is presumed to be authorized by title 25 of the *Code of Federal Regulations*, which limits the concept "Tribe" to entities *"recognized by the Secretary as eligible for the special programs and services from the Bureau of Indian Affairs."*

But native sovereignty by definition signifies independence from *"the special programs and services from the Bureau of Indian Affairs."*

For in the beginning the only jurisdiction constitutionally claimed by the British Crown and by its successor the United States was the preemptive right to purchase Indian territory when the natives were willing to sell. Then, the native nations occupying yet unpurchased territory were said to be *"domestic dependent nations"*: "domestic" in the sense of not "foreign"; "dependent" in the sense of under the United States' military protection as against others; and "nations" in the sense of being free from interference in any respect other than the restriction on alienation imported by the United States' preemptive right of purchase.

By 1871 the United States had adopted as its final solution to the Indian problem the policy of forced assimilation by incremental stages. First, the natives' cultural attachment to national independence over unpurchased territory surreptitiously was to be replaced by the fostering of native municipal government upon surveyed reservations. The "wild" Indians roaming at large would be replaced by "civilized" Indians attached to individually allotted plots and to defined common areas. Ultimately, the inherently offensive nature of municipal governments defined by racial criteria – culture differentiation having disappeared by effluxion of time and educational compulsion – would justify termination of special status based upon race alone. Racially segregated reservations eventually were supposed to phase out and racially egalitarian municipalities were supposed to phase in.

This experiment in social engineering visibly has failed. The mortality rates of native Americans demonstrate the genocidal consequence of this process of reneging upon the natives' previously established status as *"domestic dependent nations"* under natural, international and constitutional law.

The promotion of their alternative status as *"dependent Indian communities"* under federal law is the probable cause of the abridged life spans and the mental anguish that life without liberty engenders. The engine that drives this genocidal machine masquerading as the fulfillment of the so-called federal trust responsibility, is the fraudulent pretence of federal plenary jurisdiction. The fraud consists in the legal *non sequitur* that Congress, by the bootstraps operation of ordinary legislation in the absence of an enabling constitutional aggrandizement of its inceptive power, can increase the extent of the newcomers' constitutional rights in relation to the natives' constitutional rights.

If Congress could do that, the natives would have mere privileges, not constitutional rights. If that were the case the United States Supreme Court in the constitutively definitive years was wrong in categorizing the native groups as *"domestic dependent nations"* subject only to the preemptive purchase jurisdiction of the United States as the Crown's successor. But the original and authoritative precedents can not be set aside in the absence of a legislative constitutional amendment directly on point.

Assumptions and policies are not the equivalent of or a substitution for a legislative constitutional amendment. At least not in a rule of law society.

As can be seen, the essence of the Mohegan First Amendment grievance petition to the president of the United States was that the Bureau of Indian Affairs (BIA) unconstitutionally served as the United States' agent for genocide. The *modus operandi* for the crime was in the application, by the BIA, of federal law that conflicts with constitutional law. The petition pleaded with the president to bypass the BIA, which was stonewalling rather than addressing and respecting the paramount constitutional law. Lamentably, the BIA took over the file and simply began applying the federal law. It responded on behalf of the president and, instead of treating the petition as one against the application of federal legislation, treated it as an application for federal recognition under the federal legislation, thus illustrating perfectly the Mohegans essential point: that the genocide is specifically by chicanery.

In the course of misconstruing the Mohegans' petition, the BIA pointed out that some of the documents cited by the sachem in support of the tribe's oral history do in fact contain the attributed information. But the BIA also revealed that a photocopy of one archival microfilm had been altered. When drafting the petitioning letter for the sachem's signature, I had accepted the photocopy in the Mohegans' own files at face value, without going to the archives to check their copy against the original. The BIA did that checking, and the copy was discovered to have been altered.

This discrepancy and possible fraud was, in my view, devastating to the credibility of the Mohegans' petition. The fact that a historical document in support of the Mohegan oral history was altered did not, of course, prove that there were no Mohegans. But it undermined the whole point of the Indian position: the promotion of justice as the application of truth to affairs.

For me, this revelation was frustrating. The petition would have been perfectly satisfactory without the impugned document. The essence of the native position was that their oral history proved their continuity in New York, albeit as an underground society for reasons of survival in the midst of genocidal pressure. In such circumstances, the absence of non-native written records of continuity is not a problem. Such absence in itself does not establish discontinuity. It merely evidences the fact of undergroundness, which in itself is neutral to the continuity issue. The strength, for legal purposes, of the Indian position does not consist in coming up with written records that confirm their continuity as a secret society but in insisting on the international and constitutional law that fixes the onus of proof of establishing a purchase on the newcomer society. The fundamental fact is that the Indians were there first. On this basis, the opening presumption of international and constitutional law is that the natives' jurisdiction is presumed until such time as the newcomers' prove that such original jurisdiction has been surrendered by treaty. Correspondingly, the newcomers' jurisdiction is deriva- tive: presumed not to exist until established by positive evidence of purchase. The federal law that purports to shift the onus from the newcomers, of proving purchase, to the natives, of proving geographical continuity, is simply the *modus operandi* for the newcomers' genocide by chicanery, contrary to existing interna- tional and constitutional law.

Even so, the presence of altered documents was, in my opinion, fatal to the Mohegans' position as presented in the petition to the president. How could we persist in criticizing the BIA and the United States for bending or evading the whole truth if we were doing the same? I asked for and received the Mohegans' permission and instructions to withdraw the petition.

It is by no means unusual for lawyers to discover half way through a case that a client has not been 100 per cent open in every respect about the facts or the ev- idence of the facts. In this particular instance I believe that the oral history as re- counted by the sachem and others in the tribe, and by the general histories of the region, is true. But still, the case was tainted. There was no way of knowing for a certainty how the alteration of the impugned document had occurred or with what intent. It could have been done by the sachem's ancestors, who made changes to conform with the numbers of the tribe as they knew them to be true. But it could also have been done by the sachem or another person for the purpose of fraudulently bolstering the written record corroborating the oral history.

If the latter were the situation, I would not have a great deal of difficulty un- derstanding how such a thing might occur. The fraud of the newcomer society has been, unconstitutionally, to shift the burden of proof from itself, of proving purchase, to the Indians, of proving geographical continuity. Precisely because of the newcomers' premature occupation of the Indians' country prior to pur- chase, the Indians were driven underground, if not killed or driven out. In these circumstances, there is virtually no direct evidence in the form of written records recording the Indians' continuity, as Indians. When the census enumerators in preceding times inquired about race or ethnicity, the Indians survived by con- cealing their Indianness.

The temptation for a sachem or other tribal member who is trying to identify the people and lead them out of anonymity to pad the written record so that it sup- ports the oral history of continuity is as strong as it is understandable. It is partic- ularly so in circumstances where, as here, the BIA will otherwise get away with perfecting the crime of genocide against humanity. If the sachem himself had done the alteration, it would have been a classically "Indian Trickster" function. The great hunters achieved success in the hunt in part by means of stealth, of de- ception. The means, of tricking the animal spirit to gift the animal body to the hunter, justified the ends – the survival of the hunter. To placate the animal spirit, ceremonies were held later to expiate and justify the means: they took the form of an affirmation of the spiritual identity of all beings, so that exchanging the life of one body to sustain the life of another was not only acceptable but natural.

When I withdrew the Mohegans' petition to the president, I had also to withdraw the litigation I had commenced to complement that petition. By that point the trial judge in the litigation had, in any event, evaded the fundamental jurisdiction issue. He held that the tribe had not drafted a complaint that "stated a case" within the jurisdiction of the federal court system of the United States. To do so, he said, the tribe would have to identify a breach by the United States of the constitutional, treaty, or federal law of the United States, and, in consequence, seek declaratory relief. The sachem's statement of claim did precisely that. The trial judge could not see it and held that no case had been stated. So the tribe appealed the trial judge's ruling to the United States Court of Appeals for the Second Circuit, in essence asking the higher court to read the material and, having done so, to resist compounding the wilful blindness to which the trial judge had succumbed.

The trial judge had added that, in his view, he had no jurisdiction to consider the case because, under federal law, exclusive original juridiction over Indians was given to the BIA instead of to the courts. Here, again, I would have thought that the complaint as drafted had clearly identified the international and constitutional law legislation and precedents that rendered null and void the said federal law depriving the courts of jurisdiction to address the question of those courts' own jurisdiction. After all, the whole point of the complaint had been that the assumption of federal jurisdiction prior to treaty is *prima facie* contrary to the 1832 precedent in the Supreme Court of the United States of *Worcester v. Georgia*, and, arguably, establishes the stonewalling of the international and constitutional law by the premature application of federal law as the *modus operandi* for genocide by chicanery in America. Therefore, the tribe appealed on this ground also.

Just a few weeks before the appeal was to have been heard, the BIA notified me of the discrepancy involving the altered documents. The appeal was based in part on the same evidence as the petition to the president. Like a house of cards, when the census document was discredited, the whole edifice of proceedings tumbled down as well. Thus, in addition to withdrawing the petition, I sought and was given instructions from the tribe to withdraw the appeal.

A third proceeding had been built on the same petition and also was withdrawn – the application of the tribe that its ancestral river, the Hudson, be accepted as a heritage river under the auspices of the American Heritage Rivers Initiative Executive Order of 11 September 1997. The tribe's application, dated 19 September 1997, was submitted to President Clinton:

In our Native Way, there is no such thing as coincidence. Our *1st Amendment Petition of 20 August 1997* pleaded personally with you, Mr President, to end the era of the genocide of our Native Nation. To us, the *American Heritage Rivers Executive Order of 11 September 1997* is part of the answer. In your Newcomer Way, our Hudson River native homeland was converted from paradise to wasteland. Your ecocide of our native land meant the genocide of our native people. But the *American Heritage Rivers Order of 11 September 1997* means the night of ecogenocide is over. The millennium of healing has dawned. In a sense, the Creator's tracing of the circumference of the Circle of Life has passed the farthest point, and begun the journey home.

In our Native Way, we *are* our valley. We are the autochthonous people: our culture, that which makes us *us*, springs directly from the Mother Earth that births us and that sustains us. The brooks and streams of our Hudson River drainage basin are capillaries. Schodac Island is the heart. But the mind, the mind is Liberty Island. For in our Native Way, the Great Law is Respect. For all things. And liberty means respect. There is no such thing as coincidence. The mind and heart of our native nation and the mind and heart of America are one. When the waters that flow past Schodac Island wash untainted at the shore upon which rests the Statue of Liberty, we all, natives and newcomers alike, will be free, and healthy, together. And when the mind and heart of America in this way have become free and pure, the body politic that is the world can have hope.

For America's is the last empire. And the artery of the last empire is in the empire State. From this juncture in history America will lead all people of the world, not just herself and her own people, out of the era of empires, into the new millennium of unity and equality based upon our Native Way: Respect. In our *1st Amendment Petition of 20 August 1997* we asked you, Mr President, to let us *"fulfill our rightful role as participants in the life of the Hudson River valley. We are the valley's original inhabitants."* We repeat that request, now, by asking that you accept the Hudson River drainage basin into the *American Heritage Rivers Initiative*, and recognize a role for us. In our Native Way, we have a gift for you – the Unity Paddle.

Our hope is that you will choose to give it a home on Liberty Island. On its handle a red arm and a black arm rise intertwining, to blend with a yellow arm and a white arm descending from the other end, all reaching into a sacred copper coil of spirit being. *Beloved's* Baby Suggs *"learned from her sixty years as a slave and ten years free: that there was no bad luck in the world but white people – They don't know when to stop."* The *American Heritage Rivers Executive Order of 11 September 1997* signifies that America has learned. Thank you for accepting our gift, for listening, and for understanding.

In sum, with the exposure of the existence of the altered documents, the work of the preceding two years was wiped out. The Mohegans and I started over with a blank slate. On this basis I was then instructed to draft a test case that would focus on one issue only: the natives' alleged right in international and constitutional law to independant and impartial third-party adjudication as recognized and affirmed in the 1704 precedent of *Mohegan Indians v. Connecticut*. The feeling of the natives was that, without third-party adjudication, they were defeated before starting.

In order to focus the third-party adjudication issue, I was instructed to restrict it to a small and clearly defined geographical compass: specifically, to Liberty Island. Accordingly, I issued in the federal district court for the southern district of New York a fresh complaint alleging that "a federal question arises in relation to Liberty Island in virtue of a conflict of laws, between the constitutional law *prima facie* protecting Indian liberty upon arguably unceded territory and the premature and therefore derogating application thereupon of federal and state law, as to the resolution of which conflict of laws court jurisdiction vests to make a declaration." The complaint submitted that, "by operation of constitutional law, plaintiff has standing to sue as a class of 'Indians or any of them,' entitled, as such, to third-party adjudication, relative to Indian liberty in relation to Liberty Island, since, from all that appears, the island has not been purchased from the Indians and therefore is reserved for the Indians. On it, the Statue of Liberty, which belongs to the United States, faces Europe and promises liberty, while her back is turned upon native American liberty. She trespasses, and stands as a constant reminder of genocide in America, thereby causing the plaintiff class the civil injury 'serious bodily or mental harm.' Liberty will be when America is true: to justice, and to the judicial function." On this factual basis, the fresh complaint asked the federal district court for "a declaration of the remedy of third-party adjudication in relation to Liberty Island and the right thereupon of Indian liberty, which, for constitutional law purposes, is to say the native sovereignty interest of exclusive jurisdiction and possession pending cession thereof to the United States."

By this time the Mohegans of the Hudson River drainage basin had naturalized me as a citizen of their tribe. This was done, in part, so I could represent the tribe in various legal proceedings – and counter the chicanery whereby the judges refuse to address the law unless it is presented by a member of the local bar association. At the same time, the membership criteria in the local bar associations introduce such severe conflict of interest guidelines as to preclude any member being ready, willing, and able to represent the Indians on the issue involved. Making me a tribal member meant that I should be able to address the courts as an Indian of the tribe suing *pro se* (without legal representation). Not that I necessarily needed to speak to the courts: the facts and the law relevant to the jurisdiction issue are perfectly suited to being dealt with entirely in writing, and the written material in *pro se* actions can be signed by any member to which the tribe agrees according to its own rules. Making me a spokesperson for the litigation purposes simply allowed the tribe to put me forward as one of the named *pro se* plaintiffs, available to answer the court's questions, if any, arising out of the written material.

Prior to the *Liberty Island* case, the Mohegans and I had attempted to intervene in the *Ellis Island* case between New Jersey and New York, then pending before the Supreme Court of the United States. In that case the two states were disputing which of them has the better right of jurisdiction to which portions of the island. A contract had been made between the state litigants in 1834 dealing with the jurisdiction issue, but since then the island had grown by the addition of land fill, leading to a dispute over the intent and effect of the 1834 contract.

The Mohegans application to intervene sought to apprise the Supreme Court of the United States of the law which established that either or both of the states, or the United States federal government, must prove, before an independant and impartial third-party adjudicator, that the island has been validly purchased from the Indians. Until proof of purchase is made, by operation of the paramount international and constitutional law, neither state can have jurisdiction. The island remains Indian territory and is legally subject to the natives' liberty and possession, with which the newcomer governments and ordinary courts are precluded from interfering.

The Supreme Court of the United States, without giving reasons, refused to allow the Mohegans to intervene in the *Ellis Island* case, and on this basis decided the jurisdiction issue between the states as if there were no competing Indian jurisdictional interest precluding both states' jurisdiction. The failure to give reasons was not exceptional. The Supreme Court never gives reasons for denying leave to intervene, just as it does not provide reasons for denying leave to appeal. Thus, there is no way of knowing why the court declined to let the natives have a say in the *Ellis Island* case.

After this refusal, the Mohegans went to Liberty Island, both to protest the Supreme Court's decision denying them a fast track on the jurisdiction/genocide issue and to assert a presence. The island on which the Statue of Liberty sits is in the same legal position as Ellis Island so far as aboriginal rights are concerned, both islands being unceded Indian territory. The protest was to have been covered by German national television. But the evening before the protest, German TV was contacted by someone in the U.S. Justice Department who apparently recommended that the event not be covered. German TV did not show up, nor did any of the American media. The Mohegans were not allowed to protest in public sight near the Statue of Liberty, but were ushered politely onto a small pebble beach among some government staff houses at the other end of the island.

The United States' attorney general applied to have the *Liberty Island* action struck down, on the basis that federal law had not been complied with. The Mohegans answered that they agreed that federal law had not been complied with, but that federal law is irrelevant, in light of the anterior and superior international and constitutional law. And so, as always, the same issue presented itself. Like Canada, the United States sought to suppress the international and constitutional law on the basis of applying conflicting federal and state law, as if the international and constitutional law did not exist. The United States used the same technique – chicanery – to avoid the issue.

Occasionally, there is understanding. On 30 November 1997, under the heading "Painful Observance," the *Rutland Herald* of Vermont editorialized:

Legend has it that the Pilgrims' first Thanksgiving in Plymouth, Mass., in 1621 was a great harvest and feast, enabled by local Indians who taught the settlers how to coax sustenance from the fields and forests of their new home.

On Thanksgiving Day 376 years later, members of the United American Indians of New England were arrested by Plymouth police. They had been attending an annual event on Cole's Hill, overlooking Plymouth Rock, and decided to march downtown. They lacked a permit, and when police stopped them, a confrontation occurred. Twenty-five people were hauled to jail. Some witnesses said the police sprayed Mace into the crowd.

Whether the charges of police brutality are accurate or not, the name of the protesters' annual Thanksgiving observation is poignant, and painful. They call it a National Day of Mourning.

If history told a different tale, that title might seem overly dramatic. But the story of what the European settlers did to the people on this continent when they arrived is distressing in the extreme. It is a sad reflection on the human character that history provides many parallels, and no exaggeration to say that one of them is the Nazi Holocaust that erased six million European Jews just over 50 years ago.

The Holocaust occurred in a compressed period of time. The virtual annihilation of countless tribes and nations of Native Americans, by contrast, took some 300 years. But it was scarcely less purposeful, and arguably more successful. For there has been no widespread effort to restore what was taken from the Indians. Nor has there been much attempt to atone for the horror's perpetrated upon them.

Simply put, the European newcomers declared war on those who were already here. Acquisitive pioneers desired their lands and the treasures and resources thereon, and they took them. Such thievery was made U.S. policy by the Indian Removal Act of 1830. It authorized the resettlement of 70,000 Southeastern Cherokees, Seminoles and others to Oklahoma in a forced migration – with death from starvation and freezing temperatures a constant companion. It was known as the Trail of Tears.

Where riches were not suspected – in Arizona, for example – the Indians were largely left alone. But when gold was found there in the 1860s, the tribes of that region were massacred and driven from their homes to a reservation in the eastern part of the territory.

It would be naive to claim that all the wrongs in a centuries-long warfare between settlers and natives were committed by one side. But the difference between usurper and usurped was stark, and so was the difference between their fates.

The descendants of one side celebrate Thanksgiving; the other, a Day of Mourning. It remains a wide gulf for us to bridge.

Apparently, some editors or journalists in the United States are farther ahead than in Canada in their understanding of the fact of genocide against native people, and sensitive to the problem of psychological denial by those in legal and political authority. As this article evidences, the American people in general not only know but seem ready to acknowledge that the Indian Removal Act and the "Trail of Tears" was one of the history's most well-documented studies in the systematic methodology of intentional genocide. It is conceivable that the judges, or at least one member of the bench, will be willing to address the law that is essential to healing the wound left as legacy to that experience both to the native people and to the rule of law.

When I was in California in relation to the involvement of some California Indians as interested parties in the *Liberty Island* complaint, the final piece of the puzzle fell into place for me as to why Congress in 1871 enacted the clause in the Appropriations Act reneging on the international and constitutional law recognized by the Supreme Court in *Worcester v. Georgia* in 1832. Between 1773 and 1823, Spain claimed what is now southern California, to a point just north of San Francisco Bay, by virtue of what Chief Justice Marshall described in *Worcester* as the doctrine of discovery. Spain was bound by the same international and constitutional law as bound all European nations and, as their successor, the United States. Sir Francis Drake claimed California for England, but the overlap between the claims of Spain and England was of no consequence to the Indians, since all European claims were "blank pieces of paper" so far as the rights of the natives are concerned. All discovery conferred was the jurisdiction to purchase, if and when the natives were ready to sell, and, pending sale, the natives were not "to be molested or disturbed."

The international and constitutional law jurisdiction to purchase the California (and Nevada, Arizona, New Mexico, and Utah) territory was ceded by Spain to Mexico in 1823, and, in 1848, by Mexico to the United States by the Treaty of Guadalupe Hidalgo – in the same way that jurisdiction relative to British North America south of Canada had been ceded by Britain to the United States by the Peace of Paris in 1783. In 1850 California became a state. The next year the United States negotiated eighteen treaties purchasing California from the California natives, pursuant to the United States' international and constitutional law jurisdiction. These treaties reserved 8.5 million acres for the natives. Gold fever intervened and hotter heads prevailed. California lobbied the US Senate, which refused to ratify these treaties. It would seem that California was concerned that some of the gold might turn out to be on the reservations. California's antidote for that possibility was to deny the Indians any jurisdictional and land rights whatsoever – to turn the clock back to *Inter Cetera, 1493*, before its repeal by *Sublimus Deus, 1537*, which is to say to deny the humanity of the natives in favour of treating them as animals, without souls, and, correspondingly, without the attributes of the human condition: original jurisdiction and possession. That might have been legal if the international and constitutional law had not previously been ascertained to the very opposite effect. In sum, under pressure from California, the United States reneged on the previously established international and constitutional law without taking the appropriate due process steps to repeal it. The United States simply placed itself outside the rule of law, and sat by while California passed overtly genocidal domestic legislation, such as that making Indians without property indentured servants, or, for all practical purposes, slaves.

In 1853 the United States created mission reservations at Hoopa Valley, Round Valley, and Tule River. And in 1880 she began the process of creating rancherias, by purchasing land and setting it apart as reservation trust land. In 1952 US Public Law 280 supposedly made all state laws of general application *prima facie* applicable to Indians (the same as section 88 of the 1952 Indian Act did in Canada). All this domestic legislation activity was premised on the unconstitutional assumption that there was no Indian jurisdiction and possession which had to be purchased before federal and state (or in the instance of Canada, provincial) jurisdiction and possession could be acquired. All this domestic legislative activity simply turned a blind eye on the centuries of international and constitutional legal tradition preceding and following *Worcester v. Georgia*.

In sum, the California solution to the "Indian problem" was to perfect the crime of genocide by chicanery, in virtue of the big lie: the willful blindness of the newcomers' legal and political establishment to the international and constitutional law. There was no place to which the natives could turn. They were being dispossessed, dehumanized, murdered, and enslaved because of the criminal conspiracy of the lawyers, judges, police, and politicians of the federal and state levels of newcomer society acting in concert. The left hand was washing the right in the blood of innocents, with the army at the ready to massacre and round up any natives who might, preferring death to the unconstitutional denial of their liberty, presume to meet California's and the United States' illegal force with the Indians' common law remedy of self-help in defence of their blindsided international and constitutional law jurisdiction and possession. The army's involvement was styled a "just war" against Indian terrorism.

The role of California is pivotal in North America. United States' policy was dictated by it, and Canada followed suit. The gold rush led to the United States' unconstitutional Appropriations Act of 1871 (and in Canada to the equally unconstitutional *Indian Act of 1880*), as if by those acts of ordinary domestic legislation the United States (and Canada) could repeal the previously established international and constitutional law, simply by ignoring it. By their bootstraps, the United States and Canada pulled their constitutional jurisdiction to purchase, up to plenary jurisdiction. In the way they made a casualty of the rule of law and precipitated the genocide of the natives.

After commencing the *Liberty Island* case, I was drawn back to Canada to begin two complementary cases based on the same law. One of these cases hailed from Saskatchewan, the other from Ontario. Whether the rule of law would be upheld in either the United States or Canada, in the aboriginal rights and genocide context, would depend on what happened.

CHAPTER 17

Law Society of Upper Canada v. Bruce Clark

My two citizen's arrest endeavours, one with the Ontario police officer and the other with the British Columbia Court of Appeal panel hearing the *Delgamuukw* case, eventually became the basis of a decision by the Law Society of Upper Canada that I be reprimanded for a disciplinary offence. Before deciding on a reprimand for these so-called offences, the Law Society threw out some twenty-five other complaints by judges that I had insulted them by alleging their assumption of jurisdiction to be treasonable, fraudulent, and complicitous in genocide.

On 19 June 1996 the Law Society in the case of *Law Society of Upper Canada v. Bruce Clark* decided as follows:

Mr. Clark has devoted his career to the advancement of the cause of native rights in Canada. He has studied the subject at the graduate school level, and has obtained a Master of Arts degree in History and a Ph.D. in Jurisprudence as a result of his studies in the field of native rights.

For a period of seven years, Mr. Clark lived on a native reserve. He is the author of two academic texts on the subject of the rights of the indigenous people in Canada.

All of the particulars in the complaint relate to Mr. Clark's relentless attempts to advance a single legal argument on his natives clients' behalf.

Although space does not permit a complete summary of Mr. Clark's argument, it is based upon the proposition that certain native lands (or "hunting grounds") have never been properly surrendered to the Crown. It follows, he contends, that the Canadian courts have no jurisdiction over indigenous people who reside on the unsurrendered lands. Mr. Clark argues that statutes of Canada and the provinces do not apply to indigenous people who live on the unsurrendered lands, and that the affected indigenous people have a right of access to an independent and impartial third party court – to adjudicate the law ...

Mr. Clark goes on to contend that the extraterritorial assumption by the non-native Canadian domestic courts, of jurisdiction over indigenous people living on hunting grounds prima facie constitutes "misprision of treason" and "misprision of fraud" within the meaning of paragraph 6, Part IV of the Royal Proclamation of 1763, which has never been repealed. He adds that the use of the legal term of art "misprision" in the order-in-council relieves his clients of the need to prove intent.

Finally, Mr. Clark argues, by usurping jurisdiction over indigenous people living on unsurrendered hunting grounds, the Canadian government, the legal establishment and the domestic courts are contributing to and are complicit in the genocide of indigenous people. (The term genocide is defined in the Concise Oxford Dictionary as the "extermination of a race".)

As the hearing panel pointed out, and as mentioned above, it is this argument that is at the root of the complaint of professional misconduct that the panel and Convocation were called upon to deal with ...

The discipline hearing panel accepted that Mr. Clark is remarkably knowledgeable in the area of native rights, and that the views that he espouses are honestly and sincerely held. It is accepted also that he believes that his comments and conduct as particularized in the complaint were intended to advance the cause of justice and the rule of law.

The panel also observed in its report that "all of the members of the panel were impressed with the solicitor's presentation, his thoughtful remarks to us, his commitment to his cause, and the obvious sincerity of his beliefs". It acknowledged that Mr. Clark has made very significant family and financial sacrifices in pursuit of his quest for justice for his clients. The panel also recorded its belief that Mr. Clark has much to offer the legal profession ...

In recommending that Mr. Clark's right to practise law be terminated, the discipline hearing panel explained that it made its recommendation "very reluctantly", and "primarily because of the finding that the solicitor is ungovernable". It added that while some or most of the allegations would not in themselves justify the ultimate penalty of disbarment, the cumulative effect of them, coupled with the finding of ungovernability, left the panel with little choice ...

As mentioned above, the discipline hearing panel acknowledged that Mr. Clark's argument (as summarized above) is at the root of the complaint of professional misconduct that the discipline hearing panel and Convocation have been called upon to adjudicate.

Mr. Clark's argument is anything but frivolous. It is the product of intensive study, and reflects a belief that Mr. Clark sincerely holds.

It would be difficult to disagree with Mr. Clark's assertion that the issue that his argument raises is "constitutionally critical". Again, the discipline hearing panel found that Mr. Clark honestly believes that the comments and conduct particularized in the complaint – which are an outgrowth of his argument – were intended to advance the cause of justice and the rule of law.

The "genocide" of which Mr. Clark speaks is real, and has very nearly succeeded in destroying the Native Canadian community that flourished here when European settlers arrived. No one who has seen many of our modern First Nation communities can remain untouched by this reality.

Mr. Clark is not making the kind of arguments that fall to most of us daily in our courts; much of the ordinary work of lawyers relates to the interpretation of a will, the proper understanding of a contract, the ownership of a piece of land, or individual culpability for crime. The issue Mr. Clark raises is one of great significance for the entire people – and for all of us. His commitment to the argument and his conviction respecting its correctness cannot be questioned ...

The nature of Mr. Clark's argument is such that the persistent refusal of the courts – he states, without contradiction, that he has attempted to raise this argument some forty-one times – itself in part engenders his fixed and firm conclusion that his argument is correct. The issue has not been determined by any Court ...

It is important to our decision that the use of what would in most other circumstances rightly be regarded as extravagant, disrespectful and discourteous language, in Mr. Clark's case emanated directly from the legal argument that he was vigorously advancing on behalf of his clients. In attempting to resolve the tension between vigorous advocacy in the face of judicial resistance and the duty to treat the tribunal with courtesy and respect, much will depend on the context.

We are sympathetic, moreover, to Mr. Clark's assertion that the courts have been unwilling to listen to his argument. Though he must accept part of the responsibility for this, it is apparent on the record that he has been prevented by the courts on a number of the occasions in issue from effectively presenting the argument summarized above. Our finding may well have been different if Mr. Clark, having been given a full opportunity to develop his argument, had persisted in attempting to argue a point after the court had ruled against him. Again, the Law Society must promote, rather than inhibit, the right and duty of advocates to protect their clients' interests without unwarranted interference.

The lawyer's duty to resolutely advance every argument the lawyer thinks will help the client's case is of fundamental importance to the proper functioning of our judicial system. Failures to carry that duty are more prevalent within the system of justice and more harmful to that system than are overzealousness and failures to treat the courts with courtesy and respect. Where the duties do come into conflict, Convocation should be reluctant to find that overzealousness constitutes professional misconduct ...

We also note that the advocacy in question here took place in the context of a serious argument on an issue of public importance. The Law Society's concurrent jurisdiction to discipline lawyers for excesses in advocacy should be reserved for particularly serious and harmful violations.

It is necessary, in the light of the values expressed above, to examine the charges brought against Mr. Clark that deal with the question of improper advocacy.

We do not find his letters abusive or offensive. Nor do we find his statements intemperate or unsupported by the facts to sustain the argument. Indeed, throughout he has begged to be allowed to develop facts to sustain the argument. It is impossible to say there was no reasonable basis in evidence for the legal positions he asserted; he has always been prepared to make a thorough and comprehensive argument in each case. There is an entire absence of evidence that the documentation he delivered from a Native tribunal came from a "bogus court"; native tribunals are commonplace throughout Canada and there was simply no evidence about the composition or authority of this one. Though that documentation was intended to influence proceedings in relation to outstanding criminal charges, it was part of a legitimate argument relating to the jurisdiction of the Court before which Mr. Clark was appearing. Indeed, each of the statements alleged to be intemperate and unjustified flow logically and properly from the submissions he was making respecting jurisdiction ...

Convocation considers the panel's finding of ungovernability to be unsustainable in this case.

Mr. Clark cannot be considered to be ungovernable in the sense in which that term is usually used in discipline proceedings. Though not determinative, it is important that there was no evidence before either the panel or Convocation that he has been disciplined previously since his call to the bar in 1971, almost 25 years ago. The panel recognized that Mr. Clark has been of previous good character.

In the proceedings before the discipline hearing panel and in Convocation, Mr. Clark readily admitted the facts and documents on which the complaint was based. The panel made a point of mentioning in its report that all of the members of the panel were impressed by Mr. Clark's presentation, his thoughtful remarks to the panel, his commitment to his cause, and the obvious sincerity of his beliefs. Convocation was similarly impressed.

The panel based its finding of ungovernability on the fact that Mr. Clark would not undertake to refrain from repeating the conduct that brought him before the Law Society. The panel attached to its report a letter from the Law Society's counsel dated April 21, 1994 and Mr. Clark's reply to that letter dated April 25, 1994. In his reply, Mr. Clark stated that though he had no intention of revisiting his clients' "allegation of law" at the trial level in Canada, he was not prepared to undertake not to repeat the argument that he has been advancing in proceedings that were then pending in the Supreme Court of Canada. Nor was he willing to undertake not to repeat his argument in support of a petition that had been submitted to the Queen, or before "any other appellate or international tribunal that may have or may come to have jurisdiction over genocide".

Particularly in light of our finding that Mr. Clark is not guilty of professional misconduct in respect of many of the particulars referred to in the complaint, we do not think that Mr. Clark's refusal should make him vulnerable to a finding that he is not governable by the Law Society. Indeed, in our view, the Law Society has come quite close to asking Mr. Clark to refrain from making an argument that he believes to be both well founded in law and in the interest of his clients.

The solicitor is not ungovernable. He simply does not agree with the characterization of his conduct by counsel for the Law Society, nor that of the courts that have refused to rule on it, and he will not give up his argument at least until some court has ruled on it.

The paradox is that although the Law Society vindicated what I had said and turned back the judges' attempt to have me disbarred for raising the law they preferred not to have to address, it gave my detractors one small bone on which to gnaw. It decided that I should be reprimanded for seeking to inaugurate the two citizen's arrests of the Ontario police officer and the British Columbia panel of judges. Yet, ironically, the Law Society agreed with me that the genocide was a fact and that the judges should address the law. Apparently, in Ontario, it is all right to speak against genocide, but not physically to act to apprehend it.

When on 23 April 1998 the reprimand was eventually administered in Convocation of the Law Society, I applied by telephone from New York to be permitted to receive it by conference call rather than be present in Toronto in person before the assembled benchers (the lawyers who are elected by the profession to oversee the profession's interests as a self-governing body). The treasurer of the Law Society, the chief executive officer, was to administer the reprimand. He absented himself from the hearing of my motion to be present by phone rather than personally on the ground that that he was on the original panel that had recommended my prosecution and disbarment. I do not know why he felt this fact should disqualify him from being present on the motion. In any event, he did step out of the room for the hearing of motion. I then explained to the benchers who remained in the room that the reason I could not be present before them was because I was not safe from arbitrary arrest, conviction, and imprisonment in Canada because of fallout from the Gustafsen Lake contempt of court charges, and that it was more important to the integrity of the rule of law that I complete my present duties on behalf of the Mohegans of New York (see chapter 16) than be a political prisoner in Canada.

The Law Society staff lawyer was asked to respond to my submission. She said she did not feel the Law Society should be aiding and abetting a fugitive from justice. I was invited to reply, and pointed out that the staff lawyer's response illustrated the Society's continuing wilful blindness to the law and the corresponding persecution of me as the law's messenger. I had complained of arbitrary arrest by Canadian authorities who were perpetrating a crime, and she had treated this concern as an admission of wrongdoing on my part, not theirs. The Law Society decided, nevertheless, to accept my proposal for a reprimand by conference call and invited the treasurer back into the room to administer it then and there. The reprimand was to effect that I was an utter disgrace to the bar and that, if ever he were to learn that I had transgressed again, the penalty would be much more severe.

When the report of my conviction for contempt of court in British Columbia was published in the Canadian media in February 1997, the Law Society disciplinary staff, which had been disappointed by Convocation's decision of 19 June 1996 in its endeavour to have me convicted and disbarred for raising the law in court, immediately opened a fresh disciplinary file against me on the basis of the contempt conviction. I was so advised at the time, and in response I pointed out that I welcomed the process, as it would give me the opportunity to attempt once again to force the Law Society to address the law that judges convicting me had ignored. I advised that my defence to this new disciplinary charge would be that I had been convicted without arraignment, plea, trial, or opportunity to present a defence, and that, if the Law Society wanted to add double jeopardy to this heady stew of injustice, to proceed with dispatch. The reason I wished the matter expedited was that, when I applied to the Law Societies of the other Canadian provinces for occasional appearance certificates permitting me to appear as legal counsel elsewhere than in Ontario, those other Law Societies were informed that I was either under investigation or under charge. On this basis, the other Law Societies usually refused my request, and the judges of those other provinces refused to allow me to speak in court, thereby continuing to evade the law that otherwise I would place before them. The staff lawyers of the Law Societies thus achieved, for practical purposes, the disbarment that the Ontario Law Society's official decision of 19 June 1996 precluded for legal purposes.

The Law Society's original letter of 21 April 1994 had offered not to disbar me if I would agree never again to raise the law to which the complaining judges had taken umbrage and to apologize to them for having raised it. In a letter dated 25 April 1994 I declined to comply with this extortion and challenged the Society to get on with trying to disbar me. I wrote three further letters to the Society, but there was no response.

April 13, 1998

This will confirm that I will be on telephone conference stand-by again on April 23, 1998 relative to the reprimand.

With respect to the possibility of the new complaint mentioned in your letter of January 13, 1998 please either proceed with dispatch or confirm that the investigation file has been closed. As I have attempted on several previous occasions to explain in correspondence with Ontario's law society, the delay in proceeding constitutes complicity in genocide albeit with apparent immunity to the perpetrators such as yourself. The fact of each outstanding investigation file is used by law societies elsewhere to withhold occasional appearance certificates. The consequence, since my practice is restricted to the genocide issue, is that I am de facto although not de jure disbarred by the perpetrators, and the genocide that is aided and abetted by the legal establishment's procedural stonewalling of the law continues.

April 23, 1998

I have your letter dated April 17, 1998. You misrepresent the facts by stating that "this investigation has not been disclosed to other Law Societies and will not be a matter of public record until the Complaint is issued." Please stand corrected by reading our society's certificates of standing that have been issued to me since the investigation began and my letters complaining of the appearance upon such certificates of the fact of the investigation in progress.

Please also review all of the correspondence in relation to all of the past complaints and investigations against me. You will see that I have been seeking all along to lay a complaint against our law society and the members of its disciplinary staff for their complicity in genocide. All along my endeavours in this respect have been stonewalled.

Yet, as Convocation held on June 19, 1996 in complaint D36/94 being Law Society of Upper Canada v. Bruce Clark:

> The 'genocide' of which Mr Clark speaks is real, and has very nearly succeeded in destroying the Native Canadian community that flourished here when European settlers arrived ... We are sympathetic, moreover, to Mr Clark's assertion that the courts have been unwilling to listen to his argument.

The *New York Times* "International Section" of January 13, 1996 had an article entitled 'Berlin Journal: Exoneration Still Eludes An Anti-Nazi Crusader.' It concerned Carl von Ossietzky who won the 1935 Nobel Peace Prize. He was convicted and imprisoned for opposing as unconstitutional some of the practices introduced into Germany's domestic legal system by the Third Reich, spent time in jail, and died of mistreatment in 1938. The article noted:

> The German judicial system has never faced the facts of its role in the Nazi period ... The judiciary considers itself a nonpolitical branch of Government and has never looked self-critically at what it did in the service of an unjust regime ...

The article "Defending the Indefensible" in the *New York Times Magazine* for April 19, 1998 contains the following passage relative to a current trial in progress in The Hague of crimes related to genocide in Bosnia:

> International-law experts say it isn't clear whether such intent is necessary to convict, because Kovacevic is accused not of genocide itself but of complicity in genocide. It might be enough to show that he deliberately contributed to the crime even though he may not have had genocidal intent, said Diane Orentlicher, a professor at American University's Washington College of Law and director of its War Crimes Research Office. 'Suppose someone built a gas ovens knowing how they'd be used in the Holocaust, but didn't carry out the gassings himself,' Orentlicher hypothesized. "He might not have shared Hitler's genocidal intent, but might well be liable to punishment as an accomplice to genocide."

The courts still "have been unwilling to listen to my argument," although I am continuing in my endeavours to have the law addressed, just as you are continuing in the endeavours to have the law's message pre-empted by prosecuting me for spurious complaints.

I repeat, I wish to register a complaint against the Secretary as our society's representative as a class, and against you personally, for complicity in genocide in consequence of the past and continuing efforts to stonewall the law precluding genocide.

April 23, 1998

Subsequent to my earlier letter today seeking to lay a complaint, my motion for administration of the reprimand by telephone was heard. During the course of the hearing of the motion I learned from comments by the Acting Treasurer Mr McKenzie that the present Treasurer of the Law Society, Mr Strosberg, personally was on the discipline committee that recommended the prosecution of me for a raft of alleged offences, all but two of which were eventually thrown out by Convocation. As to those which were thrown out, I have to repeat, convocation upheld the propriety of my conduct on the grounds inter alia that:

> The "genocide" of which Mr Clark speaks is real, and has very nearly succeeded in destroying the Native Canadian community that flourished here when European settlers arrived ... We are sympathetic, moreover, to Mr Clark's assertion that the courts have been unwilling to listen to his argument.

But for the fact that the courts and the law society jointly are committing complicity in the said genocide by stonewalling the addressing of the law precluding it, I would proceed in the courts against Mr Strosberg for malicious prosecution in aid of complicity in genocide. In lieu, I have to insist that my complaint against the law society for its complicity be processed as against Mr Strosberg both personally and as representative of the profession. For this reason, I have now to withdraw as being redundant the complaint as against you or the Secretary, in favour of proceeding against Mr Strosberg.

Although I received no response whatsoever to my complaint that the treasurer of the Law Society, as representative of all its members, was implicated in the ongoing genocide of the native people, the Disciplinary Committee of the Law Society eventually made another decision and recommendation concerning me. In December 1998 the committee held and recommended as follows:

REPORT

Complaint DI 10/98 was issued on July 16, 1998 against Bruce Allan Clark alleging that he was guilty of conduct unbecoming a barrister and solicitor.

The matter was heard in public on November 3, 1998 before this Committee composed of Bradley H. Wright, Chair, Elvio L. DelZotto, Q.C. and Nora Angeles. The Solicitor did not attend the hearing nor was he represented. Elizabeth Cowie appeared on behalf of the Law Society.

DECISION

The following particulars of conduct unbecoming a barrister and solicitor were found to have been established:

Complaint DI 10/98

2. a) On or about February 20, 1997, he was found guilty of contempt of court by the Honourable Judge N. Friesen of the Provincial Court of British Columbia, Criminal Division;

   b) on or about February 21, 1997, he was convicted by the Honourable Judge T.C. Smith in the Provincial Court of British Columbia, Criminal Division, that he on or about the 15th day of September, 1995, at or near the District of 100 Mile House, in the Province of British Columbia, did resist a peace officer, engaged in the execution of his duty, contrary to Section 129(a) of the Criminal Code.

RECOMMENDATION AS TO PENALTY

The Committee finds Bruce Allan Clark guilty of conduct unbecoming a barrister and solicitor and recommends that he be disbarred and struck off the Rolls.

REASONS FOR RECOMMENDATION

1. The Member was called to the Bar on March 26, 1971. He is presently residing in Granville, New York and refuses to return to Canada. Service was properly effected. We were advised by duty counsel that the Member had declined the assistance of duty counsel other than to inform us that the Member would not appear before us and was content to rely solely on the motion material he had previously filed. There is no agreed statement of facts.

2. It is not contested by the Member that he was convicted of contempt of court and of resisting a police officer as set out in Particulars 2(a) and 2(b) respectively of Complaint DI 10/98. The Member appealed his conviction for contempt of court to the British Columbia Court of Appeal which unanimously dismissed the appeal on March 14, 1997 (The Court of Appeal's Oral Reasons for Judgment were filed before us as Exhibit 3, Tab I 1).

3. The Committee accepts that, absent compelling circumstances of mitigation (not present here), contempt of court and resisting a police officer are sufficiently serious as to constitute conduct unbecoming a barrister and solicitor. To understand the Committee's recommendation of disbarment, it is necessary to understand the background to this matter.

4. The Oxford English Dictionary ("OED") contains the following definitions:

"Genocide"   Annihilation of a race.

"Misprision"   A wrong action or omission, specifically, a misdemeanour or neglect of duty on the part of a public official.

"Misprision of Treason"   An offence or misdemeanour akin to treason or felony, but not liable to the capital penalty. Later misunderstood as meaning only concealment of a person's knowledge of treasonable actions or designs.

"Treason"   2. Law. (a) High t. Violation of a subject of his allegiance to his sovereign or to the state.

Osborn's Concise Law Dictionary, Sixth Edition, contains the following definitions:

"Actus non tacit reum, nisi mens sit rea"   The act itself does not constitute guilt unless done with a guilty intent. [Often shortened to "actus reus" or "guilty act".]

"Mens rea"   An evil intention, or a knowledge of the wrongfulness of an act.

"Misprision of Treason"   Where a person who knows that some other person has committed high treason does not within a reasonable time give information thereof to a judge of assize or justice of the peace.

5. The Member has for many years accused a great number of people, including judges, benchers, and police officers, of the crimes, *inter alia*, of genocide, misprision of treason, and treason. His argument is based on an assertion that an edict issued by Queen Anne of Great Britain in 1708 in respect of a dispute between an aboriginal population in Connecticut and the Connecticut colonial government applies to modern Canadian constitutional law. Every one of the many duly constituted Canadian courts and tribunals, including the Supreme Court of Canada, to which he has presented his argument, has rejected it. The Member claims that the courts have failed to hear him. This is not so. They have heard him, but they have rejected his argument. He does not accept the rulings.

6. The Member did not attempt, in an effort to justify his conduct, to adduce before us any evidence, credible or otherwise, of the crimes that he asserts have been committed. It is patent that the judiciary, benchers, and police of this country have not engaged in genocide or treason, and cannot, therefore, have engaged in misprision or misprision of treason. There is neither the *actus reus* nor the *mens rea* on their part to annihilate a race or betray our country. We add ourselves to the list of courts and tribunals who reject the Member's argument.

7. As a result of the Member's behaviour arising in 1992, Complaint D36/94 was issued against him. The Member appeared before a Committee of Convocation in December 1994 and April 1995. The Report and Decision of that Committee was issued on July 10, 1995 recommending his disbarment. On July 6, 1995, the Supreme Court of Canada refused the Member leave to appeal the case of *R v. Williams* (1994) 52 B.C.A.C. 296 in which the Member had challenged the jurisdiction of Canadian courts. On November 23, 1995, Convocation ordered that the Member be reprimanded rather than disbarred. The Reasons of Convocation were issued on June 19, 1996. The reprimand was finally administered in February 1998 by teleconference because of the Member's refusal to attend in person.

8. The Member perpetrated the acts that were to result in the convictions against him for contempt of court and assaulting a police officer before Judge Friesen of the Provincial Court of British Columbia, sitting in 100 Mile House, on September 15, 1995, i.e., two months after (1) a Committee of Convocation had recommended the Member's disbarment and (2) leave to appeal *Williams* (supra) had been refused.

9. On September 15, 1995, the Member tried to portray himself before Judge Friesen as counsel for several accused in a bail hearing in a highly-charged matter known as the "Gustafsen Lake Standoff". Judge Friesen refused to recognize him because he was not listed on the court docket. The Member then used a vulgar expression, termed Judge Friesen's court "a kangaroo court", spoke loudly and aggressively, flung papers which struck the court reporter on the arm and face, and assaulted a police officer by making contact

with his leg or groin. Judge Friesen cited the Member for contempt and later scheduled a hearing of the matter. The Member undertook to appear before Judge Friesen on the contempt matter and on that basis was permitted to leave. The Member breached his undertaking by failing to appear; instead, he sent a letter in which he challenged the jurisdiction of the court. The court was forced to issue a bench warrant. The Member was not detained until well over a year later.

10. Upon learning of the convictions in British Columbia for contempt of court and resisting a police officer, the Society issued Complaint DI 10/98 against the Member. He then brought a motion (1) claiming an abuse of process and (2) seeking to attend the hearing by conference call. On September 29, 1998, a Committee of Convocation comprised of Daniel Murphy, Chair, Susan Elliott, and Michael Adams heard his motions. A transcript of the hearing was entered before us as Exhibit 1, Tab 1.

11. The motions Committee considered whether the events leading to Complaint DI 10/98 may have been dealt with in Complaint D3 6/94. Referring to the facts underlying DI 10/98, Ms. Elliott stated the following at Exhibit 1, Tab 1, Page 33, line 6, et seq.:

Well, our main concern is that these facts, the underlying facts, have been rolled up in a Convocation matter already. I think that's our overwhelming concern. Even though the convictions weren't entered, the facts, the basis for them was certainly I don't know if the transcript will help you much because I think we can agree that the essence of these facts were rolled up in all the other facts before Convocation and that disturbs us, for lack of a better word.

12. Speaking to the Society's counsel, Mr. Adams and Ms. Elliott stated the following at Exhibit 1, Tab 1, Page 40, Line 3, et seq.:

(Mr. Adams) I believe the question we put to you was that the conduct that occurred in B.C. was inseparable from the conduct for which he [the Member] received discipline before Convocation in 1995 ...
(Ms. Elliott) That's my concern.

13. The motions Committee then heard submissions from the Society's counsel and concluded that the material facts leading to Complaint DI 10/98 had not been before Convocation during its deliberations in Complaint D3 6/94 in November 1995 such that Complaint DI 10/98 was not an abuse of process. By November 1995, the Member had only been cited for contempt and resisting a police officer, but not yet convicted. The Committee then heard and denied his motion to attend the full hearing by teleconference.

14. The Chair of the motions Committee advised the Member that his motions had been denied and that the hearing would proceed before another committee, and urged him to appear before the new committee or at least have counsel who could make representations on his behalf Whereupon the Member advised the motions Committee at Exhibit 1, Tab 1, Page 48, line 6, et seq. as follows:

I can tell you that I have no intention of doing that. I am content with the matter going to Convocation on the basis of the affidavit material I've filed and I'm also content, sir, that if you and the Law Society of Upper Canada have such a different value system than I do, you may as well get on to it. I don't really belong with you crowd ... I have nothing further to say. I'm content with the matter being disposed of in absentia and I have no desire to appear further before the committee ... I'm asking this committee of its own motion to recommend that Convocation commission an inquiry of the Law Society's ongoing misprision of treason and fraud and complicity in genocide ...

15. We agree with the findings of the motions Committee. As of the date of the proceedings before us, the Member had not filed an appeal of the motions Committee's rulings. The Member has now widened his accusations of genocide to include the Society. We were unruffled by that accusation and it played no part in our deliberations.

16. It is helpful to quote *passim* from the Reasons for Judgment of Judge Friesen in *Regina v. Bruce Clark* in the contempt of court matter released on February 21, 1997 (Exhibit 3, Tab 8, pp 5 and 11–13):

In 25 years on the Bench I had never witnessed such anger and violence, except by mentally ill persons ...

In these rare "in the face of the court" contempt citations, when a contemnor is arrested, he is brought back from cells at the first opportunity to show cause why he should not be cited. After a brief cooling-off period, the contemnor is usually regretful. An apology is encouraged and accepted. There is then no further penalty and no criminal record associated with the citation.

This is not such a case. Clark deliberately challenged the authority of this court in a most contemptuous, discourteous and angry manner accompanied by some violence. In this way he attempted to intimidate the court to accept his legal argument – an argument which has been rejected on some 40 consecutive attempts.

Despite time in custody, and having had the last 16 months to think about this matter while at large, Clark shows little remorse. He portrays himself as a "prisoner of war", as a "Solhenitzyn" contemned (sic) to a psychiatric ward for speaking the truth. He calls himself a "fugitive *for* justice" [emphasis is in the original] while at large on a warrant for his arrest for contempt and assault.

He continues to refuse to accept rulings of our courts.

The Law Society of Upper Canada held extensive disciplinary hearings in April 1995. Clark was found guilty of many charges by a panel, was considered ungovernable, and faced disbarment. On review, another panel reversed most of the findings and found him guilty of only a few charges, and governable. Surprisingly, and regrettably, the Law Society of Upper Canada seemed to condone much of Clark's hectoring as "zealous" advocacy – necessary because judges did not give him a proper audience, or consider his argument. *That is a false premise* [bold emphasis is in the original]. Judges have listened patiently and carefully to his argument. Must a court listen to the same legal argument for the 41st time when that argument has been heard, considered and rejected 40 consecutive times at all levels in Canada?

As already mentioned, the Supreme Court of Canada refused to hear the *Williams*, (supra) appeal. Clark then had another setback on September 12, 1995 in the Supreme Court of Canada. He refused to accept these rulings. On September 15, 1995, three days later, he added some violence to his submission in 100 Mile House.

After September 15, 1995, Clark continued his campaign to argue his rejected thesis in the courts. In *R. v. Ignace et al* (Prov. Ct. (sic) B.C. 100 Mile House #5786 Oct. 6 '95) in another matter (Clark again made his complete submission in his application to appear as counsel in the Gustafsen Lake case), Barnett J. ended his reasons by saying:

"— I am convinced that two propositions are clear beyond all doubt.
First, Mr. Clark, contrary to his statements, is not a friend of any court in British Columbia, or the Supreme Court of Canada. His writings and remarks are beyond being merely scandalous and outrageous. The Chief Justice of Canada was absolutely correct when he told Mr. Clark on September 12, [1995] that:

'LAMER C.J.: I must say, Mr. Clark, that in my 26 years as a judge I have never heard anything so preposterous and presented in such an unkind way. To call the judges of the Supreme Court of Canada and the nine hundred and seventy-five (975) High Court judges of Canada accomplices to genocide is something preposterous. I do not accept that and think you are a disgrace to the bar.'

Second, Mr. Clark apparently knows essentially nothing about the conduct of a criminal trial in Canada. He has repeatedly asked this court to make orders that it cannot possibly make, and he has repeatedly protested orders that this court must make. The various documents filed by Mr. Clark in this court, the Supreme Court of British Columbia, and the Court of Appeal are, in large part, an utter farrago of nonsense ..."

Lamer, C.J. made the above comments to Clark only three days before he (Clark) appeared before me in 100 Mile House; Barnett J. made his comments three weeks later. After evading the warrant for his arrest for 16 months, he continues his attack on the courts in a most contemptuous way. The apology for having spoken a few ill-chosen words does not purge his profound, intractable continuing contempt. He clearly intends to continue his campaign to scandalize the courts as soon as he is released ...

... In my view, his intransigent contempt for all Canadian Courts, his deception, and his willingness to resort to violence in the face of the court also jeopardizes the legitimate aspirations and interests of the aboriginal cause ... The imposition of the conditional sentence is inappropriate in these circumstances.

... I impose a prison sentence of three months.

17. Judge Friesen's expression of regret over the Society's handling of Complaint D3 6/94 played no part in our determinations.

18. It is also helpful to quote *passim* from the unanimous Oral Reasons for Judgment of the British Columbia Court of Appeal in *Regina v. Bruce Clark* released on March 14, 1997 (Exhibit 3, Tab I 1, pp 5–1 1):

... the appellant was not convicted of contempt until ... some 17 months after the contemptuous conduct occurred. The time lapse was due almost entirely to the breach by the appellant of his solemn undertaking given both in writing and verbally, to appear and be dealt with ...

... There is a surprising aspect to the appeal and even to the fact of an appeal. It is that the appellant had admitted to the Provincial Court Judge 17 months earlier that his conduct constituted contempt ...

There can be no doubt that the events occurred in a duly constituted court or that the Provincial Court Judge was clothed with the authority to conduct bail hearings. If there ever was any uncertainty about jurisdiction, and I do not think there was, it was put to rest by R v. *Williams* (1994) 52 B.C.A.C. 296, leave to appeal to the Supreme Court of Canada refused on July 6, 1995 ... two months before the 100 Mile House episode ...

It is notable, I think, in this case that there is no suggestion that the appellant was unfairly treated. There could hardly be. At every stage of the show cause hearing he was offered assistance. He had every opportunity to give and lead evidence. He had the right of cross-examination and the opportunity to tender documentary exhibits and to make submissions. He enjoyed every element and ingredient of a fair hearing and even to the extent that the Crown was moved to observe in its factum that "an examination of the transcripts reveals ... that Judge Friesen treated the Appellant with courtesy and patience throughout". In my opinion, that is a fair and accurate observation ... there are no grounds here to support a bias allegation ...

In my opinion, no impartial reviewer of the record in this case would come to any other conclusion than that the appellant was properly convicted of contempt in the face of the court. It is my further opinion that the same impartial reviewer would inevitably come to the conclusion that the requirements of natural justice and procedural fairness were met at every stage of the proceedings.

The appellant is in the position he now finds himself as a consequence of his own conduct. He cannot reasonably expect to be exonerated by seeking to indict the trial judge and the process that brought him to book.

19. The Member's conduct before Judge Friesen was outrageous. He acted in serious contempt of court and never expressed genuine and full remorse. He resisted a police officer, this time involving more than a technical touching, but a kick to the leg or groin. He breached his undertaking to a judge to reappear at the contempt hearing. He remained at large for more than a year.

20. The Member refuses to accept the consistent rejection of his legal argument by several courts at several levels. Instead, he spreads his accusations of egregious crimes to any-

one with whom he disagrees. He demonstrably does not respect the rule of law or his obligation to be governed by the Society.

21. The Member's conduct does not involve financial defalcation and no one doubts the sincerity with which he believes in his Queen Anne argument. Nevertheless, his conduct is so unbecoming a member of the legal profession and so consistently flouts the proper authority of the courts and his governing body that the Committee is compelled to conclude that he is ungovernable, not only by the Society but by the Canadian courts, and should be disbarred. It is unfortunate for the Member that his career must end in this fashion, but end it must. If he wishes to pursue his argument further, it is recommended that he do so as a private citizen, and not as a member of the Law Society of Upper Canada.

ALL OF WHICH IS RESPECTFULLY SUBMITTED.
DATED this 17th day of December, 1998.

/s/ _____

Bradley H. Wright, Chair

I received this decision from the Discipline Committee of the Law Society of Upper Canada recommending my disbarment for "conduct unbecoming" a lawyer on Christmas Eve, 1998. Lamentably, for Margaret and me, I had not prepared myself. I had let hope sneak in and persuaded myself that the committee members would read the law and critique the Law Society's own complicity in the genocide, instead of reacting punitively against the messenger. I went down to the bar in the Indian hotel in Saskatchewan where we were staying and had three double vodkas and three pints of beer chasers in half an hour, while I struck up a friendship, I thought, with a couple of young oil pipeline workers.

I escaped from the task of facing what the discipline committee had said in its report by running from it – into bravado, perhaps, into ego, certainly, as a hail-fellow-well-met rather than a-disgrace-to-the-bar. The pipeline workers were the same age as my own sons, and I remember telling them of my own experiences as a pipeline worker when I was putting myself through law school. I knew the lingo, was one the boys, was buying my new pals the beer, when one said to the other, "this fag." I tried to explain that my camaraderie was limited to that. Then I went to get us more beers and must have pissed someone else off. I remember a blow to the side and then waking in snow, trying to get air through a spasm that froze my body's trunk. The next thing I can remember is waking with Margaret in our room, and several broken ribs that made moving for several weeks very difficult.

"I guess you kicked ass pretty good last night, eh, Bruce," she said. The pain when I started to laugh was like having the wind knocked out of me all over again. We talked. We analyzed. "You were very angry when you read the committee's report," she said, explaining why she had let me go without her. At first I disagreed, believing that what I had been feeling had been despair rather than anger. But gradually I realized that ego, and my protection of it when it gets puffed up, is a serious problem for me. We made some life decisions over the next few weeks while I was healing, and I resolved not to drink again. We realized that ego is all that stands in the way of being united with each other, with nature, or God, or however else the other, outside the ego, may be described. As petty as it sounds, I stopped wearing the eyeglasses that the newspapers had spoken off so disparagingly during the Gustafsen Lake events. The glasses were said to be confrontational. This cosmetic change seemed an important symbol in letting the ego go. The glasses had become a set of armour that perhaps made others react in kind, and so prevented them from addressing the law of which I was a messenger. As Margaret put it, I had been "the man who kicks ass (his own) and wears armour (magnetic, attracts bullets)."

By the end of month I responded to the committee's finding that I was guilty of "conduct unbecoming" a lawyer and should for this reason be disbarred. I filed a Notice of Disagreement (footnotes omitted) in the following terms:

THE LAW SOCIETY OF UPPER CANADA

IN THE MATTER OF the *Law Society Act*;

AND IN THE MATTER OF Bruce Allan Clark of the City of Granville, NY, a Barrister and Solicitor.

NOTICE OF DISAGREEMENT

Grounds

1. The committee made the same error as the judge registering the contempt conviction, and for the same reason.

2. The error consists in the finding that the courts have rejected the barrister's jurisdiction argument on its merits, as contrasted with evading it.

3. The reason for the said error is the profound conflict of interest under which the courts and the law society labour, as witness the committee's peremptory acquittal of the legal establishment of complicity in misprision of treason, fraud and genocide.

DISPOSITION SOUGHT

4. That the Law Society address the legislation and precedents which the courts and the committee to this juncture have evaded and, having done so, do discipline itself for "conduct unbecoming," beginning with a public apology to the aboriginal people of Canada.

DATED December 30, 1998.

/s/ _____

Bruce Allan Clark

CHAPTER 18

Epitaph for a Dead Lawyer Walking

On Easter Sunday morning, 4 April 1999, Margaret and I went to a local coffee shop in Ottawa where the cappuccinos are 99 cents each and the newspapers are free to read. As I looked over the *Ottawa Citizen*, I suddenly stopped at a large Reuters picture of me under the caption: "Rogue lawyer runs out of arguments: Bruce Clark's Canadian courtroom career was effectively killed 10 days ago when he was disbarred in Ontario." Stunned, I read on:

Bruce Clark, the renegade lawyer who spent two decades cultivating militant native clients across Canada with arguments dating back to the 1700s, has used up his ninth legal life.

Ten days ago, he was disbarred in Ontario. The ruling effectively kills the Canadian courtroom career of the only lawyer on the planet to combine a banker's suit, PhD, cone-head haircut, Star Wars glasses, and self-penned writs to arrest judges hearing his cases.

A disciplinary panel, reviewing Mr. Clark's 1997 convictions for contempt of court and resisting a police officer (during a court hearing for five charged in the 1995 Gustafsen Lake armed stand-off in British Columbia), found him ungovernable and guilty of "conduct unbecoming a barrister and solicitor."

The Law Society of Upper Canada panel also cited scathing accounts of his courtroom conduct from Supreme Court Justice Antonio Lamer, a dismal 0-for-40 record in native land claim cases he argued, his 16-month flight from Canada while facing criminal charges, and his claim that virtually all of Canada's judges, police and governments are guilty of treason and genocide against native peoples.

But in the murky world of guerrilla politics, Mr. Clark's disbarment may enhance his hallowed status among a minority of native activists. A self-declared exile and "fugitive for justice" who moved to the rural town of Granville, New York, last year, he refused to attend his Ontario disbarment hearing.

Instead, he filed a sheaf of papers constituting what one respected aboriginal historian has called "a never-ending argument in search of a client."

They relate to a 1704 British Privy Council judgment on the legality of land expropriations against the Mohegan Indians in what was then the British colony of Connecticut. It ruled that British colonial courts were intrinsically biased against aboriginal peoples in land claims cases, and that just decisions could only be made by a special constitutional court created in the name of the Queen of England.

That court was never convened. The Mohegans lost their land. And the 1704 Privy Council ruling was decisively forgotten as the British colonized much of North America during the next two centuries.

Mr. Clark, who unearthed the case during research for his PhD in law in Scotland, immediately seized on the potential legal implications: much of North America may have been illegally seized from aboriginal peoples. And if that were established as a matter of law, native treaties, forced reservation status, and land claim settlements covering most of the continent and hundreds of native bands, were potentially void.

It was an argument many aboriginal leaders wanted to hear. Mr. Clark quickly gained near-celebrity status on both sides of the Canada–U.S. border for his startling legal discovery. Many were impressed by his flashes of legal brilliance, personal charm, and unwavering commitment to native rights. He is the author of two authoritative books on aboriginal law.

Even his critics agree he gave up a lucrative law practice, huge home and private airplane in the 1970s to champion the native cause – at one time from the very log cabin the Indian imposter Grey Owl used as part of his own mythology. Since 1995, Mr. Clark, his wife Margaret, three children and a menagerie of pets have lived in impoverished circumstances, often smuggled like illegal aliens into native villages from northern New Brunswick to the B.C. coast.

But some native rights activists and native lawyers who were once allies of Mr. Clark became adversaries after he repeatedly lost land claim cases, ignited courtroom fracases, and aligned himself with militants who set up armed barricades and attempted to serve subpoenas, make arrests or seize historical documents in the name of "aboriginal courts" conceived by Mr. Clark.

The more charitable critics say Mr. Clark is the biggest liability to the legal merits of the 1704 case because that message has become inseparable from an obsessive, in-your-face messenger with a taste for martyrdom.

"A lot of aboriginal people agree with his arguments, but not with his tactics," says David Nahwegahbow, an Anishnabe (Ojibway) lawyer in Ottawa who is president of the Indigenous Bar Association of Canada. "He hurts the arguments in the long run. He has divided communities."

Those less charitable say his embattled image and charismatic promises of sweeping legal victories have derailed a dozen land claim settlements – and helped escalate land-claim legal costs in Canada – by splitting native band loyalties and triggering competing claims.

Recently, he filed a surprise case on behalf of a dissident native faction in northern Ontario. The 1704 case is cited as the leading legal grounds for the lawsuit. It pits Mr. Clark and a militant minority against the Ontario and federal governments – as well as the elected Longlac chief and council.

"He's a dangerous item. He ends up creating internal turmoil. That's happened like clockwork in every community he's gone to," says Peter Di Gangi, an Ottawa-based researcher and policy analyst who has advised native groups across Canada since 1981. Several have been convulsed with bitter in-fighting triggered by Mr. Clark's tactics, he says.

"He's been bad for public optics, for (native) relations with governments, and for native communities themselves. Whenever he leaves, there's a mess to clean up."

The bottom line, Mr. Nahwegahbow says, is that Mr. Clark hasn't won a single land claim case on behalf of native clients during the past two decades. Meanwhile, the Supreme Court of Canada's landmark *Delgamuukw* decision has affirmed aboriginal rights to self-government and land use across Canada – and effectively achieved much of what Mr. Clark's native apostles could have hoped to attain from a favourable ruling on the 1704 Connecticut case.

Ironically, Mr. Clark once briefly represented one of the 75 Gitskan chiefs who fought the *Delgamuukw* case through two decades of setbacks and appeals before the Supreme Court ruled in their favour. Stuart Rush, an aboriginal lawyer in Vancouver who was lead counsel on the case, says he and native leaders were appalled by Mr. Clark's guerrilla tactics.

"We were arguing the case at appeal when Bruce Clark showed up, out of the blue, and purported to arrest the four Appeal Court judges for genocide and crimes against aboriginal people," recalls Mr. Rush. "One judge ordered him taken away by the bailiff. We will never know what effect that had (the appeal was lost, but superseded by the Supreme Court decision), but it sure left a bad impression."

Mr. Rush contends that Canadian courts at all levels have properly dismissed Mr. Clark's 1704 legal argument, because it demands that aboriginal title claims be adjudicated at a non-existent court in England – and ignores the Canadian Constitution.

"His whole argument is misplaced and wrong in law. Canada is the only place this can be settled. Yet some of his native clients have gone to jail because of a vain, discreditable argument. He wasn't helping them."

Mr. Clark also argued – and lost – the original Temagami land claim case in northern Ontario. He left after new lawyers were hired to salvage the land claim on appeal, then returned to advise a small faction of militant dissidents to pursue a competing land claim case.

It has gone nowhere. So have attempts to win similar land claim efforts in the Maritimes, northern Quebec, the upper Ottawa valley, British Columbia, and in the U.S.

In September 1995, Mr. Clark finally got a chance to argue his 1704 case at the Supreme Court of Canada. He used most of 45 minutes to excoriate Chief Justice Lamer – and the Canadian judicial system – for fraud, chicanery, treason and genocide. It took a mere two minutes for the court to dismiss his case.

"I must say, Mr. Clark, that in my 26 years as a judge I have never heard anything so preposterous and presented in an unkind way," said Chief Justice Lamer. "To call the judges of the Supreme Court of Canada and the 975 High Court judges of Canada accomplices to genocide is something preposterous. I do not accept that and think you are a disgrace to the bar. The various documents filed in this court, the Supreme Court of British Columbia, and the Court of Appeal are, in large part, an utter farrago of nonsense."

Only three days later, Mr. Clark burst into a courtroom in north central British Columbia, pushing a cart laden with papers relating to the 1704 case. He demanded to represent five native people charged in the Gustafsen Lake standoff. When the judge resisted his arguments, Mr. Clark threw a stack of legal papers at him, and was tackled by police while condemning the hearing as a "kangaroo court."

That scene triggered charges of contempt and resisting arrest. Mr. Clark fled Canada for Amsterdam, where he publicly vowed never to return. (Sixteen months later he returned to Canada. He was convicted on both charges, lost an appeal on the contempt charge, and was sentenced to three months in jail).

Improbably, his fugitive status increased his cachet among some militant natives, but also within pockets of arch-conservative, anti-government activists such as Parliament Hill crusader Glen Kealey and white supremacist defender Doug Christie.

The 1995 criminal charges were laid against Mr. Clark two months after a disciplinary panel of the Law Society of Upper Canada recommended that he be disbarred for professional conduct charges dating back to 1992. The evidence in that hearing was virtually identical to that used in the 1999 hearing in which he lost his legal licence to practise.

But in 1995, Mr. Clark had an extraordinary ally in Clayton Ruby, a left-wing Toronto lawyer and native rights advocate. He almost single-handedly reversed the initial Law Society recommendation, defending Mr. Clark as a merely over-zealous champion of an oppressed native minority. Mr. Ruby co-authored a report which concluded that while Mr. Clark was guilty on three counts of professional misconduct, he deserved only a formal reprimand.

"I read that report carefully," says Mr. Di Gangi, who works directly with native groups across Canada. "Clayton Ruby didn't look at the damage Mr. Clark did to the communities. He ignored the impacts on (Mr. Clark's) own native clients."

Nevertheless, Mr. Ruby's defence of Mr. Clark was adopted by the Law Society governors. Then Mr. Clark refused to appear for his reprimand, leaving no doubt in letters to the Law Society that he was resolutely unrepentant. That prompted a new Law Society panel to review his case and overturn the 1995 reversal engineered by Mr. Ruby, an influential Law Society governor.

Mr. Clark, who could not be contacted for a Citizen interview, still has no apparent misgivings about the scrappy tactics, courtroom confrontations and single-minded conviction which has underpinned his crusade. In a final letter to the Law Society he concluded:

"I really don't belong with your crowd. I have nothing further to say. I am content with the matter being disposed of in absentia. I have no further desire to appear before the committee. I am asking this committee of its own motion to recommend that (the Law Society governors) commission an inquiry of the Law Society's ongoing treason and fraud and complicity in genocide."

Paul McKay, *Citizen* Reporter

I responded by delivering to the newspaper that same day the following letter, which it declined to print or to answer privately:

Dear Mr Editor:

It is true that I have on behalf of native clients on 40 or so occasions attempted to raise in Canadian courts the legal issue of court jurisdiction in relation to boundary and jurisdictional disputes between native and newcomer governments. On each such occasion I filed, or attempted to file, a legal brief referencing international and Canadian constitutional law legislation and precedents which *prima facie* establish that the conventional assumption by federal and provincial courts of that particular jurisdiction is not only illegal, but criminally so.

What is false is the suggestion that the Canadian courts have on those 40 occasions addressed the said issue, legislation and precedents. Instead, the courts held that it was not necessary for them to address the legislation and precedents because, they said, the issue itself had been thoroughly canvassed and the position for which my clients contended had been authoritatively rejected by the British Columbia Supreme Court and Court of Appeal in *Delgamuukw v. AGBC.*

Subsequently, on September 12, 1995, the Supreme Court of Canada in the *Delgamuukw* case itself refused to address the issue, legislation and precedents because, it said, the issue had not even been raised in the British Columbia Supreme Court and Court of Appeal. And the Supreme Court said it did not want to consider such an important constitutional question of first instance in the absence of lower court input directly on point.

It is true that subsequent to September 12, 1995 I have been imprisoned in both a mental asylum for the criminally insane and in an ordinary prison and, according to your article at least, disbarred for continuing to attempt to raise same issue, legislation and precedents. (I have not myself officially been notified of the disbarment, but will be contacting the law society to determine the accuracy of this aspect of your article). Contrary to what the Supreme Court had held on September 12, 1995, the judge imprisoning me in the asylum and the jail for the events on September 15, 1995, held that the issue, legislation and precedents had been addressed and rejected 40 times, including pre-eminently in the *Delgamuukw* case.

What is false, therefore, is the impression left that the convicting court (and the Law Society if the reported disbarment is accurate) constitutes a legitimate reaction against a lawyer's irresponsible hectoring in relation to a patently settled issue.

One function of responsible newspapers like the *Ottawa Citizen* is, specifically by remarking untruth, to apprehend or at least to inhibit injustice as the application of untruth to affairs. To this end may I suggest that you ask the author of the article to go back to his sources, specifically for the purpose of asking them to produce transcripts of the 40 cases in which the issue, legislation and precedents were supposedly dealt with on their merits and rejected, as contrasted with stonewalled.

The remainder of the article is so replete with factual errors as to make rebuttal like pinning jelly to the wall. For example, the article reports that I "threw a stack of legal papers at" a judge. As to this allegation the presiding judge of the court in question in a court transcript (copy of pertinent pages enclosed) subsequent to the supposed event said:

CLARK: [My previously-filed affidavit attested] "Said aggressive manner of filing arises since when the court on the 15th day of September, 1995, first appeared reticent to file the material, I proceeded to file it aggressively by flinging it onto the desk surface of the court clerk, who had hesitated to take it from my hand."

And I believe the verb that I took exception to was your Honour's use of the word – that I had said I had "dropped" it – if I had said that I would be lying. I didn't use the word "drop" because I didn't drop it. I did what I said I did. And when I say the desk surface you can see that the desk surface is raised, so it seems now that when I did that onto the high desk surface it slid off and would strike her at a high point on the body. It was – it hit the top surface.

JUDGE: Yes, I think this is a good time to indicate that all the reports throughout the last year and a half, whatever, indicate that you were throwing papers at me. At no time did I ever feel that you were throwing papers at me.

CLARK: And I think if one reads the –

JUDGE: I don't know how that got into the news media.

CLARK: There was an awful lot that got into the newspapers about that whole transaction that are similarly inaccurate.

JUDGE: All right. Could you take that document from ...

Rather than belabour each and every error concerning my supposed misconduct, and by doing so obscure the more important underlying issue concerning justice and the rule of law, might I suggest that you contact McGill-Queen's University Press for a reviewer's copy of my (in press) book *Justice in Paradise* (October 1999). There is another side to this whole story, and it is far more important than me. The real story involves the integrity of the rule of law, and Canada's great destiny to help lead the world to an era of justice as the application of truth to affairs.

Though I may be disbarred, oddly enough I continue to think I am and always will be a true friend of the courts and the lawyers who serve in them, though (apparently) no longer a member of that club. Friends do not let friends continue making an assumption the application in practice of which *prima facie* constitutes misprision of treason and fraud at constitutional law and, arguably, complicity in genocide at international law.

I am enclosing a copy of an affidavit filed by my native clients in the recent court case in Ottawa referenced in the article. It was prepared in anticipation of my potential disbarment. I did not introduce the conflict into native society between the *Indian Act* system and the native traditionalists. The federal government introduced the conflict over a century ago. All that I have done is to identify, for the traditionalists in native society, the newcomers' own international and constitutional law that establishes the criminal character of the premature application of the *Indian Act* to arguably unceded Indian territory.

The informants identified in the *Ottawa Citizen* article make or have made a living in whole or in significant part acting for and being paid pursuant to the arguably unconstitutional *Indian Act* system and, correspondingly, by steering native clients away from the native sovereignty issue under the existing international and constitutional law that is being blindsided and stonewalled by the legal establishment and news media.

Yours very truly,
Bruce Clark

I also wrote to the Law Society of Upper Canada and received the following replies, to which I in turn replied.

April 6, 1999

Law Society of Upper Canada
Toronto, Ontario

RE: DI 10/98

Dear Madam Clerk:

The newspaper article by Rod McKay, "Rogue lawyer runs out of arguments," *Ottawa Citizen*, April 4, 1999, A 3, *inter alia* reported "Bruce Clark's courtroom career was effectively killed 10 days ago when he was disbarred in Ontario." Have I in fact been disbarred? Please reply, by fax, today.

Very truly yours,
Bruce Clark

April 6, 1999

Dear Mr. Clark:

I am in receipt of your faxed letter of today's date. When your matter came before Convocation on March 25, 1999 Convocation adopted the Report and Decision of the Discipline Committee dated December 17, 1998 and accepted its recommendation that you be disbarred. A copy of the Order of Convocation will be forwarded to you by registered mail shortly.

Yours very truly,
/s/
_____
Clerk to the Discipline Committee

April 19, 1999

Dear Sir:

Enclosed please find a true copy of the Order of Convocation dated march 25, 1999 and a Notice of Right to Appeal.

Yours very truly,
/s/
_____
Clerk to the Discipline Committee

Enclosure:

THE LAW SOCIETY OF UPPER CANADA

IN THE MATTER OF THE *Law Society Act*;

AND IN THE MATTER OF Bruce Allan Clark, of the City of Granville, NY, a Barrister and Solicitor (hereinafter referred to as "the Solicitor").

ORDER

CONVOCATION of the Law Society of Upper Canada, having read the Report and Decision of the Discipline Committee dated December 17, 1998, in the presence of Counsel for the Society, the Solicitor not being in attendance, but assisted by Duty Counsel, wherein the Solicitor was found guilty of conduct unbecoming a barrister and solicitor and having heard counsel aforesaid;

CONVOCATION HEREBY ORDERS that Bruce Allan Clark be disbarred as barrister, and that his name be struck off the Roll of Solicitors, that his membership in the said Society be cancelled, and that he is hereby prohibited from acting or practising as a barrister and solicitor and from holding himself out as a barriter and solicitor.

DATED this 25th day of March, 1999.
/s/
_____
Acting Treasurer
/s/
_____
Secretary

April 21, 1999

Clerk to the Discipline Committee
Law Society of Upper Canada

RE: DI 10/98

Dear Madam Clerk:

Earlier today I received your letter dated 19 April 1999 enclosing Disbarment Order dated 25 March 1999.

Please confirm that there is not a mistake on the face of the order. It indicates that Convocation read the Report of the Discipline Committee but not my written Reply in Several Documents. If there is a mistake, Convocation should reconvene to address my Reply. If there is no mistake, the Order should be amended to reflect the true basis upon which the decision was taken.

Very truly yours,
Bruce Clark

My Reply, which, from all that presently appears, was not addressed by Convocation before arriving at the decision to disbar me, included all the material that was before the Discipline Committee and quoted previously, plus the following Several Documents.

AFFIDAVIT #1

I, Bruce Allan Clark, barrister and solicitor, MAKE OATH AND SAY:

1. The admissible evidence relative to the events giving rise to the convictions is recorded in the transcript of proceedings in provincial court for September 15, 1995 (Tab 8 pp. 3–4). I accused (p. 4 lines 7–14) the provincial court judge unconstitutionally, treasonably, fraudulently and genocidally of assuming jurisdiction in relation to territory not proven to have been purchased by the crown from the Indians. Immediately I made that accusation I was assaulted at the counsel table (p. 4 lines 26–7) by the police and when I asked the presiding judge to order the assault to cease he instead ordered the assaulting officer to arrest me (lines 28–31). The other facts alleged in the prosecution brief are hearsay, embellishments, exaggerations and outright lies.

2. The said accusation was and remains true. The law involved is international as well as constitutional. International law is regarded as foreign law and, as such, is a matter for sworn testimony by expert witnesses. I have read for master's and doctoral degrees the thesis for each of which focused this law, and its constitutional ramifications, and on this basis I am qualified to testify.

The international law was settled by the papal bull *Sublimus Deus, 1537* (Tab 14 p. 4) which *inter alia* enacted "that the Indians are truly men ... and that they may and should, freely and legitimately, enjoy their liberty and possession of their property ... should the contrary happen, it shall be null and of no effect." This was implemented by the constitutional law's stipulation that the sole original jurisdiction of the newcomer governments in North America is to "purchase" Indian territory, and thereby to acquire "plenum dominium" (plenary jurisdiction). Schedule "A", *infra*, p. 6. The jurisdiction to purchase was made exclusive, in exchange for which exclusivity the newcomer government is under the fiduciary duty of protecting that territory against invasion prior to purchase. Schedule "B", *infra*, pp. 7–14.

The constitutional common law implementing this international law legislatively was confirmed as early as 1684, when chapter 8 of the New York Colonial Laws entitled *An Act to Prevent Deceit and Forgeries* enacted that every purchase of land must "be done by Deed in writting under ye hand and Seale of the Grantor & delivery ... PROVIDED that no Conveyance Deed or Promise shall be of any fforce or Vallidity nor shall the Grantor be Compelled to acknowledge the same if it were obtained by Illegall violence Imprisonm't or any kind of fforcable Compulsions called Duress any thing to the Contrary hereof notwithstanding." Chapter 9 entitled *An Act Concerning Purchasing of Lands from the Indians* added that "noe Purchase of Lands from the Indians shall bee esteemed a good Title without Leave first had and obtaineid from the Governour."

As to whether any particular purchase is invalid because signed under duress or a misrepresentation of the law made by a fiduciary, or both, the *Order in Council (Great Britain) of March 1704* in re *Mohegan Indians v. Connecticut* (Tab 15 pp. 4–6, 48–54) constitutionally confirmed that the native nations have the quasi-sovereign right to independent and impartial third-party adjudication in the international arena. In that case the legislation of the newcomer government that established the newcomer government's domestic court system was held to be inapplicable to territory in relation to which the native interest allegedly had not been purchased, precisely because until the validity of the purchase is proven the only jurisdiction that constitutionally exists is the jurisdiction to purchase, and that precludes the application to the territory of the legislation setting up the newcomer courts the same as it precludes all other newcomer legislation. The 1704 order in council constitutionally enacted that newcomer domestic legislation to the contrary is "illegal and void."

When the *Royal Proclamation of 1763* (Tab 14 pp. 6–7) constitutionally organized the courts for what is now Canada it expressly placed those courts' jurisdiction "under such Regulations and Restrictions as are used in other Colonies," thus applying to Canada the same jurisdictional law as previously held to be applicable in the older British colonies. See also, Foster, Tab 15 pp. 54–7. Similarly, when the proclamation constitutionally organized Canada's original land granting power it placed that jurisdiction on the same footing as in the older colonies, being extended to "such Lands, Tenements and Hereditaments, as are now or hereafter shall be in Our Power to dispose of." The lands not yet within the newcomer governments' constitutional power of disposition were the yet unpurchased Indian territories. Section 109 of Canada's *Constitution Act, 1867* confirmed that pending the Indian purchase the crown's title to territory is held "subject to" the Indian "Interest", and section 129 confirmed that this constitutional balance was not subject to change in the absence of a duly enacted constitutional amendment. The *Order in Council (Can.), 1875*

(Tab 14 pp. 10–14) and section 35(*1*) of the *Constitution Act, 1982* reconfirmed this "existing" law.

3. Secondly, I am qualified by personal observation to bear witness to the treasonable, fraudulent and genocidal breach and suppression of the said law by the Canadian legal establishment. For the past 25 years I have studied and experienced first-hand the relationship between natives and newcomers. For 10 of those years I lived upon Indian reservations. I observed and now do bear witness to "serious bodily or mental harm" being inflicted upon the native people as "a national, ethnical, racial or religious group" contrary to article 2(*b*) of the *Convention for the Prevention and Punishment of the Crime of Genocide, 1948* (Tab 13 pp. 69–70) by the said legal establishment's stonewalling of the law. Paragraphs 1 and 2 of part 2 and paragraphs 1–5 of the 1763 proclamation constitutionally preclude as "Pretence" and "Fraud and Abuse" the assumption, first, of court jurisdiction, and, secondly, of land granting jurisdiction, relative to territory not "ceded to or purchased by" the crown. Paragraph 6 of part 4 of the proclamation constitutes the said fraudulent assumption of the crime of misprision of treason. On 20 occasions since 1990 I applied to the Supreme Court of Canada for leave to appeal the ignoring of the law and the fact of genocide by lower courts. Leave was denied on each occasion, on the ground that no issue of "importance" within the meaning of s. 40(1) of the *Supreme Court Act* had been identified. Instead of addressing the law as it is already written, the said Supreme Court in the recent line of 1990s British Columbia cases running from *Van der Peet* to *Delgamuukw* has indicated that it proposes to re-write the law, on a case-by-case basis, as part of an ongoing exercise to reconcile the natives' priority of occupation with the crown's claim of sovereignty, as if the reconciliation did not already exist in the form of a general law of universal application.

The institutionalized injustice attributable to ignoring the law, as it is written, accompanies the native people from the cradle and hastens their introduction to the grave. The horrific statistics of death rates in native communities are attributable to despair of justice manifested in alcoholism, addictions and violence, as the native people's legal sovereignty is held in contempt and they are forced, generation after generation, powerlessly to watch the destruction of the mother earth and, with her, of their culture which springs directly from her, and gives them their identity and reason for being.

4. The crucial passages from the constitutive precedents are recorded in the annexed schedule "A". Passages from secondary precedents are recorded in the annexed schedule "B". Now aside from these there have been many cases in both Canada and the United States (whose constitutional law shares the same root) which have *assumed*, without ever questioning the assumption, newcomer court jurisdiction. But assumptions can not repeal previously established international and constitutional law. A court can declare constitutional common law when an issue is raised for the first time but once an issue has been declared, whether by statute or a previous court judgment, the issue as settled can only thereafter be changed legislatively by a properly enacted constitutional amendment. As the preeminent jurist E.V. Dicey said in his celebrated Harvard Law School Lecture series on

the foundations of Anglo-American jurisprudence, portions of which were included in his subsequently (1920) published treatise entitled *Lectures on the Relation between Law and Public Opinion in England in the Nineteenth Century* (at page 483):

Judge-made law is subject to certain limitations. It can not openly declare a new principle of law: it must always take the form of a deduction from some legal principle whereof the validity is admitted, or the application or interpretation of some statutory enactment. It can not override statutory law. The courts may, by a process of interpretation, indirectly limit or possibly extend the operation of a statute, but they can not set a statute aside. Nor have they in England ever adopted the doctrine which exists, one is told, in Scotland, that a statute may be obsolete by disuse. It can not from its very nature override any established principle of judge-made law.

5. As appears at Tab 13 p. 46, three days before the events described in paragraph 1 above the Supreme Court of Canada in the matter of *Delgamuukw v. AGBC* confirmed that the said accusation presented not only a constitutional question, but one of first impression so far as the Canadian courts are concerned. And on June 19, 1996 in *Law Society of Upper Canada v. Bruce Clark* Convocation held in respect of the same accusation:

Mr. Clark's argument is anything but frivolous. It is the product of intensive study… It would be difficult to disagree with Mr. Clark's assertion that the issue that his argument raises is "constitutionally critical." Again, the discipline hearing panel found that Mr. Clark honestly believes that the comments and conduct particularized in the complaint – which are an outgrowth of his argument – were intended to advance the cause of justice and the rule of law. The "genocide" of which Mr. Clark speaks is real, and has very nearly succeeded in destroying the Native Canadian community that flourished here when European settlers arrived. No one who has seen many of our modern First Nation communities can remain untouched by this reality.

The Law Society's disciplinary staff and those benchers approving the prosecution of the present complaint apparently disagree with the supreme court and convocation and agree instead with the said provincial court, which the prosecution brief (pp. 5–6) sympathetically quotes as settling that I do not "respect our Constitution and the institutions of democracy" but rather do "attempt to destroy them", and that:

Surprisingly, and regrettably, the Law Society of Upper Canada seemed to condone much of what Clark's hectoring as "zealous advocacy" – necessary because judges did not give him a proper audience, or consider his argument. *That is a false premise.* Judges have listened patiently and carefully to his argument. Must a court listen to the same legal argument for the 41st time when that argument has been heard, considered and rejected 40 consecutive times at all levels in Canada?

The answer to that rhetorical question is: no, of course not, if it were indeed true that the "argument has been heard, considered and rejected 40 consecutive times at all levels in Canada." But the judge's statement is unsupported, and insupportable. The use by him of underlining and bold type neither erases the supreme court's recognition that the argument presents a (still unaddressed) constitutional question of first impression, nor negates convocation's finding that the law must eventually be addressed on its merits if Canada is going to earn and keep its status as a rule of law society.

6. The onus is not upon me to establish the truth of the said accusation, but, rather, upon the prosecution to establish its falsity. *Standing Committee on Discipline v. Yagman*, 55 F.3d 1430, 1438–42, 1445 (USCA 9th Cir. 1995):

> ... attorneys may be sanctioned for impugning the integrity of judge or the court only if their statements are false; truth is an absolute defence. *See, Garrison v. Louisiana*, 379 US 64, 74 (1964). Moreover, the disciplinary body bears the burden of proving falsity. *See, Philadelphia Newspapers, Inc. v. Hepps*, 475 US 767, 776–77 (1986); *Porter*, 766 P.2d at 969 ... A statement of opinion based upon fully disclosed facts can be punished only if the stated facts are themselves false and demeaning ... the fact remains that the Standing Committee bore the burden of proving Yagman had made a statement that falsely impugned the integrity of the court. By presuming falsity, the district court unconstitutionally relieved the Standing Committee of its duty to produce evidence on and element of its case. Without proof of falsity, Yagman's "drunk on the bench" allegation, like the statements discussed above, cannot support the imposition of sanctions for impugning the integrity of the court ... The standard announced in these cases is a demanding one: Statements may be punished only if they "constitute an imminent, not merely a likely, threat to the administration of justice. The danger must not be remote or even probable, it must immediately imperil." *Craig* [*v. Harney*, 331 US 367] at 376 ... In an oft-quoted passage, the Court noted that "the law of contempt is not made for the protection of judges who may be sensitive to the winds of public opinion. Judges are supposed to be men of fortitude, able to survive in a hardy climate." *Id* ... We can't improve on the words of Justice Black in *Bridges* [*v. California*, 314 US 252] at 270–71 (footnote omitted):

> > The assumption that respect for the judiciary can be won by shielding judges from published criticism wrongly appraises the character of American public opinion. For it is a prized American privilege to speak one's mind, although not always with perfect good taste, on all public institutions. And an enforced silence, however limited, solely in the name of preserving the dignity of the bench, would probably engender resentment, suspicion, and contempt much more than it would enhance respect.

7. Unless the prosecution can discharge the said burden of proving falsity, which has not even been attempted, the present complaint must permanently be stayed as a possible suppression of a truth, which precludes justice as the application under the rule of law of

truth to affairs, which negates the law society's duty to uphold the public interest in the implementation of those values and standards.

/s/
_____

Bruce Allan Clark

Sworn before me this 30th day
of July, 1998.
/s/
_____

Notary Public

AFFIDAVIT #2

I, Bruce Allan Clark, barrister and solicitor, MAKE OATH AND SAY:

1. Agents who are not members of the Law Society of British Columbia can appear at bail hearings in that Province. Judge Friesen's refusal to allow me to address his bail court was not because I was not a member of the Law Society of British Columbia. That was his pretext. He had met *ex camera* with police in advance of the bail hearing. Upon his instructions (which later he denied), the police first tried to block my entry into the locked courtroom, and then, while I was addressing the court, the police began assaulting me by pushing me from behind into the counsel table. I asked Judge Friesen to order the assault to cease. Instead, to preempt my statements in court on my native clients' behalf that the courts' assumption of jurisdiction constitutes "Misprision of Treason" and "Fraud" contrary to the *Royal Proclamation of 1763* and "Complicity in Genocide" contrary to articles 2(b) and 3(e) of the *Convention for the Prevention and Punishment of the Crime of Genocide, 1948,* he ordered my arrest and removal.

2. "Conduct" by definition and in general includes "statements" and "actions". The criminal charges against me, above all, concern my statements. My actions, standing alone, would not have been proceeded against. As appears from the following references to the transcripts of court proceedings, but for my said statements my actions would have been excused at the show cause hearing in exchange for my apology, which I did make, but which was not accepted, expressly and explicitly because I declined to recant my statements, which I refused to do because those statements were relevant, true and crucial to the integrity of the rule of law and to my clients' legal position.

Transcript of October 18, 1995 before Friesen, PCJ, in re *R. v. Clark: "Any thought that the contempt charge might be withdrawn, vanished* when he refused to accept the jurisdiction of the court, *and declined to apologize"* [emphasis added].
Reasons for Judgment of February 21, 1997 by Friesen, PCJ, in re *R. v. Clark. "Clark's attack was not just against me or the provincial court, but rather against the entire institution of the Canadian judiciary ... The apology for having spoken a few ill-chosen words does not purge his profound, intractable continuing contempt. He clearly intends*

to continue his campaign to scandalize the courts as soon as he is released ... The penalty must serve to deter him."

3. On the eve of the events in the bail court hearing set for Friday, September 15, 1998, I learned that some 500 police surrounding my 18 native clients (children included) were on the brink of mounting an all-out armed assault with military armoured vehicles. (The police plan to storm the camp subsequently was detailed in the ensuing trials of the Gustafsen Lake natives in the Supreme Court of British Columbia.)

After years of seeing the law stonewalled in the courts by being rejected without ever being addressed, my clients had made it clear to the Canadian public that they would come out voluntarily if, but only if, some court agreed in principle to address the law concerning court jurisdiction in relation to yet unceded Indian territory, such as the territory at Gustafsen Lake. Previously, the police had undertaken to ensure that I would be with my clients as they came out and at their bail hearings. I had discussed with the police the fact that the standoff would end immediately I relayed to my clients inside the encampment the anticipated decision of the Supreme Court of Canada on September 12th to address the jurisdicion issue in the context of the *Delgamuukw* case. When I had gone into the camp with police consent I had asked the clients to come out on the basis of my opinion that on September 12th the Supreme Court would likely agree to address the jurisdiction issue as a pure law matter going to its own jurisdiction, since leave to appeal has already been granted in *Delgamuukw* and since I was now acting for one of the appellants in that case. But the clients at Gustafsen Lake decided to stay in the camp until I confirmed to them, on or shortly after the 12th, after the Supreme Court had in fact decided in principle to address the issue and the law.

On the 12th I advised the Supreme Court, once again, not only of the jurisdiction issue, but that the court's agreement in principle to address the issue and the law would end the Gustafsen Lake standoff peaceably, whereas the court's refusal to address the issue and the law would *de facto* sign my clients' death warrant at Gustafsen Lake, for those clients would likely be murdered by police who themselves had no jurisdiction. The Supreme Court refused, once again, to address the issue and the law.

Up until that time the police had held off storming the camp, since it was apparent that their jurisdiction in the unceded Indian territory might soon be addressed in the Supreme Court of Canada. When the Supreme Court on the 12th, once again, refused to address the jurisdiction issue, it was apparent to the police that the likelihood of the issue being addressed, ever, in accordance with the rule of law, was virtually non-existent in Canada. The point is that the Supreme Court instructed me to raise the issue first at the trial level, as if I had not already done that on some 40 previous occasions, and as if it were not already clear from some 20 previous applications for leave to appeal not only that the lower courts would never address the issue but that the Supreme Court would never address it until it had been addressed in the lower courts. The message, between the lines, sent to the police by the Supreme Court on September 12th was clear and plain: proceed by *force majeure* regardless of the jurisdiction issue and regardless of the deaths that were probable. The 'orders', in effect, were given to commit genocide by 'killing' within the meaning of article 2(*a*) of the genocide convention were, in this sense, to all intents and purposes given by the Supreme Court of Canada on September 12th. There was no doubt that the police would 'just follow orders,' which is how genocide always works.

Therefore, on September 14th, the police breached their earlier undertaking to give me access to my clients. The police refused to let me see or speak with my clients any longer, some few clients having just come out of the camp and being now in custody. As of the evening of September 14th the risk became real, and high, that the police would kill at least some of my clients and their children remaining in the camp over the weekend of September 15th, unless, as a last desperate resort, I could persuade the bail court near Gustafsen Lake on September 15th to say, in principle, that the said law would be addressed. The transcript of the Supreme Court hearing on September 12th (pp. 16–17, 21) says:

Chief Justice: *If you* [Bruce Clark] *had decided to initiate or if you decide tomorrow morning to initiate in the Supreme Court of British Columbia an action for declaratory relief saying that the British Columbia courts have no jurisdiction, that is a different matter and you could be arguing to the judge that, well, this is an issue that has never been tried and I want a declaratory, but we are talking about doing this within the four (4) corners of this appeal. And what you have against you is that, while you might have a good point to argue in the British Columbia Court of Appeal, this is not the place to start the thing and this is certainly not the way of doing it along with them. In other words they do not want to be in the same courtroom with you because you are saying they should not be in the courtroom.*

Mr. Bruce Clark: *On July 6* [1995]*, your Lordship refused leave to appeal on the same point of law pursuant to s. 40(1) of the* Supreme Court Act, *the sole test for which is whether the issue is of importance. You, my Lord, have already decided this issue is not of sufficient importance to occupy the Court's time. For you now to say that it is realistically open to Xsgogimlahxa to commence a separate action and to work his way through the court system, as was done on those eleven (11) other applications is blatant chicaneries* [sic: chicanery].

Chief Justice Lamer: *I must remind you, Mr. Clark, that I do not intend to tolerate such language on the part of any counsel including yourself.*

Mr. Bruce Clark: *Nor, sir, do I intend to tolerate treason, fraud and complicity in genocide against our Constitution and against the aboriginal peoples of this country ...*

Chief Justice Lamer: *Proceed, proceed.*

Mr. Bruce Clark: *If my client's point ultimately is vindicated, this Court does not have jurisdiction. The remaining plaintiffs will then have an informed option. That informed option will permit them either to say "We will take that route". That is the probability because at that point their native sovereignty would be – they would not only have land jurisdiction but they would have court jurisdiction. They would have the greatest of all possible forms of native sovereignty. On the other hand, they may be advised by their lawyers to waive the right to dispute the court jurisdiction, essentially to treat the non-native tribunals as a form of arbitration and in an informed fashion attorn to the jurisdiction of this tribunal. That would be their choice at that time but it would be an informed choice. And as members of the legal profession, the duty is to make sure that the client is put in the position of making that type of choice.*

Those are my submissions, my Lord. Thank you ...

Chief Justice Lamer: *There is no doubt that it is a constitutional issue. If it is a constitutional issue that we decide to entertain, then it flows from that that we should state a constitutional question to send notice outside so that they intervene but therefore this takes us to the fundamental question, Do we want to entertain, and why should we, in your view entertain a constitutional question of nature when that question was not raised below? ... the fact of the matter is that we do not have the benefit of the Supreme Court of British Columbia and the Court of Appeal. Earlier on this morning at 10: 00 a.m., in a case from Quebec, I refused to state a constitutional question because it was being raised before us for the first time.*

Mr. Bruce Clark: *What the courts below said in all of the eleven (11) cases that this Court recently on July 6 refused leave* [to appeal] *on was basically that, regardless of the truth of what I was alleging on behalf of my clients, the issue was of such momentous concern, was of such momentous importance to Canada that nobody but the highest Court in the land was going to touch it. On July 6 it gets to the highest Court in the land and that Court says the issue is of no importance and leave to appeal is denied. The reason this Court must address the issue is because the rule of law hangs in the balance ... I wish to argue that the crime of genocide never occurs unless the court system of the country in which it is occurring is complicitous. Right now, the world more than any other single advance needs a breakthrough on the crime of genocide and the crime of ecocide and I am suggesting that this Court can light a candle for all humanity to follow. Alternatively, it can engage in chicaneries and not address the point. It can soar or it can plummet. There is no in between ... Your jurisdiction* [is] *as guardians of the sacred trust of civilization.*

Chief Justice Lamer: *Oh my God. I did not swear to that. I just swore to be a judge and try to do my best according to the rule of law.*

Mr. Bruce Clark: *It fell upon you, whether or not you realized it. That is the duty under which you labour.*

Chief Justice Lamer: *I must say, Mr. Clark, that in my twenty six (26) years as a judge I have never heard anything so preposterous and presented in such an unkind way. To call the judges of the Supreme Court of Canada and the nine hundred and seventy five (975) High Court judges of Canada accomplices is something preposterous. I do not accept that and I think you are a disgrace to the bar. The point is you have my opinion and you are lucky I am just proceeding to opinions at this stage. I will hear from you on the motion. Is that all you have to say on the constitutional question? ...*

Mr. Bruce Clark: *... So we have a classic situation of the truth versus political opportunism. In theory, the function of the rule of law and therefore of this Court above all* *courts is to get at the truth, the whole truth and nothing but the truth regardless of any political opportunism, regardless of personal offence. This Court is supposed to be above such petty considerations.*

The remedy specifically therefore is not to ask this Court to address the constitutional question as such but to ask this Court to address the law which indicates that this Court ought in justice to refer it to an independent and impartial third party tribunal, and in the meantime to make sure that more lives are not lost on the basis of the arguably erroneous assumption that this Court and hence the Royal Canadian Mounted Police or other police forces have jurisdiction. Indian people allegedly are murdered by police who in the event may turn out to have been there fraudulently, treasonably and genocidally, not legally.

In the material that is filed it appears:

Each and every of the petitioners ... attests that in consequence of the aforesaid (treasonable and fraudulent) usurpation by the domestic Crown Courts in relation to Hunting Grounds, the members of the tribal system to which he or she belongs have been and are being subjected to "serious mental harm" within the meaning of article 2(b) of the above mentioned Convention, to prejudiced rates of mortality, and, furthermore, to "killing" within the meaning of article 2(a) of the said Convention.

Those are my submissions, my Lords ...

Chief Justice Lamer: ... *Today we are not here to decide whether there is a jurisdictional issue to the merits. It is to decide if you can raise the jurisdictional issue in the manner you have ... How do you bring your clients within the four (4) walls of this courtroom without proceeding through the Supreme Court of British Columbia, the Court of Appeal and then to us? ... The fact that we might be concerned about something does not grant us jurisdiction. The only point I am putting to you and I think my colleagues agree with me on this is that we are not a court of original jurisdiction such as the Supreme Court of British Columbia ... We are all of the view that there is no foundation whatsoever for these two (2) motions and they are accordingly dismissed with costs.*

4. When I went to the bail court on September 15th it was apparent that the police and judge had conspired to preclude me and therefore the jurisdiction issue and the law addressing it from entering the courtroom, in favour of employing *force majeure* regardless of the law. After I was arrested on the 15th, the medicine man who had been instructing me and my clients did go into the camp on the 16th and told the clients to come out, which they did, thus forestalling the bloodshed. At the trial of the Gustafsen Lake defendants in British Columbia the evidence included police videos of themselves (made and retained for police academy training purposes) in which *inter alia* the following statements are recorded (referenced on Gustafsen Lake trail transcript for January 6, 1997):

"*Smear campaigns are our specialty.*" Per: Staff Sergeant Peter Montague, Chief Media Liaison Officer.

"Is there anyone who can help us with our smear and disinformation campaign." Per: Sergeant Denis Ryan. Addressing the Police Management Team overseeing the Gustafsen Lake event.

"Kill this Clark and smear the prick and everyone with him." Per: Sergeant Denis Ryan. Ditto.

In conformity with the "smear campaign" policy, the police publicly described my native clients as "terrorists" at the time of the Gustafsen Lake events, thus prejudging and preempting the jurisdiction issue as well as distributing criminally false hate literature. And while the subsequent trial of those clients was in progress, that same instruction was published widely by the national media. Shortly thereafter the engine of the car being used by my wife to attend the trial in British Columbia was sabotaged and exploded in flames. On the assumption that the police did not do this themselves, apparently or at least arguably the publication of the said police instruction incited some other persons to take this action. In a little town on the Gaspé Peninsula in Quebec called Matapédia there was, and perhaps still is, a police memo in the format of a wanted poster describing me as someone to whom was paid $5 million by the Bulgarian government to undermine the "stability" of Canadian society. The only cited "evidence" of this (utterly absurd and totally insupportable fantasy) was the fact I visited Bulgaria and published a book entitled *Native Liberty, Crown Sovereignty.* Presumably, if such hysterical, false and malicious hate literature is posted in the village of Matapédia, it has been distributed widely across Canada, and the police generally in Canada take it as a given that I am some kind of intellectual quasi-terrorist. Whatever I may be charged with, and regardless of how untenable the pretext may be, there is no prospect of a fair trial for me anywhere in Canada, since, as Judge Friesen and Chief Justice Lamer have indicated, there is a settled *a priori* notion that I am trying to destroy the Canadian state by making supposedly self-evidently "preposterous" statements, which, to them, apparently justifies their refusal to address the law on which I rely, and their right to publish unsubstantiated and false facts about me.

5. There is no way that I can bring reason into the process. The legal establishment, and the national media, misrepresent the issue and the circumstances, as part of their own self-serving psychological denial of the truth of my statements. For example, at the bail hearing before Judge Friesen I filed a 33 page motion record by flipping it onto the desk surface of the Court Clerk while I was being assaulted by the police as above described. The national media (absurdly) reported this as me throwing papers at the judge and hitting him in the chest. Later, the judge tried to pretend I had intended to assault the Clerk and ended up doing 'violence' to her when the motion record that I filed skidded across her desk surface. I was paraded not just in handcuffs but in leg irons and chains through the media scrum through the public access door of courthouse, rather than through the prisoner access door at the rear. Over the weekend of September 16th, in addition to personal indignities, I was deprived by the police of any sleep. On Monday the 18th I was remanded in custody (for 30 days though returned with a clean bill of mental health after 7 days) to a facility for the criminally insane, as a person whose statements challenging his jurisdiction

on behalf of my clients caused the judge to conjecture that I was suffering from delusional paranoia. The jurisdictional issue and the law in relation to it was never addressed at any stage of the Gustafsen Lake proceedings. As always, convictions were registered in that law's absence, which, historically, has been and continues to be the genocide's *modus operandi* since the latter half of the 19th century in North America. These incidents illustrate the tip of an iceberg of a self-serving systematic obstruction of justice by the legal establishment, about which I have written a more detailed book which soon will be published by the academic press in Canada and the United States.

6. In the preceding paragraph I remarked the imperviousness of the legal system to "reason." What I mean to signify is that I have experienced, and am experiencing, firsthand, the phenomenon of the institutionalized structural injustice with which the native people have had to cope. The law is simple, clear and plain. Ever since the enactment of the papal bull *Sublimus Deus* in 1537, the international and constitutional law has had one unbroken theme: the Indians were in occupation first and are human beings, with souls, and therefore we, the newcomers, may not, legally at any rate, occupy their territory and assume jurisdiction there, as if they were nothing more than animals without souls; rather, we must recognize their humanity by purchase of their territory, as the precondition to our own occupation and assumption of jurisdiction. That is the international law which the crown confirmed and re-created as constitutional law, in virtue of its claim of sovereignty upon the discovery and conquest of North America. There has never been a repeal of this international and constitutional law. Tracing its continuity was the subject of my masters and doctoral research, the organization and expression of which I have successfully defended in the academic arena in Canada and in Scotland. The legal instruments in which the jurisdiction issue and the related crimes of misprision of treason and fraud and complicity in genocide are constituted are set out with particularity in the application for leave to appeal at Tab 13 of the Exhibit Book on this disciplinary proceeding.

7. From living upon Indian reservations for so many years, I have learned that the aboriginal people, or at least some of them, have always known this, just as they also know that there is no justice for them in the newcomers' court system. For the newcomers' lawyers, judges and police will not allow the law into their courtrooms: they are labouring under a profound conflict of interest. The lawyers, judges and police spearheaded the premature occupation of, and assumption of jurisdiction in, the yet unceded Indian territories, *en masse*, in the heyday of rampant racism and imperialism that was the latter half of the 19th century. Newcomer society omitted not only first to purchase the Indian territories before occupying them, but, more significantly from the perspective of the rule of law, neglected also to repeal the constitutional law stipulating purchase as the legal precondition to occupation. Historically, when the Indians objected to this illegality their words were ignored, and their actions to draw attention to the illegality were treated as criminal breaches of the peace.

8. What I have done over the past 8 years is to step into the shoes of some natives who, like their ancestors, have tried to have these words heard. And I have taken actions to draw attention to the words, when the words were ignored. For when the words are ignored, the

consequence for the aboriginal people, or at least a part of that sub-culture, is 'serious bodily or mental harm' within the meaning of article 2(b) of the *Convention for the Prevention and Punishment of the Crime of Genocide, 1948,* which is to say a form of "genocide." And the ignoring of the law's words, and the criminalization of actions taken to breakthrough the stonewall of willful deafness, constitutes "complicity in genocide" within the meaning of article 3(e) of the said convention. At the end of each day what we in Canadian society are left with is a legacy that denies the humanity of the aboriginal people and in the process destroys hope for justice as the application under the rule of law of truth to affairs. The genocide's *modus operandi* – ignoring the words and criminalizing the actions – is what accounts for statistics of mortality from unnatural causes that differentiates native society from non-native society. The human spirit is crushed by the institutionalized suppression of truth. The only remedy, that I can see in any event, is to remove the basis for the genocidal *angst* created by the institutionalized injustice. This can occur in one of two modes: respect the law, as it is written, or change the law by due process of a constitutional amendment. Only thus will the era of genocide be over and the rule of law rehabilitated, in the best interest of all people, in justice.

9. Repeatedly over the past 8 years I have asked the Law Society to investigate not just me, but itself, and, having done the latter, apprehend its own and its members' complicity in the aforementioned crimes-in-progress. All such requests have been stonewalled. Most recently, the annexed letters to the Law Society dated January 14, 1998, April 13, 1998, April 23, 1998, and a second also dated April 23, 1998, set out with particularity the evidence and I repeat under oath the contents of those letters as being relevant to this discipline proceeding. Instead of helping me to uphold rule of law, over the past 8 years the discipline staff of the law society consistently has participated in the harassment and destruction of me professionally, while at the same time aiding and abetting the crimes of misprision of treason and fraud and complicity in genocide, by turning a blind eye to the legal professions' role in the premature invasion of the unceded Indian territories, and the ensuing suppression of the natural, international and constitutional law which precludes the said invasion. In consequence, I have been driven into exile to escape persecution because I make statements in courts of law concerning the law, the truth of which statements I fully can substantiate. The perpetrators of the crimes identified in the statements, the judges and lawyers and police, are the very ones who are persisting in the persecution, while at the same time refusing to address the underlying, and infinitely more important to the rule of law, jurisdictional and criminal law issues.

10. If I believed that appearing in person before the Disciplinary Committee, as contrasted with consenting to a hearing *in absentia* or making myself fully available by conference calls, would advance the interest of justice as the application under the rule of law of truth to affairs, I would not hesitate so to appear, regardless of the personal risk. But I believe that at this time I can be of greater service to my clients, to my country, and to the legal profession, by staying away, and out of Canadian jails. The rule of law intransigently is in abeyance in Canada, and in consequence I have been demonized and criminalized and thereby neutralized in this country. But if the jurisdictional issue is addressed in the United

States, as it may be in consequence of my work here on behalf of the Mohegan descendants of the absolutely pivotal 1704 precedent on the jurisdiction issue, namely the case of *Mohegan Indians v. Connecticut*, there is at least a hope that Canada will benefit from the example. My feeling and belief is that if the truth can come out somewhere in North America, once out, its exposition will lead to the rehabilitation of the rule of law everywhere, and therefore to the human achievement of justice as the application of truth to affairs. The only hope left, that I can see at any rate, that the rule of law will be rehabilitated in Canada regardless of what eventually transpires here in the United States, is that the Law Society of Upper Canada will seize this disciplinary proceeding against me as an opportunity. An opportunity to fulfil the society's mission to uphold the rule of law, which can never be achieved so long as the truth about the law continues to be sidelined and stonewalled. Unless the Law Society of Upper Canada now will take upon itself the role of investigating its own complicity, and therefore by necessary implication the judges' and the police's, I do not know of any alternative institution in our society to which to have recourse. For I believe that I have exhausted all other conceivable legal avenues, from motions before judges such as that filed before Judge Friesen in the present proceeding, to the attempted citizen's arrests of judges and police (for which I was convicted and reprimanded by the Law Society previously, even though the Law Society recognized the fact of the genocide and the fact that the judges still have not addressed the law). I do not know of any remaining and yet untried means of inaugurating legal process into the legal truth of the said legal statements, that I am professionally obliged and legally entitled to put forward on behalf of my native clients, who continue to be the victims of the legal establishment's ongoing unconstitutional assumption of jurisdiction which *prima facie* constitutes misprision of treason and fraud and arguably constitutes complicity in genocide.

11. The legal establishment's problem is that there is not, even arguably, a basis for refuting the truth of my statements precisely because the existing law is so extraordinarily simple, clear and plain. Even so, the obscene absurdity, now, is that the case of *R v. Bruce Clark*, wherein I was convicted of contempt by a jurisdiction-less newcomer court sitting in unceded Indian territory, by a judge who refused to address constitutional law refuting his assumption of jurisdiction, presently is being treated in Canada as if it were a precedent establishing newcomer court jurisdiction upon such territory, on the basis of Judge Friesen's bare-faced lie that the jurisdiction issue was addressed on its merits on some 40 different previous occasions when I had raised it before other Canadian courts. Yet on every single such previous occasion the issue was stonewalled, rather than addressed, and therefore the international and constitutional law legislation bearing directly upon that issue consistently has been evaded. Thus, as always in the situation where genocide is in progress, the "big lie" is its tool. Here the wielder of the tool is the court system, whose task it is to uphold the rule of law that its actions are trashing, and for this reason the casualty of this particular big lie is not just the native victims of the genocide in question, but the rule of law itself, and therefore all people, for justice depends upon the application under the rule of law of truth to affairs. No judge in Canada, so far, has addressed those instruments. The Supreme Court of Canada has some 20 times ruled that the jurisdiction

issue and judicial complicity in those crimes is not important and has denied leave to appeal, so avoiding publicly addressing the said law. That holding is so self-evidently exculpatory and fraudulent as to constitute evidence of the judges' criminal intent. For if those instruments did not say what I say they say, the judges would, long ago, have addressed the issue and the wording of the constitutive instruments which resolve the issue, and on that basis identified my error in law.

12. The discipline staff's present pretext seems to be that my *actions* were "unbecoming", in circumstances where the court record makes apparent that it was my *statements* that constituted the "unforgivable" essence the problem. Thus, rather than address the message that I bear and can prove, the legal establishment continues, as witness the present disciplinary proceeding, to intimidate and to neutralize the messenger, and thereby to suppress the exposition of the truth. Even if my actions, standing alone, have been un- . conventional, the question whether this has been 'unbecoming' can not, legitimately, be addressed in isolation from the truth of my statements. For if my statements are true, or even arguable – that judges and lawyers and police unconstitutionally are committing misprision of treason and fraud and complicity in genocide – then unusual, and perhaps even desperate, steps are justified to apprehend this profoundly serious assault upon the integrity of the rule of law.

/s/
_____

Bruce Allan Clark

Sworn before me this 4th day
of September, 1998.
/s/
_____

Notary Public

LAW SOCIETY OF UPPER CANADA

IN THE MATTER OF THE *Law Society Act*;

AND IN THE MATTER OF Bruce Allan Clark, of the City of Granville, NY, a Barrister and Solicitor.

FACTUM OF SOLICITOR

ISSUE

1. From the solicitor's perspective the issue is whether discipline counsel and those instructing her should be indicted for malicious prosecution that aids and abets the Canadian legal establishment's crime in progress of complicity in genocide, a concomitant of which issue is whether the charge against the solicitor should be dismissed as an abuse of process.

FACT

2. At all material times the solicitor acted either as agent or as counsel for natives who were defending the integrity of the rule of law against the non-native legal establishment's self-interested refusal to address the law indicting it for misprision of treason and fraud and complicity in genocide in virtue of its unconstitutional assumption of jurisdiction over natives in relation to arguably unceded territory.

LAW

3. The law was settled internationally by *Sublimus Deus, 1537* and the *Convention for the Prevention and Punishment of the Crime of Genocide, 1948* and constitutionally by *Mohegan Indians v. Connecticut, 1704* and far from being repealed or purportedly judicially overruled (as if that were constitutionally possible) has since legislatively been saved and judicially evaded.

ARGUMENT

4. The charges against the solicitor are intended to suppress truth and therefore are at variance with the Law Society's mission to protect the public interest in the implementation of justice as the application of truth to affairs under the rule of law.

DISPOSITION REQUESTED

5. The solicitor respectfully asks that the society address the legislation and precedents identified above and then discipline itself for "conduct unbecoming" beginning with a public apology to the aboriginal people of Canada; or, alternatively, to postpone disbarment until after final disposition of the accompanying motion record and factum in 99CV9070 *Ginoogaming Nation (Long Lake #58) v. Canada and Ontario.*

DATED: February 26, 1999.   Respectfully
submitted,

                                             /s/ _____

                                             Bruce Clark

In that last document, dated 26 February 1999, I begged the Law Society to let the native people in Ontario have at least one meaningfully complete day in court at which their jurisdiction argument might at last be presented and defended, by me, the only lawyer, from all that appears, who is ready, willing, and able to carry out that particular legalistic function.

Up to that juncture I had opposed the attempt to disbar me on the ground that it constituted an endeavour to pre-empt from public scrutiny in court the jurisdiction argument that previous courts had consistently evaded on any number of pretexts. Now I pleaded with the Law Society, in the alternative, to go ahead and disbar me, but subject only to these clients having this one last chance to have their side addressed. Ample historical precedents exist to argue that even if the

Law Society disagreed with my clients and me on the law, the Society was duty bound to uphold my clients' right to have their say. The general adage is that justice must not only be done but be seen to be done. In the aboriginal rights context, the Royal Proclamation of 1763 expressed this general constitutional legislative intent even more strongly: it had been enacted because a recognition of aboriginal rights was inherently "just and reasonable" and because the crown's specific intent was "to the end that the Indians may be convinced of our Justice and Determined Resolution to remove all reasonable Cause of Discontent." Or, as the Supreme Court of Canada held in *Ontario v. Canada* (1895), the Indians must be treated by the crown's legal establishment with "not only justice, but generosity."

Instead, the Law Society moved quickly to head off my native clients' argument by making my disbarment immediate, thereby virtually assuring that the case would be thrown out without the issue being addressed.

The Law Society endorsed, without separate reasons, the committee's report that these clients' legal argument had been addressed on its merits and rejected by the courts on some forty previous occasions. The committee had referred to and adopted the blatantly transparent lie by the judge who used that as an excuse for convicting me for criminal contempt of court. Neither that judge nor the committee referred to and quoted the supposed previous judicial analyses in any of the supposed forty cases. There are, of course, none.

I pointed this fact out in my reply documents filed with the Law Society. But the documents were apparently never read by the Law Society, or, if read, were disregarded without reasons.

The Indians will try to go it alone, in accordance with their affidavit that I filed on their behalf just before the disbarment took effect.

AFFIDAVIT APPENDED TO REPLY TO CANADA

We, Rayno Fischer, Frances Abraham, Alec Fischer, Agnes Fischer, Charlotte Legarde, Mabel Finlayson, Christine Shebagabow, William Legarde and George Muckaday, TO THE BEST OF OUR KNOWLEDGE, INFORMATION AND BELIEF MAKE OATH AND SAY:

1. We are the family heads of the family hunting grounds territories of the Ginoogaming Nation (Long Lake #58) and, as such, we are the plaintiff, the traditional aboriginal government of the native nation of the Long Lake drainage basin, and we give this affidavit in reply to Canada's motion to strike down our statement of claim and to evade or delay the addressing of the law concerning the preliminary and indeed only issue: court jurisdiction relative to native versus newcomer jurisdictional disputes.

2. Our statement simply says, in legal language, what the native elders before us and their elders before them have always said. We Indians were on this land first and the taking of it from us by the newcomers destroys us contrary to the great law of respect, which we believe binds the newcomers no less than it does us and all other life forms.

3. We have always known that we are beat before we start in the courts of the newcomers, precisely because those courts are the newcomers' creations. Not ours. And also not independent and impartial third-party courts which are neither native nor newcomer.

4. We believe our legal counsel Bruce Clark when he tells us that the law of the newcomers says the same thing as the great law of respect; and that, correspondingly, we are entitled to independent and impartial third-party adjudication in accordance with the rule of law, which is what he says was confirmed for international and constitutional law purposes by the *Order in Council (Great Britain) of 9 March 1704* in the matter of *Mohegan Indians v. Connecticut.*

5. It seems natural law to us that Canada is supposed to protect our unceded lands against the province of Ontario. Our understanding of oral history is that the kings and queens of England promised that the crown would always protect Indians from injustice. And we believe Bruce Clark when he tells us that section 109 of the *Constitution Act, 1867* confirms that the province's claims are "subject to" our unceded Indian "Interest."

6. We believe him when he says that section 91(24) put onto Canada the duty of "Protection" that Bruce says was promised Indians by the *Royal Proclamation of 1763.* And we understand that section 90 entrusted to Canada the power to disallow any provincial legislation that pretended to make us "subject to" the province rather than the other way round as guaranteed by section 109.

7. We also know that Canada and her courts and Ontario and her courts have broken faith with the Indian people and the rule of law, by helping each other to assume jurisdiction over our lands without first purchasing them from us as required by the great law of respect and the *Royal Proclamation of 1763.* The result has been and continues to be the ecocide of our lands and waters and genocide of our people.

8. We have the impression that Canada and the lawyers and judges in Ontario would like to get rid of our counsel Bruce Clark. We believe the reason is to steer us to other lawyers who may well be at least as "able" as Dr Clark, but who are not "ready" in terms of preparation or "willing" in terms of courage to speak the whole truth about the law and the newcomers' criminal breaches of it. We believe that we would be better off with no lawyer than with a lawyer labouring under a conflict of interest.

9. If we are denied the services in court of our counsel of choice then we will represent ourselves *pro se*, in which event we do not wish to attend for oral argument against lawyers and do therefore waive our right to be present if oral arguments are scheduled by the court.

10. If we act *pro se* we rest our case upon the written words filed on our behalf by Bruce Clark, all of which we adopt as our own.

11. And we rely upon this our affidavit, read in light of those written words, as our argument.

12. Our address for service if we act *pro se* will remain c/o Bruce Clark, ...

/s/
_____

Rayno Fischer

/s/
_____

Alec Fischer

/s/
_____

Frances Abraham

/s/
_____

Agnes Fischer

/s/
_____

Charlotte Legarde

/s/
_____

Christine Shebagabow

/s/
_____

Mabel Finlayson

/s/
_____

William Legarde

/s/
_____

George Muckaday

JOINTLY AND SEVERALLY SWORN BEFORE ME
at the Hamlet of Caramat, in the District of Thunder Bay,
this 15th day of March 1999.
Roger C. McCraw
Justice of the Peace
N.W.R. Prov. of Ont.

CONCLUSION

For humankind to progress, North American society must rehabilitate the rule of law domestically. The first stage in any such rehabilitation is to address the international and constitutional law, as it is written, without restricting the focus to the federal, state, and provincial law that conflicts with and is overridden by the international and constitutional law. Until the judiciary addresses the higher law, there is no prospect that the law can rule.

If and when the rule of law is rehabilitated, North American society can and should debate the appropriateness of the international and constitutional law, as it presently is written. That law was premised on the segregation of society into racially defined enclaves, which may be an outmoded concept. If so, the concept should be repealed, or a phasing-out process inaugurated, by way of revising the international law conventions concerning the rights of indigenous peoples, and by way of amending the complementary constitutional law of the United States and Canada.

The great challenge, the one for which a structural solution must be found if civilization is to progress beyond its present condition, is how to make the world's judiciary apply the law, whatever the law, as it is written. Segregation versus integration is and will remain an ongoing debate. The final solution is not in how the balance is resolved for the time being in any given generation, but in the structural integrity of the judicial branch. It is to this end that the world needs an international court to judge the national judges. If the latter can be kept true to the great principles of the law on which humankind has reached consensus, such as the law precluding genocide, there will be no genocide, for it will be apprehended domestically. If the national judges cannot be controlled, however, there is no point in having an international penal court to try others. This is the lesson to be learned from the legacy of genocide in North America.

The reserve system fosters an artificial and unreal illusion of separateness and inequality or privilege. It fosters a form of race capital in which natives are encouraged to expect a return on their genetic investment and to feel defrauded when its dividends are not materially satisfying. In the end, it is all built on a lie: that natives and newcomers are so fundamentally different as to require separate legal regimes based on race for their governance. It would be better for the existing law to be acknowledged until it is changed to accommodate the factual reality of modern and future society. For once existing law is acknowledged, the task of reforming it can begin.

At the present time the international and constitutional law indicates, first, that natives have the right of territorial jurisdiction until they voluntarily relinquish it; and, second, the corresponding remedy of third-party adjudication relative to the question of whether they have in fact relinquished the right in any particular region. But the legal establishment of the United States and Canada stonewalls the issue and therefore the legislation and precedents that resolve it. The rule of law cannot function when the law is pre-empted from consideration. And when the rule of law is precluded, structurally, justice as the application of truth to affairs joins it in the waste bin.

Canada is negotiating agreements with natives which, once concluded, become constitutionally entrenched pursuant to section 35(1) of the *Constitution Act, 1982*. Each of these agreements permanently assigns territorial jurisdiction to bodies politic, membership in which is based on race. By this means, racial segregation for legal purposes is entrenched constitutionaly. No less ruefully, these agreements are being negotiated on the basis of a fraudulent misrepresentation of law: that the natives do not have recourse to the remedy of third-party adjudication if and when the negotiations reach an impass. Worse, the native negotiators represent the present generation of collaborating natives, whose history has been to aid and abet the ethnic cleansing of the "all my relations" culture in favour of materialistic facsimiles of the dominant culture. In this skewed process, both the rule of law and the vindication of the wisdom of the elders is precluded. A few profit; humankind does not.

The United States's fraud is more in-your-face. Since 1871 it has refused to engage in the pretence of negotiating at all. Like Canada, it invades and then dictates terms of settlement, as if there had been a repeal of the international and constitutional law as recognized and affirmed in the formative years by the Supreme Court. Each year, Congress debates or manoeuvres behind the scenes for an end to the special status and privileges that earlier Congresses and courts supplied as palliatives to substitute for the previously established rights and remedies of international and constitutional law.

Native culture in its essential sense, of fidelity to the principles of sharing and respect, was characterized by the conservation of natural resources. This was so because of native religious inhibitions and the lack of the technological capacity to exploit. Now, with only a few individual heroic exceptions, the ancient values of sharing and respect among natives, and the inhibitions and technology underpinning them, appear to have been replaced by what Keynes identified as the universal human condition: the quest to satisfy infinite wants. Baby Suggs said troubles exist because the white race doesn't know when to stop. But maybe the problem is the human race.

My own experience has been that the native governments and organizations with enough money to wage the legal contest vindicating the aboriginal right of third-party adjudication ultimately prefer to spend it on personal consumption, rather than on advancing the principle of justice as the application of truth to affairs. Indeed those native governments and organizations have an interest in common with the non-native legal establishment in positively evading truth. It indicts them for acting in concert to suppress, with genocidal consequence, the previously established native culture under which greed was tempered. Rather than force themselves to address the international and constitutional law that indicts them for their role in the genocide, the natives who profit cooperate with the non-native legal establishment to perpetuate a genocidal system of race-based Indian governments and organizations, under the fraudulent pretence they are protecting the very native culture they are destroying.

Over and above accountability for complicity in genocide, the risk presented by third-party adjudication to those natives who profiteer is that the existing international and constitutional law, once perceived and declared by the third-party adjudicator, will be seen for what it is: a legal regime that segregates on the basis of race. Any such regime arguably is inherently illegal in a world based on the principle of human equality for legal purposes, as ours is supposed to be en route to becoming. When what the existing law actually says is recognized, it will at that instant also be seen that the existing law deserves to be repealed, as an anachronism. But until the repeal has occurred, by due process, the rule of law requires that the existing law be respected, not suppressed by the legal establishment.

In contrast with the *profiteering* natives, some culturally *native* natives are willing to risk the exposition and reform of the existing law in consequence of third-party adjudication, but they have neither the means nor the connections to fight the legal fight, particularly now that I have been disbarred. Under the present regime, their essential values of sharing and respect are trodden down, and they feel as crushed as their values. Change introduces hope for the resurrection of those values, under some new regime, one possibly not dominated by the profiteering natives and the corrupt legal establishment.

Since the fraud occurs under the auspices of federal law and treaty law, in wilful blindness to the paramount and conflicting international and constitutional law, the rule of law and justice as the application of truth to affairs are being destroyed along with the few remaining culturally native natives. From this perspective, the average person is being victimized as well. The common person has an interest in justice and the rule of law. Yet critics of the native rights industry and the legal establishment are smeared and discredited on the grounds that to argue against the existing and future race-based government system is itself racist.

I think we all, not only natives and newcomers but all persons on earth, will have either to evolve to a condition above the one we presently occupy, perhaps by resorting to the underused portions of our massive human brains, or we all will eventually overconsume nature and destabilize, and perhaps even destroy, ourselves in the process. The limitation on our consumption can, and indeed threatens to, occur under an heretofore unparalleled imperial tyranny, wherein the strong will continue culling the competing weaker consumers of nature's increasingly scarce resources on the basis of a biased legal establishment's perversion of the integrity of the rule of law. The globe becomes the new Indian country, awaiting the further extension of the North Atlantic nations' *lebensraum* and genocide by chicanery.

Alternatively, universal human equality can exist pursuant to a democratic system of global justice as the application of truth to affairs. That, to me at any rate, would be paradise: the place at which sharing and respect intersect with justice under the rule of law, based on the principle of third-party adjudication.

Humankind can learn from the experience of genocide by chicanery in North America a lesson of structural significance not only to the prevention of that crime in future eras and in other parts of the world, but also to the integrity of the rule of law and the achievement of justice generally. The spirits of the victims perhaps can be left in peace, if not requited, by the acceptance of their tragic gift of this lesson to all the generations yet unborn, and to the shared and respected creation.

ACKNOWLEDGMENTS

Although I have not named names, for fear of missing the point that all the players are stock characters in a scenario only too familiar to the human condition, there are some names that must be acknowledged, for these are not standard people by any measure.

Tsemhu'qw and Lahalus are the Lil'Wat names of Harold "Chubb" Pascal and his wife, Loretta, whose courage matches their convictions and whose convictions, in a profoundly unjust legal system, have brought them great suffering, but greater and more lasting honour. They also oversaw my formal adoption into the Lil'Wat nation, witnessed by other traditionals of native nations from the four surrounding directions, at which I was given the name W'lawpsh – meaning bighorn ram that watches for danger and leaps from crag to crag.

The "Wolverine" is the *nom de guerre* acquired by the Shushwap William "Jones" Ignace during the course of the armed standoff at Gustafsen Lake in the summer of 1995. His wife, Flo, stood beside him and shared the burden. Like Tsemhu'qw and Lahalus, they are among the last of the North American native warriors who have sacrificed themselves as defenders of the physical integrity of the land, water, and air for the sake of the spiritual integrity of all beings.

James "O.J." Pitawanakwat is an Ojibway from Manitoulin Island who stood with the Wolverine and Flo at Gustafsen Lake and, with them, was unjustly jailed for persevering for justice under the rule of law.

Verna Friday is a Temagami elder, strong and brave and doubly resilient for carrying the same burden as any other warrior while harbouring, as native women must and do, the native culture. Because of them, this culture still lives, despite the adversity of 500 years of genocide designed to eradicate it. Steve Snake, Verna's partner, is an artist whose sensitivity is matched with the valour that he and Verna together symbolize.

Shelagh Franklin is a non-native woman warrior for justice as the application of truth to affairs. She is ready to stand or fall in the cause of others, including her daughter Possum, the beginning of the seven generations that will follow her.

John Shafer is a true believer in justice, a tireless worker without compensation or credit, who has devoted his life to this cause.

The Mohawk-Cree Dacajeweiah (Splitting-the-Sky), or "Doc," or John Hill, sets an example, writing his memoirs, proving that the pen can be personally more healing and publicly mightier than the sword for the native people in their struggle for justice. Sandra, his wife, and their children, Angela, Dylan, Rainbow, and Ché-Thunder, have stood by him and helped him to stand when the fatigue from injustice might have swamped lesser or lonelier men.

Tthowgwelth (Sound-of-Many-Copper-Shields), or Lavina White, and Bill Lightbowm are, respectively, a Haida princess and a Kootenai warrior, blessed with many children and grandchildren. Throughout their lives they have selflessly served the native people of British Columbia and justice in general.

Andrea Bear-Nicholas and her husband, Daryl Nicholas, are distinguished Maliseet elders, resident in that native nation's ancestral homeland, what newcomers call New Brunswick, and are, respectively, an accomplished historian and a ground-breaking native language teacher.

The Mohawk-born, Navajo-naturalized, Hopi-messenger Craig Carpenter and his German wife, Silke von Manowski, together shelter and spread the gospel of the spirit present in all things. Wah-Hay-Low (traditional chief) Willard Rhoades and Mildred, his wife, respectively of the Itsatawi and Wennemem bands of the Pitt River tribe, embody, epitomize, and carry on the trust and hope of native Californians, as does their friend, the Achomawi Vernon Johnson.

I also pay tribute to Chief Denton George and his councillors of the Ochapowace First Nation in Saskatchewan and their elder-adviser Joe Crowe of the neighbouring Kahkewistahaw First Nation; and the several native elders who are the heads of the traditional family hunting grounds territories of the Ginoogaming First Nation (Longlake 58) and their trusted assistant Bernard Abraham.

Ron Roberts, Tim Stoddard, Eddie Vangelder, Ray Lake, and the other Mohicans of the Hudson River drainage basin in New York and Vermont bravely, in the *Liberty Island* case, carry the torch lit by their ancestors for all indigenous people in 1704 in the case of *Mohegan Indians v. Connecticut*. Tom Fennell, an Irish-American, honourably and selflessly has worked with these Mohicans in their endeavour to salvage, and rebuild from the ashes of genocide, their native identity, culture, and environment.

The Lil'Wat medicine man (though he might decline the honour of that label, he lives the reality) Johnny Jones offered his native life to the newcomers' bulldozer poised to break in upon sacred ground. He and his newcomer wife, Liz, and their young daughters, epitomize living the life of sharing and respect.

In spite of the stranglehold that the legal establishment has over events, there beats in North America a heart of goodness – the ethic of the average people, the public, which, given the opportunity, would like to see the golden rule of "doing onto others" followed in practice: the reciprocation of sharing and respect. Because I am Web illiterate I had no idea until recently just how much work in keeping with that generous ideology had been done by so many people: those who, though anonymous, maintained a watch on the Internet.

As I pay homage to and am inspired by the courage and integrity of every one of these persons, I also recognize these same qualities in my wife, Margaret, and our children, David, Zoë, and Beau – my family, solace, and fulfilment. During the Gustafsen Lake affair I asked Margaret and each of the children individually whether it was appropriate for me to go into the encampment, given the possibility that I might die there, along with those inside, for our defence of the rule of law, and whether the family wished to be together. Each person thought deeply, and each had distinct reasons both for and against the proposition. We all decided to make the commitment, not necessarily for Indians or for anyone else's cause, but for our own personal sense of honour and love and hope. Not to kill but, if necessary, to be killed.

The director of McGill-Queen's University Press, Philip Cercone, showed compassion for the plight of our family when times were darkest and encouraged me to write about, rather than be smothered by, the overwhelming injustice that had befallen us. Marketing manager Bruce Walsh was able to capture the essence of the book in a few well-chosen words. Finally, I would also like to thank my editor, Rosemary Shipton, who, as Margaret identified, has proved to be both a convergent and a divergent thinker in her substantive and line edit of the book.

My mother and I on my fourth birthday.

Margaret and I on our wedding day: forever in blue jeans.

My first summer on Bear Island.

Margaret, Zoë, and David picking blueberries on Bear Island.

"Native and Newcomer." On the left is Charlene Mathias, my son David's Indian friend on Bear Island. In the background is the former Hudson's Bay Company factor's house in which the Temagamis let my family live on the island.

Our neighbour Yvonne Katt taking care of Beau in our house on Bear Island.

Margaret's parents, Bill and Lucy Book, visit us on Bear Island.

My favourite office on Bear Island, outside the house in front of the fire, where I worked during the day reading law and in the evenings reading bedtime stories. Here David has already checked out.

David, Zoë, and Beau in our mobile vehicle on Bear Island. There were no cars on the island, so this transportation worked for kids, groceries, wood, and other supplies.

Margaret, our kids, and hiking and picnicking friends on the peak of the lookout tower mountain on Bear Island.

Bottom row, seated left to right Verna Friday and her uncle Philip Potts, the father of the former Temagami chief Gary Potts. *Back row, standing left to right* Verna's brother Tommy Friday and sister Michelle O'Leary. The Friday-Potts clan were originally Crees from James Bay who married into the Temagami Nation at the turn of the twentieth century. Philip tried with great patience to teach me something of trapping and understanding nature.

Tsemhu'qw, Lahalus, Margaret, and I at the train station in The Hague, where we went to try to deal with the International Court of Justice. The picture frame was lying abandoned beside the track. We were used to being framed as criminals in Canada and seized the chance to illustrate the point.

Tsemhu'qw and Lahalus at the Lil'Wat road blockade on 6 November 1990, the day of the mass arrests of Lil'Wats for criminal contempt of court. This was Harold and Loretta's twenty-fifth anniversary and Loretta still thanks Harold for his thoughfulness in providing her with "silver bracelets" (handcuffs).

Top row, left to right Flora Sampson; her husband, William "Jones" Ignace, a.k.a. the Wolverine; Dacajeweiah, or John "Splitting-the-Sky" Hill; his wife, Sandra Bruderer; and their children Rainbow, Dylan, Ché-Thunder, and Angela.

Tthowgwelth (Sound-of-Many-Copper-Shields) or Lavina White, Haida princess, and her grandson Anthony, taken in British Columbia.

Chief Denton George of the Ochapowace First Nation, taken in Saskatchewan.

A moment of relaxation in the spring of 1997 at the Upsalquitch River in New Brunswick, as I worked for the Listuguj Mi'cmaqs.

APPENDIX

CONTENTS

INTRODUCTION   265

LIBERTY ISLAND CASE

Petitions to the President   267

  August 20, 1997   267

  September 19, 1997   274

  January 7, 1998   275

Complaint to the Court   284

Motion by the United States to Dismiss the Complaint   285

Reply to United States' Motion   289

PLAINS CASE

Claim to the Court   291

Motion by Canada to Dismiss the Claim   292

Reply to Canada's Motion   293

Motion by Saskatchewan to Dismiss the Claim   295

Reply to Saskatchewan 's Motion   301

Motion by Indians for Immediate Judgment   304

Motion by Indians for Court to Listen to Bruce Clark on the Law   305

Court Decision Refusing to Listen   309

Indian Appeal from the Refusal   310

Court Decision Dismissing the Claim   312

Indian Appeal from the Dismissal   315

Response of Canada to the Appeal from the Refusal to Listen   316

Response of Canada to the Appeal from the Dismissal of the Claim 319

Court of Appeal Decisions 321

Application by Indians to Supreme Court for Leave to Appeal 322

NOTES: INTERNATIONAL AND CONSTITUTIONAL LAW 325

Introduction

It has been a literary trade adage that the rule of law as actually practised, and as recorded in court documents, is not a topic amenable to public consumption; that legal language, and legal arguments, are opaque and therefore of marginal, if any, interest to all but academics and professional jurists. In part at least this has been because academics and lawyers as a class are trained to write formulaicly, precisely so they can understand each other wherever they may practise, local idiosyncrasies and communication conventions notwithstanding. The jargon is universal, and its universality serves a sensible purpose. But it can become a code, and in doing so defeat another, perhaps even more important, purpose. For the rule of law belongs to the people, not to the professionals, whose sacred trust is only to administer or comment upon the rule. The rule of law is a servant of the people, not a master over them; and, to serve, it must be understood by the people at large.

Fortunately, significant progress is being made in connection with the democratization of the rule of law. With the O.J. Simpson trial and the attempted impeachment of President Clinton, millions of ordinary folk were invited into the legal strategies as they evolved, much as if the people were on the prosecution and defence teams, almost as lawyers or at least as intimate observers. Mass brain damage did not result. To the contrary, the public was found to have a large capacity for seeing through the language and the arguments to the points that the lawyers' and the commentators' words and arguments either made clear or obscured, as the tactic might be.

In this book I have made some quite specific allegations concerning what "the law" actually says. But "the law," at any given time and place, consists in the words of the legislation and the precedents that record it. It does not consist in what a lawyer or other commentator says it says. Since "the law" belongs to the people, they should decide for themselves whether it really says what I, for example, have in this book said it says. They should have the opportunity to read, and to compare, what the law says as I quote it as against what it says as quoted by other lawyers or commentators who may have a contrasting perspective.

For these reasons I have prevailed upon my publisher to allow me to include a detailed appendix of court case documents. One set concerns the Liberty Island case pending in the United States; the other is the Plains case in Canada. They put the basic law in practical contexts.

As prelude to the Liberty Island case documents, I have included a set of petitions to President Clinton concerning the real "last of the Mohicans," a group into which I have been adopted as a citizen. The ancestors of this particular group took the brunt of the trauma of the British invasion of North America. An overview of their story is recounted in the appended petitions that I prepared for the purpose of the Mohicans' avoiding the necessity of litigation. The fact that this attempt was to no avail set the stage for a series of court cases in both the United States and Canada, beginning with the Liberty Island case.

The Canadian case that follows adopts the same law as is set out in the Liberty Island case, that law being the constitutive legislation and precedents for British North America in general. The appended Canadian court documents then proceed to add additional Canadian content, which itself is of interest to the United States' legal context. For the Supreme Court of the United States has equated that country's post-independence constitutional law with the pre-revolutionary law established by Great Britain, and Canada has continued this law. Now, things equal to the same thing are equal to each other. So, the United States' law and the Canadian law, being both equal to the same British colonial law, are equal to each other. Different labels, same contents.

The proof is to be found in the words and arguments of the attorneys general and the courts of the United States and Canada. As will be seen, they have not yet identified and quoted any legislation or precedents that are capable of contradicting the law I have quoted. Instead, they have evaded the issue – or so it seems to me. The reader will, I hope, judge for her- or himself.

As you read, bear in mind the constitutional injunction that no government "do presume upon any *Pretence* whatever to grant" lands before purchasing them from the Indians. Then imagine a marine drill sergeant repeatedly yelling in your face that he "can not hear you" each and every time you point out the simple, and obvious, fact that governments are in breach of the injunction. If you can see that picture you can, as through Indian eyes, see "justice" as it is practised in the courts of the United States and Canada.

Liberty Island Case

August 20, 1997

Re: Mohegan Renaissance in the Hudson Valley Homeland: The Problem of Genocide Attributable to the Eclipse of Justice in America and the Solution of Third-Party Adjudication

Dear President Clinton:

Pursuant to the *1st Amendment* right *"to petition the Government for a redress of grievances"* I am writing to request a letter from you acknowledging the existence of the Western Mohegan Tribe & Nation of New York so that we can fulfill our rightful role as participants in the life of the Hudson River valley. We are the valley's original inhabitants, witnesses to its conversion from paradise to wasteland, and now to the beginnings of its return to ecological health, as its economy shifts from industrial to recreational tourism.

I am not writing so that this native nation can become a welfare recipient of programs and services under federal law. These we do not want and will not accept. I am writing so that we can regain our liberty under anterior and superior natural, international and constitutional law, and on the basis of that liberty to work in harmony with the newcomers for a better future for us all in this society of natives and newcomers and their reviving nature-based economy.

According to our oral history the Mohegan tribe originally consisted of the council fires of 9, later 8, autonomous Mohegan nations, all of whom annually met at a great council fire on Schodac Island just south of the present city of Albany near the center of the Hudson River drainage basin, our ancestral homeland.

My ancestor the famous Mohegan sachem Uncas although in later life achieving notoriety for his political and military exploits in Connecticut was himself born by the Hudson River.

Oftentimes our several Mohegan nations were given different names by different outside groups encountering them, such as the Dutch or the English or even neighboring native tribes. For example, the Smithsonian Institution's *Handbook of American Indians* (1907) gives 49 different phonetic renditions for us ranging from the Dutch-speakers term "Mahicans" to the English-speakers "Mohegans" both meaning "Wolf People," and including the "Pequots" meaning "Destroyers," who speak the identical and unique Y-dialect of the Algonkian linguistic family.

In consequence of the trauma of the European invasion a diaspora of much of our Mohegan tribe occurred. Some members migrated or fled eastward down the Connecticut River system immediately to the east of the Hudson River drainage basin, into Connecticut and Massachusetts. From thence some others carried on eventually to Wisconsin. Some individuals blended with adjacent and distant native peoples and acquired citizenship in other native nations. Other Mohegans stayed behind in what is now New York State, but went underground into anonymity for reasons of survival.

I am the sachem for those who stayed, whom I represent both by birthright and by confirmation.

We style ourselves the "Western Mohegan Tribe & Nation of New York" in order to avoid being confused with those of us who established alternative homelands elsewhere.

Many of my ancestors became ministers, preachers and professionals. Publicly we blended with the newcomers. Privately we held our Indian meetings in the Indian Way and never forgot who we were and are. For example, the 1928–30 diary of my aunt Mary records the fact that her father (my grandfather) was grand sachem of the "*Mohegan Tribe and Nation NY Conn Ma Vt*" and that when he sojourned in the territories of his fellow Mohegans in Connecticut he sat with them in their councils. Similarly, when the sachems of any of the Mohegan nations of Connecticut visited here in New York they could sit with us in our council.

Our oral history of continuity in New York State is at least in part confirmed by the *New York Census of 1845* which at one page identifies the "*Mohegan tribe New York*" as consisting in some "*154*" persons and on another page enumerates among the "*Distinctive populations*" a total of "*54*" as "*New York Mohegans.*"

Later, in the above mentioned diary for 1928 the "*Mohegan Trible Rolls*" for the "*Granville, Hebron, Hartford, Wells, Troy, Catskill, Hudson, Ulster, Utica, Falton, Johnstown*" portion of the "*Mohegan Tribe and Nation NY Conn Ma VT*" enumerates 152 persons as constituting the "*Mohegan Tribe NY.*" It lists the "*Mohegan Village and Towns*" as "*Scodiac Troy Warcnawonknong (Salem) Mamekoting (Hebron) Lake Austin (Chilohocki).*"

Even as late as 1928 the newcomers were still trying to remove us from our homeland in New York. The December entry in the above mentioned diary for that year also identifies the "*Mohegan tong*" names for 10 Mohegan "*clans*" and that "*our great great grand Father was from Uncas*" and that "*Local People want too take everyone who is Mohegan away just for there land dad said the govenor of New York will always help the Mohegan tribe because we have save this Country from the French ...*"

Again, the February 1929 diary entry records comments by a "*Chief Tepec*" in New Jersey who: "*talks of a time when he was a boy and his Mother and Father told him about the wars his Father and great grand Father all those men were Mohegan Sachames Owaneco Uncas and many more our great great great grand Father was with President Washington at the Crossing. the Mohegan People kept our Country being in hands of the French. We have always been helping the English and Colonist to keep Freedom for all Americans. dad said that our family in New York are the last of the real Mohegan People.*"

Similarly, the diary entry for April 2, 1930 records: "*The Mohegan people are going to demand payment for all the lands we own. New York still owes the Mohegans for many thousands of acres of land we have land in almost every County from here too New York City.*"

My grandfather Arthur E. Smith, a full blood Mohegan resident all his life in New York State, wrote *Rural Legends* published by John B. Alden Company in New York in 1892. His poems "In the Adirondacks," "Beside the Hudson," "When I go Home Again," "Ode" and "Hudson River" concern our connection with the Hudson River homeland, the geno-cidal pressure on our people, the ecocidal pressure on our lands and waters, and our de-fence of American liberty.

According to the oral history of my family our particular ancestors assisted the new-comer Americans to survive and eventually to flourish in the Hudson River valley and also in New England, from the earliest times to and including the *Pequot War of 1637, King Philip's War of 1676*, the *Revolution* and the *War of 1812*. For example, on July 22, 1979 my aunt Mary wrote the local historian and Justice of the Peace Harold Craig of Hebron NY and informed him: "*I also have a Cote of Arm's from England in 1664 or 1665.*" The coat of arms which hung over my grandfather's bed was given to our family in consider-ation of our role as a military ally of the British against the French and their Indian allies.

Thus, Mr President, our oral history confirms the existence and continuity of the West-ern Mohegan Tribe & Nation of New York from time immemorial. Furthermore, so far as the written archival record of the newcomers is concerned to the extent that records do ex-ist they corroborate our oral history, or at least are not inconsistent with our oral history.

Now I have specifically to address the topic of the legal remedy secured to the Mohe-gans for the protection of our particular aboriginal rights. I say our "particular" aboriginal rights because we were highly regarded by the British and later by the Americans for the help we gave them as against other Indians, and I am not aware of any other native group that either was so consistently a faithful ally of the newcomers or that was acknowledged by the them to have the same legal remedy as my grandfathers and grandmothers secured for us Mohegans.

In the 1600s a Connecticut branch of our tribe made a treaty with the then royal colony of Connecticut relative to the Indian title to lands acquired by them through intermarriage with and/or conquest of the peoples who were aboriginal to that region. Subsequently a disagreement arose over whether that treaty had been intended by the parties to be as Con-necticut contended, an outright sale of land entitling Connecticut to re-sell or give the land to settlers, or as the Mohegans contended a deed in trust for Connecticut to hold the land to protect it against newcomer settlement and incursions by other Indians. Connecticut en-acted legislation dealing with the land as if that colony and its courts did have jurisdiction over it, and regarded that legislation as determinative on the ground of crown sovereignty, in any event of the contractual intent.

The Mohegans applied to Queen Anne for relief. It was held that the Connecticut legis-lation could not bind the land or the native people upon it until it was first established that the natives had sold the land to the Crown. As for the crucial question – who gets to de-cide? – Queen Anne enacted that the Connecticut Court was not sufficiently independent and impartial to be conceded that jurisdiction, without risking the integrity of the rule of law.

In order avoid that mischief the Queen in Council constitutionally adopted and applied the rule of law's essential principle – third-party adjudication – for which purpose she con-stituted a standing Court, the commissioned members of which at any given time would exclude judges appointed by either of the two governments who are competing for juris-diction.

The guarantee to the Mohegans of the remedy of third-party adjudication has never since been repealed. Subsequent to the *Revolution* and the *Peace of Paris of 1783* the Su-preme Court of the United States confirmed that the international law and constitutional law rights previously conceded to natives by Great Britain were in no way impaired or prejudiced in consequence of the fact that the United States became the successor and heir of the Crown's rights.

My native nation believes that the rule of law is critical to the society of natives and newcomers. And we submit that the extent to which the United States respects the rule of law at home, particularly when it comes to apprehending genocide, is critical to the whole world, for all nations in the global village are led in the human rights field by the United States.

The existing natural, international and constitutional law which this great country confirmed following its *Revolution* still forbids the taking of land in the absence of an Indian treaty, regardless of the statement to the contrary made by the federal *Appropriations Act of 1871*. *Sublimus Deus, 1537* legislatively settled that since the native Americans are human beings with souls rather than animals without souls, therefore as a matter of natural, international and constitutional law the newcomer Americans can acquire territorial jurisdiction if but only if they purchase the native Americans' original jurisdiction; and that should the natives' jurisdiction be usurped, their property confiscated or their persons enslaved, such usurpation, confiscation or enslavement is illegal. The *Declaration of Independence* confirmed and still confirms that when natural law (represented by the inalienable rights to life, liberty and the pursuit of happiness) conflicts with international and constitutional law (represented by the legal parameters of the mercantile system and the British-made colonial constitutions), the latter must be understood as being subject to the former.

In point of fact, however, there was never any conflict between natural law on the one hand, and international and constitutional law on the other hand. The international and constitutional law as ascertained by the original and authoritative precedent *Worcester v. Georgia* 5 Peters 1 (1832) incorporates natural law.

In sum, the native Americans' life, liberty and pursuit of happiness continues to shelter under the consensus of natural, international and constitutional law that precludes usurpation, confiscation and enslavement by newcomer Americans.

Contrary to law the Puritans of New England in the *Pequot War of 1637* and *King Philip's War of 1676* established a practice of usurpation, confiscation and enslavement of genocidal consequence for the native Americans.

Congress's *Appropriations Act of 1871* ostensibly legitimized that practice by inventing the doctrine of plenary federal jurisdiction in the aboriginal rights context. Pursuant to that doctrine Congress purported to, but could not legally have, repealed the United States' legal obligation to purchase rather than to usurp or confiscate, and thereby implicitly repealed the native Americans' previously vested natural, international and constitutional law right to life, liberty and the pursuit of happiness.

But it is legally impossible for an act of Congress to repeal a previously vested natural, international and constitutional law right in the absence of an empowering constitutional amendment. And it is equally impossible for subsequent judicial decisions to overrule a constitutional principle previously settled by an original and authoritative precedent.

To recapitulate: for natural, international and constitution law purposes the *Order in Council (Great Britain) of 9 March 1704* in the matter of *Mohegan Indians v. Connecticut* confirmed my ancestors' remedy of third-party adjudication vis-à-vis jurisdictional disputes with the newcomers' governments and courts as the rule of law remedy for the protection of our vested aboriginal right not to have our jurisdiction usurped, our territory confiscated or our liberty denied. Even so, on July 3, 1997 the New York Supreme Court denied my nation the said remedy on the ground "*The court disagrees with the defendant's argument that this court does not have jurisdiction over this matter. The Western Mohegan tribe is not federally recognized and, therefore, jurisdiction over this controversy is not preempted by the federal government. Since the bingo games are taking place in the Vil-*

lage of Granville, Washington County, State of New York, this court does have jurisdiction over the within lawsuit."

Thus the New York court chose not publicly to address the natural, international and constitutional law legislation and precedents that I identified and produced. Rather than do so, the court mistakenly assumed that I was relying on federal law to preempt the state court's jurisdiction. I was not, as so assumed, ever, relying upon federal law. To the contrary, I identified and produced for the court natural, international and constitutional law that conflicts with and is paramount over the federal law concerning gaming.

More importantly, I identified for the court the natural, international and constitutional law that not only preempts the court's assumption of jurisdiction over the application of law issue, but indicts that assumption as judicial complicity in genocide. The court did not in its reasons for judgment acknowledge the existence of the identified natural, international and constitutional law going to the issue of the court's jurisdiction, preferring the pretence that my objection to jurisdiction was based upon federal law.

The court's phrase *"federal recognition"* is the key to comprehending precisely how the genocide of native Americans today is implemented by the United States. The executive, legislative and judicial branches of the newcomers' federal and state governments advertise themselves – to themselves and to the world – as human rights practitioners in virtue of their acknowledgment of native American sovereignty. But when any given native American nation seeks actually to implement the ostensibly acknowledged native sovereignty, the native nation is met by a Catch-22 of genocidal consequence.

As a matter of bureaucratic assumption and convention, the adjective *"federal"* in the crucial phrase *"federal recognition"* is taken to signify that the recognition specifically be by the federal Bureau of Indian Affairs (BIA) or Congress. That signification imports the act of state doctrine: the legal principle which holds that no legal remedy attaches to any given right unless the government chooses in addition to acknowledge the status of the entity to assert that right. More simply put, the United States says: we respect the native sovereignty of those native nations that we recognize as native nations. It is just that we do not actually acknowledge any native groups as "nations." We have not done so since the *Appropriations Act of 1871* precluded the making of Indian treaties. that by definition recognize native groups as "nations."

From 1871 to the present, *"federal recognition"* bureaucratically has in fact been extended only to those native groups that relinquish their national status and accept in its place municipality status. This pre-condition to *"federal recognition"* is presumed to be authorized by title 25 of the *Code of Federal Regulations*, which limits the concept *"Tribe"* to entities *"recognized by the Secretary as eligible for the special programs and services from the Bureau of Indian Affairs."*

But native sovereignty by definition signifies independence from *"the special programs and services from the Bureau of Indian Affairs."*

For in the beginning the only jurisdiction constitutionally claimed by the British Crown and by its successor the United States was the preemptive right to purchase Indian territory when the natives were willing to sell. Then, the native nations occupying yet unpurchased territory were said to be *"domestic dependent nations"*: "domestic" in the sense of not "foreign"; "dependent" in the sense of under the United States' military protection as against others; and "nations" in the sense of being free from interference in any respect other than the restriction on alienation imported by the United States's preemptive right of purchase.

By 1871 the United States had adopted as its final solution to the Indian problem the policy of forced assimilation by incremental stages. First, the natives' cultural attachment to national independence over unpurchased territory surreptitiously was to be replaced by the fostering of native municipal government upon surveyed reservations. The "wild" Indians roaming at large would be replaced by "civilized" Indians attached to individually allotted plots and to defined common areas. Ultimately, the inherently offensive nature of municipal governments defined by racial criteria – culture differentiation having disappeared by effluxion of time and educational compulsion – would justify termination of special status based upon race alone. Racially segregated reservations eventually were supposed to phase out and racially egalitarian municipalities were supposed to phase in.

This experiment in social engineering visibly has failed. The mortality rates of native Americans demonstrate the genocidal consequence of this process of reneging upon the natives' previously established status as "*domestic dependent nations*" under natural, international and constitutional law.

The promotion of their alternative status as "*dependent Indian communities*" under federal law is the probable cause of the abridged life spans and the mental anguish that life without liberty engenders. The engine that drives this genocidal machine masquerading as the fulfillment of the so-called federal trust responsibility is the fraudulent pretence of federal plenary jurisdiction. The fraud consists in the legal *non sequitur* that Congress, by the bootstraps operation of ordinary legislation in the absence of an enabling constitutional aggrandizement of its inceptive power, can increase the extent of the newcomers' constitutional rights in relation to the natives' constitutional rights.

If Congress could do that, the natives would have mere privileges, not constitutional rights. If that were the case the United States Supreme Court in the constitutively definitive years was wrong in categorizing the natives' legal status as "*domestic dependent nations*" subject only to the preemptive purchase jurisdiction of the United States as the Crown's successor. But the original and authoritative precedents can not be set aside in the absence of a legislative constitutional amendment directly on point.

Assumptions and policies are not the equivalent of or a substitution for a legislative constitutional amendment. At least not in a rule of law society.

Since 1704 my native nation has been vested not only with the right of native sovereignty subject only to the newcomers' preemptive power relative to purchase, but with the legal remedy of third-party adjudication to protect that right. There is no other way that the right can be a right, as contrasted with a privilege. If the right were subject to jurisdiction of the courts constituted by the newcomers – who *prima facie* and in blindness to the natural, international and constitutional law are usurping our native jurisdiction and confiscating our native territory and thereby denying our life, liberty and pursuit of happiness, if not literally any longer murdering or enslaving us – the right would be a right without the remedy of third-party adjudication, which constitutes an oxymoron.

Where, as in the situation in which my native nation presently finds itself, the oxymoron is institutionalized such that there is no mechanism for insisting that the legislation and precedents that constitute the law be addressed and respected, the rule of law does not operate, and liberty does not exist.

My request of you, Mr President, in addition to writing a letter recognizing us is that you order the executive branch to cooperate with this native nation, to the extent jointly of submitting along with us to independent and impartial third-party adjudication or arbitration the jurisdictional dispute between your nation and mine. I believe that by doing so you will not only relieve this native nation of the genocidal pressure that bears down upon it, but you will rehabilitate the integrity of the rule of law for America and for humankind.

This native nation does not want the "*special programs and services*" offered by the BIA. We want to retain our liberty under natural, international and constitutional law rather than sell our liberty for "*special programs and services*" under federal law. We do not want to relinquish our natural, international and constitutional law status as a "*domestic dependent nation*" by accepting mere "*dependent Indian community*" status under the federal law that conflicts with the international and constitutional law. Therefore, we are not willing to attorn to the genocidally illegal assumption of jurisdiction over us by the United States pursuant to the spurious doctrine of federal plenary jurisdiction, by implicitly accepting the application of federal law by applying for "*federal recognition*" under 25 CFR in order to secure the "*special programs and services*" on offer.

To do so would be to relinquish our native sovereignty under natural, international and constitutional law, in favor of accepting delegated municipal government type powers subject to federal jurisdiction. We have pointedly avoided doing that for 400 years.

Recently we have begun to make progress with the government of the State of New York, toward negotiating a modern government-to-government solution that builds a better future for natives and newcomers living symbiotically with the ecology of the Hudson River drainage basin. We wish to entrench this mutually beneficial relationship, and therefore we take cognizance of section 7(*a*) of Chapter 26 of the *Consolidated Laws*, Laws 1909 chapter 31, entitled *Indian Law*, which provides: "*No purchase or contract for the sale of lands of Indians in this state shall be valid unless made under the authority, and with the consent of the legislature.*"

That provision appears to be based upon the 13 original states doctrine, which arguably conflicts with the reference that "*No State shall enter into any Treaty*" contained in section 10.1 of the *Constitution*. We do not want to negotiate with the State of New York only to have the United States abuse its protection obligation by attacking the symbiotic relationship established between the State and the Western Mohegan Tribe & Nation of New York. We believe that your confirmation of our previously recognized status under natural, international and constitutional law will assuage the reasonable concerns of both the State of New York and this native nation in this connection.

These are the reasons, then, that I request from you (*a*) a letter recognizing the domestic dependent nation status of the Western Mohegan Tribe & Nation of New York under natural, international and constitutional law and (*b*) instructions to the Bureau of Indian Affairs that it cooperate either to settle jurisdictional disputes with this nation without litigation or, if litigation is necessary, that same be submitted for independent and impartial third-party adjudication or arbitration.

We believe that every day that passes while the United States equivocates upon this request will aid and abet genocide contrary to the provisions of the *Genocide Convention Implementation Act of 1987 (the Proxmire Act)*. We respectfully submit that such equivocation is tantamount to a failure to protect us against invasion, which is the one and only obligation the United States owes us.

Thank you for reading and for understanding our position, and for acting with dispatch on behalf of this native nation, the State of New York, the United States and the rest of the global village for whom the United States sets the example and in whose mutual best interest it is to uphold the integrity of the rule of law and to apprehend genocide.

Very truly yours,

/s/ _____

Ronald Roberts
Sachem
Concurring:

/s/ _____

Bruce Clark, LLB, MA, PhD
Attorney General

September 19, 1997

Re: Mohegan Renaissance in the Hudson Valley Homeland: The Candidacy of the Hudson River under the American Heritage Rivers Executive Order of 11 September 1997.

Dear President Clinton:

In our Native Way, there is no such thing as coincidence. Our *1st Amendment Petition of 20 August 1997* pleaded personally with you, Mr President, to end the era of the genocide of our Native Nation. To us, the *American Heritage Rivers Executive Order of 11 September 1997* is part of the answer.

In your Newcomer Way, our Hudson River native homeland was converted from paradise to wasteland. Your ecocide of our native land meant the genocide of our native people. But the *American Heritage Rivers Order of 11 September 1997* means the night of ecogenocide is over. The millennium of healing has dawned. In a sense, the Creator's tracing of the circumference of the Circle of Life has passed the farthest point, and begun the journey home.

In our Native Way, we *are* our valley. We are the autochthonous people: our culture, that which makes us *us*, springs directly from the Mother Earth that births us and that sustains us. The brooks and streams of our Hudson River drainage basin are capillaries. Schodac Island is the heart. But the mind, the mind is Liberty Island. For in our Native Way, the Great Law is Respect. For all things. And liberty means respect. There is no such thing as coincidence.

The mind and heart of our native nation and the mind and heart of America are one. When the waters that flow past Schodac Island wash untainted at the shore upon which rests the Statue of Liberty, we all, natives and newcomers alike, will be free, and healthy, together.

And when the mind and heart of America in this way have become free and pure, the body politic that is the world can have hope. For America's is the last empire. And the artery of the last empire is in the empire State. From this juncture in history America will lead all people of the world, not just herself and her own people, out of the era of empires, into the new millennium of unity and equality based upon our Native Way: Respect.

In our *1st Amendment Petition of 20 August 1997* we asked you, Mr President, to let us *"fulfill our rightful role as participants in the life of the Hudson River valley. We are the valley's original inhabitants."* We repeat that request, now, by asking that you accept the Hudson River drainage basin into the *American Heritage Rivers Initiative*, and recognize a role for us.

In our Native Way, we have a gift for you – the Unity Paddle. Our hope is that you will choose to give it a home on Liberty Island. On its handle a red arm and a black arm rise intertwining, to blend with a yellow arm and a white arm descending from the other end, all reaching into a sacred copper coil of spirit being. *Beloved's* Baby Suggs *"learned from her sixty years as a slave and ten years free: that there was no bad luck in the world but white people – They don't know when to stop."* The *American Heritage Rivers Executive Order of 11 September 1997* signifies that America has learned.

Thank you for accepting our gift, for listening, and for understanding.

Very truly yours,

/s/
_____

Ronald Roberts
Sachem
Concurring:

/s/
_____

Bruce Clark, LLB, MA, PhD
Attorney General

Re: Supplement to Petitions
Dear President Clinton:

Recapitulation

Previously we submitted to you two (related) petitions. The first was by letter dated August 20, 1997, entitled "*1st Amendment Petition for a Redress of Grievances.*" It was for federal recognition. When read in light of the second petition dated September 19, 1997 and which concerns the *American Heritage Rivers Initiative Executive Order of 11 September 1997*, it will be apparent to you that the first petition was not for the usual sort of federal recognition. The "usual sort" of federal recognition is for the purpose of applying for "*the special programs and services from the Bureau of Indian Affairs*" referred to in s. 151.2(*b*) of Title 25 of the *Consolidated Federal Regulations* as being available to "*reorganized*" governments, such as those contemplated by the federal *Reorganization Act of 1934*. There is another, and contrasting, sort of federal recognition. It concerns us specifically as an original, or traditional, or hereditary Indian government – that has never been "*reorganized*" – but which, rather, continues from time immemorial. Our original government pre-dates the very existence of the federal government of the United States. Our original government does not, as such, enjoy federal law rights, but, rather does enjoy international and constitutional law rights that are both anterior and superior to federal law rights. Our original right as an original Indian government, quite simply and straightforwardly, as the *Royal Proclamation of 1763* confirms, is the right not to be: "*molested or disturbed in the Possession of such Parts of* [the United States's] *Dominions and Territories as not having been ceded to or purchased by* [the United States] *are reserved to* [the Indians] *as their Hunting Grounds.*"

Furthermore, for the better protection of our original right we specifically and uniquely enjoy the remedy of third-party adjudication, as contrasted with having to attorn to the jurisdiction of the courts of the federal or state governments that we believe are in breach of our original right: *Order in Council (Great Britain) of 9 March 1704* in the matter of *Mohegan Indians v. Connecticut.*

Our second petition to you was submitted under letter dated September 19, 1997 pursuant to the *American Heritage Rivers Initiative Executive Order of 11 September 1997*. It incorporates our nomination packet dated October 2, 1997 relative to the Hudson River, the artery of the original homeland of our original government.

When you have read both petitions in light of each other you will see that we are offering contractually to relinquish the original right and remedy identified by our first petition, for the purpose specifically of advancing the ideal identified in our second petition. That ideal is the same as the legislative intent of the said *American Heritage Rivers Initiative Executive Order of 11 September 1997*. It is to regenerate the ecological and economic health of our shared homeland.

Subsequent to both petitions the Director of the Office of Tribal Government in the Bureau of Indian Affairs asked us whether we wanted to make use of the Bureau's facilities relative to federal recognition. We replied in the affirmative, provided it was understood that until we have made an agreement with you, Mr President, we will continue as an original government to assert our original right and remedy for the purpose of making that agreement in accordance with the letter of the international and constitutional law and the spirit of the *American Heritage Rivers Initiative Executive Order of 11 September 1997*.

Litigation

Court Minutes in the constitutionally formative years on either side of the 1664 cession of New Netherland to Great Britain make apparent that purchase from the Indians was a precondition to newcomer possession and jurisdiction; and, furthermore, that the evidence of valid purchase endemically is wanting, in terms of basic contract law. This fact is what prompted the *Royal Proclamation of 1763* legislatively to acknowledge and enact for constitutional law purposes: "*And whereas great Frauds and Abuses have been committed in purchasing Lands of the Indians to the great Prejudice of our Interests and to the great Dissatisfaction of the said Indians; In order therefore to prevent such Irregularities for the future and to the end that the Indians may be convinced of our Justice and determined Resolution to remove all reasonable Cause of Discontent We do with the Advice of our Privy Council strictly enjoin and require that ... if at any Time any of the said Indians should be inclined to dispose of the said Lands the same shall be Purchased ... at some public Meeting or Assembly of the said Indians to be held for that Purpose ...*"

Native Americans were not prejudiced for legal purposes by the *Declaration of Independence*, the Revolution, the *Peace of Paris*, the *Constitution* or any duly enacted *Constitutional Amendment*.

In any litigation over the Hudson River drainage basin before an independent and impartial third-party tribunal such as required by the *Order in Council (Great Britain) of 9 March 1704* in the matter of *Mohegan Indians v. Connecticut*, the City of New York, the State of New York the United States of America and their assignees would not be capable of establishing a good and valid root underlying their assumption of beneficial possession and jurisdiction, to any but rare portions of the Hudson River drainage basin.

In consequence, litigation would be protracted and destructive of possessions, jurisdictions, race relations, the ecology and the economy. The first issue in relation to any such litigation would be the identity of the adjudicator. The original government of our ancestors knew better than to attorn to the jurisdiction of the courts of our jurisdictional competitors. Our ancestors used "*Indian conferences,*" which is to say our own courts, upon the basis of whose adjudications we sought assistance for enforcement purposes; but we never did accept the jurisdiction of our competitors' courts; and should never be forced to, so long at least as America is true to herself, the soul of which is justice strictly in accordance with the rule of law.

The ragged condition of jurisdiction and possession in the Hudson River drainage basin is not lost upon this native tribe and nation, whose ancestral homeland this region constitutes. It is common knowledge that even as to Manhattan Island it is at least arguable that the original tribal jurisdiction and possession has never legally been purchased as required by the international and constitutional law identified in our earlier petitions to you, Mr President. As to Manhattan itself, it is now conventional wisdom that: "*The commonly alleged price – $24, or $26 – is almost surely fiction. And to mode of payment, in beads and tools, is an educated guess. Finally, it is fair to surmise that the Indians did not think they were selling the island, but only granting rights to use it. They had no concept of land ownership ... There is no record. A forgery has been widely reproduced, but the only credible documentation is a letter from Peter Jansen Schagen, an official of the West India Company in Amsterdam, to the States General in the Hague in November 1626. He relays news from an unidentified source on a ship just in from New Amsterdam, that* 'our people ... have purchased the island Manhattan from the Indians for the value of 60 guilders; – tis 11,000 morgens in size.' *That would be 22,000 acres, but it can't be right. Even today, with much landfill, Manhattan is only 15,000 acres. But that is the least of what is unclear* *in this history. The Schagen letter lay undiscovered in Dutch archives until the 1840's. Until then, there was no history of anyone buying Manhattan. When the letter surfaced, it was simply assumed that Minuit was the first governor and, therefore, that he had made the purchase. But documents discovered in 1910 revealed that Verhulst preceded him in office and was instructed to establish a fort on the Delaware or the Hudson, by purchase if necessary ... The true story of the Manhattan purchase is an exercise in weeding myth from fact.*"

Similarly, Governor's Island or Paggank, "*situated over against the island of Manahatas, between the North and East Rivers of New Netherlands*" purportedly was purchased by Wouter Van Twiller from "*Cakapetijno and 1 Indian*" under a deed "*Dated June 16, 1637.*" Upon the index for the abstract of title, however, the endorsement appears: "*Governor's Island. This purchase annulled July 1, 1652 by Director Genl in Council of New Netherlands.*"

At this stage of our research it appears at least arguable that, like Manhattan Island, Governor's island also remains unceded Indian territory, the original purchase being void *ab initio* and no subsequent valid Indian deed being in evidence.

In contrast with the land mass of the Hudson River drainage basin the offshore has not, even arguably, been ceded to or purchased by the United States. For example, in 1807 the United States purchased from the Indian nations occupying the Lake Huron drainage basin the offshore, from land's edge to the lake's international boundary with Canada, the lands themselves having been purchased by separate instruments. Although there are some potentially valid Indian deeds for portions of the *lands* in the Hudson River drainage basin there is no counterpart, so far at least as we are aware, of a treaty for the *offshore* of the Hudson River and its salt water estuary.

Two basic rules of construction concern the burden of proof in any potential action. *Contra proferentes* stipulates that when a document has gone missing its contents are presumed against the interest of the party in whose possession and control the document was at the time of its disappearance. Secondly, where the relationship between the parties is of a *fiduciary* character the presumption is against the interest of the trustee and in favor of the interest of the *cestui que trust.* At all material times all title documents have been in the possession and control exclusively of the United States and its predecessors, all of whom occupy the position of trustee as holder of the fee and preemptive right of purchase subject only to the Indians' interest as first governments and beneficial occupants.

The fact that we are aware of the ragged condition of jurisdictional and possessory pretensions in our ancestral homeland is not, however, the same thing as saying that we wish politically to confront or legally to litigate. The opposite is our approach, and always has been the Native Way of the Mohegan people.

Settlement

At the outset one must be belay confusion potentially resulting from the different phonetic renditions attributed to the aboriginal presence. The first syllable is an "*uh*" sound. In 1854 an expatriate named John Quinney whose ancestors had become Christianized and emigrated to Wisconsin explained: "*About the year 1645, and when King Ben, the last of the hereditary chiefs of the Muh-he-con-new Nation, was in his prime, a Grand Council was convened of the Muh-he-con-new tribe, for the purpose of conveying from the old to the young men, a knowledge of the past ...*"

That reference to "King Ben" was to my ancestor Ben Uncas who is identified in the genealogical data already disclosed with our first petition to you. In order to understand events in the 17th and 18th centuries, it is necessary to appreciate that from the perspective of my particular ancestors, this was an era of sustained terrorism of genocidal consequence to us. In order to survive, some of our relatives succumbed to the non-natives' unconstitutional policy of concentration, conversion and removal and left the Hudson River homeland region.

My family and others sought safety in the hinterland of the homeland, in what is now the Granville region of New York in the foothills of the Green Mountains of Vermont, the tribe's traditional threshold.

In 1754 the Mohegan named Aupaumut recounted: "*The etymology of the word Muh-heakunnuck, according to original signifying, is great waters or sea, which are constantly in motion, either flowing or ebbing. Our forefathers asserted, that their ancestors were emigrated from the west by north of another country; they passed over the great waters, where this and the other country is nearly connected, called Ukhkokpeck; it signifies snake water, or water where snakes abounded; that they lived by side of great water or sea, from whence they derive the name of Muhheakunnuk nation. Muhheakunneuw signifies a man of the Muhheakunnuk tribe. Muhheakunneyuk is a plural number. We understand that they were more civilized than what Indians are now in the wilderness; as it was said that they lived in towns, and were very numerous, until their arose a mighty famine which obliged them to disperse throughout the regions of the wilderness for sustenance, and at length they lost their former way of living, and apostatized. As they were coming from the west, they found many great waters, but none of them flowing and ebbing like Muhheakunnuk until they came to Hudson's River; then they said to one another, this is like Muhheakunnuk our nativity. And when they found grain was very plenty in that country, they agreed to kindle fire and hang a kettle, whereof they and their children after them might dip out daily refreshment.*"

In 1819 the historian John Heckewelder confirmed the oral history of New England and the Middle Colonies as follows: "*This was the case of the Mahicanni or Mohicans, in the east, a people who by intermarriages had become a detached body, mixing two languages together and out of the two forming a dialect of their own: choosing to live by themselves they crossed the Hudson River, naming it Mahicannituck River after their assumed name, and spread themselves over all that country which now composes the eastern states. New tribes again sprung up from them who assumed distinct names.*"

The previously mentioned Mohegan John Quinney further elaborated upon the oral history as understood in the 18th century, as follows: "*A great people came from the North-West; crossed over the salt-waters, and after long and weary pilgrimages (planting many colonies on their track), took possession, and built their fires upon the Atlantic coast, extending from the Delaware on the south, to the Penobscot in the north. They became, in the process of time, divided into different tribes and interests; all, however, speaking one common dialect. This great confederacy, comprising Delawares, Munsees, Mohegans, Narragansetts, Pequots, Penobscots, and many others ... held its Council once a year, to deliberate on the general welfare. Patriarchal delegates from each tribe attended, assisted by priests and wise men ... The policy and decisions of this Council were every where respected and inviolably observed ... The tribe, to which your speaker belongs, and of which there were many bands, occupied and possessed the country from the sea-shore, at Manhattan, to Lake Champlain. Having found the ebb and flow of the tide, they said: 'This is Muh-he-con-new – like our waters, which are never still.' From this expression, and by this name, they were afterwards known until their removal to Stockbridge in the year 1730. Housatonic River Indians, Mohegan, Manhattas, were all names of bands in different localities, but bound together, as one family, by blood, marriage, and descent.*"

The annual tribal "*Council*" to which that teller of that oral history referred took place on what is now known as Schodack Island at Albany, to where the tide reaches. Here, the tribe met each year at the full council of 9 fires to affirm and to renew the ties that bound, until the cycle was broken by the European invasion and reign of terror. This special place was called "*Maghtequack*" signifying the place of red soil, where all the council fires of all the tribe's nations came together at the Great Council Fire of the tribe. This was the place a part of which (supposedly) was sold to the non-natives by the (alleged) Indian purchase of October 17, 1730 in Rensselaer County. The same term Maghtequack is used at the head of the tide on the St. John River in New Brunswick, there in conjunction with "*Ek-pah-a-kw*" which signifies a place where salt and fresh waters meet. William Commanda, the 84 year old keeper of the Algonkian wampum belts, and who resides north of Ottawa, Canada, points out on the oldest belt that the first symbol represents the Muh-he-con-new, the genesis in the east of the Algonkian peoples.

The Hudson River salt water estuary is as important to Native American history as is Plymouth Rock and the Statue of Liberty are to Newcomer American history, perhaps more so.

Maghtequack at Schodack Island is just inside the tribe's door on the Hudson, where in one sense the tribe was born in the east. It is the womb to which return and renewal is made. At its threshold, to the immediate north, is the Granville region of New York and Vermont, just south and west of Lake Champlain. This is the reason, according to my family tradition, we hid where we did, when so many others of our tribe were removed to other parts of America, such as Wisconsin. The door is crucial because the renaissance of the ecology and economy of our Hudson River homeland depends upon us re-entering, to re-light the Great Council Fire at Maghtequack. This is why we stayed and hid, and waited, precisely where we did. The mid-18th century Moravian Missionary Rev. J. Christopher Pyrlaeus mentioned the oral history regarding the door as follows: "*The old and intelligent Mahicanni, whose forefathers inhabited the country on the east side of the North River, gave many years since the following account ... They said that their grandfather (the Leni Lanape), and the nations or tribes connected with them, were so united, that whatsoever nation attacked the one, it was the same as attacking the whole; all in such cases would unite and make a common cause. That the long house (council house) of all those who were of the same blood, and united under this kind of tacit alliance, reached from the head of the tide, at some distance above where Gaaschtinick [Albany] now stands, to the head of the tide water on the Potomack. That at each end of this house there was door for the tribes to enter at. That the Mengwe [Mohawks] were in no way connected to those who has access to this house; but were looked upon as strangers.*"

It would be a tragic mistake, in our view, to re-enter the door and re-kindle the great council fire in the Hudson River drainage basin with the wrong underlying philosophy and attitude: the way of thinking that has been made the norm for the "*reorganized*" Indians, as contrasted with the original way of Indian thinking. This is the reason that we think it so very important that our position is based on succession from and the philosophy of the original hereditary and traditional government, rather than upon the philosophy inculcated by long adherence to the ways of governing and thinking insisted upon by the Bureau of Indian Affairs. The consequence, in terms of philosophy and attitude, of the process of conversion, concentration and removal has been profound. The reorganized philosophy and attitude dwells upon blood connections and reservations, which is to say upon the racial and physical segregation of human beings. That is not the traditional Mohegan Way, which is to love all and share with all, as the creator shared and instructed us from time immemorial.

When all the apparatus, doubts and fears of the age of magic and superstition have been set aside, and we are left with the soul alone of our Mohegan philosophy and religion, it is simple. It is an abiding belief in respect for all things as the imperative of being, and in law as the application of respect to affairs. It is an abiding belief in truth as the summit of being, and in justice as the application of truth to affairs.

We would hope and trust that as we enter the 21st century the Bureau of Indian Affairs and the Council on Environmental Quality can and will work together with our original traditional government, as the BIA does with the reorganized elective governments. This is the reason that we wish to assert our original right and remedy so as to advance the legislative intent of the *American Heritage Rivers Initiative Executive Order of 11 September 1997*. It is the original way.

This does not mean that we do not know who we are, or that we can not provide genealogies that illustrate and substantiate our oral history. Accompanying this supplementary petition is a set of our genealogical charts, tracing descent to those Mohegans still residing in New York State as at 1861, and that set of persons in turn is traced virtually to the time of first contact with European civilization. Even so, genealogy charts do not alone define a tribe or nation: all they can define is a racial group. Since the original Mohegan Way and religious belief in unity was national, not racial, our tribe and nation regularly accepted into citizenship persons even of European descent, not only by adoption of children but also by marriage, and even naturalization. We want our tribe and nation, in principle, to continue to be open to all who reside in our homeland.

It is true that, even so, we want to give our blood relatives a special chance to join in the economy as equals. But we do not want them to be paid on the basis of blood, rather than on the basis of work. And we want our work to advance the stewardship obligation that the creator reposes in humans resting upon the creation.

Above all, we do not wish to hide any longer. When I was growing up my Aunt Mary told me to look into the names, and some day I would know who I was. My mother's brother's name is Edward S. Smith. The "S." stands for "Sacnu." She did not do it for me, but she led me, eventually, to spell Sacnu backwards: Uncas. In every generation since the removal we have hidden, not only from others, but even from ourselves, except when people were thought ready to know, as I have been made to know. This is not to say that every child and every man knows. The knowledge was kept in the women's circle. My mother and her sisters knew, as did the women before them. But it was not safe to tell the children, lest they blurt out their Indianness in the schoolyard and bring the reign of terror back. I do not know for certain, but I suspect that there may have been generations when the women did not even dare to tell the man who they had made Sachem of the fact, for his own safety. The circumspect way in which my mother and aunts led me to the knowledge, but never thrust it upon me, lest I was not ready and it was not in the Creator's time, is simply part of the reality forced upon the original people by the policy of conversion, concentration and removal.

Our tribe's council of women elders and my grandmother Emma together with her daughters including my mother chose me, and groomed me as Sachem in the original way, as re-affirmed by our full council in later years. Our original government does not have elections and vote in the reorganized way that is modeled on non-native municipal governments, but in its own way. As to the original way Aupaumit as at 1854 said: *"Our ancestors' Government was a democratical. They had a Wi-gow-wauw, or Chief Sachem, successively, as well as other nations had, chosen by the nation, whom they looked upon as conductor and promoter of their general welfare, and rendered him obedience as long as he behaved himself agreeably, to the office of a Sachem. And this office was hereditary by lineage of a female's offspring, but not on the man's line, but on woman's part. That is, when Wi-gow-wauw is fallen by death, one of his Nephews (if he has any) will be appointed to succeed his Uncle, and not any of his sons ... The Sachem always have Woh-weet-quan-pe-chee, or Councilors, and one Mo-quau-pauw, or Hero, and one Mkhoo-que-thoth, or Owl, and one Un-nuh-kau-kun, or Messenger, or Runner; and the rest of the men are called young men."*

My mother Francis was a princess of the tribe. She was full-blooded Mohegan. My mother's brother Edmund Sacnu Smith was Sachem before me. In 1976 the town of Rupert, Vermont, which is 6 miles south of Granville, New York published a pamphlet entitled *Some Historic Sites of Rupert, Vermont, This Bicentennial Year 1776–1976.* It notes (pp. 18, 19): *"We now cross the Indian River, so named because the Indians camped nearby ... There was an Indian's wigwam on the flat below where the sawmill stood. The old Indian preacher Occum preached at his house and Mr Hayes, in his youth, preached there."* The reference to *"Indian River"* is to the same river upon the banks of which I now reside. The reference to *"The old Indian preacher Occum"* is to Uncas's (himself a 1751 descendant of "King Ben" Uncas) aunt's son, and therefore a relative of mine.

The Mohegan preacher Samson Occam was the founder of Dartmouth College, where his picture still hangs. Some of his people are buried in the local area. His mother was Sary Occam who was sister to Uncas, and she was married to a Montauk Mohegan on Long Island, where her husband worked on whaling ships. The Reverend Occam came here to preach is because this is where some of his Indian people lived. Some others of his people joined the Brotherton Movement and emigrated to the western states of Michigan and Wisconsin, as part of the continuing removal process. Another one of my relatives, George Carson Smith, my grandfather's brother, ended up also in Michigan.

Times, nevertheless, have changed. The original government is not in a position, today, to govern all the humans in the original homeland. It is not ready, not willing and not able to govern the millions of people who are now part of our valley. The original government's role, for the future, rather, will if permitted be that of a conscience, a helper and a worker in the ecological and economic regeneration of this region. Which is a matter, we believe, not for litigation but rather for settlement by contractual arrangement or treaty with the United States and the State of New York, the modern successors to government over our homeland, in accordance with the philosophy and attitude shared by the original government and by the United States and New York as expressed by the *American Heritage Rivers Initiative Executive Order of 11 September 1997.*

Future

President Lincoln's *Emancipation Proclamation* heralded the beginning of the end of segregation for legal purposes on the basis of race. In 1871 President Grant suspended this beneficial process vis-à-vis Native Americans, as contrasted with African-Americans. His letter to the Senate and House of Representatives of January 30th enunciated the policy motivating the (unconstitutional) termination by Congress later that year of the treaty-based original system of Indian government in favor of promoting the assumption by Congress of plenary jurisdiction and the fostering of Indian governments reorganized on the more "civilized" white model: *"This is the first indication of the aborigines desiring to adopt our form of government, and it is highly desirable that they become self-sustaining, self-relying, Christianized, and civilized. If successful in this their first attempt at Territorial government, we may hope for a gradual concentration of other Indians in the new Territory. I therefore recommend as close an adherence to wishes as is consistent with safety ... It is confidently hoped that the policy now being pursued toward the Indian will fit him for self-government and make him desire to settle among people of his own race where he can enjoy the full privileges of civil and enlightened government."*

President Grant's goal plainly was stated on the occasion of this Second Inaugural Address on March 4, 1873: *"by a humane course, to bring the aborigines of the country under the benign influences of education and civilization. It is either this or war of extermination. Wars of extermination, engaged in by people pursuing commerce and all industrial pursuits, are expensive, even against the weakest people ..."*

By the time of the Clinton Presidency, American society had matured, so as now to be on the brink of ending racial segregation for legal purposes, even as against the native Americans. We believe that the *American Heritage Rivers Initiative Executive Order of 11 September 1997* provides a vehicle for completing the paradigm shift. For, as we see things at any rate, that executive order fully embraced the philosophy of stewardship, which itself is the essence of the philosophy of the original Native Way. In the result, as never before in her history America is poised to mature ethically no less than ecologically and economically.

We read, for example, in the *New York Times* on Sunday the 28th of December 1997 that Boston Harbor is, with help of the aquaculture research of the Massachusetts Institute of Technology, ready to introduce profitable fish factories to take advantage of the fact that: *"aquaculture has grown to a $30 billion industry worldwide, helping to meet an international demand for seafood that is projected to rise by 19 million tons to 91 million tons within the next 15 years."*

The Muh-he-con-new want to see their great tidal basin made ready to participate in that burgeoning market. That was our great river's traditional role – to feed the inhabitants of the valley – and that condition can be brought back under the auspices of the Native Americans' principle of respect as reiterated by the above mentioned executive order of President Clinton.

Similarly, the tourism industry is also poised exponentially to grow in the area, especially, of eco-tourism. The same edition of the *New York Times* explained: *"The world tourism industry will expand so fast between now and 2020 that 'it will not only be the world's biggest industry, it will be the largest by far the world has ever seen,' according to a new study by the World Tourist Organization ... According to its projections, issued at an October assembly in Istanbul, there will be 1.6 billion international tourist arrivals in 2020, nearly triple the current number. These tourists will spend more than $2 trillion for their vacations, up from $399 billion in 1995."*

The Muh-he-con-new want to see their great tidal basin made ready to participate in that burgeoning market, as well. That too was our great river's traditional role – to nurture the spirits of the people who live in and come to our valley – and that condition can also be enhanced under the auspices of the Native Americans' principle of respect as reiterated by the above mentioned executive order of President Clinton. We envisage constructing villages that portray the Mohegan culture, and places to which people of all races can resort to connect with nature, not just as an adjunct to the tourist economy but as thing good in itself for the human spirit. We envisage a university facility on Governor's Island, connected by monorail to Brooklyn, and dedicated to the cross-discipline and cross-cultural studies of anthropology, ethics, ecology and economics.

We believe that no region on earth is more worthy of benefiting from the regeneration of America than the region constituted by Muhheakunnuck, which includes not only the sea at the City but the sky in the Catskill Mountains, inside the door of the Muhheakunneyuk's spiritual long house at Schodack Island by Albany.

In the immediate future the surest source of capital with which to realize these ecological and economic aspirations is gaming, but with a New York difference, better, bolder, maybe even bigger. This we propose to carry out with the cooperation and sharing of the non-native governments that share political responsibility for the best interests of all the people of the Hudson River drainage basin. We envisage Governor's Island as the base of operations, connecting to aquaculture, hydroponic agriculture and tourism throughout the region.

In the slightly longer range future we can envisage, and wish the federal, state and municipal governments to reflect upon with us, other mutual advantages of maintaining the principle of our original government jurisdiction. For example, a portion of America's financial capital today goes offshore, to places of independent jurisdiction such as Switzerland, the Cayman Islands and so on. To a degree the benefit of that capital is, in consequence, lost to America, in terms at least of local works. By returning Governor's Island to its original jurisdiction an offshore financial capacity can be established virtually onshore, with significant benefit for the Hudson River drainage basin, the ultimate beneficiary of the stewardship obligation of the original Muh-he-con-new government.

At first impression it might appear to the legal advisers of the federal, state and municipal governments that, rightly or wrongly, the legal structure in fact irremediably has calcified around the 19th century policy of extermination or assimilation. President Grant's policy of extermination-or-assimilation (with racial segregation on reservations in the meantime) obviously conflicts with Chief Justice Marshall's perception of the constitutional right of the original Native American governments not to be interfered with in terms either of possession or jurisdiction until the United States has with the Indians' consent exercised the preemptive right of purchase. Nevertheless Supreme Court decisions in the 20th century might appear, in effect, to have endorsed the President and overridden the Chief Justice.

Based upon a liberal interpretation of the federal commerce power the Court has, in general, endorsed the concepts of *eminent domain* and *plenary jurisdiction*, while at the same time periodically re-affirming the seemingly inconsistent concept *Indian sovereignty* in constitutional law. Eminent domain and plenary jurisdiction are greater powers than the mere preemptive right of purchase allowed to the United States by the Chief Justice.

We do not believe that a scrutiny of the cases supports the contention that the view of Chief Justice Marshall has been overruled. No American case has ever addressed the *Order in Council (Great Britain) of 9 March 1704* in the matter of *Mohegan Indians v. Connecticut.* If and when the Court does, in future, address that constitutive instrument, an endeavor will have to be made to reconcile the specific view of the law as taken by Chief Justice Marshall and the Order in Council, with the Court's own endorsement in general of eminent domain, plenary jurisdiction and Indian sovereignty. The reconciliation represents opportunity.

Eminent domain and plenary jurisdiction are appropriate concepts vis-à-vis the relationship between the United States and the *reorganized* Indian governments. Those governments were designed to discharge the functions of municipal institutions. Municipal institutions by definition are subordinate to the federal level.

Eminent domain and plenary jurisdiction are not appropriate vis-à-vis the relationship between the United States and the *original* Indian government of the Muh-he-con-new. The *original* Indian government was designed to exercise complete sovereignty, subject, as Chief Justice Marshall and the order in council when read together make apparent, only to the exclusive federal right to purchase a relinquishment by the original government of its sovereign power.

The point is that it is not difficult to reconcile eminent domain and plenary jurisdiction with Indian sovereignty and the right of preemption. The concepts exist in relation to dif-

ferent Indian constituencies. And different territories. The reorganized Indian governments have municipal powers and federal benefits and programs on reservations. The
original Indian governments have sovereign powers, but no federal benefits and programs,
on territory that has never been ceded to or purchased by the United States and set apart as
reservation land.

We seek federal recognition for the purposes not of perpetuating the illusion of advantages under the racial segregation policy saved for Indians in 1871 as an exception to the
general emancipation and which is still administered under the general marching orders of
the Bureau of Indian Affairs. Instead, we want to negotiate a new and mutually beneficial
contractual or treaty solution, one that may provide a model for the beginning of the end of
segregation on the basis of race, in favor of catching the stewardship wave together as one,
united, people.

Very truly yours,
/s/
_____

Sachem
Golden Eagle, Ron Roberts
Concurring
/s/
_____

Attorney General
Bruce Clark, LLB, MA, PhD

COMPLAINT TO THE COURT

98 CIV. 8194
JUDGE McKENNA

_____

UNITED STATES DISTRICT COURT
FOR THE
SOUTHERN DISTRICT OF NEW YORK

_____

Timothy J. Stoddard and Bruce Clark, Vernon T. Johnson, Craig Carpenter, Willard W. Rhoades and Mildred A. Rhoades representing Indians or any of them, the class constituted by operation of the
constitutional law

Plaintiff

v.

The United States of America

Defendant

_____

COMPLAINT

_____

Pro se

_____

Plaintiff alleges:

1. A federal question arises in relation to Liberty Island in virtue of a conflict of laws, between the constitutional law *prima facie* protecting Indian liberty upon arguably un-ceded territory and the premature and therefore derogating application thereupon of federal and state law, as to the resolution of which conflict of laws court jurisdiction vests to make a declaration pursuant to Title 28 United States Code §§1331 and 2201.

2. By operation of constitutional law[1] plaintiff has standing to sue as a class of "Indians or any of them,"[2] entitled, as such, to third-party adjudication,[3] relative to Indian liberty in relation to Liberty Island, since, from all that appears, the island has not been purchased from the Indians and therefore is reserved for the Indians. On it, the Statue of Liberty, which belongs to the United States, faces Europe and promises liberty, while her back is turned upon native American liberty. She trespasses, and stands as a constant reminder of genocide in America, thereby causing the plaintiff class the civil injury "serious bodily or mental harm."[4] Liberty will be when America is true: to justice,[5] and to the judicial function.[6]

Plaintiff seeks:

3. A declaration of the remedy of third-party adjudication in relation to Liberty Island and the right thereupon of Indian liberty, which, for constitutional law purposes, is to say the native sovereignty interest of exclusive jurisdiction and possession pending cession thereof to the United States.

THE FOREGOING IS SWORN TO BE TRUE UNDER PAIN AND PENALTY BOTH OF DIS-TURBING THE GREAT SPIRIT'S NATURAL ORDER BASED UPON TRUTH AND OF ALL SANCTIONS PROVIDED BY POSITIVE LAW AGAINST THE ADVANCEMENT OF UN-TRUTH.

November 11, 1998.

/s/
_____
Timothy J. Stoddard
(MOHEIGAN
HUDSON RIVER INDIANS, NEW YORK)

/s/
_____
Vernon T. Johnson
(ACHOMAWI BAND
PITT RIVER TRIBE, CALIFORNIA)

/s/
_____
WAH-HAY-LOW Willard W. Rhoades
(ITSATAWI BAND
PITT RIVER TRIBE, CALIFORNIA)

Plaintiff, *pro se*, per:

/s/
_____
Bruce Clark
(BY NATURALIZATION)

/s/
_____
Craig Carpenter
(MOHAWK/NAVAHO
RUNNER FOR HOPI NATION)

/s/
_____
Mildred A. Rhoades
(WENNEMEM BAND
WINTU TRIBE, CALIFORNIA)

MOTION BY UNITED STATES TO DISMISS THE COMPLAINT

UNITED STATES DISTRICT COURT SOUTHERN DISTRICT OF NEW YORK

_____

Timothy J. Stoddard, Bruce Clark, Vernon) T. Johnson, Craig Carpenter, Willard W. Rhoades and Mildred Rhoades,

Plaintiffs

98 Civ. 8194 (LMM)

– against –

v

                                                    NOTICE OF MOTION

The United States of America,
                              Defendant.

PLEASE TAKE NOTICE that, upon the accompanying memorandum of law and all prior papers and proceedings had herein, the undersigned moves this Court before the Honorable Lawrence M. McKenna for an order dismissing the complaint pursuant to *Federal Rules of Civil Procedure* 12(b)(1) and 12(b)(6).

PLEASE TAKE FURTHER NOTICE that plaintiffs must serve their answering papers, if any, on counsel for the defendant within ten business days of receipt of this notice of motion.

MEMORANDUM OF LAW IN SUPPORT OF
GOVERNMENT'S MOTION TO DISMISS THE COMPLAINT

Defendant the United States of America, by its attorney, Mary Jo White, United States Attorney for the Southern District of New York, respectfully submits this memorandum of law in support of its motion to dismiss the complaint pursuant to Rules 12(b)(1) and 12(b)(6) of the *Federal Rules of Civil Procedure*.

PRELIMINARY STATEMENT

Six individuals, each one claiming to have an Indian ancestry or tribal affiliation, have brought this class action lawsuit purporting to represent a group of persons defined as "Indians or any of them." Complaint, p. 1. Plaintiffs assert that Liberty Island, which is located in New York Harbor and owned by the United States, was never properly purchased from the Indians by the United States and therefore "is reserved for the Indians." *Id.*, p. 1. For their relief, plaintiffs seek from this Court a declaration that they are entitled to "third-party adjudication" – *i.e.*, adjudication by some entity independent of the federal judiciary – of their land dispute with the United States. *Id.*, p. 2. They apparently do not want this Court itself to adjudicate the merits of their claim.

The complaint should be summarily dismissed. As a threshold matter, nothing in the complaint indicates that plaintiffs have standing to petition for "third-party" adjudication of their claim to Liberty island. Due to plaintiffs' failure to plead facts establishing their standing, this Court lacks subject matter jurisdiction over the complaint. Plaintiffs also fail to state a claim on which relief can be granted, despite the volume of arcane, centuries-old legal citations attached to their complaint.

ARGUMENT

I
Plaintiffs Lack Standing

A. The Doctrine of Standing

Standing to litigate a dispute "is an essential and unchanging part of the case-or-controversy requirement of Article III" of the Constitution. *Lujan v. Defenders of Wildlife*, 504 US 555, 560 (1992). Because standing is an Article III requirement, federal subject matter jurisdiction does not exist in its absence. *Raines v. Byrd*, 117 S. Ct. 2312, 2317 (1997). As with every required element of federal subject matter jurisdiction, the plaintiff bears the burden of establishing the basis of his or her standing.

The "irreducible minimum" of the doctrine of standing is the requirement that "the party who invokes the court's authority ... show that he personally has suffered some actual or threatened injury as a result of the putatively illegal conduct of the defendant ..." *Valley-Forge College v. Americans United*, 454 US 464, 472 (1982) (citation and internal quotation marks omitted). This actual or threatened injury must be concrete, particularized and either ongoing or imminent; speculative or hypothetical claims of harm do not suffice. *Lujan*, 504 US at 560. Moreover, a plaintiff generally must assert his own legal rights and interests, and cannot rest his claim to relief on the legal rights or interests of third parties. *Valley-Forge*, 454 US at 474 (citation and internal quotation marks omitted).

B. Plaintiffs Lack Standing

Plaintiffs in this case have not met their burden of pleading facts showing that they have standing to litigate the legitimacy of the United States's ownership of Liberty Island. In suing the United States on behalf of themselves and all "Indians or any of them," plaintiffs are implicitly claiming that they and the members of the would-be class were the original aboriginal owners of Liberty Island to whom the island should now be returned. But plaintiffs plead no facts to support their claim of original ownership of Liberty island. And for good reason: Federal-law provides that Indian tribes, not individual Indians, are the sole proper claimants to Indian tribal lands, owing to the fact that Indian tribes, not individual Indians, are deemed to have been the original "owners" of aboriginal land in North America. See *Golden Hill Paugussett Tribe of Indians v. Weicker*, 839 F. Supp. 130, 133 (D. Conn. 1993) (holding that "[n]either individual Indians, nor groups of Indians that possess no tribal status, have standing to sue for tribal land ..."), *remanded*, 39 F. 3d 51 (2d Cir. 1994); *see also Tee-Hit-Ton Indians v. United States*, 348 US 272, 279 (1955) ("It is well settled that in all the States of the Union the *tribes* who inhabited the lands of the States held claim to such lands after the coming of the white man ...") (emphasis added). Plaintiffs do not claim to be an Indian tribe, much less the specific Indian tribe that allegedly originally owned Liberty Island. *See* Complaint, p. 2 (plaintiffs list various disparate tribal affiliations). Indeed, plaintiffs do not bother in their complaint even to identify the tribe that originally owned Liberty Island. Nor do plaintiffs claim that they have been authorized by this (unidentified) original-owning tribe to represent its interests in this lawsuit.

In failing to make such allegations, plaintiffs fail to allege that they have been deprived of something to which they are personally entitled. The have failed to allege that *their* ownership interests, as opposed to *someone else's*, have been impinged upon. Plaintiffs therefore have no standing to prosecute this lawsuit. *See, e.g., Raines*, 117 S. Ct. at 2318–2322 (where complained-of legislation harmed only Congress's institutional interests and not the personal rights of individual members of Congress, and where individual members had not shown that they were authorized by Congress to represent its institutional interests, individual members could not attack complained-of legislation in federal court).

II

Plaintiffs Fail to State a Claim

A. No Law Entitles Plaintiffs to the Remedy They Seek

In addition to lacking standing, plaintiffs lack a legally cognizable claim for relief. As noted above, the sole remedy plaintiffs seek in this case is an order from the Court requiring the United States to submit to the jurisdiction of some unspecified adjudicators body which is independent of the federal judiciary for the purpose of litigating plaintiffs' claim to Liberty Island. Plaintiffs base this claim for relief on the argument that "whenever two quasi-sovereign bodies politic litigate, the court system of neither can assume jurisdiction. There must be either a consent by one party to the other's court, or both must accept a third-party tribunal as an outside referee." Complaint, p. 31.

Plaintiffs have no legal right to have an "outside referee" adjudicate their land claim against the United States. To begin with, the federal courts themselves undoubtedly can "assume" jurisdiction over the subject matter of plaintiffs' claim to Liberty Island, since plaintiffs base that claim on the United States Constitution. *See* 28 USC § 1331 (note that plaintiffs' base their claim both on express constitutional provisions and on legal authority which they assert is implicitly incorporated into the Constitution. *See* Complaint, pp. 3–27.) Moreover, even if the federal courts did not have subject matter jurisdiction over plaintiffs' land claim, this would not mean that jurisdiction over the subject matter of plaintiffs' claim exists in another, non-federal forum. Plaintiffs identify no statute pursuant to which the United States has waived its sovereign Immunity from suit in such other forum. Absent such a waiver of its sovereign immunity, the United States cannot be forced to subject itself to suit by plaintiffs in a third-party forum. *See United States v. Sherwood*, 312 US 584, 586 (1941) ("The United States, as sovereign, is immune from suit save as it consents to be sued ... and the terms of its consent to be sued in any court define that court's jurisdiction to entertain the suit.").

Because plaintiffs do not have a legal right to the sole remedy they seek, their complaint fails to state a claim on which relief can be granted and should be dismissed pursuant to *Federal Rule of Civil Procedure* 12 (b) (6)

B. On Its Merits, Plaintiffs' Constitutionally-Based Claim to Liberty Island Fails to State a Claim on Which Relief Can Be Granted

In the event this Court were to interpret the complaint as requesting *this Court* to adjudicate the merits of plaintiffs' claim to Liberty Island, the complaint should still be dismissed for failure to state a claim because none of the "Constitutional" authority cited by plaintiffs entitles them to ownership of Liberty Island.

Plaintiffs contend that certain pre-Constitution edicts by the Pope, Great Britain and the colony of New York, as well as the Declaration of Independence, are incorporated into the Constitution and support their claim. *See* Complaint, pp. 3–9. Plaintiffs are wrong: None of these authorities is incorporated into the Constitution. *See Golden Hill*, 839 F. Supp. At 137–38 (rejecting proposition that Constitution incorporated British Royal Proclamation of 1763; noting that the Constitution established the supremacy of "United States law"); *Shuttlesworth v. Housing Opportunities Made Equal*, 873 F. Supp. 1069, 1079–80 (SD Ohio 1994) (holding that Section 1983 plaintiff's reliance on the guarantees enunciated in the Declaration of Independence did not state a claim under federal law).

Plaintiffs also rely on certain actual provisions of the Constitution. They invoke the Thirteenth Amendment, which outlawed slavery. But that amendment has no bearing on plaintiffs' claim, which essentially alleges an unjust taking of property by the United States, not enslavement. Plaintiffs invoke the Fourteenth Amendment, but that amendment applies to the states only, not to the Federal Government. *Noel v. Chapman*, 508 F.2d 1023, 1026 n.2 (2d Cir. 1975). Oddly, plaintiffs fail to invoke the only part of the Constitution which is conceivably relevant – the Takings Clause of the Fifth Amendment. But even if plaintiffs did invoke that clause, it would not avail them. The Supreme Court held long ago that Indians have no claim under the Fifth Amendment to possessory or ownership interests in land taken by the United States unless Congress has by treaty or other agreement declared that Indians were to hold the land permanently. *See Tee-Hit-Ton Indians*, 348 US at 285 ("Indian occupation of land without government recognition of ownership creates no rights against taking or extinction by the United States protected by the Fifth Amendment or any other principle of law."); *see also id.* at 277–78. Because plaintiffs have not identified in their complaint any past congressional recognition of Indian ownership rights respecting Liberty Island, the Fifth Amendment affords them no basis for relief.

CONCLUSION

For all of the foregoing reasons, the motion by the United States to dismiss the complaint for lack of subject matter jurisdiction and failure to a state a claim on which relief can be granted should be granted.

Dated: New York, New York

> January 15, 1999
> MARY JO WHITE
> United States Attorney for the
> Southern District of New York
> By: */s/*
> _____
>
> AMY BENJAMIN
> Assistant United States Attorney

REPLY TO UNITED STATES' MOTION

UNITED STATES DISTRICT COURT
SOUTHERN DISTRICT OF NEW YORK

_____

Stoddard v. USA   98 CV 8194 (LMM)

_____

PLAINTIFF'S MEMORANDUM OF LAW IN REPLY TO DEFENDANT'S MOTION TO DISMISS THE COMPLAINT

1. The defendant's motion is to dismiss for a supposed failure on the part of the plaintiff:
   (a) to plead facts, or
   (b) to state a claim,
capable of satisfying the burden upon an Indian plaintiff under federal Indian law.

2. The plaintiff agrees with the defendant that the plaintiff has not pleaded facts or stated a claim capable of satisfying the burden upon an Indian plaintiff under federal Indian law.

3. The case for the plaintiff, however, is that the application of federal Indian law to arguably unceded territory such as Liberty Island is genocidally unconstitutional to all Indians including the plaintiffs.

4. The defendant's motion and brief do not address the constitutional law upon which the facts as pleaded and claim as stated in the complaint are relevant and sufficient.

5. The defendant's motion and brief illustrate the *modus operandi* for the genocide identified in the complaint: willful blindness to the constitutional law, in favor of applying federal law as if there were no constitutional law precluding the application.

DATED: New York, New York
   January 25, 1999

Plaintiff, *pro se*, per:

/s/
_____
Timothy J. Stoddard

/s/
_____
Vernon T. Johnson

/s/
_____
WAH-HAY-LOW Willard W. Rhoades

/s/
_____
Bruce Clark

/s/
_____
Craig Carpenter

/s/
_____
Mildred A. Rhoades

Plains Case

3759/98
Pro se

IN THE COURT OF QUEEN'S BENCH
JUDICIAL CENTER OF REGINA

BETWEEN:

Ochapowace First Nation

PLAINTIFF

AND:

Canada and Saskatchewan

DEFENDANTS

CLAIM

1. The Plaintiff is an Indian nation of the Treaty 4 region.

2. The Defendants' judicial, executive and legislative branches assume jurisdiction to apply federal and provincial law to the said region, as if there were no constitutional law[7] native sovereignty precluding this.

3. Native oral history is that the said treaty as explained and understood at the time of signing was intended to reinforce and protect the said native sovereignty, and, if that is not what the treaty's words in English say, then its words must be rectified so as to conform to the contractual intent.

4. The consequence of the said assumption is serious bodily or mental harm within the meaning of article 2(b) of the *Convention for the Prevention and Punishment of the Crime of Genocide, 1948*.

5. For constitutional law purposes, the Indians' remedy of third-party adjudication in relation to the right of native sovereignty was recognized in the 18th[8] century and affirmed in the 19th[9] century; and, on the 12th day of September 1995 in the matter of *Delgamuukw v. AGBC*, the Supreme Court of Canada invited the testing of the constitutional law continuity of the said remedy in this the 20th century, specifically by way of the commencement of an action for "declaratory relief"[10] before a Canadian court of general and original jurisdiction.

6. The Plaintiff therefore seeks a declaration acknowledging its remedy of independent and impartial third-party adjudication.

DATED December 7, 1998.   Ochapowace First Nation, per:
                                           /s/
                                           _____
                                           Chief Denton George
                                           /s/
                                           _____
                                           Councilor Louis Kenny

MOTION BY CANADA TO DISMISS THE CLAIM

                                                              3759/98
                                                              Pro se

                        IN THE COURT OF QUEEN'S BENCH
                           JUDICIAL CENTER OF REGINA
        BETWEEN:
                           Ochapowace First Nation
                                                         Respondent
                                                         (Plaintiff)
        AND:
                                    Canada
                                                         Applicant
                                                         (Defendant)
                                      and
                                 Saskatchewan
                                                         Respondent
                                                         (Defendant)

NOTICE OF MOTION

TAKE NOTICE that an application will be made to the presiding judge in chambers at the Court House, 2425 Victoria Avenue, Regina, Saskatchewan, on Thursday the 7th day of January, 1999, at ten o'clock in the forenoon or so soon thereafter as counsel may be heard on behalf of the defendant Canada, for the following relief:

(a) an order pursuant to Rule 173(b) of the *Queen's Bench Rules* striking out the Statement of Claim in this action, on the grounds that it consists largely of immaterial assertions of propositions of law and quotations from judicial decisions and is unnecessarily prolix; or

(b) in the alternative, an order pursuant to Rule 534, extending the time for delivery of a defence by Canada to a date 60 days after the filing of the decision of this Honourable Court upon the present motion; and

(c) such further and other relief as to this Honourable Court may seem just and expedient.

THE GROUNDS for this application are:

(a) Rule 139 requires that every pleading contain and contain only a statement in summary form of the material facts relied upon. The Statement of Claim in this action incorporates, as annotations, extensive discussions of legal arguments and quotations from judicial decisions and other authorities. The defendant should not be required, in its Statement of Defence, to respond to the 65 pages of citations and commentary which appear to be incorporated by reference in the Statement of Claim.

AND FURTHER TAKE NOTICE that in support of this application will be read this Notice of Motion with proof of service, the pleadings and proceedings had and taken herein, and such further and other material as counsel may advise and this Honourable Court may allow.

DATED at Saskatoon, Saskatchewan, this 23rd day of December, 1998.

/s/
_____

Mark R. Kindrachuk
of Counsel for the defendant Canada

WRITTEN SUBMISSIONS OF THE APPLICANT

1. This is an application by the defendant Canada for an order pursuant to Rule 173(b) of the *Queen's Bench Rules* striking out the Statement of Claim in this action, on the grounds that it consists largely of immaterial assertions of propositions of law and quotations from judicial decisions and is unnecessarily prolix.

2. Rule 139(l) provides as follows:
"Every pleading shall contain *and contain only* a statement *in a summary Form* of the material facts on which the party pleading relies for his claim or defence, but not the evidence by which the facts are to be proved. A pleading shall be a brief as the nature of the case will permit." [emphasis added]

3. The function of pleadings is to define with precision and accuracy the issues in controversy between the litigants. A defendant is entitled to know what is that the plaintiff asserts against him or her, and the plaintiff is entitled to know the nature of the defence raised in answer to the claim.
Romanic v. Hartman (1986) 51 Sask. R. 169 at p. 171 (Q.B.)
Piché v. Big "C" First Nation, (1994), 121 Sask. R. 20 (Q.B.)

4. Allegations which are immaterial and unnecessary may be struck out.
Romanic v. Hartman, supra.
Hutchinson v. Saskatoon Funeral Home Co. Ltd. (1985), 41 Sask. R. 119 (Q.B.)

5. The Statement of Claim in this action incorporates, as annotations, extensive discussions of legal arguments and quotations from judicial decisions and other authorities. Although this material does contain statements of fact, these are intermingled with argument and submissions of law. It is respectfully submitted that the Statement of Claim as a whole is far from the "statement in a summary form of the material facts" which is required by Rule 139(1).

6. The defendant should not be required, in its Statement of Defence, to respond to the 65 pages of citations and commentary which appear to be incorporated by reference in the Statement of Claim. The defendant is entitled to have the plaintiff's cases put in an intelligible form to which it can plead in reply.

All of which is respectfully submitted.

Dated at Saskatoon, Saskatchewan, this 23rd day of December, 1998.

/s/
_____

Mark R. Kindrachuk
of Counsel for the defendant Canada

REPLY TO CANADA'S MOTION

3759/98
Pro se

IN THE COURT OF QUEEN'S BENCH
JUDICIAL CENTER OF REGINA

BETWEEN:

Ochapowace First Nation

RESPONDENT
(PLAINTIFF)

AND:

Canada

APPLICANT
(DEFENDANT)

and

Saskatchewan

RESPONDENT
(DEFENDANT)

REPLY RE CANADA'S MOTION TO STRIKE

1. Far from being "prolix" as alleged in the applicant's 1st paragraph the operative part of the Statement of Claim consists in 5 concise, simple and straightforward allegations of fact all contained within the compass of a single page. This manifestly satisfies the requirement identified at applicant's paragraph 2 that the pleading "contain a statement in summary form of the material facts on which the party pleading relies." To this juncture, therefore, the pleading is eminently familiar in form.

2. But the pleading goes on to provide particulars of the law upon which rests the relevancy and sufficiency of the said facts. Now in the vast majority of cases one does not plead law, not because one may not, but because it is not generally necessary. The basics elements of the various causes of action, such as those for example in contract and tort, are well understood and do not need repetition. However, no such understanding can be presumed in the *sui generis* instance of aboriginal rights.

3. First, as held by the Supreme Court of Canada on December 11, 1997 in *Delgamuukw v. AGBC* (at paragraph 75) "The content of common law aboriginal title, for example, has not been authoritatively determined by this Court ..."

4. But the problem goes much deeper than the ostensibly unsettled nature of the legal parameters of the cause of action. For you see, when the law was created, so many centuries ago, the natives and newcomers were in a vastly different position than that which informs present attitudes. Then, it made sense for the whole continent to be recognized as constitutionally reserved for the Indians except to the extent purchased from them, and to concede to this concept of native sovereignty the corresponding right of third-party adjudication, which is all that the present action is concerned with. But this constitutional law, though never repealed, was ignored in practice by the application, regardless of purchase, of non-native domestic law, to such an extent for so long a time and with such vast consequences that today conventional wisdom *assumes* that the non-native courts and governments have original rather than derivative jurisdiction.

5. In these circumstances, if one were to plead facts without at the outset stipulating the correct legal standard by which to assess their relevancy and sufficiency, the party adverse in interest and the court spontaneously would apply the erroneous assumption, and on this basis tend to want to strike the pleading as frivolous, vexatious or not disclosing a cause of action, or even as scandalous.

6. In short, this case is not really about the facts. Rather, it is about the more preliminary issue of who has jurisdicion to adjudicate the facts. Far from not being "intelligible" as contended at applicant's 6th paragraph, this issue is clear and plain. Therefore, the applicant's motion is disingenuous and against good faith. It is not that the applicant does not comprehend either the facts or the legal issue, but wishes to evade the latter.

7. The consequence of the motion is delay, which *prima facie* prolongs the era of genocide identified as a fact at paragraph 4 of the claim. At the same time as the applicant seeks to delay the civil law resolution of the court jurisdiction issue, the applicant presses on

with the prosecution and persecution of the plaintiff in the Saskatchewan Provincial Court case of *R. v. Ochapowace Band and others*. This duplicity exquisitely illustrates the historical *modus operandi* for the said genocide: the stonewalling of the constitutional law which precludes the assumption of jurisdiction, while pressing ahead with criminal sanctions based upon that very assumption. This entails the use of the criminal law process to commit genocide in willful blindness to the constitutional law precluding the assumption of any jurisdiction, to the profound prejudice of the rule of law no less than to the devastation of native society.

8. The respondent agrees with the applicant's allegation at paragraph 3 that the "function of the pleadings is to define with precision and accuracy the issues." The issue is court jurisdiction. The Statement of Claim has defined that issue "with precision and accuracy."

9. The respondent asks the court to refuse the applicant any extension of time and instead to grant the prior motion of the Ochapowace First Nation for summary judgment on the preliminary point of jurisdictional law alone.

All of which is respectfully submitted.

DATED January 6, 1999.

Ochapowace First Nation
per:
/s/
_____

Chief
/s/
_____

Councilor

MOTION BY SASKATCHEWAN TO DISMISS THE CLAIM

3759/98
Pro se

IN THE COURT OF QUEEN'S BENCH
JUDICIAL CENTER OF REGINA

BETWEEN:

Ochapowace First Nation

Respondent
(Plaintiff)

AND:

Saskatchewan

Applicant
(Defendant)

and
Canada

Respondent
(Defendant)

NOTICE OF MOTION

TAKE NOTICE that an application will be made to the presiding Judge in Chambers at the Court House in Regina, Saskatchewan on Thursday the 7th day of January, 1999 at ten o'clock in the forenoon or so soon thereafter as counsel can be heard on behalf of the Applicant for an Order pursuant to Queen's Bench Rule 173 that the Statement of Claim in this action be struck out in its entirety on the following grounds:

(a) that the Statement of Claim does not set out the factual or legal basis upon which the Plaintiffs claim to be entitled to "independent and impartial third-party adjudication" of their assertions of sovereignty and, therefore, discloses no reasonable cause of action within the meaning of subsection (a) of Rule 173;

(b) that the Statement of Claim contains numerous references to case law, historical evidence and irrelevant matters which are not properly a part of pleadings and which are immaterial and redundant and which make the Statement of Claim unnecessarily prolix, all within the meaning of subsection (b) of Rule 173; and

(c) that the Statement of Claim seeks a declaration that the Plaintiffs are entitled to "independent and impartial third-party adjudication" of their assertions of sovereignty; however, as no domestic court can question the sovereignty of the Crown, this Court does not have the jurisdiction to authorize such an adjudicative process and, therefore, the Statement of Claim discloses no reasonable cause of action within the meaning of subsection (a) of Rule 173, is scandalous, frivolous and vexatious within the meaning of subsection (c) of Rule 173 and is an abuse of the process of the Court within the meaning of subsection (e) of Rule 173.

AND FURTHER TAKE NOTICE that in support of this application will be read the pleadings and proceedings taken herein to date and such further and other material as counsel may advise and this Honourable Court may allow.

DATED at Regina, Saskatchewan this 29th day of December, 1998.

/s/

P. Mitch McAdam
Counsel for the Attorney
General for Saskatchewan

BRIEF OF LAW

I. FACTUAL BACKGROUND

1. The Plaintiffs are an Indian Band (also known as a First Nation). They are a party to Treaty No. 4 and have a reserve near Broadview, Saskatchewan. They issued a Statement of Claim on December 7, 1998. In the Statement of Claim, the Plaintiffs allege that they are a sovereign, independent nation with jurisdiction over the entire Treaty 4 territory. They say that no federal or provincial laws apply within this territory. They say that their sovereignty was confirmed by the terms of Treaty No. 4. They also allege that the assumption of jurisdiction over this land by Canada and Saskatchewan constitutes the crime of genocide contrary to the United Nations' *Convention for the Prevention and Punishment of the Crime of Genocide.*

2. The Plaintiffs, however, do not seek a declaration from this Court affirming their sovereignty. Rather, they seek a declaration that they are entitled to "independent and impartial third-party adjudication" with respect to this issue.

3. The Statement of Claim was served on Canada and Saskatchewan by facsimile transmission on December 10, 1998. Canada responded by making an application to strike out the Statement of Claim pursuant to Queen's Bench Rule 173. Canada's Notice of Motion was served on December 23rd. Saskatchewan followed suit and made a similar application to strike out the Statement of Claim. Saskatchewan's Notice of Motion was served on December 30th.

II. THE SASKATCHEWAN APPLICATION

4. Saskatchewan has applied to have the Statement of Claim struck out under Queen's Bench Rule 173, which reads as follows:

173. The Court may at any stage of an action order any pleading or any part thereof to be struck out, with or without leave to amend, on the ground that

(a) it discloses no reasonable cause of action or defence, as the case may be;

(b) it is immaterial, redundant or unnecessarily prolix;

(c) it is scandalous, frivolous or vexatious;

(d) it may prejudice, embarrass or delay the fair trial of the action;

(e) it is otherwise an abuse of the process of the court;

and may order the action to be stayed or dismissed or judgment to be entered accordingly or may grant such order as may be just. Unless otherwise directed, the offending party shall pay double the costs to which the other party would otherwise be entitled.

5. The grounds of Saskatchewan's application are both procedural and substantive. Three separate grounds are set out in the Notice of Motion. They are:

1. that the Statement of Claim does not set out the factual or legal basis upon which the Plaintiffs claim to be entitled to "independent and impartial third-party adjudication" of their assertions of sovereignty and, therefore, discloses no reasonable cause of action within the meaning of subsection (a) of Rule 173;

2. that the Statement of Claim contains numerous references to case law, historical evidence and irrelevant matters which are not properly a part of pleadings and which are immaterial and redundant and which make the Statement of Claim unnecessarily prolix, all within the meaning of subsection (b) of Rule 173; and

3. that the Statement of Claim seeks a declaration that the Plaintiffs are entitled to "independent and impartial third-party adjudication" of their assertions of sovereignty; however, as no domestic court can question the sovereignty of the Crown, this Court does not have the jurisdiction to authorize such an adjudicative process and, therefore, the Statement of Claim discloses no reasonable cause of action within the meaning of subsection (a) of Rule 173, is scandalous, frivolous and vexatious within the meaning of subsection (c) of Rule 173 and is an abuse of the process of the Court within the meaning of subsection (e) of Rule 173.

III. LEGAL ARGUMENT

A. Ground One

6. A Statement of Claim should clearly and precisely set out the question in controversy. A Defendant is entitled to know the case that he must meet. The Statement of Claim must be sufficiently precise to give the Defendant fair warning of what is being claimed and the basis upon which it is being claimed so that the Defendant will not be taken by surprise later in the proceedings. These are fundamental rules of pleading.

Duchane v. Davies (1983) 29 Sask. R. 57 (C.A.), at p. 68.

7. In this case, the Plaintiffs claim that they are entitled to "independent and impartial third-party adjudication" with respect to-their assertions of sovereignty. However, the Statement of Claim does not clearly disclose the factual or legal basis of this claim. The Plaintiffs do not say whether this alleged "right" to third-party adjudication arises from the common law, a statute, international law or some other source. Without this information, it is impossible for the Defendant to respond to the claim. Without this information, a reasonable cause of action has not been pled.

8. The Plaintiffs' Statement of Claim is only one page long. However, attached to the Statement of Claim as "footnotes" are approximately 60 pages of single spaced text. These footnotes contain references to case law, historical documents, legal commentaries, similar claims being advanced in other jurisdictions and include excerpts from a hearing before the Supreme Court of Canada and a hearing before the Law Society of Upper Canada. The basis of the Plaintiffs' claim may be set out somewhere in these footnotes. However, it is submitted that a Defendant should not be required to sort through voluminous

material in an attempt to ascertain the basis of a Plaintiff s claim. The Plaintiff is obligated to set out that claim clearly. If the Plaintiff fails to do so, the Defendant is entitled to have the Statement of Claim struck out.

B. Ground Two

9. According to Queen's Bench Rule 139, a Statement of Claim should contain only a concise summary of the material facts on which the Plaintiff relies. The Statement of Claim should not set out the evidence that the Plaintiff intends to rely upon to establish those facts. Also, the Statement of Claim should set out the points of law upon which the Plaintiff is relying. However, it should not contain the full legal argument that the Plaintiff will make to support his legal assertions.

10. It is submitted that the footnotes that are attached to the Statement of Claim in this case clearly offend these rules. The footnotes consist largely of case summaries and editorial comments. This material should be set out in the Brief of Law to be filed at trial. It should not be set out in the Statement of Claim. The footnotes also contain numerous references to evidence such as the report of Chief Justice Elmsley dated October 22, 1798. Finally, much of the material set out in the footnotes appears to be irrelevant to the legal claims being advanced such as the excerpts from the transcript of the hearing before the Supreme Court of Canada with respect to the motion to state a constitutional question in *Delgamuukw v. British Columbia* and the excerpts from the transcript of the disciplinary hearing of Bruce Clark before the Law Society of Upper Canada. While the issue raised by this case formed part of the background to those proceedings, they are neither legal determinations of the issue nor are they evidence with respect to the issue. Therefore, they are simply irrelevant and should not be referred to in the Statement of Claim.

C. Ground Three

11. The first two grounds advanced by Saskatchewan for striking out the Statement of Claim are procedural in nature. The last ground is substantive. It is the position of Saskatchewan that even if the Plaintiffs' claim was properly pleaded, it is not one that can be entertained by the Court.

12. The Plaintiffs allege that they are a sovereign, independent nation and that no federal or provincial laws apply to the Treaty 4 territory. They do not ask the Court directly for a declaration to this effect. Rather, they ask for a declaration that they are entitled to "independent and impartial third-party adjudication with respect to this issue." Presumably, the effect of this adjudication, if the Plaintiffs were successful, would be some sort of enforceable order declaring that the Plaintiffs are a sovereign, independent nation and that the Treaty 4 territory should no longer be considered to be within the geographical confines of either Canada or the Province of Saskatchewan. It is the position of Saskatchewan that this Court could not directly make any such order. It is also the position of Saskatchewan that this Court cannot make any order authorizing an adjudicative process that could lead to such a determination. The Court cannot do indirectly what it cannot do directly.

13. The test for striking out a Statement of Claim is that the claim must be clearly without merit. The action must be certain to fail. The Province acknowledges that the Court will not strike out a Statement of Claim if there is any doubt whatsoever about the outcome of the case. However, where a claim is obviously bad, a Defendant is entitled to have the Statement of Claim struck out in order to avoid the expense, delay and inconvenience of defending the action.

Hunt v. Carey Canada Inc., [1990] 2 S.C.R. 959.

14. It is a long-standing and well-entrenched constitutional principle that no domestic court has authority to question the sovereignty of the Crown. In *Delgamuukw v. British Columbia,* Wallace J.A. described the principle as follows:

It is beyond the competence of a municipal court to question the validity of the acquisition of sovereignty over new territory which is an act of state.

> *Delgamuukw v. British Columbia,* [1993] 5 W.W.R.
> 97 (B.C.C.A.) at p. 198; appeal allowed [1997] 3
> S.C.R. 1010, without discussion of this point.
> See also: *Mabo v. Queensland,* [1992] 107 A.L.R. 1
> (H.C.), at p. 51.
> *Sobhuza II v. Miller,* [1926] A.C. 518 (P.C.), at p. 525.

15. The Supreme Court affirmed that the Crown has asserted sovereignty over Aboriginal
people in Canada in *R. v. Sparrow,* wherein Dickson C.J. and La Forest J. stated:

> It is worth recalling that while British policy toward the native population was based on
> respect for their right to occupy their traditional lands, a proposition to which the *Royal
> Proclamation of 1763* bear witness, there was from the outset never any doubt that sov-
> ereignty and legislative power and indeed the underlying title, to such lands vested in
> the Crown.

> *R. v. Sparrow,* [1990] 1 S.C.R. 1075, at p. 1103.

16. There can be no question that the Crown has asserted sovereignty over the Treaty 4
territory. The majority of this land was purchased from the Hudson's Bay Company by the
Canadian Government in 1869. The newly acquired lands were admitted into Confederation by the terms of the *Rupert's Land and North-Western Territory Order* in 1870. This
Order specifically provided that from and after July 15, 1870 the Parliament of Canada
had "full power and authority to legislate for the future welfare and good governments of
the new Territory." There is nothing in the Order which suggests that Parliament's jurisdiction with respect to unceded Indian lands is contingent upon obtaining a surrender of
the Indian's interest or is in any way limited. While the Order specifically provides that
Canada shall settle the claims of the Indians to compensation for lands required for settlement, this provision merely recognizes the Indians' interest in their traditional lands in
conformity with the long-standing practice of the British Crown. It in no way derogates
from the plenary jurisdiction granted to Parliament by the Order.

> *Rupert's Land and North-Western Territory Order,* R.S.C. 1985,
> Appendix II, No. 9.

17. The *Rupert's Land and North-Western Territory Order* is part of the *Constitution of
Canada.* According to section 52(l) of the *Constitution Act, 1982,* the *Constitution of Canada* is the supreme law of Canada and any law that is inconsistent with the provisions of
the Constitution is, to the extent of the inconsistency, of no force or effect.

> *Constitution Act, 1982,* R.S.C. 1985,
> Appendix II, No. 44.

18. The Government of Canada subsequently entered into Treaties with the Indians inhabiting the newly acquired territories. These Treaties were known as the "numbered treaties". Their terms were all very similar. In each case, the Indians surrendered their
Aboriginal title to the lands that they traditionally occupied in order to allow settlement by
Canadians and Europeans to take place and to pave the way for the transcontinental rail-
way. In exchange, the Crown promised the Indians a number of things including reserve
lands, annual payments, assistance with the transition to an agricultural economy and
hunting, fishing and trapping rights. Treaty No. 4 was entered into in 1874. It encompasses
much of the land in what is now southern Saskatchewan.

19. The Plaintiffs have alleged in their Statement of Claim that Treaty No. 4 confirmed
their sovereignty over their traditional lands. It is the position of Saskatchewan that the
Treaty was not required in order for the Canadian Government to obtain sovereignty over

the Indian lands. That sovereignty was already an established fact and had been since July 15, 1870. The Treaty neither surrendered Indian sovereignty nor affirmed Indian sovereignty. The Treaty simply dealt with the surrender of the Indian interest in their traditional lands.

20. Nevertheless, the terms of the Treaty clearly acknowledge the sovereignty of the Crown. The Indians specifically promised to "conduct and behave themselves as good and loyal subjects of Her Majesty the Queen" and to "obey and abide by the law". The relevant provisions from the Treaty read as follows:

> And the undersigned Chiefs and Headmen on their own behalf, and on behalf of all other Indians inhabiting the tract within ceded, do hereby solemnly promise and engage to strictly observe this Treaty, and also to conduct and behave themselves as good and loyal subjects of Her Majesty the Queen.
>
> They promise and engage that they will, in all respects, obey and abide by the law: that they will maintain peace and good order between each other, and between themselves and other tribes of Indians, and between themselves and others of Her Majesty's subjects, whether Indian, Half-breeds or whites, now inhabiting, or hereafter to inhabit, any part of the said ceded tract; and that they will not molest the person or property of any inhabitant of such ceded tract, or the property of Her Majesty the Queen, or interfere with or trouble any person passing or travelling through the said tract or any part thereof; and that they will assist the officers of Her Majesty in bringing to justice and punishment any Indian offending against the stipulations of this Treaty, or infringing the laws in force in the country so ceded.

> Treaty No. 4 made between Her Majesty the Queen
> and the Cree, Saulteaux and other Indians at
> Qu'Appelle on September 15, 1874
> (Queen's Printer and Controller of Stationery, 1966).

21. The Province of Saskatchewan was created in 1905. By virtue of section 3 of the *Saskatchewan Act,* the Province has all of the same legislative powers as the original Provinces of Confederation possessed by virtue of the terms of the *Constitution Act, 1867* subject to certain exceptions which are not relevant to these proceedings. The plenary jurisdiction which had theretofore been vested in Parliament was after 1905 divided between Parliament and the provincial legislature. After 1905 the Province had constitutional authority to make certain laws applicable to the Treaty 4 territory.

> *Saskatchewan Act,* R. S. C. 1985, Appendix II, No. 2
> 1. *Constitution Act, 1867,* R.S.C. 1985, Appendix II, No. 5.

22. While the basis of the Plaintiffs' claim to be entitled to "independent and impartial third-party arbitration" of their claim to sovereignty is not clear, it appears from some of the material set out in the footnotes to the Statement of Claim that the genesis of the claim is an Order-in-Council dated March 9, 1704. This Order-in-Council was issued in connection with a land controversy between the Mohegan Indians and the Colony of Connecticut. It has no constitutional status in Canada. It is not referred to in the schedule of constitutional instruments referred to in section 52(2)(b) of the *Constitution Act, 1982.* Therefore, this Order-in-Council cannot override or annul the clear provisions of the *Constitution Act, 1867; the Rupert's Land and North-Western Territory Order,* and the *Saskatchewan Act,* (all of which are constitutional instruments) which grant legislative jurisdiction over the Treaty 4 territory to both Parliament and the provincial legislature. Even if the Order-in-Council dated March 9, 1704 had the effect that the Plaintiff says it has and applied to the lands in question, it has clearly been repealed by these constitutional provisions.

23. Arguments similar to those raised by the Plaintiffs have been made in the courts in the past and have been universally rejected. For example, in *R. v. Williams* and *R. v. Ignace,* the British Columbia Court of Appeal held that Aboriginal people are subject to the jurisdiction of the courts with respect to criminal offences and offences under provincial laws even though the offences occurred on land which had not been surrendered or ceded to the Crown by Treaty. In Saskatchewan, a group known as the Dene Sovereign has been advocating in court that it is a sovereign, independent nation and that its members are not subject to any federal or provincial laws. This argument has been rejected by various levels of court on numerous occasions.

> *R. v. Williams,* [1995] 2 C.N.L.R. 229, (B.C.C.A.).
> *R. v. Ignace,* [1998] 156 D.L.R. (4th) 713, (B.C.C.A.).
> *R. v. Chief,* [1997] 4 C.N.L.R. 212 (Sask. Q.B.).
> *R. v. Kahpeechoose,* [1997] 4 C.N.L.R. 215 (Sask. Prov. Ct.).

IV. NATURE OF RELIEF SOUGHT

24. The Applicant requests that the Statement of Claim be struck out in its entirety, without leave to amend, and that the action be dismissed with double costs.

ALL OF WHICH IS RESPECTFULLY SUBMITTED.

DATED at Regina, Saskatchewan this 30th day of December, 1998.

/s/
_____

P. Mitch Mc

AdamCounsel for the Attorney General for Saskatchewan

REPLY TO SASKATCHEWAN'S MOTION

3759/98

Pro se

IN THE COURT OF QUEEN'S BENCH
JUDICIAL CENTER OF REGINA

BETWEEN:

Ochapowace First Nation

RESPONDENT
(PLAINTIFF)

AND:

Saskatchewan

APPLICANT
(DEFENDANT)

and
Canada

RESPONDENT
(DEFENDANT)

REPLY RE SASKATCHEWAN'S MOTION TO STRIKE

1. Paragraph's (*a*) and (*b*) of Saskatchewan's notice of motion raise the same grounds as those raised in Canada's motion to strike and the respondent therefore adopts and repeats the reply to Canada's motion.

2. Paragraph (*c*) of Saskatchewan's notice of motion raises an additional ground and the balance of this reply is to it. The basis for this ground is the statement "no domestic

court can question the sovereignty of the crown," as if the Statement of Claim's request that the Court of Queen's Bench recognize the constitutional law confirming the native nations' sovereign right to third-party adjudication were tantamount to asking the court to "question the sovereignty of the crown." Saskatchewan has entirely missed the point, which is that the crown exercised its original claim of sovereignty by enacting constitutional law that is constitutive of the jurisdiction of the governments and courts of Canada and Saskatchewan. Correspondingly, this native nation does not ask to court "to question the sovereignty of the crown," but, to the contrary, to address the constitutive legislation and precedents that evidence the constitutional implementation of that sovereignty.

3. When that has been done it will be comprehended that the legislative and executive branches of Canada and Saskatchewan, and, correspondingly, the courts constituted and staffed by them, do not really exercise sovereign powers, at least not in the absolute sense. Rather, they exercise constitutionally defined jurisdictions which, by nature, are circumscribed and limited, not only by each other's counterbalancing constitutional jurisdiction but also by the native nations' counterbalancing constitutional jurisdiction as against both of theirs. Saskatchewan's fundamental error consists in her assumption that she and Canada are absolutely sovereign entities, when at law they are only sovereign within their constitutionally assigned respective fields of jurisdiction, the same as the plaintiff native nation is sovereign within its constitutionally protected field of jurisdiction. Saskatchewan and Canada can no more override the natives' jurisdiction than each other's, at least not without a constitutional amendment.

4. Saskatchewan's brief of law in support of her motion raises (at paragraph 14) the "act of state" doctrine, as if every purported exercise of jurisdiction by Canada and Saskatchewan in relation to natives were an act of state, unrestricted, as such, by constitutional law provisions. Again, Saskatchewan has missed the point. When the crown inceptively claimed sovereignty several centuries ago it constitutively exercised that claim by enacting constitutional law which created jurisdictions. Saskatchewan and Canada are entitled to exercise those jurisdictions. They are not, however, entitled in effect to turn back the clock and masquerade as if they were "the Crown" prior to the constitution.

5. Saskatchewan's said brief adds (at paragraph 15) that "there was from the outset never any doubt that sovereignty and legislative power and indeed the underlying title, to such lands vested in the Crown." That is the threshold. It begs the question of what, precisely, "the Crown" did in terms of exercising the said "sovereignty" and "underlying title." This is the question answered by the Statement of Claim's footnoted particulars.

6. For present purposes what is relevant is that by section 109 of the *Constitution Act, 1867* "the Crown" constitutionally assigned the said "underlying title" to the Provinces "subject to" the Indian "Interest," thereby confirming the constitutional paramountcy of the latter over the former. And by section 91(24) "the Crown" assigned to the federal government the jurisdiction to purchase the said "Interest." As to whether and to what extent a purchase has been made, that is a matter for independent and impartial third-party adjudication: *Order in Council (Great Britain) of 9 March 1704* in the matter of *Mohegan Indians v. Connecticut.*

7. Saskatchewan's said brief submits (at paragraph 16) "There can be no question that the Crown has asserted sovereignty over the Treaty 4 territory." Certainly, the Crown, as indicated above, "asserted sovereignty" over the whole of British North America, inclusive of the Treaty 4 region. But Saskatchewan then improperly treats the 1869 Hudson Bay purchase and the *Rupert's Land and North-Western Territory Order* in 1870 as if those instruments effectively repealed the phrase "subject to" in section 109 of the *Constitution Act, 1867.* Constitutionally, however, no such repeal of the previously established constitutional law can be so implied. There was never any "plenary jurisdiction granted to Parlia-

ment by the Order" as pretended by Saskatchewan. All that occurred was that the Hudson's Bay Company transferred the "underlying title" to Canada "subject to" the Indian "Interest" and thereafter Canada was empowered to negotiate for a purchase extinguishing (or varying) the said Indian interest. As to purchased portions, certainly, Canada's jurisdiction is indeed plenary. Just as certainly, as to yet unpurchased portions it remains "subject to" the Indian interest. In 1930 Canada transferred the underlying title to Saskatchewan, "subject to" the Indian "Interest" in any yet unpurchased portions.

8. In contrast with the claim's contention (at paragraph 3) that Treaty 4 was affirmative of native sovereignty, Saskatchewan's said brief (at paragraphs 19–20) construes the treaty as an extinguishment of native title and an affirmation of federal and provincial plenary jurisdiction. This conflict is identical to that presented on the facts in *Mohegan Indians v. Connecticut* in 1704. The principle of constitutional law settled by that precedent is that this issue of fact must go to independent and impartial third-party adjudication. This principle is not only the law, but necessary to the integrity of the rule of law. If at the outset the jurisdiction issue were to be conceded to the courts of either of the contesting sides to the dispute, the jurisdiction issue would by that very concession have been prejudged. As David Hume said of the principle of third-party adjudication:

Nothing is more certain than that men are, in great measure, governed by interest, and that even when they extend their concern beyond themselves it is not any great distance ... indifferent persons ... Here then is the origin of civil government and society.

9. In terms alone of pure reason, it is apparent that once the humanity of the natives was acknowledged with the enactment of *Sublimus Deus, 1537*, the decision in *Mohegan Indians v. Connecticut, 1704* was predetermined. Since the natives are human beings they are social beings, with institutions of law and government that characterize the human condition. Moreover, as officially observed by the Secretary of State for the Colonies "a steady and uniform attachment to, and love of Justice and Equity is one their first principles of Government." Therefore it is not in terms of *reason* that the non-native legal establishment is resistant to addressing the precedents and legislation which establish the natives' constitutional right to third-party adjudication, but rather *sentiment*: the feeling that while it would be unjust to insist that, whenever native and newcomer governments jurisdictionally conflict, the natives' courts should adjudicate, it makes comfortable sense to insist that the newcomer courts enjoy that racist monopoly.

10. The solution offered by reason to this inconsistency is the constitutionally recognized device of third-party adjudication, which removes, as the *Royal Proclamation of the 1763* said (in the purchase context) any apprehension that "the Indians may" not "be convinced of our Justice and determined Resolution to remove all reasonable Cause of Discontent."

11. Saskatchewan's said brief misrepresents (at paragraph 23) that "Arguments similar to those raised by the Plaintiffs have been made in the courts in the past and have been universally rejected," and, in support, has cited a series of cases supposedly doing the rejecting, preeminently the *Williams* and *Ignace* cases. But the courts below in *R. v. Williams* and *R. v. Ignace* declined to address the natives' court jurisdiction argument, on the ground that it supposedly had already had been considered and rejected on its merits by the courts below in the case of *Delgamuukw v. AGBC*. The Supreme Court of Canada refused leave to appeal in both *Williams* and *Ignace*, but, in *Delgamuukw* itself, went on to hold that the latter case is irrelevant to the jurisdiction argument, since that argument was never even raised in the courts below let alone considered on its merits and rejected.

12. The supposed precedent value of cases such as *R. v. Williams* and *R. v. Ignace* was reduced to zero when the Supreme Court acknowledged the irrelevancy of *Delgamuukw v. AGBC*, since all that those other cases did was to apply *Delgamuukw*, as if it were the determinative precedent.

13. The truth is that the precedents and legislation bearing upon the jurisdiction issue, and identified in the particulars of the constitutional law provided in the Statement of Claim, have not yet directly and squarely been addressed and analysed by any Canadian court, and in that sense the case at bar genuinely is one of first instance.

14. This is not to say that the issue is controversial, open to go either way. The said precedents and legislation are not only clear and plain but monolithic. They have not been rendered or enacted by federal or provincial courts or legislatures. Rather, the said precedents and legislation have been rendered and enacted, and thus given constitutional force and effect, by the Judicial Committee of the Privy Council and by the King in his Imperial Privy Council and Parliament, the architects of the Canadian constitution. If the rule of law is to have any meaning in Canada beyond that of an extension of tooth and claw by which raw power dominates regardless of truth, the Canadian courts will acknowledge themselves bound by the existing constitutional law.

15. The respondent respectfully asks the court for summary judgment on the preliminary point of jurisdictional law alone.

All of which is respectfully submitted.

DATED January 6, 1999.   Ochapowace First Nation
                                                per:
                                                /s/
                                                _____
                                                Chief
                                                /s/
                                                _____
                                                Councilor

MOTION BY INDIANS FOR IMMEDIATE JUDGMENT

                                                            3759/98
                                                            Pro Se

IN THE COURT OF QUEEN'S BENCH
JUDICIAL CENTER OF REGINA

BETWEEN:

                        Ochapowace First Nation
                                        PLAINTIFF/APPLICANT

AND:

                        Canada and Saskatchewan
                                        DEFENDANTS/RESPONDENTS

NOTICE OF MOTION

TAKE NOTICE that the Plaintiff applies at the same time and place as the motions of Canada and Saskatchewan to strike the statement claim, namely Thursday January 7, 1999 at 10: 00 a.m., for summary judgment upon the question of law alone identified by the Statement of Claim and Notice of Constitutional Question and, while reserving the right to make written reply, declines in addition to appear for the purpose of oral argument.

DATED December 7, 1998.   Ochapowace First Nation, per:
                                               /s/
                                               _____
                                               Chief
                                               /s/
                                               _____
                                               Councilor

MOTION BY INDIANS FOR COURT TO LISTEN
TO BRUCE CLARK ON THE LAW

3759/98
Pro se

IN THE COURT OF QUEEN'S BENCH
JUDICIAL CENTER OF REGINA

BETWEEN:

Ochapowace First Nation

PLAINTIFF/APPLICANT

AND:

Canada and Saskatchewan

DEFENDANTS/RESPONDENTS

NOTICE OF MOTION

TAKE NOTICE that the plaintiff on January 21, 1999 at 10: 00 a.m. or so soon thereafter as the matter can be heard the plaintiff will apply in chambers to have the court accept Bruce Clark, LL.B., M.A., Ph.D., as the plaintiff's *pro se* representative in these proceedings.

AND TAKE NOTICE that the grounds for the motion are:

1. The sole issue in the present action is court jurisdiction relative to native versus new-comer jurisdictional disputes over the territorial continuity of the native sovereignty for which the plaintiff contends;

2. A concomitant of the international and constitutional law identified in the claim's footnoted particulars is that by operation of law all Saskatchewan lawyers are in a pro-found conflict of interest which precludes any of them from representing the plaintiff herein on the said sole issue;

3. From all that appears the only scholar who has completed masters and doctoral the-ses into the precedents and legislation bearing directly upon the said issue is Bruce Clark, LL.B., M.A., Ph.D.;

4. The said Bruce Clark has been naturalized as a citizen of the plaintiff pursuant to the contended for native sovereignty and the plaintiff wishes to have him represent it as its spokesperson in these *pro se* proceedings but does not wish him to be a made a member, even occasionally, of the Saskatchewan bar and so placed under the said conflict of interest; and

5. If this Honourable Court will not hear from the said Bruce Clark as the plaintiff's *pro se* representative then the plaintiff respectfully asks the court to make its decision upon the basis of the plaintiff's written materials delivered to date, including the affidavit in support of this motion, and without further argument or submissions from the plaintiff.

AND TAKE NOTICE that in support of the motion the plaintiff relies upon the accompa-nying affidavit of Denton George dated January 18, 1999.

DATED the 18th day of January, 1999.

Ochapowace First Nation, *pro se*
Per:
/s/
_____

Chief Denton George

AFFIDAVIT

I, Denton George, of Whitewood, Saskatchewan, MAKE OATH AND SAY:

1. I am the Chief of the Ochapowace First Nation and as such have knowledge of the matters as to which deposition is made herein and the contents of the accompanying notice

of motion and materials previously delivered herein by the plaintiff are true to the best of my knowledge, information and belief. Moreover, I am advised and verily believe when, on Thursday January 7, 1999 the presiding judge adjourned the 3 motions before the court that day to January 21, 1999, he indicated that, because of the length of the particulars of the law determining the relevancy and sufficiency of the pleaded facts in the Statement of Claim, unless changes were made to the said Statement the court would be inclined peremptorily to look favourably upon the motions to strike and to dismiss the motion for judgment. He also indicated that the court was inclined to address the native sovereignty issue, but recommended in that connection retaining Saskatchewan counsel to re-do the claim rather than proceeding *pro se*.

2. As to the latter point, the plaintiff's said Statement and subsequent documents herein have been drafted by Bruce Clark, LL.B., M.A., PH.D. in consultation with the plaintiff's Saskatchewan legal counsel, who declined to appear as counsel of record in part at least because of what the said particulars of law have to say against the lawyers and the judges for their implication in the misprision of treason and fraud and complicity in genocide attributable to the unconstitutional assumption of jurisdiction over the aboriginal people. Ochapowace respects the position of the said Saskatchewan law firm and has made inquiries for alternatives, but is advised and verily believes that there is no person other than the said Bruce Clark who is at this time both willing and competent adequately to present and to defend the Ochapowace legal argument.

3. For these and the other reasons identified in its written replies to Canada's and Saskatchewan's motions, Ochapowace does not believe any changes to its Statement of Claim are in its best interests. However if otherwise the court were going to refuse to address claim at all, then Ochapowace would have to consent to the striking of all but the style of cause and the single page of facts headed "Claim." In that event Ochapowace will continue to rely upon the portions struck, read in conjunction with Ochapowace's replies to both motions to strike, as its brief of law and argument throughout the proceedings. You see, Ochapowace wants the portion struck to remain part of the court record for appeal purposes, or at least for posterity if the information is eventually suppressed or ignored in the resulting judgments due to the profound conflict of interest under which the newcomer judiciary and bar labour.

4. If the court wishes to avail itself of the opportunity to question Bruce Clark for clarification on the substance of the claim or brief of law, as the case may be, Ochapowace will make him available as its *pro se* representative. But if the court does not wish to take advantage of this particular opportunity fully to inform itself of the law, Ochapowace respectfully is content with resting its case on the written materials delivered to date, including this affidavit.

5. I am advised and verily believe that before closing there is one final word to be said concerning Saskatchewan's (erroneous) contention that, contrary to the Supreme Court's holding in *Delgamuukw v. AGBC*, the native sovereignty issue supposedly was disposed of in the Supreme Court by that court's denial of leave to appeal in *R. v. Williams* and in *R. v. Ignace*, as if denial of leave to appeal were the equivalent of a dismissal of appeal once granted. This ties in the with Supreme Court's (equally erroneous) comment in *Delgamuukw* that (at paragraph 75) "The content of common law aboriginal title, for example, has not been authoritatively determined by this Court ..." In fact, the said content was "authoritatively determined" in the Supreme Court case of *Church v. Fenton* (1878), 28 UCCP 384, 388, 399, aff'd (1879), 4 OAR 159, aff'd 5 SCR 239. In this, the trial court held:

The British Crown has invariably waived its right by conquest over all lands in the Province until the extinguishment of what the Crown has been pleased to recognize as the Indian title, by a treaty of surrender of the nature of that produced in this case; until such extinguishment of that title the Crown has never granted such lands ...

As early as 1837 was passed the Act 7 Wm. IV ch. 118 entitled "*An Act to provide for the disposal of the public lands in this Province*," &c. That was an Act passed for the management and sale of the portion of the lands vested in Her Majesty which consisted of Crown lands, clergy reserves, and school lands, the proceeds arising from the sale of which were to be accounted for as forming part of public revenue through the commissioner of Crown lands and the receiver-general.

This Act did not affect the lands vested in Her Majesty in which the Indians were interested, either as lands appropriated for their residence, as to which there had been no treaty of surrender for the purpose of extinguishing the Indian title, nor lands as to which there had been a surrender of such title, but in the proceeds arising from the sale of which the Indians being interested, the sale and management of them was retained in the Indian Department.

This term or designation "Public Lands," as applied to those lands the proceeds arising from the sale of which constituted part of the public revenue of the Province, has ever since been maintained in various Acts of the Legislature, viz., 2 Vic. ch. 15; 4 & 5 Vic. ch. 100; 16 Vic. ch. 159, and 23 Vic. ch. 2.

In contrast with *R. v. Williams* and *R. v. Ignace* upon which Saskatchewan relies, leave to appeal to the Supreme Court was not denied in *Church v. Fenton* but rather was granted, and the trial judgment eventually was affirmed on its merits. These cases represent the option: *Church v. Fenton* is the constitutional law; *R. v. Williams* and in *R. v. Ignace* is the unconstitutional assumption.

6. In 1878 *Church v. Fenton* thus effectively confirmed the *Order in Council (Canada) of 23 January 1875* (cited and quoted at pp. 8–11 of the Statement of Claim). Recall, the said order confirmed that the crown has no constitutional jurisdiction to grant land prior to an Indian treaty surrendering the Indian "Interest" "subject to" which the crown holds the underlying title as confirmed by section 109 of the *Constitution Act, 1867*. In spite of the 1879 Supreme Court's affirmation on appeal of that principle as expressed in *Church v. Fenton*, commencing in 1880 the federal government legislatively set in motion a policy designed to legitimize the provincial theft of the Indian interest, by breaking down Indian culture and therefor resistance, as follows:

The Indian Act, 1880, s. 72. Whenever the Governor in Council deems it advisable for the good government of a band to introduce the system of chiefs, he may by Order in Council provide that the chiefs of any band of Indians shall be elected, as hereinafter provided, at such time and place as the Superintendent-General may direct; ... Provided always, that all life chiefs now living shall continue to hold the rank of chief until death or resignation, or until their removal by the Governor for dishonesty, intemperance, immorality or incompetency: Provided also, that in the event of His Excellency ordering that the chiefs of a band shall be elected, then and in such case the life chiefs shall not exercise the powers of chiefs unless elected under such order to the exercise of such powers.

An Act further to amend "The Indian Act, 1880," SC 1884, c. 27, s.

1. Whoever induces, incites or stirs up any three or more Indians, non-treaty Indians or half-breeds apparently acting in concert, –

(*a.*) To make any request or demand of any agent or servant of the Government in a riotous, routous, disorderly or threatening manner, or in any manner calculated to cause a breach of the peace; or

(*b.*) To do an act calculated to cause a breach of the peace, –
Is guilty of a misdemeanor, and shall be liable to be imprisoned for any term not exceeding two years, with or without hard labor.

s. 3. Every Indian or other person who engages in or assists in celebrating the Indian festival known as the "Potlatch" or in the Indian dance known as the "Tamanawas" is guilty of a misdemeanor, and shall be liable to imprisonment for a term of not more than six months nor less than two months in any gaol or other place of confinement; and any Indian or other person who encourages, either directly or indirectly, an Indian or Indians to get up such a festival or dance, or to celebrate the same is guilty of a like offence, and shall be liable to the same punishment.

Those patently unconstitutional and genocidal *Indian Act* amendments are the "legislation" to which Prime Minister Sir John A. Macdonald referred in the *Return to an Order of House of Commons*, dated May 2, 1887 (20b) at 37 in a Memorandum dated January 3, 1887, as follows:

The great aim of our legislation has been to do away with the tribal system and assimilate the Indian people in all respects with the other inhabitants of the Dominion, as speedily as they are fit for the change.

To ensure that no one assisted the natives in bringing forward the constitutional law precluding this genocidal federal policy the government supplemented the reign of terror with legislation suppressing a counter-struggle by lawyers on behalf of the Indians:

An Act to amend the Indian Act, SC 1926–27, c. 32, s. 6. The said Act is amended by inserting the following section immediately after section one hundred and forty nine thereof: –
"149A. Every person who, without the consent of the Superintendent General expressed in writing, receives, obtains, solicits or requests from any Indian any payment or contribution or promise of any payment or contribution for the purpose of raising a fund or providing money for the prosecution of any claim which the tribe or band of Indians to which such Indian belongs, or of which he is a member, has or is represented to have for the recovery of any claim or money for the benefit of the said tribe or band, shall be guilty of an offence and liable upon summary conviction for each such offence to a penalty not exceeding two hundred dollars and not less than fifty dollars or to imprisonment for any term not exceeding two months."

7. The constitutional law recognized and affirmed by the said 1875 Canadian order in council and the said 1879 Supreme Court affirmation in *Church v. Fenton*, was re-confirmed by the Imperial Privy Council in *St. Catherine's Milling & Lumber Co. v. The Queen* (1888), 14 AC 46, 51, 53, 54, 55, 60 (JCPC) (Claim, pp. 12–14), *AG Ont. v. AG Can.*, [1897] AC 199, 205, 210–11 (JCPC) (Claim p. 14), *Ontario Mining Co. v. Seybold*, [1903] AC 73, 79 (JCPC) (Claim p. 14), *AG Can. v. AG Ont.*, [1910] AC 637, 644, 646 (JCPC) (Claim p. 14) and *R. v. Ontario & Minnesota Power Co.*, [1925] AC 196, 197 (JCPC) (Claim, p. 14).

8. Historically this continuity of the constitutional law was paralleled by an equal continuity of the genocidally unconstitutional federal policy introduced by section 72 of *The Indian Act, 1880*. The problem, today, as epitomized by *R. v. Williams* and *R. v. Ignace*, is that attitudes are informed by the policy and the domestic legislation implementing it, in

blindness to the constitutional law precluding it. This is a problem not just for native people, but for all people, whose paramount interest is in the integrity of the rule of law, even more than in stealing the land and the jurisdiction of the natives. This is not a complex problem, but it is a persistent problem because the non-native legal establishment refuses to address the law since it labours under the profound conflict of interest attributable to its implication in the ongoing genocide.

9. I am advised and verily believe that the only hope for justice as the application of truth to affairs lies in breaking the genocidally unconstitutional interpretive monopoly assumed by the newcomers' courts contrary to the fundamental common law principle of third-party adjudication recognized and affirmed by *Mohegan Indians v. Connecticut*.

SWORN BEFORE ME at the City of
Regina, Province of Saskatchewan
this 18th day of January, 1999.

/s/

Denton George

/s/

A Commissioner etc.

COURT DECISION REFUSING TO LISTEN

3759/98

IN THE QUEEN'S BENCH
JUDICIAL CENTER OF REGINA

Between:

Ochapowace First Nation

Plaintiff

– and –

Canada and Saskatchewan

Defendants

JUDGMENT   BARCLAY J.

January 29, 1999

The plaintiff, Ochapowace First Nation, (the "Band") applies to the court for directions as to whether Bruce Clark LL.B. may represent the Band in this action.

Mr. Clark is a member of the Ontario bar. However, he is not in good standing as he has not paid his current membership fees. Mr. Allan Snell, who represented the Law Society of Saskatchewan at the hearing, indicated that once Mr. Clark satisfies the Law Society of Saskatchewan that he is a member of the Law Society of Ontario in good standing, and applies for an occasional appearance certificate and pays a fee of $100.00, he would be entitled to appear as counsel for the Band in this action. I understand that Mr. Clark will not make the necessary application.

Section 30 of *The Legal Profession Act*, SS 1990, c. L-10.1, prohibits Mr. Clark from acting as counsel for the Band unless he is granted a practicing certificate by the Law Society of Saskatchewan: See also *Atamanchuk v. DeBruin and Smithwick's Physiotherapy* (1992), 106 Sask. R. 288 (Sask. QB).

The Saskatchewan Court of Appeal in *Kieling et al. v. Saskatchewan Wheat Pool* (1992), 105 Sask. R. 11 also held that a party cannot bring a representative action unless represented by a lawyer.

The application by the Band is dismissed. Costs shall be in the cause.

BARCLAY J.
Judge

INDIAN APPEAL FROM THE REFUSAL

Appeal No. 3187
Pro Se

IN THE COURT OF APPEAL FOR SASKATCHEWAN

Between

Ochapowace First Nation

Appellant (Plaintiff)

– and –

Canada and Saskatchewan

Respondents (Defendants)

NOTICE OF APPEAL

TAKE NOTICE

1. THAT Ochapowace First Nation the above named Appellant hereby appeals to the Court of Appeal from the judgment of the Honourable Mr Justice Barclay issued on the 29th day of January, 1999.

2. THAT the whole judgment is being appealed.

3. THAT the appeal is taken on the following grounds:

3.1. Although interlocutory as to form the judgment in substance constitutes a final disposition of the native sovereignty/jurisdiction issue being litigated.

3.2. The application was for a direction indicating the court below's consent to Bruce Clark addressing the court in the action as a naturalized citizen of the *pro se* plaintiff speaking to his own Indian interest, both as of right and on the ground that the conflict of interest under which lawyers labour in relation to the said issue being litigated precludes representation by any counsel who is a member (whether permanent or temporary) of the Saskatchewan bar.

3.3. The court below misconstrued the application as if it were for Bruce Clark to appear in an agency capacity as counsel, and on this erroneous basis applied the *Legal Profession Act* of Saskatchewan, thereby prejudging the native sovereignty issue against the Plaintiff on the merits for all purposes in the action and thus rendering further proceedings redundant.

3.4. In addition, the court below gratuitously introduced a Catch-22 of genocidally unconstitutional consequence. The learned judge held that "a party cannot bring a representative action unless represented by a lawyer," thereby signaling that the action must be dismissed because framed *pro se,* in circumstances where representation by a lawyer is precluded by the above mentioned structural conflict of interest. This illustrates, exquisitely, the *modus operandi* for the genocide by chicanery identified in the *pro se* claim: the native right is, with genocidal consequence, frustrated by the chicanery of denying a remedy, without ever addressing the settled law constitutionally both constituting the right and correspondingly guaranteeing the remedy of independent and impartial third-party adjudication in relation to the right.

4. THAT even if the judgment under appeal were not final and leave to appeal were therefore required, the merit to the appeal, the significance of the issue to the practice, the significance of the issue to the action and the effect of the potential delay on the progress of the action, all cry out for retroactive leave to appeal as a matter of course in light of the purpose and application of the *Court of Appeal Rules* as set forth in Rule 3 and 4. Since genocide and the integrity of the rule of law hang in the balance, delay is legally unconscionable and morally reprehensible. The Court of

Appeal has jurisdiction under section 6 of the *Court of Appeal Act* to address the third-party adjudication remedy attributable to the native sovereignty/jurisdiction issue on its merits, as a question of pure law alone which was preempted by the court below.

5. THAT the Appellant requests the following relief: a declaration of the Plaintiff's remedy of third-party adjudication as prayed for in the claim.

6. THAT the Appellant's address for service is ...
    The lawyer in charge of the file is: not applicable. The appeal, like the action, is *pro se*.

7. THAT the Appellant requests that this appeal be heard at Regina, Saskatchewan and there disposed of without delay on an expedited emergency basis as a written appeal without hearing oral argument from the Appellant.

DATED at Regina, Saskatchewan, this 2nd day of February, 1999.

Ochapowace First Nation, per:

/s/
_____

Chief

/s/
_____

Councilor

WRITTEN ARGUMENT OF *PRO SE* APPELLANT IN LIEU OF FACTUM

Part I. Introduction

1. Appellant native nation sued for recognition by declaration of its *prima facie* remedy of independent and impartial third-party adjudication in relation to a native sovereignty/jurisdiction dispute with the Defendants, on the grounds

   (*a*) the 1704 precedent *Mohegan Indians v. Connecticut* confirmed that remedy;

   (*b*) the *Royal Proclamation of 1763 prima facie* rendered the ignoring of that remedy by crown courts the judicial crimes of misprision (no proof of *mens rea* required) of treason and fraud; and

   (*c*) the *Convention for the Prevention and Punishment of the Crime of Genocide, 1948* arguably rendered the said ignoring complicity in crimes related to genocide.

Part II. Jurisdiction and Standard for Review

2. As a court of general jurisdiction the Court of Queen's Bench *prima facie* has inherent jurisdiction to address the question of its own and by implication its inferior courts' subject-matter and territorial jurisdiction.

3. *Attorney General of Ontario v. Attorney General of Canada* (1895), 25 SCR 434, 535: [The courts] would with the consent of the Crown and of all our governments strain to their utmost limit all ordinary rules of construction or principles of law – the governing motive being that in all questions between Her Majesty and "Her faithful Indian allies" there must be on her part, and on the part of those who represent her, not good faith, but more, there must be not only justice, but generosity.

Part III. Summary of the Facts

4. The Appellant's claim supported by its submissions of record on the several interrelated motions affirm the unquestioned and unquestionable fact that the Appellant is a native tribe or nation in a native sovereignty/jurisdiction dispute with the Respondents and the courts constituted by them. As to such dispute, the Appellant sought recognition by declaration of its remedy of third-party adjudication.

Part IV. Points in Issue

5. Court jurisdiction relative to the said dispute, which is to say the applicability of the principle of constitutional law settled by *Mohegan Indians v. Connecticut.*

Part V. Argument

6. The argument is set out at paragraphs 3 and 4 of the Notice of Appeal. If *stare decisis* governs, there is no case capable in good faith of being argued against the applicability of the principle of constitutional common law settled by *Mohegan Indians v. Connecticut.* Willful blindness to this existing law negates the rule of law by rendering the courts of Canada and Saskatchewan accomplices in misprision of treason, fraud and crimes related to genocide.

Part VI. Relief

7. A declaration confirming the Appellant's international and constitutional law remedy of third-party adjudication.

Part VII. Authorities

8. Particulars of the international and constitutional law informing and continuing the principle of constitutional law settled by *Mohegan Indians v. Connecticut* are set out in the claim and the written submissions constituting the complete court file in the court below, as reproduced in the Appeal Book.

Part VIII. Estimated Time for Hearing

9. Appellant waives the right to make oral argument and oral reply. No time is required by Appellant at any hearing. The appeal rests on the Appeal Book and this Written Argument in Lieu of Factum.

DATED at Regina, Saskatchewan, this 2nd day of February, 1999.

Ochapowace First Nation, per:

/s/
_____

Chief

/s/
_____

Councilor

COURT DECISION DISMISSING THE CLAIM

Q.B.G.   A. D. 1998
No. 3759   J. C. R.

IN THE QUEEN'S BENCH
JUDICIAL CENTRE OF REGINA

BETWEEN:

OCHAPOWACE FIRST NATION

PLAINTIFF

and

CANADA AND SASKATCHEWAN

DEFENDANTS

No one appearing on behalf of Ochapowace First Nation
(written submissions having been filed)
Mark R. Kindrachuk   for the defendant, Canada
P. Mitch McAdam   for the Attorney General for Saskatchewan
FIAT   ZARZECZNY J.

February 9, 1999

[1] Canada and Saskatchewan apply to strike out tile statement of claim issued by the Ochapowace First Nation dated December 7, 1998. The statement of claim is one page long and consists of six paragraphs. It provides as follows:

CLAIM

1. The Plaintiff is an Indian nation of the Treaty 4 region.

2. The Defendants' judicial, executive and legislative branches assume jurisdiction to apply federal and provincial law to the said region, as if there were no constitutional law' native sovereignty precluding this.

3. Native oral history is that the said treaty as explained and understood at the time of signing was intended to reinforce and protect the said native sovereignty, and, if that is not what the treaty's words in English say, then its words must be rectified so as to conform to the contractual intent.

4. The consequence of the said assumption is serious bodily or mental harm within the meaning of article 2(b) of the *Convention for the Prevention and Punishment of the Crime of Genocide, 1948.*

5. For constitution law purposes, the Indians' remedy of third-party adjudication in relation to the right of native sovereignty was recognized in the 18th century and affirmed in the 19th century; and, on the 12th day of September 1995 in the matter of *Delgamuukw v. AGBC*, the Supreme Court of Canada invited the testing of the constitutional law continuity of the said remedy in this the 20th century, specifically by way of the commencement of an action for "declaratory relief" before a Canadian court of general and original jurisdiction.

6. The Plaintiff therefore seeks a declaration acknowledging its remedy of independent and impartial third-party adjudication.

DATED December 7, 1998.   Ochapowace First Nation, per:

/s/
_____

Chief-Denton George

/s/
_____

Councilor-Louis Kenny

[2] Attached to the statement of claim is a 26 page document which might best be described as a research paper to which in turn is attached a 35 page appendix which appears to be a complaint similar to the claim filed by the plaintiff in this case filed against the United States of America in the United States District Court for the Southern District of New York to which is further attached another substantial research document.

[3] In total there are approximately 60 pages of mostly single spaced text attached to the claim.

[4] The defendants' motion to strike is made pursuant to Rule 173 of *The Queen's Bench Rules* with additional reliance placed upon Rule 139(l).

[5] These rules provide as follows:

173. The court may at any stage of an action order any pleading or any part thereof to be struck out, with or without leave to amend, on the ground that:

(a) it discloses no reasonable cause of action or defence, as the case may be;

(b) it is immaterial, redundant or unnecessarily prolix;

(c) it is scandalous, frivolous or vexatious;

(d) it may prejudice, embarrass or delay the fair trial of the action;

(e) it is otherwise an abuse of the process of the Court;

and may order the action to be stayed or dismissed or judgment to be entered accordingly or may grant such order as may be just. Unless otherwise directed, the offending party shall pay double the costs to which the other party would otherwise be entitled.

139(l). Every pleading shall contain and contain only a statement in a summary Form of the material facts on which the party pleading relies for his claim or defence, but not the evidence by which the facts are to be proved. A pleading shall be as brief as the nature of the case will permit.

[6] In the cases of *The Attorney General of Canada v. Inuit Tapirisat of Canada and the National Anti-poverty Organization*, [1980] 2 S.C.R. 735 and *Hunt v. Carey Canada Inc.*, [1990] 2 S.C.R. 959, the Supreme Court of Canada directed that pleadings should only be struck in plain and obvious cases where it is beyond doubt that the pleadings do not meet the minimum requirements of pleadings at law. Such cases include circumstances where a statement of claim discloses no reasonable cause of action. (To similar effect see the Saskatchewan Court of Appeal decision in *Sagon v. Royal Bank of Canada, et al.* (1992), 105 Sask. R. 133 (C.A.)).

[7] In the case of *Sandy Ridge Sawing Ltd. v. Norrish and Carson* (1996), 140 Sask. R. 146 (Q.B.), it was held that the onus is upon a plaintiff to state sufficient facts to establish the requisite legal elements for a cause of action, otherwise the claim should be struck. Pleadings which are immaterial, redundant or unnecessarily prolix or that may tend to prejudice, embarrass or delay a fair trial of an action should be struck (see *Romanic v. Hartman*, [1986] 5 W.W.R. 610 (Sask. Q. B.)).

[8] In an application to strike pleadings (and in particular statements of claim) the only documents to be considered are the notice of motion, the statement of claim and any particulars which may have been furnished pursuant to a demand for particulars (*Bank of Montreal v. Schmidt et al.* (1989), 75 Sask. R. 157 (Sask. C.A.)).

[9] In determining this application I have considered not only the statement of claim filed by the Ochapowace First Nation but additionally, to the extent it may be said that the addendum and/appendix might be incorporated by reference therein (and without determining whether or not in fact the latter constitute a part of the statement of claim or not) I am unable to conclude that the plaintiff has met the minimum requirements of the rules and principles of law applicable to pleadings as I have reviewed them.

[10] The pleadings as filed do not disclose a reasonable cause of action or the material facts upon which the plaintiff relies to support its claim as required by Rules 139(l) and 173(a). If one did regard the addendum and appendix to the statement of claim as being incorporated into it by reference then a large bulk of it is clearly immaterial and unnecessarily prolix.

[11] The pleadings in a case particularly the statement of claim and statement of defence, are the foundations upon which the parties proceed to an adjudication of legal rights, duties and obligations. The Rules of Court which are applicable to all parties seeking the determination of rights from the Court govern the requirements of these pleadings. It is the plaintiff in this case that has invoked the application of the Rules of Court by its filing of a statement of claim in the first instance. It is therefore the plaintiff that has the initial responsibility to meet the fundamental requirements which the rules impose, namely, to identify the cause(s) of action, the relief sought and the minimum facts upon which such cause(s) of action and relief are based.

[12] The statement of claim and attached materials filed by the Ochapowace First Nation aver to or hint at broad claims of sovereignty both territorial and institutional. If, as can only presently be speculated, such important and fundamental issues are indeed intended to be raised by the plaintiff in an action before the Court, the plaintiff must accept the responsibility for itself and all of its members to present its claim to the Court in such a fashion so as to identify clearly the claim(s) being made and the factual basis for those claims consistent with the requirements of the Rules of Court and proper practice. It may be that the plaintiff cannot do so without obtaining the advice and counsel of a lawyer qualified to practice in Saskatchewan.

[13] The applications made by Canada and Saskatchewan to strike the claim are granted but without prejudice to the right of the Ochapowace First Nation to bring a statement of claim properly raising the claims, facts and the relief requested from the Court intended to be raised by the current documents.

[14] In view of the granting of the motion to strike the claim, the motion by the plaintiff for summary judgment must of necessity be dismissed.

[15] If the applicants seek costs with respect to these applications that matter may be spoken to by arrangement with the local registrar.

/s/ _____

Mr Justice Zarzeczny

INDIAN APPEAL FROM THE DISMISSAL

Appeal No. 3198

IN THE COURT OF APPEAL FOR SASKATCHEWAN

Between

Ochapowace First Nation

Appellant (Plaintiff)

– and –

Canada and Saskatchewan

Respondents (Defendants)

NOTICE OF APPEAL

TAKE NOTICE

1. THAT Ochapowace First Nation the above named Appellant hereby appeals to the Court of Appeal from the judgment (by fiat) of the Honourable Mr Justice Zarzeczny dated the 4th day of February, 1999 and issued and entered the 9th day of February, 1999.

2. THAT the whole judgment is being appealed.

3. THAT the Appellant cross-references and relies upon the Appeal Book and Written Argument in CA3187/99 [the earlier appeal].

4. THAT this appeal is taken on the ground that even if the Statement of Claim were not in every way necessary and appropriate given the extraordinary need to account for the law rendering the pleaded facts not only relevant but sufficient, since the Appellant consented to deleting the entire Statement of Claim except for the single page containing a concise statement of material facts alone there was no legitimate basis for striking the claim (albeit without prejudice to re-filing). Furthermore, since the court has indicated that a *pro se* action supposedly is not permissible for a native nation, and since the uncontradicted evidence is that representation by counsel is precluded by the nature of the issue being litigated, the achievement of the striking is to perfect by chicanery the newcomer court system's genocidally unconstitutional usurpation of jurisdiction relative to arguably unceded territory.

5. THAT the Appellant requests the following relief: a declaration of the Plaintiff's remedy of third-party adjudication as prayed for in the claim.

6. THAT the Appellant's address for service is: ...The lawyer in charge of the file is: not applicable. The appeal, like the action, is *pro se*.

7. THAT the Appellant requests that this appeal be heard at Regina, Saskatchewan and there disposed of without delay on an expedited emergency basis as a written appeal without hearing oral argument from the Appellant.

DATED at Regina, Saskatchewan, this 8th day of February, 1999.

Ochapowace First Nation, per:

/s/

Chief

/s/

Councilor

RESPONSE OF CANADA TO THE APPEAL FROM THE REFUSAL TO LISTEN

C.A. No. 3187

IN THE COURT OF APPEAL FOR SASKATCHEWAN

BETWEEN:

OCHAPOWACE FIRST NATION

APPELLANT (Plaintiff)

and

CANADA AND SASKATCHEWAN

RESPONDENTS (Defendants)

FACTUM ON BEHALF OF THE RESPONDENT, CANADA

I. INTRODUCTION

1. This is an appeal from a decision of Barclay J. in chambers, dismissing an application by the appellant for leave to have Bruce Clark appear and make representations on its behalf, not as a lawyer but as the appellant's *"pro se* representative."

II. JURISDICTION AND STANDARD OF REVIEW

2. The decision which the appellant seeks to appeal is an interlocutory decision. As a result, the appellant should have obtained leave before filing its Notice of Appeal.

   The Court of Appeal Act, R. S. S. 1978, c. C-42, s. 6

   Thompson Lands Ltd. v. Henry Kelly Tractor Ltd. (1984), 34 Sask. R. 246 at pp. 249–250 (C.A.)

3. However on 9 February 1999, after the Notice of Appeal in this matter was filed, Zarzeczny J. made an order striking out the Statement of Claim in this action, and the appellant has also appealed from this order. Under Rule 12 of the *Court of Appeal Rules,* the appellant would be entitled to include its appeal from the interlocutory order of Barclay J. in its appeal from the final order, in any event. As a result, the fact that this appeal was not properly commenced does not appear to be of any practical consequence.

4. The decision of Barclay J. was made in the discretionary exercise of the inherent jurisdiction of the court to regulate its own practice. It is submitted that the Court of Appeal should only intervene to set aside the decision below if it concludes that Barclay J. failed to appreciate the extent of his discretion or misdirected himself in its exercise.

   Govan Local School Board v. Last Mountain School Division No. 29 of Sask., [1991] 6 W.W.R. 150 (Sask. C.A.), *per* Vancise J.A. at p. 156.

   Abse v. Smith, [1986] 1 Q.B. 536 (C.A.), *per* Sir John Donaldson M.R. at pp. 554–555.

III. FACTS

5. The appellant commenced an action in the Court of Queen's Bench on 7 December 1998, claiming a declaration "acknowledging its remedy of independent and impartial third-party adjudication."

6. The respondents moved to strike out the Statement of Claim.
7. The appellant moved for "summary judgment." In the appellant's Notice of Motion, the appellant indicated that it did not wish to present oral argument in support of this motion.
8. The appellant also made an application to have the court accept Bruce Clark as its "pro se representative" and hear oral submissions from Mr. Clark. The appellant indicated that Mr. Clark had been naturalized as a citizen of the Ochapowace First Nation, and that it wished him to appear as its spokesperson without having been admitted to the Saskatchewan Bar. In the appellant's estimation, it could not be represented by a member of the Bar because this would give rise to a conflict of interest.
9. All of these motions came before Barclay J. in chambers on 21 January 1999. Barclay J. decided to deal first with the motion for leave to have Mr. Clark appear, and adjourned the other motions to be dealt with after this initial matter was decided. Mr. Clark appeared before Barclay J., and in response to questions from the court, Mr. Clark indicated that while he had been admitted to the Bar of Ontario, he was not a member in good standing of that or any Bar, as he had not paid his current membership fee.
10. On 29 January 1999, Barclay J. delivered a decision dismissing the appellant's application for leave to have Mr. Clark appear. The written reasons delivered by Barclay J. set out two propositions in support of this decision:
    (a) Under s. 30 of *The Legal Profession Act, 1990*, S.S. 1990–91, c, L-10. 1, Mr. Clark is prohibited from acting as counsel for the appellant unless he is granted a practicing certificate by the Law Society of Saskatchewan; and
    (b) Under Rule 10 of the *Queen's Bench Rules*, a party who acts in a representative capacity must be represented by a lawyer.

IV. POINTS IN ISSUE

11. The respondent respectfully submits that the issue raised by this appeal is not "court jurisdiction relative to the … dispute", as is contended by the appellant. The respondent says that the only issue raised by this appeal is whether, in response to the application before him, Barclay J. exercised the inherent jurisdiction of the Court of Queen's Bench to regulate its own process in accordance with the parameters which that court has adopted in the *Queen's Bench Rules* to govern the exercise of that jurisdiction.

V. ARGUMENT

12. It is clear that the Court of Queen's Bench has the inherent jurisdiction to regulate its own practice, and, in particular, to control the categories of person who can appear before the court as advocates.
    Shinkaruk Enterprises Ltd. v. Commonwealth Insurance Co. (1994), 22 C.C.L.I. (2d) 209 (Sask. C.A.)
    Awmanchuk v. Debruin (1992), 106 Sask. R. 288 (Q.B.)
    Professional Sign Crafters (1988) Ltd. v. Wedekind (1994), 19 Alta. L.R. (3)d) 53 (Q.B.)
    Abse v. Smith. supra, at pp. 552–556
13. Section 10 of the *Queen's Bench Rules,* which describes and defines the circumstances in which a person may appear in court on behalf of a party to litigation, has been made in the exercise of this inherent jurisdiction and the authority conferred by s. 89 of *The Queen's Bench Act*, R.S.S. 1978. c. Q-1.
14. Barclay J. appears to have approached the question on the basis that he would not allow Mr. Clark to appear because this would give rise to a breach of s. 30 of *The Legal Profession Act*. The reasons delivered by Barclay J. do not indicate explicitly whether he regarded this simply as a circumstance which influenced the way in which he would exercise his discretion, or whether he concluded that he had no authority to

permit Mr. Clark to appear because of the statutory prohibition. In *Professional Sign Crafters (1988) Ltd. v. Wedekind, supra,* the Alberta Court of Queen's Bench decided that a similar provision in section 103 of *The Legal Profession Act* of Alberta did not limit the exercise of the court's inherent jurisdiction to control the right of audience.

15. It is submitted that there is nothing in the decision of Barclay J. which necessitates the conclusion that he considered that the provisions of *The Legal Profession Act* were determinative of the matter before him. His reasons suggest only that he regarded the statutory prohibition as a relevant consideration (which it certainly was).

16. Barclay J. also referred to Rule 10 of the *Queen's Bench Rules*. It is evident that he was perplexed by the questions of the same kind as those raised by this court in *Ochapowace First Nation v. A.(V)*, [1995] 3 W.W.R. 32 (Sask. C.A.). at p. 40:

> First, it is unclear as to what sort of legal entity made this application. Was it a statutory body created by the *Indian Act, R.S.C. 1985. c. 1–5.* with only the powers conferred by that Act, or was it the approximately 1,000 members of the Band bringing a representative action, or was it something else?

17. The individual members of the Ochapowace First Nation are not named as plaintiffs in the Statement of Claim. The claim appears to be made on behalf of all of the members of the appellant. As a result, it is submitted that it was reasonable for Barclay J. to conclude, as he apparently did, that the action was a representative action in substance, if not in name, and that Rule 10(1) therefore required the appellant to be represented by a lawyer. In this respect, Barclay J. simply applied the rule which the court has adopted to govern the exercise of its inherent jurisdiction, in circumstances to which the policy considerations underlying the rule had clear application.

   Kieling v. Saskatchewan Wheat Pool (1991), 96 Sask. R. 134 (Q.B.) at pp. 135–136, (1992), 105 Sask. R. 11 (C.A.) at pp. 12–13

18. There is some authority for the proposition that an Indian band can sue or be sued in its own name, at least with respect to matters falling within the statutory authority conferred by the *Indian Act*. However, it is not clear whether this means that an Indian band is an entity with legal personality.

   Kucey v. Peter Ballantyne Band Council, [1987] 3 W.W.R. 438 (Sask. C.A.)
   King v. Gull Bay Indian Band (1983), 38 C.P.C. 1 (Ont. Dist. Ct.)
   Springhill Lumber Ltd. v. Lake St. Martin Indian Band (1985), 6 Man. R. (2d) 231 (Q.B.); reversed on other grounds (1986), 38 Man. R. (2d) 157 (C.A.)
   Bannon v. Pervais, [1990] 2 C.N.L.R. 17 (Ont. Dist. Ct.)
   Clow Darling Ltd. v. Big Trout Lake Band, [1990] 4 C.N.L.R. 7 (Ont. Dist. Ct.)

19. However, even if the appellant in this case is regarded as in some way analogous to a corporation, so that Rule 10(2) of the *Queens Bench Rules* could have some application, its representation by a non-lawyer remains a matter which is controlled by the discretion of the court.

20. The decision made by Barclay J. was made in the exercise of the inherent jurisdiction of the Court over its own process and practice. As was said by Sir John Donaldson M. R. in *Abse v. Smith, supra,* at p. 555:

> It is for the judges of the High Court to regulate the practices of the High Court and for the judges of this court to regulate those of the Court of Appeal. The only concern of this court with the practices of the High Court is in an appellate capacity, namely to consider whether individual judges of the High Court are correctly ap-

plying the general practices of that court, subject always to their discretion to depart therefrom in appropriate circumstances.

21. It is respectfully submitted that there is nothing in the decision of Barclay J. to suggest that he made any error of law or misdirected himself as to the principles which should govern the exercise of his discretion, and accordingly that there is no basis upon which his decision should be reversed by this honourable Court.

VI. RELIEF

22. The respondent therefore submits that this appeal should be dismissed.

All of which is respectfully submitted.

Dated at Saskatoon, Saskatchewan, this 16th day of February 1999.

/s/
_____
Mark R. Kindrachuk
of Counsel for the respondent
(defendant), Canada

RESPONSE OF CANADA TO THE APPEAL FROM THE DISMISSAL OF THE CLAIM

C.A. No. 3198

IN THE COURT OF APPEAL FOR SASKATCHEWAN

BETWEEN:

OCHAPOWACE FIRST NATION

APPELLANT (Plaintiff)

and

CANADA AND SASKATCHEWAN

RESPONDENTS (Defendants)

FACTUM ON BEHALF OF THE RESPONDENT, CANADA

I. INTRODUCTION

1. This is an appeal from a decision of Zarzeczny J. in chambers, ordering that the Statement of Claim filed by the appellant be struck out, without prejudice to the right of the appellant to bring a new Statement of Claim properly raising the claims intended to be raised by it, and dismissing the appellant's motion for summary judgment.

2. Before filing the Notice of Appeal in this case, the appellant filed a Notice of Appeal challenging an earlier interlocutory decision in the same proceedings. The appellant filed an Appeal Book in that earlier appeal without first obtaining the agreement of the respondents as to its contents. The appellant has now filed an Appeal Book in this appeal which includes only the decision appealed from, the Notice of Appeal, and the appellant's written submissions in the court below.

3. In order to avoid confusion, this factum will refer to the Appeal Book in the first appeal as "Appeal Book I" and to the Appeal Book filed in this appeal as "Appeal Book II".

II. JURISDICTION AND STANDARD OF REVIEW

4. The respondent submits that this case falls within the general right of appeal conferred by section 6 of *The Court of Appeal Act,* R.S.S. 1978, c. C-42, and that the applicable standard of review is correctness in law.

III. SUMMARY OF FACTS

5. ment of Claim consists of one page of numbered paragraphs, followed by 65 pages of annotations which consist of discussions of legal arguments, quotations from judicial

decisions and other authorities, and copies of legal submissions filed in other court proceedings. The relief sought by the appellant was a declaration "acknowledging its remedy of independent and impartial third-party adjudication."

6. Both respondents moved to strike out the Statement of Claim pursuant to Rule 173 of *The Queen's Bench Rules.*

7. The appellant moved for "summary judgment".

8. These applications were heard by Zarzeczny J. in chambers on 4 February 1999. on 9 February 1999, Zarzeczny J. delivered a fiat directing that the Statement of Claim be struck out, but without prejudice to the right of the Ochapowace First Nation to bring a statement of claim properly raising the claims, facts and the relief requested from the Court. The appellant's motion for summary judgment was dismissed.

IV. POINTS IN ISSUE

9. The following issues are raised by this appeal:
   (a) Was the learned judge in chambers correct in concluding that the Statement of Claim should be struck out because it does not disclose a reasonable cause of action or the material facts upon which the appellant relies, as required by Rules 139(l) and 173(a) of *The Queen's Bench Rules?*
   (b) Was the learned chambers judge correct in dismissing the appellant's motion for summary judgment?

V. ARGUMENT

1. The learned chambers judge correctly concluded that the Statement of Claim should be struck out because it does not identify the cause of action, the relief sought and the minimum factual basis for the cause of action.

10. The function of pleadings is to define with clarity and precision the question in controversy between litigants. A defendant is entitled to know what it is that the plaintiff asserts against him or her, and the plaintiff is entitled to know the nature of the defence raised in answer to the claim.
    Ducharme v. Davies (1983), 29 Sask. R. 54, *per* Cameron J.A. at pp. 68–69 (C.A.)
    Romanic v. Hartman (1986), 51 Sask. R. 169 at p. 171 (Q.B.)
    Piché v. Big "C" First Nation (1994), 121 Sask. R. 20 (Q.B.)

11. Rule 139(l) of *The Queen's Bench Rules* provides as follows:
    Every pleading shall contain *and contain only* a statement *in a summary form* of the material facts upon which the party pleading relies for his claim or defence, but not the evidence by which the facts are to be proved. A pleading shall be as brief as the nature of the case will permit. [emphasis added]

12. Allegations which are unnecessary and immaterial may be struck out.
    Romanic v. Hartman, supra
    Hutchinson v. Saskatoon Funeral Home Co. Ltd. (1985), 41 Sask. R. 119 (Q.B.)

13. The Statement of Claim in this case is embarrassing because, as the learned judge in chambers indicated, it is unclear whether the 65 pages of annotations should be considered as incorporated by reference, and therefore as part of the Statement of Claim.

14. It is respectfully submitted that the learned chambers judge was correct in concluding that if the annotations are not part of the Statement of Claim, the Statement of Claim should be struck out because it fails to set out the claim being made and the factual basis for that claim.

15. If the annotations are part of the Statement of Claim, the Statement of Claim should be struck out because it consists largely of discussions of points of law and legal submissions. The respondent should not be required, in its Statement of Defence, to reply to the 65 pages of citations and commentary which are set out in the annotations.

2. The learned chambers judge correctly concluded that the appellant's motion for summary judgment should be dismissed.

16. It is apparent that if the Statement of Claim is struck out, the motion for summary judgment must necessarily be dismissed, as was observed by the learned chambers judge.

17. Even if the Statement of Claim is not struck out, it is submitted that there is no basis upon which the appellant can claim to be entitled to a summary determination of this action before the defendants have pleaded in response to the Statement of Claim.

18. The appellant's Notice of Motion gives no indication of the rule of court or statutory provision upon which the motion is based. This is contrary to the requirements of Rule 441B of *The Queen's Bench Rules,* and is unsatisfactory because it compels the respondent to guess at the intended basis for the motion.

19. The only procedure for "summary judgment" is that provided by Part IX of *The Queen's Bench Rules.* This procedure clearly has no application to the present case, since it is available only where the claim is for a debt or liquidated demand (Rule 129).

20. Rule 188 permits an application for the preliminary determination of a point of law. This procedure is inappropriate here, since it requires an agreed statement of facts, or at least an undisputed factual basis which is apparent from the record.
Goertz v. Zmud (1995), 137 Sask. R. 289 (C.A.)

21. The same considerations apply to Rule 264, which empowers the court to make an order stating a special case for determination.

22. Finally, Rule 247 permits an application for judgment on admissions made by an opposing party. This clearly can have no relevance to the present case, where Statements of Defence remain to be delivered.

VI. RELIEF

23. The respondent respectfully submits that this appeal should be dismissed with costs.

All of which is respectfully submitted.

Dated at Saskatoon, Saskatchewan, this 16th day of February, 1999.

/s/
_____

Mark R. Kindrachuk
of Counsel for the respondent
(defendant), Canada

[Note: Saskatchewan's response was the same as Canada's]

COURT OF APPEAL DECISIONS

Appeal #3187

IN THE COURT OF APPEAL FOR SASKATCHEWAN

OCHAPOWACE FIRST NATION

APPELLANT

– and –

CANADA and SASKATCHEWAN

RESPONDENT

COUNSEL

Mr. P.M. McAdam for the respondent Saskatchewan
Mr. M.R. Kindrachuk for the respondent Canada
No one appearing on behalf of Ochapowace First Nation

DISPOSITION

Upon a careful examination of all the material filed, as well as the reasons for decision given by Mr Justice Barclay, we can find no reversible error made by him. The appeal must, accordingly, be dismissed. The Government of Canada will have its costs in the usual way. In respect of the Government of Saskatchewan, there will be no costs, since none were asked for.
APRIL 8, 1999.
REASONS BY: The Honourable Mr. Justice Sherstobitoff
IN CONCURRENCE: The Honourable Mr. Justice Tallis
                                         The Honourable Mr. Justice Gerwing

                                                              Appeal #3198

IN THE COURT OF APPEAL FOR SASKATCHEWAN
OCHAPOWACE FIRST NATION
                    APPELLANT

– and –

CANADA and SASKATCHEWAN
                    RESPONDENT
COUNSEL

Mr. P.M. McAdam for the respondent Saskatchewan

Mr. M.R. Kindrachuk for the respondent Canada

No one appearing on behalf of Ochapowace First Nation

DISPOSITION

Upon a careful examination of all the material filed, as well as the reasons for decision given by Mr Justice Zarzecny, we can find no reversible error made by him. The appeal must, accordingly, be dismissed. The Government of Canada will have its costs in the usual way. In respect of the Government of Saskatchewan, there will be no costs, since none were asked for.
APRIL 8, 1999.
REASONS BY: The Honourable Mr. Justice Sherstobitoff
IN CONCURRENCE: The Honourable Mr. Justice Tallis
                                         The Honourable Mr. Justice Gerwing

APPLICATION BY INDIANS TO SUPREME COURT FOR LEAVE TO APPEAL

IN THE SUPREME COURT OF CANADA
(On Appeal from the Court of Appeal for the Province of
Saskatchewan)

Between

Ochapowace First Nation

                                              Applicant
                                              (Plaintiff,
                                              Moving Party
                                     and Responding Party)

And

Canada and Saskatchewan

                                              Respondents
                                              (Defendants,
                                              Responding Parties
                                       and Moving Parties)

APPLICATION FOR LEAVE TO APPEAL
(FOR THE PURPOSE OF STATING A CONSTITUTIONAL QUESTION)
Section 40(*1*) of the *Supreme Court Act*
Rules 23(*1*) and 32(*1*)(*b*) of the *Rules of the Supreme Court*
NOTICE OF APPLICATION FOR LEAVE TO APPEAL

TAKE NOTICE that the applicant will apply to this Court pursuant to section 40(*1*) of the *Supreme Court Act* and rule 23(*1*) of the *Rules of the Supreme Court* for an order granting leave to appeal against the Court of Appeal's dismissal on 8 April 1999 of the applicant's appeals against the Court of Queen's Bench's order dated 29 January 1999 and judgment dated 9 February 1999.

AND FURTHER TAKE NOTICE that the documents identified in the Table of Contents [the documents reproduced above] will be referred to in support of such application for leave.

AND FURTHER TAKE NOTICE that the said application for leave shall be made on the ground the judgments below constitute a fraudulent and treasonable pretence and complicity in genocide.

DATED April 8, 1999, by Ochapowace First Nation *pro se*, per the following members each as to his own beneficial interest in the aboriginal right:

/s/   /s/
_____   _____
Chief Denton George   Councilor Louis Kenny

NOTICE OF APPLICATION TO STATE A CONSTITUTIONAL QUESTION

TAKE NOTICE that the applicant will apply to the Chief Justice or a judge pursuant to rule 32(*1*)(*b*) of the *Rules of Supreme Court* for an order stating the following constitutional question:

Do the phrases "under such Regulations and Restrictions as are used in other Colonies" and "reserved to" as used in the *Royal Proclamation of 1763*, when read in conjunction with the terms "subject to" and "Interest" as used in section 109 of the *Constitution Act, 1867*, signify that the remedy of third-party adjudication, as recognized by the *Order in Council of 9 March 1704* in the matter of *Mohegan Indians v. Connecticut*, is an "existing aboriginal right" within the meaning of section 35(*1*) of the *Constitution Act, 1982*, so that the jurisdiction of the respondents' judges and courts under the domestic legislation enacted pursuant to sections 92(*14*), 96 and 101 of the *Constitution Act, 1867* is inoperable relative to the Indians pending such third-party adjudication of the fact of territorial crown "Purchase" from the Indians within the meaning of the *Royal Proclamation of 1763*?

AND FURTHER TAKE NOTICE that the accompanying notice of application for leave to appeal will be referred to in support of this application.

AND FURTHER TAKE NOTICE that this application shall be made on the same ground as the said application for leave to appeal.

DATED April 8, 1999, by Ochapowace First Nation *pro se*, per the following members each as to his own beneficial interest in the aboriginal right:

/s/   /s/
_____   _____
Chief Denton George   Councilor Louis Kenny

MEMORANDUM OF ARGUMENT

PART I: FACT[11]

1. Applicant native government per its members Chief Denton George, Councilor Louis Kenny and Attorney General Bruce Clark each as to his own beneficial interest in

the aboriginal right sought a declaration recognizing the aboriginal rights remedy of third-party adjudication in relation to a boundary and jurisdictional dispute with the respondent newcomer governments.[12]

PART II: POINT IN ISSUE

2. Is the said remedy an "existing aboriginal right"[13] "subject to"[14] which the respondents' judges and courts exercise jurisdiction, as questioned in the accompanying notice of application to state a constitutional question?

PART III: ARGUMENT

3. Leave should be granted if the issue to be raised on the proposed appeal is of public importance.[15]

4. On September 12, 1995 in *Delgamuukw v. AGBC* the Court held that it is, but declined to address it then because it had not previously been raised in that case. The Court recommended seeking declaratory relief in a fresh action.[16]

5. But when this was done the courts below perversely evaded the issue by pretending:

(a) that Ochapowace First Nation was seeking to have Bruce Clark address the issue as if he were an agent rather than a member of the nation speaking in elation to his own beneficial interest;[17] and

(b) that the fact of the governmental jurisdictional dispute was not clearly and plainly identified in the claim or, if it was, that the issue of third-party adjudication in relation to that fact was preempted from consideration by a series of cases applying the said case of *Delgamuukw v. AGBC* as if that case were a precedent on that issue.[18]

6. By operation of law each of the said evasions constitutes a "Pretence" that *prima facie* consummates "Misprision of Treason and Frauds and Abuses"[19] and, arguably, inflicts "serious bodily or mental harm" resulting in "Genocide," a culling of a "part" of "a national, ethnical, racial or religious group," namely, those particular aboriginal people who insist upon their full measure of liberty free from newcomer government and court meddling upon the basis of premature assumptions of jurisdiction.[20] Judicial *mens rea* need not be proven relative to "Misprision;"[21] and in relation to "Complicity in Genocide" is evidenced by the judges' willful blindness to the issue, legislation and precedents.

7. At the jurisprudential level, therefor, the "importance" within the meaning of section 40(*1*) of the *Supreme Court Act* of the proposed appeal is as a test case for measuring the integrity of the "rule of law" within the meaning of the *Constitution Act, 1982* upon which the basis of absolute respect for which Canada is supposed to be constituted as a state.[22] Is law the art of the possible in this country? which is to say might is right. Or does justice here consist in the application of truth to affairs? which is to imply, and perhaps risk the maxim *fiat justitia, ruat coelum* (let justice[23] be done, though the heavens fall.)

PART IV: ORDER REQUESTED

10. Leave to appeal to state the constitutional question.

DATED April 8, 1999, by Ochapowace First Nation *pro se*, per the following members each as to his own beneficial interest in the aboriginal right:

/s/ _____   /s/ _____

Chief Denton George   Councilor Louis Kenny

NOTES: INTERNATIONAL AND CONSTITUTIONAL LAW

I PARTICULARS OF THE CONSTITUTIONAL LAW UPON WHICH RESTS THE RELE-
VANCY AND SUFFICIENCY OF THE COMPLAINT:

A. NATURAL AND INTERNATIONAL LAW INCORPORATED INTO THE CONSTITU-
TIONAL LAW:

Sublimus Deus, 1537 (papal bull). "We ... consider, however, that the *Indians are truly
Men* ... we define and declare by these letters, or by any translation thereof signed by
any notary public and sealed with the seal of any ecclesiastical dignitary, to which the
same credit shall be given as to the originals, that notwithstanding whatever may have
been said to the contrary, the said Indians ... are by no means to be deprived of their
liberty or the *possession* of their property ...; and that they may and should, freely and
legitimately, enjoy their liberty and possession of their property; nor should they be in
any way enslaved; *should the contrary happen, it shall be null and of no effect.*" [em-
phasis added]

Declaration of Independence, 1776: "When in the Course of human events, it becomes necessary for one People to dissolve the Political Bands which have connected
them with another, and to assume among the Powers of the Earth, the separate and
equal Station to which *the Laws of Nature and of Nature's God* entitle them, a decent
Respect to the Opinions of Mankind requires that they should declare the causes
which impel them to the Separation. We hold these Truths to be self-evident, that *all
Men are created equal*, that they are endowed by their Creator with certain unalienable
Rights, that among these are Life, *Liberty*, and the Pursuit of Happiness – That to secure these Rights, Governments are instituted among Men, deriving their just Powers
from *the Consent of the Governed ...*" [emphasis added]

B. PRE-INDEPENDENCE LEGISLATION INCORPORATED INTO THE CONSTITUTIONAL
LAW:

An Act to prevent deceit and forgeries, NYCL, c. 8 (1684)."For the preventing of many
deceits and fforgerys which may happen through the artifice of wicked and evil
minded people Be it Enacted by this Generall Assembly and by the authority of the
same that no bargain sale Mortgage or grant of any house or Land within this Province
shall be holden good in Law Except ye same be done by Deed in writting under ye
hand and Seale of the Grantor & delivery and possession given in part in the name of
the whole by the said Grantor or his attorney so authorized under hand and seale and
unless ye said Deeds be acknowledged by the said Grantor before one of the Judges of
Oyer and Terminer and Generall Goale Delivery within one yeare after sealing thereof
and Recorded as is prescribed in an Act Intitled, An Act to prevent ffrauds in convey-
encing of Lands made this present session of Assembly ... PROVIDED Also and Be it
ffurther Enacted by the authority aforesaid that no Conveyance Deed or Promise shall
be of any fforce or Vallidity nor shall the Grantor be Compelled to acknowledge the
same if it were obtained by Illegall violence Imprisonm't or any kind of fforcable
Compulsions called Duress any thing to the Contrary hereof notwithstanding."

An Act concerning purchasing of lands from the Indians, NYCL, c. 9 (1684). "BEE itt
Enacted by this Gen'll Assembly and by the authority of the same that from hencefor-
ward noe Purchase of Lands from the Indians shall bee esteemed a good Title without
Leave first had and obtaineid from the Governour signified by a Warrant under his
hand and Seale and entered on Record in the Secritaries office att New Yorke and Satisfaction for the said Purchase acknowliged by the Indians from whome the Purchase

was made which is to bee Recorded likewise which purchase soe made and prosecuted and entered on Record in the office aforesaid shall from that time be Vallid to all intents and purpoases."

Order in Council (Great Britain) of 9 March 1704 in the matter of *Mohegan Indians v. Connecticut.* Affirmed by *Order in Council (Great Britain) of 23 January 1773.* "On perusal and Consideration of the Case annexed it doth not appear to me that the Lands now claimed by the Indians were intended to pass or could pass to the Corporation of the English Colony of Connecticut or that it was intended to Dispossess the Indians who before and after the Grant were the owners and possessors of the same and therefore what the Corporation hath done by the Act mentioned in the Case is an apparent Injury to them and Her Majesty notwithstanding the powers granted to that Corporation, there not being any words in the Grant to exclude Her Majesty, Her Majesty may Lawfully erect a Court within that Colony to do Justice in this matter and in the erecting of such Court may reserve an Appeal to Her Majesty in Council & may command the Governors of that Corporation not to oppress those Indians or deprive them of their right but to do them right notwithstanding the Act made by them to dispossess them which I am of opinion was illegal and void."

The preceding *Order in Council of 1704* is discussed in Joseph H. Smith, *Appeals to the Privy Council from the American Plantations,* New York, Columbia University Press, 1950, excerpts, pp. 417–25, 461–63. "UP TO THIS POINT we have dealt with the regulatory and procedural aspects of what may be described as the ordinary appellate jurisdiction of the Privy Council as the court last instance in the judicial hierarchy of the several dominions of the crown. There remains to be considered the jurisdiction which was exercised exceptionally, in the sense that it depended upon particular commission. The exercise of this power was unusual, since it involved controversies between units which were politically independent of each other, but were in some wise in subjection to the crown. *** The controversies which we are about to discuss all related to disputed boundaries, a subject matter of the greatest jurisdictional significance and the parties in the several causes, with one exception, were of equal capacity. The exception was the case between the Mohegan Indians and the colony of Connecticut, once described as 'the greatest cause that ever was heard at the Council Board.' This litigation, which dragged on for decades, is properly considered in connection with the intercolonial boundary disputes, since the plaintiff tribe was recognized to possess attributes of internal sovereignty sufficient at least to maintain and prosecute an action. *** As to proceeding in the English courts, Yorke was of opinion the common law courts could not exercise jurisdiction. If a point of equity were involved, the Chancery Court might take cognizance and compel the parties resident within the realm to perform its decree ... Despite the earlier settlement of the Pennsylvania-Maryland boundary, recognition of the original jurisdiction of the Privy Council in the eighteenth century as a procedural possibility came late, so that royal commissions with appeals reserved were employed in the majority of the judicial settlements of disputed colonial boundaries ... Later, in 1773, it was alleged that 'in every question of boundary between two colonies, the King, in Privy Council, exercises original jurisdiction on the principles of feudal sovereignty. There can be no other tribunal.' *** ... In conclusion, it can be said that of the procedural alternatives available to the Council – original jurisdiction by the King in Council, concilar appeal from the judgment of a colonial court, and issuance of a commission under the Great Seal with an appeal reserved to the King in Council – only the last was important.

THE MOHEGAN INDIANS V. CONNECTICUT

With this discussion of the jurisdictional basis, let us examine specific cases. The first cause to occupy our attention is the prolonged controversy between the Mohegan Indians and the colony of Connecticut ... *** ... in 1703 Owenco on behalf of the Mohegans petitioned the Queen in Council, setting forth that by order of the General Court [of Connecticut] the tribe had been deprived of a tract of land reserved to them by treaty, that application for redress had been made to the Connecticut government ... *** Upon query to the Board of Trade, Attorney General Northey stated that it do not appear that the lands claimed by the Mohegans were intended to pass to the corporation under the charter. In the absence of excluding words in the charter the Queen might lawfully erect a court within the colony to do justice in the matter, reserving an appeal to the Queen in Council. A commission was accordingly advised to issue ... *** Although the General Court was ignorant of the powers granted to the commission, it appointed a committee to appear before the commissioners. This committee was instructed to show the unreasonableness of the Mohegan claims if the court were one of inquiry, but to protest and withdraw if judicial determination of titles was attempted. When the royal commissioners assembled at Stonington, Connecticut, in August, 1705, the colony representatives, perceiving the latter intent, protested against the legality of such determination. It was insisted that such action was contrary to law, to the royal intent, to the colony charter, and to the rights of subjects throughout the dominions. Notwithstanding this objection and some interference with the proceedings, the commissioners proceeded to hear the complaint *ex parte*. On August 24, 1705, the commissioners, accepting *in toto* Mohegan interpretation of the above events, gave judgment that Oweneco and the Mohegans be restored to possession of four tracts of land of which they had been unjustly deprived, with costs ... in fact, the judgment was never executed. Although greatly alarmed by the trial of freeholds by commissions without jury or legal process, the colony at first doubted the value of an appeal ... Nevertheless, on February 14, 1705/6, Sir Henry Amherst, the Connecticut agent, presented to the Queen in Council an appeal from the commission determination ... *** On February 20 the Committee [of appeal] ordered that a copy of the petition and appeal be transmitted to the Mohegan agent to answer, and that the appeal be heard the first week after Easter ... ***The Committee upheld the propriety of the commission, since frequent treaties revealed that the Mohegans were a sovereign nation ... *** However, the Committee finally advised that as much of the sentence as awarded costs should be reversed and that a commission of review should be issued for reviewing the residue of the sentence ... ***For some years the controversy remained in abeyance ... ***To establish his claims to recompense and guardianship, Mason, accompanied by the usurped Mahomet, in 1735 journeyed to England, where the Duke of Newcastle was memorialized by Mahomet upon the failure to enforce the earlier commission determination and upon the injuries received by the Mohegans at the hands of the Connecticut subjects. The Board of Trade at first intended to represent that the 1705 judgment be executed or cause shown, but upon discovery of the appeal therefrom, it advised the granting of a new commission of review invested with the same authority and power for rehearing and determining all matters in dispute as were granted by the earlier unexecuted commission ... *** After the issuance of the commission, Connecticut sought to improve its position by securing from Ben Uncas releases of all rights accruing under the 1705 judgment and of all other claims to the controverted lands. On May 24, 1738, the commissioners, ... convened at Norwich,

Connecticut ... neither the Indians nor Samuel Mason, the son of the late John Mason and their alleged guardian, were granted a hearing, on the ground that Ben Uncas was the rightful sachem. The New York members, being dissatisfied with such proceedings, filed their protest against them and withdrew. The Rhode Island commissioners proceeded in the hearing, declaring Ben Uncas rightful sachem and admitting his releases made subsequent to the issuance of the commission. Thereupon, the remaining commissioners reversed the 1705 judgment, except as to one tract, the so-called 'Mohegan fields,' still in tribal possession. Although denied an appeal by the commissioners, Samuel and John Mason, both sons of the late guardian, appealed directly to the King in Council from this judgment, while the New York members, Daniel Horsmanden and Philip van Cortland, made separate return. Despite objection by the Connecticut agent, this representation elicited conciliar approval, the proceedings were set aside on July 31, 1740, and a new commission of review was ordered to pass under the Great Seal ... *** [1743] ... Ben Uncas was then allowed to lay before the court what he had to offer, mainly a disclaimer of the lands in controversy ... The numerous tenants in possession of controverted lands, being summoned by the commissioners, entered a plea to the jurisdiction, alleging a commission to determine individual land titles in a course of equity to be contrary to the laws of England, and of Connecticut, and to the colony charter. Demurrer being made to this plea, it was overruled. Commissioner Horsmanden was of the opinion that the Indians were a distinct people, that the property of the soil was in the Indians, and that royal charters did not *ipso facto* impropriate lands delimited therein to subjects until fair and honest purchases were made from the natives. A dispute as to property in lands between a distinct people and English subjects could not be determined by the laws of England, but only by the law of nature and nations. And it was upon this foundation that these commissions had issued. President Colden dissenting, stated that the Mohegans were not a separate or sovereign state, but were subjects of England ... *** On August 16 a new decree was accordingly made, to the effect that the August 24, 1705, determination of the commission be repealed and declared null and void, excepting that part of the decree that concerned the 'sequestered lands' confirmed to the Mohegans by a May, 1721 assembly act, which was affirmed. *** ... the petition and the appeal was not entered at the Council Office until July, 1746. Referred to the Committee, the appeal remained dormant until 1756, due to lack of funds to prosecute it, Connecticut endeavoring to prevent the crown financing of the appeal. *** ... After a further period of dormancy the respondent tenants entered their appearance to the appeal in December, 1769. *** ... the Committee proceeded to hear the cause on the merits in June, 1770 ... *** ... it was not until December 19, 1772, that the Committee reported, advising affirmation of the judgment of the 1743 commissioners. The Order in Council followed on January 15, 1773. Thus, sixty-nine years after the date of the issuance of the first commission the cause came to a definitive termination. This case affords an extreme example of the difficulties faced in enforcing and unpopular adjudication against a colony enjoying quasi-sovereignty. Yet the cause is distinguishable in its difficulties in that one party, the Mohegans, although juristically regarded as sovereign, did not enjoy *de facto* sovereignty. *** ... From this and the three other causes [*Massachusetts v. New Hampshire*; *Massachusetts v. Rhode Island*; and *New York v. New Jersey*] it is evident that commission and appeal procedure might prove cumbersome, dilatory, and expensive. Interference with successful operation by colonial recalcitrance was more difficult to overcome than in ordinary appeals from the established courts. But the imperial authorities adhered to the commission and appeal as a procedural device, and such procedure did meet with some, if not unqualified, success in settling intercolonial boundary controversies. The solution which the Privy Council hit upon for the settlement of the several causes here discussed possessed a significance far beyond the immediate circumstances of its use. There can be little doubt but that the method evolved for the settlement of disputes between states under the Articles of Confederation derived from the conciliar employment of the commission for intercolonial controversies. The conduct of proceedings in the Connecticut-Pennsylvania (1782) illustrates how the details of the commission procedure persisted. More far-reaching even than these effects was the influence of colonial experience upon the revival of international arbitration at the instance of the United States after 1783. For this John Jay, who had been a clerk of the New York-New Jersey boundary commission, who became Secretary for Foreign Affairs, and who later negotiated the celebrated treaty of 1794, was largely responsible. There is no more striking instance of the adaptation and remolding of a legal institution, and while the United States may properly pride itself upon its achievement in reviving the use of international arbitration, a share of the credit should not be gainsaid the Privy Council."

Royal Proclamation (Great Britain) of 7 October 1763. "And whereas it is just and reasonable and essential to our Interest and the Security of our Colonies that the several Nations or Tribes of Indians with whom We are connected and who live under our Protection should not be molested or disturbed in the Possession of such Parts of Our Dominions and Territories as not having been ceded to or purchased by Us are *reserved to them or any of them* as their Hunting Grounds. – We do therefore with the Advice of our Privy Council declare it to be our Royal Will and Pleasure that no Governor or Commander in Chief ... do presume upon any *Pretence* whatever to grant Warrants of Survey or pass any Patents for Lands ... upon any Lands whatever which not having been ceded to or purchased by Us as aforesaid are reserved to the said Indians or any of them. And We do further strictly enjoin and require all Persons whatever who have either wilfully or inadvertently seated themselves ... upon any ... Lands which not having been ceded to or purchased by Us are *still* reserved to the said Indians as aforesaid forthwith to remove themselves from such Settlements. And whereas *great Frauds and Abuses* have been committed in purchasing Lands of the Indians to the great Prejudice of our Interests and to the great Dissatisfaction of the said Indians In order therefore to prevent such Irregularities for the future and to the end that the Indians may be convinced of our Justice and determined Resolution to remove all reasonable Cause of Discontent We do with the Advice of our Privy Council strictly enjoin and require that ... if at any Time any of the said Indians should be inclined to dispose of the said Lands the same shall be Purchased ... at some public Meeting or Assembly of the said Indians to be held for that Purpose ..." [emphasis added]

Royal Regulation (Spain), 1772, s. 6. "With the nations that remain quiet or neutral there will be maintained the best treatment and communication, overlooking some of their faults and lesser excesses, and endeavoring to induce them by good example to admit missionaries and to submit to my authority; ... In no case shall the Indians arrested be sent into servitude as has illegally been done in the past; instead they will be treated and assisted as prescribed for prisoners of war."

C. POST-INDEPENDENCE LEGISLATION INCORPORATED INTO THE CONSTITUTIONAL LAW:

Constitution, 1789. "Art.1.Sec.2.Par.3 ... excluding Indians not taxed ..." [*i.e.*, from the enumeration for the franchise relative, by implication, to the purchased territory, as to which region alone the *Constitution's* primary *raison d'être* is relevant; *i.e.,* the apportionment of jurisdiction as between the federal and state levels of domestic government and the apparatus for domestic government at the federal level.]

"Art.1.Sec.8. The Congress shall have the power ... Par.3. To regulate commerce with foreign nations, and among the Indian tribes."

"Art.2.Sec.2.Par.2. He [the president] shall have power, by and with the advice and consent of the senate, to make treaties, provided two-thirds of the senators present concur."

Thirteenth Amendment, 1865. "Sec.1. Neither slavery nor involuntary servitude, except as a punishment for crime whereof the party shall have been duly convicted, shall exist within the United States, or any place within their jurisdiction."

"Sec.2. Congress shall have power to enforce this article by appropriate legislation." [These two sections illustrate the constitutionally required means for repealing or rendering illegal an institution expressly authorized by, or at least implicitly countenanced by, the *Constitution*, such means being by constitutional amendment. The alternative is not permissible, being a judicial declaration that events have superseded the former constitutional law countenancing of an institution, because the courts' function is to declare the law as it is written rather than as it should be written. See, *infra*, PARTICULARS OF THE CONSTITUTIONAL LAW CONCERNING THE NATURE OF THE JUDICIAL FUNCTION.]

Fourteenth Amendment, 1868. "Sec.2 ... excluding Indians not taxed ..." [*cf.,* above, *Constitution, 1789*, Art.1.Sec.2.Par.3. The constitutional law class "Indians not taxed," being those Indians occupying yet unpurchased territory, remain outside the franchise enumeration. Which is logical, since those particular Indians still enjoy native sovereignty under constitutional law in relation specifically and only to such yet unpurchased territory, rather than benefit from the non-native sovereignty in relation to territory which, in contrast, has been purchased from the Indians pursuant to Art.2.Sec.2.Par.2, which allots to the president "power, by and with the advice and consent of the senate, to make treaties, provided two-thirds of the senators present concur." Pending purchase, federal jurisdiction in relation to Indians upon the yet unpurchased territory is the jurisdiction expressly conferred by Art.1.Sec.8, namely the jurisdiction of Congress "To regulate commerce with foreign nations, and among the Indian tribes." This express constitutional jurisdiction to make treaties, and regulate commerce, does not confer plenary jurisdiction pending treaty, but, rather, precludes it, since the expression of the lesser specific power by necessary implication excludes the greater general power. See also, S. McSloy, "Back to the Future: Native American Sovereignty in the 21st Century," *New York University Review of Law & Social Change*, 20: 2: 1993 at 217–302. McSloy affirms the absence of a basis in the *Constitution* for the modern conventional assumption of federal plenary jurisdiction in relation even to territory not yet purchased from the Indians.]

D. POST-INDEPENDENCE CONSTITUTIONAL LAW PRECEDENTS:
Marshall v. Clark, 1 KY 77, 80–1 (CA 1791). "The dormant title of the Indian tribes remained to be extinguished by government, either by purchase or by conquest, and when that was done it enured to the benefit of the citizens who had previously acquired a title from the crown, and did not authorize a new grant of the lands as waste and unappropriated ... the Indian title did not impede either the power of the legislature to grant the land to the officers and soldiers, or the location of the lands on trea-

sury warrants, the grantee in either case must risk the event of the Indian claim, and yield to it if finally established, or have the benefit of a former or future extinction thereof."

Hughes v. Dougherty, 1 Yeat's 497, 498 (PA CA 1791). "The settlement on this land was against the law. It was an offense which tended to involve the country in blood."

Plumstead v. Rudebagh, 1 Yeat's 502, 504 (PA SC 1791). "In 1761, the soil belonged to the aborigines."

Weiser v. Moody, 2 Yeat's 127, 127–8 (PA SC 1796). "We are no enemies to bona fide improvements, restricted within rational limits. But these were never deemed to extend beyond the lands purchased from the Indians. Such a system would be wild, as well as highly impolitic, and would tend to deluge the country in blood, by provoking the savage nations to hostilities ... [If a grant to a third party was made] with full knowledge [of the unsurrendered Indian possession] ... The patent would enure to the benefit of the grantee, when the lands afterwards came to be purchased from the Indians." [Otherwise, the grant was absolutely null and void as made by mistake or deception.]

Sherer v. McFarland, 2 Yeat's 224, 225 (PA SC 1797). "[The colonial governments] bought the land from the natives, and gave them valuable considerations therefor. Herein they evinced a strong sense of moral honesty, as well as sound extended policy."

Strother v. Cathey, Morgan's 1 NC 162, 168 (SC 1807). "[An Indian treaty is a] relinquishment of that possessory right which alone had been yielded to the Indians."

Fletcher v. Peck, 6 Cranch's 87, 121 (SC 1810). "[The Indian interest] is certainly to be respected by all courts."

New Jersey v. Wilson, 7 Cranch's 164, 166 (SC 1812). "Every requisite to the formation of a contract is found in the proceedings between the then colony of New Jersey and the Indians."

Thompson v. Johnson, 6 Binney's 68, 68 (PA SC 1813). "[Grants] for lands not purchased of the Indians, and which the proprietaries [William Penn and others] did not know at the time of granting to be within the Indian limits, pass no rights."

Meigs v. McLungs Lessee, 9 Cranch's 11, 17 (SC 1815). "The treaty is the contract of both parties."

Johnson v. McIntosh, 8 Wheaton's 543, 574, 592, 597 (SC 1823). "[The Indians] were admitted to be the rightful occupants of the soil, with a legal as well as a just claim to retain possession of it, and to use it to their own discretion. [The Indian interest] is certainly to be respected by all courts. [Regarding the *Royal Proclamation of 1763*] The authority of this proclamation, so far as it respects this continent, has never been denied."

Arnold v. Mundy, 6 NJ 1, 83 (SC 1821). "[New Jersey] did not drive out the natives, but by a peaceable purchase became possessed of their rights to the soil, ..."

Danforth v. Wear, 9 Wheaton's 673, 675 (SC 1824). "As to lands surveyed within the Indian boundary, this Court has never hesitated to consider all such surveys and grants as wholly void."

Cornet v. Winton, 2 Yerger's 129, 130 (TN CA 1826). "[The proposition] that the Indians were mere savage beasts without rights of any kind, have long since been exploded, as the result of avarice, fraud and rapacity; and that those who have acted upon them are at this day deemed by the people of the United States more savage and cruel than those they have despoiled ... [The Indians have] acknowledged rights ... which the courts of justice are bound to regard ... And what is this Indian title? ... the right to use and occupy it within their own territorial limits, unmolested by our citizens."

Lee v. Glover, 8 NY 189, 189 (SC 1828). "... if it be Indian property in land, it is protected by our constitution and laws."

Cherokee Nation v. Georgia, 31 Pet. 1, 16, 17, 48, 49, 55, 58, 71 (SC 1831). "They may, more correctly perhaps, be denominated domestic dependent nations ... [The Indians have] an unquestionable, and heretofore unquestioned right to the lands they occupy ... Indians have absolute rights of occupancy to their lands as sacred as the fee simple, absolute of the whites ... this occupancy belongs to them as a matter of right, and not by mere indulgence. They cannot be disturbed in the enjoyment of it, or deprived of it, without their free consent, or unless a just and necessary war should sanction their disposition ... These grants [to third parties prior to treaty] have been understood by all to convey a title to the grantees, subject only to the Indian right of occupancy ... The treaties made with this [Indian] nation purport to secure it certain rights. These are not gratuitous obligations assumed on part of the United States. They are obligations paid by the Indians by cession of part of their territory ... a contract ... The contract is made by way of treaty."

United States v. Arredondo, 31 US 691, 712–13 (1832). "... it is the usage of all the civilized nations of the world, when territory is ceded, to stipulate for the property of its inhabitants. An article to secure this object, so deservedly held sacred, in the view of policy, as well as of justice and humanity is always required and is never refused ... The instructions of the King to his governors are the supreme law of the conquered colony; ... call it by whatever name – a royal order – an ordinance – a cedula – a decree of council – or an act of an authorized officer – if made or promulgated by the king, by his consent or authority, it becomes as to the persons or subject-matter to which it relates, a law of the kingdom."

Worcester v. Georgia, 6 Pet. 515,541,544,546,549,560,581 (SC 1832). "[Discovery] could not affect the rights of those already in possession ... It gave THE EXCLUSIVE RIGHT TO PURCHASE, but did not found that right on a denial of the right of the possessor to sell ... The United States SUCCEEDED to all the CLAIMS of Great Britain, BOTH TERRITORIAL AND POLITICAL; BUT NO ATTEMPT, so far as is known, has been made TO ENLARGE THEM ... [The first crown grants] were well understood to convey the title which, according to the common law of European sovereigns respecting America, they might rightfully convey, and no more. This was the exclusive right of purchasing such lands as the natives were willing to sell. The crown could not be understood to grant what the crown DID NOT AFFECT TO CLAIM; ... these grants asserted a title against Europeans only, and were blank pieces of paper so far as the rights of the natives were concerned ... The Indian nations possessed a full right to the lands they occupied, until that right should be extinguished by the United States, with their consent ... it is the King's order ... to forebear all encroachments on the territories allotted to them. Far from asserting any right of DOMINION OVER THEM, Congress resolved," that the securing and preserving the friendship of the Indian nations appears to be a subject of the utmost moment to these colonies. " ... Have the numerous treaties which have been formed with them ... been nothing more than an idle pageantry? ... Except by compact we have NOT EVEN CLAIMED a right of way through Indian lands ... What is a treaty? The answer is, it is a compact formed between two nations or communities, having the right of self government. [Emphasis and double emphasis added.]"

Mitchel v United States, 9 Peter's 711, 745, 746, 749, 755 (SC 1835). "[The Indians have] a perpetual right of possession ... [which] could not be taken without their consent ... [because] The King waived all rights accruing by conquest or cession, and thus most solemnly acknowledged that the Indians had rights of property they could cede or reserve, and that the boundaries of his territorial and proprietary rights should be such, and such only as were stipulated by these treaties. This brings into practical operation another principle of law settled and declared in the case of *Campbell v. Hall*, that the proclamation of 1763, which was the law of the provinces ceded by the treaty of 1763, was binding upon the king himself, and that a right once granted by a proclamation could not be annulled by a subsequent. It cannot be necessary to inquire whether these rights secured by a treaty approved by a king are less sacred than under his voluntary proclamation ... The proclamation of 1763 was undoubtedly the law of the province till 1783: it gave direct authority to the Governors of Florida to grant crown lands, subject only to such conditions and restrictions as they or the King might prescribe. These lands were of two descriptions: such as had been ceded to the king by the Indians, in which he had full property and dominion, and passed in full property to the grantee; and those reserved and secured to the Indians, in which their right was perpetual possession, and his the ultimate reversion in fee, which passed by the grant, subject to the possessory right ... This proclamation was also the law of all the North American colonies in relation to crown lands."

Harris v. Doe, 4 Blackf. 412, 414 (IN SC 1837). "This treaty ... is obligatory as public law, but also partakes of the character of a contract."

Clark v. Smith, 38 US 195, 201 (1839). "The colonial charters, a great portion of the individual grants by proprietary and royal governments, and still a greater portion by the States of this Union after the Revolution, were made for lands within the Indian hunting grounds. North Carolina, and Virginia, to a great extent, paid their officers and soldiers of the revolutionary war, by such grants; and extinguished the arrears due the army by similar means. It was one of the great resources that sustained the war, not only by these states but others. The ultimate fee (encumbered with the Indian right of occupancy) was in the crown previous to the Revolution, and in the states of the union afterwards, and subject to grant."

Georgia v. Canatoo, 31 Washington National Intelligencer 1, 9–10, 16, 24 (GA SC 1843). "I therefore conclude that whatever right the Indians held to their land, they hold the same right to every thing which falls within its legal definition; and this brings us to consider, secondly the nature of their title ... Their occupant title is unlimited as to time, and not to end without their consent. Great Britain never took one foot of their land by force: she chose rather to adopt a more enlarged and liberal policy ... private property is sacred ... Great Britain, greatly to the praise of her justice and humanity, chose to respect them in that light. Their rights must be respected."

Coleman v. Tish-Ho-Mah, 4 Smedes & M 40, 48 (MS CA 1844). "Before the treaty the land belonged to the Choctaws as a nation. It was regarded as their common property from generation to generation, ... The parties to the treaty held the whole property in these lands, the one the right of occupancy, the other the fee, ..."

Stockton v. Williams, 1 MI 546, 560 (SC 1845). "Here then were two parties capable of contracting; the one having the legal title and ultimate right to the land which was the subject of the contract; the other having the right of possession or occupancy, which has always been respected."

Fellows v. Lee, 5 Denio's 628, 628 (NY CA 1846). "... the Indian title to lands is an absolute fee, and that the preemption right conceded to Massachusetts, is simply a right to acquire by purchase from the Indians their ownership of the soil, whenever they should choose to sell it."

Ogden v. Lee, 6 Hill's 546, 548 (NY SC 1846). "The European governments whose people discovered and made settlements in North America, claimed the sovereignty and of the country, and the ultimate title, but not the immediate right of possession, to

all lands within their respective limits ... It is true, that the British crown granted charters and issued patents for large tracts of land before the Indian right had been extinguished; and these instruments purported to convey the property in fee ... But these
grants were not intended to convey, and the grantees never pretended that they had acquired an absolute fee in the land. They neither took nor claimed any thing more than
the ultimate fee, or the right of dominion after the Indian title should be extinguished."
Webster v. Reid, 1 IA 467, 476 (SC 1846). "A more difficult question growing out of
this treaty of 1824, relates to the title which the half breeds acquired by the treaty.
They were to hold 'by the same title, and in the same manner as other Indian lands are
held.' From this it has been contended that the half breeds were to hold this land in the
same manner in all respects as though they were a nation by themselves, including the
qualified right of sovereignty. We do not think this is a correct view of the subject. The
treaty of 1824 conferred upon the half breeds the right of private property in the lands,
not that of sovereignty over them."
Montgomery v. Ives, 13 Smedes & M 161, 171, 174–5, 177, 179 (MS CA 1849). "After
the war of 1756, by the treaty concluded in 1763, Spain ceded to Great Britain, Florida
Fort St. Augustin, the Bay of Pensacola, and all that she possessed on the continent of
North America, to the east or south-east of the river Mississippi. At the same time,
France also ceded to Great Britain the whole of New France, and all of that portion of
the province of Louisiana, lying upon the east side of the Mississippi river, except the
island of New Orleans. Great Britain, by these concessions, became the owner, subject
to the Indian right of occupancy of all the land between the Mississippi river and the
Atlantic ocean ...

Let us refer to the proclamation of George III, already referred to, as having been
made on the 7th of October, 1763. 5 Hall Law Journal, 405; 1 Lourie, State Papers, 30.
By that proclamation, four distinct and separate governments were created and established within the countries and islands, then recently ceded and confirmed to Great
Britain by the treaty of Paris. These were Quebec, East Florida, West Florida, and
Granada. The limits of each of these were practically defined. We have no concern
with any of them but West Florida, and of this, it is enough to say, that its northern
boundary was fixed at latitude 31 north. This proclamation then goes on to declare,
among other things, '*that it is just, and reasonable, and essential to our interest, and
the security of our colonies, that the several nations or tribes of Indians, with whom
we are connected, and who live under our protection, should not be molested or disturbed, in the possession of such parts of our dominions and territories, as not having
been ceded to, or purchased by us, are reserved to them, or any of them, as their hunting grounds.*'

It then goes on to declare, that no governor, in any of the said provinces, shall presume, '*upon any pretence whatever, to grant warrants of survey, or pass any patents
for lands, beyond the bounds of their respective governments, as described by their
commissions.*' It further declares, '*that, for the present, all the lands not included
within the limits of said new governments, shall be reserved under the sovereignty,
protection and dominion of the crown, and forbids all purchases and settlements beyond those limits, without special leave and licence first obtained.*' It goes on still
farther to declare a principle which seems to have been adhered to ever since, '*that
no private person do make any purchase of any land from any Indians, but that the
same shall be purchased only for the government, in the name of the sovereign, at
some public meeting of the Indians.*' This principle, the offspring of a just and
enlightened policy, became incorporated into the intercourse of England, with the

Indian tribes, and has been adopted and pursued by our own government, in all its transactions with them.

The Indian title to the country in which this tract of land lies, was not then extinguished. In point of fact, it was not extinguished until May 1777, when the Choctaws relinquished their title to it, by a treaty at Mobile with the British superintendent of Indian affairs. ...

Unless we hold that the extension of the limits of Florida, by the commission to her governor, which took place some years before this relinquishment by the Indians, abrogate the provision in the proclamation against grants of land to which the Indian title had not been extinguished, to the extent of the new bounds, we must hold that the grant to Campbell in 1772, had in itself no intrinsic validity, because the lands were not subject to be granted, until their title was relinquished. On this part of the proclamation of 1763, the Supreme Court of the United States say, '*This reservation is a suspension of the powers of the royal governor, within the territory reserved.*' *Fletcher v. Peck*, 6 Cranch, 142. It is because of this suspension, which existed at the date of this grant, that we think it has no intrinsic validity. It is an established principle in our jurisprudence, that a grant of land on which the Indian title has not been extinguished, is void. *Danforth v. Wear,* 9 Wheat. 676.

In the war between the French and the Natchez tribe of Indians, which terminated about the year 1730, in the extinction of that tribe, the Choctaws were the allies of the French, and gave them very efficient aid. It is probable from the fact of the treaty made by the British with them at Mobile, in 1777, before mentioned, that they succeeded to and occupied the hunting grounds of the Natchez, in virtue of the conquest. They do not appear to have been ceded to any one. 1 Martin's Hist. Louisiana, 280–287; 1 Monette, 274. Be this as it may, when the prohibition on the governor of West Florida, to grant lands beyond the limits of his province as then fixed, is established in 1763, it becomes incumbent on those claiming under this grant, to show that the prohibition has been removed ...

... the British grant did not of itself confer a valid title on the grantee ...

I concur in holding that the grant from the British governor of West Florida, dated 11th February, 1772, to the ancestor of the plaintiffs below, was invalid for want of power in the governor to make it. This result seems to follow, whether the land in dispute was or was not, at the date of the grant, within the limits of West Florida."

Gaines v. Nicholson, 9 How. 356, 365 (1850). "No previous grant of Congress could be paramount, according to the rights of occupancy which this government has always conceded to the Indian tribes within her jurisdiction. It was so much carved out of the territory ceded, and remained to the Indian occupant, as he had never parted with it. He holds, strictly speaking, not under the treaty of cession, but under his original title, confirmed by the government in the act of agreeing to the reservation."

Rowland v. Ladiga's Heirs, 21 AL 9, 28 (SC 1852). "Before the treaty the ultimate fee simple to the land was vested in the General Government. This at least was the policy adopted by our Government in reference to Indian lands. The Indians were allowed the right of possession, but not the right of disposition – that right, or the ultimate fee, was claimed by the Government of the United States. The Indians however had an interest in the soil, and that interest was the right to occupy and enjoy, and the Government of the United States has never assumed to deprive them of that right, except by contract founded on sufficient consideration."

Dred Scott v. John F.A. Sandford, 19 How. 393, [per Taney, CJ] 403, 405, 407, 420, 426, 432, 435, 449, 450, [per Nelson, J] 460, [per Daniel, J] 480, 483, 484, 485, [per Camp-

bell, J] 495, 501, 506, 508–09, 513, [per Catron, J] 520, [per McLean, J, dissenting] 531, 532, 533, 538, 546, 548, [per Curtis, J, dissenting] 571, 575, 578, 588 (SC 1857).
[per Taney, CJ]

[403] ... our duty [is] to decide whether the facts stated in the plea are or are not sufficient to show that the plaintiff is not entitled to sue as a citizen in a court of the United States ... The question is simply this: can a negro, whose ancestors were imported into this country, and sold as slaves, become a member of the political community formed and brought into existence by the Constitution of the United States, and as such become entitled to all the rights and privileges, and immunities, guaranteed by that instrument to the citizen?

One of which rights is suing in a court of the United States in the cases specified in the Constitution.

It will be observed, that the plea applies to that class of persons only whose ancestors were negroes of the African race, and imported into this country, and sold, and held as slaves. The only matter before the court, therefore, is, whether the descendants of such slaves, when they become emancipated, or who are born of parents who had become free before their birth, are citizens of a State, in the sense in which the word citizen is used in the Constitution of the United States. And this being the only matter in dispute on the pleadings, the court must be understood as speaking in this opinion of that class only, that is, of those persons who are the descendants of Africans who were imported into this country, and sold as slaves.

The situation of this population was altogether unlike that of the Indian race. The latter, it is true, formed no part of the colonial communities, and never amalgamated with them in social connections or in government. But although they were uncivilized, they were yet a free and independent people, associated together in nations or tribes, and governed by their own laws. Many of these political communities were situated in territories to which the white race claimed the ultimate right of dominion. But that claim was acknowledged to be [404] subject to the right of the Indians to occupy it as long as they thought proper, and neither the English nor colonial Governments claimed or exercised any dominion over the tribe or nation by whom it was occupied, nor claimed the right to the possession of the territory, until the tribe or nation consented to cede it. These Indian Governments were regarded and treated as foreign Governments, as much as if an ocean had separated the red man from the white; and their freedom has constantly been acknowledged, from the time of the first emigrants to the English colonies to the present day, by the different Governments which succeeded each other. Treaties have been negotiated with them, and these Indian political communities have always been treated as foreigners not living under our Government. It is true that the course of events has brought the Indian tribes within the limits of the United States under the subjection to the white race; and it has been found necessary, for their sake as well as our own, to regard them as in a state of pupilage, and to legislate to a certain extent over them and the territory they occupy. But they may, without doubt, like the subjects of any other foreign Government, be naturalized by the authority of Congress, and become citizens of a State, and of the United States; and if an individual should leave his nation or tribe, and take up his abode among the white population, he would be entitled to all the rights and privileges which would belong to an emigrant from any other foreign people ...

[405] It is not the province of the court to decide upon the justice or injustice, the policy or impolicy, of these laws. The decision of that question belonged to the political or law-making power; to those who formed this sovereignty and framed the Constitu-

tion. The duty of the court is, to interpret the instrument they have framed, with the best lights we can obtain on the subject, and to administer it as we find it, according to its true intent and meaning when it was adopted.

[407] It is difficult at this day to realize the state of public opinion in relation to that unfortunate race, which prevailed in the civilized and enlightened portions of the world at the time of the Declaration of Independence, and when the Constitution of the United States was framed and adopted. But the public history of every European nation displays it in a manner too plain to be mistaken.

They had for more than a century before been regarded as beings of an inferior order, and altogether unfit to associate with the white race, either in social or political relations; and so far inferior, that they had no rights which the white man was bound to respect; ...

[Ed. commentary: Thus, to this juncture, the Supreme Court has settled that, in contrast with native Americans, African Americans inceptively had no constitutionally recognized rights. The Court's ensuing conclusion, as will be seen, is that a constitutional law *status quo* once established thereafter is subject to constitutional amendment (as occurred in the African American context with the *13th Amendment, 1865*), but not to alteration pursuant to domestic law initiatives by the legislative, executive or judicial departments of government.]

[420] Congress might ... have authorized the naturalization of Indians, because they were aliens and foreigners. [Ed. note: see, *Act of June 2, 1924*, 49 Stat. 253, subsequently purporting to extend to Indians the privileges of United States' citizenship. *Query*: was it *ultra vires* Congress to extend citizenship to Indians in relation to yet unpurchased territory, to which Congressional jurisdiction does not run at constitutional law pending territorial purchase by the United States? In other words can Congress unilaterally extend the privileges of citizenship to one specific class of quasi-foreigners, when the *Constitution* itself withheld such status?] But, in their untutored and savage state, no one would have thought of admitting them as citizens in a civilized community. And, moreover, the atrocities they had but recently committed, when they were the allies of Great Britain in the Revolutionary war, were yet fresh in the recollection of the people of the United States, and they were even guarding themselves against the threatened renewal of Indian hostilities. No one would have supposed then that any Indian would ask for, or was capable of enjoying, the privileges of an American citizen, and the word was not used with any particular reference to them.

Neither was it used with any reference to the African race imported into or born in this country; because Congress had no power to naturalize them, and therefore there was no necessity for using particular words to exclude them ...

[426] No one, we presume, supposes that any change in public opinion or feeling, in relation to this unfortunate race, in the civilized nations of Europe or in this country, should induce the court to give to the Constitution a more liberal construction in their favor than they were intended to bear when the instrument was framed and adopted. Such an argument would be altogether inadmissible in any tribunal called upon to interpret it. If any of its provisions are deemed unjust, there is a mode prescribed in the instrument itself by which it may be amended; but while it remains unaltered, it must be construed now as it was understood at the time of its adoption ... Any other rule of construction would abrogate the judicial character of this court, and make it the mere reflex of the popular opinion or passion of the day. This court was not created by the Constitution for such purposes. Higher and graver trusts have been confided to it, and it must not falter in the path of duty.

... And upon a careful consideration of the subject, Dred Scott was not a citizen of Missouri within the meaning of the Constitution of the United States, and not entitled as such to sue in its courts; ...

[432] The act of Congress, upon which the plaintiff relies, declares that slavery and involuntary servitude, except as punishment for crime, shall be forever prohibited in all that part of the territory ceded by France, under the name of Louisiana, ... And the difficulty which meets us at the threshold of this part of the inquiry is, whether Congress was authorized to pass this law under any of the powers granted to it by the Constitution; for if the authority is not given by that instrument, it is the duty of this court to declare it void and inoperative, and incapable of conferring freedom upon any one who is held as a slave under the laws of any one of the United States ...

[435] ... this Government was to be carefully limited in its powers, to exercise no authority beyond those expressly granted by the Constitution, or necessarily to be implied from the language of the instrument, and the objects it was intended to accomplish; ...

[449] It has no power of any kind beyond it; and it cannot, when it enters a Territory of the United States, put off its character, and assume discretionary or despotic powers, which the Constitution denied to it ...

[450] ... and the Federal Government can exercise no right power over his person or property beyond what the instrument confers, nor lawfully deny any right which it has reserved ... And no laws or usages of other nations, or reasoning of statesmen or jurists upon the relations of master and slave, can enlarge the powers of the Government, or take from the citizens the rights they have reserved.

[452] Upon these considerations, it is the opinion of the court that the act of Congress which prohibited a citizen from holding and owning property of this kind in the territory of the United States north of the line mentioned, is not warranted by the Constitution, and is therefore void; ...

[per Nelson, J]

[460] Every State or nation possesses an exclusive sovereignty and jurisdiction within her own territory; and, her laws affect and bind all property and persons residing within it ... And it is equally true, that no State or nation can affect or bind property out of its territory, or persons not residing within it. [Ed. commentary: By analogy, this observation underscores the jurisdictional significance of the constitutional law's affirmation of the sovereignty of the native nations pending purchase. Native sovereignty is anterior and superior, and therefore precludes the application, to unpurchased territory, of State and federal law promulgated pursuant to State and federal sovereignty. Otherwise, the very concept of native sovereignty is and always has been an oxymoron.]

[per Daniel, J]

[480] ... to change or to abolish a fundamental principle of the society, must be the act of the society itself – of the *sovereignty*; and that none other can admit to the participation of that high attribute.

[483] ... each nation should be left in the peaceable enjoyment of that liberty which she inherits from nature ... Power or weakness does not produce any difference. A small republic is no less sovereign than the most powerful kingdom ...

[484] and no one nation is entitled to dictate a form of government or religion, or a course of internal policy, to another.

[485] Sovereignty, independence, and a perfect right of self-government, can signify nothing less than a superiority to and an exemption from all claims of extraneous power, however expressly they may be asserted, and render all attempts to enforce

such claims merely attempts at usurpation. [Cross-reference, *Worcester v. Georgia*, 6 Pet. 515, 581 (SC 1832). "What is a treaty? The answer is, it is a compact formed between two nations or communities, having the right of self government."]
[per Campbell, J]
[495] In 1788, Congress directed General Washington to continue his remonstrances to the commander of the British forces respecting the permitting negroes belonging to the citizens of these States to leave New York, and to insist upon the discontinuance of that measure.
[501] But the recognition of a plenary power in Congress to dispose of the public domain, or to organize a Government over it, does not imply a corresponding authority to determine the internal policy, or to adjust the domestic relations, or the persons who may lawfully inhabit the territory in which it is situated. A supreme power to make needful rules respecting the public domain, and a similar power of framing laws to operate upon persons and things within the territorial limits where it lies, are distinguishable by broad lines of demarcation in American history. This court has assist to define them. In Johnson v. McIntosh, (8 Wheat., 595 – 543,) they say: "According to the theory of the British Constitution, all vacant lands are vested in the Crown; and the exclusive power to grant them is admitted to reside in the Crown, as a branch of the royal prerogative. All that lands we hold were originally granted by the Crown, and the establishment of a royal Government has never been considered as impairing its right to grant lands within the chartered limits of such colony." And the British Parliament did claim a supremacy of legislation coextensive with the absoluteness of the dominion of the sovereign power over the Crown lands. The American doctrine, [is] to the contrary, ...
[Ed. commentary: Here, this learned judge of the Supreme Court of the United States has contrasted the view of plenary jurisdiction, as conceived by the Crown, with the view of it as conceived by America. The Crown argued, this judge contends, that plenary jurisdiction was unlimited. (Actually, as Chief Justice Marshall stated in 1832 *Worcester v. Georgia*, the Crown never claimed plenary jurisdiction vis-a-vis unpurchased Indian territory, as to which the Crown's claim at constitutional was limited to the exclusive jurisdiction to purchase.) America proved, contrary to the Crown's argument, by the success its revolution and the Crown's agreement at the Peace of Paris in 1783, that plenary jurisdiction (subject as recognized in *Worcester v. Georgia* to the yet unpurchased Indian interest), inherently and by nature is circumscribed by the constitutional rights of the inhabitants of British America, whose constitutional rights can not be taken away, upon the pretext of the Crown's plenary jurisdiction, without their consent. This, then, is the legal significance of the assertion in the *Declaration of Independence* that "Governments are instituted among Men, deriving their just Powers from the Consent of the Governed." This is the single most important observation of law in human history, for upon its vindication turned the creation, and subsequent triumph of the United States of America, and therefore of liberty and justice. In support of his said observation, the learned judge cited *Johnson v. McIntosh. Johnson v. McIntosh*, 8 Wheaton's 543, 574, 592, 597 (SC 1823) also held: "[The Indians] were admitted to be the rightful occupants of the soil, with a legal as well as a just claim to retain possession of it, and to use it to their own discretion. [The Indian interest] is certainly to be respected by all courts. [Regarding the *Royal Proclamation of 1763*] The authority of this proclamation, so far as it respects this continent, has never been denied." The crucial point, relevant to the native sovereignty issue, is that just as the Crown's plenary jurisdiction was proven by America to be subject to the constitutional rights of the

American colonists, so also is America's plenary jurisdiction subject to the Indians' rights that the constitutional law has recognized as being inherent.]

[506] This [the inflation of federal plenary jurisdiction] proceeds from a radical error, which lies at the foundation of much of this discussion. It is, that the Federal Government may lawfully do whatever is not directly prohibited by the Constitution. This would have been a fundamental error, if not amendments to the Constitution had been made. But the final expression of the will of the people of the States, in the 10th amendment, is, that the powers of the Federal Government are limited to grants of the Constitution.

[508] In Pollard's Lessee v. Hagan, (3 How., 212,) the court say: 'The United States have no constitutional capacity to exercise municipal [509] jurisdiction, sovereignty, or eminent domain, within the limits of a State or elsewhere, except in cases where it is delegated [Ed. commentary: as, for example, where delegated by Indian treaty of purchase extinguishing the previously established native sovereignty and possession under constitutional law], and the court denies the faculty of the Federal Government to add to its powers by treaty or compact [Ed commentary: for which reason the benefit of an Indian treaty should accrue to the State, not to the federal government, when the State's radical fee is relieved, by Indian treaty, of the previously established native sovereignty and possession under constitutional law.]'

[513] ... a power to make rules and regulations respecting the public domain does not confer a municipal sovereignty over persons and things upon it.

[per Catron, J]

[520] The King of Great Britain, by his proclamation of 1763, virtually claimed that the county west of the mountains had been conquered from France, and ceded to the Crown of Great Britain by the treaty of Paris of that year, and he says: 'We reserve it under our sovereignty, protection and dominion, for the use of the Indians. This country was conquered from the Crown of Great Britain, and surrendered to the United States by the treaty of peace of 1783.'

[per McLean, J, dissenting]

[531] But it is said, if the court, on looking at the record, shall clearly perceive that the Circuit Court had no jurisdiction, it is a ground for the dismissal of the case. This may be characterized as rather a sharp practice, and one which seldom, if ever, occurs. No case was cited in the argument as authority, and not a single case precisely in point is recollected in our reports. The pleadings do not show a lack of jurisdiction. This want of jurisdiction can only be ascertained by a judgment on demurrer to the special plea. No such, case, it is believed can be cited ... Under such circumstances, the want of jurisdiction must be so clear as to not admit of doubt. Now, the plea which raises the question of jurisdiction, in my judgment, is radically defective ... Being born under our Constitution and laws, no naturalization is required, as one of foreign birth, to make him a citizen. The most general and appropriate definition of the term citizen is a "freeman." Being a freeman, and having his domicil in a State different from that of the defendant, he is a citizen within the act of Congress, and the courts of the union are open to him.

[532] No injustice can result to the matter, from an exercise of jurisdiction in this cause. Such a decision does not in any degree affect the merits of the case; it only enables the plaintiff to assert his claims to freedom. If the jurisdiction be ruled against him, on the ground that he is a slave, it is decisive of his fate.

[533] In the argument, it was said that a colored citizen would not be an agreeable member of society. This is more a matter of taste than of law.

[538] All slavery has its origin in power, and is against right.

[546] If the great and fundamental principles of our Government are never to be settled, there can be no lasting prosperity. The Constitution will become a floating waif on the billows of popular excitement.

[558] Does not the master assent to the law, when he places himself under it in a free State?

[Curtis, J, dissenting]

[571] ... the question is, whether any person who is of African descent, whose ancestors were sold as slaves in the United States, can be a citizen of the United States. If any person can by such a citizen, this plaintiff has the right to the judgment of the court that is so; for no cause is shown why he is not, except his descent and the slavery of his ancestors.

[575] ... In some of the original thirteen States, free colored persons, before and at the time of the Constitution were citizens of those States.

[576] Did the Constitution deprive them of their citizenship?

[578] ... the only power expressly granted to Congress to legislate concerning citizenship, is confined to the removal of the disabilities of foreign birth.

[588] ... as the plea to the jurisdiction in this case shows no facts, except that the plaintiff was of African descent, and his ancestors were sold as slaves, ... these facts are not inconsistent with his citizenship in the United States, ..."

Minter v. Shirley, 3 MS 376, 384 (SC 1871). "... the government never regarded the absolute title to the soil as resting in the United States, as the proprietors in fee, until ceded by the Indians. Nor did they undertake to dispose of them by grants until the acquisition of the Indian title."

Holden v. Joy, 84 US 211, 244 (1872). "Their title was absolute, subject only to the preemptive right of purchase acquired by the United States as the successors to Great Britain."

Wood v. Missouri, K. & T. Ry. Co., 2 KS 248, 264 (SC 1873). "It will generally be conceded that the Indians have the power by treaty to sell."

United States v. 43 Gallons of Whisky, 93 US 188, 196 (1876). "This right could only be extinguished by voluntary surrender to the government."

Butz v. Northern Pacific Railroad, 119 US 55, 67–8 (1886). "Whilst claiming a right to acquire and dispose of the soil, the discoverers recognized a right of occupancy or usufructory right in the natives. They accordingly made grants of lands occupied by the Indians, and these grants were held to convey a title to the grantees, subject only to the Indian right of occupancy ... This right of occupancy was protected by the political power and respected by the courts until extinguished; when the patentee took the unencumbered fee."

Eastern Band of Cherokees v. United States, 117 US 288, 294 (1886). "... by treaties with them from time to time their title and interest were ceded to the United States."

St. Catherines Milling & Lumber Co. Ltd. v. The Queen, (1888), 14 AC 46, 53–55, 60 (JCPC). "Whilst there have been changes in the administrative authority, there has been no change since the year 1763 in the character of the interest which its Indian inhabitants had in the lands surrendered by the treaty. The ceded territory was the time of the [Canadian] union, land vested in the Crown, subject to 'an interest other than that of the Province in the same' within the meaning of sect. 109 [of Canada's *Constitution Act, 1867*]; ... The legal consequences of the treaty [subsequent to the said Canadian union] ... opened up [the land] for settlement, immigration, and such other purpose as to Her Majesty might seem fit ... [T]here has been all along vested in the

Crown a substantial and paramount estate underlying the Indian title, which became a
PLENUM DOMINIUM [plenary jurisdiction] whenever that title was surrendered or otherwise extinguished." [emphasis and double emphasis added]
United States v. Shoshone Tribe, 304 US 111, 116 (1938). "Grants of land subject to
the Indian title by the United States, which has only the naked fee, would transfer no
beneficial interest."

2 PARTICULARS OF THE CONSTITUTIONAL LAW CONCERNING STANDING TO SUE:
"Or *any* of them," the phrase, is from the *Royal Proclamation of 1763*, *supra*, which
recognized and affirmed the colonial era's common law perception that, pending purchase, the constitutional law is indifferent to *which* Indians. Relative to yet unpurchased territory the constitutional common law recognized the presumptive continuity
of native sovereignty *per se*, which concept, by definition of terms, runs with the land,
and precludes the application to the land of non-native domestic law pending purchase. The sole constitutionally recognized non-native jurisdiction in relation to unpurchased territory is the two powers expressly conceded by the *Constitution* to
Congress and the president: namely, to regulate trade *with* the Indians pursuant to the
commerce clause (Art. 1, Sec. 8, Par. 3), and to purchase territory *from* the Indians
pursuant to the treaty clause (Art. 2, Sec. 2, Par. 2).
Because native sovereignty under constitutional law is a concept that by nature runs
with the land, it exists in any event of actual inhabitation. There is no concept of es-
cheat, for example, for lapse of actual Indian inhabitation, and certainly not for a lapse
arguably attributable to the constitutionally premature occupation of unpurchased territory by non-native society, for that would be contrary to the axiom of equity that parties may not profit from their own wrongdoing. Correspondingly there is no onus in
relation to constitutional law native sovereignty upon the "Indians or any of them" to
prove continuity of occupation, or any particular character of occupation.
    The fact that territory is, by operation of law, constitutionally reserved for "Indians
or any of them," does not mean that "any of them" have jurisdiction to sell it. The
"purchase" has to be made from those particular Indians in occupation, or at least
those who have the best right to occupation. Territory is reserved for the racial or political class "Indians or any of them," until purchase, which shall be made from that particular sub-set of the class as is in occupation or has the best right to be in occupation,
those whose ancestors had a connection with the particular land. In this sense, the Indian interest in unpurchased territory is both national and individual.
    Consider an analogy. Suppose it is not the Hudson River national homeland of the
Muh-he-kuns that becomes occupied by a foreign people contrary to the great law of respect. Suppose, instead, the illegally occupied country is the United States of America;
and the invaders, all the while paying lip service to the great law, take the land, rather
than purchase it. What remains of America, after the taking, lives on in the hearts of a
handful of surviving individual Americans. Because it is not safe for them to communicate, or because each is unaware of the survival of the others, years and decades pass
without the individuals communicating. They die, and thereafter their descendants shelter the memory of America in isolation. Suppose, then, the reign of terror seems to pass.
The descendants come out of anonymity. They meet each other. They seek to combine
to raise once again the American flag, as of legal right. Do they or "any of them" have
standing to raise the law that was overlooked for so long, on the demonstrably true
ground it was never repealed by due process? And when the flag is once again raised,
do not the particular individuals whose particular ancestors occupied the particular
tract, over which the flag waves, have the best particular right physically to occupy

once again that particular tract? And if there are no descendants of that particular tract, is it not the legacy of the country and therefore all who are the country?

Historically, nevertheless, the denial of standing to sue has sometimes been the means to frustrate access to the rule of law, and thereby to aid and abet racially motivated genocide. See, as to Africans Americans, *Dred Scott v. John F.A. Sandford*, 19 How. 393 (SC 1857), *supra*; and, as to native Americans, *Cherokee Nation v. Georgia*, 31 Pet. 1, 16 (1831), *infra*.

In *Dred Scott*, standing to sue was denied African Americans suing for recognition of their alleged right to freedom, on the ground that only citizens and foreigners can sue in federal courts, and African Americans were said to be neither in the eye of the constitutional law. The *Dred Scott* case contrasted the African American situation with that of the native Americans, whom it acknowledged do have such constitutional rights, in virtue of their priority of occupation and the conventions of international and constitutional law prevalent at the time when the constitutional law was adopted. Though the native Americans also are not citizens, but rather are foreigners, said the court in *Dred Scott*, they have always been conceded native national sovereignty as foreigners, and further, Congress constitutionally has jurisdiction to naturalize Indians, although not blacks.

Yet, in *Cherokee Nation v. Georgia*, direct access was denied native Americans to the Supreme Court, as a court of original jurisdiction, on the ground that they were not foreigners, but rather, "They may, more correctly perhaps, be denominated domestic dependent nations."

In any event, the era ended, of using standing to sue as the basis for frustrating access to the rule of law by means of blocking access to the federal courts. In the instance of African Americans it ended with the enactment in 1865 of the *13th Amendment*.

In the instance of native Americans, it ended either with the congressional *Act of June 2, 1924* extending citizenship to Indians, or, alternatively with the conjunction, on October 5, 1998, of *United States v. Washington,* 384 F.Supp. 312, 327, 328, 339, 379, 405, 406, 414 (1974) and *Jota v. Texaco Inc.*, as explained *infra*.

In anticipation of the fuller explanation which follows in the next endnote, these two last-mentioned cases collectively recognize that where there is a civil right, in which the federal government is implicated, the federal court system will ensure there is a meaningful remedy, either before an alternative third-party to whose jurisdiction the federal government will agree to subject itself, or, failing the availability of such a third-party, before the federal courts themselves.

In sum, no longer is racially motivated genocide in America legally possible in virtue of a remedy hiatus.

Royal Proclamation of 1763: "... Indians ... should not be molested or disturbed in the Possession of such Parts of Our Dominions and Territories as not having been ceded to or purchased by Us are reserved to them *or any of them*." [emphasis added]

Worcester v. Georgia, 6 Pet. 515, 541, 544, 546, 549, 581 (SC 1832): "[Discovery] ... gave the exclusive right to purchase ... The United States *succeeded* to all the claims of Great Britain, both territorial and political; but no attempt, so far as is known, has been made *to enlarge* them ... Far from asserting any right of dominion over them, ... Except by compact we have not even claimed a right of way through Indian lands." [emphasis added]

Mitchel v. United States, 9 Pet. 711, 745, 746, 749, 755 (SC 1835): "This proclamation was also the law of all the North American colonies in relation to crown lands."

St. Catherines Milling & Lumber Co. Ltd. v. The Queen, (1888), 14 AC 46, 53–55, 60 (JCPC): "Whilst there have been changes in the administrative authority, there has been no change since the year 1763 in the character of the interest which its Indian inhabitants had in the lands surrendered by the treaty. The ceded territory was the time of the [Canadian] union, land vested in the Crown, subject to 'an interest other than that of the Province in the same' within the meaning of sect. 109 [of Canada's *Constitution Act, 1867*]; ... The legal consequences of the treaty [subsequent to the said Canadian union] ... opened up [the land] for settlement, immigration, and such other purpose as to Her Majesty might seem fit ... [T]here has been all along vested in the Crown a substantial and paramount estate underlying the Indian title, which became a *plenum dominium* [plenary jurisdiction] whenever that title was surrendered or otherwise extinguished." [emphasis added]

3 PARTICULARS OF THE CONSTITUTIONAL LAW CONCERNING THIRD-PARTY ADJUDICATION:

"Third-party adjudication" is the structural pre-condition to the rule of law. In Roman law, this concept was expressed by the axiom: "*nemo potest esse simul actor et judex* (no one can be at the same time suitor and judge)." David Hume (*Theory of Politics: Containing a Treatise on Human Nature, and thirteen of the Essays, Moral, Political and Literary*, Toronto, Nelson, 1951, F. Watkins, ed., pp. 81, 84) said:

> Nothing is more certain than that men are, in a great measure, governed by interest, and that even when they extend their concern beyond themselves, it is not any great distance ... The only difficulty, therefore, is to find out this expedient, by which men cure their natural weakness and lay themselves under the necessity of observing the laws of justice and equity ... But this being impractical with respect to all mankind, it can only take place with respect to a few, whom we immediately interest in the administration of justice. These persons we call civil magistrates, kings and their ministers, our governors and rulers, who being indifferent persons to the greatest part of the state, have no interest, or but a remote one, in any act of injustice; and being satisfied with their part in society, have an immediate interest in every execution of justice which is so necessary to the upholding of society. Here then is the origin of civil government and society.

In terms of political application, whenever two quasi-sovereign bodies politic litigate, the court system of neither can assume jurisdiction. There must be either a consent by one party to the other's court, or both must accept a third-party tribunal as an outside referee.

Since Indians enjoy native sovereignty in relation to yet unpurchased territory, therefore the constitutional common law settled that they are entitled to third-party adjudication, when in competition with newcomer society as to whether the native sovereignty has been extinguished. *Mohegan Indians v. Connecticut* (1704 aff'd 1773), *supra*.

In consequence, Indians are entitled to ask the federal courts to declare the paramountcy of the Indian jurisdictional and possessory interest in arguably unpurchased territory, as against the competing non-native interest represented by the United States. An aspect of the Indian interest is the remedy in relation to it of independent and impartial third-party adjudication at constitutional and international common law, as implicitly confirmed by the equation made in *Worcester v. Georgia*, between aboriginal rights before and after the War of Independence. But if the United States will not consent to abide by the decision of an independent and impartial third-party adjudicator, in the international arena, rather than leave the Indians at the mercy of the United States' overwhelming coercive force, and without a effective rule of law remedy at all, the federal courts will step into this breach in the integrity of the fabric of the rule of law. *Jota v. Texaco Inc.*, (1998), *infra*.

In historical perspective, the Indians' previously established constitutional and international law remedy of third-party adjudication was forgotten in the aftermath of the War of Independence. Some Indians, specifically in *Cherokee Nation v. Georgia*, tried to get the U.S. Supreme Court to step into the third-party adjudicator shoes formerly worn by the British Privy Council, but the Supreme Court declined such jurisdiction, on the ground that its original jurisdiction extended only to "foreign" nations, which it held the Indians were not. For want of an efficient and effective rule of law remedy, thereafter the Indian native sovereignty interest was ignored, in practice. State and federal law came to be applied universally. The constitutional law protecting the Indians' jurisdiction and possession was never repealed, but, rather, simply blindsided.

The federal government unconstitutionally established an alternative regime of federal law, upon which reliance has since been placed by many Indians to secure some alternative Indian rights and privileges, in lieu of the pragmatically unenforceable constitutional law Indian interest in jurisdiction and possession pending purchase under the constitutional law doctrine of native sovereignty.

The remedy hiatus era relative to the still unrepealed native sovereignty interest in yet unpurchased territory may have expired with the decision on 5 October 1998 in the matter of *Jota v. Texaco Inc.*

Mohegan Indians v. Connecticut, 1704, aff'd 1773.

Cherokee Nation v. Georgia, 31 Pet. 1, 16 (1831). "They may, more correctly perhaps, be denominated domestic dependent nations."

United States v. Washington, 384 F.Supp. 312, 327, 328, 339, 379, 405, 406, 414 (1974), aff'd 520 F.2nd 676 (9th Cir. 1975), cert. denied 423 US 1086 (1976). "Plaintiffs seek a declaratory judgment pursuant to 28 U.S.C. §§ 2201 and 2202 concerning off reservation treaty fishing rights … The case area … includes the Puget Sound watershed, the watersheds of the Olympic Peninsula north of the Grays Harbor watershed and the off-shore adjacent to those areas … Venue is properly laid before this court under 28 U.S.C. § 1391(b). Jurisdiction is alleged as to all tribes under one or more of the following provisions: 28 U.S.C. §§ 1345, 1331, 1343(3) and (4), and 1362. All of these allegations were conceded by all defendants, subject to their contention that exclusive jurisdiction to hear and determine the issues in this case is in the Indian Claims Commission … and Games' denial of jurisdiction as to the Puyallup Tribe. This Court has previously held and hereby affirms that both of these contentions are without merit and denied … The basis of this ruling is the indisputable and unqualified duty of every federal circuit or trial judge, despite academic and personal misgivings, to enforce and apply every principle of law as it is directly stated in a decision of the United States Supreme Court … The membership of the Stillaguamish Tribe is determined in accordance with the tribal Constitution and Bylaws which have been approved by the tribe but have not been approved by a representative of the Secretary of the Interior. The Stillaguamish Tribe is not recognized as an Indian governmental entity by the federal government. Its enrollment has not been approved by the Secretary of the Interior or his representative and the tribe does not have a reservation. The Stillaguamish Tribe presently has about 94 members … The Plaintiffs are entitled to injunctive relief against the continuance and repetition of acts or omissions declared by these Conclu-

sions of Law to be in violation of the treaty-secured rights of the Plaintiff tribes and
their members."

Jota v. Texaco Inc., 5 October 28, 1998, 2d Cir., docket Nos. 97–9102,–9104,–9108,
pp. 10, 13–14. [In this case, Peruvian and Ecuadorian indigenous persons sued Texaco
in the district court, relative to alleged environmental depredations arising in Peru and
Ecuador in consequence of corporate decisions made in the United States. The district
court dismissed on preliminary jurisdictional grounds: *forum non conveniens*, comity
conflict, and absence of an indispensable party. Ecuador delivered an affidavit in support of an intervention application, averring:

"[t]he intervention ... does not under any concept damage the sovereignty of the Republic of Ecuador, instead it looks to protect the interests of the indigenous citizens of
the Ecuadorian Amazon who were seriously affected by the environmental contamina-
tion attributed to the defendant company ... "

In *Jota*, the court of appeals enunciated a jurisprudential principle of general application to the issue of court jurisdiction, in light of which that case was remitted for reconsideration by the court below.]

"'Through a discretionary inquiry, the court determines where litigation will be
most convenient and will serve the ends of justice.' *PT United Can Co. v. Crown Cork
& Seal Co.*, 138 F.3d 65, 73 (2d Cir.1998). '[I]n order to grant a motion to dismiss for
forum non conveniens, a court must satisfy itself [among other things] that the litigation may be conducted elsewhere against all defendants.' *Id.* ...

Accordingly, dismissal for forum non conveniens is not appropriate, at least absent a
commitment by Texaco to submit to the jurisdiction of the Ecuadorian courts for purposes of this action. *Cf. In re Union Carbide Corp. Gas Plant Disaster*, 809 F.2d 195,
203–04 (2d Cir.1987) (affirming dismissal for forum non conveniens that was condi-
tioned upon defendant's consent to personal jurisdiction in India; such conditions 'are
not unusual and have been imposed in numerous cases where the foreign court would
not provide an adequate alternative in the absence of such a condition').

... The plaintiffs ... argue ... violation of the law of nations. [note] We express no view
on whether the plaintiffs have alleged conduct by Texaco that violates the law of nations ... *Cf. Kadic v. Karadzic*, 70 F.3d 232, 241–44, 250 (2d Cir.1996) (upholding jurisdiction over ATA claim against individual for alleged violations of law of nations
involving genocide, war crimes, and violations of humanitarian law, and rejecting forum non conveniens defense in suit against individual alien)."

4 PARTICULARS OF THE GENOCIDAL CHARACTER OF THE INJURY:
"Serious bodily of mental harm," the phrase, is from article 2(b) of the *Convention for
the Prevention and Punishment of Genocide, 1948*.

At the heart of the constitutional law herein before identified, is a simple but fundamental recognition: the Indians were and are human beings, to be respected as such,
for legal purposes. The respect is demonstrated, specifically, by that law's stipulation
of purchase as the precondition to the assumption by the United States of domestic territorial jurisdiction and possession. The alternative to this respect for the Indians' human condition, is contempt for it, which is precisely what is evidenced by United
States' assumption of domestic jurisdiction and possession in any event of purchase.
Such contempt is the predominant fact of American history, in spite of the law's stipulation for respect.

Once the United States acquired overwhelming force, it abused it, by taking instead
of purchasing, without ever bothering to amend or repeal by due process the previously established constitutional law necessitating purchase. This denial of the law

holding in respect the Indians' humanity denied the Indians' humanity, like was done to the slaves.

This contempt by the United States both for the Indians' humanity and the integrity of the rule of law is epitomized by the Statue of Liberty's implicit promise, to the European immigrants, of the Indians' territory, upon which Europeans may have their liberty at the cost of the Indians' liberty.

This profound injustice accounts for the disproportionate statistics of mortality rates and the indicia of despair, the evidence of social malaise uniquely inflicting the Indian sub-culture in the land of the free.

Convention for the Prevention and Punishment of the Crime of Genocide, 1948.
"Art.2. In the present Convention, genocide means any of the following acts committed with intent to destroy, in whole or in part, a national, ethnical, racial or religious group, as such: (b) Causing serious bodily or mental harm to members of the group; ..."

5 PARTICULARS OF THE MEANING OF JUSTICE:
Ralph Waldo Emerson, *Essays,*

On Character, New York, Thomas Y. Crowell Company, 1926, p. 329. Truth is the summit of being: justice is the application of it to affairs. All individual natures stand in a scale, according to the purity of this element in them. The will of the pure runs down from them into other natures, as water runs down from a higher into a lower vessel. This natural force is no more to be withstood, than any other natural force. We can drive a stone upward for a moment into the air, but it is yet true that all stones will forever fall; and whatever instances can be quoted of unpunished theft, or of a lie which somebody has credited, justice must prevail, and it is the privilege of truth to make itself believed.

6 PARTICULARS OF THE NATURE OF THE JUDICIAL FUNCTION:
The judicial function is to declare and apply the law as it is written, not as the judges feel it should be written, for that would be the rule of men, not the rule of law.
Dred Scott v. Sandford, 19 How. 393 (SC 1857), *supra.*
E.V. Dicey, *Lectures on the Relation between Law and Public Opinion in England in the Nineteenth Century,* London, Macmillan, 1920, p. 483. "Judge-made law is subject to certain limitations. It can not openly declare a new principle of law: it must always take the form of a deduction from some legal principle whereof the validity is admitted, or the application or interpretation of some statutory enactment. It can not override statutory law. The courts may, by a process of interpretation, indirectly limit or possibly extend the operation of a statute, but they can not set a statute aside. Nor have they in England ever adopted the doctrine which exists, one is told, in Scotland, that a statute may be obsolete by disuse. It can not from its very nature override any established principle of judge-made law."

7 *See,* the particulars of the constitutional law in the (annexed) District Court for the Southern District of New York Complaint 98 CIV. 8194 (LMM) (NOTES 2–6 ABOVE) supplemented by the following additional specifically Canadian content. In overview, for constitutional law purposes the constitutive 1832 American case of *Worcester v. Georgia* and the complementary constitutive 1888 Canadian case of *St. Catherines Milling & Lumber Co. Ltd. v. The Queen* confirmed the continuity of Great Britain's previously established constitutional law jurisdictional reconciliation of newcomer and native sovereignty. Those precedents held that throughout North America, new-

comer legislative and executive jurisdiction is derivative, the constitutional means of derivation being territorial purchase from the Indians. Correspondingly, the *Order in Council of 9 March 1704* in the matter of *Mohegan Indians v. Connecticut* recognized the remedy of independent and impartial third-party adjudication. The territorial jurisdiction of the newcomer courts constituted pursuant to newcomer legislative and executive acts may not be assumed, for that would be to prejudge the derivation issue being litigated.

Treaty of 1752. Between the Crown and Some Nova Scotia Native Nations. "THAT all Disputes whatsoever that may happen to arise between the Indians now at Peace and others His Majesty's Subjects in this Province shall be tryed in his Majesty's Courts of Civil Judicature, where the Indians shall have the same benefit, Advantage and Privileges as any others of His Majesty's Subjects."

[Ed. commentary: The reason the local crown governor contracted for court jurisdiction is that constitutionally the assumption without authorization of such jurisdiction is precluded by the *Order in Council (Great Britain) of 9 March 1704* in the matter of *Mohegan Indians v. Connecticut.*]

Campbell v. Hall (1774), 98 ER 848, 898 (JCPC). "[I]f the King has power (and when I say the King, I mean in this case to be understood 'without concurrence of Parliament') to make laws for a conquered country, this being a power subordinate to his own authority, as a part of supreme Legislature in Parliament, he can make none which are contrary to fundamental principles; ..."

Chief Justice John Elmsley, *Report to the Executive Council of Upper Canada dated October 22, 1798*, PAC, RG1, E1, V46, State Book "B", pp. 210–14. "It is no secret to any person at all acquainted with the present state of Indian Affairs that the aborigines of this Part of His Majesty's American Dominions are beginning to appreciate their lands not so much by the use which they themselves are in the habit, or are capable of making of them themselves, as by the value at which they are estimated by those who purchase them, and either cultivate them, or dispose of them in their natural state. It is equally notorious, that if the Indians wanted penetration to make the discovery, there are a great many persons of European origin who have attached themselves to the several Tribes which surround us, and who will not fail to inform them that the value of any article depends as much upon its importance to the purchaser, as on its usefulness to the present possessors.

But if this were doubtful now, when the lands purchased from the Indians are distributed among His Majesty's Subjects at a Fee hardly exceeding the prime cost of them, it cannot possibly remain so when the Indians discover as they unquestionably will, that the purchases made from them are to be converted into a source of Revenue to ourselves – slow as their progress is towards civilization they are perfectly apprised of the value of money and of its use in maintaining them in those habits of indolence and intemperance to which most of them are more or less inclined.

In order therefore to exercise that foresight which our Indian neighours are beginning to learn, and in which it certainly cannot be our interest to promote their improvement, we submit for your Honour's consideration the propriety of suspending the promulgation of the plan which has been laid down for us until we can make a purchase sufficiently large to secure for us the means of extending the population and encreasing the strength of the Provinces so far as to enable us before our stock is exhausted to dictate instead of soliciting the terms on which future acquisitions are to be made."

William Blackstone. *Commentaries on the Laws of England. Book the Forth.* 16th ed. London. A. Strahan. 1825. Pages 74–5, 119–22. "The third general division of crimes

consists of such as more especially affect the supreme executive power, or the king and his government; ... and these may be distinguished into four kinds; 1. Treason. 2. Felonies injurious to the king's prerogative. 3. *Praemunire.* 4. Other misprisions and contempts. Treason, *proditio,* in its very name (which is borrowed from the French) imports a betraying, treachery, or breach of faith. It therefore happens only between allies, ...
THE fourth species of offences, more immediately against the king and government, are entitled misprisions and contempts.
MISPRISIONS (a term derived from the old French, *mespris,* a neglect or contempt) are, in the acceptation of our law, generally understood to be all such high offences as are under the degree of capital, but nearly bordering thereon: ... Misprisions are generally divided into two sorts; negative, which consist in the concealment of something which ought to be revealed; and positive, which consists in the commission of something which ought not to be done.
I. OF the first, or negative kind, is what is called *misprision of treason*; consisting in the bare knowledge and concealment of treason, without any degree of assent thereto: for any assent makes the party a principal traitor; as indeed the concealment, which was construed aiding and abetting, did at common law: ...
II. MISPRISIONS, which are merely positive, are generally denominated *contempts* or *high misdemeanors*; of which
1. THE first and principle is the *mal-administration* of such high officers, as are in public trust and employment. ... misprisions are, in general, such contempts of the executive magistrate, as demonstrate themselves by some arrogant and undutiful behavior towards the king and government. These are
2. CONTEMPTS against the king's *prerogative.* As, by refusing to assist him for the good of the public; ... Or, by disobeying the king's lawful commands; whether by writs issuing out of his courts of justice, ... or proclamation, ... Disobedience to any of these commands is a high misprision and contempt; ..."
Cameron v. Kyte (1835), 12 ER 678, 682 (JCPC). "If a Governor had, by virtue of that appointment, the whole sovereignty of the Colony delegated to him as a Viceroy, and represented the King in the government of that Colony, there would be good reason to contend that an act of sovereignty done by him would be valid and obligatory upon the subject living within his government, provided the act would be valid if done by the Sovereign himself ... But if the Governor be an officer, merely with a limited authority from the Crown, his assumption of an act of sovereign power, out of the limits of the authority so given to him, would be purely void, and the Courts of the Colony over which he presided could not give it any legal effect. We think the office of the Governor is of the latter description, for no authority or dictum has been cited before us to show that a Governor can be considered as having the delegation of the whole Royal power, in any colony, as between him and the subject, when it is not expressly given by his commission. And we are not aware that any commission to colonial governors conveys such an extensive authority ..."
Bown v. West (1846), 1 E & A 117, 118 (UC). "The government, we know, always made it their care to protect the Indians, so far as they could, in the enjoyment of their property, and to guard against them being imposed upon and dispossessed by the white inhabitants ... we cannot be supposed to be ignorant of the general policy of the government, in regard to the Indians, so far as has been manifest from time to time by orders of council and proclamations, of which all people were expected and required to take notice."
Constitution Act, 1867. "s. 90. The following Provisions of this Act respecting the Parliament of Canada, namely, – the Provisions relating to the Appropriation and Tax

Bills, the Recommendation of Money Votes, the Assent to Bills, the *Disallowance of Acts*, and the Signification of Pleasure on Bills reserved, – shall extend and apply to the Legislatures of the several Provinces as if the Provisions were re-enacted and made applicable in Terms to the respective Provinces and the Legislatures thereof, with the Substitution of the Lieutenant Governor of the Province for the Governor General, of the Governor General for the Queen and for a Secretary of State, of One Year for Two Years, and of the Province for Canada. [Emphasis added.]

s. 91. It shall be lawful for the Queen, by and with the Advice and Consent of the Senate and House of Commons, to make Laws for the Peace, Order, and Good Government of Canada, in relation to all Matters not coming within the Classes of Subjects by this Act assigned exclusively to the Legislatures of the Provinces; and for the greater Certainty but not so as to restrict the Generality of the foregoing Terms of this Section, it is hereby declared that (notwithstanding anything in this Act) the exclusive Legislative Authority of the Parliament of Canada extends to all Matters coming within the Classes of Subjects next herein-after enumerated; that is to say, –

(*24*) Indians, and Lands reserved for the Indians.

s. 92. In each Province the Legislature may exclusively make Laws in relation to Matters coming within the Classes of Subjects next herein-after enumerated; that is to say, –

(*13*) Property and Civil Rights in the Province.

(*14*) The Administration of Justice in the Province, including the Constitution, Maintenance, and Organization of Provincial Courts, both of Civil and of Criminal Jurisdiction, and including Procedure in Civil Matters in those Courts.

s. 109. All Lands, Mines, Minerals and Royalties belonging to the several Provinces of Canada, Nova Scotia, and New Brunswick at the Union, and all Sums then due or payable for such Lands, Mines, Minerals or Royalties, shall belong to the several Provinces of Ontario, Quebec, Nova Scotia, and New Brunswick in which the same are situate or arise, *subject to* any Trusts existing in respect thereof, and to any *Interest* other than that of the Province in the same. [Double emphasis added.]

s. 129. Except otherwise provided by this Act, all Laws in force in Canada, Nova Scotia, or New Brunswick at the Union, and all Courts of Civil and Criminal Jurisdiction and all legal Commissions, Powers, and Authorities, and all Officers, Judicial, Administrative, and Ministerial, existing therein at the Union, shall continue in Ontario, Quebec, Nova Scotia, and New Brunswick respectively, as if the Union had not been made; subject nevertheless (*except* with respect to such as are enacted by or exist under Acts of the Parliament of Great Britain or of the Parliament of the United Kingdom of Great Britain and Ireland,) to be repealed, abolished, or altered by the Parliament of Canada, or by the Legislature of the respective Province, according to the Authority of the Parliament or of that Legislature under this Act. [Double emphasis added.]"

[Ed. commentary: The legislative intent of this 1867 act was to apportion the crown's jurisdiction as between the federal and provincial levels. As to yet unpurchased Indian territory, crown jurisdiction constitutionally was conceived to consist in the jurisdiction to purchase, and thereby to acquire plenary jurisdiction. Section 91(*24*) allotted the said jurisdiction to purchase to the federal level; whereas section 109 allotted crown land to the provincial level. Section 109 recognized and affirmed that the crown's claim of jurisdiction pending purchase constitutionally remains "subject to" the unpurchased Indian "Interest": epitomized by the *Royal Proclamation's* earlier affirmation that the Indians "should not be molested or disturbed" in relation to "such parts of Our Dominions and Territories as, not having been ceded to purchased by Us,

are reserved for them or any of them as their Hunting Grounds." Section 129's "except" clause precluded the federal and provincial governments from enlarging their field of jurisdiction vis-à-vis the said Indian "Interest." There has been no subsequent repeal of this set of constitutional checks and balances. The jurisdiction and mandatory formula to enact such a repeal was patriated by the *Constitution Act, 1982.*]
Connelly v. Woolrich (1867), 11 LCJ 197, 205–7; affirmed (1869) RLOS 253 (CA), 356–7 [Emphasis the Court's] "... will it be contended that the territorial rights, political organization such as it was, or the laws of the Indian tribes, were abrogated – that they ceased to exist when these two European nations began to trade with the aboriginal occupants? In my opinion, it is beyond controversy that they did not – that so far from being abolished, they were not even modified in the slightest degree in regard to the civil rights of the natives. As bearing upon this point, I cannot do better than to cite the decision of a learned and august tribunal – the Supreme Court of the United States. In the celebrated case of *Worcester against the State of Georgia*, (6th Peters Reports, pages 515–542), Chief Justice Marshall – perhaps one of the greatest lawyers of our times – in delivering the judgment of the Court, said:

America, separated from Europe by a wide ocean, was inhabited by a distinct people, divided into separate nations, independent of each other and of the rest of the world, having institutions of their own, and governing themselves by their own laws. It is difficult to comprehend the proposition, that the inhabitants of either quarter of the globe could have rightful original claims of dominion over the inhabitants of the other, or over the lands they occupied; *or that the discovery of either by the other should give the discoverer rights in the country discovered, which annulled the pre-existing rights of its ancient possessors.*

After lying concealed for a series of ages, the enterprise of Europe, guided by nautical science, conducted some of her adventurous sons into this western world. They found it in the possession of a people who had made small progress in agriculture or manufactures, and whose general employment *was war, hunting and fishing.*

Did these adventurers, by sailing along the coast, and occasionally landing on it, acquire for the several governments to whom they belonged, or by whom they were commissioned, a rightful property in the soil, from the Atlantic to the Pacific; or rightful dominion over the numerous people who occupied it? Or has nature, or the Creator of all things, conferred these rights over hunters and fishermen, *on agriculturalists and manufacturers*?

But power, war, conquest, give rights, which, after possession, are conceded by the world; and that can never be controverted by those on whom they descend. We proceed, then, to the actual state of things, having glanced at their origin, because holding it in our recollection might shed some light on existing pretensions.

The great maritime powers of Europe discovered and visited different parts of this continent at nearly the same time. The object was too immense for any of them to grasp the whole; and the claimants too powerful to submit to the exclusive or unreasonable pretensions of any single potentate. To avoid bloody conflicts, which might terminate disastrously to all, it was necessary for the nations of Europe to establish some principle which all would acknowledge, and which should decide their respective rights as between themselves. This principle, suggested by the actual state of things, was, 'that discovery gave title to the government by whose subjects or by whose authority it was made, against all other European governments, which title might be consummated by possession.' Johnson vs. McIntosh, 8 Wheaton's Rep., 543.

This principle, acknowledged by all Europeans, because it was in the interest of all to acknowledge it, gave to the nation making the discovery, as its inevitable consequence, the sole right of acquiring the soil and of making settlements on it. It was an exclusive principle which shut out the right of competition among those who had agreed to it; *not one which could annul the previous rights of those who had not agreed to it*. It regulated the right given by discovery among the European discoverers, *but could not affect the rights of those already in possession, either as aboriginal occupants*, or as occupants by virtue of a discovery made before the memory of man. It gave the exclusive right to purchase, but did not found that right on a denial of the right of the possessor to sell.

The relation between the Europeans and the natives was determined in each case by the particular government which asserted and could maintain this pre-emptive privilege in the particular place. The United States succeeded to all, the claims of Great Britain, both territorial and political; but no attempt so far as is known, has been made to enlarge them. So far as they existed merely in theory, or were in their nature only exclusive of the claims of other European nations, they still retain their original character, and remain dormant. So far as they have been practically exerted, they exist; are asserted by the one, and admitted by the other.

Soon after Great Britain determined upon planting colonies in America, the king granted charters to companies of his subjects who associated for the purpose of carrying the views of the crown into effect, and of enriching themselves. The first of these charters was made *before possession* was taken of any part of the country. They purport, generally, to convey the soil, *from the Atlantic to the South Sea*. This soil was occupied by numerous and warlike nations, equally willing and able to defend their possessions. The extravagant and absurd idea, that the *feeble settlements made on the sea coast, or the companies under whom they were made, acquired legitimate power by them to govern the people or occupy the lands from sea to sea, did not enter the mind of any man*. They were well understood to convey the title which, according to the common law of European sovereigns respecting America, they might rightfully convey, and no more. This was the right of purchasing such lands as the natives were willing to sell. The crown could not be understood to grant what the crown did not affect to claim; nor was it so understood.********
Certain it is, that our history furnishes no example, from the first settlement of our country, *of any attempt on the part of the crown to interfere with the internal affairs of the Indians*, farther than to keep out the agents of foreign powers, who, as traders or otherwise, might seduce them into foreign alliances. The king purchased their lands when they were willing to sell, at a price they were willing to take; but never coerced a surrender of them. *He also purchased their alliance and dependence by subsidies; but never intruded into the interior of their affairs, or interfered with their self government, so far as respected themselves only.*
Though speaking more particularly of Indian lands and territories, yet the opinion of the Court as to the maintenance of the laws of the Aborigines, is manifest throughout. The principles laid down in this judgment, (and Mr. Justice Story as a member of the Court concurred in this decision), admit of no doubt.

[The Court of Appeal of Lower Canada affirmed the preceding judgment, and added the following.] "Even the United States are careful to acquire the Indian title, either by purchase or by other conventional means, before occupancy can be allowed, or public grants made."

Order in Council (Canada) of 23 January 1875. Endorsed "*Approved*" and signed by
the Governor General of Canada, the Lord Dufferin, 25 January 1875. "The Committee of the Privy Council have had under consideration the Report, hereunto annexed,
from the Honourable the Minister of Justice, to whom was referred with the other Acts
passed by the legislature of the Province of British Columbia in the 37th year of Her
Majesty's Reign the following Act, which was assented to by the Lieut Governor on
the 2d March 1874 viz: No 2 intitled: "An Act to amend and consolidate the Laws affecting Crown Lands in British Columbia" and they respectfully submit their concurrence in the views and recommendations set forth in the said Report, and advise that a
copy be transmitted to the Right Honourable H.M. Secretary of State for the Colonies
& to the Lieut Governor of British Columbia.

[p. 1 of Report] *Department of Justice.* Ottawa, 19th January 1875.

The Undersigned has the honour to report:

That of the Acts passed by the Legislature of the Province of British Columbia in the
37th year of Her Majesty's reign and assented to on the 2nd March 1874 is the following:
*No 2 intitled 'An Act to amend and consolidate the Laws affecting Crown Lands in
British Columbia.'*

The title of the Act explains its objects.

[p. 3] ... the words 'Crown Lands' may, for the purposes of this memorandum, be
considered to mean all lands in the Province vested in the Crown of which no grant
had been made.

[p. 7] ... The undersigned refers to the Order in Council under which the Province of
British Columbia was admitted into the Dominion, and particularly the 13thSection as
to the Indians which is as follows:

> The charge of the Indians, and the Trusteeship and management of the lands re-
> served for their own use and benefit, shall be assumed by the Dominion Govern-
> ment, and a policy as liberal as that hitherto pursued by the British Columbia
> Government shall be continued by the Dominion [p. 8] Government after the Union.
> To carry out such policy, tracts of land of such extent as it has hitherto been the prac-
> tice of the British Columbia Government to appropriate for that purpose shall from
> time to time be conveyed by the Local Government to the Dominion Government, in
> trust for the use and benefit of the Indians on application of the Dominion Govern-
> ment; and in case of disagreement between the two Governments respecting the
> quantity of such tracts of land to be so granted, the matter shall be reserved for the
> decision of the Secretary of State for the Colonies.

[p. 9] ... having regard to the known existing and increasing dissatisfaction of the Indian
Tribes of British Columbia at the absence of adequate reservations of lands for their use,
and at the liberal appropriation for those in other parts of Canada upon surrender by
Treaty of their territorial rights, and the difficulties which may arise from the not improbable assertion of that [p. 10] dissatisfaction by hostilities on their part, the undersigned
deems it right to call attention to the legal position of the Public Lands of the Province.

The Undersigned believes that he is correct in stating, that with one slight exception
as to land in Vancouver Island surrendered to the Hudson's Bay Company which
makes the absence of others the more remarkable no surrenders of lands in that Province have ever been obtained from the Indian Tribes inhabiting it, and that any reservations which have been made, have been arbitrary on the part of the Government and
without the assent of the Indians themselves, and although the policy of obtaining sur-

renders at this lapse of time and under the altered circumstances of the Province
[p. 11] may be questionable, yet the Undersigned feels it his duty to assert such legal
or equitable claim as may be found to exist on the part of the Indians.

There is not a shadow of doubt that, from the earliest times, England has always felt
it imperative to meet the Indians in Council and to obtain surrenders of tracts of Canada as from time to time such were required for the purpose of settlements.

The 40th article of the Treaty of Capitulation of the City of Montreal, dated 8th September 1760, is to the effect that:

'The Savages or Indian allies of His Most Christian Majesty shall be maintained in
the lands they inhabit [p. 12] if they chose to remain there.'

The Proclamation of King George III 1763, erecting within the Countries and Islands, ceded and confirmed to Great Britain by the Treaty of the 10thFebruary 1763,
four distinct Governments styled Quebec, East Florida, West Florida and Granada,
contains the following clauses:

[Here, at p. 12 to 21 this Report quotes verbatim the 'Indian part' of the proclamation
reproduced above, from 'Whereas it is just and reasonable' to 'in order to take their
trial for the same.' The only parts reproduced now are the parts underlined by the Minister of Justice and Deputy Minister in the original.]

[p. 13] ... *such parts of our dominions and territories as,* not having been ceded to or
purchased by Us, are reserved to them, or any of them as their hunting grounds; ...

[p. 14] ... *or upon* any lands whatever, which not having been ceded to or purchased
by us, as aforesaid, are reserved to the said Indians, or any of them ...

[p. 16] ... *And we do further strictly enjoin and require all persons whatsoever, who
have either wilfully or inadvertently seated themselves upon any lands within the
Countries above described, or upon any other lands,* which not having been ceded to
or purchased by us, *are reserved to the said Indians as aforesaid, forthwith to remove
themselves from such settlements* ...

[p. 21] It is not necessary now to inquire whether the lands [p. 22] to the west of the
Rocky Mountains and bordering on the Pacific Ocean form part of the lands claimed
by France, and which, if such claim were correct, would have passed by cession to England under the Treaty of 1763; or whether the title of England rests on any other
ground; nor, is it necessary to consider whether that Proclamation covered the land
now known as British Columbia. It is sufficient for the present purposes to ascertain
the policy of England in relation to the acquisition of the Indian territorial rights, and
how entirely that policy has been followed to the present time, except in the [p. 23] instance of British Columbia.

It is also true that the Proclamation of 1763, to which allusion has been made, was
repealed by the Imperial Statute 14 George III, Ch: 83, known as 'The Quebec Act'
but that Statute merely, so far as regards the present case, annuls the Proclamation,

so far as the same relates to the Province of Quebec and the Commission and authority thereof, under the authority whereof the Government of the said Province is
at present administered

and the Act was passed for the purpose of effecting a change in the mode of the
Civil Government of the [p. 24] administration of Justice in the Province of
Quebec.

The Imperial Act 1821, 1st & 2nd George 4, Ch: 66 for regulating the Fur Trade and
establishing a Criminal and Civil jurisdiction within certain parts of North America,

legislates expressly in respect to that portion of the Continent which is therein spoken of as 'the Indian territories', and by the Imperial Act 1849, 12 & 13 Vic: Ch: 48 'An Act to provide for the administration in Vancouver's Island', the last mentioned Act is recited and it is added in recital that

> for the purpose of the colonization of *that part of the said Indian Territories* [p. 25] called Vancouver's Island, it is expedient that further provision should be made for the administration of justice therein.

The Imperial Act 1858, 21 and 22 Vic: Ch: 98, 'An Act to provide for the Government of British Columbia' recites,

> that divers of Her Majesty's subjects and others have, by the license and consent of Her Majesty, resorted to and settled on certain *wild and unoccupied territories on* the North West Coast of North America now known as 'New Caledonia' from and after the passing of the Act to be named British Columbia and the Islands adjacent &c

[p. 26] The determination of England, as expressed in the Proclamation of 1763 that the Indians should not be molested in the possession of such parts of the dominions and territories of England as, not having been ceded to the King, are reserved to them, and which extended also to the prohibition of purchase of lands from the Indians, except only by the Crown itself – at a public meeting or assembly of the said Indians to be held by the Governor or Commander in Chief has, with slight alterations, been continued down to the present time, either as the settled policy of Canada [p. 27] or by Legislative provision of Canada, to that effect, and it may be mentioned that, in furtherance of that policy, so lately as in the year 1874, treaties were made with various tribes of Indians in the North West Territories, and large tracts of lands, lying between the Province of Manitoba and the Rocky Mountains, were ceded and surrendered to the Crown, upon conditions of which, the reservations of large tracts for the Indians and the granting of annuities and gifts annually, formed an important consideration: and, in various parts of Canada, from the Atlantic to the Rocky Mountains, large and valuable tracts of land [p. 28] are now reserved for the Indians, as part of the consideration of their ceding and yielding to the Crown their territorial rights in other portions of the Dominion.

Considering, then, these several features of the case, – that no surrender or cession of their Territorial rights, whether the same be of a legal or equitable nature, has been ever executed by the Indian Tribes of the Province; that they allege that the reservations of land made by the Government, for their use have been arbitrarily so made and are totally inadequate to their support and [p. 29] requirements, and without their assent – that they are not averse to hostilities in order to enforce rights, which it is impossible to deny them, – and that the Act under consideration not only ignores those rights, but expressly prohibits the Indians from enjoying the rights of recording or pre-empting Lands, except by consent of the Lieutenant Governor, – the Undersigned feels that he cannot do otherwise, than advise that the Act [No. 2: the BC Public Lands Act] in question is objectionable, as tending to deal with Lands which are assumed to be the absolute property of the Province, an assumption which completely ignores, – as applicable to the Indians of [p. 30] British Columbia, – the honour and good faith with which the Crown has in all other cases, since its sovereignty of the territories in North America dealt with their various Indian Tribes.

The Undersigned would also refer to the B.N.A. Act 1867 Sec. 109, applicable to British Columbia, which enacts in effect that, all lands belonging to the Province, shall belong to the Province 'subject to any trust existing in respect thereof, and to any interest other than that of the Province in the same.'

That which has been ordinarily spoken of as the 'Indian Title' must, of necessity, consist in some species of interest in the lands of [p. 31] British Columbia. If it is conceded, that they have not a freehold in the soil but that they have an usufruct, – a right of occupation, or possession of the same for their own use, then it would seem that these Lands of British Columbia are subject, if not to a 'trust existing in respect thereof,' at least to 'to an Interest other than that of the Province alone.'

The Undersigned, therefore, feels it incumbent upon him to recommend that this Act should be disallowed, ..."

[p. 35] Signed by Deputy Minister of Justice of Canada and endorsed "*I concur*" and signed by the Minister of Justice of Canada.

Church v. Fenton (1878), 28 UCCP 384, 388, 399, affirmed (1879), 4 OAR 159, affirmed 5 SCR 239. "The British Crown has invariably waived its right by conquest over all lands in the Province until the extinguishment of what the Crown has been pleased to recognize as the Indian title, by a treaty of surrender of the nature of that produced in this case; until such extinguishment of that title the Crown has never granted such lands ...

As early as 1837 was passed the Act 7 Wm. IV ch. 118 entitled '*An Act to provide for the disposal of the public lands in this Province,*' &c. That was an Act passed for the management and sale of the portion of the lands vested in Her Majesty which consisted of Crown lands, clergy reserves, and school lands, the proceeds arising from the sale of which were to be accounted for as forming part of public revenue through the commissioner of Crown lands and the receiver-general.

This Act did not affect the lands vested in Her Majesty in which the Indians were interested, either as lands appropriated for their residence, as to which there had been no treaty of surrender for the purpose of extinguishing the Indian title, nor lands as to which there had been a surrender of such title, but in the proceeds arising from the sale of which the Indians being interested, the sale and management of them was retained in the Indian Department.

This term or designation 'Public Lands,' as applied to those lands the proceeds arising from the sale of which constituted part of the public revenue of the Province, has ever since been maintained in various Acts of the Legislature, viz., 2 Vic. ch. 15; 4 & 5 Vic. ch. 100; 16 Vic. ch. 159, and 23 Vic. ch. 2."

St. Catherine's Milling & Lumber Co. v. The Queen (1886), 13 OAR 148, 167, 169.

... the lands were public lands which passed or remained with the Province, subject to the rights which the Indians might possess, as in my opinion they were, ...

The Indians] were the rightful occupants of the soil, with a legal as well as a just claim to retain possession of it, and to use it according to their own discretion. In a certain sense they were permitted to exercise rights of sovereignty over it. They might sell or transfer it to the sovereign who discovered it.

St. Catherine's Milling & Lumber Co. v. The Queen (1887), 13 SCR 577, 599, 608–10, 628, 631–2, 647, 652. "I am of opinion, that all ungranted lands in the province of Ontario belong to the crown as part of the public domain, subject to the Indian right of occupancy in which the same has not been extinguished, and when such right of occupancy has been lawfully extinguished absolutely to the crown, and as a consequence to the province of Ontario.

These rules of policy being shown to have been well established and acted upon, and the title of the Indians to their unsurrendered lands to have been recognized by the crown to the extent already mentioned, it may be of little importance to enquire into the reasons on which it is based. But as these reasons are not without some bearing on the present question, as I shall hereafter shew, I will shortly refer to what appears to have led to the adoption of the system of dealing with the territorial rights of the Indians. To ascribe it to moral grounds, to motives of humane consideration for the aborigines, would be to attribute it feelings which perhaps had little weight in the age in which it took its rise. Its true origin was, I take it, experience of the great impolicy of the opposite mode of dealing with the Indians which had been practiced by some of the Provincial Governments of the older colonies and which had led to frequent frontier wars, involving great sacrifices of life and property and requiring an expenditure of money which proved most burdensome to the colonies. That the more liberal treatment accorded to the Indians by this system of protecting them in the enjoyment of their hunting grounds and prohibiting settlement on lands which they had not surrendered ... was successful in its results, is attested by the historical fact that from the memorable year of 1763, when Detroit was besieged and all the Indian tribes were in revolt, down to the date of confederation, Indian wars and massacres entirely ceased in the British possessions in North America, although powerful Indian nations still continued for some time after the former date to inhabit those territories. That this peaceful conduct of the Indians is in a great measure to be attributed to the recognition of their rights to lands unsurrendered by them, and to the guarantee of their protection in the possession and enjoyment of such lands given by the crown in the proclamation of October, 1763, hereafter to be more fully noticed, is a well known fact of Canadian history which cannot be controverted. The Indian nations from that time became and have since continued to be the firm and faithful allies of the crown and rendered it important military services in two wars – the war of the Revolution and that of 1812 ... In the first settlement of the country to assert sovereignty and to put that assertion into operation would have caused war, and it is necessary to treat with the Indians from time to time in order to facilitate settlement.

To summarize ... at the date of confederation the Indians, by the constant usage of the crown, were considered to possess a certain proprietary interest in the unsurrendered lands which they occupied as hunting grounds; that this usage had either ripened into a rule of the common law as applicable to the American Colonies, or that such a rule had been derived from the law of nations and had in this way been imported into the Colonial law as applied to Indian Nations; ...

... it [the *Royal Proclamation of 1763*] gives legislative expression and force to what I have heretofore treated as depending on a regulation of policy, or at most on rules of unwritten law and official practice, namely, the right of the Indians to enjoy, by virtue of a recognized title, their lands not surrendered or ceded to the crown. ... [B]eing a legislative act having the force of a statute it has never, in my opinion, been repealed, but has, so far as it regulates the rights of the Indians in their unsurrendered lands remained in force to the present day.

It [the proclamation] was a legislative act, ... and being still in full force and vigour when the British North America Act was passed, it operated at that time as an express legislative appropriation of the land now in dispute for the use and benefit of the Indians by the designation of 'lands reserved to the Indians.' ...

Further, the third section of the act [*Quebec Act, 1774*] contains an express saving of titles to land, in words sufficiently comprehensive to include the Indian title recognized by the proclamation. Its words are:

Nothing in this act contained shall extend, or be construed to extend, to make void, or to vary or alter any right, title, or possession, derived under any grant, conveyance, or otherwise howsoever, of or to any lands within the said province, or the provinces thereto adjoining; but that the same shall remain and be in force, and have effect, as if this act had never been made.

The words 'right,' 'title' and 'possession' are all applicable to the rights which the crown had conceded to the Indians by the proclamation, and, with absolutely disregarding this 3rd section, it would be impossible to hold that these vested rights of property or possession had all been abolished or swept away by the statute. I must therefore hold, that the Quebec Act had no more effect in revoking the five concluding paragraphs of the proclamation of 1763 which relate to the Indians and their rights to possess and enjoy their lands until they voluntarily surrendered or ceded them to the crown than it had in repealing it as a royal ordinance for the government of the Floridas and Granada.
    ... any right the Indians might have previously had could not, it seems, have been affected by this act [*Quebec Act*], as by its 3rd section it is specifically provided that

'nothing in this act contained shall extend, or be construed to extend, to make void, or to vary, or alter, any right, title, or possession, derived under any grant, conveyance, or otherwise howsoever, of or to any lands within the said province, or the provinces thereto adjoining.' ...

By the Haldimand papers in the Canadian archives it appears that in December, 1766, one Philibot, having an order of His Majesty in Council, dated the 18 of June, 1766, directed to the Governor in Chief of the Province of Quebec, for a grant of 20,000 acres in the province, petitioned the Governor, praying that the grant might be assigned to him on the Restigouche at a place indicated by him, and the Committee of Council at Quebec having taken the matter into consideration reported that the lands so prayed to be granted were or were claimed to be the property of the Indians, and as such, by His Majesty's express command as set forth in his proclamation of 1763, not within their power to grant."
A G Ont. v. Francis (1889), PAO, Irving Papers, Box 43, File 42, Item 9, at 13 (High Court of Ontario). "I think that for this or a like purpose this band of Indians should be considered as standing in the same position as any other high contracting power or government, and it is a proposition of law that if an agent exceed his authority the principal is not bound. For this reason I think both the instructions and the contract must be seen in such a case."
A G Ont. v. A G Can. (1895), 25 SCR 434, 504, 535. "[The legal effect of the Robinson-Huron Treaty of 1850 was that by it] these lands were acquired by the Crown with a view to settlement, for developing mineral deposits, and for the purpose of applying the timber to purposes of utility ... [The courts] would with the consent of the Crown and of all our governments strain to their utmost limit all ordinary rules of construction or principles of law – the governing motive being that in all questions between Her Majesty and 'Her faithful Indian allies' there must be on her part, and on the part of those who represent her, not good faith, but more, there must be not only justice, but generosity."

AG Ont. v. AG Can., [1897] AC 199, 205, 210–11 (JCPC). "The beneficial interest in the territories ceded by the Indians under the treaties became vested, by virtue of s. 109, in the Province of Ontario ... The effect of the treaties was, that, whilst the title to the lands ceded continued to be vested in the Crown, all beneficial interest in them, together with the right to dispose of them, and to appropriate their proceeds, passed to the Government of the Province.

'An interest other than that of the province in the same' [within the meaning of section 109] appears to them [their Lordships] to denote some right or interest in a third-party, independent of and capable of being *vindicated in competition with the beneficial interest of* the old province. [Emphasis added].

Ontario Mining Co. v. Seybold, [1903] AC 73, 79 (JCPC). "It was decided by this board in the *St. Catherine's Milling Co.'s Case* that prior to the treaty the province of Ontario had a proprietary interest in the land, under the provisions of s. 109 of the British North America Act, 1867, subject to the burden of the Indian usufructory title, and upon the extinguishment of that title by the surrender the province acquired the full beneficial interest."

AG Can. v. AG Ont., [1910] AC 637, 644, 646 (JCPC). "[The treaty's] effect was to extinguish by consent the Indian interest over a large tract of land ... Dominion Government were indeed, on behalf of the Crown, guardians of the Indian interest."

R. v. Ontario & Minnesota Power Co., [1925] AC 196, 197 (JCPC). "In the year 1888 this Board decided in *St. Catherine's Milling & Lumber Co. v. The Queen* that by force of the surrender of 1873 the beneficial interest in the lands in Ontario comprised in that surrender was transmitted to that Province."

R. v. McMaster, [1926] Ex. 68, 73. "[An Indian treaty is] a sale or transfer of their interest in land. [It is] a formal contract."

Easterbrook v. R., [1932] 5 SCR 210, 217–18. "... the lease was ineffective and void at law ... for non-compliance with the peremptory requirements of the proclamation which have the force of statute."

R. v. Wesley, [1932] 2 WWR 337, 348, 351 (Alta. CA). "In *Dominion of Canada v. Ontario (Indian Annuities)*, [1910] AC 637, 80 LJPC 32, Lord Loreburn, L.C. giving the judgment of the Judicial Committee, in speaking of the effect of the surrender of lands by the Indians by the treaty there in question, said that 'the lands are released from the overlying Indian interest.'

It is clear that whether it be called a title, an interest, or a burden on the Crown's title, the Indians are conceded to have obtained definite rights under this proclamation in the territories therein mentioned which certainly included the right to hunt and fish at will over those lands in which they held such interest.

... [Indian treaties are] formal agreements ..."

R. v. George, [1964] 1 OR 24, 27(HC). "Throughout the *Dominion of Canada* case and the *St. Catherine's* case it is recognized that the Indians' interest was an interest that attached the land."

R. v. George, [1964] 2 OR 429, 433 (CA). "The treaty does not refer to the Proclamation in terms but historical implication impels the conclusion that what was surrendered and conveyed to the Crown by the treaty were the rights granted to them by the Proclamation to and in respect of the lands described in the treaty as being intended to be conveyed. What was preserved and confirmed to them were those same rights to and in respect of the lands reserved by the treaty and without any limitation as to time thereon."

R. v. Sikyea (1964), 46 WWR 65, 66 (NWTCA), affirmed [1964] SCR 642, 642. "Canada has treated all Indians across Canada, including those living on lands claimed by

the Hudson Bay Company, as having an interest in the lands that required a treaty to effect its surrender."
Brick Cartage Ltd. v. R., [1965] I Ex. 102, 105 (TD). "[Indians have] a possessory right in lands. [Crown title is] subject to the Indians' possessory rights. ... The Indian possessory right could only be extinguished by a formal contract."
Calder v. AGBC, [1973] SCR 313, 320, 323, 379, 389, 394, 401, 402. "[Per Judson J.] Any Canadian enquiry into the nature of the Indian title must begin with *St. Catherines Milling and Lumber Co. v. The Queen* ... It was held that the Crown had at all times a present proprietary estate, which title, after confederation, was in the Province, by virtue of s. 109 of the *B.N.A. Act*. The Indian title was a mere burden upon that title which, following the cession of the lands under the treaty, was extinguished ... [T]he fact is that when the settlers came, the Indians were there, organized in societies and occupying the land as their forefathers had done for centuries ... [Per Hall J.] ... on the point of Indian title there was no disagreement between the majority and minority views [in the Supreme Court of Canada in the *St. Catherine's* case]. Ritchie CJ for the majority agreed substantially with Strong J in this respect, saying at pp. 559–60:

> I am of opinion, that all ungranted lands in the Province of Ontario belong to the crown as part of the public domain, subject to the Indian right of occupancy in cases in which the same has not been extinguished, and when such right has been lawfully extinguished absolutely to the crown, and as a consequence to the province of Ontario. I think the crown owns the soil of all the unpatented lands, the Indians possessing only the right of occupancy, and the crown possessing the legal title subject to that right of occupancy, with the absolute exclusive right to extinguish the Indian title either by conquest or by purchase ...

It is of importance that in all those areas where Indian lands were being taken by the Crown treaties were negotiated and entered into between the Crown and the Indian tribe on land then in occupation. The effect of these treaties was discussed in by Davey JA (as he then was) for the majority in *White and Bob* and follows at p. 197:

> It was the long-standing policy of the Imperial government and of the Hudson's Bay Company that the Crown of the Company should buy from the Indians their land for settlement by white colonists. In pursuance of that policy many agreements, some very formal, some informal, were made with various bands and tribes of Indians for the purchase of their lands.

Paralleling and supporting the claim of the Nishgas that they have a certain right or title to the lands in question is the guarantee of Indian rights contained in the Proclamation of 1763.
Once aboriginal title is established, it is presumed to continue until the contrary is proven ...
It being a legal right, it could not thereafter be extinguished except by surrender to the Crown or by competent legislative authority, and then only by specific legislation."
Re Paulette's Application to File a Caveat, [1973] 6 WWR 120, 144 (NWTTD). "It seems clear to me that aboriginal rights are an interest in land: *cf. St. Catherine's Milling & Lumber Co. The Queen* (1888), 14 App. Cas. 46, 4 Cart. 107; and *Calder v. Attorney General of British Columbia*, [1973] 4 WWR I, 34 DLR (3d) 145 (Can.)"
R. v. Secretary of State for Foreign and Commonwealth Affairs, [1982] 2 All ER 118

(CA), 125. "Save for that reference in s 91(24), the 1867 Act was silent on Indian affairs. Nothing was said about the title to property in the lands 'reserved for the Indians', not to the revenues therefrom, nor to the rights and obligations of the Crown or the Indians thenceforward in regard thereto. But I have no doubt that all concerned regarded the royal proclamation of 1763 as still of binding force. It was an unwritten provision which went without saying. It was binding on the legislature of the Dominion and the Provinces just as if there had been a sentence: 'The aboriginal peoples of Canada shall continue to have all their rights and freedoms as recognized by the royal proclamation of 1763.'"
Constitution Act, 1982.

"PART II. RIGHTS OF THE ABORIGINAL PEOPLES OF CANADA.

s. 35. (*1*) The existing aboriginal and treaty rights of the aboriginal peoples of Canada are hereby recognized and affirmed.
PART V. PROCEDURE FOR AMENDING CONSTITUTION OF CANADA.
s. 38. (*1*) An amendment to the Constitution of Canada may be made by proclamation issued by the Governor General under the Great Seal of Canada where authorized by
(*a*) resolutions of the Senate and House of Commons; and
(*b*) resolutions of the legislative assemblies of at least two-thirds of the provinces that have, in the aggregate, according to the then latest general census, at least fifty per cent of the population of all the provinces."
R v. Sparrow, [1990] 1 SCR 1075, (1990), 56 CCC (3d) 263, 283 (SCC). "... while British policy towards the native population was based upon respect for their right to occupy their traditional lands, a proposition to which the Royal Proclamation of 1763 bears witness, there was from the outset any doubt that sovereignty and legislative power, and indeed the underlying title, to such land vested in the Crown: see *Johnson v. M'Intosh*, 8 Wheaton 543 (1823); see also the Royal Proclamation of 1763 itself (RSC, 1985 App. II, No. 1, pp. 4–6); *Calder* per Judson J. at p. 156, Hall J. at pp. 195, 208."
Hamar Foster, "Forgotten Arguments: Aboriginal Title and Sovereignty in *Canada Jurisdiction Act* Cases," 1992 *Manitoba Law Journal* 343–89, excerpts of which follow, from pages 353, 356–7, 360–1, 365–7, 370, 379–80, 383, 385, 388. "Transcripts of many of the *Canada Jurisdiction Act* cases do exist, and they include arguments of counsel and rulings from the bench that have been ignored or, more likely, simply forgotten. All of this evidence ... tends to show not only that many people doubted whether these statutes applied to Indians, but even whether the Imperial Parliament had any jurisdiction at all in the Indian Territories.

    In October of 1765, for example, the Superintendent of Indian Affairs, Sir William Johnson, advised the attorney general of New York that '... strictly speaking our rights of soil Extend no farther than they are actually purchased by Consent of the natives, 'tho' in a *political* sense our Claims are much more Extensive ... but these claims are kept up by European Powers to prevent the Encroachments or pretensions of each other, *nor can it be consistent with the Justice of our Constitution to extend it farther ...*'

    ... Although the right conceded to the 'discovering nation' was described as constituting a form of title, in practical terms it amounted to an exclusive right to purchase and nothing more. ... As Justice Thompson [in *Cherokee Nation*] put it, '... a weak state, that, in order to provide for its safety, places itself under the protection [*c.f. Royal Proclamation of 1763*: 'under our Protection'] of a more powerful one, without stripping itself of the right of government and sovereignty, does not cease on this account to be placed among the sovereigns who acknowledge no other power.'

... At least until treaties were entered into, the chief justice [Marshall in *Worcester*] ruled, nothing more than the unlimited right to sell land and conduct foreign relations had been lost ...

At the time the *Canada Jurisdiction Act* and the *Regulation of the Fur Trade Act* were passed, the legal doctrines enunciated by the Marshall Court possessed an even greater practical reality in the Indian Territories of British North America ... [Yet] By the late nineteenth century the concept of tribal sovereignty had lost its potency even in the United States. In Canada it almost completely disappeared.

... the mischief against which the [*Canada Jurisdiction Act*] was directed was European, not Aboriginal. It was not passed in order to apply colonial criminal law to Indians, but to enable the courts at Montréal to try Canadian traders who had committed serious offences against one another in the fur trade country, even in regions as far away as Oregon and Russian America. Empirically, four facts about the *Canada Jurisdiction Act*'s history stand out ... most important for present purposes, no one who was tried in the Canadas under the Act was a 'full-blooded' Indian.

The motives of those who lobbied for the 1803 Act are recorded ... No one spoke of using such a law against the Indian tribes; it was directed, not at the Cree or the Chipewyan or any other Indian nation, but at extending the process of the Canadian courts to traders who would otherwise have to be sent to England for trial or, more likely, who would escape punishment altogether ...

... [In] the *Report* made by the Select Committee on the Hudson's Bay Company ... Edward 'Bear' Ellice, one of the prime movers of the coalition between the North West and Hudson's Bay Companies in 1821, testified at length ... [He] knew as much about it as anyone. But nowhere in over thirty printed pages does he suggest that the statute rendered Indians subject to colonial criminal law.

... the North American governor of the Hudson's Bay Company, Sir George Simpson ... [testified] ... 'Q. What law do you consider in force in the case of the Indians committing any crime upon the Whites; do you consider that the clause in your licence to trade, by which you are bound to transport criminals to Canada for trial, refers to the Indians, or solely to the Whites – To the Whites, we conceive.' Thus the senior official in the Hudson's Bay Company not only believed that colonial criminal law had no application to disputes that involved Indians only, but he also believed that it had no application to Indians who injured or killed Europeans. This is hardly surprising. The wording of both the licence to trade and s. 3 of the *Regulation of the Fur Trade Act* required the Hudson's Bay Company to deliver into custody 'for purposes of trial all persons in their employ or acting under their authority within the said territories who should be charged with any criminal offence ...' In this respect the statutes of 1803 and 1821 followed the precedent set by the *Royal Proclamation of 1763*, and by the legislation enacted by the Imperial Parliament prior to the American Revolution, which was designed to enable colonial courts to try Europeans – not Indians – for crimes committed in the Indian Territories.

ADMITTEDLY, THE *CANADA JURISDICTION Act* is not restricted on its face ... This wording has led not only Clark but the distinguished historian A.S. Morton, to assume that Indians were subject to the Act. Concern about similar assumptions may have led the Dominion Parliament to state explicitly, in the original *Indian Act* of 1876, that the term 'person' did *not* include Indians unless the context clearly required that construction.

But no court appears to have ruled that members of the Indian nations were liable to prosecution under the *Canada Jurisdiction Act* ...

The Shawanakiskie case [1823] ... was believed to be the first of its kind [Indian kills another Indian in the town of Amherstburg, which from all that appears was ceded land no longer subject territorially to aboriginal rights]. ... Shawanakiskie therefore enjoyed a kind of diplomatic immunity. If this is a possibility that could be entertained by the authorities respecting an offence committed within a settled township in Upper Canada, how likely is it that colonial criminal law applied to Indians on unceded Indian land?

The clearest answer I have found to this question, i.e., whether the *Canada Jurisdiction Act* should be construed as having subjected the Indians of the Indian Territories to colonial criminal law, comes from a prosecution brought in Trois Rivières in 1838 ...

When defence counsel argued that the court had no jurisdiction over the accused, Chief Justice James Reid told the jury that this depended partly upon whether [the accused] Cadien was a British subject. If he were 'a mere Indian, attached to no place of residence [meaning trading post],' he was someone 'over whom no jurisdiction could be maintained.' In other words, Cadien's socio-economic affiliations with the fur trade pulled in one direction, his 'Indianness' in another. If he were simply an Indian on Indian Territory, the *Canada Jurisdiction Act* did not reach him ...

The fact remains that the only judge west of the Canadas appears to have agreed with the Court of King's Bench at Trois Rivières: in the absence of express statutory language, Indians in the Indian Country were not to be regarded as subject to colonial criminal law ...

... Over the years ... the jurisprudence confining the *Canada Jurisdiction Act* to fur traders was forgotten, and an arid and exclusive view of sovereignty unsuitable for a federation became ascendant ...

... a corollary is that what went before remains until it is specifically abrogated: only the clearest legislation, clearly communicated to those affected, can have such a fatal effect. Case law is insufficient, because of that other mystery of the common law system, the one Frederic William Maitland flagged as causing so much misunderstanding between lawyers and historians. It is that, even when judges change their minds, they simply declare the law as it has always been ...

... Clark's approach seems to have even more serious problems, because judges are unlikely to hold that imperial law forbad the colonies and later the dominion from passing legislation extinguishing title and self-government ..."

[Ed. commentary: In the last quoted sentence the author of the article has voiced the realist school of jurisprudence which holds that judges are ruled by sentiment rather than by the law as written, at least where, as in the native versus newcomer jurisdiction context, existing law and existing judicial sentiment profoundly conflict. Recall, in his article Foster has identified a body of "imperial law" which did indeed constitutionally "forbad the colonies and later the dominion from passing legislation extinguishing title and self-government," at least unless the "legislation" were to take the form of a duly enacted constitutional repeal pursuant to section 38 of the *Constitution Act, 1982* of the "subject to" clause in section 109 of the *Constitution Act, 1867*. Foster has not identified any such repeal. If Canada is a "rule of law" society, as proclaimed by its *Constitution Act, 1982*, Canada's judges have no choice: judges in a rule of law society are obliged to declare the established constitutional law, as it is written, leaving to the legislative process the task of re-writting it if that law is no longer acceptable to the society. For an alternative to the realist school of jurisprudence please see the discussion at endnotes 5 and 6 of the (appended) District Court Complaint.]

Delgamuukw v. AGBC. Supreme Court of Canada Case File 23799. Reasons for Judgment on a Motion to State a Constitutional Question. September 12, 1995. Transcription of Tapes. Pages 1, 6, 10, 11, 12, 14–18, 21–5, 27, 28, 30, 35.

"MR. BRYAN WILLIAMS, Q.C. [counsel for the Attorney General of British Columbia]: ... The co-plaintiffs, having decided to sue together, there were fifty one (51) I believe in Delgamuukw, having decided to commence and action, cannot pursue a different course and separate themselves from the other plaintiffs to obtain separate representation [*.i. e.*, legal counsel Bruce Clark] ...

MR. JUSTICE SOPINKA: ... Does the same thing apply to appeal? I mean, some people might not want to appeal. Some might want to appeal. There are differentiations made at the trial with respect to the judgment. I wonder if that rule is applied strictly in respect of appeals. Do you have to stick together throughout?

MR. BRYAN WILLIAMS, Q.C.: ... So, my Lords, what I am saying in summary on this motion is purely and simply that for an action that has gone on to trial for four (4) years, six (6) weeks in the Court of Appeal, now coming before this Court with competent counsel representing all those plaintiffs throughout the that case and to have one of the plaintiffs decide that they want to take a totally inconsistent position in this Court at this time, is simply not warranted. I submit that their motion should be struck out.

MR. STUART RUSH [counsel for the *Delgamuukw* case native appellants other than the native appellant Xsgogimlahxa, for whom Bruce Clark as counsel brings the application to state a constitutional question challenging the assumption of jurisdiction by the non-native courts relative to natives and their unceded land]: It is our position, assuming that the constitutional question notice filed by Xsgogimlahxa reflects the case which will be brought, that the case which Xsgogimlahxa seeks to bring is fundamentally different from the one that the hereditary Chiefs brought at trial and on appeal and I need only refer your Lordships to exhibit A of Mr. Bell's affidavit of September 6 and to the points in issue that were raised by the Delgamuukw appellants on this appeal and on which leave to appeal was granted. I say as well that the case that is reflected in the constitutional question that is posed by Xsgogimlahxa is not the appellants' case. It is a different case which we say should not be part of this appeal and it may well be the subject of another case for another appeal based on other facts at another time, by my Lords it is not this case. I submit further that this action was brought by the hereditary Chiefs collectively for themselves, their House members and all of the members of the Gitksan and Wet'suweten peoples. In doing so, they were and are seeking rights of title and self-government as nations. Their action is also in respect of their territory as a whole. In denying the jurisdiction of the Canadian courts to adjudicate on these issues, the applicant Xsgogimlahxa in this application to state a constitutional questions [sic] raises issues which are at odds completely with the appellants' issues and has nothing to do with the appellants' case. We say that he wishes to proceed with the case in the Canadian courts on the basis that there is no jurisdiction and a Canadian court will hear that, then the applicant should sever off from this appeal and start his own action or proceed on the basis of his own proceedings.

MR. DAVID FRANKEL, Q.C. [counsel for the Attorney General of Canada]: My Lords, ... I have nothing to usefully add to the submissions of my learned friends [*i.e.*, Mr. Bryan Williams, Q.C. and Mr. Stuart Rush].

MR. BRUCE CLARK: [counsel for the applicant Xsgogimlahxa] ... They [all the native plaintiffs] wanted and did assert jurisdiction over land. From the affidavit material filed, they were not however advised and fully informed that they had the right in addition in view of the *Mohagen* [sic: *Mohegan*] precedent to contest the jurisdiction of the non-native court system at the same time. That in my submission is crucial because, if the province of British Columbia and the dominion of Canada have legislative jurisdiction to provide for courts relative to arguably yet unseated [sic: unceded] hunting grounds, by the same token they also have jurisdiction to provide for land legislation. To grant one is to grant the other.

In this perspective, the day the writ was issued in the *Delgamuukw* case returning [sic: attorning] to the jurisdiction of the court, it is [sic: was] lost by the plaintiffs by conceding the jurisdiction of the court. By necessary implication, they conceded the jurisdiction of the legislatures that created those courts, which is to say the Indian apparent assertion of native sovereignty was scuttled by the legal profession in its presentation to the court system.

CHIEF JUSTICE LAMER: Maybe the fact that they have been unsuccessful might have something to do with the change of mind as to who has jurisdiction. We are facing a situation, as you readily admit, that by going to a court one brings oneself within the jurisdiction of that court ...

MR. BRUCE CLARK: ... jurisdiction that is inherently illegal cannot be acquired by waiver ... on the face of the [other appellants'] affidavit, coupled with my clients' affidavit, we have what appears to be a fraud upon a minority and that minority now wants to apprehend that fraud, and in arguing for the apprehension of that fraud argues that the entire system of justice and rule of law is placed on trial in consequence. The reason is, if my clients' point of law is well taken, the assumption of jurisdiction in the past and today and tomorrow *prima facie* constitutes treason and fraud and arguably complicity in genocide.

CHIEF JUSTICE LAMER: ... If you had decided to initiate or if you decide tomorrow morning to initiate in the Supreme Court of British Columbia an action for declaratory relief saying that the British Columbia courts have no jurisdiction, that is a different matter and you could be arguing to the judge that, well, this is an issue that has never been tried and I want a declaratory, but we are talking about doing this within the four (4) corners of this appeal. And what you have against you is that, while you might have a good point to argue in the British Columbia Court of Appeal, this is not the place to start the thing and this is certainly not the way of doing it along with them. In other words they do not want to be in the same courtroom with you because you are saying they should not be in the courtroom.

MR. BRUCE CLARK: On July 6 [1995], your Lordship refused leave to appeal on the same point of law pursuant to s. 40(1) of the *Supreme Court Act*, the sole test for which is whether the issue is of importance. You, my Lord, have already decided this issue is not of sufficient importance to occupy the Court's time. For you now to say that it is realistically open to Xsgogimlahxa to commence a separate action and to work his way through the court system, as was done on those eleven (11) other applications is blatant chicaneries [sic: chicanery].

CHIEF JUSTICE LAMER: I must remind you, Mr. Clark, that I do not intend to tolerate such language on the part of any counsel including yourself.

MR. BRUCE CLARK: Nor, sir, do I intend to tolerate treason, fraud and complicity in genocide against our Constitution and against the aboriginal peoples of this country ...

CHIEF JUSTICE LAMER: Proceed, proceed.

MR. BRUCE CLARK: If my client's point ultimately is vindicated, this Court does not have jurisdiction. The remaining plaintiffs will then have an informed option. That informed option will permit them either to say "We will take that route". That is the probability because at that point their native sovereignty would be – they would not only have land jurisdiction but they would have court jurisdiction. They would have the greatest of all possible forms of native sovereignty. On the other hand, they may be advised by their lawyers to waive the right to dispute the court jurisdiction, essentially to treat the non-native tribunals as a form of arbitration and in an informed fashion turn [sic: attorn] to the jurisdiction of this tribunal. That would be their choice at that time but it would be an informed choice. And as members of the legal profession, the duty is to make sure that the client is put in the position of making that type of choice.

Those are my submissions, my Lord. Thank you …

CHIEF JUSTICE LAMER: There is no doubt that it is a constitutional issue. If it is a constitutional issue that we decide to entertain, then it flows from that that we should state a constitutional question to send notice outside so that they intervene but therefore this takes us to the fundamental question, 'Do we want to entertain, and why should we, in your view entertain a constitutional question of nature when that question was not raised below?' … the fact of the matter is that we do not have the benefit of the Supreme Court of British Columbia and the Court of Appeal. Earlier on this morning at 10: 00 a.m., in a case from Quebec, I refused to state a constitutional question because it was being raised before us for the first time.

MR. BRUCE CLARK: What the courts below said in all of the eleven (11) cases that this Court recently on July 6 refused leave [to appeal] on was basically that, regardless of the truth of what I was alleging on behalf of my clients, the issue was of such momentous concern, was of such momentous importance to Canada that nobody but the highest Court in the land was going to touch it. On July 6 it gets to the highest Court in the land and that Court says the issue is of no importance and leave to appeal is denied. The reason this Court must address the issue is because the rule of law hangs in the balance … I wish to argue that the crime of genocide never occurs unless the court system of the country in which it is occurring is complicitous. Right now, the world more than any other single advance needs a break[through] on the crime of genocide and the crime of ecocide and I am suggesting that this Court can light a candle for all humanity to follow. Alternatively, it can engage in chicaneries and not address the point. It can soar or it can plummet. There is no in between … Your jurisdiction [is] as guardians of the sacred trust of civilization.

CHIEF JUSTICE LAMER: Oh my God. I did not swear to that. I just swore to be a judge and try to do my best according to the rule of law.

MR. BRUCE CLARK: It fell upon you, whether or not you realized it. That is the duty under which you labour.

CHIEF JUSTICE LAMER: I must say, Mr. Clark, that in my twenty six (26) years as a judge I have never heard anything so preposterous and presented in such an unkind way. To call the judges of the Supreme Court of Canada and the nine hundred and seventy five (975) High Court judges of Canada accomplices is something preposterous. I do not accept that and I think you are a disgrace to the bar. The point is you have my opinion and you are lucky I am just proceeding to opinions at this stage.

I will hear from you on the motion. Is that all you have to say on the constitutional question? …

MR. BRUCE CLARK: … So we have a classic situation of the truth versus political opportunism. In theory, the function of the rule of law and therefore of this Court above all courts is to get at the truth, the whole truth and nothing but the truth regardless of any political opportunism, regardless of personal offence. This Court is supposed to be above such petty considerations.

The remedy specifically therefore is not to ask this Court to address the constitutional question as such but to ask this Court to address the law which indicates that this case [sic: Court] ought in justice to refer it to an independent and impartial third party tribunal, and in the meantime to make sure that more lives are not lost on the basis of the arguably erroneous assumption that this Court and hence the Royal Canadian Mounted Police or other police forces have jurisdiction. Indian people allegedly are murdered by police who in the even[t] may turn out to have been there fraudulently, treasonably and genocidally, not legally.

In the material that is filed [as amended, it appears]: 'Each and every of the petitioners ... attests that in consequence of the aforesaid (treasonable and fraudulent) usurpation by the domestic Crown Courts in relation to Hunting Grounds, the members of the tribal system to which he or she belongs have been and are being subjected to "serious mental harm" within the meaning of article 2(*b*) of the above mentioned Convention, to prejudiced rates of mortality, and, furthermore, to "killing" within the meaning of article 2(*a*) of the said Convention'.

Those are my submissions, my Lords ...

CHIEF JUSTICE LAMER: ... Today we are not here to decide whether there is a jurisdictional issue to the merits. It is to decide if you can raise the jurisdictional issue in the manner you have ... How do you bring your clients within the four (4) walls of this courtroom without proceeding through the Supreme Court of British Columbia, the Court of Appeal and then to us? ... The fact that we might be concerned about something does not grant us jurisdiction. The only point I am putting to you and I think my colleagues agree with me on this is that we are not a court of original jurisdiction such as the Supreme Court of British Columbia ... We are all of the view that there is no foundation whatsoever for these two (2) motions and they are accordingly dismissed with costs."

Delgamuukw v. AGBC. December 11, 1997. [Final disposition of the appeal.] "[paragraph 74] I reject the submission with respect to the substitution of aboriginal title and self-government for the original claims of ownership and jurisdiction ... [paragraph 75] The content of common law aboriginal title, for example, has not been authoritatively determined by this Court ... [paragraph 77] This defect in the pleadings prevents this Court from considering the merits of this appeal."

Law Society of Upper Canada v. Bruce Clark. Unreported. Reasons for Judgment of Convocation. June 19,1996. "There is no dispute as to the essential facts. The solicitor's position before Convocation on the merits of the complaints was set out by him in writing:

Cumulatively these materials demonstrate the domestic legal establishment's criminal modus operandi: first, that establishment prematurely (prior to cession or purchase) invaded the Indians' yet unsurrendered Hunting Grounds, in the result establishing by force majeure an interpretive monopoly over the legal process; second, it implemented that monopoly by condoning the non-natives' physical dispossession of the Indians, specifically by criminalizing, under ultra vires domestic legislation, Indian resistance. This modus operandi is the cause. The effect is the ongoing genocide of the Indians upon their yet unsurrendered Hunting Grounds.

The constitutional legislation upon which the Indian resistance movement relies not only renders the aforesaid domestic legislation ultra vires but in addition enacts that the implementation of that domestic law constitutes the precise crimes of 'Misprision of Treason' and 'Misprision of Fraud', offences in respect of which by legal definition it not necessary to adduce proof of mens rea.

The present charge brought by the Law Society against the accused of 'professional misconduct' for 'ungovernability' is a variation upon the same historic theme of employing the usurped jurisdiction to criminalize resistance. From all that appears, in virtue of a long and unique professional career involving living with the Indian people as well as reading for advanced degrees directly on point the accused is the only lawyer presently ready, willing and able to raise and to defend the point of law his Indian clients unquestionably are legally entitled to make. Since the domestic judiciary does not want to be informed by any person that they, the judges, are committing treason, fraud and genocide by stonewalling the constitutional law indicting them, the offended judges have reported the accused to the Law Society. Because the real criminals, the domestic judges, are unable to meet the constitutional law in open court they seek in this fashion to preempt that law from public awareness – by silencing its messenger – by having him disbarred. As to the truth or falseness of the point of law upon which all else turns, not only is the domestic legal establishment presumptively biased and hence disqualified upon first principles from proceeding to purport to adjudicate the point, but the constitution expressly and explicitly has constituted an unbiased alternative. This is the clear and plain consequence, and the profound jurisprudential wisdom, of the law that the legal establishment in Canada so far has stonewalled.

Furthermore, the accused's Indian clients' constitutionally entrenched due process right of access to the special constitutional Court constituted under the unrepealed Imperial Orders in Council dated 9 July 1704 and 7 October 1763 is the crucial, indeed the sine qua non, 'existing aboriginal right' within the meaning of section 35(1) of the Constitution Act, 1982. That due process right is their only genuine remedy for apprehending the ongoing genocide of which they complain.

If the accused's Indian clients are right on the law then it is clear and plain that everything said and done by the accused is reasonable, indeed conservative. Even if the clients are wrong upon the law it can not be held that the accused has committed professional misconduct, since all that he has said and done has been directed toward informing the legal establishment of the law that, at least arguably, supports his clients' position. No judge has ever 'ruled on that law'. Without exception, every single domestic judge has evaded the seminal juridical jurisdiction issue after having heard only the bare allegation of the Indians' point of law. No domestic judge has disagreed with the Indians that the constitutional legislative words say what they so clearly and plainly do say, when addressed, precisely because every domestic judge preemptively has refused to address those words. It can not be said that the accused ever 'unprofessionally' persisted with his argument *after* a ruling on the law had been made by any judge. No 'ruling' has ever been made. That is the problem: the issue itself all along has been evaded by the criminals that the law speaking to the issue indicts. The heinousness of their crimes makes any arguable breach of decorum by the accused a trivialization which, by distracting attention from the constitutionally critical issue, aids and abets the unconstitutional treason, fraud and genocide.

And in a later submission he said:

I have been excluded by the combined machinations of the law societies and domestic judges from the defence of my clients. My clients are being drawn into the courts either without legal counsel or with fostered counsel who refuse to risk the censure of contempt citations, forced mental examinations, police assaults at the counsel table and disbarment proceedings for raising the law that justifies my clients' words and deeds. Instead, the fostered lawyers attorn the clients to the jurisdiction of the domestic courts. The courts and lawyers that respectively are trying and defending my clients are thus the same as those that have for over a century treasonably, fraudulently and genocidally suppressed the indigenous peoples' lawful resistance by exercising their own usurped jurisdiction to criminalize or to allow the criminalization of that resistance.

In aid of this grotesque and obscene abuse of the legal process the Law Society is being asked to aid and abet the crimes of treason, fraud and genocide by making permanent the ostracism of me, and hence of the law which, from all that appears, I alone am at present ready, willing and able to raise and to defend. The view of the Discipline Committee was that my refusal to recant and apologize established me as being ungovernable, and that this ungovernability was contrary to the public interest. In reply, I have to argue that the Law Society should never have been attempting to 'govern' me out of telling the legal truth.

The public's interest is in the vindication of the rule of law which is based upon truth – which entails listening to and dealing with the legislative words and precedents that constitute the truth. The lie that Canada is living should be identified and corrected. For the injustice that it represents corrupts its perpetrators as well as wastes its victims. The members of the Law Society are not just lawyers but human beings who, as citizens, have a legacy to leave and children and grandchildren to whom to leave it. It is time for more of us lawyers to help Canada to face the legal truth and make a fresh start. Disbarring the messenger will not assist with this any more than will imprisoning the indigenous people who have had the conviction to speak the legally accurate truth and the courage to risk their own lives against insurmountable physical power to defend it.

The intensity of the feelings engendered in Mr. Clark can be illustrated by his comments before His Honour Judge K.J. Libby on February 26, 1992 in the Provincial Court of British Columbia:

Mr. Clark: And suppose the allegation is made to you that a holocaust and genocide are going on and the proposition will be to put before the international law that constitutes that a crime, and secondly, to put before you the context in which this allegation is made. Now we're at court. It is fair for you to say, 'I'm not going to listen to that context because I don't yet have it in writing' and it not legitimate for me to say, 'Goodness gracious, Your Honour, can't you see the fraud inherent in that position?' What you are doing is saying, 'I am going to preclude the possibility of making a finding on holocaust and genocide by precluding the evidence which substantiates it.' ...
The Court: Let's leave then World War II out of it.
Mr. Clark: We cannot leave World War II out of it. The principle of the – of – of the convention on the prevention and punishment of the crime of genocide in 1948 is the result of the lesson of World War II. I am here to prove that genocide is occurring. How in name of the supremacy of God which is engraved in the Canadian constitution, how on earth can you say, 'Let's leave then World War II out of it?' ...
The Court: Your answer is either I'm for you or I'm part of the conspiracy?

Mr. Clark: You are not for me.

The Court: Well, I –

Mr. Clark: You are either –

The Court: I accept your argument, I'm sorry, you're right.

Mr. Clark: Your are either for justice or you are part of the conspiracy.

... Mr. Clark's argument is anything but frivolous. It is the product of intensive study, and reflects a belief that Mr. Clark sincerely holds.

It would be difficult to disagree with Mr. Clark's assertion that the issue that his argument raises is 'constitutionally critical.' Again, the discipline hearing panel found that Mr. Clark honestly believes that the comments and conduct particularized in the complaint – which are an outgrowth of his argument – were intended to advance the cause of justice and the rule of law.

The 'genocide' of which Mr. Clark speaks is real, and has very nearly succeeded in destroying the Native Canadian community that flourished here when European settlers arrived. No one who has seen many of our modern First Nation communities can remain untouched by this reality.

Mr. Clark is not making the kind of arguments that fall to most of us daily in our courts; much of the ordinary work of lawyers relates to the interpretation of a will, the proper understanding of a contract, the ownership of a piece of land, or individual culpability for crime. The issue Mr. Clark raises is one of great significance for the entire people – and for all of us. His commitment to the argument and his conviction respecting its correctness cannot be questioned.

Had this activity been engendered in a context less fraught with significance and emotion, we would take a very different view of Mr. Clark's conduct.

The nature of Mr. Clark's argument is such that the persistent refusal of the courts – he states, without contradiction, that he has attempted to raise this argument some forty-one times – itself in part engenders his fixed and firm conclusion that his argument is correct. *The issue has not been determined by any Court ...*

One may well question the effectiveness of Mr. Clark's advocacy. His use of such words as 'fraud,' 'treason,' and 'genocide' is designed to shock as well as explain, but does not justify the unwillingness of many courts to hear his submissions ...

We are sympathetic, moreover, to Mr. Clark's assertion that the courts have been unwilling to listen to his argument. Though he must accept part of the responsibility for this, it is apparent on the record that he has been prevented by the courts on a number of the occasions in issue from effectively presenting the argument summarized above ..." [Emphasis added.]

8 *See*, especially, *Order in Council (Great Britain) of 9 March 1704* in the matter of *Mohegan Indians v. Connecticut*.

9 *See*, especially, *Constitution Act, 1867*, s. 109, and its phrase "subject to."

10 *Delgamuukw v. AGBC*, September 12, 1995, and its phrase "declaratory relief."

11 *See*, concerning the relevancy and sufficiency of the following single fact, the particulars of the law provided in the statement of claim and notice of constitutional question.

12 Statement of claim.

13 *Constitution Act, 1982*, section 35(*1*).

14 *Constitution Act, 1867*, section 109. *And see, Order in Council (Can.) of 23 January 1875*.

15 *Supreme Court Act*, section 40(*1*).

16 *Delgamuukw v. AGBC*. Transcript for September 12, 1995.

17 Notice of motion, affidavit, judgment and reasons below.
18 Judgment and reasons below. *But see*, *Delgamuukw v. AGBC*, September 12, 1995 and December 11, 1997.
19 *Royal Proclamation of 1763*.
20 *Convention for the Prevention and Punishment of the Crime of Genocide, 1948*, articles 2(*b*), 3(*e*), 4 and 6.
21 Blackstone, *Commentaries*.
22 *Constitution Act, 1982*, preamble.
23 The argument on the proposed appeal will be that, for legal purposes at least, "justice" is and must be the application of truth to affairs; the specific means to the achievement of which, in accordance with the "rule of law," is "third-party adjudication" such as recognized and affirmed in the aboriginal rights context by the *Order in Council (Great Britain) of 9 March 1705* in the matter of *Mohegan Indians v. Connecticut.* The verb phrase "would have been" is used since the application for leave to appeal to the Supreme Court of Canada was not in fact filed with the Court, ostensibly due to a lack of funds with which to pay the court costs. It seems that when the courts are not knocking the ball out of the natives' hands, the natives' organizations seem bent on dropping it anyway. This should not perplex. Native organizational profit is premised on the values of race politics – avarice and pettiness – the antithesis of the native cultural values of sharing and respect. The principle of third-party adjudication that the proposed appeal was designed to serve conflicts with race politics (not that the Supreme Court of Canada would have noticed an "important" enough legal issue to address in any event). In sum, the legal establishment and the existing native organizational structure are on the same side, and both know well how to play and win their game. The average people, native and newcomer alike, are on the other side, and the game is being played around them. They are unfamiliar not only with the peculiar nature of its rules but even with the fact that it is going on.

Legal Authorities

1493 Inter Cetera, 79, 208
1537 Sublimus Deus, 79, 92, 149–50, 208, 234, 245, 270, 303, 325
1543 New Laws for the Government of the Indies & the Preservation of the Indians, 149
1677 Statute of Frauds, 77
1684 An Act Concerning Purchasing of Lands from the Indians, 235–326
1684 An Act to Prevent Deceit and Forgeries, 235, 325
1704 Order in Council of 9 March 1704 in the matter of *Mohegan Indians v. Connecticut*,
     89, 91–2, 144, 159, 161, 170, 184, 189, 191, 196, 204, 235, 247, 251, 275, 276, 283,
     300, 302, 303, 310, 311, 326–9, 344, 348
1752 Treaty between the Crown and Nova Scotia Native Nations, 348
1760 Treaty of Capitulation of New France at Montreal, 150, 354
1763 Royal Proclamation, 32, 40, 45, 79–80, 91–2, 145, 150, 159, 170, 189, 197, 208,
     210, 235, 236, 251, 275, 276, 288, 299, 303, 310, 329, 331, 332, 333, 334–5, 339,
     340, 341, 342, 343, 344, 354, 355–6, 359, 360, 361
1772 Royal Regulation, 150, 329
1774 *Campbell v. Hall*, 145, 334
     Quebec Act, 354, 358
1776 Declaration of Independence, 270, 276, 288, 325, 339
1783 Peace of Paris, 276, 333, 339, 340
1789 Constitution, as amended, 43, 44, 198, 267, 273, 275, 275, 288, 289, 329–30, 340,
     342, 343
1790 Indian Non-Intercourse Act, 196
1791 *Hughes v. Dougherty*, 331
     Marshall v. Clark, 330–1
     Plumstead v. Rudebagh, 331
1796 *Weiser v. Moody*, 331
1797 *Sherer v. McFarland*, 331
1803 Canada Jurisdiction Act, 361–3
1807 *Strother v. Cathey*, 331
     Treaty at Detroit between US and Chippewas, 277
1810 *Fletcher v. Peck*, 331, 335
1812 *New Jersey v. Wilson*, 331
1813 *Thompson v. Johnson*, 331
1815 *Meigs v. McLungs Lessee*, 331

1821 An Act for Regulating the Fur Trade and Establishing a Criminal and Civil Jurisdiction within certain parts of North America, 354–5
  Arnold v. Mundy, 331
1823 *Johnson v. McIntosh*, 44, 46, 331, 339, 351, 361
  R. v. Shawanakiskie, 363
1824 *Danforth v. Wear*, 331, 331
1826 *Cornet v. Winton*, 331
1828 *Lee v. Glover*, 331
1830 Indian Removal Act, 207
1831 *Cherokee Nation v. Georgia*, 44, 45, 46, 332, 343, 344
1832 *US v. Arredondo*, 332, 339
  Worcester v. Georgia, 44, 46, 79, 197, 203, 208, 209, 270, 332, 343, 344, 351–2
1835 *Cameron v. Kyte*, 349
  Mitchel v. US, 332, 343
1837 An Act to Provide for the Disposal of Public Lands in this Province, 307, 356
  Harris v. Doe, 333
1838 *R. v. Cadien*, 363
1839 *Clark v. Smith*, 333
1843 *Georgia v. Canatoo*, 333
1844 *Coleman v. Tish-Ho-Ma*, 333
1845 *Stockton v. Williams*, 333
1846 *Bown v. West*, 349
  Fellows v. Lee, 333
  Ogden v. Lee, 333–4
1849 An Act to provide for the administration in British Columbia, 355
1850 *Gaines v. Nicholson*, 335
1857 *Scott v. Sandford* (Dred Scott case), 335–41, 343
1858 An Act to provide for the Government of British Columbia, 355
1865 Emancipation Proclamation, 281
1867 *Connelly v. Woolrich*, 351–2
  Constitution Act, 43, 170, 235, 251, 300, 302, 307, 341–2, 344, 349–51, 353–6, 359, 360, 363
  Treaty of Cession of Russian-America, 150
1870 *Rupert's Land and North-Western Territory Order*, 299, 302
1871 Appropriations Act, 46, 110, 114, 199, 208, 209, 270, 271
  Minter v. Shirley, 341
1872 *Holden v. Joy*, 341
1873 Treaty 3, 359
  Wood v. Missouri K..& T. Ry. Co., 341
1874 Treaty 4 between the Crown and Cree ..., 300, 302–3, 355
  An Act to Amend and Consolidate the Laws Affecting Crown Lands in British Columbia, 353–6
1875 Order in Council (Canada), 235–6, 307, 308, 353–6
1876 *US v. 43 Gallons of Whiskey*, 341
1879 *Church v. Fenton*, 306–7, 308, 356
1880 Indian Act, 116, 209, 307
1884 Indian Act, 307–8
1886 *Butz v. Northern Pacific Railroad*, 341
  Eastern Band of Cherokees v. US, 341
  St. Catherine's Milling & Lumber Co. v. The Queen, 356

1887 *St. Catherine's Milling & Lumber Co. v. The Queen*, 356–7

1888 *St. Catherine's Milling & Lumber Co. v. The Queen*, 308, 344, 359, 360

1889 *AG Ontario v. Francis*, 358

1895 *Ontario v. Canada*, 250, 310, 358–9

1897 *AG Ontario v. AG Canada*, 308, 359

1903 *Ontario Mining Co. v. Seybold*, 308, 359

1909 Consolidated Laws of New York, 273

1910 *AG Canada v. AG Ontario*, 359

1924 Act of June 2 (Indian Citizenship in USA), 343

1925 *R. v. Ontario & Minnesota Power Co.*, 308, 359

1926 *R. v. McMaster*, 359

     Sobhuza II v. Miller, 299

1927 Indian Act, 116

1930 Natural Resources Transfer Act, 303

1932 *Easterbrook v. R.*, 359

     R. v. Wesley, 359

1934 Indian Reorganization Act, 275

1938 *US v. Shoshone Tribe*, 342

1941 *US v. Sherwood*, 288

1948 Convention for the Prevention and Punishment of the Crime of Genocide, 32, 125, 149, 165, 170, 173, 174, 175, 236, 246, 273, 291, 296, 310, 347

1951 Indian Act, 117

1955 *Tee-Hit-Ton Indians v. US*, 287, 289

1964 *R. v. George*, 359

     R. v. Sikyea, 359–60

1965 *Brick Cartage v. R.*, 360

1973 *Calder v. AGBC*, 360, 361

     Indian Act, 186, 209

     Re Paulette's Application to File a Caveat, 360

1974 *US v. Washington*, 343, 344–5

1975 *Noel v. Chapman*, 288

1980 *AG Canada v. Inuit Tapirisat of Canada and National Anti-Poverty Organization*, 314

     Maine Settlement Act, 195

1982 Constitution Act, 170, 236, 299, 300, 1, 363

     R. v. Secretary of State for Foreign & Commonwealth Affairs, 360–1

     Valley Forge College v. Americans United, 287

1983 *Duchane v. Davies*, 297, 320

     King v. Gull Bay Indian Band, 318

1985 *Hutchison v. Saskatoon Funeral Home Co. Ltd.*, 293, 320

     Income Tax Act, 31

     Indian Act, 318

     Saskatchewan Act, 300

     Springhill Lumber Ltd. v. Lake St. Martin Indian Band, 318

1986 *Abse v. Smith*, 316, 317

     Romanic v. Hartman, 293, 314, 320

1987 *Kucey v. Peter Ballantyne Band Council*, 318

     Proxmire Act, 273

1988 *Professional Sign Crafters (1988) Ltd. v. Wedekind*, 317, 318

1989 *Bank of Montreal v. Schmidt*, 314

1990 *Bannon v. Pervais*, 318
  ClowDarling Ltd. v. Big Trout Lake Indian Band, 318
  Hunt v. Carey Canada Inc., 298, 314
  Legal Profession Act, 309, 317, 318
  R. *v. Sparrow*, 299
1991 *Govan Local School Board v. Last Mountain School Division No. 29 of Sask.*, 316
1992 *Atamanchuk v. DeBrun and Smithwick's Physiotherapy*, 309, 317
  Keiling v. Saskatchewan Wheat Pool, 309
  Lujan v. Defenders of Wildlife, 286, 287
  Mabo v. Queensland, 299
  Sagon v. Royal Bank of Canada, 314
1993 *Delgamuukw v. AGBC*, 298–9
  Golden Hill Paugussett Tribe of Indians v. Weicker, 287, 288
1994 *Piché v. Big "C" First Nation*, 293, 320
  Shinkaruk Enterprises Ltd. v. Commonwealth Insurance Co., 317
  Shuttlesworth v. Housing Opportunities Made Equal, 288
1995 *Delgamuukw v. AGBC*, 291, 298, 303, 306, 324, 364–7
  Goertz v. Zmund, 321
  Ochapowace First Nation v. A.(V.), 318
  R. *v. Williams*, 301, 303, 306, 307
  Standing Committee on Discipline v. Yagman, 238
1996 *Sandy Ridge Sawing Ltd. v. Norrish and Carson*, 314
1996 *Law Society v. Bruce Clark*, 367–70
1997 American Heritage Rivers Initiative Executive Order, 203, 274, 275, 280, 281
  Delgamuukw v. AGBC, 294, 303, 306, 367
  Raines v. Byrd, 286, 287
  R. *v. Chief*, 301
  R. *v. Kahpeechoose*, 301
1998 *Jota v. Texaco Inc.*, 343–6
  New Jersey v. New York (Ellis Island case), 44, 205–6
  R. *v. Ignace* (Gustafsen Lake case), 301, 303, 306, 307
1999 Code of Federal Regulations, 200, 275, 285
  Dan v. US, 115, 118
  Land Titles Act, 26–8, 33
  Law Society of Upper Canada v. Bruce Clark, 210–25, 298
  Public Law 280, 209
  R. *v. Bruce Clark*, 247
  Statute of the International Court of Justice, 126, 131
  Sulfur Fumes Arbitration Act, 24
  Supreme Court Act, 107–8, 117, 148, 236, 324

Index

aboriginal economy: black market in, 96, 100–1; destruction of, 6, 96; reconstruction of alternatives, 184

aboriginal rights: comparative law equation between USA and Canada based on common British colonial law to which both regimes trace, 266, 269, 272, 332, 333, 334, 341, 344; what the existing words of the international and constitutional legislation and precedents constituting such rights *literally* say, 265, 284–371

aboriginality: burden upon natives of proving, 66, 201–2; discharging the burden, 66–81; historical cartography (old maps), 75; material culture, 69; proof in terms of the continuity of linguistics, 70–1; sociological anthropology, 71–2; transportation and communication patterns, 73; *see also* burden of proof; federal Indian law; Mohicans, altered document issue

act of state doctrine, 271, 302

adhesions, to treaties, 77, 78, 82; *see also* treaties

adoption, 34, 39, 205, 257, 265

airplane, experiences owning and flying, 9

"all my relations," the benediction, 21; *see also* unity, principle of

amendments or repeal, constitutional need for rather than acting under federal law, 46, 47, 96, 117, 183, 200, 201, 209, 245, 246, 272, 302, 330

American Indian Movement, apparent legal strategy, 119–20

American Revolution, effect of on aboriginal rights, 44–7, 269, 276, 344

anarchy, view of native sovereignty as, 35, 146

arbitration, international trade strategy of native sovereigntists, *see* international trade arbitration

Arizona, 207

aspirations, professional of author, 17–18

asylum for criminally insane, referral by court of author to, 168–9

Baby Suggs, 204, 274

bear, spirit, 20, 99

Bear Island, 20–3, 48–53; aboriginal rights, 155–6; conference, 65–6; nature sovereignty, 134, 140; self-sufficiency, 54–7; traditional lifestyle, 58–9; trial, 67–81

Bended Elbow, parody of Wounded Knee, 12

black market, conflict of interest with native sovereignty, 101; native participation in, 101

blood brothers, significance, 33–4

boat crash, 3

borders, native national and family, 27; *see also* hunting grounds, family basis and legal significance

breakthrough, in author's research, 89

Bulgaria, sojourn and impressions, 134, 137–8, 141–3, 144; supposedly finances the author to destabilize North America, 244

burden of proof, land claims, 104; shifting the international and constitutional law burden on the newcomers of proving purchase to the Indians of proving aboriginality, 67–8, 96, 104, 201–2, 286–9; *see also contra proferentes*; fiduciary relationships

bush Indians, contrasted with acculturated Indians, 21–2

California, 208

canoes, material culture of, 70

car-bomb incident, 244

cautions, legal injunction device, 26–8, 360

cellmates, author and Gustafsen Lake clients, 188

Central America, sojourn, 148–52

Chee'Bai' Gin, *see* Temagamis

chicanery, governmental, 201, 202, 206, 209, 287–302; judicial, 67, 79, 104–7, 109, 205, 241, 310, 314–15, 317 citizen's arrests, of police and judges by author, 157, 161, 164, 210, 213–14, 247

civil rights movement, spillover to native rights, 12

Clinton, President, Mohican petition to, 267–84

Cochrane, trial at, 5, 157

collaborating natives, in cahoots with the legal establishment to suppress the law, 86, 93, 100, 111, 134, 140, 149, 155–7, 163, 164, 171–2, 177, 182, 185–6, 190–1, 201

collective unconscious, hypothesis of, 181

conflict of interest, legal establishment of, 25–6

conservationist ethic, of natives, 4, 23

conservatism, of native culture, 70

constitutional law, genesis and persistence of, 41–7; see also amendments or repeal

contra proferentes, rule of construction of documents, 277

costs, incidence of the burden of concerning the native sovereignty issue, 27

cowboys, and cheering for the Indians instead, 12

crimes, by author, 157, 163–4, 171

criminal law, inconsistencies of in relation to Indians, 8–9, 49, 107, 189

criminalization of protest, the technique in aid of genocide, 185, 192, 245, 329

culture shock, experience of, 12–13, 18, 51, 53, 55–7, 85

cyclic, worldview, 20–4, 52–3, 195

denial, legal establishment in, 244, 308–9

dependent Indian communities under federal law, contrast with domestic dependent nations under constitutional law, 200, 271–3

Dicey, A.V.: limitations on judicial power, 46, 236–7, 270, 272, 335–41, 347

disbarment of author: author's message is "the root" of the complaints of professional misconduct, 211, 239; Law Society of Upper Canada neglects to consider the author's defence material, 233–4, 250; silencing the message, 102–13, 158, 163–4, 177, 197, 213, 214, 239, 247

discovery, confers exclusive jurisdiction to purchase, 208; see also purchase

"disgrace to the bar," author as in view of Chief Justice of Canada, 242

domestic dependent nations, native nations as, 45, 200, 271–3, 332, 343

double standard, of Canada and USA in relation to genocide, 175, 183–4

drugs, Indian role, 96

economic pressure, on non-natives, 28–9, 32

edge effect, proliferation of biological life in transition zones, 8

Einstein, Albert: unified field theory of and the mystics, 21, 40, 181

Ellis Island case, Indian intervention in denied by US Supreme Court, 205–6

Emancipation Proclamation, 281

Emerson, Ralph Waldo: definition of justice, 39, 347

eminent domain, the concept and its constitutional inapplicability in the aboriginal rights context, 118–20, 283–4, 332, 335, 336–7, 340, 341, 360

environment, experience of depredations against, 14–15, 23–5

environmentalist movement, conflict of with native sovereignty, 174

Europe, complicity of in genocide, 173–9

European Court of Human Rights, 170, 178

evasion: aided and abetted by Law Society, 225; of the juris-

diction issue by the legal establishment, 28–30, 40, 59, 67, 68, 101–13, 177, 198, 203, 206, 266, 285–324

evolution, intellectual and institutional needed, 184, 187

expectations, of natives, 8

fatalism, in native culture, 49, 51–2

father, death of author's, 10

fear: author's of government, non-native and native lawlessness, 29, 136, 152, 164, 166, 168, 169, 178, 192, 214, 240, 243–6; natives' of genocide, 103, 162, 195, 196, 240

federal Indian law: application of as modus operandi for genocide, 201, 202, 287, 289, 291, 294–5, 318; challenge to constitutionality of in the Liberty Island case, 205, 285, 289; Indian Non-Intercourse Act of 1790, 196; irrelevance of to the native sovereignty issue, 47, 114, 115, 117, 119, 196, 198, 203, 206, 209, 269–71, 275, 289, 333–4, 344–6, 351–2, 356, 361; weapon unconstitutionally to suppress native sovereignty, 182, 186, 295

federal recognition, 275; see also recognition, federal

feminism, psychological influences of and sympathy for, 14, 16, 19–20, 53, 72, 280

fiduciary relationships: rule of construction of documents, 277, 310; status of native nations as, 336–7, 349–50, 353–6, 358–9

First British Empire, demise of, 41

fool, author as, 56, 96, 135

fraud, judicial, 61, 66–8, 74–80, 89, 90, 92, 93, 104–13, 118, 127, 133, 135, 146, 148, 156, 157, 158–9, 160, 167, 168, 171, 179, 183–6, 189, 197, 198, 209, 239, 240, 241–3, 247, 271, 309–24, 329, 348, 364–7; see also jurisdiction issue, fraudulent denials of by the Supreme Court of Canada frivolous, author's argument on jurisdiction as, 211, 212, 294, 314

funding, Indian competition for precludes a single coherent focus in Europe, 124

fur-trade records, fallibility of in historical analysis, 73

Gayanerekowa, law, 35–9

genocide: bases for allegation of, 32, 33, 58–61, 67, 85–6, 89, 92, 94, 98, 103, 108–9, 111, 133, 146, 150, 156–7, 168, 170, 173, 175–6, 178, 179, 180, 181, 182, 184, 186, 195, 200, 201, 203, 204, 205, 207, 208–9, 211, 236, 245, 246, 251, 271–2, 274, 279–80, 281–2, 284–9, 324, 346–7, 367–70; global dimension of, 124–5, 144, 182, 187, 216, 269, 271–2, 307–8; Law Society opinion that the genocide of which author speaks is real, 211; Statue of Liberty and, 285; see also Europe, complicity in genocide; Queen Elizabeth II; respect

George, Dudley, 189

gods, investing nature with, 4

Governor's Island, legal status of as Indian territory, 277

Grant, President Ulysses, 281, 283

Great Britain: legacy of, 44, 145, 200, 269, 332, 333, 334, 341; see also Queen Elizabeth II

Great Law of Peace, Iroquoian, see Gayanerekowa

gunshot incident, childhood experience of, 16–17

Gustafsen Lake crisis, 161–72, 240–5; author's arrest and imprisonment in insane asylum, 166–9; clients' instructions to depart for Europe to apprehend genocide in progress, 169–71; criminal trial and disbarment of author in consequence of, 187–9; malice of police and smear campaign, 163–4, 168–9; natives' sole demand that the jurisdiction issue be addressed, 162, 165, 240; precipitating factors, 161–2, 240

Gus-wen-tah, law, 40

Haileybury, practising in, 7, 17–18

heroism, of natives, 98, 100, 101

heterogeneity, of native culture, 6, 8

Hobbes, Thomas: life in New World society as "nasty, brutish, and short," 35, 146

Hudson River, 203–4, 267, 274; status of as Indian territory, 277, 279

Human Rights Committee of the United Nations, role of, 125, 131

human rights industry, influence of in suppressing human rights law, 100

Hume, 183, 303, 344

hunting grounds, family basis and legal significance of, 27; sociology of, 72

identity crisis, see culture shock

income tax: abuses and excesses of jurisdiction in relation to, 30–3, 93–4, 192, 329–30; Indians on unceded land constitutionally exempt from, 329–30; see also residence, prima facie illegality of non-native in the Indian territories

inconstancy, personal experience of, 82–4, 93, 97, 100, 119, 139, 141, 171–2, 173–4, 189–92, 197, 371; see also Trickster, the ethic; whiteman, as prey

injustice, as an art form and cause of genocide, 13

intent, legislative, in the constitutional law, 41–7

International Court of Justice, role of, 125–8, 131–2, 178–9

international criminal court: author's dream of Bulgaria as its venue, 143; need for, 143, 178, 179, 253–4

international law, 325, 332

international trade arbitration, a strategy for native sovereigntists, 133, 136, 139

Jackson, President, Andrew, 46, 47

Johnson, Sir William, 35

judges: duty of, 40, 46, 79, 236; limitation of power of under the rule of law, see Dicey, A.V.

Judicial Committee of the Privy Council: access to terminated, 117, 147–8; decisions of, 308; third-party adjudicator, 44, 45, 147, 161–2, 269, 304

jurisdiction, objecting to the assumption of as a legal strategy, 98, 117, 135–6

jurisdiction issue: acknowledgment of Law Society that the issue is constitutionally critical and has not been addressed by the courts, 211–12; admission by the Supreme Court of the importance of the issue, 242; fraudulent denials of by the Supreme Court of Canada, 104, 107–8, 113, 134, 157, 162, 185, 188, 189, 192, 236, 241, 247–8

jurisdictions, constitution of, 32, 43, 117, 201–2, 294, 302, 333, 341–2

"just following orders," the excuse, 165–6, 168, 241

just wars, concept of, 46, 209

justice: capricious force of nature, 4; definition, 22, 39, 181, 184, 201, 243, 247, 280, 324, 347; intent of author to advance the cause of, 211

Kenora, birth place and trial at, 6–7, 9

King Philips' War, 270

Lake Temagami, 7–8

land claims: courts' insistence on claims being brought, 109, 110; stupidity of bringing claims, 104; when fundraising for and bringing claims was a crime in Canada, 116–17, 307–8

latch-key kids, being one, 16

law, as the art of the possible, 5, 33, 79, 81, 87, 96, 128, 132, 147, 169, 196, 209, 242, 294, 303, 324

law, Indian, 145–7, 155, 180–7, 204, 250–1, 274, 276; see also Gayanerekowa

law school, experience of, 17

Law Society, definition of becoming conduct for lawyers, 84, 115, 156, 158–60, 161, 164–5, 172, 185, 188, 191, 210–25, 248; disbarring the author without considering his defence, 233–4, 246; suppressing the law in circumstances where the suppression arguably aids and abets genocide, 225, 226–51

lawyers: ascertaining personal duty and function of, 14, 16, 17, 47, 85, 247, 250; conflict of interest of in relation to native sovereignty issue, 117, 305, 306, 317

liberty: balancing against need for order, 16, 52, 98, 115, 184; in native society, 182, 198, 200, 204, 205, 209

Liberty Island, see Statue of Liberty

Lil'Wats, criminal charges against, 97–8; drama of their trial, 108–13

locus standi, see natives capacity to sue concerning genocide in North America

lying, cultural propensity, 21–2, 146

magic, presence of, 23, 70, 181; and the reticence to give names, 73

Manhattan Island, legal status of as Indian territory, 276–7

Maple Mountain, "where the spirits go," 19

maps, historical, 20

Marshall, Chief Justice John, 45–6, 283

Martin, Calvin: Indian conservation hypothesis of, 4

material success, influence of, 9, 16

media, assumptions and biases of, 95, 97, 102, 104, 135–6

methodology, the author's, 54

"might is right," 186

Mi'gmaq, 180, 189–91

mining rights, 333

misprision, significance of the term, 211, 236, 311, 324, 348–9

Mohegans, see Mohicans

Mohicans, 89, 195–209, 265–84; adoption of author as citizen of, 265–6; altered document issue, 201–2, 204, 268, 269; case against Connecticut, 89–92, 269; last of in New York and Vermont, 197; petition to the president, 198–202, 267–84; rejection of welfare economy by, 267, 271, 280; Supreme Court of New York case, 197–8, 270–1; survival strategy of precludes written records, and federal law insists on written records as a precondition to tribal recognition, 199–200, 268, 269, 271, 278

moose story, 52

Moosonee, murder at, 4–6

mystics, and Einstein's unified field, 21, 40, 181, 195

native sovereignty: author instructed to defend, 19, 96; coexistence with newcomer sovereignty, 40, 45, 329, 331, 332, 333–4, 336–7; consequences of, 32, 35, 283–4, 329; de facto negation of contrary to the rule of law, 45; definition, 45; Indian black-market conflict of interest with, 101; see also domestic dependent nations; eminent domain; evasion of the jurisdiction issue by the legal establishment; Mi'gmaq; plenary jurisdiction

natives' capacity to sue concerning genocide in North America, 335–41, 343–4; see also sovereign immunity

natural law, 185, 270, 331, 332

naturalization, as a citizen of a native nation, see adoption

nature, accommodating the power of, 49; capriciousness of, 3–4

New Yorkers, Temagami playground of, 8

Nietzsche, Friedrich, 181

night shift, the metaphor, 55

Ogoki Post, murder at, 6

Oka crisis, 95–7

opportunism, legal establishment of, 22, 33, 79, 82, 96–7, 196, 242, 324

original states doctrine, 273

paradise, defined, 22, 39, 256

Passamaquoddies, Maine, 195

Peace of Paris of 1783, 208, 269, 339

Pequot War, 270

perfect crime, identified, 92, 105, 182, 185, 197

plane crash, averting, 9

plea bargaining, pre-empting justice as the application of truth to affairs, 4

plenary jurisdiction, 209, 235, 272, 283–4, 302–3, 330, 331, 332, 334, 335, 336–7, 339–40, 342, 344; see also eminent domain

policy, not to be confused with law, 50, 86, 147, 183, 272

pollution, motivating factor behind the assertion of native sovereignty, 23–5

Pontiac, influence of, 41

potlatching, a crime in Canada, 116, 307–8

priests, as scapegoats for the deeper errors of an unjust legal system, 13, 245

prisoners of war, natives as, 329

private property in territory, introduction of the concept by the European invasion, 182

prophecies, native, 181, 195

provincial laws of general application, applicability of to federal Indians, 209; see also federal law

psychiatric assessment, of author, 168–9

purchase: non-native original jurisdiction limited to, 43, 44, 79, 95–6, 117, 133, 182, 185, 200, 202, 205, 208, 235, 270, 276, 283, 294, 325, 330, 331, 332, 333, 334, 336–7, 341, 356–7; of right of way only, 114; pre-emptive (exclusive) character of the purchase jurisdiction, 133, 200–1, 325, 341

Puritans, assault on the rule of law, 270

Quebec secession reference, Indian intervention in, 189
Queen Elizabeth II: complicity in genocide by omission to perform duty, 147, 170; petition to perform constitutionally assigned role, 144–8, 161, 163, 165, 170

race-based Indian governments, rejection of by Mohicans, 198, 204, 280, 281, 282; termination of, 200, 272
rage, judicial, 103, 118, 168, 187
rape trial, Bear Island, 49–50
recognition, federal, 275; see also act of state doctrine; federal law; fraud, judicial
"red niggers," Indians as, 162, 172
religion, native, 19–23, 39, 48–9, 99, 108, 115, 146, 274, 279; see also "all my relations"; respect; sharing; unity principle
religious orders, see priests
remuneration, author's, 29, 93, 191–2
residence, prima facie illegality of non-native residence in the Indian territories, 32, 94, 329, 334; see also income tax: abuses and excesses of jurisdiction in relation to
residential schools, author's experience of, 11–13, 169; genocidal character of, 103; symptom rather than a cause of abuse, see priests
respect, essential need for, 13, 39, 40, 107, 145–6, 181, 183, 204, 274, 280, 329, 333; see also "all my relations"; religion, native; sharing; unity principle
rights of way, 332
rule of law, 16, 26, 33, 39, 40, 44, 46, 79, 85, 92, 96–7, 102–3, 107, 109, 110, 135, 147–8, 157, 161, 162, 168–70, 173–4, 183–6, 191, 195, 196, 198, 199, 200, 201, 208–9, 210–12, 236, 267,

270, 272, 288, 308–309, 340; intent of author to protect, 211; judges accountable for degradation of, 178, 253; people own the rule of law, not the lawyers and judges, 265; see also international criminal court

Scottish hills, as therapy, 88
self-sufficiency, in native culture, 3
sentencing, of natives for crimes, 8–9
sexual power, the aboriginal ethos, 53
sharing, the native way, 184, 198, 204, 267, 275, 277, 279, 280; see also "all my relations"; religion, native way; respect; unity principle
smallpox, oral history of ethnic cleansing by gifts of infected blankets, 103
small-town life, aspiration for, 17
smear campaigns, 82–3, 93, 95–6, 100, 125, 135–6, 160, 162–5, 167, 197, 185–6, 209, 226–32, 243–4
sovereign immunity, claimed by Canada and USA in relation to international standards of human rights law, 288, 289, 298–302; see also double standard; genocide; natives' capacity to sue concerning genocide in North America; third-party adjudication
sovereignty, native, see native sovereignty
standing to sue, see natives capacity to sue concerning genocide in North America
state laws of general application, applicability of to federal Indians, 209; see also federal law
Statue of Liberty, 204–6, 274, 285, 347
succession, international and constitutional law principle of, 44, 79, 269, 270, 332, 333, 334, 341
Sudbury, childhood in, 14–15; union rivalry, 151–2
sundancing, a crime in Canada, 116, 307–8

teachers, personal influence of on author, 16
Temagamis, 19–30; Bear Island trial, 67–81; fired author, 82–5, 93; never signed a treaty, 59–61
termination, see race-based Indian governments
terra nullius, the pretext, 146
terrorism, alternative to the rule of law, 33; see also smear campaigns
third-party adjudication, 44–7, 77, 79, 85, 91–2, 96–7, 102–13, 160, 180, 182, 183, 184, 186–7, 245, 269–70, 272, 273, 275, 284–91, 294, 296, 303, 325–9, 344–6; see also fraud, judicial
throw papers at judge, nationally published lie that author did, 230–1, 244
timber, aboriginal right to cut and sell, 133; Temagami rehiring in relation to, 133–4
treason, by Canadian governments and courts, 145
treaties: contracts, 91, 114, 291, 331, 332, 333, 334, 341, 359, 360; jurisdiction of newcomer courts, 348, 353–4, 361–3; jurisdiction to make, 43, 273, 302, 330; voidability due to fraud, duress, undue influence, or failure of consideration, 184, 291, 358; see also adhesions, to treaties; purchase
treaties, jurisdictional significance of, 26, 59, 182, 333
Treaty of Guadeloupe-Hidalgo of 1848, 208
trees screaming, tradition in relation to, 181
Trickster, the ethic, 50, 202–3
truth, irrelevance in court, 5, 79, 243; peculiar propensity of bush natives to tell, 6, 8, 21–2, 74–5; relation of justice to, 40

undertakings, fraudulent breaches of by the legal establishment, 30, 76, 101, 106–7, 117–18
United Nations: role of, 125; Working Group for Indigenous People, 150–1

unity, principle of, 20–1, 181, 280, 284; *see also* "all my relations"; religion, native; respect; sharing

usufruct, the concept in relation to aboriginal rights, 89, 341

Wampum, 36–40

Washington, George, 43

welfare, natives and, 6–7; native sovereignty precludes, 271, 272–3; rejection of by Mohicans, 267, 271, 272–3, 280

White, Lavina, Sound-of Many-Copper-Shields, wisdom of, 39

white man's burden, literature of, 52

Whitehorse, childhood in, 10–11

whiteman, as prey, 49; *see also* Trickster, the ethic

World Court, *see* International Court of Justice

Wounded Knee, influence of, 12, 163